# Inside Server-Based Applications

Douglas J. Reilly

PUBLISHED BY
Microsoft Press
A Division of Microsoft Corporation
One Microsoft Way
Redmond, Washington 98052-6399



Library of Congress Cataloging-in-Publication Data
Reilly, Douglas J.
Inside server-based applications / Douglas J. Reilly.
p. cm.
Includes index.
ISBN 1-57231-817-1
1. Client/server computing. 2. Microsoft Windows (Computer file) 3. Application software--Development. I. Title.
QA76.9.C55 R448 1999
005.2'769--dc21 99-046394

Printed and bound in the United States of America.

1 2 3 4 5 6 7 8 9 MLML 4 3 2 1 0 9

Distributed in Canada by Penguin Books Canada Limited.

A CIP catalogue record for this book is available from the British Library.

Microsoft Press books are available through booksellers and distributors worldwide. For further information about international editions, contact your local Microsoft Corporation office or contact Microsoft Press International directly at fax (425) 936-7329. Visit our Web site at mspress.microsoft.com.



**Acquisitions Editor:** Ben Ryan
**Project Editors:** Mary Barnard, Molly Fulton
**Technical Editor:** Jim Fuchs

*Dedicated to my brother Bobby.*
*We lost him while I was writing this book, far too soon.*
*I miss him very much.*

# Contents

## Part III Building Windows 2000 Server Applications

# Preface

*Inside Server-Based Applications* is designed to guide you from being a server-based applications novice to becoming a server-based applications expert. I start with some general background material about server-based applications and then move into the specifics of the APIs and technologies that allow you to create useful server-based applications for Microsoft Windows 2000.

## WHO SHOULD READ THIS BOOK?

I wrote this book for the developer who wants to understand the underlying Win32 programming elements that make server-based development possible. In order to get the most from this book, you should be familiar with C++, especially the Microsoft Visual C++ programming environment. It is not essential that you have extensive experience with the Win32 API, but it won't hurt.

The Active Server Pages (ASP) and Internet Server API (ISAPI) examples in this book assume that you have some familiarity with Internet Information Server (IIS). The ASP examples also assume some familiarity with VBScript or Microsoft Visual Basic. Familiarity is not essential, however, because most of the VBScript used in the examples simply accesses methods of objects, something any C++ programmer will likely be comfortable doing. One of the examples uses JScript created on the server to be passed to the client. You'll also need to know JScript to understand the details of the example, but understanding the broader implications of creating client-side scripting and sending it to the client does not require knowledge of JScript.

Some examples use Microsoft SQL Server, both as a simple data source and as a sever-side development environment. Using SQL Server as a server-side development environment does require some understanding of SQL.

## ABOUT THE EXAMPLES AND THE COMPANION CD-ROM

One thing you will notice about the first few examples is that they are implemented as console mode applications. Console mode applications are similar to the MS-DOS text mode applications from the 16-bit world, but they have some important differences. First these are true 32-bit applications. Second these applications can call dynamic-link libraries (DLLs) and other parts of the Win32 API with few exceptions. Finally the Windows 2000 service applications that I discuss are at their heart special-purpose console mode applications.

I created all of the examples on the companion CD-ROM with Microsoft Visual Studio 6.0 and the July 1999 MSDN Library. All examples have been compiled and run on Windows 2000 using Release Candidate 1 (Build 2072). I created the ASP examples with Microsoft Visual InterDev. To run the ASP and ISAPI applications, you must have Internet Information Server (at least version 4 but preferably version 5, which comes with Windows 2000). Some of the examples use SQL Server. These examples will work just as well with the Microsoft Database Engine (which is available through *http://msdn.microsoft.com/vstudio/msde/download.asp*). Some examples use TCP/IP and thus require a functional network with TCP/IP installed and configured properly with a TCP/IP naming service of some kind (such as WINS or DNS) in place. (The readme file on the companion CD-ROM also contains a list of the software required to run the examples.)

## OVERVIEW

Chapters 1 and 2 present an overview of the requirements for server-based applications. Then, chapter by chapter, I discuss the APIs that allow Windows 2000 server-based applications to do what they must do. Chapter 3 discusses the Service API that allows you to create a true server-based application—one that can run even when no one is logged in to the server. Here I introduce a C++ class to support server-based applications. Chapter 4 is an introduction to the impersonation APIs, including the security implications of the basic question, "Who are you?" Chapter 5 discusses event logging and integrates it into the C++ class introduced in Chapter 3.

Chapter 6 uses the Remote Access Server (RAS) API to create virtual networks using standard phone lines. Chapter 7 discusses the Telephony API (TAPI) and Messaging API (MAPI), with special emphasis on the potential pitfalls when integrating these technologies into a Windows 2000 service application. In Chapter 7, I expand the C++ service class introduced earlier to support integrating COM technologies, such as MAPI, or any feature that requires an application with a message pump.

Chapter 8 discusses Open Database Connectivity (ODBC) and creates a class to exploit ODBC-compliant data sources. While there are many spiffy new technologies for database access, ODBC has the advantage of speed and widespread availability. In Chapter 8, I also introduce several classes supporting ODBC. You'll use these classes throughout the balance of the book.

Once I've discussed the basics of creating Windows 2000 server-based applications and the Win32 APIs that support them, I move into a discussion of several Web technologies that enable you to create server-based applications for the Internet age. Using ASP in Chapter 9 and ISAPI in Chapters 10 and 11, I show how you can create cutting-edge applications that take the best of traditional server-based applications and marry them to Internet technologies. Chapter 12 describes client communication using both named pipes and WinSock, implemented using Win32 events as well as I/O completion ports. Chapter 13 looks at database access again, but this time SQL Server specifically, with an eye toward fully exploiting SQL Server's server-side application support. Finally, in Chapters 14 and 15, I present an example of a network monitoring system that can function as a stand-alone service application or work in concert with Web clients, using ASP and ISAPI.

## THE WAY I WORK

One comment about the way that I work: with some notable exceptions, I do not use frameworks such as MFC and ATL, but rather I write to the Win32 API. For traditional client applications, the frameworks are often appropriate because these tools are optimized for supporting client applications. In general these frameworks are not as useful for server-based applications. There are exceptions, of course. We can use ATL to create a server-side Microsoft ActiveX control for use with ASP. There is little reason not to use ATL for this task, as the code from the ATL Object Wizard is designed for server-side use. MFC is used extensively in the ISAPI examples, and again there is no good reason not to use the MFC ISAPI extensions. The MFC ISAPI classes can operate without taking the baggage of the rest of the MFC classes along for the ride. Once you know the underlying API or technology, you will be much more effective using the frameworks when it is appropriate to use the frameworks' wrappers around the APIs and technologies. I hope you agree.

I have enjoyed writing this book about the technologies I use almost daily to create server-based applications. I hope that you will find here the grounding you need to create the reliable, robust applications required in the increasingly server-based computing environment of the twenty-first century.

# Acknowledgments

You might have noticed that this book is dedicated to my brother Bobby. He was the first person in the family to get involved with computers, and in many ways Bobby was responsible for my eventual career in computer programming. Bobby died from colon and liver cancer while I was writing this book. Shortly thereafter, during a routine screening for a minor health problem, an alert ultrasound technician noticed a spot on *my* liver.

While virtually everyone—including very good doctors in several hospitals—assured me that this was likely nothing to worry about, I worried. I also hassled one of the doctors I had been seeing for many years for the treatment of Gardner's Syndrome, the underlying condition that had killed both Bobby and my father, many years earlier. Dr. Hans Gerdes and his office assistant, Joanne Booth-Pezantez, were every bit as relentless as I was in trying to get to the bottom of this, and we did. Not long after Bobby died, I had successful liver surgery to remove two liver tumors, one malignant. Without the excellent care I received at Memorial Sloan-Kettering Cancer Center, writing this book would not have been possible.

Working with Microsoft Press has been a joy. In addition to Ben Ryan, whom I have known and worked with since before he came to Microsoft Press, the editors who worked on the book were uniformly helpful even when assaulted by my occasionally tortured prose. Kathleen Atkins, Mary Barnard, Molly Fulton, and Rebecca McKay, among others, have vastly improved and clarified my basic ideas. Jim Fuchs has been a truly amazing technical editor, not only clarifying technical points where needed but also adding insights and pushing me to improve in some areas. When I discovered a significant problem with some of the code late in the game, Jim worked to make the required changes, ensuring this would be the best book possible. Thanks to everyone at Microsoft Press!

Claire Horne of the Moore Literary Agency helped me clarify what it was I thought I had to say and presented it to several publishers until one of them agreed that there was a book in there somewhere. Thank you, Claire.

Tom Dignan of Bear Mountain Software came to my rescue as I was at sea in a pool of MAPI. When I needed insight into the inner workings of MAPI, I turned to Tom. The MAPI examples are largely drawn from code Tom kindly provided for me to use. Even the significant modifications to that code were the result of conversations with Tom. The final example in the book is a simple network monitor. For many of you, this simple example will serve as a starting point for your needs. For those of you with more complex needs, Tom's Bear Mountain Software puts out a great product named Topper that you should consider owning.

While I was writing the book, I couldn't ignore my day job. Special thanks to the folks at Home Care Information Systems (HCIS) for their kindness not only during the book-writing process but also during my illness, which was plopped right in the middle of the process. Michael Zaccardi of HCIS has the distinction of being the first person to purchase the book on line—before I even completed it. Kathy Collins and Rich Wheatley of the St. Barnabas Health Care System have continued to allow me to work on some neat projects in spite of a much-too-limited time budget. Ed Colosi and Lenny Gray have been sounding boards for many of the topics covered in this book, even in subjects beyond their special areas of expertise. Thanks all.

Family life with two teenagers can be trying in the best of circumstances. As you can gather from my brief discussion of my family's recent health problems, my children, Tim and Erin, have not had the best of circumstances. In spite of that, I am pleased to report that as of this writing they are happily in college, studying (I hope) even as I write this. Kids, I love you very much and am proud to see the grown-ups you are becoming.

Finally, this book would not have been possible without one other person in my life—my wife, Jean. I am not sure she knew what she thought she was getting into when she signed on for this marriage 21 years ago, but I bet it was a bit different from the way it turned out. She has been with me and other family members literally up and down the east coast, getting the best care we could. Many other wives would have said "Enough!" some time ago. She keeps on trucking. Here's to 100 more years, with 100-year extensions. I love you.

Douglas Reilly
*doug@accessmicrosystems.com*

# Part I

# Server Basics

# Chapter 1

# Server-Based Development

Michael J. Fox appears in a movie called *The Secret of My Success,* in which he has just arrived in New York City from Kansas. He calls home from a phone booth and assures his mother things are fine. He tells her that it is "just like Kansas." Gunfire erupts, causing him to duck for a second, and then he continues, "Yes, it is just like Kansas, only intensified." Server-based development reminds me of that quote—it is just like regular programming, only intensified.

## What Is a Server?

Before we proceed much further, some definitions are in order. Defining exactly what constitutes a server is a lot like defining what beauty is—you know it when you see it. Most programmers know what a server program is when they see it, but coming up with a definition is a little tough. Most server systems exist on a local area network (LAN) or wide area network (WAN) and communicate with clients on the same network, but not always. Even the operating system in use is no longer the marker for what a server program is; Microsoft Windows 2000 is the first generally available system in which the client operating system and the server operating system are the same (ignoring for a moment the difference between Windows 2000 Professional and Windows 2000 Server—more on that later).

Network attachment is also not a requirement for a server program. Most server programs are constructed to interact with the network environment or client workstations, but this interaction is not a requirement. As I just mentioned, Windows 2000 is constructed in a client/server fashion, with the client and the server contained in the same machine. Take a look at Figure 1-1, which shows the Windows 2000 Services applet. Looking down the list of services, we see some that are clearly network related (DHCP Client and FTP Publishing Service) as well as some that are clearly not (Event Log). Speaking of Event Log, the local machine uses this service to record informational messages, warnings, and errors. OK, the Event Log service creates a log that can also be read from another machine on the network, but that functionality is not an essential part of the service, and the service functions just fine on stand-alone machines. (How Microsoft Windows NT came to be constructed in such a way is a subject for an entirely different book—see the descriptions of *Show-Stopper* and *Inside Windows NT,* Second Edition, in the annotated bibliography—but it is important to realize that the client and the server need not be on different computers.)

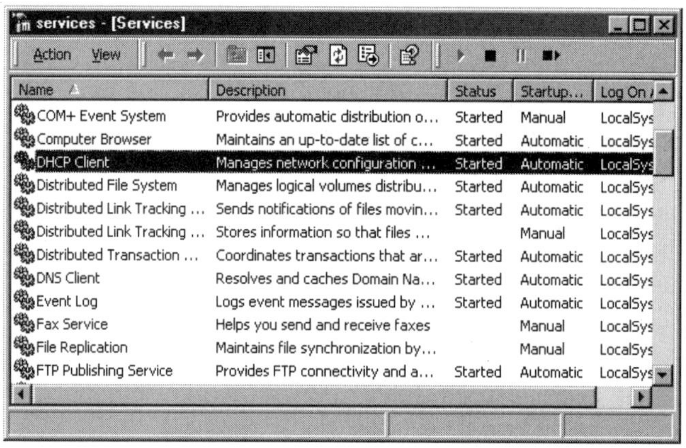


**Figure 1-1** *The Windows 2000 Services applet.*

Since we cannot rely on these criteria to define a server program—what operating system is in use, whether there is communication between a client and a server, or even whether the program is running on a network—we need another criterion. My criterion is this: a server program is a program in which the user interface (UI) does not exist or is separate from or incidental to the function of the program.

Let's consider two server programs and see how they fit this criterion. The first example is a networked MS-DOS program that monitors a virtual drive on an AS/400 midrange computer, copies and processes the files on a LAN drive, and then waits for the next file to appear. The only real user interface is a text-based display that tells the operator what the system is doing. This user interface is incidental to the main task of the server program—since there are no user options—and the messages exist solely for the operator to know whether the system is running.

The second example of a server program is Microsoft SQL Server. If you could scroll further down the list shown in Figure 1-1, you would see two entries in the services list related to SQL Server: MSSQLServer, which is the actual server program that manages the database operations, and SQLExecutive, which is a program that handles timed operations on the SQL Server database. Figure 1-2 shows the opening screen of the program that starts when you run SQL Enterprise Manager.

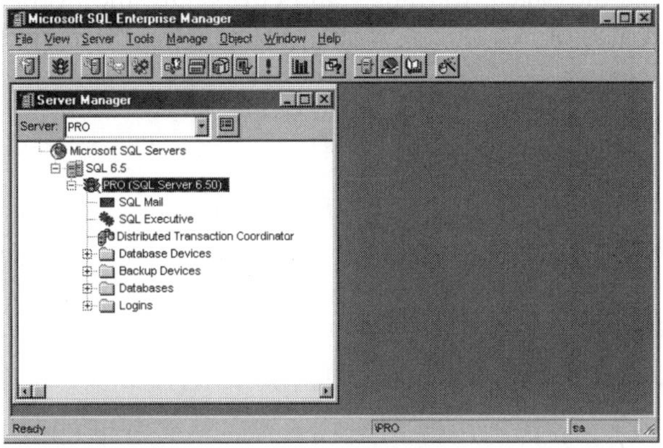


**Figure 1-2** *SQL Enterprise Manager, the user interface for SQL Server.*

This program functions as a user interface for the MSSQLServer and SQLExecutive services. Many of the operations you can perform with SQL Enterprise Manager can also be performed (albeit with greater difficulty) with command-line tools that provide essentially no user interface. Thus, SQL Server meets our test of being a server program.

## THE GROWTH OF SERVER-BASED DEVELOPMENT

Several factors have come together to make this the ideal time to study and understand the nuances of server-based development. Perhaps the most important factor is the emergence of Windows 2000 as the server of choice within many organizations. Windows 2000 provides many features that previous server operating systems did not.

Windows 2000 allows developers to write server-based systems by using the tools that they are already familiar with, such as Microsoft Visual C++, Borland C++, Microsoft Visual Basic, and Borland's Delphi. I will argue that in many cases, the tools based on Visual C++ are the most appropriate for production server systems, but for many applications Visual Basic will suffice. Visual Basic programmers out there are legion, and their work will lead to an onslaught of Visual Basic server solutions in addition to the C and C++ solutions already becoming available.

## NetWare

Novell NetWare was previously the server of choice and is still a strong force in the network operating arena. At its inception, NetWare did exactly what was needed: file and print sharing with what now seems like minimal hardware. NetWare networks frequently supported dozens of users for file and print services using Intel 486–based servers with 32 MB of RAM. However, writing a NetWare Loadable Module (NLM) was a daunting process, and NetWare never emerged as an application server for the masses.

Why was it difficult to write an NLM? Consider the environment. NLMs generally run in ring 0 of the CPU, a ring that provides no memory protection. In the early days of NetWare, running code in ring 0 was a feature rather than a bug because the Intel 80286 and 80386 processors were the most powerful microprocessors available for servers, and code executed faster when running in ring 0. As CPU speed increased, running NLMs in ring 0 became less of a benefit. NetWare 4 and later versions could run NLMs in either ring 0 or ring 3, which was slower but safer. Code running in ring 3 is less likely to bring down the entire server but can still bring down an individual application by performing tasks that in other operating systems might simply cause a resource leak.

The second problem with NetWare as an application server was the limited selection of tools available for NLM development. For a long time, only the Watcom C/C++ compiler was able to create NLMs. The Watcom C/C++ is a perfectly capable compiler, but it is not the preferred compiler for the majority of developers. Other compilers can be used for NLM development, but they still require use of the Watcom linker, making the use of any other compiler more complex. The importance of limited tool selection cannot be understated. Programmers often have near-religious attachment to their compilers and need compelling reasons to switch.

## Cracks in the Fat Client Model

The most common client/server model before the Internet explosion was the "fat client" model, in which most of the processing took place on the client computer, with only the database and some modest amount of business logic on the server. The client took care of not just the presentation of information but also decisions about what information was shown—as well as when and how information would be saved. The popular tools used for client/server development included PowerSoft, PowerBuilder, and Visual Basic. These tools left significant portions of a system's logic on the client computer.

The fat client model seemed more entrenched than ever, with ever more powerful client workstations absorbing the increasing amount of code that allowed client/server systems to function. However, about the time the Internet and soon after the local Internets, or intranets, were emerging, several cracks in the fat client model began to appear. First, the overwhelming cost of upgrading client workstations every year was taking its toll on corporate information technology (IT) budgets. Since the current year's fat client software ran slowly if at all on the previous year's PC, new client/server software meant new hardware.

Second, as users began to make use of their powerful new systems and loaded several applications on the client workstation, configuration problems that had been manageable previously became an additional drain on IT budgets. The existence of two mutually exclusive client applications (only one running on a client workstation at a time) became more than a theoretical possibility. Many hours were lost to just such situations, with dynamic-link library (DLL) conflicts the most common cause of failures. The financial burden on IT budgets, christened "Total Cost of Ownership" (TCO), brought about changes in the computer marketplace on a scale not seen since microcomputers became common in the late seventies.

## THE NEED FOR SERVER-BASED APPLICATIONS

At the same time that NetWare provided a less-than-hospitable environment for server-based development, the need for server-based applications was skyrocketing because of the Internet. The Internet is at the server-centric extreme of the client/server continuum. Contrary to the media hype of the early nineties, client/server is not a binary choice. Figure 1-3 shows the range of client-only to server-only options, with balanced client/server systems in the middle. Systems can range from stand-alone PCs in which the client does all the work to terminals connected to mainframe computers in which, except for some basic keyboard handling and display management, the server does all the work. The Internet has turned the client/server world upside-down.

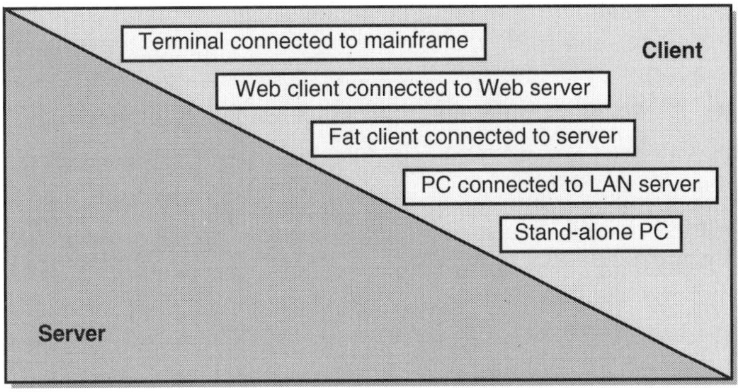


**Figure 1-3** *The client/server continuum.*

## The Internet: A Solution to TCO Problems

Begun as Arpanet during the cold war, the Internet was designed to be a decentralized system that could withstand the loss of one or more nodes, presumably during nuclear attack. After many years of use, a protocol called Hypertext Transfer Protocol (HTTP) was introduced as a way to share information in a manner different from exclusively text-based methods. HTTP was used to transmit Hypertext Markup Language (HTML) documents. HTML documents contained text and links to graphic elements and were viewed using a browser. A browser was essentially a program that converted HTML page text and instructions to a display that merged text and graphics. HTTP pages were located on what became known as the World Wide Web.

Researchers, government agencies, and educational institutions were the primary users of the Internet; for the most part, it was ignored by the general public. As information on the Internet became more consumer oriented and as modem speeds increased, more and more of the general public began to use the Internet. Just as the IBM PC brought about increasingly usable software development tools for microcomputers, the emergence of the Internet caused development tool vendors, from Borland to Microsoft to Sun Microsystems, to create tools for developing ever more powerful Internet applications.

These new Internet development tools (some client-side, some server-side) were attractive not merely to people developing Internet Web pages. Before too long, developers realized that the new Internet development technologies provided some of the solutions they sought to reduce TCO and, specifically, client-side configuration abnormalities. Although the Internet was not of immediate interest to corporate IT managers, the ideas behind the technology were. Developers had created some pretty fantastic applications on the Web, and using these applications from a 28.8-Kbps modem was, if not pleasant, at least possible. What would happen if these applications were operated not over a relatively slow phone line but rather over the overburdened corporate LAN or WAN?

## The Intranet: Bandwidth Nirvana

Applying Web technologies to common corporate IT problems created a new model that accomplished more than developers anticipated. Dubbed the "intranet," this new model simplified client-side configuration. To install an application, you merely set up a TCP/IP stack and a browser (standard equipment in current 32-bit Windows operating systems), pointed the browser at an intranet page, and added the page to the "favorite places" list. Compare this process to the nightmare some traditional application installations can become.

Once installation was simplified, a second benefit was realized: because the Internet grew up in a bandwidth-starved environment, intranet applications ran like a champ on the corporate LAN or WAN. As many industries went merger-crazy (for example, healthcare and banking), applications increasingly needed to operate efficiently in a lower-bandwidth environment. Intranet applications fit the bill.

Today additional unanticipated advantages continue to fuel the growth of intranet applications. Virtually all graduating high school and college students have at least a passing knowledge of the Web and how a browser functions as a user interface. Applications that behave as new employees expect allow training to focus on application-specific issues rather than on user interface issues. Once again, the importance of your comfort level with application tools cannot be overstated.

### Where there is an intranet, there is a server

All intranet systems have at least one thing in common: they require a server. Initially, virtually all Internet servers ran one of the several available UNIX variants that were popular in academia. Servers used Common Gateway Interface (CGI) to acquire information entered by the user at the client browser application. CGI operated in a way that is familiar to UNIX wizards, passing information by means of environment variables and command line redirection. Unfortunately, the supply of UNIX wizards is limited, and corporate IT's demand for intranet developers is seemingly unlimited. This led to a problem. Luckily for you and me, the solution is Windows NT.

## Windows 2000 Hardware Support

Microsoft had long sought to influence the Network Operating System (NOS) world, as it had done with many other operating system and application areas. LAN Manager and OS/2 were early Microsoft attempts to dethrone the leaders in the NOS market, such as Novell NetWare and Banyan VINES. Banyan became a less competitive NOS as time passed, but NetWare was a formidable product that dominated the NOS market for years in terms of sales and installed base.

As previously mentioned, a weakness of NetWare was the difficulty of developing server-based solutions. NetWare NLM development was beyond all but the most dedicated programmers, who would commonly have to move to a new set of tools for NetWare server development.

As Windows NT versions 3.5 and 3.51 became available, the need for a suitable server platform for application development reached its peak. As long as servers continued to do what they had been doing for the last decade (mostly providing printer and file sharing, with some minimal applications running on the server), NetWare was untouchable. When the rules of the game changed, however, and server-based development became more than just a convenience, Windows NT finally found its role as the premier file server for many LAN applications. Whereas sales and installed base numbers can be argued either way, the tide has turned toward Windows NT for many new server installations and for virtually all servers running nontrivial applications. Windows 2000 Server and Windows 2000 Advanced Server should speed up migration by adding improved support for today's hardware.

## WHAT MAKES SERVER-BASED DEVELOPMENT DIFFERENT?

Even if you agree that server-based development is the "next big thing" in software development, you might still wonder why server-based development deserves its own book. You aren't alone. When I first thought about server-based development as a book topic, I had to define exactly what I meant by it. My criterion for what qualifies as server-based development made it clear to me that server-based programs really are different. Recall my definition: a server program is one in which the user interface does not exist or is separate from or incidental to the function of the program. In the case of Windows 2000 Server, programs are created for an operating system that is closely related to a standard desktop operating system, using the same development tools. Let's take a look at how server-based programs differ from other programs and how their differences are handled.

### The Server Is Unattended

Think about the kinds of events that our programs deal with every day:

- A modem dials out and is unable to connect to the computer that it dials.
- The file system tries to write to a sector on the disk and does so only after a number of retries.
- A hardware device fails to initialize properly.
- A user tries but fails to log on to the system several dozen times.
- A resource error occurs. (For example, a file is opened by a different system exclusively, memory or disk space is not available, or a record in a database is locked.)

Now think about how server applications are used. Often you will not find the servers near the users, but rather locked away in wiring closets or in a computer room. Unlike users of desktop systems, users of server-based systems are isolated. If you have ever been involved in technical support, you can well imagine the conversations you have with the users of server-based systems when an error occurs:

*"Technical support, may I help you?"*
*"My ServerTron 2000 has stopped working."*
*"Do you know who was on the system when it failed?"*
*"No."*
*"Do you know when it failed?"*
*"No."*
*"Was there any error message when it happened?"*
*"No one was around—we just noticed that it was not working this morning. The system was locked up."*
*"Please hold on..."*

Obviously, we need a better way to track what is going on with a server application. I have learned from hard experience that even when a user is directly in front of a machine, getting a coherent explanation of what happened when a system failure occurred is often impossible. For server applications, the user is not a potential source of information.

In addition to the lack of user feedback regarding failures, server-based systems do not provide the chance to gather information about impending failures from users sitting at their keyboards. How many times have you decided that a computer is in an unstable state and restarted the computer at a convenient time? Isolated from the actual computer on which the server application is running, the user is less likely to see signs of impending disaster.

The solution to the problems of tracking and user isolation is event logging, which is covered in Chapter 5. The Win32 API (application programming interface) provides functions to log system warnings, events, and errors. For years, programmers have used proprietary log file formats to record system activity. This system is better than nothing, but it is still a challenge to get the kind of systemwide view of activity that is sometimes required to diagnose difficult problems.

Logging events is one thing; making that information available is another. What makes event logging difficult also makes it difficult for logged information to go where it will do some good. The Win32 API provides some functions that can make information available to people away from the keyboard. Messaging API (MAPI) and Telephony API (TAPI), both covered in detail in Chapter 7, aid the server developer by keeping an administrator aware of the state of the system. MAPI allows the system to use an e-mail system. Depending on the problem, MAPI sends a message alerting an administrator. For more immediate errors, TAPI allows a system to page an administrator regarding the problem. This kind of exception reporting allows a system administrator to be on top of system problems without being physically present.

## Resource Leaks Are Hidden Bugs

Imagine a moderately loaded server application. Now further imagine a memory leak that causes the system to allocate 1024 bytes and not release them each time the system performs a particular operation 10 times an hour. The numbers add up quickly. Do the math: 10 KB per hour times 24 hours times 7 days equals 1.68 MB of leaked memory allocations in a week. Run this software for a couple of months, and at best the machine will be thrashing; at worst it will simply stop working. If instead you have a traditional client application, 10 KB per hour times an 8-hour work day equals an 80-KB leak of memory over the course of a day. This leakage probably isn't a show-stopper, but it is surely a result of sloppy programming.

The same rule applies to system objects such as file handles, database locks, and semaphores: add a little to a little, and soon you have a big pile. Errors that in conventional systems might simply inconvenience a single user can in a server-based system stop the work of dozens or even hundreds of people. For example, resource leaks introduced by changes in a Windows NT Service Pack in the Active Server Page DLL required Microsoft to post a "hot fix" not long after the release of the service pack. The root of the problem was that Microsoft Internet Information Server (IIS) would slowly leak memory, eventually degrading performance. The details are reported in the Microsoft Knowledge Base article Q165335. The interesting point about the article is the claim, "It may take a long time for you to notice these performance problems, depending on how often the Active Server Pages are accessed." This key characteristic—the resource leak is not apparent for a long time—makes server-based development different from other types of development.

Microsoft Knowledge Base article Q150934 offers advice on creating a performance monitor log to troubleshoot resource leakage. (We don't cover this topic explicitly in this book.) Using all available tools to discover such resource leaks is required to ensure that a server application will run unattended for long periods of time. Other options for uncovering resource leakage during the development phase include bracketing resource allocations and deallocations with increments and decrements of resource usage variables that allow you to determine whether all resources are freed.

Additional programming methods, such as using C++ constructors and destructors for resource allocation and deallocation, can reduce resource leakage. C++ constructors and destructors still require that allocation and deallocation be coded properly, but properly used classes can ensure that all resources are freed when objects go out of scope. This technique is addressed in the Chapter 8 coverage of the ODBC API. Many Win32 APIs are natural fits for the constructor/destructor model. Some resources are allocated in a constructor, used by the methods of a class, and deallocated in a destructor (called when a stack-based instance of the class goes out of scope or when a heap-based instance is destroyed). This is not a perfect method and should be augmented by structured exception handling, which is another method that can reduce resource leakage.

Structured exception handling is useful for situations in which an instance of a class is created on the heap using the *new* operator. If you allocate memory on the heap and an unexpected situation occurs, you might not delete the instance of the class previously allocated. In these cases (and really for any dynamically allocated resource), you can use *try-catch* and *try-finally* blocks to ensure that the resources are freed. This method is covered in later examples.

## Multitasking Is Essential

Unlike programming for environments such as MS-DOS, server-based development demands multitasking. More than most other applications, server-based applications must be able to perform more than one task at a time, with very rare exceptions. In a traditional client-based application, an application commonly begins performing a task, displays the hourglass, and continues the task until completion. In a server application, refusing to respond to clients while performing a task is rarely acceptable.

We have come a long way since the MS-DOS/Windows 3.x days, when effective multitasking was simply not an option, or at least not a simple option. Many years ago my company developed an application in C++ for MS-DOS that needed to handle many activities at the same time: react to the user at the keyboard, redraw a high-resolution display, and, most important, respond to an outside device, in this case a box that received radio messages. The radio messages needed to be acknowledged within one-tenth of a second. Our first thought was to put a check for data on the serial port in the keyboard routine (polling while waiting for a keystroke) and sprinkle polling calls throughout the screen redraw routine. This was dismissed almost immediately because we could not guarantee that the acknowledgment would be sent in less than one-tenth of a second. Missing an acknowledgment would cause multiple copies of each message to be sent, making the system work harder than it had to.

The solution in the MS-DOS environment was to install an interrupt handler or two. Interrupts are designed to allow a program (called an interrupt service routine, or ISR) to be called asynchronously. They are commonly tied to hardware events; in this case, the event was the arrival of a character on the serial port, called a timer tick. The purpose of the first ISR was to enable us to use interrupt-driven serial communication. In this way, we could be sure that no information would be dropped because subsequent information overwrote it in the communications buffer. This serial communication placed all messages in a globally accessible queue. One problem was solved: messages were no longer missed because they were not received in time from the serial port. The next problem was acknowledging the messages. This might have been possible within the serial communications handler, but we did not want to make that ISR take too much time.

We solved the second problem by installing an additional ISR that occurred 18.2 times a second. During this ISR, we quickly sent an acknowledgment to the radio box, marked the record in the global queue as acknowledged, and returned from the interrupt. Finally, about once a minute (but not very strictly timed), we sent the messages received to a database. This was not done during any ISR since that can be a lengthy process (lengthy by ISR standards—perhaps a few seconds).

One of the lessons I learned during this process was that the globally accessible queue needed to be protected from multiple competing processes. Eventually, the solution was to move to a double-buffered queue and create a global flag that indicated when the queue was in use. In fact, guarding against data corruption was a bit more complicated than I can describe here, but suffice it to say that this sort of grungy multitasking was not elegant.

Windows 3.x provided a sort of multitasking called cooperative multitasking. While cooperative multitasking was better than nothing, it was not all that much better. Win32 provides support for preemptive multitasking, closer to the interrupt handling of the MS-DOS system mentioned in the previous paragraphs. In addition to preemptive multitasking among multiple applications, a single application can have multiple threads of execution, simply called threads. Win32 multitasking support goes far beyond just supporting threads; it implements synchronization objects that can help threads stay out of one another's way. These API features will be covered more fully in Chapter 2, and examples of multitasking can be found throughout the book.

## SERVER-BASED APPLICATIONS

Current server-based applications can be broken up into two broad classes: traditional server-based applications (often the server part of traditional client/server applications) and Web-based server applications. While they share many features, they are distinct, especially within the Win32 world. Explicit Win32 API support for traditional server-based applications is limited, although many APIs assist in developing these types of applications. Conversely, the Win32 API explicitly supports Web-based server development with the Internet Server API (ISAPI, covered briefly here and extensively in Chapter 10).

### Traditional Server-Based Systems

Traditional server-based systems are best examined by use of example. Microsoft SQL Server is a good example of a traditional server-based application. When SQL Server is used, there is most often a specialized client application that interacts with the server-side program by using one of several possible communications protocols. SQL Server supports named pipes, Windows Sockets, IPX/SPX, Banyan VINES, and

Multi protocol communications. The two most popular communications protocols for client/server development, named pipes and Windows Sockets, are covered in Chapter 12. The client communicates a request to the server (generally in the form of a string of SQL language commands), and the server processes the request and sends back a result set or an error code indicating that the request could not be processed.

Continuing with our SQL Server example, the client program could use either an Open Database Connectivity (ODBC) driver, an OLE DB driver, or the DB-Library API (dbLib) to deliver the request. The details of this communication are of little concern to the server program proper. Requests can come in simultaneously from clients using ODBC and dbLib, through named pipes and Windows Sockets. In any case, the core server application behaves the same way no matter what driver is used, delivering the result set to the client.

SQL Server is designed to use the Win32 API to allow multiple threads of execution to handle requests at the same time. In the case of SQL Server, the number of threads can be configured, as shown in Figure 1-4. A client configuration program allows each client to select any supported communications protocol on a per-client basis.

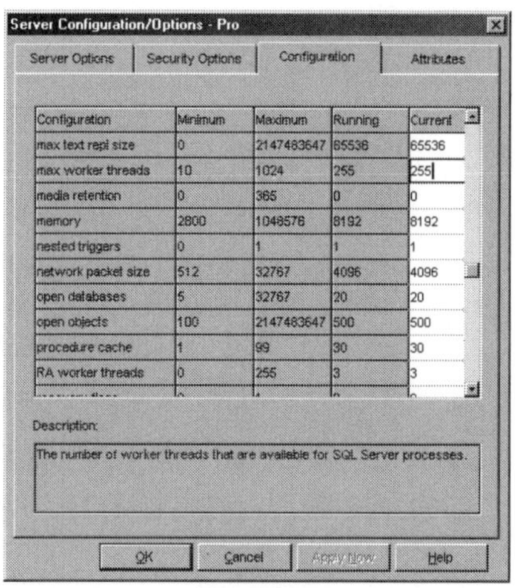


**Figure 1-4** *Microsoft SQL Server configuration dialog box, showing the configurable number of worker threads.*

## The Web-Based Server

In traditional server-based systems, the methods used to communicate between client and server are almost incidental to the server. In fact, if the developer of the system so desires, the communications component can be completely isolated for other operations, allowing the protocol used to be switched dynamically at run time. An example of a protocol-independent API can be found in my book *Win32 Client-Server Developer's Guide* (Addison-Wesley, 1996).

In Web-based servers, the protocol used is not at all incidental. A number of Internet/intranet-specific protocols are used exclusively for Web-based servers. As TCP/IP becomes the networking protocol of choice, programmers regard the exclusive use of protocols as a strength. The limited protocol choice brings us to another strength of Web-based systems.

In contrast to the huge array of client software available for traditional server-based systems, Web-based systems use a single type of universal client, the Web browser. The exclusive use of the browser as client software does limit some user interface choices. Imagine what the configuration dialog box from Figure 1-4 would look like if the client were a browser; it would be different, perhaps in some ways even inferior, but it would reveal several distinct advantages compared with using a traditional fat client application:

- *Simpler installation.* No special client-side installation is required.
- *Smaller installation.* "Universal" client software commonly takes up less space than a single traditional client software installation.
- *Accessibility of resources.* The use of the configuration utility is not limited by network location in the same way traditional client software might be. Because protocols are used by the browser, resources on the Internet are just as accessible as resources on a local network.
- *Familiar user interface.* Users are becoming more familiar with the browser user-interface model. Like it or not, this may be the user interface of the twenty-first century (or at least the first few years of the twenty-first century).

Different APIs and system structures can be used exclusively for Web-based systems. The distinction between Web-based and traditional server-based systems is much clearer when discussing Win32 servers. UNIX systems commonly use software that is much more like traditional server-based systems for interactions with Web clients.

One of the problems with using a traditional server-based system for a Web application is the nature of the interactions with Web clients: Web pages are requested by and sent to clients via a connectionless protocol, HTTP. So each transaction (a single page requested and received) is atomic, with a new "session" started when the next page is requested. This model is quite appropriate for most of the activity that takes place on the World Wide Web. The traditional way to create Web-based server applications is to call individual executable or script files when needed (for instance, when a form is filled out on the browser client). This model initiates processes each time a user selects a given control on the screen, with the process living just long enough to execute the user's request.

Unfortunately, creating a process and destroying it after handling a single request is expensive in terms of system resources. Using this model on a Web site that contains only a single infrequently used server-based application might not be a problem. Sites such as www.microsoft.com or more interactive intranet sites are another matter entirely. These sites might receive thousands or even tens of thousands of client requests that require more than the server simply returning a static HTML page.

ISAPI is Microsoft's solution to this problem. Netscape offers a similar API (the Netscape Server API, or NSAPI). The goal of both APIs is to allow existence of a process that can service multiple client requests and not require constant creation and destruction of processes. ISAPI solves the problem by specifying a predefined set of entry points in a DLL. For this method to work, the actual Web server must be told about the DLL (generally through the registry) and must load the DLL once. This single instance of the DLL is responsible for handling the requests of many clients.

An example of what can be done using ISAPI is the ASP.DLL ISAPI program that comes standard with IIS. This DLL handles the conversion of Active Server Pages (ASP) documents. When you request a page with the ASP extension (either explicitly or because an ASP file is the default page), the ASP.DLL is called and the scripting in the ASP file is executed. The result is a standard HTML document that is returned to the browser for display. The browser client knows nothing of all the activity that has gone on to return the HTML document. Active Server Pages will be covered in detail in Chapter 9.

## WIN32 SUPPORT FOR SERVER-BASED PROGRAMMING

In the computer world, an interface is a set of operating system functions that determine how your program performs its tasks. An application programming interface is analogous to a user interface. Think about how you use a word processor. When you are entering text into the computer, the UI controls how you direct the word processing program to do what you want, and the program provides feedback through the UI. For instance, the word processing program I use (Microsoft Word) initially presents me with a blank document. A menu and a toolbar appear at the top of the window, allowing me to quickly access frequently used items. (See Figure 1-5.) Just below the toolbar is a ruler control, which might be the most familiar part of the interface for those of us old enough to remember typing on a real typewriter.

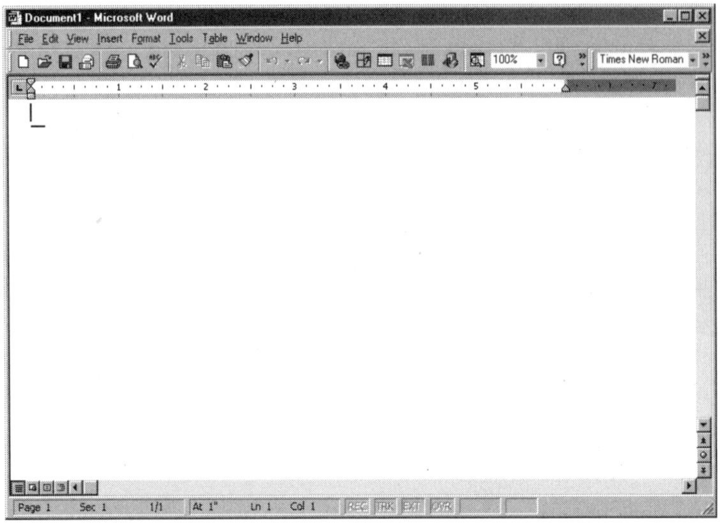


**Figure 1-5** *The Word UI.*

The program gives me feedback as I use it: I type and text appears on the screen. More subtle examples of feedback from the user interface exist as well. For example, if I were to misspell something or use a proper name like "Reilly," the program would display a squiggly red line under the word to communicate its recognition of a possible misspelling. Microsoft WordPad, the basic word processing program that ships with Microsoft Windows 2000, lacks many of these feedback features. However, its UI (shown in Figure 1-6) is very similar to that of Microsoft Word.

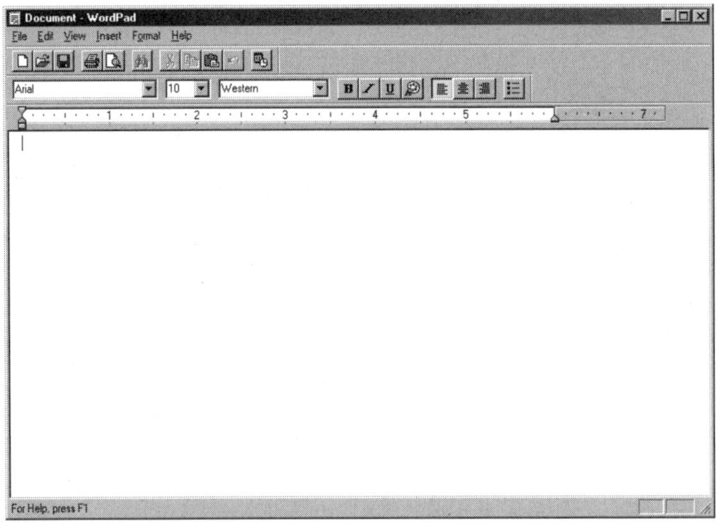


**Figure 1-6** *The WordPad UI.*

In the same way that a UI allows users to send and receive information, an API allows programmers to call a function and receive status information in a structured way. For instance, the API for the standard C run-time library provides a set of functions (such as *fopen* and *fread*) that allow the programmer to work with files. In the case of *fopen*, the function returns NULL if the file cannot be opened. The programmer can check the global variable *errno* when *fopen* returns NULL to receive feedback on why the function failed.

You've noticed that the user interfaces of similar programs, such as word processing programs like Word and WordPad, are similar. Although differences exist, similarities make switching from one program to another easier. Many APIs are also similar in external structure. Their similarity makes them convenient to use. For instance, many APIs have three phases: first you allocate and open resources; next you use the resources; and finally you close and free resources previously opened. Thus it is reasonable to generalize from one API to the next. If you have used the C run-time library functions, you should have little difficulty using a named pipe (even though a named pipe is internally very different from a file). In addition, many Windows APIs use the same kernel synchronization objects. (Kernel synchronization objects will be discussed in Chapter 2.) These objects are used in a similar manner with each API: you create or open the object, use it, and then you close the object's handle.

Many APIs support server development within Windows 2000. Some of them will be briefly mentioned here and some will receive additional coverage in later chapters. Not all the APIs we discuss will be similar. However, some of these APIs do resemble other APIs, and that can make future learning easier.

## The Console API

You probably know that you can run many MS-DOS programs in Windows 2000. You might also know that you can create 32-bit console applications. But do you know which of the following API functions cannot be called by a 32-bit console application?

*LoadLibrary*
*MessageBox*
*RegQueryValue*

OK, this is a trick question. You can call all three functions. And that is the point of this discussion: the tasks performed by a Windows 2000 service can be accomplished by a console application. One of the best ways to start creating a service is to create a console application that has the required functionality before converting the application to a service.

You can use the Microsoft Visual C++ new application wizard to create a basic framework for console applications. Within the framework created by the wizard, you can use the C run-time library functions to print messages to the console, which allows you to display messages similar to the way MS-DOS text-based programs do.

## The Service API

Given that a console application can perform the tasks of a service, why bother converting a console program to a service? First and foremost, a server application often needs to run on a server computer that might be locked away somewhere in a computer room. Probably no one will be present at the console of the machine to run the server application if the machine is restarted. In the "good old days" of MS-DOS systems, you could work around this (and I actually did) by making sure that the Autoexec.bat file set up any necessary conditions (such as network connections) and then started the server application. Unfortunately, Windows 2000 might not be able to set up all of these necessary conditions. Windows 2000 provides an alternative method of performing such a task; this method is a service. Windows 2000 makes it easy to automatically restart a service after a computer server restarts.

You create a service using the service API. Two service API functions—the service main function and the control handler function—allow a program to register as a service with the Service Control Manager (SCM). Further, the program can run under the authority of the system account or another user's account. (Programs that run under the authority of another account have the access rights of that account.)

## The Impersonation API

The service API allows a service to work under the authority of the system account or some other user account. However, imagine you were creating a service that would read and write files on the server. If the service was running under the system account's authority or a user account with administrative authority, it could clearly access all the files on the server. This situation might be appropriate in some cases, but what if you wanted to give users different authorities?

One option would be to create a security system for your application that would allow you to specify the rights for each user based on the directory where the files are located. This would not be a trivial undertaking; it would require administrators of the system to methodically set up security for each of the users who will act as clients connected to the server. Fortunately, we can avoid this kind of redundant work because there is a better way to give users authorities—impersonation.

Several APIs support impersonation. Much like guests at a costume party, the services can put on different user "masks" when required and operate on resources as if they were being run by other users. This ability to impersonate another user and then allow the operating system to do its normal rights checking could be duplicated programmatically if programmers tested the rights of the user on the client machine for each operation. Impersonation is much better because the check is done by the operating system at the time of each request.

## The Event Logging API

Event logging allows programs—not merely servers—to log events as special system supported files. In fact, most entries in the event log of a normal Microsoft Windows NT system will be service-related messages. The event logging API allows for more than just message logging. The messages can be retrieved from the local machine or, with proper authority, from a remote machine. In addition, you can save messages in different languages. This is clearly a better method of handling error messages than the humble *printf* statement.

## RAS, MAPI, and TAPI

Remote Access Service (RAS) is software that allows remote clients to access a network server by means of a modem. RAS allows you to connect to a remote computer and its network as if your computer were on the remote computer's LAN.

TAPI allows you to use a computer to interact with the telephone. Using TAPI, you can dial or answer the phone, as well as retrieve caller ID information about incoming calls. Advanced support for call-center operations is also available. Of course, you could try to manually interact with the serial ports, but TAPI provides a more integrated solution.

MAPI supports applications that need to send and receive e-mail. Why might a server need to send or receive e-mail? Well, for instance, imagine a hospital financial system that tracked billing exceptions. A good implementation of this system might mail a report of outstanding exceptions to the responsible parties each evening.

> **NOTE** Some competing e-mail options might be worth consideration today: Post Office Protocol (POP) and Simple Network Mail Protocol (SNMP) are both noteworthy. We will not be covering these options.

## Database Connectivity

Eventually, your server will need to connect to a database. The differences in performance between the various options and the stated direction of Microsoft for database access from Win32 platforms means you have a lot of decisions to make. We'll examine two popular database connectivity options: Open Database Connectivity (ODBC) and Active Data Objects (ADO).

ODBC is a long established option for database access. Most databases are accessible through one or more ODBC drivers. In addition, many tools exist for manipulating ODBC-compliant databases, including Microsoft Access and Seagate Crystal Reports. Visual C++ also has support within MFC for ODBC compliant databases.

ADO provides a more object-oriented method of data access. The Connection and Recordset objects, among others, allow for connection to databases and the retrieval of records. This model is frequently used with some of the technologies related to Microsoft Visual Basic such as VBScript, but Visual C++ programmers have other reasonable alternatives.

## Active Server Pages

Strictly speaking, Active Server Pages (ASP) is not an API, but it does provide support for the creation of server applications. ASP is supported by IIS on Windows 2000; on Windows 98, it is supported by means of a similar system known as Personal Web Server. Whereas ASP is primarily for use on Windows 2000, it is also available from third-party vendors for UNIX.

ASP is server-side script that gets executed on the server with the intent of delivering HTML content to the browser. The script is often VBScript, though JScript (Microsoft's version of JavaScript) is supported as well. VBScript is a simplified version of Visual Basic that supports much of the same functionality as Visual Basic, with some important exceptions. The chief difference is that you don't need to type variables—every variable is a variant. In addition to script running directly, it can use compiled components for augmentation by creating objects based on ActiveX controls.

## The Internet Server API

The Internet Server API (ISAPI) is Microsoft's solution for creating high-performance Web applications. In the UNIX world, Internet server applications are almost invariably Common Gateway Interface (CGI) applications. Grady Booch, father of the Unified Modeling Language and author of many books on object-oriented analysis and design, says CGI is "The Duct Tape of Web development" (Software Development Conference, May, 1999). CGI is a standard for interfacing a Web browser with an external application. When the user enters a URL that points to a CGI script, the browser executes the script. The information from the browser, including the URL typed into the address bar (and information entered in any HTML form) is passed to the CGI program. The CGI program then generates HTML output and sends it to the standard output using *printf* and similar functions.

This approach is problematic for several reasons. The most significant is that spawning a new process each time a user request comes in is fairly expensive, limiting the scalability of the server program. In addition, no explicit support exists for programs to parse the incoming information.

ISAPI is the solution for Web developers who work on Windows 2000 using IIS. ISAPI allows the creation of DLLs that export specific functions and can be called by IIS when required. The ISAPI DLL is loaded into the memory of IIS and, once used, remains loaded until IIS is unloaded.

### ISAPI extensions

ISAPI supports two distinct interfaces that allow creation of very different applications. The first is an ISAPI extension. ISAPI extensions are DLLs that are called in the same way as CGI programs: as part of a URL or as a default action for a particular site. For example, imagine an ISAPI extension named GETINFO.DLL that exposes a single function named *GETNIC*. If the DLL is stored on a machine named PRO, the following URL calls the ISAPI extension, loading the DLL into the IIS memory space if required:

*http://pro/getinfo.dll?getnic*

This process is a huge improvement over CGI, and it can often offer impressive improvement over alternatives such as ASP.

### ISAPI filters

ISAPI filters are similar to ISAPI extensions in the way they are implemented, but their functionality differs significantly. While ISAPI extensions duplicate functionality that could also be provided by CGI or ASP, ISAPI filters provide functionality that cannot be easily duplicated other ways.

Like ISAPI extensions, ISAPI filters are DLLs, but unlike extensions they are never called directly. Instead, every call to the Web server where the filter is installed passes through the filter, presuming that the filter has told IIS that it wants receive the particular notification.

What are ISAPI filters good for that ISAPI extensions, ASP, or CGI are not? One primary use for filters is to create custom user authentication. Since every session generates one notification that allows the ISAPI filter to authenticate the user, custom operations can be performed. Other common uses include the compression and encryption of content.

## Communication APIs

Virtually no server is an island. Thus, in addition to RAS, TAPI, and MAPI, which are often used to communicate with remote clients, other protocols exist that allow the server to communicate with local clients. (Using RAS to establish the network connection, these APIs can be used to communicate with more remote clients as well.) Note that while we will be developing servers, it is not uncommon for a "server" to be in the role of "client" with respect to other systems. An example of this situation is a communication server in a healthcare organization that needs to communicate with a central hospital system. From the perspective of the end users of the communication server, the server is a server. However, to the central hospital system, the communication server is in fact a client. We will be covering communication APIs in Chapter 12, but they are not the central thrust of this book. Other books specifically dealing with the client/server interaction offer more complete coverage.

### TCP/IP

The Internet has made TCP/IP almost a household name. When we use TCP/IP these days we are usually using some "well known" protocol such as HTTP, FTP, or even Telnet, but our own servers will often need to communicate to clients using our own custom server.

TCP/IP is normally accessed using sockets, a common UNIX API suite that allows both clients and servers to communicate with each other. Windows 2000 supports Windows Sockets (commonly referred to as Winsock), a modified version of the standard sockets API. Winsock is a superset of the standard UNIX sockets, which emphasizes support for the cooperative multitasking model used by Windows 3.x. We will primarily cover those parts of Winsock that are appropriate for serious Windows 2000 server development.

### Named pipes

Named pipes is an alternative to TCP/IP. In some cases named pipes offers significant advantages, while in others it can create an application that is slower than it otherwise would be if it used TCP/IP. Using named pipes is similar to working with files, which is not surprising, since named pipes is actually implemented as a file system. If you search the registry on a Windows 2000 machine for NPFS (Named Pipes File System), you will see it listed along with the other file systems.

Named pipes is an authenticated protocol, which presents both some challenges and some opportunities. Regarding the challenges, services accepting named pipe connections must take special care and allow the service to run under the local system account. As for opportunities, named pipes allows for convenient impersonation, using the *ImpersonateNamedPipeClient* function. Named pipes can be about as fast as TCP/IP on a local area network, although my experience is that establishing the connection can take longer than TCP/IP. Over a wide area network, the speed difference becomes more noticeable and TCP/IP generally comes out on top.

> **NOTE** Named pipes has one unusual feature. If a client and a server are located on the same machine, a *local pipe* is used. This arrangement offers outstanding performance and would always be my choice when the client and server can be or might be located on the same machine.

When choosing communications protocols it is important to consider whether your testing requires that you use a Windows 95 or 98 machine as a "server." If it does, TCP/IP is the only choice between these two protocols. Only Windows NT or Windows 2000 can act as a server for named pipes.

# A PEEK AT SQL SERVER

Before you create a world-class server that will run on Windows 2000, you should first examine an existing server. An excellent example is Microsoft SQL Server. We of course do not have access to the details of the implementation of SQL Server, nor do we have the source code. So, how can we gather information?

The best way is to install and configure the server because the configuration options provide insight into the design process. Notice the way the server allows clients to communicate with it. Figure 1-7 illustrates the options that are available for the client, including the ability to select communications over named pipes or TCP/IP. Although implementation differences exist between the two protocols, the server and client software mask those differences.

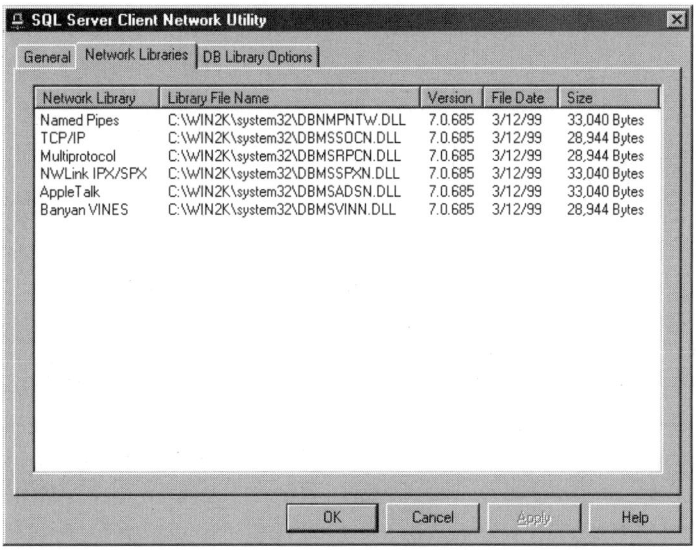


**Figure 1-7** *SQL Server options available for the client.*

Also, notice that SQL Server implements a complex model for handling clients. The common models for servers are single threaded (serializing access to the server), one thread per client (appropriate for some servers with few simultaneous clients), or N-clients per thread. Figure 1-8 illustrates the SQL Server configuration screen that allows selection of the maximum number of worker threads, implying that SQL Server uses the N-threads per client model.

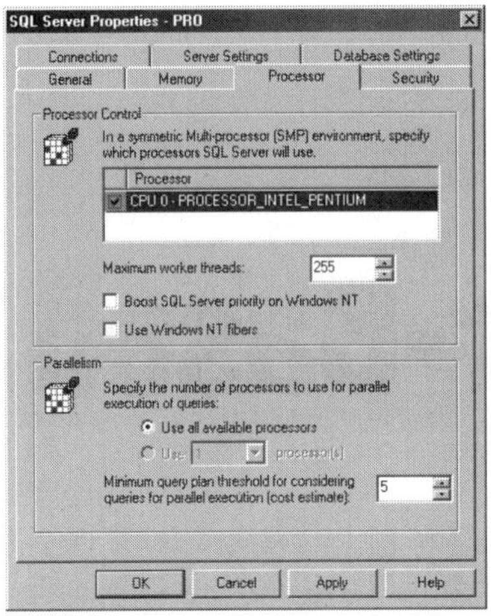


**Figure 1-8** *SQL Server configuration screen.*

# CONCLUSION

How different is server-based development from traditional client-side software development? In general, it is very different—but different does not imply worse. The requirements are merely diverse and in some ways more intense.

The differences between traditional client development and server development are changing the world of software development. First, servers must run unattended, a requirement that means server applications must find alternative ways to handle and report problems. Second, resource leaks are hidden bugs that are much more likely to be revealed by server applications than by traditional client-based applications; resource leaks are not obscured by the on/off cycle common with client-based applications. Finally, multitasking is essential for most developers of server-based applications.

The resulting systems can be the antidote for what ails corporate IT professionals and independent software vendors alike. By moving more functionality to powerful microprocessor-based PC servers, the total cost of ownership for client PCs can decrease, while the server still remains less remote than the glass houses of yesterday's mainframes. Perhaps as the newer Web-based systems become fully deployed, client/server systems will finally begin to realize the promise of free software movement to clients, with minimal client intervention.

*Chapter 2*

# Server-Based Development 101

This chapter will provide you with the theoretical underpinnings required for production of robust and reliable server-based systems. In many respects, the knowledge required to develop server-based systems is the same knowledge required to develop traditional client-side systems. Although important differences exist between client-side and server-based systems, most folks capable of constructing one can also construct the other.

The key issues covered in this chapter are multitasking, resource sharing, and user authentication. Client/server communication is another significant element of server-based development that will be addressed, though not extensively. (See the Annotated Bibliography for client/server communication resources.)

## MULTITASKING BASICS

Multitasking is the ability of a computer program to perform—or seem to perform—more than one task at a time. While multitasking can take many forms, cooperative multitasking (CM) and preemptive multitasking (PM) are two distinct models commonly used today. Most systems are moving toward the preemptive multitasking model.

Just as the assumptions about stand-alone applications were invalidated by LAN support requirements, multitasking invalidates programs that make assumptions about local resources. The issues involved are not terribly dissimilar: stand-alone applications were designed as if no other competing computers existed, and programs today often presume a static path of operations in which resources global to the program can still be used without concern for contention.

## Cooperative Multitasking

The first multitasking model is cooperative multitasking; CM was used in Microsoft Windows prior to Windows NT and Windows 95. The use of CM implied a certain model of Windows programming that is still employed, though often hidden beneath an application framework (Microsoft Visual C++ and Microsoft Foundation Classes) or a visual programming model (Microsoft Visual Basic or Borland Delphi).

As the name implies, CM requires the cooperation of the programs involved. However, more than mere resource sharing, cooperation enables a program to take an active part in making the system available to other programs. At the heart of any Windows 3.x program is a message pump routine that resembles the following:

```
while (GetMessage(&msg,NULL,0,0))
{
    TranslateMessage(&msg);
    DispatchMessage(&msg);
}
```

All three function calls are Windows API functions—not your own. How does your code run? *DispatchMessage* calls a window procedure that you have written if the message received is destined for the window associated with that message procedure.

However, the call to *GetMessage* does more than simply get the next message for your program to process. It also returns control to Windows, which allows other programs to run if no messages are available for your program or if the messages waiting are low priority (such as requests to paint the screen or timer notifications). Periodically calling *GetMessage* is more than a requirement for your program to get its next message; it is critical to the correct functioning of the entire Windows system. Note that Windows 3.x device drivers do gain control without calling *GetMessage*, *PeekMessage*, or *WaitMessage*.

The CM model requires the cooperation of every program in the system. Each program can behave as if it is the only program running between calls to *GetMessage* or between calls to another function that yields control to Windows. Of course, it is possible that you will discover one program that will not work and play well with others. This is the problem with the CM model.

If you have used Windows 3.x for any period of time, you have seen the symptoms of this problem. You initiate a task, the hourglass cursor appears, and you wait. You wait for an awfully long time. Hardware interrupts are not disabled because your mouse moves and the Num Lock light toggles when you press the Num Lock key. The machine seems to be doing something, but the task never seems to complete. You have discovered the chink in cooperative multitasking armor: CM requires cooperation, and sometimes we write programs that refuse to cooperate. When this situation occurs in Windows 3.0, the machine always requires a reboot. In Windows 3.1 and later, you have one last chance to recover by pressing Ctrl-Alt-Delete; if the system is suffering because of a program that is not relinquishing control, you are given a chance to close the offending application and continue. Of course, all your unsaved work is lost.

Understanding why Windows 3.x used this model requires an understanding of the hardware limitations that existed when Windows was first envisioned. The first version of Windows to receive widespread use was Windows 386, which became available shortly before Windows 3.0. The determining factor that made the CM model attractive was the necessity of running Windows on both a 386 and a 286. CM allowed multiple programs to work with very little overhead imposed by the multitasking model.

Other popular systems have used CM for the same reasons. NetWare uses a CM model, though the model is implemented in such a way that it imposes less structure on programs written for that platform. Dozens of NetWare function calls can yield control to the operating system. This requires that NetWare NLM programmers know which calls can yield control so they can ensure that any necessary events take place without operating system intervention.

## Preemptive Multitasking

CM is sometimes called nonpreemptive multitasking to contrast it with the other major model: preemptive multitasking. PM seems much simpler on the surface, but its implementation is often more complex at the operating system level and can create unforeseen problems for the application programmer.

The basic premise of PM is that a scheduler at the operating system level controls how long each process is allowed to operate. The amount of time is often called a time slice. After the time slice is up, another program is allowed to function and the original program waits for the scheduler to allow it to operate again. This seems like a more reasonable model of operation than the CM model. Problems, however, await the unaware.

Imagine you have two operations: one in a function *dothis* and the other in a function *dothat*. Consider the following code:

```
dothis();
dothat();
```

You cannot be sure that these operations will be performed in their entirety without other processes taking control. If *dothis* operates on some globally available resource (for instance, a file or a device), you cannot be assured that *dothat* will get to the resource before some other process operates on it. This is a major departure from the model that presumes the program operating is in total control of the machine.

## MULTITHREADING

In addition, many processes can contain multiple threads of execution. A thread is a lightweight process, meaning that it is similar to a process but shares resources such as global data with other threads. It is useful to think of the relationship between processes and threads as illustrated in Figure 2-1.

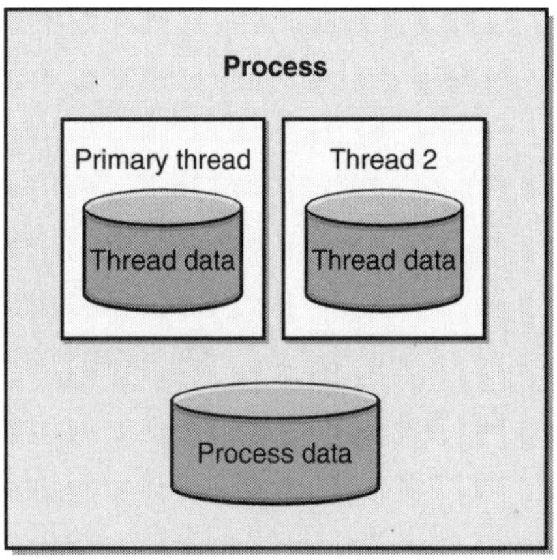


**Figure 2-1** *The relationship between processes and threads.*

Each process contains some global information and at least one thread. In many respects, this single thread is no different from other threads that the application may generate. However, one significant difference exists: when the primary thread exits, the entire process ends (including any currently operating threads).

Although they are efficient, multiple-threaded programs are more difficult to create and debug than single-threaded programs. The reason is that in most cases, multiple single-threaded processes will not be operating on exactly the same resources at exactly the same time. This is precisely what multiple threads within a single process often need to do. For example, one or more threads might try to access a global variable at the same time.

Other problems exist as well. Imagine that the following brief code segment exists in a function that is called from multiple threads:

```
// A global variable...
extern long numProcessed=0;
// Function declarations...
```

```
void DoInitialStuff(void);
void DoOtherProcessing(struct THING *thing);

// A function called by multiple threads...
ProcessThing(struct THING *thing)
{
    if (numProcessed==0)
    {
        DoInitialStuff();
    }
    numProcessed++;
    DoOtherProcessing(thing);
}
```

We can see from the code that some initial processing must be done only once when the first object is processed. In isolation from other code operating at the same time, the *DoInitialStuff* function will run only once. However, with multithreaded programs, we cannot assume that code will operate in such isolation. Imagine two threads calling *ProcessThing* at about the same time. Normally, not more than one thing is happening at exactly the same time (with symmetric multiprocessing [SMP] support, this is not always true—more on that later), but there is no assurance that each thread will perform *ProcessThing* as an atomic unit. So given two threads calling *ProcessThing*, the following order of execution is possible:

| ***Thread 1*** | ***Thread 2*** |
|---|---|
| 1. `if (numProcessed==0)` (Evaluates TRUE) | |
| | 2. `if (numProcessed==0)` (Evaluates TRUE) |
| 3. `DoInitialStuff();` (Do work that should be done only once) | |
| | 4. `DoInitialStuff();` (Do work that should be done only once) |

SMP machines create a more complex situation with a much smaller margin of error. Given more than one processor, an SMP operating system such as Windows 2000 will actually execute more than a single instruction at the same instant. In the previous case, the calls to check on the number of records processed or the calls to *DoInitialStuff* could happen at exactly the same instant.

The previous example presumes global variables; however, these variables do not need to be of truly global scope. They could be static members of a class, or perhaps even other types of resources. For instance, some code might operate under the assumption that it is safe to write to and read from a file local to the system in which the operation is taking place (for example, an INI file located in the Windows directory). This might have been a reasonable assumption in the past if the program ensured that only a single instance of itself was running. Given the multithreaded scenario, it is not sufficient to ensure that a single instance of the program is running. Of course, other problems with this kind of model exist as well, and examples less contrived than this one abound. What programmers need is some way to coordinate the sharing of resources among multiple threads and processes.

## SYNCHRONIZATION OBJECTS

The process of coordinating resource use among multiple threads is known as *synchronization*. Basically, a thread synchronizes itself with other threads by putting itself to sleep until the operating system signals it to wake up by means of a synchronization object. (A sleeping thread does not execute and is therefore very efficient.)

The Win32 API provides several synchronization objects. Of these, the easiest to use is the critical section. The others are kernel objects and include events, mutexes, semaphores, and waitable timers.

### DON'T ROLL YOUR OWN

While it might be tempting to "roll your own" synchronization objects, don't. These objects may appear simple, but it is difficult to properly synchronize access to code using variables not under operating system control. For instance, you might try the following construction:

```
BOOL gate1=FALSE;
BOOL gate2=FALSE;
if (gate1==FALSE)
{
    gate1=TRUE;
    if (gate2==FALSE)
    {
        gate2=TRUE;
        // Do something protected...
    }
}
```

Code such as this is very problematic. For example, there is no guarantee that the first test of gate1 will be performed atomically with the setting of gate1 in the next line. All manner of race conditions could result from this kind of code. If you are interested in more information, refer to Andrew Tanenbaum's *Modern Operating Systems* (Prentice-Hall, 1992).

The kernel objects differ from critical sections because they can be used across process boundaries. The flip side of this benefit is that these objects require a switch from user mode to kernel mode to function, which makes them slower than critical sections. A distinguishing feature of two of the kernel object types (events and semaphores) is that they allow resource counting, while critical sections and one of the other object types (mutexes) allow only for exclusive access. Table 2-1 summarizes the differences among the synchronization objects.

**TABLE 2-1**
**SYNCHRONIZATION OBJECTS**

| *Name* | *Cross Process* | *Resource Counting* |
|---|---|---|
| Critical section | No | No |
| Event | Yes | Not automatically |
| Mutex | Yes | No |
| Semaphore | Yes | Yes |
| Waitable timer | Yes | No |

Cross-process object types are by definition slower than critical sections, which exist within a single process space. Note also that use of cross-process objects requires that a name be given to the object when it's created. Also, these named objects—along with memory-mapped files—share a common name space. Trying to create a named synchronization object will fail if an object of that name already exists, even if the name is for a different type of object. Thus, a naming convention for these objects might be important for larger projects.

> **NOTE** The name space limitation can be used to your advantage. If you want to be sure that only one instance of your application is running on a system at once, have each instance try to create an instance of a specific, kernel-based synchronization object with a specific name. The first instance of the program will be able to create the program, but subsequent instances will not. This can be a more reliable way to sense the running of the application than checking window titles or classes.

## Critical Sections

The critical section is an extremely efficient way to synchronize global resource use among multiple threads, and it is often the easiest method to understand. The example beginning on page 30 can be rewritten to operate safely in the multithreaded world as follows:

```
// A global variable...
extern long numProcessed=0;
```

*(continued)*

```
// Function declarations...
void DoInitialStuff(void);
void DoOtherProcessing(struct THING *thing);
// A critical section variable...
CRITICAL_SECTION CriticalSection;


WinMain()
/* Or some other function that is called before
 additional threads are created */
{
    InitializeCriticalSection(&CriticalSection);
    // Other work, create and use other threads...

    // Eventually, before exiting...
    DeleteCriticalSection(&CriticalSection);
}

// A function called by multiple threads...
ProcessThing(struct THING *thing)
{
    EnterCriticalSection(&CriticalSection);
    if (numProcessed==0)
    {
        DoInitialStuff();
    }
    numProcessed++;
    LeaveCriticalSection(&CriticalSection);
    DoOtherProcessing(thing);
}
```

This code could be fine-tuned—especially if *DoInitialStuff* takes a long time to complete—but it will work properly with multiple threads executing it (assuming that *DoOtherProcessing* does not access global resources).

In general, the less done within the critical section the better. In the example above, *DoInitialStuff* acts as a choke point, causing all threads calling *ProcessThing* to wait until the call to *DoInitialStuff* returns and the *numProcessed* variable is properly incremented. In this example, that would not be too heavy a burden since there is only a single call to *DoInitialStuff*. In other circumstances, a critical section might cause all processing to be serialized, thus losing some of the benefits of multithreading.

Before it is used, a critical section must be initialized by a call to *InitializeCriticalSection*. Before the application terminates, the critical section must be deleted by a call to *DeleteCriticalSection*:

```
VOID InitializeCriticalSection(LPCRITICAL_SECTION lpCriticalSection);
VOID DeleteCriticalSection(LPCRITICAL_SECTION lpCriticalSection);
```

In general, it is safest to call these functions in the application initialization and termination code, to ensure that no other threads are active.

Between the return from the call to *EnterCriticalSection* and the call to *LeaveCriticalSection*, any other threads calling *EnterCriticalSection* using the same critical section object will be blocked. *EnterCriticalSection* does not return until the calling thread is the only thread with ownership of the critical section. This blocking process is a problem addressed by other functions not shown in the above example.

> **NOTE** MFC users take special note. Even though the *Lock* member function of the *CCriticalSection* class can take a single parameter, tantalizingly named *dwTimeout*, this parameter is ignored, and *Lock* is a blocking function, just like *EnterCriticalSection* in the native Win32 API.

### Blocking functions and deadlock potential

Blocking functions create several potential problems. The first of these occurs when the function simply does not return because a resource required for it to return is not available. For instance, if you use a critical section to synchronize access to a file shared by multiple threads, the thread using the file (and thus owning the critical section) may not be able to continue and may put up a dialog box for the user to make a decision. If the user is not sitting at the terminal, the thread will not give up the critical section, meaning that other threads waiting for the same critical section (to gain access to the shared resource) will be blocked. Of course, this example is silly—you should never place user interface code within a critical section—but less contrived instances of deadlock with blocking functions abound.

For example, a problem arises when multiple resources are needed and the order in which they are requested differs in different threads. In the following case, thread A has critical section 1 and is waiting for critical section 2, and thread B has critical section 2 and is waiting for critical section 1. The following code illustrates the potential problem:

```
CriticalSection CS1;
CriticalSection CS2;
⋮
// In WinMain or a similar function...
InitializeCriticalSection(&CS1);
InitializeCriticalSection(&CS2);
⋮

int ThreadA()
{
    EnterCriticalSection(&CS1);
    EnterCriticalSection(&CS2);
```

*(continued)*

```
    // Do some work....
    LeaveCriticalSection(&CS2);
    LeaveCriticalSection(&CS1);
    return(0);
}

int ThreadB()
{
    EnterCriticalSection(&CS2);
    EnterCriticalSection(&CS1);
    // Do some work....
    LeaveCriticalSection(&CS1);
    LeaveCriticalSection(&CS2);
    return(0);
}
```

In this admittedly contrived example, the following sequence of operations is possible:

| *Thread A* | *Thread B* |
|---|---|
| 1. `EnterCriticalSection(&CS1);` | |
| | 2. `EnterCriticalSection(&CS2);` |
| 3. `EnterCriticalSection(&CS2);` Deadlock! | 4. `EnterCriticalSection(&CS1);` Deadlock! |

In reality, the resource contention is generally less obvious, and the possibility for deadlock is real. Deadlocks result when two threads, processes, or users are each waiting for a resource held by the other. The code above could be rewritten in the following manner, and a deadlock would not occur:

```
CriticalSection CS1;
CriticalSection CS2;
⋮
// In WinMain or a similar function...
InitializeCriticalSection(&CS1);
InitializeCriticalSection(&CS2);
⋮

int ThreadA()
{
    EnterCriticalSection(&CS1);
    EnterCriticalSection(&CS2);
    // Do some work....
    LeaveCriticalSection(&CS2);
    LeaveCriticalSection(&CS1);
    return(0);
}
```

```
int ThreadB()
{
    EnterCriticalSection(&CS1);
    EnterCriticalSection(&CS2);
    // Do some work....
    LeaveCriticalSection(&CS2);
    LeaveCriticalSection(&CS1);
    return(0);
}
```

Here each thread is allocating resources in a set order. (In this example, CS1 is always entered before CS2.) Even in a complex system, allocating all resources in the same order in all threads is a good way to avoid deadlocks. Although that is not always possible, in a system that will be heavily dependent upon exclusive use of resources, it is worth consideration.

Many systems use what Andrew Tanenbaum describes as the "Ostrich Algorithm" for handling deadlocks. (The algorithm simply ignores the problem.) This makes a great deal of sense for some systems. If a failure resulting from deadlocks occurs once every two years and the system goes down every month for some other reason (such as compiler errors or hardware failures), the failure that occurs every two years is not critical and is possibly not worth programming against. Many systems in widespread use are potentially in danger of deadlocks occurring, but the practical risk is small. Of course, if the system is running a nuclear power plant or monitoring a life support system, the stakes of the game increase drastically.

### Server-based deadlocks

Servers are likely to acquire resources on behalf of clients. A common example is a database server. Because the clients requesting resources have no way to detect a deadlock themselves, servers require an additional level of deadlock detection: they must track the exclusive resources used by the clients as new requests come in.

Here's an example of deadlock in a server-based system: Client A requests the record for Douglas Reilly for an edit and gets the record with a lock. Client B requests the record for Erin Reilly for edit and gets the record with a lock. Next, Client A requests the record for Erin Reilly for edit and tries to acquire the record with a lock. Client B now requests the record for Douglas Reilly for edit and tries to acquire the record with a lock. Presuming the request for a lock is a blocking operation, the clients will be deadlocked. Further, the clients cannot really know in advance when the records they are requesting are locked unless they each try to acquire locks by using a nonblocking function.

The previous example is not entirely unreasonable or contrived. For instance, consider a person's record in a medical system. If Douglas Reilly is the guarantor of payment for Erin Reilly, it is reasonable to think that different parts of the system might access this information in different orders. A clinical user might get to Erin's record and then want to get to the guarantor's record; a financial system user might start with the guarantor's record and then need to get to the patient's record.

The solution for a server-based system is to track what clients have which records locked and, when a new request to lock a record fails, scan the lock table for the client holding the lock on the requested record. When Client B tries to access Douglas Reilly's record, the lock will fail. Further checking will allow the server to determine that Client A is holding a lock on Douglas Reilly and also waiting for a lock on Erin Reilly, and that Client B already has Erin Reilly's record locked. In this case, the blocking functions for each client can return an error indicating that a deadlock has occurred, and each client can take whatever action is appropriate.

The important part of this discussion is that the deadlock can be detected in the example above only because there is a central authority on the activity of the clients: the server process. A similar system that uses client-based database engines (for example, using Access MDB files or dBase files) cannot detect deadlocks so easily.

### Other critical section functions

There are several other critical section functions that can help with the blocking problems mentioned in the previous sections. The first and most important function is *TryEnterCriticalSection*. *TryEnterCriticalSection* takes a pointer to a critical section object, but unlike *EnterCriticalSection*, this function will not block. The return value is nonzero if the critical section was entered successfully or 0 if the critical section was owned by another thread. This function is not available in Windows 9x and is available only in Windows NT 4.x or later. Its limited availability prevents MFC from directly offering full support for *CriticalSection* object functionality.

Using *TryEnterCriticalSection*, we could rewrite the example on page 34 as follows:

```
⋮
// A function called by multiple threads...
ProcessThing(struct THING *thing)
{
    while (TryEnterCriticalSection(&CriticalSection)==0)
    {
        // Do some other work, or exit the function and return
        // a value indicating that we cannot get CriticalSection
    }
   if (numProcessed==0)
    {
        DoInitialStuff();
    }
    numProcessed++;
    LeaveCriticalSection(&CriticalSection);
    DoOtherProcessing(thing);
}
```

In this example, we have control over what to do in case we cannot acquire the resource we need. In addition to the examples of possible actions presented in the code comment, we could even display a dialog box that allows the user to cancel the operation. If we do that, we must be certain that we will not simply continue through the code as if we did get the critical section.

Two functions—*InitializeCriticalSectionAndSpinCount* and *SetCriticalSectionSpinCount*—can be used to set a spin count for the critical section. To understand the implications of a spin count, you must understand what happens inside the operating system when a thread calls *EnterCriticalSection*. If the critical section is already owned by another thread, the operating system calls *WaitForSingleObject*, which does not return until the other thread relinquishes control of the critical object. We will discuss *WaitForSingleObject* in detail later in this chapter, but for now, suffice it to say that calling *WaitForSingleObject* is a relatively expensive operation. Imagine a system with a couple of processors and a number of threads that serializes access to a shared resource. If the threads are very busy, a multiprocessor system might keep this critical section owned by one or another of the threads almost constantly. In this case, threads constantly calling *WaitForSingleObject* can be a nontrivial drain on system resources.

The spin count of a critical section object can come into play on multiprocessor systems when a thread tries to acquire a critical section and the section is already owned by another thread. Rather than immediately making a call to *WaitForSingleObject*, the operating system will "spin" (repeatedly try to get ownership of the critical section) the number of times specified by the spin count. If the object becomes free during the spinning, a call to *WaitForSingleObject* is unnecessary. (The Visual C++ online help indicates that the heap manager uses a spin count of about 4000; that setting gives optimal performance in most worst-case scenarios.)

*SetCriticalSectionSpinCount* and *InitializeCriticalSectionAndSpinCount* are prototyped as follows:

```
DWORD SetCriticalSectionSpinCount(
    LPCRITICAL_SECTION lpCriticalSection, DWORD dwSpinCount);
BOOL InitializeCriticalSectionAndSpinCount(
    LPCRITICAL_SECTION lpCriticalSection, DWORD dwSpinCount);
```

*InitializeCriticalSectionAndSpinCount* takes the pointer to a critical section object just like *InitializeCriticalSection*, but it also expects a parameter specifying the spin count. *SetCriticalSectionSpinCount* takes the same parameters as *InitializeCriticalSectionAndSpinCount*, though the critical section should be initialized by calling *InitializeCriticalSection* before you pass it to *SetCriticalSectionSpinCount*.

**NOTE** The use of the spin count functions has two significant restrictions. First, these functions have meaning only on multiprocessor systems. Second, the functions require Windows NT 4.0 Service Pack 3 or later in order to function.

## Events

Events are objects used to signal that some event has taken place. For instance, a program might use an event object to allow a group of threads to know that some action has taken place. The threads can then act on that knowledge. As with all kernel-based synchronization objects, the general sequence of events is that the object is created or opened, used, and then closed (using *CloseHandle*). Events are more flexible than the other synchronization objects and can be of special value for developers of server applications.

Even the call to *CreateEvent* is a little busier than the other *Create...* calls. The function prototype is as follows:

```
HANDLE CreateEvent(LPSECURITY_ATTRIBUTES lpEventAttributes,
    BOOL bManualReset, BOOL bInitialState, LPCTSTR lpName);
```

The first parameter, *lpEventAttributes*, is a pointer to a security attribute. Windows 9x programs do not use it, but this will be described in more detail later. The *bManualReset* parameter is a flag used to indicate whether the event should require a manual reset. If this parameter is FALSE, the event, once signaled, will automatically reset to nonsignaled. The flag's broader implications will be discussed shortly. The third parameter is *bInitialState*. This specifies whether the object should be created signaled or nonsignaled. Finally, the *lpName* parameter allows the event to be named, which is useful for events that need to be detected in other applications. If this parameter is NULL, the event is created without a name. Programs within the same process can use the handle returned by *CreateEvent* to access the event. Another process accesses the event using *OpenEvent* and the returned handle. In any case, the handle should be closed using *CloseHandle*, or the handle will be freed automatically when the process exits. As with all of the kernel-based synchronization objects, the object is destroyed when the last handle to it is closed.

> **NOTE** For Windows NT 4 Terminal Server Edition Service Pack 4 or later, or Windows 2000 Terminal Server Edition, the *lpName* parameter for all of the kernel-based synchronization object creation functions can signal whether the name should be global to the machine or global only to the session. If you prefix a name with "Global\" the object is created global to the machine; if you prefix the name with "Local\" the object is created just for one user's session.

The *bManualReset* parameter also affects the way that multiple threads react when they are waiting for an event to be signaled. If it is TRUE and multiple threads are waiting for the event to be signaled, all threads are notified of the state change when the event is signaled, and the threads are responsible for resetting the event. If it is FALSE, only a single thread is notified and the event is automatically reset to an unsignaled state. This can be useful when a program needs to have a single thread act on some event. An example would be preparing a queue of threads to perform some activity and having a single thread react to each event. The changes to the Win32 API in Windows 2000 allow more elegant solutions to thread pooling, but this remains an option.

## Mutexes

The name "mutex" comes from the object's allowance of mutual exclusive access to a shared resource. A mutex is signaled when it is not owned by any thread; it is unsignaled when a thread owns it. For instance, if multiple threads or processes are sharing memory, they might agree to use a mutex to control access to that memory. This one-of-a-kind access to a resource is called serialization. Serialization can be a good thing when needed, but it can also cause a bottleneck in a server application.

A mutex must first be created using the *CreateMutex* function:

```
HANDLE CreateMutex(LPSECURITY_ATTRIBUTES lpMutexAttributes,
    BOOL bInitialOwner, LPCTSTR lpName);
```

Once again, *lpMutexAttributes* is the security attribute. If the second parameter, *bInitialOwner*, is TRUE, the calling thread will own the mutex if it is created. The third parameter is the name of the mutex if it is to be shared among processes. If it is not to be shared among processes, this parameter can be NULL. As with other kernel-based synchronization objects, the *lpName* parameter is used to allow other processes or threads to open the object using the *OpenMutex* function:

```
HANDLE OpenMutex(DWORD dwDesiredAccess, BOOL bInheritHandle,
    LPCTSTR lpName);
```

The first parameter, *dwDesiredAccess*, is a set of flags that specify the access to the object that is required. These flags are specified in the Visual C++ online help for each of the object types. The second parameter, *bInheritHandle*, specifies whether the mutex should be inheritable by processes created by the *CreateProcess* function. The third parameter, *lpName*, is the name that must exactly match the name of a mutex previously created by *CreateMutex*.

Once a mutex is created or opened, a thread can use one of the *Wait* functions to gain ownership of the mutex. The exception occurs when the mutex is created with *bInitialOwner* set to TRUE. Once the task that needs to be serialized has been completed, the mutex can be released by calling *ReleaseMutex*, a function that takes a single parameter, which is the handle to the mutex object. A thread that has ownership of the mutex object can reacquire ownership by calling one of the *Wait* functions, but it must call *ReleaseMutex* once for each call to a *Wait* function.

## Semaphores

Unlike a mutex, a semaphore object allows a number of threads to share ownership of a resource. This kind of metered access is useful for resources that are shareable but not limitlessly so. For example, a server that does calculations might know that it can support, at most, 10 clients during any given moment. You can restrict access to the server by creating a semaphore that allows a maximum of 10 shared owners. The eleventh thread will discover that it cannot gain partial ownership of the semaphore and can refuse the client or make the client wait. The semaphore can then be passed to one of the *Wait* functions so that the thread will become active when one of the other threads releases its partial ownership.

To create a semaphore object, you call the *CreateSemaphore* function:

```
HANDLE CreateSemaphore(LPSECURITY_ATTRIBUTES lpSemaphoreAttributes,
    LONG lInitialCount, LONG lMaximumCount, LPCTSTR lpName);
```

Once again, the first parameter, *lpSemaphoreAttributes*, is the security attribute. The second parameter, *lInitialCount*, is a long value that must be greater than or equal to 0 and less than or equal to the third parameter, *lMaximumCount*, which must be greater than 0. Often the two count values are the same. The final parameter, *lpName*, is the name used to allow other processes to open the semaphore.

The initial and maximum count values make a semaphore different from a mutex. These are used to allow more than a single "owner" of the semaphore, although ownership does not fully describe why semaphores are used. (Most likely, someone will set the initial count to something other than the maximum count when the semaphore is created before the metered resource is ready for use.)

A semaphore maintains an internal count of the maximum number of threads that can own the semaphore and a count of the number of threads that currently own the semaphore. The count for the number of owning threads—initially set to the value of *lInitialCount*—is decremented each time you call one of the *Wait* functions. When the count reaches 0, all *Wait* calls fail until you call *ReleaseSemaphore,* which increments the count of the number of owning threads:

```
BOOL ReleaseSemaphore(HANDLE hSemaphore, LONG lReleaseCount,
    LPLONG lpPreviousCount);
```

*ReleaseSemaphore* allows you to do more than simply increment the count of owning threads. In addition to the semaphore handle, *lReleaseCount* is the count of the number to add to the current internal count of the semaphore, and returns in *lpPreviousCount* a pointer to the count before the release operation takes place. As with other kernel-based synchronization objects, the *lpName* parameter is used to allow other processes or threads to open the object. In this case, *OpenSemaphore* is used:

```
HANDLE OpenSemaphore(DWORD dwDesiredAccess, BOOL bInheritHandle,
    LPCTSTR lpName);
```

The first parameter, *dwDesiredAccess*, is a set of flags that specify the access to the object that is required. These flags are specified in the Visual C++ online help for each of the object types. The second parameter, *bInheritHandle*, specifies whether the mutex should be inheritable by processes created by the *CreateProcess* function. The third parameter, *lpName*, is the name, which must exactly match (including case) the name of a semaphore previously created by *CreateSemaphore*.

> **NOTE** Other Win32 functions seem to expose some of the same functionality that semaphores do. These other functions provide interlocked access to long variables, which ensures that the operations on the variable are performed in an atomic fashion. In other words, the operations are completely finished as a unit. For instance, *InterlockedIncrement* increases the value of the variable pointed to by the single parameter to the function. Several other functions are available, including *InterlockedCompareExchangePointer* for Windows NT 4 and later and Windows 98. How do these functions differ from semaphores? For one thing, they generally will not work between processes, though they can if the variable being atomically incremented is in shared memory. In general, if you are just manipulating a shared variable, the interlocked functions might be appropriate. However, whenever the possible end result of some operation is the need to wait for another thread or process, a semaphore is preferable.

## Waitable Timers

A waitable timer is a kernel object that signals itself at a specific time or at regular intervals and can be shared by multiple threads. To create a waitable timer object, you call the *CreateWaitableTimer* function:

```
HANDLE CreateWaitableTimer(
    LPSECURITY_ATTRIBUTES lpWaitableTimerAttributes,
    BOOL bManualReset, LPCTSTR lpName);
```

The first parameter, *lpWaitableTimerAttributes*, is the security attribute. The second parameter, *bManualReset,* indicates whether the timer should be triggered just once or repeatedly. The final parameter, *lpName*, is the name used to allow other processes to open the waitable timer.

You can retrieve the handle of an existing waitable timer by calling *Open-WaitableTimer*:

```
HANDLE OpenWaitableTimer(DWORD dwDesiredAccess, BOOL bInheritHandle,
    LPCTSTR lpName);
```

The first parameter, *dwDesiredAccess*, is a set of flags that specify the access to the object that is required. These flags are specified in the online Visual C++ help for each of the object types. The second parameter, *bInheritHandle*, specifies whether the object should be inheritable by processes created by the *CreateProcess* function. The *lpName* parameter is the name, which must exactly match (including case) the name of a waitable timer previously created by *CreateWaitableTimer*.

You set a waitable timer using *SetWaitableTimer*:

```
BOOL SetWaitableTimer(HANDLE hTimer, const LARGE_INTEGER *pDueTime,
    LONG lPeriod, PTIMERAPCROUTINE pfnCompletionRoutine,
    LPVOID lpArgToCompletionRoutine, BOOL fResume);
```

The *hTimer* parameter is the handle from *CreateWaitableTimer* or *Open-WaitableTimer*. The second parameter is *pDueTime*, a pointer to a 64-bit value representing the time the object is to be signaled (in 100-nanosecond intervals from January 1, 1601) if the value is positive. If the value is negative, it represents the number of 100-nanosecond intervals to wait before the object should be signaled. The format of this parameter is the same as that of the *FILETIME* structure; *pDueTime* can also be thought of as simply a quad word. The third parameter, *lPeriod*, specifies a period, in milliseconds, between activations of the timer. If *lPeriod* is 0, the timer is signaled once; otherwise, the timer is signaled every *lPeriod* milliseconds. The fourth and fifth parameters specify a completion routine and the argument to be passed to the completion routine. The completion routine is called when the timer is signaled.

Timers can be canceled by a call to *CancelWaitableTimer*, a function that takes a handle to a waitable timer as its single parameter:

```
BOOL CancelWaitableTimer(HANDLE hTimer);
```

## *Wait* Functions and Thread Synchronization

Now that we've seen the synchronization objects, let's examine the functions that allow you to wait for them. Six functions allow your program to wait for one of these synchronization objects to be signaled. Their descriptions and distinguishing features are presented in Table 2-2. For more detailed information, refer to the examples using the *Wait* functions in the communication examples in Chapter 12, or see the Microsoft Platform Software Development Kit (SDK) documentation. The following synchronization objects have two states: signaled and unsignaled. The *Wait* functions, in general, wait for one or more objects to become signaled.

**TABLE 2-2**
**WAIT FUNCTIONS FOR USE WITH SYNCHRONIZATION OBJECTS**

| *Name* | *Number of Objects to Wait For* | *Special Features* |
|---|---|---|
| *WaitForSingleObject* | 1 | None |
| *WaitForSingleObjectEx* | 1 | Optionally returns when I/O completion routine or asynchronous procedure call is queued to thread |
| *WaitForMultipleObjects* | Multiple (caller specifies) | None |
| *WaitForMultipleObjectsEx* | Multiple (caller specifies) | Optionally returns when I/O completion routine or asynchronous procedure call is queued to thread |
| *MsgWaitForMultipleObjects* | Multiple (caller specifies) | For use in threads that create windows |
| *MsgWaitForMultipleObjectsEx* | Multiple (caller specifies) | Optionally returns when I/O completion routine or asynchronous procedure call is queued to thread, for use in threads that create windows |

In general, we will ignore the *MsgWait* functions. Server applications do not usually create windows, so understanding the details of these functions is unnecessary. For server applications, we can create fairly simple programs that provide any user interface we might need by using one of the *Wait* functions, which are prototyped as follows:

```
WaitForSingleObject(HANDLE hHandle,DWORD dwMilliseconds);
WaitForMultipleObjects(DWORD nCount,CONST HANDLE *lpHandles,
    BOOL fWaitAll,DWORD dwMilliseconds)
DWORD WaitForSingleObjectEx(HANDLE hHandle, DWORD dwMilliseconds,
    BOOL bAlertable);
DWORD WaitForMultipleObjectsEx(DWORD nCount,
    CONST HANDLE *lpHandles, BOOL fWaitAll, DWORD dwMilliseconds,
    BOOL bAlertable);
```

*WaitForSingleObject* is a relatively simple function that takes two parameters: *hHandle* is the handle of the object to wait for, and *dwMilliseconds* is the number of milliseconds to wait for the handle to become signaled. If *dwMilliseconds* is 0, the function tests the handle's state and immediately returns WAIT_TIMEOUT if the object is unsignaled. If the object is signaled, WAIT_OBJECT_0 is returned. If *dwMilliseconds* is INFINITE, the function does not return until the object is signaled. For any other value of *dwMilliseconds*, the function waits until the object is signaled or the time-out expires. For instance, if *dwMilliseconds* is 1000, the function waits up to 1 second if the object does not become signaled. The normal return values from the *Wait* functions are listed in Table 2-3.

**TABLE 2-3**
**RETURN VALUES FROM THE *WAIT* FUNCTIONS**

| *Return Value* | *Description* |
|---|---|
| WAIT_FAILED | Call failed; call *GetLastError* to get more details. |
| WAIT_ABANDONED_0 to WAIT_ABANDONED_0 + (object count –1) | The object being waited for was a mutex, and the object was not released before the thread owning it was terminated. Ownership of the mutex is granted to the calling thread, and its state is unsignaled. |
| WAIT_OBJECT_0 to WAIT_OBJECT_0 + (object count –1) | Object specified is in the signaled state. |
| WAIT_TIMEOUT | The object is unsignaled, and the time-out specified has expired. |

*WaitForMultipleObjects* behaves in a manner similar to *WaitForSingleObject*, but it has the ability to wait for more than a single object. The count of objects is passed in *nCount*, and *lpHandles* points to an array of handles that will be tested for signaled state. If *fWaitAll* is TRUE, the function returns only if all objects passed are signaled or the time specified by *dwMilliseconds* has expired. If *fWaitAll* is FALSE, the function returns if any of the objects become signaled before the time-out with the return code WAIT_OBJECT_0 plus the zero-based index of the object whose state changed.

The wait functions that end in *Ex* all support the return from the function if an I/O completion routine or an asynchronous procedure call (APC) is queued to the thread. This extension will be discussed in greater detail when I/O completion ports are discussed in Chapter 13.

## CREATING A NEW THREAD

Now that we can synchronize threads, we need to be able to create them. Several families of functions create, manage, and end a thread in a program. Before deciding which family of functions to use, you need to determine exactly what kind of program you plan to write, as well as how many threads you plan to create.

## Thread Creation Functions

For a pure Win32 application that does not use any C run-time library functions, the *CreateThread* and *ExitThread* functions can be used to create and end, respectively, a thread.

```
HANDLE CreateThread(LPSECURITY_ATTRIBUTES lpThreadAttributes,
    DWORD dwStackSize, LPTHREAD_START_ROUTINE lpStartAddress,
    LPVOID lpParameter, DWORD dwCreationFlags, LPDWORD lpThreadId);

VOID ExitThread(DWORD dwExitCode);
```

You should not need to explicitly call *ExitThread* since it is called whenever a thread created by *CreateThread* returns, but some of the documentation from Microsoft recommends that *ExitThread* be called explicitly where possible.

You won't use these functions if you are using functions in the C run-time library or if you are using MFC. Use of MFC is beyond the scope of this discussion, but issues related to use of the C run-time library could be significant in the context of server development.

Some standard C run-time library functions (for instance, *malloc, fopen*) cause allocation of a C run-time library per-thread data block. The *CreateThread/ExitThread* pair do not properly free this block if allocated, and the possibility exists of a memory leak of about 70–80 bytes for each thread terminated with *ExitThread* that uses C run-time library functions. Recall from the Chapter 1 discussion of the Microsoft bug report related to ASP.DLL that even very minor memory leaks can create problems in long-running services. Note that the general perception is that C run-time library functions will not work at all if *CreateThread* is used rather than the C run-time library *_beginthreadex* function. In reality, according to Microsoft Knowledge Base article ID Q104641, the only function that cannot be used in a thread created by *CreateThread* is the *signal* function.

The alternative for threads that must use the C run-time library functions is a pair of functions named *_beginthreadex* and *_endthreadex*.

```
HANDLE _beginthreadex(void * lpThreadAttributes,
    unsigned dwStackSize,
    unsigned (__stdcall *start_address)(void *) lpStartAddress,
    void * arglist, unsigned initFlag, unsigned * thrdaddr);

VOID _endthreadex(unsigned retval);
```

Another family of thread creation/termination functions is *beginthread/endthread*. These functions are less like the standard Win32 counterparts; the most significant difference is that *beginthread* does not take a security attributes parameter. The similarity of function parameters will make it easier to switch from one thread creation family to another, so we will use the *beginthreadex/_endthreadex* functions when C run-time library support is required.

**NOTE** For multithreaded projects, be sure you change the code generation options in the Project Settings dialog box to use the multithreaded C run-time library.

After discussing the basics of multithreaded applications, let's take a look at a rather contrived example that will allow us to see threads in action. As with all examples in the book, this example is also on the companion CD.

## A Multithreaded Example Program

This example program is simple: it creates five threads from the primary thread in a simple 32-bit console-mode application. Console-mode applications will be discussed in more detail later in this book, but for now, just think of them as simple 32-bit programs that allow use of Win32's full range of functionality. Each of the five threads waits indefinitely for ownership of a mutex created in the *main* function before the threads are created. When a thread gains ownership of the mutex, it holds the mutex for some period of time and then releases it. Each thread monitors a global variable, synchronized by a critical section, to determine whether it should terminate. The global variable is set when the user presses a key. We will use the *_beginthreadex/_endthreadex* pair since we are using standard C run-time library functions. The code is in Listing 2-1.

**Thread Creation and Thread Synchronization Functions**

```
#include <stdio.h>
#include <conio.h>
#include <windows.h>
#include <process.h>

CRITICAL_SECTION csExit;
BOOL exitNow=FALSE;
HANDLE hMutex;

unsigned __stdcall SecondThreadFunc(void* pArguments);
int main(int argc, char* argv[]);

unsigned __stdcall SecondThreadFunc(void* pArguments)
{
    int threadNum;
    threadNum=*((int *)pArguments);
    printf("In thread %d...\n",threadNum);
```

**Listing 2-1**

```
    while (TRUE)
    {
        WaitForSingleObject(hMutex,INFINITE);
        Sleep(1000*threadNum);
        EnterCriticalSection(&csExit);
        if (exitNow)
        {
            printf("\nThread %d GONE!",threadNum);
            _endthreadex(0);
        }
        LeaveCriticalSection(&csExit);
        ReleaseMutex(hMutex);
        printf("\nThread %d still going",threadNum);
    }
    return 0;
}

int main(int argc, char* argv[])
{
    int loop;
    int threadCount[5];
    unsigned threadID[5];

    InitializeCriticalSection(&csExit);
    __try
    {
        for (loop=0 ; loop<5 ; loop++)
        {
            threadCount[loop]=loop+1;
            _beginthreadex(NULL,
                           0,
                           &SecondThreadFunc,
                           &threadCount[loop],
                           0,
                           &threadID[loop]);
        }
        getch();
        EnterCriticalSection(&csExit);
        exitNow=TRUE;
        LeaveCriticalSection(&csExit);
    }
    __finally
    {
        DeleteCriticalSection(&csExit);
    }
    return 0;
}
```

When the program is run, it gives you feedback as each thread is started and as each thread is testing for the *exitNow* flag to be set, and it reports whether it is still running. You will notice that when you run this program, the performance is a bit choppy. That is something that you may find in many multithreaded applications. The synchronization objects that have been discussed and used in this example are useful for their intended purpose, but if there is a reasonable alternative, you should be careful to avoid using resources that need to be shared. Wherever possible, try to use constructs that allow server clients to operate without interactions with other clients, such as requiring waits for availability of shared resources.

# Part II

# Windows 2000 as a Server Platform

*Chapter 3*

# The Service API

What separates a file server from an application server is the server's ability to safely and reliably run applications without the intervention of a user. While it is possible to run an application on a Microsoft Windows 98 workstation and make it available on a peer-to-peer network, this is not an ideal environment. Running an application on a real server allows the program to perform the work closer to the data and then allows that processing to be shared among many clients.

Certainly you could cobble together something on Windows 98 that looks and acts an awful lot like a server application. For instance, the Microsoft Database Engine (MSDE) can run on platforms ranging from Windows 95 to Windows 2000. In many respects, the functionality is the same on all of these platforms, and you might be tempted to consider the potential operating systems to be equals in terms of hosting applications. This would be a mistake.

Aside from the differences in threading and application partitioning, another big difference between the various 32-bit Windows platforms is the availability on Windows 2000 of the Service API, which I will discuss next.

## WHAT IS THE SERVICE API?

The Service API consists of a set of functions and a couple of callback functions that must be supported. Together these functions allow an application to run independent of any logged-on user. This is not common to the entire Windows family of operating systems. For instance, the MSDE running on a Windows 9x machine is not available to users if no one is logged on to the workstation. This limited ability of Windows 9x workstations to make applications available to other users is probably reasonable for applications that make minimal demands and are run for a few desktops physically near each other. This breaks down, however, when the application to be served is used by a large number of users distributed over a wide area who are unlikely to be located near the application server. In this case, the ability to run independent of the currently logged-on user is essential.

At its heart, a service application supports at least three functions:

- **The *main* function** This is just a standard *main* function with arguments like any console mode Win32 application. The *main* function must call certain functions in a timely manner.
- **The *ServiceMain* function** This is the entry point for the service. The *ServiceMain* function must have the following prototype, though it can have a different name:

```
VOID WINAPI ServiceMain(
    DWORD dwArgc,     // Number of arguments
    LPTSTR *lpszArgv  // Array of argument string pointers
);
```

  One interesting feature of *ServiceMain* is that it takes the same arguments as a traditional C/C++ *main* function.
- **The control handler function** This function receives requests for the service. The control handler function must have the following prototype, though it can have a different name:

```
DWORD WINAPI HandlerEx(
    DWORD dwControl,      // Requested control code
    DWORD dwEventType,    // Event type
    LPVOID lpEventData,   // Event data
    LPVOID lpContext      // User-defined context data
);
```

Note that this function prototype has superseded the previous *Handler* prototype that expected only a single *dwControl* parameter. The old-style control handler function can still be specified for compatibility and is the only option for Windows NT 4 and earlier, but the new-style function is preferred for Windows 2000 service applications. Listing 3-1 will use the *Handler* function. Later examples in this book will use the new form of the control handler function. The *HandlerEx* function is primarily useful for services that need to manage multiple services from a single control handler or for a service that needs to react to device notifications.

Before we look at an example, we need to answer one question: if a service is running when no one is logged on, under whose authority does the service run?

## WHO RUNS THE SERVICE?

A key component of the Win32 security model in Windows 2000 is that every process runs under the authority of some user. This is required so that upon each request to the operating system, the security on the object that is being requested can be tested against the rights of the current user or the groups the current user belongs to. If this is how security is handled, how do services run when no one is logged on?

The answer is a little more complicated than it might seem. Generally, the service runs in the context of the System account, a special account that has godlike powers on the machine that houses the account but cannot cross the wire and access resources on any other machine. It is obvious from that description that running under the System account is not always a perfect solution, since sometimes your service might want to cross the wire and gain access to resources on another machine. For instance, a service that does file backups might want to back up files on remote servers if the tape drive hardware exists on only one of several machines requiring backups.

> **NOTE** While testing some of the programs in this chapter, I discovered that the System account has no power beyond the machine it resides on. As a matter of course, I was compiling some of the service applications on the server. Installing them from the directory where they were created on the server was not a problem. Actually *starting* the service was a problem. In retrospect, it is clear why: the System account could not access the executable on the remote server. In general, of course, no service—even one that is running under a properly authorized account—should be run from a server. With most automatically started services, it would be difficult to reliably ensure that the service application residing on the server will be available when the service tries to start.

The solution to this problem is the ability to run a service within the context of a user account rather than the context of the System account. This can be accomplished programmatically as well as through the user interface. Figure 3-1 shows the property sheet for a service, which you can use to set the user name and password for the user account a service should run under.

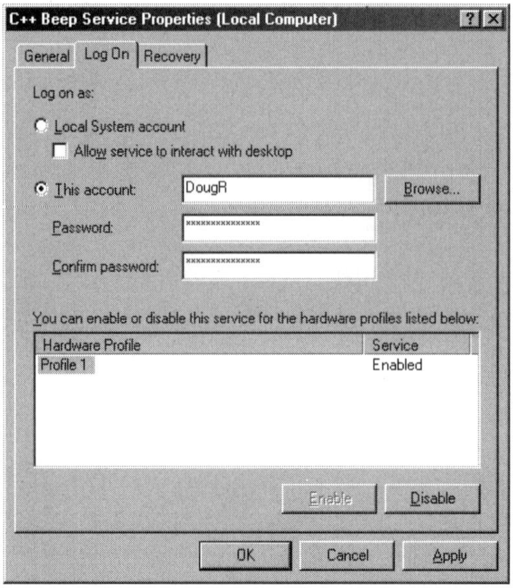


**Figure 3-1** *Setting the user context for a service in Windows 2000.*

Services are managed by the Service Control Manager (SCM). The SCM maintains a database of services, controls their installation, and starts them up at boot time or upon demand. Many operations on services require the handle of the SCM, and the SCM of remote machines can also be opened on the machine where the request for the handle takes place.

# HELLO, SERVICE API WORLD!

Listing 3-1, the *HelloService* example, contains the world's simplest—and perhaps dumbest—service. The service will do nothing more than beep once per second. Other than being quite annoying, this service will also allow you the opportunity to have concrete proof that the service is running—even when no user is logged on to the system.

> **NOTE** The key feature of this service is, of course, the annoying beep that takes place every second or so. So if you are testing this on a machine, it is obviously critical that the speaker is working correctly. Obvious, of course, to everyone but me while I was debugging this code. After many exotic attempts at diagnostics (some of which left artifacts in the final program), I ran the service on another machine. To my horror, it worked perfectly the first time. On further inspection, the audio driver on the initial test machine was not working. The lesson to be learned is that even when you're working on advanced programming problems, making sure the simplest things operate is critical.

**HelloService.cpp**

```
#include "stdafx.h"

SERVICE_STATUS          ServiceStatus;
SERVICE_STATUS_HANDLE   ServiceStatusHandle;

VOID WINAPI ServiceMain(DWORD argc, LPTSTR *argv);

VOID WINAPI Handler(DWORD dwControl);
DWORD ServiceInitialization(DWORD argc, LPTSTR *argv,
    DWORD *specificError);
VOID logError(char *text);

FILE *log;
char diag[255];
BOOL isRunning = false;

int main(int argc, char* argv[])
{
    SERVICE_TABLE_ENTRY DispatchTable[] =
    {
        { "BeepService", ServiceMain },
        { 0,             0 }
    };

    sprintf(diag, "Log opened\n");
    logError(diag);

    if (argc>1 && !(stricmp(argv[1], "-i")))
    {
        char szBuffer[255];
        char szPath[MAX_PATH];

        sprintf(diag, "In install leg\n");
        logError(diag);
        SC_HANDLE scmHandle = OpenSCManager (NULL, NULL,
            SC_MANAGER_ALL_ACCESS);

        if (scmHandle == NULL) // Perform error handling.
        {
            sprintf(diag, "BeepService OpenSCManager error = %d\n",
                GetLastError());

            logError(diag);
        }
        SC_HANDLE scHandle;
```

**Listing 3-1** *(continued)*

**Listing 3-1** *continued*

```
        GetModuleFileName(GetModuleHandle(NULL), szPath,MAX_PATH);
        // Why do we do this? The path may contain spaces.
        //  If it does, the path must be quoted.
        strcpy(szBuffer, "\"");
        strcat(szBuffer, szPath);
        strcat(szBuffer, "\"");
        printf("\nInstalling service %s", szPath);

        scHandle = CreateService (scmHandle, "BeeperService",
            "Beeper Service For Test", SERVICE_ALL_ACCESS,
            SERVICE_WIN32_OWN_PROCESS,
            SERVICE_DEMAND_START,
            SERVICE_ERROR_NORMAL,
            szBuffer, NULL, NULL, NULL, NULL, NULL);

        if (scHandle == NULL) // Process error
        {
            sprintf(diag, "BeepService CreateService error = %d\n",
                GetLastError());
            logError(diag);
        }

        CloseServiceHandle(scHandle);
        CloseServiceHandle(scmHandle);
    }
    else if (argc>1 && !(stricmp(argv[1], "-u")))
    {
        SC_HANDLE scmHandle = OpenSCManager (NULL, NULL,
            SC_MANAGER_ALL_ACCESS);

        if (scmHandle == NULL) // Perform error handling.
        {
            sprintf(diag, "BeepService OpenSCManager error = %d\n",
                GetLastError());

            logError(diag);
        }
        SC_HANDLE scHandle;

        scHandle = OpenService(scmHandle, "BeeperService",
            SERVICE_ALL_ACCESS);
        DeleteService(scHandle);
        printf("\nBeeperService uninstalled...");
    }
    else
```

```
    {
        sprintf(diag, "About to start service control...\n");
        logError(diag);
        if (!StartServiceCtrlDispatcher(DispatchTable))
        {
            sprintf(diag,
                "BeepService StartServiceCtrlDispatcher error = %d\n",
                GetLastError());
            logError(diag);
        }
    }
    return 0;
}

// A trivial logging function. Event logging will be added in
//  Chapter 5.
VOID logError(char *text)
{
    log = fopen("c:\\service.log", "a+t");
    if (log)
    {
        fprintf(log, text);
        fclose(log);
    }
    return;
}

VOID WINAPI ServiceMain(DWORD argc, LPTSTR *argv)
{
    DWORD status;
    DWORD specificError;

    ServiceStatus.dwServiceType        = SERVICE_WIN32_OWN_PROCESS;
    ServiceStatus.dwCurrentState       = SERVICE_START_PENDING;
    ServiceStatus.dwControlsAccepted   = SERVICE_ACCEPT_STOP;
    ServiceStatus.dwWin32ExitCode      = 0;
    ServiceStatus.dwServiceSpecificExitCode = 0;
    ServiceStatus.dwCheckPoint         = 0;
    ServiceStatus.dwWaitHint           = 0;

    ServiceStatusHandle = RegisterServiceCtrlHandler(
        "BeepService",
        Handler);

    if (ServiceStatusHandle == (SERVICE_STATUS_HANDLE)0)
    {
```

*(continued)*

**Listing 3-1** *continued*

```
        sprintf(diag,
            "BeeperService RegisterServiceCtrlHandler failed %d\n",
            GetLastError());
        logError(diag);
        return;
    }

    // Initialization code goes here.
    status = ServiceInitialization(argc, argv, &specificError);

    // Handle error condition
    if (status != NO_ERROR)
    {
        ServiceStatus.dwCurrentState       = SERVICE_STOPPED;
        ServiceStatus.dwCheckPoint         = 0;
        ServiceStatus.dwWaitHint           = 0;
        ServiceStatus.dwWin32ExitCode      = status;
        ServiceStatus.dwServiceSpecificExitCode = specificError;

        SetServiceStatus (ServiceStatusHandle, &ServiceStatus);
        return;
    }

    // Initialization complete--report running status.
    ServiceStatus.dwCurrentState       = SERVICE_RUNNING;
    ServiceStatus.dwCheckPoint         = 0;
    ServiceStatus.dwWaitHint           = 0;

    if (!SetServiceStatus(ServiceStatusHandle, &ServiceStatus))
    {
        status = GetLastError();
        sprintf(diag,
            "BeeperService SetServiceStatus error %ld\n", status);
        logError(diag);
    }
    isRunning = true;

    sprintf(diag, "Just before processing loop...\n");
    logError(diag);
    // This is where the service does its work.
    // First we display a message on the desktop, just because we can!
    MessageBox(NULL, "Hello Service World", "BeeperService",
        MB_OK | MB_SERVICE_NOTIFICATION | MB_ICONINFORMATION);
    while (1)
    {
        Beep(2000, 200);
```

```
        Sleep(1000);
        if (isRunning == false)
        {
            break;
        }
    }

    ServiceStatus.dwCurrentState = SERVICE_STOPPED;
    // Send current status.
    if (!SetServiceStatus(ServiceStatusHandle, &ServiceStatus))
    {
        status = GetLastError();
        sprintf(diag,
            "BeeperService SetServiceStatus error %ld\n", status);
        logError(diag);
    }

    return;
}

// Stub initialization function.
DWORD ServiceInitialization(DWORD argc, LPTSTR *argv,
    DWORD *specificError)
{
    // Just return for now...
    return(NO_ERROR);
}

VOID WINAPI Handler(DWORD dwControl)
{
    DWORD status;

    sprintf(diag, "In to service control...\n");
    logError(diag);
    switch(dwControl)
    {
        case SERVICE_CONTROL_PAUSE:
        // Do whatever it takes to pause here.
            ServiceStatus.dwCurrentState = SERVICE_PAUSED;
            break;

        case SERVICE_CONTROL_CONTINUE:
        // Do whatever it takes to continue here.
            ServiceStatus.dwCurrentState = SERVICE_RUNNING;
            break;
```

*(continued)*

**Listing 3-1** *continued*

```
        case SERVICE_CONTROL_STOP:
        // Do whatever it takes to stop here.
            sprintf(diag, "Stopping...\n");
            logError(diag);
            ServiceStatus.dwWin32ExitCode = 0;
            ServiceStatus.dwCurrentState  = SERVICE_STOP_PENDING;
            ServiceStatus.dwCheckPoint    = 0;
            ServiceStatus.dwWaitHint      = 0;

            isRunning = false;

            if (!SetServiceStatus(ServiceStatusHandle,
                &ServiceStatus))
            {
                status = GetLastError();
                sprintf(diag,
                    "BeeperService SetServiceStatus error %ld\n",
                    status);
                logError(diag);
            }
            sprintf(diag,
                "BeeperService leaving handler \n", 0);
            logError(diag);
            return;

        case SERVICE_CONTROL_INTERROGATE:
        // Fall through to send current status.
            break;

        default:
            sprintf(diag,
                "BeeperService unrecognized control code %ld\n",
                dwControl);
            logError(diag);
    }

    // Send current status.
    if (!SetServiceStatus(ServiceStatusHandle, &ServiceStatus))
    {
        status = GetLastError();
        sprintf(diag,
            "BeeperService SetServiceStatus error %ld\n", status);
        logError(diag);
    }
    return;
}
```

The *main* function of a server application often serves multiple purposes. Notice first that the bulk of the *main* function is an *if...else if...else* statement that does different things based on the arguments (if any) that are passed to the program. The actual program can be run directly from the command line with an argument of *–I* to install the service or *–U* to uninstall the service. Alternatively, the service can be started by the SCM. One interesting implementation note is that it is critical to check the argument count (*argc*) before checking *argv[1]*. In a C or C++ program that is run from the command line, *argv[0]* traditionally would contain the name of the program being run (often containing the full path name); *argv[1]* would therefore at least be a NULL that could safely be tested. This is not the case when a service is started.

An array of SERVICE_TABLE_ENTRY structures is declared and allocated at the beginning of the *main* function. Each element of the array contains the name of the service (BeeperService in this example) as well as the name of the service main function (in this case *ServiceMain*). The second entry in the array contains two zeros, indicating the end of the array. If multiple, independent services needed to be run using this single service application, there would be multiple nonzero entries followed by the all-zero entry.

The first lines of code past the initializations are used for some simple message logging. When running, a service application cannot simply use *printf* statements to show errors. While use of a message box is possible, it is generally better not to display error messages that way, since it is possible no user will be present at the server. The *logError* function is a simple function that just sends a line of text to a file used to log errors. There is a much better way to record errors and events in the life of the service, which I'll cover in Chapter 5.

## Installing the Service

If the first argument to the program is *–I*, the service should be installed. The first Win32 Service API function called is *OpenSCManager*. The prototype for this function is

```
SC_HANDLE OpenSCManager (
    LPCTSTR lpMachineName,    // Pointer to machine name string
    LPCTSTR lpDatabaseName,   // Pointer to database name string
    DWORD dwDesiredAccess     // Type of access
);
```

The first argument, *lpMachineName*, specifies the machine where the SCM should be opened. If this is NULL, the current machine's SCM is opened. The *lpDatabaseName* parameter is odd. The only documented value for this parameter is SERVICES_ACTIVE_DATABASE, and if this parameter is NULL, SERVICES_ACTIVE_DATABASE is assumed. The final parameter, *dwDesiredAccess*, specifies the access to the SCM required. This parameter has a number of possible values, including values that will allow locking of the database, enumeration of services, and so on. The generic rights (discussed in the next chapter) are mapped to combinations of the SCM rights. In this example (and in most cases) SC_MANAGER_ALL_ACCESS is requested and granted. You can find details on the possible rights in the SDK documentation.

## Using *CreateService* to Install the Service

To actually install the service, you must call *CreateService*. This function takes many parameters:

```
SC_HANDLE CreateService(
    SC_HANDLE hSCManager,          // Handle of SCM database
    LPCTSTR lpServiceName,         // Name of service to start
    LPCTSTR lpDisplayName,         // Display name
    DWORD dwDesiredAccess,         // Type of access to service
    DWORD dwServiceType,           // Type of service
    DWORD dwStartType,             // When to start service
    DWORD dwErrorControl,          // Severity of service failure
    LPCTSTR lpBinaryPathName,      // Name of binary file
    LPCTSTR lpLoadOrderGroup,      // Name of load ordering group
    LPDWORD lpdwTagId,             // Receives tag identifier
    LPCTSTR lpDependencies,        // Array of dependency names
    LPCTSTR lpServiceStartName,    // Service account name
    LPCTSTR lpPassword             // Account password
);
```

The first parameter is the handle returned from *OpenSCManager*. The next two parameters are the service name and the display name, respectively. It is useful to make the actual service name short and leave out any spaces, since this is the name used if the service is started using the NET START command from the command prompt. The display name is used by the user interface to display the name of the service. The *dwDesiredAccess* parameter specifies the access to the service that is requested. The constant STANDARD_RIGHTS_REQUIRED includes DELETE, READ_CONTROL, WRITE_DAC, and WRITE_OWNER rights. SERVICE_ALL_ACCESS includes all of these rights plus many rights regarding querying, enumerating, and controlling the service. The generic rights are also mapped to reasonable values, as detailed in the SDK documentation. The simple beep service created by the *HelloService* program in Listing 3-1 uses SERVICE_ALL_ACCESS. The *dwServiceType* parameter specifies the type of service from among the options shown in Table 3-1.

This book will not cover kernel or file system drivers, which extend far beyond the scope of this volume.

The SERVICE_INTERACTIVE_PROCESS flag requires some explanation. Services commonly have no way to interact with the currently logged-on user. Generally this is a good thing, because there is no assurance that a user will be at the server console. At times, however, interaction with the user might be required. For these situations,

**TABLE 3-1**
**VALUES FOR THE *DWSERVICETYPE* PARAMETER**

| *Service Type* | *Description* |
|---|---|
| SERVICE_WIN32_OWN_PROCESS | Specifies a service that runs within its own process. |
| SERVICE_WIN32_SHARE_PROCESS | Specifies a service that shares its process space with other services. |
| SERVICE_KERNEL_DRIVER | Specifies a driver service. |
| SERVICE_FILE_SYSTEM_DRIVER | Specifies a file system driver. |
| SERVICE_INTERACTIVE_PROCESS | Enables a service that is SERVICE_WIN32_OWN_PROCESS or SERVICE_WIN32_SHARE_PROCESS to interact with the desktop. Valid only if the service is running in the security context of the System account. This constant is ORed with the SERVICE_WIN32_xxx constant. |

the Windows 2000 development team provided the SERVICE_INTERACTIVE_PROCESS flag. Even this option has some important restrictions. First, this flag is only usable if the service is working under the context of the System account. Furthermore, even if the service installation has requested interactive rights, there is a key in the registry named *NoInteractiveServices* that controls the effect of the SERVICE_INTERACTIVE_PROCESS flag. This key is found at

```
HKEY_LOCAL_MACHINE\SYSTEM\CurrentControlSet\Control\Windows
```

The default value is 0, meaning that services can interact with the user if this value is set. If this value is nonzero, no service started subsequently—regardless of the *dwServiceType* requested—will be allowed to run interactively. Thus, if the service is for a mass distribution, it is wiser to create a client process that can interact with the service—perhaps by setting registry values read by the service or by directly communicating with the service through a named pipe or a TCP/IP port. Chapter 12 will use named pipes to interact with a variant of the simple beep service created in Listing 3-1.

There is one other possible way to interact with the user. The *MessageBox* Win32 API function has the following prototype:

```
int MessageBox(
    HWND hWnd,          // Handle of owner window
    LPCTSTR lpText,     // Text in message box
    LPCTSTR lpCaption,  // Message box title
    UINT uType          // Message box style
);
```

This function should be familiar to you, but the MB_SERVICE_NOTIFICATION flag that can be ORed into the *uType* parameter is likely not as familiar. There is also an MB_SERVICE_NOTIFICATION_NT3X flag that should be used if the service application will be running on Windows NT 3.x. Although Windows NT 3.51 (the last of the 3.x Windows NT line) is quite old now, it is still often used by some of the multiuser systems, such as Citrix Version 1.8. When this flag is set, the *hWnd* parameter must be NULL so that the message box will be visible on the user's desktop.

The next parameter is *dwStartType*. This parameter can be set to SERVICE_AUTO_START to start the service automatically upon system startup, to SERVICE_DEMAND_START to allow the service to be started manually as needed, and to SERVICE_DISABLED to indicate that the service is disabled. Other flags detailed in the Win32 SDK allow different starting methods for drivers.

The *dwErrorControl* parameter specifies how the system should behave if an error occurs while starting the service during system startup. SERVICE_ERROR_IGNORE logs the failure of the service in the event log (discussed in the next chapter) but otherwise continues. SERVICE_ERROR_NORMAL causes the error in starting the service to be logged as well, but also places an error dialog informing the user that the service has failed to start. This is the most common—and generally the most appropriate—setting for all but the most mission-critical service applications.

SERVICE_ERROR_SEVERE causes the error to be logged, and if the system is being started with the last known good configuration, startup continues. If the system is not starting up using the last known good configuration, the system is restarted using the last known good configuration. SERVICE_ERROR_CRITICAL behaves similarly to SERVICE_ERROR_SEVERE, except that if the error occurs and the system is already being started using the last known good configuration, the startup operation fails. If a server is dedicated to a single service, it might be appropriate to use one of the last two values for *dwErrorControl*, because if the service fails to start, server availability is not important.

Commonly, *argv[0]* of the *argv* array of pointers passed to *main* contains the path of the program that is running. This method of getting the path is not as safe and sure as the *lpBinaryPathName* argument. Instead, the following line of code is used to get the path of the executable to install:

```
GetModuleFileName(GetModuleHandle(NULL), szPath, MAX_PATH);
```

*GetModuleHandle* is a Win32 API function that returns a module handle for the module name passed as its only parameter. In the *HelloService* program, NULL is passed so that the module handle returned is for the file used to create the calling process. This returned value is passed to the Win32 API function *GetModuleFileName*, along with a pointer to a character buffer—*szPath* in the beep example—and the length of the buffer, MAX_PATH. *GetModuleFileName* returns the full path name of the module referenced by the module handle passed as its first parameter. This path is copied to another buffer, *szBuffer*, with leading and trailing quotes. If the module file name contains spaces, the quotes are mandatory, and it does no harm to add quotes around the string if there are no spaces.

The next three parameters to *CreateService* work together to handle service dependencies that can occur when one service relies on another service. For example, Microsoft Knowledge Base article Q177681 describes a problem in which a service might fail because UNC names that need to be resolved using Domain Name Service (DNS) are being used before the *LMHOSTS* service is started. The solution in this case is to add the *LMHOSTS* service to the *DependsOnService* registry entry at

```
HKLM\SYSTEM\CurrentControlSet\Services\LanManWorkstation
```

This will let the system know that the *LMHOSTS* service needs to be started for the *LanManWorkstation* service to work properly. In other cases, the service that is being installed will know that it is directly dependent on some other service. For instance, a service might require Microsoft SQL Server to properly initialize. In this case, *MSSQLServer* can be added to the double-NULL-terminated list pointed to by the *lpDependencies* argument to *CreateService*. A double-NULL-terminated list is an array of characters in which text values are usually entered, each separated by a NULL, with the last entry followed by two NULLs. Setting this kind of registry entry will be explored in Chapter 12. A somewhat more complicated method for controlling the load order of services is provided by the *lpLoadOrderGroup* and *lpdwTagId* parameters. In general, these parameters are used for drivers rather than service applications and are fully documented in the Win32 SDK.

The final two *CreateService* parameters are used for a user name and a password for an account to start the service, with NULL being used for both *lpServiceStartName* and *lpPassword* to indicate that the System account should be used. Remember that if the service is to be interactive, as specified by SERVICE_INTERACTIVE_PROCESS included in the *dwServiceType* parameter, these entries *must* be NULL. Also, if the service supports more than a single service by using the SERVICE_WIN32_SHARE_PROCESS flag in the *dwServiceType* parameter, these entries must be NULL to ensure that the System account is used.

If the handle returned by *CreateService* is non-NULL, the service has been successfully installed. All that remains is to close the handles that were opened using *OpenSCManager* and *CreateService*. Note that in the installation section of the *main* routine, *printf* is used to display a progress message. Since the *HelloService* program is a service, is *printf* allowed? In this case, yes, because the application is running as a standard Win32 console mode application in the installation portion or, as we will see, the uninstallation portion of the *main* routine.

## Using *DeleteService* to Uninstall the Service

If *–U* is passed as the first parameter to the service program, the code to uninstall the service is run. This code is similar to—but much simpler than—the installation routine. After the call to *OpenSCManager*, the uninstallation section of *main* calls *OpenService*, which has the following prototype:

```
SC_HANDLE OpenService (
    SC_HANDLE hSCManager,     // Handle of service control manager
                              //  database
    LPCTSTR lpServiceName,    // Pointer to name of service to start
    DWORD dwDesiredAccess     // Type of access to service
);
```

The *hSCManager* parameter is the handle returned by *OpenSCManager*. The *lpServiceName* parameter is the name specified previously as the *lpServiceName* parameter in the call to *CreateService*. The *dwDesiredAccess* parameter specifies the access to the service requested, in the same format as *CreateService*.

Once the handle of the service is returned from *OpenService*, you can pass it to *DeleteService*. If the return value is nonzero, the service has been deleted.

## Starting the Service

If neither *–I* nor *–U* is passed as an argument on the command line, the service assumes that it should start running and the following code segment is run:

```
sprintf(diag,"About to start service control...\n");
logError(diag);
if (!StartServiceCtrlDispatcher(DispatchTable))
{
    sprintf(diag,
        "BeepService StartServiceCtrlDispatcher error = %d\n",
        GetLastError());
    logError(diag);
}
```

If a service is actually being started by the SCM, the only duty of the *main* function is to call the Win32 API function *StartServiceCtrlDispatcher*. This function takes a single argument, a pointer to a SERVICE_TABLE_ENTRY array. (This is the array initialized at the top of the *main* function.) Once *StartServiceCtrlDispatcher* is called, *main* has served its purpose.

## Inside *ServiceMain*

The *ServiceMain* function is responsible for getting the service running when the service application is started by the SCM. *ServiceMain* first initializes some elements of the *ServiceStatus* structure declared at the top of Listing 3-1.

```
ServiceStatus.dwServiceType        = SERVICE_WIN32_OWN_PROCESS;
ServiceStatus.dwCurrentState       = SERVICE_START_PENDING;
ServiceStatus.dwControlsAccepted   = SERVICE_ACCEPT_STOP;
ServiceStatus.dwWin32ExitCode      = 0;
ServiceStatus.dwServiceSpecificExitCode = 0;
ServiceStatus.dwCheckPoint         = 0;
ServiceStatus.dwWaitHint           = 0;
```

The *dwControlsAccepted* parameter allows the service to specify which actions it will process. Many services also accept pause requests by ORing SERVICE_ACCEPT_PAUSE_CONTINUE into *dwControlsAccepted*. The service can also specify that it wants to be notified of a system shutdown by ORing SERVICE_ACCEPT_SHUTDOWN into *dwControlsAccepted*. Several additional notifications supported in Windows 2000 allow a service to be notified of parameter changes (SERVICE_ACCEPT_PARAMCHANGE), network binding changes (SERVICE_ACCEPT_NETBINDCHANGE), hardware profile changes (SERVICE_ACCEPT_HARDWAREPROFILECHANGE), and power status events (SERVICE_ACCEPT_POWEREVENT). The *dwWaitHint* parameter allows the service to specify, in milliseconds, how long it expects to take before the next call to notify the SCM of its status. If the time elapses without any notifications, the SCM can assume that an error has occurred.

Once the required *ServiceStatus* elements have been initialized, the service must call *RegisterServiceCtrlHandler* for Windows NT or Windows 2000 or *RegisterServiceCtrlHandlerEx* on Windows 2000. This call should take place before the service executes any initialization code that could be time-consuming. The *HelloService* code that calls *RegisterServiceCtrlHandler* is shown here:

```
ServiceStatusHandle = RegisterServiceCtrlHandler(
    "BeepService",
    Handler);

if (ServiceStatusHandle == (SERVICE_STATUS_HANDLE)0)
{
    sprintf(diag,
        "BeeperService RegisterServiceCtrlHandler failed %d\n",
        GetLastError());
    logError(diag);
    return;
}
```

*RegisterServiceCtrlHandler* is called with the name of the service and the address of the handler function. *RegisterServiceCtrlHandlerEx* takes the same parameters, except the handler function must accept four parameters rather than one and returns a DWORD value that indicates whether an error has occurred. This code logs an error if the handle returned by *RegisterServiceCtrlHandler* is NULL.

In Listing 3-1, *ServiceInitialization* is called next. This is not a Win32 API function, but instead a convenient way to place initialization code outside the *ServiceMain* function. If the *ServiceInitialization* function returns an error condition, the *dwCurrentState* element of the *ServiceStatus* structure is set to SERVICE_STOPPED with error codes set to indicate the problem *ServiceInitialization* encountered, and the Win32 API function *SetServiceStatus* is called.

```
BOOL SetServiceStatus (
    SERVICE_STATUS_HANDLE hServiceStatus, // Service status handle
    LPSERVICE_STATUS lpServiceStatus      // Pointer to status
                                          //  structure
);
```

*SetServiceStatus* is called frequently while a service is being stopped, started, or paused. This lets the SCM know the current status of the service, allowing the SCM to report this information back to the user via the appropriate user interface.

If the *ServiceInitialization* call returns NO_ERROR, the beep service sets *dwCurrentState* to SERVICE_RUNNING and calls *SetServiceStatus* again to indicate that the service is operational. Note that up to this point, no actual service has taken place. The service is running, but beyond the boilerplate code that installs, uninstalls, and runs the service, we've seen no hint of the service's real purpose.

The actual work of the beep service is simple: Display a message box and then start beeping about once per second.

```
// This is where the service does its work.
MessageBox(NULL, "Hello Service World", "BeeperService",
    MB_OK | MB_SERVICE_NOTIFICATION | MB_ICONINFORMATION);
while (1)
{
    Beep(2000,200);
    Sleep(1000);
    if (isRunning == false)
    {
        break;
    }
}
```

The processing loop checks the status of the BOOL flag *isRunning*. When the flag becomes false, the service exits. This is a reasonable action for a simple test application because we are not allowing anything but the stopping of the service. No pause or continue is possible.

Once the beep service exits the processing loop, the final step is to call *SetServiceStatus* one more time to let the SCM know that the service has stopped. Skipping this final step will result in the service stopping, but the SCM will register an error stopping the service.

> **NOTE** What happens when a service is paused? Should all operations immediately stop? Should ongoing operations continue to completion but no additional work commence? The answers depend on the duration of the operations involved, as well as the criticality of the processing, and the decision is left completely to the developer. If a service were controlling some materials processing that would cause a large amount of waste if the processing were stopped in the middle, running a particular batch to completion in the event of a pause request would be reasonable. If a service were servicing a client and the average client connection was on the order of several seconds, continuing processing for existing clients would likely make sense. On the other hand, if the service is a database engine or a Web server, pausing only new connections while allowing ongoing connections might not make sense. In the final analysis, the developer must control the semantics of pausing, and should of course document the effects of the pause operation so that the user of the service can react appropriately in the event that service stops responding.

The *Handler* function in this example is pretty plain vanilla in its behavior. In the *HelloService* example, the only special handling is for the SERVICE_CONTROL_STOP case of the *switch* statement. One problem with the code is the handling of the SERVICE_CONTROL_PAUSE case and the SERVICE_CONTROL_CONTINUE case of the *switch* statement. For instance, if there were code that began the pausing of the service, that code could be run twice if two pause commands were sent within the time it takes for the system to pause. This is not a problem in the Windows 2000 user interface, as the pause button is commonly disabled after a pause request is made. However, services can be controlled by other applications, and those applications might not be so considerate. The C++ Beep Service example later in this chapter will solve these problems and a few others.

# A C++ FRAMEWORK FOR WINDOWS 2000 SERVICES

While the program in Listing 3-1 is a workable Windows NT and Windows 2000 service, much of the code is boilerplate and can be used by other services. Boilerplate code is ideal for a C++ class that cleanly encapsulates the code while exposing event handlers that can be overridden to provide custom functionality. You can see the first C++ class for Windows 2000 Services in the MSDN documentation in an article by Nigel Thompson called "Creating a Simple Windows NT Service in C++." The class used by the C++ Beep Service example later in this chapter was developed independent of Nigel's example, but certainly no one writing a C++ class for Windows NT or Windows 2000 services should do so without reading Nigel's article.

## Writing a C++ Class for Windows 2000 Services Is Harder Than It Looks

Upon first examination, a C++ class seems perfect for solving the problem of creating a service application. There are, however, a couple of problems, all of which center around implementation details of C++ classes. Imagine a simple C++ class that only contains the two callback functions that must be implemented for a Windows 2000 service.

```
class CSillyService {
    DWORD WINAPI HandlerEx(DWORD dwControl, DWORD dwEventType,
        LPVOID lpEventData, LPVOID lpContext);
    VOID WINAPI ServiceMain(DWORD dwArgc, LPTSTR *lpszArgv);
};
```

The code fragment above declares the two callback functions required for a Windows 2000 service application. Unfortunately, these functions will not work. Internally, every member function or method of a C++ class has an implicit parameter named *this* that is a pointer to the specific instance of the class. One of the purposes of the implicit *this* pointer is to allow the methods of a class to dereference the data elements of the class. So while the function declarations look as if they meet the requirements of the service API, they do not.

How, then, can a method of a class be used as a callback function? I oversimplified the example above. All normal class methods have an implicit *this* parameter. However, classes can have *static* methods and data elements. For a static data element, there is one and only one copy of the element for all instances of the class. Only static methods can act on static data elements, and the static methods have no concept of *this*. Chapter 8 will introduce an ODBC class that makes extensive use of static class members, which also come in handy in creating a service class.

Rewriting the *CSillyService* class to use static methods (which will meet the API requirements for parameters) gives us the following fragment of a class declaration:

```
class CPPService {
<;$VE>
    static DWORD WINAPI HandlerEx(DWORD dwControl,
        DWORD dwEventType, LPVOID lpEventData,
        LPVOID lpContext);
    static VOID WINAPI ServiceMain(DWORD dwArgc,
        LPTSTR *lpszArgv);
    static CPPService *m_this;
};
```

While the loss of the *this* pointer as an implicit but undeclared parameter eliminates one problem of using a C++ class to create a service, it creates another. Because the static member functions have no concept of *this*, the class must artificially provide it by means of a data member named *m_this* that is a static pointer to a *CPPService* object. The *m_this* pointer is set in the constructor and then used within the static methods to dereference specific data members of an instance of the class. Thus, static class member variables are similar to global variables, but are local to the class.

While this seems like a win-win situation, problems remain. First and foremost, the *CPPService* class is limited to supporting service applications that contain a single service, because all instances of the class would share a single *m_this* pointer. This is seldom a significant problem, but if you have a set of services that should be controlled independently yet share much common code, and so would be natural candidates for inclusion in a single large service application, *CPPService* might not be sufficient. For the vast majority of cases, however, the limitation of a single service within the application will not be a significant drawback.

How much smaller would a service application using the C++ class be than the *HelloService* program? Compare the code in Listing 3-1 to the following code in Listing 3-2.

**CPPBeepService.cpp**

```
#include "stdafx.h"

CBeepService::CBeepService(char *tsvcName, char *tdispName,
    DWORD tsvcStart) : CPPService(tsvcName, tdispName, tsvcStart)
{
    ;
}

BOOL CBeepService::OnInit(DWORD *status)
{
    logError("OnInit");
    *status = 0;
    return true;
}

void CBeepService::Run()
{
    while (m_isRunning)
    {
        if (m_isPaused == false)
        {
            Beep(2000, 200);
        }
        Sleep(1000);
    }
    return;
}
```

**Listing 3-2** *(continued)*

**Listing 3-2** *continued*

```
int main(int argc, char* argv[])
{
    CBeepService MyBeepService("CBeepService", "C++ Beep Service");
    // Have we handled the arguments and done an install or uninstall?
    if (MyBeepService.ParseArguments(argc, argv) == false)
    {
        // If not, start the service running...
        MyBeepService.StartService();
    }

    return 0;
}
```

Listing 3-1 contains 275 lines of code, while Listing 3-2 contains 40 lines of code. If you keep in mind the credo of the high-quality coder—the best code is that which does not need to be written—you'll understand that this reduction in code is important. Interestingly, the size of the debugged version of the executable generated from the code in Listing 3-2 is about 15 percent smaller than the executable generated from the code in Listing 3-1. (The class declaration for the *CBeepService* class is in the stdafx.h file of the CPPBeepService project on the book's companion CD-ROM.) The class declaration is simple, showing how the base class needs to be used to implement a new service with minimal code.

```
class CBeepService : public CPPService
{
public:
    CBeepService(char *tsvcName,char *tdispName,
        DWORD tsvcStart = SERVICE_DEMAND_START);
    virtual BOOL OnInit(DWORD *status);
    virtual void Run();
};
```

## Implementing the C++ Service Class

Obviously, there is no free ride, and obviously, the code must be somewhere. In the *CPPService* class, however, the code can be created once and used by many different services without inadvertently modifying the code during a copy-and-paste session. Just as important, if a bug is discovered in the core code that resides in the base class, it can be fixed once, and with a recompile, all applications using the code can be corrected at once.

The *CPPService* class handles most of the housekeeping associated with installing, uninstalling, and operating a service. The class provides the callback functions as static member functions and provides many virtual functions that allow descendant classes to provide handlers for many of the events that take place. The one virtual function that will almost always be overridden is *Run*. This function is called by *ServiceMain* and should contain the actual functionality of the service.

To get an overview of the structure of the class that implements most of the service functionality, look at Listing 3-3, the header file for the *CPPService* class.

**CPPService.h**

```
#define SERVICE_CONTROL_USER 128

VOID StartThisService(char *serviceName);

class CPPService {
public:
    CPPService(char *tsvcName, char *tdispName,
        DWORD tsvcStart = SERVICE_DEMAND_START);
    virtual ~CPPService();
    BOOL IsInstalled();
    BOOL Install();
    BOOL UnInstall();
    BOOL StartService();
    void SetStatus(DWORD dwControl);
    BOOL Initialize();
    BOOL ParseArguments(int argc, char *argv[]);
    char *ServiceName()
    {
        return serviceName;
    }
    void SetUserAndPassword(char *user = NULL,
        char *pwd = NULL);
    virtual void OnInstall();
    virtual void OnUninstall();
    virtual BOOL OnInit(DWORD *status);
    virtual void Run();
    virtual void OnStop();
    virtual void OnPause();
    virtual void OnContinue();
    virtual BOOL OnUserControl(DWORD dwControl);
    virtual void OnParamChange();
    virtual void OnNetBindAdd();
    virtual void OnNetBindRemove();
    virtual void OnNetBindEnable();
    virtual void OnNetBindDisable();
#ifdef _WIN2K_COMPAT
    virtual void OnDeviceEvent(DWORD dwEventType,
        LPVOID pvEventData);
    virtual void OnPowerEvent(DWORD dwEventType,
        LPVOID pvEventData);
    virtual void OnHardwareProfileChange(DWORD dwEventType);
```

**Listing 3-3** *(continued)*

**Listing 3-3** *continued*

```
#endif
protected:
    SC_HANDLE m_scmHandle;
    SC_HANDLE m_scHandle;
    SERVICE_STATUS ServiceStatus;
    SERVICE_STATUS_HANDLE ServiceStatusHandle;
    static CPPService *m_this;
    char serviceName[128];
    char serviceDisplayName[128];
    VOID logError(char *msg);
    FILE *log;
    char m_diag[255];
    DWORD m_svcStartType;
    DWORD m_status;
    BOOL m_isRunning;
    BOOL m_isPaused;
#ifdef _WIN2K_COMPAT
    static DWORD WINAPI HandlerEx(DWORD dwControl,
        DWORD dwEventType, LPVOID lpEventData,
        LPVOID lpContext);
#else
    static VOID WINAPI Handler(DWORD dwControl);
#endif
    static VOID WINAPI ServiceMain(DWORD dwArgc,
        LPTSTR *lpszArgv);

};
```

Notice a few things about this class declaration. First, the *#define* of SERVICE_CONTROL_USER lets the class know that service control requests greater than or equal to 128 are user-defined control codes that an application can use to control the service. This is standard for all Windows 2000 services. Second, the class can be compiled for either Windows NT or Windows 2000, depending on the _WIN2K_COMPAT macro being defined. Note that the older style of functions will work on either Windows NT or Windows 2000. The functional difference is the availability of three additional virtual functions that allow the service to react to device events, power events, and hardware profile changes. The other noteworthy change in service support in Windows 2000 is the availability of a context pointer sent to *HandlerEx*. Because of the way the service class is implemented, the context pointer, which allows the *HandlerEx* function to distinguish between multiple services, is not terribly useful.

The class constructor for *CPPService* accepts several parameters:

```
CPPService(char *tsvcName, char *tdispName,
    DWORD tsvcStart = SERVICE_DEMAND_START);
```

The first two parameters are the service name and the display name. The third optional parameter allows the service to be installed to start either on demand or automatically. The constructor presented in full below first copies the arguments to class member variables. Many functions within the *CPPService* class require the handle of the SCM, so the constructor gets the handle of the SCM by calling *OpenSCManager*. The *m_this* pointer is set to point to this instance of the class, and *m_isRunning* and *m_isPaused* are set to *false*. These two Boolean variables are used to let the service know whether it is currently running or paused. Finally, the *ServiceStatus* structure is initialized.

```
CPPService::CPPService(char *tsvcName,char *tdispName,
    DWORD tsvcStartType)
{
    strncpy(serviceName, tsvcName, 128);
    strncpy(serviceDisplayName, tdispName, 128);
    m_svcStartType = tsvcStartType;
    m_scmHandle = OpenSCManager(NULL, SERVICES_ACTIVE_DATABASE,
        SC_MANAGER_ALL_ACCESS);
    if (m_scmHandle == NULL)
    {
        printf("\n OpenSCManager error %d ", GetLastError());
    }
    m_scHandle = 0;
    m_this = this;
    m_isRunning = false;
    m_isPaused = false;

    ServiceStatus.dwServiceType        = SERVICE_WIN32_OWN_PROCESS;
    ServiceStatus.dwCurrentState       = SERVICE_START_PENDING;
    ServiceStatus.dwControlsAccepted   =
        SERVICE_ACCEPT_STOP | SERVICE_ACCEPT_PAUSE_CONTINUE;
    ServiceStatus.dwWin32ExitCode      = 0;
    ServiceStatus.dwServiceSpecificExitCode = 0;
    ServiceStatus.dwCheckPoint         = 0;
    ServiceStatus.dwWaitHint           = 0;
}
```

*ParseArguments* uses the same logic from the *main* function in Listing 3-1. Commonly, as in Listing 3-2, *ParseArguments* should be called from the *main* function of the service. If *ParseArguments* returns *false*, there are no recognizable arguments on the command line and the service should be started using the *CPPService* member function *StartService*.

The *Run* virtual function is overridden in Listing 3-2 and provides the same functionality as the much longer program in Listing 3-1. The *Run* function controls the beeping and is controlled by the *m_isRunning* and *m_isPaused* member variables:

```
void CBeepService::Run()
{
    while (m_isRunning)
    {
        if (m_isPaused == false)
        {
            Beep(2000, 200);
        }
        Sleep(1000);
    }
    return;
}
```

Any function performed by the overridden *Run* method should perform its task as efficiently as possible. For example, if the *Sleep* line were moved inside the loop controlled by the *m_isPaused* variable, it would use much more processing time than would normally be required. When testing a service, it is useful to look at the Processes tab of the Task Manager to see the amount of memory and the percentage of the processor a service is using in all of its possible states, as shown for the *CBeepService* in Figure 3-2. Of course, the service does *not* show up on the Applications tab of the Task Manager.

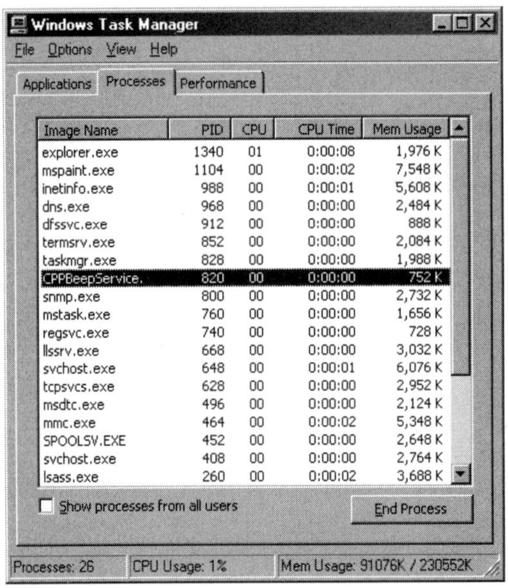


**Figure 3-2** *The Task Manager in Windows 2000 showing information on* CBeepService.

Listing 3-4 is the implementation of the *CPPService* class. Most of this code is similar in function to the code in Listing 3-1, but structured so that it can be used more generically.

**CPPService.cpp**

```
#include "Stdafx.h"

CPPService* CPPService::m_this = NULL;

VOID StartThisService(char *serviceName)
{
    SERVICE_STATUS ssStatus;
    DWORD dwOldCheckPoint;

    SC_HANDLE schSCManager =
        ::OpenSCManager(NULL,    // Local machine
        NULL,                    // ServicesActive database
        SC_MANAGER_ALL_ACCESS); // Full access

    printf("\nStarting Service...\n");
    SC_HANDLE schService = OpenService(
        schSCManager,          // SCM database
        TEXT(serviceName),     // Service name
        SERVICE_ALL_ACCESS);
    if (schService == NULL)
    {
        printf("\nCan't open service...last error = %d",
            GetLastError());
        return;
    }
    if (!StartService(
        schService,    // Handle of service
        0,             // Number of arguments
        NULL))         // No arguments
    {
            printf("\nStart Service failure...");
        return;
    }
    else
    {
        printf("Service start pending\n");
    }
    // Check the status until the service is no longer start pending.
    if (!QueryServiceStatus(
        schService,   // Handle of service
        &ssStatus))   // Address of status information
```

**Listing 3-4** *(continued)*

**Listing 3-4** *continued*

```
    {
        printf("\nError in Query Service Status");
        return;
    }

    // Some services take a long time to start, so there is
    //  an elaborate mechanism to handle that. This is not
    //  very useful with the example services provided but
    //  could be more so for more complex services.
    while (ssStatus.dwCurrentState == SERVICE_START_PENDING)
    {
        // Save the current checkpoint.
        dwOldCheckPoint = ssStatus.dwCheckPoint;
        // Wait for the specified interval.
        Sleep(ssStatus.dwWaitHint);      // Check the status again.
        if (!QueryServiceStatus(
            schService,   // Handle of service
            &ssStatus))   // Address of status information
        {
            break;
        }
        // Break if the checkpoint has not been incremented.
        if (dwOldCheckPoint >= ssStatus.dwCheckPoint)
        {
            break;
        }
    }
    if (ssStatus.dwCurrentState == SERVICE_RUNNING)
    {
        printf("\nService Started\n");
    }
    else
    {
        printf("  Current State: %d\n",
            ssStatus.dwCurrentState);
        printf("  Exit Code: %d\n", ssStatus.dwWin32ExitCode);
        printf("  Service Specific Exit Code: %d\n",
            ssStatus.dwServiceSpecificExitCode);
        printf("  Check Point: %d\n", ssStatus.dwCheckPoint);
        printf("  Wait Hint: %d\n", ssStatus.dwWaitHint);
    }
    CloseServiceHandle(schService);
    CloseServiceHandle(schSCManager);
}
```

```
CPPService::CPPService(char *tsvcName, char *tdispName,
    DWORD tsvcStartType)
{
    strncpy(serviceName,tsvcName,128);
    strncpy(serviceDisplayName,tdispName,128);
    m_svcStartType = tsvcStartType;
    m_scmHandle = OpenSCManager(NULL,SERVICES_ACTIVE_DATABASE,
        SC_MANAGER_ALL_ACCESS);
    if (m_scmHandle == NULL)
    {
        printf("\n OpenSCManager error %d ",GetLastError());
    }
    m_scHandle = 0;
    m_this = this;
    m_isRunning = false;
    m_isPaused = false;

    ServiceStatus.dwServiceType        = SERVICE_WIN32_OWN_PROCESS;
    ServiceStatus.dwCurrentState       = SERVICE_START_PENDING;
    ServiceStatus.dwControlsAccepted   =
        SERVICE_ACCEPT_STOP | SERVICE_ACCEPT_PAUSE_CONTINUE;
    ServiceStatus.dwWin32ExitCode      = 0;
    ServiceStatus.dwServiceSpecificExitCode = 0;
    ServiceStatus.dwCheckPoint         = 0;
    ServiceStatus.dwWaitHint           = 0;
}

CPPService::~CPPService()
{
    if (m_scmHandle != 0)
    {
        ::CloseHandle(m_scmHandle);
    }
    if (m_scHandle != 0)
    {
        ::CloseHandle(m_scHandle);
    }
}

BOOL CPPService::ParseArguments(int argc, char **argv)
{
    BOOL result = false;
    if (argc>1 && !(strnicmp(argv[1], "-i", 2)))
```

*(continued)*

**Listing 3-4** *continued*

```
    {
        if ((Install()))
        {
            printf("\n%s installed!", ServiceName());
        }
        else
        {
            printf(
                "\n%s NOT installed!  Last error %d",
                ServiceName(), GetLastError());
        }
        result = true;
    }
    else if (argc>1 && !(strnicmp(argv[1], "-u", 2)))
    {
        if ((UnInstall()))
        {
            printf("\n%s uninstalled!", ServiceName());
        }
        else
        {
            printf(
                "\n%s NOT uninstalled!  Last error %d",
                ServiceName(), GetLastError());
        }
        result = true;
    }
    return result;
}

VOID CPPService::logError(char *text)
{
    log = fopen("c:\\service.log", "a+t");
    if (log)
    {
        fprintf(log, "%s\n", text);
        fclose(log);
    }
    return;
}

BOOL CPPService::Install()
{
    char szPath[MAX_PATH];
    char szBuffer[MAX_PATH+2];
    BOOL result = true;  // Default to success
```

```
    GetModuleFileName(GetModuleHandle(NULL), szPath,MAX_PATH);
    // Why do we do this? The path may contain spaces.
    //  If it does, the path must be quoted.
    strcpy(szBuffer, "\"");
    strcat(szBuffer, szPath);
    strcat(szBuffer, "\"");
    printf("\nInstalling service %s", szPath);

    m_scHandle = CreateService(m_scmHandle, serviceName,
        serviceDisplayName, SERVICE_ALL_ACCESS,
        SERVICE_WIN32_OWN_PROCESS,
        m_svcStartType,
        SERVICE_ERROR_NORMAL, szBuffer,
        NULL, NULL, NULL, NULL, NULL);

    if (m_scHandle == NULL) // Process error
    {
        DWORD lastError;
        LastError = GetLastError();
        if (lastError == 1073) // Service already installed
        {
            sprintf(m_diag, " CreateService error ="
                Service Already Installed (1073)\n");
        }
        else
        {
            sprintf(m_diag, " CreateService error = %d\n",
                lastError);
        }
        printf("%s\n", m_diag);
        logError(m_diag);
        result = false;
    }
    OnInstall();
    return result;
}

BOOL CPPService::StartService()
{
    SERVICE_TABLE_ENTRY DispatchTable[] = {
        {serviceName, CPPService::ServiceMain},
        {NULL, NULL}
    };

    BOOL b = ::StartServiceCtrlDispatcher(DispatchTable);
    return b;
}
```

*(continued)*

**Listing 3-4** *continued*

```
BOOL CPPService::UnInstall()
{
    m_scHandle = OpenService(m_scmHandle, serviceName,
        SERVICE_ALL_ACCESS);
    if (m_scHandle != NULL)
    {
        DeleteService(m_scHandle);
        printf("\n%s uninstalled...", serviceName);
        CloseHandle(m_scHandle);
        m_scHandle = 0;
        OnUninstall();
        return(true);
    }
    printf("\nOpen Service error: %d ", GetLastError());
    return(false);

}

void CPPService::SetStatus(DWORD dwControl)
{
    ServiceStatus.dwCurrentState        = dwControl;
    ServiceStatus.dwCheckPoint          = 0;
    ServiceStatus.dwWaitHint            = 0;

    if (!SetServiceStatus (ServiceStatusHandle, &ServiceStatus))
    {
        m_status = GetLastError();
        sprintf(m_diag,
            " %s SetServiceStatus error %ld dwControl = %d\n",
            serviceName,m_status,dwControl);
        logError(m_diag);
    }

}

VOID WINAPI CPPService::ServiceMain(DWORD argc, LPTSTR *argv)
{
    BOOL initStat;
    DWORD specificError;
    CPPService *thisPtr;

    thisPtr = m_this;
```

```
#ifdef _WIN2K_COMPAT
    char szContext[255];
    strcpy(szContext, thisPtr->ServiceName());
    thisPtr->ServiceStatusHandle = RegisterServiceCtrlHandlerEx(
        thisPtr->ServiceName,
        HandlerEx,
        &szContext);
#else
    thisPtr->ServiceStatusHandle = RegisterServiceCtrlHandler(
        thisPtr->serviceName,
        Handler);
#endif
    if (thisPtr->ServiceStatusHandle == (SERVICE_STATUS_HANDLE)0)
    {
        sprintf(thisPtr->m_diag,
            " RegisterServiceCtrlHandler failed %d\n",
            GetLastError());
        thisPtr->logError(thisPtr->m_diag);
        return;
    }

    thisPtr->SetStatus(SERVICE_START_PENDING);
    // Initialization code goes here.

    initStat = thisPtr->OnInit(&specificError);

    // Handle error condition.
    if (initStat == false)
    {
        thisPtr->SetStatus(SERVICE_STOPPED);
        sprintf(thisPtr->m_diag,
            "OnInit failed initStat = %d...\n", initStat);
        thisPtr->logError(thisPtr->m_diag);
        return;
    }

    thisPtr->SetStatus(SERVICE_RUNNING);
    thisPtr->m_isRunning = true;


    sprintf(thisPtr->m_diag,
        "Just before processing loop...\n");
```

*(continued)*

**Listing 3-4** *continued*

```
    thisPtr->logError(thisPtr->m_diag);
    // This is where the service does its work.

    thisPtr->Run();

    // Send current status.
    thisPtr->SetStatus(SERVICE_STOPPED);

    return;
}

#ifdef _WIN2K_COMPAT
DWORD WINAPI CPPService::HandlerEx(DWORD dwControl,
    DWORD dwEventType, LPVOID lpEventData,
    LPVOID lpContext)
{
    DWORD status = SERVICE_RUNNING;
    CPPService *thisPtr;

    thisPtr = m_this;

    sprintf(thisPtr->m_diag,
        "In to service control...\n");
    thisPtr->logError(thisPtr->m_diag);
    switch(dwControl)
    {
        case SERVICE_CONTROL_PAUSE:
        // Do whatever it takes to pause here.
            sprintf(thisPtr->m_diag, "Pausing...\n");
            thisPtr->logError(thisPtr->m_diag);
            if (!(thisPtr->m_isPaused))
            {
                thisPtr->m_isPaused = true;
                thisPtr->OnPause();
                status = SERVICE_PAUSED;
            }
            break;

        case SERVICE_CONTROL_CONTINUE:
        // Do whatever it takes to continue here.
            sprintf(thisPtr->m_diag, "Continuing...\n");
            thisPtr->logError(thisPtr->m_diag);
            if (thisPtr->m_isPaused)
```

```
        {
            thisPtr->OnContinue();
            thisPtr->m_isPaused = false;
            status = SERVICE_RUNNING;
        }
        break;

    case SERVICE_CONTROL_STOP:
    // Do whatever it takes to stop here.
        sprintf(thisPtr->m_diag, "Stopping...\n");
        thisPtr->logError(thisPtr->m_diag);
        if (thisPtr->m_isRunning)
        {
            thisPtr->OnStop();
            status = SERVICE_STOP_PENDING;
            thisPtr->m_isRunning = false;
        }

        thisPtr->SetStatus(status);
        sprintf(thisPtr->m_diag,
            " BeeperService Leaving Handler \n",0);
        thisPtr->logError(thisPtr->m_diag);
        return;

    case SERVICE_CONTROL_PARAMCHANGE:
        thisPtr->OnParamChange();
        break;

    case SERVICE_CONTROL_NETBINDADD:
        thisPtr->OnNetBindAdd();
        break

    case SERVICE_CONTROL_NETBINDDELETE:
        thisPtr->OnNetBindDelete();
        break

    case SERVICE_CONTROL_NETBINDREMOVE:
        thisPtr->OnNetBindRemove();
        break

    case SERVICE_CONTROL_NETBINDENABLE:
        thisPtr->OnNetBindEnable();
        break
```

*(continued)*

**Listing 3-4** *continued*

```
        case SERVICE_CONTROL_NETBINDDISABLE:
            thisPtr->OnNetBindDisable();
            break

        case SERVICE_CONTROL_DEVICEEVENT:
            thisPtr->OnDeviceEvent(dwEventType,
                lpEventData);
            break;

        case SERVICE_CONTROL_POWEREVENT:
            thisPtr->OnPowerEvent(dwEventType,
                lpEventData);
            break;

        case SERVICE_CONTROL_HARDWAREPROFILECHANGE:
            thisPtr->OnHardwareProfileChange(dwEventType);
            break;

        case SERVICE_CONTROL_INTERROGATE:
        // Fall through to send current status.
            break;

        default:
            if (dwControl >= SERVICE_CONTROL_USER)
            {
                if (!thisPtr->OnUserControl(dwControl))
                {
                    sprintf(thisPtr->m_diag,
                        " %s Unhandled control code %ld\n",
                        thisPtr->ServiceName(),
                        dwControl);
                    thisPtr->logError(thisPtr->m_diag);
                }
                else
                {
                    sprintf(thisPtr->m_diag,
                        " %s Unrecognized control code %ld\n",
                        thisPtr->ServiceName(),
                        dwControl);
                        thisPtr->logError(thisPtr->m_diag);
                }
                break;
            }
    }
```

```
    // Send current status.
    thisPtr->SetStatus(status);
    return 0;
}
#else
VOID WINAPI CPPService::Handler(DWORD dwControl)
{
    DWORD status = SERVICE_RUNNING;
    CPPService *thisPtr;

    thisPtr = m_this;

    sprintf(thisPtr->m_diag,
        "In to service control...\n");
    thisPtr->logError(thisPtr->m_diag);
    switch(dwControl)
    {
        case SERVICE_CONTROL_PAUSE:
        // Do whatever it takes to pause here.
            sprintf(thisPtr->m_diag,
                "Pausing...\n");
            thisPtr->logError(thisPtr->m_diag);
            if (!(thisPtr->m_isPaused))
            {
                thisPtr->m_isPaused = true;
                thisPtr->OnPause();
                status = SERVICE_PAUSED;
            }
            break;

        case SERVICE_CONTROL_CONTINUE:
        // Do whatever it takes to continue here.
            sprintf(thisPtr->m_diag,
                "Continuing...\n");
            thisPtr->logError(thisPtr->m_diag);
            if (thisPtr->m_isPaused)
            {
                thisPtr->OnContinue();
                thisPtr->m_isPaused = false;
                status = SERVICE_RUNNING;
            }
            break;

        case SERVICE_CONTROL_STOP:
        // Do whatever it takes to stop here.
```

*(continued)*

**Listing 3-4** *continued*

```
            sprintf(thisPtr->m_diag,
                "Stopping...\n");
            thisPtr->logError(thisPtr->m_diag);
            if (thisPtr->m_isRunning)
            {
                thisPtr->OnStop();
                status = SERVICE_STOP_PENDING;
                thisPtr->m_isRunning = false;
            }

            thisPtr->SetStatus (status);
            sprintf(thisPtr->m_diag,
                " BeeperService leaving handler \n",0);
            thisPtr->logError(thisPtr->m_diag);
            return;

        case SERVICE_CONTROL_PARAMCHANGE:
            thisPtr->OnParamChange();
            break;

        case SERVICE_CONTROL_NETBINDADD:
            thisPtr->OnNetBindAdd();
            break;

        case SERVICE_CONTROL_NETBINDDISABLE:
            thisPtr->OnNetBindDisable();
            break;

        case SERVICE_CONTROL_NETBINDREMOVE:
            thisPtr->OnNetBindRemove();
            break;

        case SERVICE_CONTROL_NETBINDENABLE:
            thisPtr->OnNetBindEnable();
            break;

        case SERVICE_CONTROL_INTERROGATE:
            // Fall through to send current status.
            break;

        default:
            if (dwControl >= SERVICE_CONTROL_USER)
            {
                if (!thisPtr->OnUserControl(dwControl))
```

```
                {
                    sprintf(thisPtr->m_diag,
                        " %s Unhandled control code %ld\n",
                        thisPtr->ServiceName(),
                        dwControl);
                    thisPtr->logError(thisPtr->m_diag);
                }
                else
                {
                    sprintf(thisPtr->m_diag,
                        " %s Unrecognized control code %ld\n",
                        thisPtr->ServiceName(),
                        dwControl);
                    thisPtr->logError(thisPtr->m_diag);
                }
                break;
            }
    }

    // Send current status.
    thisPtr->SetStatus(status);
    return;
}
#endif

// Virtual functions; generally overridden if needed.
BOOL CPPService::OnUserControl(DWORD dwControl)
{
    logError("OnContinue");
    return false;
}

void CPPService::OnContinue()
{
    logError("OnContinue");
    return;
}

void CPPService::OnPause()
{
    logError("OnPause");
    return;
}
```

*(continued)*

**Listing 3-4** *continued*

```
void CPPService::OnStop()
{
    logError("OnStop");
    return;
}

void CPPService::OnInstall()
{
    logError("OnInstall");
    return;
}

void CPPService::OnUninstall()
{
    logError("OnUninstall");
    return;
}

BOOL CPPService::OnInit(DWORD *status)
{
    logError("OnInit");
    *status = 0;
    return true;
}

void CPPService::OnParamChange()
{
    logError("OnParamChange");
    return;
}

void CPPService::OnNetBindAdd()
{
    logError("OnNetBindAdd");
    return;
}

void CPPService::OnNetBindRemove()
{
    logError("OnNetBindRemove");
    return;
}
```

```
void CPPService::OnNetBindEnable()
{
    logError("OnNetBindEnable");
    return;
}

void CPPService::OnNetBindDisable()
{
    logError("OnNetBindDisable");
    return;
}

void CPPService::Run()
{
    while (m_isRunning)
    {
        Sleep(1000);
    }
    return;
}

#ifdef _WIN2K_COMPAT

void OnDeviceEvent(DWORD dwEventType, LPVOID pvEventData)
{
    logError("OnDeviceEvent");
    return;
}

void OnPowerEvent(DWORD dwEventType, LPVOID pvEventData)
{
    logError("OnPowerEvent");
    return;
}

void OnHardwareProfileChange(DWORD dwEventType)
{
    logError("OnHardwareProfileChange");
    return;
}

#endif
```

Most of the functions in Listing 3-4 are base virtual functions that do little more than log that they were called. Each of the virtual functions is called where appropriate by the code within *CPPService*. For instance, the *Handler* and *HandlerEx* functions call the *OnUserControl* method in the default case of the *select* statement controlled by *dwControl*. If the service will allow a service control function to send user-defined control codes to the service to implement service-specific actions, this function should be overridden in the derived class to handle those service-specific control codes. Chapter 12 will show an alternative way of controlling services by using named pipes.

## One More Enhancement

An additional desirable feature is the ability of the service to start as it is installed. This is especially handy if a service should start automatically as the server starts. With the *CPPService* class as currently implemented, that would require the user to restart the server or use the Computer Management tool to manually start the service. Listing 3-4 contains a nonmember function named *StartThisService*. This function takes as its single parameter the name of the service to start. It then performs some standard operations, including calling *OpenSCManager* to get the handle of the SCM and calling *OpenService* to get the handle of the service. *StartService* is called to actually start the service.

Once the start has been requested, the function enters a loop to wait for the service to load or fail.

```
while (ssStatus.dwCurrentState == SERVICE_START_PENDING)
{
    // Save the current checkpoint.
    dwOldCheckPoint = ssStatus.dwCheckPoint;
    // Wait for the specified interval.
    Sleep(ssStatus.dwWaitHint);          // Check the status again.
    if (!QueryServiceStatus(
            schService,    // Handle of service
            &ssStatus))    // Address of status information
    {
        break;
    }
    // Break if the checkpoint has not been incremented.
    if (dwOldCheckPoint >= ssStatus.dwCheckPoint)
    {
        break;
    }
}
```

```
if (ssStatus.dwCurrentState == SERVICE_RUNNING)
{
    printf("\nService Started\n");
}
else
{
    printf("  Current State: %d\n", ssStatus.dwCurrentState);
    printf("  Exit Code: %d\n", ssStatus.dwWin32ExitCode);
    printf("  Service Specific Exit Code: %d\n",
        ssStatus.dwServiceSpecificExitCode);
    printf("  Check Point: %d\n", ssStatus.dwCheckPoint);
    printf("  Wait Hint: %d\n", ssStatus.dwWaitHint);
}
```

The *while* loop tracks the checkpoint set by the service and sleeps the number of milliseconds specified by the wait hint set by the service. If the time elapses without the service having changed the checkpoint value, the function assumes the service has failed to start and generates error information that will detail the reason for the failure.

To allow the *CPPBeepService* class to start the service upon installation, the *OnInstall* virtual function is overridden and *StartThisService* is called with the name of the service. There are some limitations to how services can be started that make implementing this separate function preferable to including the functionality directly in the class. Furthermore, the function can be used to start any arbitrary service, not just the service represented by the class.

# CONCLUSION

Most services need to communicate with the outside world, either as part of their basic operations or for configuration purposes. Some communications protocols present special problems for services, and the *CPPService* class will be extended to allow multiprotocol communications to take place.

The Service API is one of the features that sets Windows 2000 apart from its siblings in the Microsoft Windows family of operating systems. The code presented in this chapter will be the basis of many of the examples in upcoming chapters, especially Chapters 5, 12, and 14.

What enhancements to this code will take place in the following chapters? First and foremost, true event logging will be added. For test purposes, the simple ASCII log in these examples will suffice, but for reliable logging of events that allow access from remote servers as well as support for multiple languages, we'll use the Windows 2000 Event Log service.

*Chapter 4*

# Impersonation APIs

Who are you? This question is more than just a song by The Who. Who you are, or who the user of your service is, can make a difference in how a server should react. Let's say you have a database server that accesses files on the server on behalf of the user at the client workstation. Usually the server has full access rights to all of the resources on the server, such as files and the registry. Should the server use all of those rights on behalf of any user who happens to connect? Probably not.

Once you've decided that the server should not simply allow its clients to have free reign of the system, you must decide how to restrict the client's access to resources on behalf of the server. Several possibilities exist, and most servers use some or all of these methods to allow or disallow access to resources.

One common method for restricting a client's access to resources on a server is to set up a user database specific to the server. Using this database, an administrator can assign or deny permissions, perhaps on a directory-by-directory basis or by using some other method to divide permissions. One example of this is Microsoft SQL Server's use of its own database for users and their rights. For example, in most cases, the system administrator has administrative rights and can assign or deny rights to individual databases by using those rights.

Another common method for assigning rights for incoming clients within a server application is to leverage the user database of the network operating system. For example, when you set up Microsoft SQL Server security, you are presented with a dialog much like the one in Figure 4-1.

The Security section of the dialog allows the selection of two types of authentication. The first option uses both the SQL Server user database and the user accounts from Microsoft Windows NT for authentication. The second option only allows use of the Windows NT user database. These options are roughly comparable to the two options we have discussed.

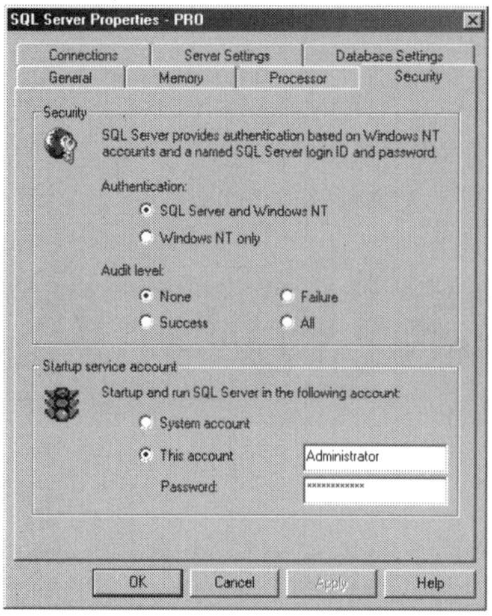


**Figure 4-1** *Dialog to set up Microsoft SQL Server 7.0 security.*

Once you know who is asking for a resource, how do you decide whether access should be permitted? While it might seem simpler to use a database provided by the application—and in some cases this is the only way to provide the level of control required—with Windows 2000 there is another way.

# WINDOWS 2000 SECURITY OVERVIEW

In Chapter 3, while discussing the service API and its implementation, I mentioned the fact that any process on a Windows 2000 system *must* run under the context of some user. In the case of services, this user is often the System account. The System account has almost total rights on the server in question and no rights beyond that single server. This is a good time to discuss exactly what we mean when we say "user contexts" and "user rights."

The core of Windows 2000 security is the Security Descriptor (SD). An SD contains a header, an owner, a group, a Discretionary Access Control List (DACL), and a System Access Control List (SACL). The owner of the SD is the Security ID (SID) of the user or group that owns the resource being protected by the SD. A SID is essentially a pointer to a variable length structure that represents the user or group. This structure should never be directly manipulated, but rather treated as a token representing the user or group.

> **NOTE** A SID represents the user, rather than any text representation of the user or group's name internally. Therefore, if a user is deleted from a Windows 2000 system and then added back, there is no chance that the new user will have any of the rights of the previously deleted user with the same name.

The group in an SD is the group that the secured object belongs to. This group is not used in the context of Active Directory security. DACLs and SACLs contain

Access Control Entries (ACEs) that describe who has what rights to the object being secured. Figure 4-2 shows how ACEs are represented in the user interface when looking at permissions for a directory on a Windows 2000 server.

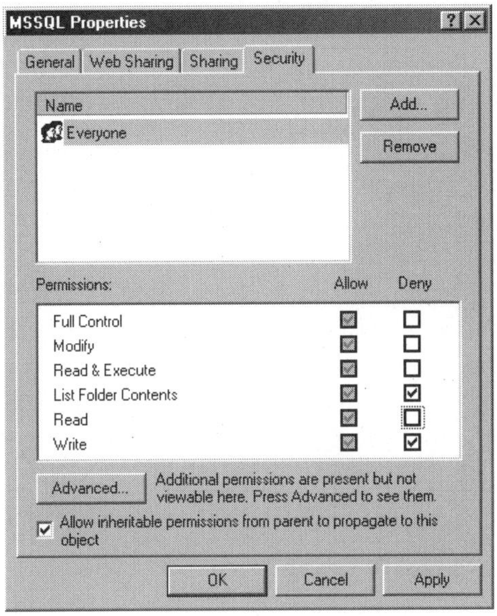


**Figure 4-2** *Rights as seen through the Windows 2000 user interface.*

In general, Windows 2000 security is as simple as that. An object has an SD associated with it, and that SD has a list of which users or groups have which rights to the object. The details of implementation are, unfortunately, much more complex, and beyond the scope of this book. *Windows NT Security* by Nik Okuntseff (R&D Books, 1997), listed in the annotated bibliography at the end of the book, covers Windows NT security, and many of the same concepts carry through to Windows 2000.

## IMPERSONATION BASICS

Let's assume that we are creating a server application that will access certain directories on behalf of the clients using the server. One example of this kind of application is Internet Information Server (IIS). Depending on certain security settings (which I'll discuss later in this chapter), IIS has two choices:

- It can act under the authority of a single user that has been configured as a system "user" with the necessary rights to access the required directories.
- It can act as an authenticated user who has a user account on the Windows 2000 server or Windows NT domain or Active Directory.

When using the second method, does IIS need to check every request to explicitly verify permission? Quite simply, the answer is no.

I have no access to the source code for IIS, but I imagine the IIS developers use impersonation to allow the server to behave as if the client user were actually making the request directly. This is a clean way to enforce security, and at the application level most of the effort involves beginning the impersonation and then simply doing what the application would normally do. Normal error handling will catch the errors that could occur when the user being impersonated does not have authority on the server to perform the requested task. Allowing the standard Windows 2000 security model to handle enforcement of permissions is an ideal way of ensuring the correct access for all clients. I don't have the source code for Microsoft SQL Server either, but based on information in *Inside Microsoft SQL Server 7.0,* by Ron Soukup and Kalen Delaney (Microsoft Press, 1999), we can see that the mechanism used internally for much of the client/server communication uses Remote Procedure Calls (RPC). I would presume that since using the Windows 2000 user authentication is one option, SQL Server uses the RPC impersonation functions that I discuss in the next section.

# CLASSES OF IMPERSONATION

In general, the Win32 API has two sets of functions that allow impersonation of clients. The first set of functions is based on some token or connection representing the client; the second set is based on some concrete knowledge of the client and a way to authenticate as if the server process were the client. The first set of functions is easier to use and has the added bonus of being the easiest to administer. Of course, this set of functions is not necessarily the best solution for all systems just because it is easier to use.

## Impersonation Based on a Connection

The easiest way to impersonate a client is to leverage what the system knows about a client and use that knowledge as the basis for impersonating the client. Three Win32 functions allow this to occur:

```
BOOL ImpersonateNamedPipeClient (
    HANDLE hNamedPipe   // Handle of a named pipe
);
BOOL DdeImpersonateClient(
    HCONV hConv         // Handle to DDE conversation
);
RPC_STATUS RPC_ENTRY RpcImpersonateClient(
    RPC_BINDING_HANDLE  BindingHandle
);
```

Dynamic Data Exchange (DDE) and RPC are beyond the scope of this book, but impersonation for DDE and RPC follows the same model as named pipe impersonation. Named pipes will be covered in more detail in Chapter 12. For this discussion, the named pipe handle can simply be seen as a black box. There are also impersonation methods associated with some COM interfaces, notably *IServerSecurity*. At their core, these methods employ RPC impersonation when used by Distributed COM. RPC impersonation is also beyond the scope of this book, but you can find out more about it in some of the books listed in the bibliography.

In named pipe impersonation, the server first obtains a named pipe handle, often after a call to *ConnectNamedPipe*. Once *ConnectNamedPipe* returns successfully, the named pipe handle can be used in a call to *ImpersonateNamedPipeClient*. Once that call is made, the server application can make calls on behalf of the client. What happens if the client does not want to allow the server to use its identity?

In the case of a named pipe, the client makes a connection using the *CreateFile* function. The flags that you send to that function control the level of impersonation allowed. These flags are covered in the SDK documentation for *CreateFile*, but in general, the client can choose to allow or disallow any impersonation on the part of the server or even allow or prevent the server's discovery of the identity of the client. The client can even allow impersonation only on remote systems. Clients usually do not manipulate these settings, and the client and server are often created together to allow them to work cooperatively. For the examples in this chapter, let's assume that the client will have allowed impersonation, though checking the return code from *ImpersonateNamedPipeClient* will, of course, allow detection of a client who doesn't want to allow impersonation.

Once the named pipe client has been impersonated, what is the next step? Most often, the program can simply do what it had planned to do and remain secure in the knowledge that if it performs an operation not allowed for the client being impersonated, the Win32 function will fail—commonly with an error 5 (access denied). When the impersonation is complete, the server can simply call the *RevertToSelf* Win32 API function, with the following simple prototype:

```
BOOL RevertToSelf(VOID);
```

If RPC was being used rather than a named pipe, either *RpcRevertToSelf* or *RpcRevertToSelfEx* is called instead. Chapter 12 will cover the use of *ImpersonateNamedPipeClient* in more detail in conjunction with communication APIs.

## Impersonation Based on Information About the Client

A second way to impersonate a client is to know the client's user name and password. This obviously presents a problem: the server must somehow track the user names and corresponding passwords of the users involved. There is no easy way to directly determine the password of a user, since that information is not stored in an accessible way within a Windows 2000 system. If a system is administered so that passwords must be changed periodically, tracking user names and passwords can be even more difficult.

Keep in mind the preceding warnings about the difficulty of this type of impersonation. The way to impersonate some user whose user name and password you have is with the function *LogonUser*, using the prototype below:

```
BOOL LogonUser (
    LPTSTR lpszUsername,     // String that specifies the user name
    LPTSTR lpszDomain,       // String that specifies the domain or
                             //  server
    LPTSTR lpszPassword,     // String that specifies the password
    DWORD dwLogonType,       // Specifies the type of logon operation
    DWORD dwLogonProvider,   // Specifies the logon provider
    PHANDLE phToken          // Pointer to variable to receive token
                             //  handle
);
```

If you search the Usenet Win32 programming newsgroups for "LogonUser," you will see more than a hundred matches, indicating that this function causes more than its share of problems for users. I will discuss some of the potential problems with using *LogonUser* after a brief description of the parameters.

The first three parameters are pointers to strings containing the user name, domain, and password respectively. The *dwLogonType* parameter contains the type of logon operation to be performed. Table 4-1 explains the possible values of this parameter as well as the implications of each type of logon.

The implications of the various logon types go beyond the simple selection of an appropriate logon type. Each type requires specific rights on the part of the user being passed to *LogonUser*. Unfortunately, the documentation is a bit sparse on specifics. In general, if *LogonUser* fails, the reason for the failure is the absence of the required rights.

The *dwLogonProvider* parameter tells *LogonUser* which logon provider to use. There are specific providers for Windows NT versions 3.5 and 4, as well as a Windows 2000 provider, identified as LOGON32_PROVIDER_WINNT50. You'll have virtually no reason to use any of these. Instead, use the default provider LOGON32_PROVIDER_DEFAULT. This provides maximum compatibility with future Windows releases.

Listing 4-1 is a simple console mode application named logonuser.exe that uses *LogonUser* to obtain a token for another user and then creates a process—whoami.exe—on behalf of the new user that operates in the context of the new user.

**TABLE 4-1**
**VALUES FOR THE *DWLOGONTYPE* PARAMETER**

| *Value* | *Description* |
|---|---|
| LOGON32_LOGON_BATCH | Intended for batch servers whose processing will not involve direct interaction with a user. Requires that user has "Log on as a batch job" rights. |
| LOGON32_LOGON_INTERACTIVE | Intended for users who will be interactively using the machine—for instance, being logged on to a terminal server. This method will cache logon information. |
| LOGON32_LOGON_SERVICE | Intended for service type logon. The user account must have the "Log on as service" privilege enabled. |
| LOGON32_LOGON_NETWORK | Intended for high-performance servers that authenticate clear text passwords. This type of logon has several limitations. First, the function will return an impersonation token, which, for instance, cannot be used directly with the *CreateProcessAsUser* Win32 API function. Second, even if the conversion from an impersonation token to a primary token is done, any process created with that converted token cannot access network resources. |

The whoami.exe application is another simple console mode application that only prints the name of the user, in this case proving that the process is being created as the new user. Listing 4-2 is the source code for whoami.exe. Figure 4-3 illustrates the results when I ran whoami.exe, showing that I am currently logged on as the administrator. Next I ran logonuser.exe, which first logs on the user *tester* and then creates a process named *tester* that prints "Hello tester!", indicating that this process is running in the context of the user passed to *LogonUser*.

**LogonUser.cpp**

```
#include "stdafx.h"

int main(int argc, char* argv[])
{
    HANDLE h;
    BOOL ret;
```

**Listing 4-1** *(continued)*

**Listing 4-1** *continued*

```
    DWORD dwCreationFlags = 0;
    STARTUPINFO startupInfo;
    PROCESS_INFORMATION processInformation;

    // Obviously, the first three parameters to LogonUser should be
    //  modified for the particular user.
    ret = LogonUser("tester", "ACCESS", "test",
        LOGON32_LOGON_BATCH,
        LOGON32_PROVIDER_DEFAULT, &h);
    printf("Hello World!  Ret = %d\n", ret);
    printf("Last Error %d\n", GetLastError());
    memset((void *)&startupInfo, '\0', sizeof(STARTUPINFO));
    memset((void *)&processInformation, '\0',
        sizeof(PROCESS_INFORMATION));
    ret = CreateProcessAsUser(h, "whoami.exe",
        NULL, NULL, NULL, FALSE,
        dwCreationFlags, NULL, NULL,
        &startupInfo, &processInformation);
    // Wait until the created process exits to make sure
    //  whoami.exe exits first.
    WaitForSingleObject(&processInformation.dwProcessId, 1000);
    CloseHandle(h);
    CloseHandle((HANDLE)processInformation.dwProcessId);
    CloseHandle((HANDLE)processInformation.dwThreadId);
    return 0;
}
```

**WhoAmI.cpp**

```
#include "stdafx.h"

int main(int argc, char* argv[])
{
    char lpBuffer[255];
    DWORD nSize = 255;
    GetUserName(lpBuffer, &nSize);
    printf("Hello %s!\n", lpBuffer);
    return 0;
}
```

**Listing 4-2**

The *CreateProcessAsUser* Win32 API function is virtually identical to the *CreateProcess* function, with the addition of the handle to the token that is retrieved by calling *LogonUser* or one of the impersonation functions.

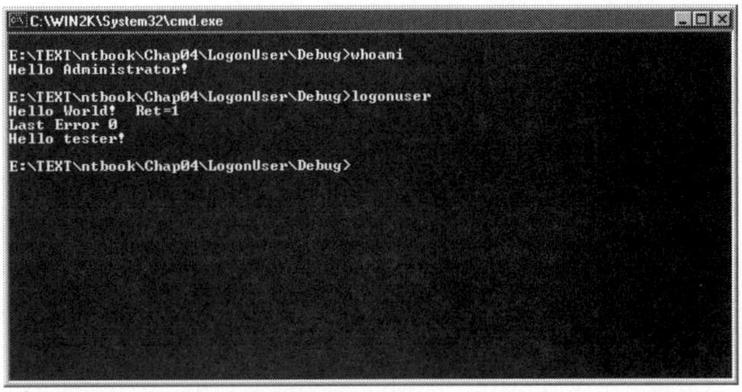


**Figure 4-3** *Testing the* LogonUser *Win32 API function.*

## Protecting Server-Specific Resources

What if the service needed to protect a resource that was not natively protected by the operating system? NTFS disk volumes and registry keys have SDs associated with them, but other server-specific resources might not. Is there a way to use the information stored in the Windows 2000 user database to grant or deny access to server-specific resources? Thankfully, the answer is yes.

Internally, the Win32 functions use a function called *AccessCheck* to determine whether a given user has the proper authority to perform a given operation. *AccessCheck* is a complicated function that has the following prototype:

```
BOOL AccessCheck(
    PSECURITY_DESCRIPTOR pSecurityDescriptor, // Security descriptor
    HANDLE ClientToken,                 // Handle to client access
                                        //  token
    DWORD DesiredAccess,                // Requested access rights
    PGENERIC_MAPPING GenericMapping,    // Map generic to specific
                                        //  rights
    PPRIVILEGE_SET PrivilegeSet,        // Receives privileges used
    LPDWORD PrivilegeSetLength,         // Size of privilege-set buffer
    LPDWORD GrantedAccess,              // Retrieves mask of granted
                                        //  rights
    LPBOOL AccessStatus                 // Retrieves results of access
                                        //  check
);
```

The first parameter, *pSecurityDescriptor*, is a pointer to a security descriptor—a structure I described earlier in the chapter. Generally, SDs are filled in by the operating system and obtained from the operating system, but they can also be created by an application to describe who has rights to an application-provided resource. (I'll discuss this later in the chapter.) The second parameter, *ClientToken*, is an impersonation token. This token can be obtained from *ImpersonateNamedPipeClient* or any of the other impersonation functions. There are specific access levels to the underlying token that the handle must have. These access levels are described in some detail in the MSDN documentation.

The *DesiredAccess* parameter contains the rights that should be tested for by *AccessCheck*. *GenericMapping* is a structure that maps object-specific rights to a set of generic rights. Generic rights include read, write, execute, and all. All Windows 2000 objects have a set of rights associated with them. Many objects will require only the generic rights for reading, writing, and executing. For some objects, additional rights are needed. For example, the registry needs to have rights defined for setting a key, creating a subkey, enumerating subkeys, and so on. A directory or a file has no need for these rights. By the same token, the execute right is meaningful for a file but has no meaning in regard to registry keys. Windows 2000 uses a unified security model; all objects are therefore protected by the same security system. This model created the need to map a specific set of rights to some generic rights. Note that all objects have all the generic rights, so even a registry key has the execute right, although the right is generally not used.

Interestingly, Windows 2000 continues the practice of making registry security settings somewhat obscure to the average user. Run REGEDIT on a Windows 2000 machine and you can search high and low and not find a trace of information on permissions for the keys displayed. You must run REGEDT32 to do that, just as on Windows NT 4. Once on the registry key in question, select "Permissions…" from the Security menu. If you assign a user or group "Special Access," the dialog in Figure 4-4 will appear, enumerating the various rights that can be assigned to registry entries.

Why is this hidden in the less commonly used REGEDT32? In general, the registry seems to have been created as an effort to avoid the random tinkering that INI files were subject to. Placing security settings in an "advanced" registry tool probably seemed like a reasonable way to prevent users from hurting themselves.

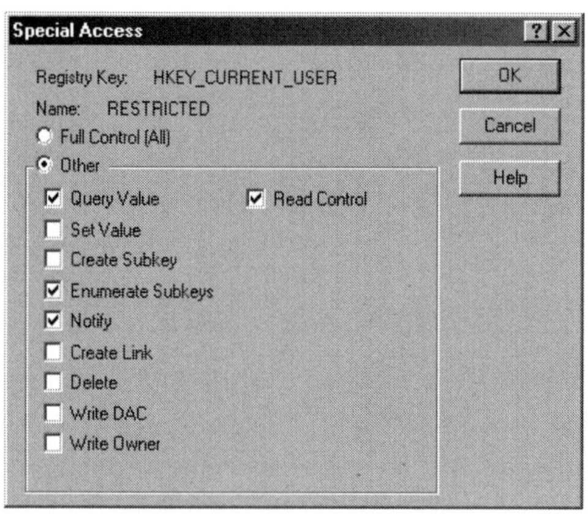


**Figure 4-4** *Dialog to set registry permissions.*

*PrivilegeSet* points to a PRIVILEGE_SET structure that contains a count of the privileges, a bitflag specifying if all specified privileges are needed, and a pointer to an array of LUID_AND_ATTRIBUTES structures. The LUID_AND_ATTRIBUTES structures contain a locally unique identifier (LUID) and its attributes, represented by up to 32 one-bit flags. *PrivilegeSetLength* specifies the size, in bytes, of the buffer pointed to by *PrivilegeSet*.

*GrantedAccess* and *AccessStatus* together provide the results of the function call. If the requested access is allowed, the DWORD pointed to by *AccessStatus* is set to TRUE; otherwise it is set to FALSE. If the function fails (indicated by a return value of zero), *GrantedAccess* is not set, and you can presume that whatever value was there before the call will remain. In case of a zero return value, *GetLastError* will return the error that caused the failure.

## Putting Impersonation and Custom Security Together

Given the availability of the *AccessStatus* function, how do you build custom security for objects within an application? There are three basic steps, but as the code to follow shows, there are also many complications.

1. The application must create an SD and a DACL for the object to be secured. The DACL will need to have an access-allowed ACE for each user or group who needs to have access to the secured portion of the server. The SD, by default, is not something that can be persisted to disk, but can be made storable through a call to *MakeSelfRelativeSD*, a Win32 API function covered in the SDK documentation.
2. The application must get the client's token. One method to do this is to use *LogonUser*, as shown in Listing 4-1. Another way to obtain the token is to use one of the impersonation functions.
3. *AccessCheck* must be called with the client token and the SD constructed in step 1.

Listing 4-3 shows the code for a simple application. This application creates its own SD for a resource it will check for rights. It then logs on as another user by using *LogonUser* and checks that user's SD.

**CheckSecurity.cpp**

```
// CheckSecurity.cpp: Modeled after code in MSDN article Q171273
//

#include "stdafx.h"

#define READ        1
#define WRITE       2
```

**Listing 4-3** *(continued)*

**Listing 4-3** *continued*

```
#define EXECUTE     4
#define BUF_SIZE    256

void main(int argc, char* argv[])
{

    PSECURITY_DESCRIPTOR pSD;

    // User/SID Variables:
    DWORD       cbBuffer = BUF_SIZE;
    PSID        pUserSid;

    // ACE variables:
    DWORD               dwAccessMask = READ | WRITE;
    PACL                pACL;
    DWORD               dwACLSize;

    // AccessCheck variables:
    DWORD               dwAccessDesired;
    PRIVILEGE_SET       PrivilegeSet;
    DWORD               dwPrivSetSize;
    DWORD               dwAccessGranted;
    BOOL                bAccessGranted = FALSE;
    GENERIC_MAPPING     GenericMapping;

    // Used to lookup account name, LogonUser
    char         szSystem[BUF_SIZE];
    char         szAccountName[BUF_SIZE];
    char         szDomain[BUF_SIZE];
    char         szPassword[BUF_SIZE];
    DWORD        cBytesSID = BUF_SIZE;
    DWORD        cBytesDomain = BUF_SIZE;
    HANDLE       hUser;
    BOOL         ret;
    SID_NAME_USE SidUser;

    // Obviously, these should be modified for the particular user.
    strcpy(szSystem, "DUAL");
    strcpy(szDomain, "DUAL");
    strcpy(szAccountName, "tester");
    strcpy(szPassword, "test");
```

```
pUserSid = (PSID)LocalAlloc(LPTR, BUF_SIZE);
if (LookupAccountName(szSystem, szAccountName, pUserSid,
    &cBytesSID, szDomain, &cBytesDomain, &SidUser) == 0)
{
    printf("Error %d LookupAccountName\n", GetLastError());
}

pSD = LocalAlloc(LPTR, SECURITY_DESCRIPTOR_MIN_LENGTH);
if (!InitializeSecurityDescriptor(
    pSD,SECURITY_DESCRIPTOR_REVISION))
{
    printf("Error %d:InitializeSecurityDescriptor\n",
        GetLastError());
}

//
// Compute size needed for the ACL.
//
dwACLSize = sizeof(ACCESS_ALLOWED_ACE) + 8 +
    GetLengthSid(pUserSid) - sizeof(DWORD);
//
// Allocate memory for ACL.
//
pACL = (PACL)LocalAlloc(LPTR, dwACLSize);

//
// Initialize the new ACL.
//
if (!InitializeAcl(pACL, dwACLSize, ACL_REVISION2))
{
    printf("Error %d:InitializeAcl\n", GetLastError());
}

//
// Add the access-allowed ACE to the DACL.
//
if(!AddAccessAllowedAce(pACL, ACL_REVISION2,
    dwAccessMask, pUserSid))
{
    printf("Error %d:AddAccessAllowedAce",
        GetLastError());
}
```

*(continued)*

**Listing 4-3** *continued*

```
//
// Set our DACL to the SD.
//
if (!SetSecurityDescriptorDacl(pSD,
    TRUE,
    pACL,
    FALSE))
{
    printf("Error %d:SetSecurityDescriptorDacl",
        GetLastError());
}

//
// AccessCheck is picky about what is in the SD. Set
//  the group and owner using our convenient SID.
//
SetSecurityDescriptorGroup(pSD, pUserSid, FALSE);
SetSecurityDescriptorOwner(pSD, pUserSid, FALSE);

// Here we log on as the user specified above...
ret = LogonUser(szAccountName, szDomain, szPassword,
    LOGON32_LOGON_INTERACTIVE,
    LOGON32_PROVIDER_DEFAULT, &hUser);

// ...and then impersonate that user.
ImpersonateLoggedOnUser(hUser);

dwAccessDesired = READ;

memset(&GenericMapping,0xff, sizeof(GENERIC_MAPPING));
GenericMapping.GenericRead = READ;
GenericMapping.GenericWrite = WRITE;
GenericMapping.GenericExecute = EXECUTE;
GenericMapping.GenericAll = READ | WRITE | EXECUTE;

//
// This only does something if we want to use generic access
//  rights, such as GENERIC_ALL, in our call to AccessCheck.
//  (We are not using generic access rights.)
//
MapGenericMask(&dwAccessDesired, &GenericMapping);
dwPrivSetSize = sizeof(PRIVILEGE_SET);
```

```
    //
    // Make the call.
    //
    if(!AccessCheck(pSD,
        hUser,
        dwAccessDesired,
        &GenericMapping,
        &PrivilegeSet,
        &dwPrivSetSize,
        &dwAccessGranted,
        &bAccessGranted))
    {
        printf("Error in AccessCheck : %d\n", GetLastError());
    }
    else
    {
        if (bAccessGranted)
        {
            printf(" Access was granted using mask %lx\n",
                dwAccessGranted);
        }
        else
        {
            printf("Access was NOT granted!\n");
        }
    }
    RevertToSelf();
    LocalFree(pACL);
    LocalFree(pSD);
    LocalFree(pUserSid);

}
```

First some strings are initialized to allow the program to log on as and impersonate another user. Next the SID for that account is looked up, using *LookupAccountName*. This function accepts a series of parameters, most of which are self-explanatory.

```
BOOL LookupAccountName(
    LPCTSTR lpSystemName,  // Address of string for system name
    LPCTSTR lpAccountName, // Address of string for account name
    PSID Sid,              // Address of security identifier
```

*(continued)*

```
    LPDWORD cbSid,          // Address of size of security identifier
    LPTSTR ReferencedDomainName,
                            // Address of string for referenced
                            //  domain
    LPDWORD cbReferencedDomainName,
                            // Address of size of domain string
    PSID_NAME_USE peUse     // Address of SID-type indicator
);
```

The *lpSystemName* parameter can be used to specify a system where the account name will be looked up. This parameter can be NULL to have the lookup take place on the local machine. The *Sid* parameter points to a buffer that will hold the SID for the account if the function succeeds. A PSID is typedefed as a PVOID in the standard Windows header files, meaning that there is nothing to be derived from the value pointed to—it should be accepted as an opaque handle. The *peUse* parameter is a pointer to a SID-type indicator. The value pointed to by this parameter will be set to equal one of the values in an enumerated type that includes such values as *SidTypeUser*, *SidTypeGroup*, *SidTypeDomain*, and so on. In Listing 4-3, the account name being looked up is a user, so *SidTypeUser* is returned.

We allocate some buffers using *LocalAlloc* and then initialize them using Win32 API functions. The SD is initialized through a call to *InitializeSecurityDescriptor*, and an ACL is initialized using *InitializeAcl*. We now call *AddAccessAllowed*, adding an ACL record for the user we are trying to impersonate by using the access mask previously set to READ | WRITE. Next we set the SD ACL through a call to *SetSecurityDescriptorAcl*. We then set some additional fields in the SD as required by *AccessCheck*.

We log on as the user for whom we have the SID and then we set generic mappings to the mapping flags we have previously set. The generic mappings are then mapped using *MapGenericMask*. Finally, we can make the call to *AccessCheck* that determines whether the user has the access required—READ access in our example. Of course, since we have just manually set the SD we already know that the access is allowed, but we check for either function failure or an indication that the user does not have access to the right we are requesting. We could have also requested what the maximum access allowed was instead of checking for a particular right by passing MAXIMUM_ALLOWED as the access desired in the *dwAccessDesired* parameter to *AccessCheck*.

## CONCLUSION

Windows 2000 security is both simple and complex. It is simple in that virtually nothing is required to take advantage of it because the security is tightly tied to the operating system. It is complex because it allows you to reference the built-in security system to leverage the existing system. That, however, requires more than a cursory understanding of the operating system.

In between simple and complex is the ability to impersonate another user. If a server is accessing existing Win32 objects—such as directories, files, and registry entries—the server application can take on the cloak of another user and use the simple part of Windows 2000 security to perform the task at hand. And if the application needs to go further—to control access to server-specific resources—the tools are there to allow that, albeit at the cost of some additional complexity.

*Chapter 5*

# Event Logging

In Chapter 3, the Service API was described as one of the features that separates a file server from an application server, since it has the ability to reliably run applications on the server without the intervention of a user. Event logging can help applications that are written using the Service API to operate reliably. It allows service applications to record activities that might not be witnessed by an end user.

When an application uses event logging, the information saved can be read in a reliable way from either the machine on which the event took place or—with proper authority—from a remote machine. Figure 5-1 shows the Windows 2000 Event Viewer displaying the system log.

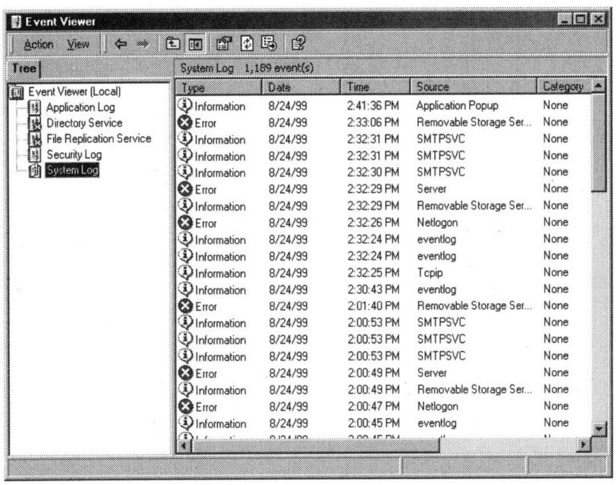


**Figure 5-1** *Viewing the system event log on Windows 2000.*

The left pane of the Event Viewer contains a tree showing all of the possible event logs that can be viewed. The right pane contains the events of the currently selected log, in this example the system log. In addition to some text information on the messages, icons indicate the severity of the event: Informational, Warning, or Error. If you double-click one of the messages, the details of the event are displayed in a dialog, as shown in Figure 5-2.

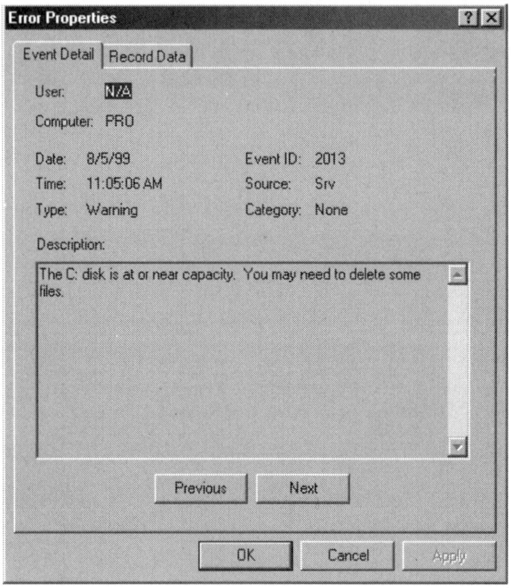


**Figure 5-2** *Viewing the details of a system event on Windows 2000.*

One problem with logging events that are handled by the event log on Windows 2000 is having to deal with an ever-growing file. Notice that in Figure 5-1 the event count on the frame indicates 1189 events in the log. This is not a terribly busy server—you could expect a very busy server to generate a lot more messages. If the number of messages is allowed to grow unchecked, the event log could quickly overtake the entire hard disk. Let's take a look at the Event Viewer main screen. If you right-click one of the logs in the left pane and select Properties from the context menu, you are presented with a dialog like that in Figure 5-3.

This dialog displays information on the location and current size of the selected log and allows you to set the size of the log. More important, the behavior of the log—as far as reuse of space—can be configured. The radio button group in the dialog presents three options: Overwrite Events As Needed allows the log to grow to the specified size and then overwrite the oldest events as needed. Overwrite Events Older Than *n* Days allows events older than the specified number of days to be overwritten automatically. Do Not Overwrite Events (Clear Log Manually) prevents events from ever being overwritten, implying that the administrator is required to clear the event log manually, perhaps after backing it up.

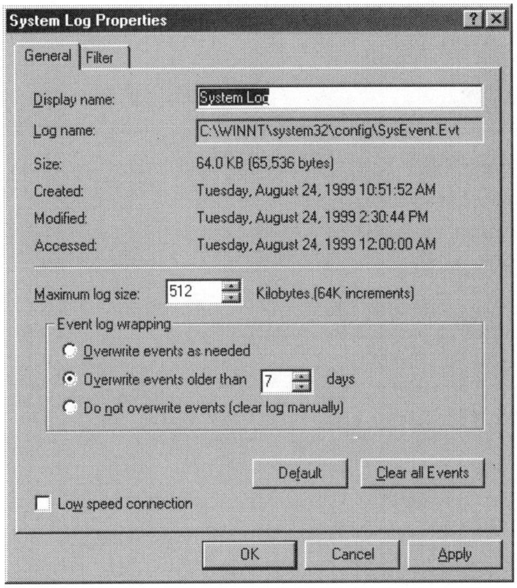


**Figure 5-3** *Viewing the properties of a system log on Windows 2000.*

The event log is perhaps one of the most underutilized features of Windows 2000. Part of the problem is that the key event that might help resolve a system problem is buried in the myriad innocuous messages commonly found in the event log. For instance, one user reported to me that his machine was locking up for no apparent reason. Dialing into the network, I was able to connect to the remote log. By using information about the date and time of several lockups, I was able to determine that the system had reported an overheating problem at approximately the time of the error. I requested that the user vacuum the vents in the front and back of the machine. This resolved the issue, leaving him to wonder what magic allowed me to see the dust without ever leaving my house.

In the same dialog as shown in Figure 5-3, there is another tab named *Filter*. That tab, shown in Figure 5-4, allows you to select event log records using a number of criteria, including date and time, severity type, and so forth.

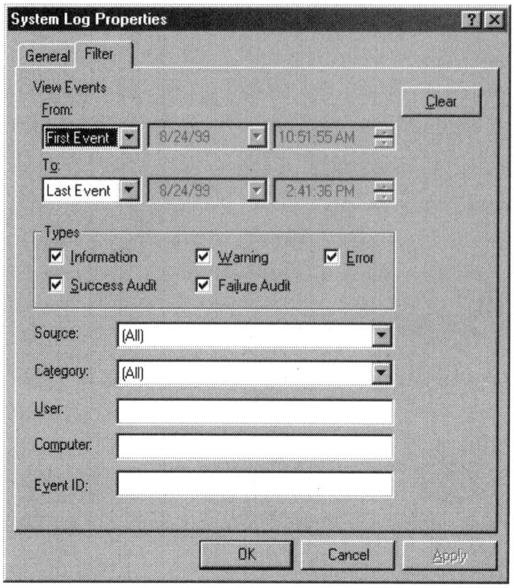


**Figure 5-4** *The Filter tab of the System Log Properties dialog.*

You've seen that you can automate the management of the event log and view the log from remote machines. In addition, the event log is designed from the ground up to work with multiple languages. The base text of a message is retrieved by the event log as a resource and can be localized for any supported language.

# THE EVENT LOGGING API

Of course, more important than the ability to use the Windows 2000 user interface to view events is the ability to add events to the event log from within a service application. Adding events to the event log can be a fairly complex process. Figure 5-5 shows this process at a very high level, without detailing the complexities.

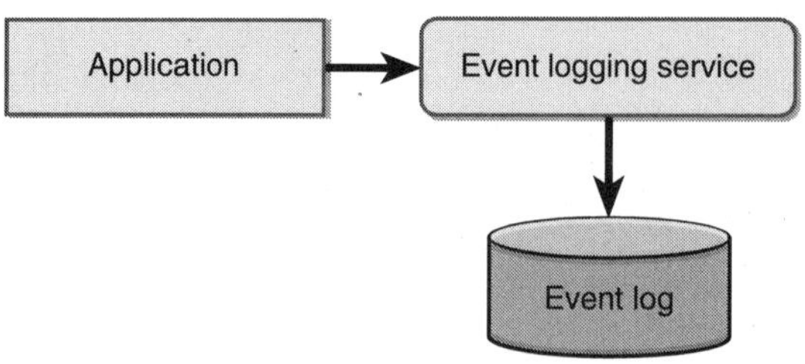


**Figure 5-5** *The process for adding events to the event log.*

The application does not write directly to the event log, but instead sends a request to the Windows 2000 EventLog service. The EventLog service in turn writes the message to the event log. Take another look at Figure 5-2. The message displayed in the event properties dialog is "The C: disk is at or near capacity. You may need to delete some files." Now take a look at Figure 5-3. We can see that the system event log is in a file named C:\Winnt\System32\Config\Sysevent.evt. Searching this file for the word "near" results in no match. You'll understand why this happens once I've explained the process involved in writing event log records.

## Writing Events to the Event Log

An application cannot simply call the *ReportEvent* Win32 API function with a character pointer and have the text logged. Creating entries in the event log involves several steps:

1. Create a message resource that can be linked into the application.
2. Create a registry entry that identifies the application that will be the source of the events and the type of events that will be submitted.
3. Call the *RegisterEventSource* Win32 API upon entry to the application.
4. Call the *ReportEvent* Win32 API to report the event, passing only the replaceable parameters required by the message mask created for the particular event, as specified by the message string.

   I'll go through these steps in more detail in the next few paragraphs.

### Creating the Resource

To create the resource, we need to create a file that can be fed to the resource compiler to generate the message resource. The file needs to have one multiline entry for each possible message, as in the following example:

```
MessageId=100
SymbolicName=EVMSG_INSTALLED
Language=English
The %1 service was installed.
.
```

The *MessageID* is commonly specified only for the first entry, with each additional entry automatically assigned a *MessageID* value one greater than the entry before it. The program uses the symbolic name to internally identify the message. Finally, the language is specified, followed by the text to be used for that message in the specified language. Note that additional languages and messages could have been specified if multiple languages were to be supported. Note also that the message text uses replaceable parameters in the form of *%n*, where *n* is the number of the parameter. Because of the format of this file, you should follow a couple of commonsense rules to make your life easier:

- Do not begin a text line with a period, as the message compiler uses a period at the start of a line to signal the end of an entry.
- If an entry must contain a percent sign (%), you must use an additional percent sign as an escape character before the percent sign. For example, if the text means "Drive %1 is more than 95% full.", you need to say "Drive %1 is more than 95%% full."

All the examples in this book will follow these rules. Listing 5-1 shows CppSvcMsg.mc, a message file for use in the *CppService* class first introduced in Chapter 3. Listing 5-2 shows CppSvcMsg.h, one of the files created when CppSvcMsg.mc is run through the message compiler.

**CppSvcMsg.mc**

```
MessageId=100
SymbolicName=EVMSG_INSTALLED
Language=English
The %1 service was installed.
.
MessageId=
SymbolicName=EVMSG_REMOVED
Language=English
The %1 service was removed.
.
MessageId=
SymbolicName=EVMSG_STARTED
Language=English
The service was started.
.
MessageId=
SymbolicName=EVMSG_STOPPED
Language=English
The %1 service was stopped.
.
MessageId=
SymbolicName=EVMSG_DEBUG
Language=English
Debug: %1
.
```

**Listing 5-1**

**CppSvcMsg.h**

```
//
//  The 32-bit values are laid out as follows:
//
//   3 3 2 2 2 2 2 2 2 2 2 2 1 1 1 1 1 1 1 1 1 1
//   1 0 9 8 7 6 5 4 3 2 1 0 9 8 7 6 5 4 3 2 1 0 9 8 7 6 5 4 3 2 1 0
//  +---+-+-+-----------------------+-------------------------------+
//  |Sev|C|R|     Facility          |               Code            |
//  +---+-+-+-----------------------+-------------------------------+
//
//  where
//
//      Sev - is the severity code
//
//          00 - Success
//          01 - Informational
//          10 - Warning
//          11 - Error
//
//      C - is the Customer code flag
//
//      R - is a reserved bit
//
//      Facility - is the facility code
//
//      Code - is the facility's status code
//
//
// Define the facility codes.
//


//
// Define the severity codes.
//


//
// MessageId: EVMSG_INSTALLED
//
// MessageText:
//
// The %1 service was installed.
//
#define EVMSG_INSTALLED                  0x00000064L
```

**Listing 5-2** *(continued)*

**Listing 5-2** *continued*

```
//
// MessageId: EVMSG_REMOVED
//
// MessageText:
//
// The %1 service was removed.
//
#define EVMSG_REMOVED                    0x00000065L

//
// MessageId: EVMSG_STARTED
//
// MessageText:
//
// The service was started.
//
#define EVMSG_STARTED                    0x00000066L

//
// MessageId: EVMSG_STOPPED
//
// MessageText:
//
// The %1 service was stopped.
//
#define EVMSG_STOPPED                    0x00000067L

//
// MessageId: EVMSG_DEBUG
//
// MessageText:
//
// Debug: %1
//
#define EVMSG_DEBUG                      0x00000068L
```

The last message in the file, identified as EVMSG_DEBUG, is useful for debugging. This message takes a single parameter and will allow you to write arbitrary strings to the event log.

### Creating a Registry Entry for the Event Source

Once the *mc* file, the *rc* file, and the *h* file have been added to the project, the project needs to be modified to create a registry entry identifying the application that will be creating the messages. The applications reading the event log use this entry to piece together the actual text of the message as intended by the developer, even though the actual verbiage is not captured in the event log file. The registry needs to have a key added under

```
HKLM\SYSTEM\CurrentControlSet\Services\EventLog\Application
```

The key needs to be the name of the application. Values under this key include the following:

- *EventMessageFile*, which contains the name of the file containing the message resource, often the application's executable file.
- *TypesSupported*, a bit flag specifying the types of messages that the application will generate, including EVENTLOG_ERROR_TYPE, EVENTLOG_WARNING_TYPE, and EVENTLOG_INFORMATION_TYPE.

Two additional values for *TypesSupported* are EVENTLOG_AUDIT_SUCCESS and EVENTLOG_AUDIT_FAILURE, which are commonly used when writing to the security log. Several less common registry entries can be added. Each is fully described in the Win32 SDK documentation. The registry entries need to be entered only once. Within a service, this is usually done during the installation process. Note that, commonly, the entries are *not* deleted during uninstallation, since the events that exist in the log cannot be properly displayed if the registry entries are missing. This implies that the service application generating event log entries will remain on the disk in the location specified in the *EventLog* registry entry.

### Calling *RegisterEventSource*

Once the registry entry is made, the Win32 API function *RegisterEventSource* can be called. This function has the following prototype:

```
HANDLE RegisterEventSource(
    LPCTSTR lpUNCServerName,  // Server name for source
    LPCTSTR lpSourceName      // Source name for registered handle
);
```

The first parameter, *lpUNCServerName*, is the Universal Naming Convention (UNC) name of the server. UNC names are names in the form of \\Server\Share\Path. In this case, the UNC name needs only to reference the server name. If this parameter is NULL, the event source is registered on the local machine. The second parameter, *lpSourceName*, is the event source name and must correspond to the name of the registry key created to represent the application in the registry entry mentioned earlier. If the source name is not found, entries are still made to the application event log. However, their later interpretation will be much more difficult. Upon success, this function returns a handle that can be used with the *ReportEvent* Win32 API function described in the next section. A corresponding Win32 API function—*DeregisterEventSource*—takes as its only parameter the handle returned from *RegisterEventSource*.

### Calling *ReportEvent*

As needed, the application can now call *ReportEvent*, which is a function with the following prototype:

```
BOOL ReportEvent(
    HANDLE hEventLog,    // Handle returned by RegisterEventSource
    WORD wType,          // The type of event to log
    WORD wCategory,      // Event category
    DWORD dwEventID,     // Event identifier
    PSID lpUserSid,      // User security identifier (optional)
    WORD wNumStrings,    // Number of strings to merge with message
    DWORD dwDataSize,    // Size of binary data, in bytes
    LPCTSTR *lpStrings,  // Array of strings to merge with message
    LPVOID lpRawData     // Address of binary data
);
```

The first parameter is the handle returned by *RegisterEventSource*. The second parameter, *wType*, is the type of event being logged. A more accurate name for this parameter might have been *severity*. The values include EVENTLOG_ERROR_TYPE, EVENTLOG_WARNING_TYPE, EVENTLOG_INFORMATION_TYPE, EVENTLOG_AUDIT_SUCCESS, and EVENTLOG_AUDIT_FAILURE. The *wCategory* parameter specifies the event category, which can have any value and is commonly set to 0. The fourth parameter, *dwEventID*, is the event identifier, which corresponds to one of the values set in the message file. This parameter will almost always be a value that you define in your application. If the user generating the event is important, the next parameter, *lpUserSid*, must be the Security ID (SID) of the user. This can be NULL if user information is not required. In a service application run under the System account, the user is rarely specified unless the service is using impersonation.

The final four parameters allow the program to send the strings used as replicable parameters in the message strings, as well as any raw data that could be useful to further understand the event. The *wNumStrings* parameter contains the number of strings passed in the *lpStrings* parameter, which should be at least the highest placeholder number in the message string. For instance, if a message string referred to by the *dwEventID* parameter is "Drive %1 has only %2 bytes of free space out of %3 total bytes on the volume", there should be three strings in the array of strings pointed to by *lpStrings*. The *dwDataSize* parameter contains the number of bytes pointed to by *lpRawData*. Even if the value of *wNumStrings* or *dwDataSize* is 0, *lpStrings* and *lpRawData* must either be valid pointers or NULL.

*ReportEvent* returns a nonzero value if the event entry was written to the log or 0 if an error occurred. As with virtually all Win32 functions, if an error occurs, calling *GetLastError* will return the error code for the last failed call.

## Adding Event Logging to *CPPService*

I introduced the *CPPService* class in Chapter 3 along with a simple example that built upon the framework named *CPPBeepService*. The base class had a simple method named *logError* for logging events to a standard MS-DOS sequential file. This method took as its single parameter a character pointer to the message to write to the file. The updated version of this class will add a method named *LogEvent*, which will accept seven parameters. The first is *wType*, a WORD value that corresponds to the type or severity of the event. The second parameter is *dwEventID*, the event identifier from the message file. The remaining five parameters are strings with default values of NULL. These will be the values passed to *ReportError* to fill in the placeholders in the messages. (Passing five individual strings rather than passing an array of character pointers is a concession to ease of use.) Of course, if the need arose for more than the five replaceable parameters, they could be added to the class with minimum effort.

The steps required for adding event logging are the four steps listed earlier on page 119. First the message script is added to the project. The message compiler is a command line tool that generates the header file containing the event IDs and the constants defined for the C++ program. In this example, the command line to generate CppSvcMsg.h is

```
mc cppsvcmsg.mc
```

The resulting header file is included in the stdafx.h file as follows:

```
// ...other code
#include <stdio.h>
#include <windows.h>
#include "CPPService.h"
// Added for Chapter 5
#include "CppSvcMsg.h"
// ...more code
```

Note that this example is used throughout the rest of the book. Changes to the code are noted in the chapter in which they are added. As you look at more complete examples later in the book, you can identify where each feature was added.

The next step is to create the appropriate registry entries to register the event source. As I mentioned in the service discussion, this is commonly done as the service is installed. Rather than doing this in the *OnInstall* method of each descendent class, the base class handles the registry entries in the *Install* method. The code to do so (shown on the following page) is added to the *Install* method of *CPPService*.

```
// Added for Chapter 5
strcpy(szKey,
    "SYSTEM\\CurrentControlSet\\Services\\EventLog\\Application\\");
strcat(szKey, ServiceName());
if (::RegCreateKey(HKEY_LOCAL_MACHINE,
    szKey, &hKey) != ERROR_SUCCESS)
{
    return FALSE;
}

// Add the event ID message file (in this case, the EXE file).
::RegSetValueEx(hKey,
    "EventMessageFile",
    0,
    REG_EXPAND_SZ,
    (CONST BYTE*)szPath,
    strlen(szPath) + 1);

// Set the supported types flags.
DWORD dwData = EVENTLOG_ERROR_TYPE | EVENTLOG_WARNING_TYPE |
    EVENTLOG_INFORMATION_TYPE;

::RegSetValueEx(hKey,
    "TypesSupported",
    0,
    REG_DWORD,
    (CONST BYTE*)&dwData,
    sizeof(DWORD));
::RegCloseKey(hKey);
// End added for Chapter 5
```

The code uses the standard Win32 Registry API functions, which are documented in the Win32 SDK. First the key is created, and then two values are added—a REG_EXPAND_SZ or NULL-terminated string for the *EventMessageFile* value, and a REG_DWORD four-byte unsigned value for *TypesSupported*.

Once the registry entries are in place, you can call *RegisterEventSource*. You can call *RegisterEventSource* within the *Initialize* method, but it makes a bit more sense to integrate it into the *LogEvent* method. In this chapter's version of the *CPPBeepService* service, I first added the declaration for the *LogEvent* method to the *CPPService* class declaration and then added the implementation to CPPService.cpp. The implementation of *LogEvent* follows:

```
// Added for Chapter 5
BOOL CPPService::LogEvent(WORD wType, DWORD dwEventID,
    const char *ps1,
    const char *ps2,
    const char *ps3,
```

```
    const char *ps4,
    const char *ps5)
{
    WORD wNumStrings;
    const char *pStrings[5];

    if (m_EventHandle == 0)
    {
        m_EventHandle = ::RegisterEventSource(NULL,
            ServiceName());
    }
    if (m_EventHandle != 0)
    {
        wNumStrings = 0;
        if (ps1 != 0)
        {
            pStrings[wNumStrings] = ps1;
            wNumStrings++;
            if (ps2 != 0)
            {
                pStrings[wNumStrings] = ps2;
                wNumStrings++;
                if (ps3 != 0)
                {
                    pStrings[wNumStrings] = ps3;
                    wNumStrings++;
                    if (ps4 != 0)
                    {
                        pStrings[wNumStrings] = ps4;
                        wNumStrings++;
                        if (ps5 != 0)
                        {
                            pStrings[wNumStrings] = ps5;
                            wNumStrings++;
                        }
                    }
                }
            }
        }
        ::ReportEvent(m_EventHandle, wType, 0, dwEventID, NULL,
            wNumStrings, 0, pStrings, NULL);

        return true;
    }
    return false;
}
// End added for Chapter 5
```

If *m_EventHandle* is 0, *RegisterEventSource* is called. If *m_EventHandle* is not 0, the function enters a loop that builds the *pStrings* array based on the values passed to the function. The *logError* method is then remapped to a call to *LogEvent* as follows:

```
VOID CPPService::logError(char *text)
{
    // Added for Chapter 5
    LogEvent(EVENTLOG_INFORMATION_TYPE, EVMSG_DEBUG,
        (const char *)text);
    // Removed for Chapter 5
//      log = fopen("c:\\service.log", "a+t");
//      if (log)
//      {
//          fprintf(log, "%s\n", text);
//          fclose(log);
//      }
    return;
}
```

Once this is done, the service, when restarted, will begin logging events to the event log rather than to the simple MS-DOS sequential file of the previous version. The complete source for the modified *CPPService* class is presented in Listings 5-3 (CppService.cpp) and 5-4 (CppService.h). The complete project is on the companion CD-ROM.

**CppService.cpp**

```
#include "Stdafx.h"

CPPService* CPPService::m_this = NULL;

VOID StartThisService(char *serviceName)
{
    SERVICE_STATUS ssStatus;
    DWORD dwOldCheckPoint;

    SC_HANDLE schSCManager =
        OpenSCManager(NULL,          // Local machine
            NULL,                    // ServicesActive database
            SC_MANAGER_ALL_ACCESS); // Full access

    printf("\nStarting Service...\n");
    SC_HANDLE schService = OpenService(
        schSCManager,           // SCM database
        TEXT(serviceName),      // Service name
        SERVICE_ALL_ACCESS);
```

**Listing 5-3**

```
if (schService == NULL)
{
    printf("\nCan't Open Service...Last Error=%d",
        GetLastError());
    return;
}
if (!StartService(
        schService,  // Handle to service
        0,           // Number of arguments
        NULL) )      // No arguments
{
    printf("\nStart Service failure...");
    return;
}
else
{
    printf("Service start pending\n");
}
// Check the status until the service is no longer start pending.
if (!QueryServiceStatus(
        schService,   // Handle to service
        &ssStatus) )  // Address of status information
{
    printf("\nError in Query Service Status");
    return;
}

// Some services take a long time to start, so there is
//  an elaborate mechanism to handle that.  This is not
//  very useful with the example services provided, but
//  could be more so for more complex services.
while (ssStatus.dwCurrentState == SERVICE_START_PENDING)
{
    // Save the current checkpoint.
    dwOldCheckPoint = ssStatus.dwCheckPoint;
    // Wait for the specified interval.
    Sleep(ssStatus.dwWaitHint);
    if (!QueryServiceStatus(     // Check the status again.
        schService,   // Handle to service
        &ssStatus) )  // Address of status information
    {
        break;
    }
```

*(continued)*

**Listing 5-3** *continued*

```
        // Break if the checkpoint has not been incremented.
        if (dwOldCheckPoint >= ssStatus.dwCheckPoint)
        {
            break;
        }
    }
    if (ssStatus.dwCurrentState == SERVICE_RUNNING)
    {
        printf("\nService Started\n");
    }
    else
    {
        printf("  Current State: %d\n", ssStatus.dwCurrentState);
        printf("  Exit Code: %d\n", ssStatus.dwWin32ExitCode);
        printf("  Service Specific Exit Code: %d\n",
            ssStatus.dwServiceSpecificExitCode);
        printf("  Check Point: %d\n", ssStatus.dwCheckPoint);
        printf("  Wait Hint: %d\n", ssStatus.dwWaitHint);
    }
    CloseServiceHandle(schService);
    CloseServiceHandle(schSCManager);
}


CPPService::CPPService(char *tsvcName, char *tdispName,
    DWORD tsvcStartType)
{
    strncpy(serviceName, tsvcName,128);
    strncpy(serviceDisplayName, tdispName, 128);
    m_svcStartType = tsvcStartType;
    m_scmHandle = OpenSCManager(NULL, SERVICES_ACTIVE_DATABASE,
        SC_MANAGER_ALL_ACCESS);
    if (m_scmHandle == NULL)
    {
        printf("\n OpenSCManager error %d ", GetLastError());
    }
    m_scHandle = 0;
    m_this = this;
    m_isRunning = false;
    m_isPaused = false;
    // Added for Chapter 5
    m_EventHandle=0;

    ServiceStatus.dwServiceType         = SERVICE_WIN32_OWN_PROCESS;
    ServiceStatus.dwCurrentState        = SERVICE_START_PENDING;
```

```
    ServiceStatus.dwControlsAccepted    = SERVICE_ACCEPT_STOP |
        SERVICE_ACCEPT_PAUSE_CONTINUE;
    ServiceStatus.dwWin32ExitCode       = 0;
    ServiceStatus.dwServiceSpecificExitCode = 0;
    ServiceStatus.dwCheckPoint          = 0;
    ServiceStatus.dwWaitHint            = 0;
}

CPPService::~CPPService()
{
    if (m_scmHandle != 0)
    {
        ::CloseHandle(m_scmHandle);
    }
    if (m_scHandle != 0)
    {
        ::CloseHandle(m_scHandle);
    }
}

BOOL CPPService::ParseArguments(int argc, char **argv)
{
    BOOL result = false;
    if (argc>1 && !(strnicmp(argv[1], "-i", 2)))
    {
        if ((Install()))
        {
            printf("\n%s installed!", ServiceName());
        }
        else
        {
            printf(
                "\n%s NOT installed!  Last error %d",
                ServiceName(), GetLastError());
        }
        result = true;
    }
    else if (argc>1 && !(strnicmp(argv[1], "-u", 2)))
    {
        if ((UnInstall()))
        {
            printf("\n%s Uninstalled!", ServiceName());
        }
```

*(continued)*

**Listing 5-3** *continued*

```
        else
        {
            printf(
                "\n%s NOT uninstalled!  Last error %d",
                ServiceName(), GetLastError());
        }
        result = true;
    }
    return result;
}

VOID CPPService::logError(char *text)
{
    // Added for Chapter 5
    LogEvent(EVENTLOG_INFORMATION_TYPE, EVMSG_DEBUG,
        (const char *)text);
    // Removed for Chapter 5
//    log = fopen("c:\\service.log", "a+t");
//    if (log)
//    {
//        fprintf(log, "%s\n", text);
//        fclose(log);
//    }
    return;
}

BOOL CPPService::Install()
{
    char szPath[MAX_PATH];
    char szBuffer[MAX_PATH+2];

    // Added for Chapter 5
    char szKey[256];
    HKEY hKey = NULL;
    // End added for Chapter 5

    BOOL result = true;  // Default to success

    GetModuleFileName(GetModuleHandle(NULL), szPath,MAX_PATH);
    // Why do we do this?  The path may contain spaces.
    //  If it does, the path must be quoted.
    strcpy(szBuffer, "\"");
    strcat(szBuffer, szPath);
    strcat(szBuffer, "\"");
    printf("\nInstalling service %s", szPath);
```

```
m_scHandle = CreateService (m_scmHandle, serviceName,
    serviceDisplayName, SERVICE_ALL_ACCESS,
    SERVICE_WIN32_OWN_PROCESS,
    m_svcStartType,
    SERVICE_ERROR_NORMAL, szBuffer,
    NULL, NULL, NULL, NULL, NULL);

if (m_scHandle == NULL) // Process error
{
    DWORD lastError;
    lastError = GetLastError();
    if (lastError == 1073) // Service already installed
    {
        sprintf(m_diag,                 " CreateService error ="
            " Service Already Installed (1073)\n");
    }
    else
    {
        sprintf(m_diag, " CreateService error = %d\n",
            lastError);
    }
    printf("%s\n", m_diag);
    logError(m_diag);
    result = false;
}

// Added for Chapter 5
strcpy(szKey,
    "SYSTEM\\CurrentControlSet\\Services\\"
    "EventLog\\Application\\");
strcat(szKey, ServiceName());
if (::RegCreateKey(HKEY_LOCAL_MACHINE, szKey,
    &hKey) != ERROR_SUCCESS)
{
    return FALSE;
}

// Add the event ID message file (in this case, the EXE file).
::RegSetValueEx(hKey,
    "EventMessageFile",
    0,
    REG_EXPAND_SZ,
    (CONST BYTE*)szPath,
    strlen(szPath) + 1);
```

*(continued)*

**Listing 5-3** *continued*

```
    // Set the supported types flags.
    DWORD dwData = EVENTLOG_ERROR_TYPE | EVENTLOG_WARNING_TYPE |
        EVENTLOG_INFORMATION_TYPE;

    ::RegSetValueEx(hKey,
        "TypesSupported",
        0,
        REG_DWORD,
        (CONST BYTE*)&dwData,
        sizeof(DWORD));
    ::RegCloseKey(hKey);
    // End added for Chapter 5

    OnInstall();
    return result;
}

BOOL CPPService::StartService()
{
    SERVICE_TABLE_ENTRY DispatchTable[] = {
        {serviceName, CPPService::ServiceMain},
        {NULL, NULL}
    };

    BOOL b = ::StartServiceCtrlDispatcher(DispatchTable);
    // Added for Chapter 5
    if (b)
    {
        // No strings needed for this message...
        LogEvent(EVENTLOG_INFORMATION_TYPE,EVMSG_STARTED);
    }
    // End added for Chapter 5
    return b;
}



BOOL CPPService::UnInstall()
{
    m_scHandle = OpenService(m_scmHandle, serviceName,
        SERVICE_ALL_ACCESS);
    if (m_scHandle != NULL)
    {
        DeleteService(m_scHandle);
        printf("\n%s uninstalled...", serviceName);
```

```
        CloseHandle(m_scHandle);
        m_scHandle = 0;
        // Added for Chapter 5
        LogEvent(EVENTLOG_INFORMATION_TYPE, EVMSG_REMOVED,
            ServiceName());
        // End added for Chapter 5
        OnUninstall();
        return(true);
    }
    printf("\nOpen Service error: %d ", GetLastError());
    return(false);

}


void CPPService::SetStatus(DWORD dwControl)
{
    ServiceStatus.dwCurrentState          = dwControl;
    ServiceStatus.dwCheckPoint            = 0;
    ServiceStatus.dwWaitHint              = 0;

    if (!SetServiceStatus (ServiceStatusHandle, &ServiceStatus))
    {
        m_status = GetLastError();
        sprintf(m_diag,
            " %s SetServiceStatus error %ld dwControl=%d\n",
            serviceName, m_status, dwControl);
        logError(m_diag);
    }

}

VOID WINAPI CPPService::ServiceMain(DWORD argc, LPTSTR *argv)
{
    BOOL initStat;
    DWORD specificError;
    CPPService *thisPtr;

    thisPtr = m_this;

#ifdef _WIN2K_COMPAT
    char szContext[255];
    strcpy(szContext, thisPtr->ServiceName());
```

*(continued)*

**Listing 5-3** *continued*

```
    thisPtr->ServiceStatusHandle =
        RegisterServiceCtrlHandlerEx(
            thisPtr->ServiceName,
            HandlerEx,
            &szContext);
#else
    thisPtr->ServiceStatusHandle =
        RegisterServiceCtrlHandler(
            thisPtr->serviceName,
            Handler);
#endif
    if (thisPtr->ServiceStatusHandle == (SERVICE_STATUS_HANDLE)0)
    {
        sprintf(thisPtr->m_diag,
            " RegisterServiceCtrlHandler failed %d",
            GetLastError());
        thisPtr->logError(thisPtr->m_diag);
        return;
    }

    thisPtr->SetStatus(SERVICE_START_PENDING);
    // Initialization code goes here.

    initStat = thisPtr->OnInit(&specificError);

    // Handle error condition
    if (initStat == false)
    {
        thisPtr->SetStatus(SERVICE_STOPPED);
        sprintf(thisPtr->m_diag, "OnInit failed initStat=%d...",
            initStat);
        thisPtr->logError(thisPtr->m_diag);
        return;
    }

    thisPtr->SetStatus(SERVICE_RUNNING);
    thisPtr->m_isRunning = true;


    sprintf(thisPtr->m_diag, "Just before processing loop...\n");
    thisPtr->logError(thisPtr->m_diag);
    // This is where the service does its work.

    thisPtr->Run();
```

```
    // Send current status.
    thisPtr->SetStatus(SERVICE_STOPPED);

    return;
}

#ifdef _WIN2K_COMPAT
DWORD WINAPI CPPService::HandlerEx(DWORD dwControl,
    DWORD dwEventType, LPVOID lpEventData, LPVOID lpContext)
{
    DWORD status = SERVICE_RUNNING;
    CPPService *thisPtr;

    thisPtr = m_this;

    sprintf(thisPtr->m_diag, "IN to service Control...\n");
    thisPtr->logError(thisPtr->m_diag);
    switch(dwControl)
    {
        case SERVICE_CONTROL_PAUSE:
        // Do whatever it takes to pause here.
            sprintf(thisPtr->m_diag, "Pausing...\n");
            thisPtr->logError(thisPtr->m_diag);
            if (!(thisPtr->m_isPaused)
            {
                thisPtr->m_isPaused = true;
                thisPtr->OnPause();
                status=SERVICE_PAUSED;
            }
            break;

        case SERVICE_CONTROL_CONTINUE:
        // Do whatever it takes to continue here.
            sprintf(thisPtr->m_diag, "Continuing...\n");
            thisPtr->logError(thisPtr->m_diag);
            if (thisPtr->m_isPaused)
            {
                thisPtr->OnContinue();
                thisPtr->m_isPaused = false;
                status = SERVICE_RUNNING;
            }
            break;
```

*(continued)*

**Listing 5-3** *continued*

```
        case SERVICE_CONTROL_STOP:
        // Do whatever it takes to stop here.
            sprintf(thisPtr->m_diag, "Stopping...\n");
            thisPtr->logError(thisPtr->m_diag);
            if (thisPtr->m_isRunning)
            {
                thisPtr->OnStop();
                status = SERVICE_STOP_PENDING;
                thisPtr->m_isRunning = false;
            }

            thisPtr->SetStatus (status);
            sprintf(thisPtr->m_diag,
                " BeeperService Leaving Handler \n",0);
            thisPtr->logError(thisPtr->m_diag);
            return;

        case SERVICE_CONTROL_PARAMCHANGE:
            thisPtr->OnParamChange();
            break;

        case SERVICE_CONTROL_NETBINDADD:
            thisPtr->OnNetBindAdd();
            break

        case SERVICE_CONTROL_NETBINDDELETE:
            thisPtr->OnNetBindDelete();
            break

        case SERVICE_CONTROL_NETBINDREMOVE:
            thisPtr->OnNetBindRemove();
            break

        case SERVICE_CONTROL_NETBINDENABLE:
            thisPtr->OnNetBindEnable();
            break

        case SERVICE_CONTROL_NETBINDDISABLE:
            thisPtr->OnNetBindDisable();
            break

        case SERVICE_CONTROL_DEVICEEVENT:
            thisPtr->OnDeviceEvent(dwEventType, lpEventData);
            break;
```

```
        case SERVICE_CONTROL_POWEREVENT:
            thisPtr->OnPowerEvent(dwEventType, lpEventData);
            break;

        case SERVICE_CONTROL_HARDWAREPROFILECHANGE:
            thisPtr->OnHardwareProfileChange(dwEventType);
            break;

        case SERVICE_CONTROL_INTERROGATE:
        // Fall through to send current status.
            break;

        default:
            if (dwControl >= SERVICE_CONTROL_USER)
            {
                if (!thisPtr->OnUserControl(dwControl))
                {
                    sprintf(thisPtr->m_diag,
                        " %s Unhandled control code %ld\n",
                        thisPtr->ServiceName(),
                        dwControl);
                    thisPtr->logError(thisPtr->m_diag);
                }
            }
            else
            {
                sprintf(thisPtr->m_diag,
                    " %s Unrecognized control code %ld\n",
                    thisPtr->ServiceName(),
                    dwControl);
                    thisPtr->logError(thisPtr->m_diag);
            }
            break;
    }

    // Send current status.
    thisPtr->SetStatus (status);
    return 0;
}
#else
VOID WINAPI CPPService::Handler(DWORD dwControl)
{
    DWORD status = SERVICE_RUNNING;
    CPPService *thisPtr;

    thisPtr = m_this;
```

*(continued)*

**Listing 5-3** *continued*

```
    sprintf(thisPtr->m_diag, "IN to service Control...\n");
    thisPtr->logError(thisPtr->m_diag);
    switch(dwControl)
    {
        case SERVICE_CONTROL_PAUSE:
        // Do whatever it takes to pause here.
            sprintf(thisPtr->m_diag,"Pausing...\n");
            thisPtr->logError(thisPtr->m_diag);
            if (!(thisPtr->m_isPaused))
            {
                thisPtr->m_isPaused = true;
                thisPtr->OnPause();
                status=SERVICE_PAUSED;
            }
            break;

        case SERVICE_CONTROL_CONTINUE:
        // Do whatever it takes to continue here.
            sprintf(thisPtr->m_diag, "Continuing...\n");
            thisPtr->logError(thisPtr->m_diag);
            if (thisPtr->m_isPaused)
            {
                thisPtr->OnContinue();
                thisPtr->m_isPaused = false;
                status=SERVICE_RUNNING;
            }
            break;

        case SERVICE_CONTROL_STOP:
        // Do whatever it takes to stop here.
            // Removed for Chapter 5
//              sprintf(thisPtr->m_diag, "Stopping...\n");
//              thisPtr->logError(thisPtr->m_diag);
            if (thisPtr->m_isRunning)
            {
                thisPtr->OnStop();
                // Added for Chapter 5
                thisPtr->LogEvent(
                    EVENTLOG_INFORMATION_TYPE,
                    EVMSG_STOPPED,
                    thisPtr->ServiceName());
                // End added for Chapter 5
                status = SERVICE_STOP_PENDING;
```

```
                thisPtr->m_isRunning = false;
            }

            thisPtr->SetStatus (status);
            sprintf(thisPtr->m_diag,
                " BeeperService Leaving Handler \n",0);
            thisPtr->logError(thisPtr->m_diag);
            return;

        case SERVICE_CONTROL_PARAMCHANGE:
            thisPtr->OnParamChange();
            break;

        case SERVICE_CONTROL_NETBINDADD:
            thisPtr->OnNetBindAdd();
            break;

        case SERVICE_CONTROL_NETBINDDISABLE:
            thisPtr->OnNetBindDisable();
            break;

        case SERVICE_CONTROL_NETBINDREMOVE:
            thisPtr->OnNetBindRemove();
            break;

        case SERVICE_CONTROL_NETBINDENABLE:
            thisPtr->OnNetBindEnable();
            break;

        case SERVICE_CONTROL_INTERROGATE:
        // Fall through to send current status.
            break;

        default:
            if (dwControl >= SERVICE_CONTROL_USER)
            {
                if (!thisPtr->OnUserControl(dwControl))
                {
                    sprintf(thisPtr->m_diag,
                        " %s Unhandled control code %ld\n",
                        thisPtr->ServiceName(),
                        dwControl);
                    thisPtr->logError(thisPtr->m_diag);
                }
```

*(continued)*

**Listing 5-3** *continued*

```
            }
            else
            {
                sprintf(thisPtr->m_diag,
                    " %s Unrecognized control code %ld\n",
                    thisPtr->ServiceName(),
                    dwControl);
                    thisPtr->logError(thisPtr->m_diag);
            }
            break;
    }

    // Send current status.
    thisPtr->SetStatus (status);
    return;
}
#endif

// Virtual functions, generally overridden if needed.
BOOL CPPService::OnUserControl(DWORD dwControl)
{
    logError("OnContinue");
    return false;
}

void CPPService::OnContinue()
{
    logError("OnContinue");
    return;
}

void CPPService::OnPause()
{
    logError("OnPause");
    return;
}

void CPPService::OnStop()
{
    logError("OnStop");
    return;
}
```

```
void CPPService::OnInstall()
{
    logError("OnInstall");
    return;
}

void CPPService::OnUninstall()
{
    logError("OnUninstall");
    return;
}

BOOL CPPService::OnInit(DWORD *status)
{
    logError("OnInit");
    *status = 0;
    return true;
}

void CPPService::OnParamChange()
{
    logError("OnParamChange");
    return;
}

void CPPService::OnNetBindAdd()
{
    logError("OnNetBindAdd");
    return;
}

void CPPService::OnNetBindRemove()
{
    logError("OnNetBindRemove");
    return;
}

void CPPService::OnNetBindEnable()
{
    logError("OnNetBindEnable");
    return;
}
```

*(continued)*

**Listing 5-3** *continued*

```
void CPPService::OnNetBindDisable()
{
    logError("OnNetBindDisable");
    return;
}

void CPPService::Run()
{
    while (m_isRunning)
    {
        Sleep(1000);
    }
    return;
}

#ifdef _WIN2K_COMPAT

void OnDeviceEvent(DWORD dwEventType, LPVOID pvEventData)
{
    logError("OnDeviceEvent");
    return;
}

void OnPowerEvent(DWORD dwEventType, LPVOID pvEventData)
{
    logError("OnPowerEvent");
    return;
}

void OnHardwareProfileChange(DWORD dwEventType)
{
    logError("OnHardwareProfileChange");
    return;
}

#endif

// Added for Chapter 5
BOOL CPPService::LogEvent(WORD wType, DWORD dwEventID,
    const char *ps1,
    const char *ps2,
    const char *ps3,
    const char *ps4,
    const char *ps5)
{
    WORD wNumStrings;
    const char *pStrings[5];
```

```
    if (m_EventHandle == 0)
    {
        m_EventHandle = ::RegisterEventSource(NULL,
            ServiceName());
    }

    if (m_EventHandle != 0)
    {
        wNumStrings = 0;
        if (ps1 != 0)
        {
            pStrings[wNumStrings] = ps1;
            wNumStrings++;
            if (ps2 != 0)
            {
                pStrings[wNumStrings] = ps2;
                wNumStrings++;
                if (ps3 != 0)
                {
                    pStrings[wNumStrings] = ps3;
                    wNumStrings++;
                    if (ps4 != 0)
                    {
                        pStrings[wNumStrings] = ps4;
                        wNumStrings++;
                        if (ps5 != 0)
                        {
                            pStrings[wNumStrings] = ps5;
                            wNumStrings++;
                        }
                    }
                }
            }
        }
        ::ReportEvent(m_EventHandle, wType, 0, dwEventID, NULL,
            wNumStrings, 0, pStrings, NULL);

        return true;
    }
    return false;
}
// End added for Chapter 5
```

**CppService.h**

```
#define SERVICE_CONTROL_USER 128

VOID StartThisService(char *serviceName);

class CPPService {
public:
    // Added for Chapter 5
    BOOL LogEvent(WORD wType, DWORD dwEventID,
        const char *ps1 = 0,
        const char *ps2 = 0,
        const char *ps3 = 0,
        const char *ps4 = 0,
        const char *ps5 = 0);

    CPPService(char *tsvcName, char *tdispName,
        DWORD tsvcStart = SERVICE_DEMAND_START);
    virtual ~CPPService();
    BOOL IsInstalled();
    BOOL Install();
    BOOL UnInstall();
    BOOL StartService();
    void SetStatus(DWORD dwControl);
    BOOL Initialize();
    BOOL ParseArguments(int argc, char *argv[]);
    char *ServiceName()
    {
        return serviceName;
    }
    void SetUserAndPassword(char *user = NULL,
        char *pwd = NULL);
    virtual void OnInstall();
    virtual void OnUninstall();
    virtual BOOL OnInit(DWORD *status);
    virtual void Run();
    virtual void OnStop();
    virtual void OnPause();
    virtual void OnContinue();
    virtual BOOL OnUserControl(DWORD dwControl);
    virtual void OnParamChange();
    virtual void OnNetBindAdd();
    virtual void OnNetBindRemove();
    virtual void OnNetBindEnable();
    virtual void OnNetBindDisable();
```

**Listing 5-4**

```
#ifdef _WIN2K_COMPAT
    virtual void OnDeviceEvent(DWORD dwEventType,
        LPVOID pvEventData);
    virtual void OnPowerEvent(DWORD dwEventType,
        LPVOID pvEventData);
    virtual void OnHardwareProfileChange(DWORD dwEventType);
#endif
protected:
    SC_HANDLE m_scmHandle;
    SC_HANDLE m_scHandle;
    // Added for Chapter 5
    HANDLE m_EventHandle;

    SERVICE_STATUS ServiceStatus;
    SERVICE_STATUS_HANDLE ServiceStatusHandle;
    static CPPService *m_this;
    char serviceName[128];
    char serviceDisplayName[128];
    VOID logError(char *msg);
    FILE *log;
    char m_diag[255];
    DWORD m_svcStartType;
    DWORD m_status;
    BOOL m_isRunning;
    BOOL m_isPaused;
#ifdef _WIN2K_COMPAT
    static DWORD WINAPI HandlerEx(DWORD dwControl,
        DWORD dwEventType,
        LPVOID lpEventData, LPVOID lpContext);
#else
    static VOID WINAPI Handler(DWORD dwControl);
#endif
    static VOID WINAPI ServiceMain(DWORD dwArgc,
        LPTSTR *lpszArgv);

};
```

**NOTE** Once the service is restarted, it is possible that rather than the properly formatted message, you will see a message indicating that the message file cannot be found, such as "The description for event ID (<####>) in Source (<application name>) could not be found. It contains the following insertion string(s):". This could be because the resources have not been properly added to the project. However, even if you've done everything correctly, this message can still appear. The solution is to stop and restart the event logging service. This restart is required because the event logging service caches the DLLs it loads for event sources.

## Reading Events from the Event Log

Reading events from the event log is also a bit more complicated than just reading a log file. Figure 5-6 shows the general structure.

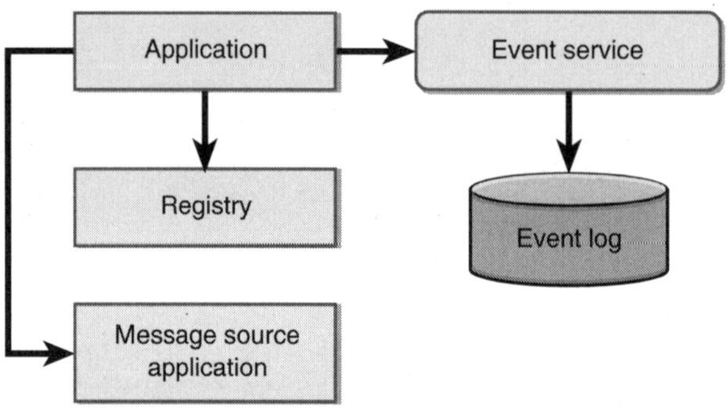


**Figure 5-6** *The process used to read events to the event log.*

As I mentioned previously, when an event is written to the log, the actual text of the message as it appears in the Event Viewer is not stored. Instead, only the parameters that get filled in to the message text are saved in the log. So, to actually read the message in the same way that the event viewer application does, you must take several steps:

1. Open the event log using the *OpenEventLog* Win32 API function and read the events using the *ReadEventLog* Win32 API function.
2. Read the registry to determine the event source for the event that was read.
3. Load the message text from the event source application, and then format the string using *FormatMessage*.

*OpenEventLog* is a simple function that accepts two parameters:

```
HANDLE OpenEventLog(
    LPCTSTR lpUNCServerName,  // Pointer to server name
    LPCTSTR lpSourceName      // Pointer to source name
);
```

The *lpUNCServerName* parameter is either the name of the server or NULL for the local machine. The *lpSourceName* parameter is the name of the log to read, which is often "Application". This function returns a handle that is used in a call to *ReadEventLog*. *ReadEventLog* has the following prototype:

```
BOOL ReadEventLog(
    HANDLE hEventLog,                // Handle to event log
    DWORD dwReadFlags,               // How to read log
    DWORD dwRecordOffset,            // Offset of first record
    LPVOID lpBuffer,                 // Buffer for read data
    DWORD nNumberOfBytesToRead,      // Bytes to read
```

```
    DWORD *pnBytesRead,              // Number of bytes read
    DWORD *pnMinNumberOfBytesNeeded  // Bytes required
);
```

The first parameter, *hEventLog*, is the handle returned by *OpenEventLog*. The parameter *dwReadFlags* specifies how the log is read. EVENTLOG_SEEK_READ allows a specific log record to be specified in the *dwRecordOffset* parameter, while EVENTLOG_SEQUENTIAL_READ reads sequentially from the last record read. One of two additional flags can be specified: EVENTLOG_FORWARDS_READ, which causes the log to be read in chronological order, and EVENTLOG_BACKWARDS_READ, which causes the log to be read in reverse chronological order. The *lpBuffer* parameter points to the buffer that will be filled with an EVENTLOGRECORD structure. The *nNumberOfBytesToRead* parameter specifies the number of bytes contained in the buffer. *ReadEventLog* will place as many complete EVENTLOGRECORD structures as will fit into the buffer passed on each call. The *pnBytesRead* parameter points to the number of bytes actually read when the function returns. If the function returns 0 (indicating an error has occurred) and *GetLastError* returns ERROR_INSUFFICENT_BUFFER, the last parameter points to the number of bytes required to read the next log entry.

Once the buffer passed to *ReadEventLog* is filled in and no error has occurred, there is at least one event record in the buffer. Thus, there is a *while* loop that is controlled by the return from *ReadEventLog* and an inner loop controlled by the reading of the buffer. The following code snippet shows the general process used:

```
while (ReadEventLog(h,
    EVENTLOG_FORWARDS_READ |
    EVENTLOG_SEQUENTIAL_READ,
    0,            // Ignored for sequential reads
    pevlr,
    BUFFER_SIZE,
    &dwBytesRead,
    &dwMinNumberOfBytesNeeded))
{
    // Loop through the returned buffer...
    while (dwBytesRead > 0)
    {
        char szPath[255];
        DWORD cbData;
        // Code for processing each record
        //  omitted for clarity.
            dwBytesRead -= pevlr->Length;
            pevlr = (EVENTLOGRECORD *)
            ((LPBYTE) pevlr + pevlr->Length);
    }

    pevlr = (EVENTLOGRECORD *) &bBuffer;
}
```

The outer loop terminates when there are no more records to read. The inner loop terminates when *dwBytesRead* drops to 0.

Each record is processed when it is placed into the EVENTLOGRECORD. For the simple example that follows, the processing involves displaying some of the raw data—for instance, the event ID, the event source, and the source. With the source, the DLL or executable file that contains the resource for the message text can be read. The registry reads in this code are the opposite of some of the registry code used during the installation of *CPPService*.

```
memset(&szKey[0],'\0',255);
strcpy(szKey, "SYSTEM\\CurrentControlSet\\"
    "Services\\EventLog\\Application\\");
strcat(szKey, (LPSTR) ((LPBYTE) pevlr +
    sizeof(EVENTLOGRECORD)));
if (::RegOpenKey(HKEY_LOCAL_MACHINE, szKey,
    &hKey) != ERROR_SUCCESS)
{
    printf("\nGetLastError()=%d ", GetLastError());
    return;
}
cbData = 255;
// Read the event ID message file (in this case, the EXE file).
::RegQueryValueEx(
    hKey,
    "EventMessageFile",
    0,
    NULL,
    (unsigned char *)szPath,
    &cbData);
```

The registry key that contains information about the event source is opened and read. Specifically, *EventMessageFile* is read. Next, the path returned from this entry is passed to *LoadLibraryEx*, a Win32 API function that loads a DLL or EXE file, with two parameters not used by *LoadLibrary*. This is required because the third parameter allows *LoadLibraryEx* to *not* resolve DLL references, which are not necessary to get at the message resource contained in the file.

> **NOTE** All examples in this text are on the local machine. I cannot overemphasize the difficulty of doing this on a remote machine. From the standpoint of the local machine, the path to the DLL or EXE file containing the message text is a local path. To use *LoadLibraryEx* from a remote machine, you must find a way to get the UNC path to the module. Although there is no perfect way to do this, Chapter 14 offers a possible solution.

*FormatMessage* is commonly used to format error messages based on the return from *GetLastError*:

```
DWORD FormatMessage (
    DWORD dwFlags,        // Source and processing options
    LPCVOID lpSource,     // Pointer to message source
    DWORD dwMessageId,    // Requested message identifier
    DWORD dwLanguageId,   // Language identifier for
                          //  requested message
    LPTSTR lpBuffer,      // Pointer to message buffer
    DWORD nSize,          // Maximum size of message buffer
    va_list *Arguments    // Pointer to array of message inserts
);
```

In Listing 5-5, *dwFlags* is set to FORMAT_MESSAGE_FROM_HMODULE to indicate that the message should be formatted from a handle to a module and—if there are insertion strings—ORed with FORMAT_MESSAGE_ARGUMENT_ARRAY. The *lpSource* parameter is a handle to a module, returned from *LoadLibraryEx*. The *dwMessageId* parameter is set to the *EventID* element of the EVENTLOGRECORD structure. The *dwLanguageId* parameter is a DWORD that is created in this example by using the MAKELANGID macro. If this parameter is set to 0, specific rules in the Win32 SDK indicate how the language will be resolved. The *lpBuffer* parameter points to the buffer that will receive the formatted message, and *nSize* contains the size of the buffer. In Listing 5-5, the buffer used is a local buffer, but flags to *FormatMessage* tell it to allocate the buffer to the appropriate size and set the passed pointer to that value. *Arguments* is an array of pointers that contains the strings used in conjunction with the message string, allowing *FormatMessage* to replace *%n* with the appropriate argument.

**ReadEvents.cpp**

```
// ReadEvents.cpp : Read events from the Application event log.
//

#include "stdafx.h"

#define BUFFER_SIZE 1024

void DisplayEvents()
{
    HANDLE h;
    HMODULE hm;
    EVENTLOGRECORD *pevlr;
    BYTE bBuffer[BUFFER_SIZE];
    DWORD dwBytesRead;
    DWORD dwMinNumberOfBytesNeeded
```

**Listing 5-5** *(continued)*

**Listing 5-5** *continued*

```
DWORD dwThisRecord = 0;
char szKey[255];
HKEY hKey = NULL;

// Open the Application event log.

h = OpenEventLog(NULL, "Application");
if (h == NULL)
 {
    printf("Could not open the Application event log.");
    return;
 }

pevlr = (EVENTLOGRECORD *) &bBuffer;


// Opening the event log positions the file pointer for this
//  handle at the beginning of the log. Read the records
//  sequentially until there are no more.
// A single read can get more than a single record.

while (ReadEventLog(h,
    EVENTLOG_FORWARDS_READ |
    EVENTLOG_SEQUENTIAL_READ,
    0,          // Ignored for sequential reads
    pevlr,
    BUFFER_SIZE,
    &dwBytesRead,
    &dwMinNumberOfBytesNeeded))
{
    // Loop through the returned buffer...
    while (dwBytesRead > 0)
    {
        char szPath[255];
        DWORD cbData;

        printf("%04d  Event ID: 0x%08X ",
            dwThisRecord++, pevlr->EventID);
        printf("EventType: %d Source: %s  \n",
            pevlr->EventType, (LPSTR) ((LPBYTE) pevlr +
            sizeof(EVENTLOGRECORD)));
        // Now we need to actually get the text so that we
        //  can actually display the message text.
```

```
memset(&szKey[0], '\0', 255);
strcpy(szKey, "SYSTEM\\CurrentControlSet\\"
    "Services\\EventLog\\Application\\");
strcat(szKey, (LPSTR) ((LPBYTE) pevlr +
    sizeof(EVENTLOGRECORD)));
if (::RegOpenKey(HKEY_LOCAL_MACHINE,
    szKey, &hKey) != ERROR_SUCCESS)
{
    printf("\nGetLastError()=%d ", GetLastError());
    return;
}
cbData = 255;
// Read the event ID message file
//  (in this case, the EXE file).
::RegQueryValueEx(
    hKey,
    "EventMessageFile",
    0,
    NULL,
    (unsigned char *)szPath,
    &cbData);

printf("\t%s \n", szPath);
hm = LoadLibraryEx(szPath, NULL,
    DONT_RESOLVE_DLL_REFERENCES);
if (hm != 0)
{
    char buffer[1024];
    char *pStr;
    char *pStrs[255];
    DWORD dwFlags = FORMAT_MESSAGE_FROM_HMODULE;
    if (pevlr->NumStrings)
    {
        int loop;
        pStr = (char *)pevlr+pevlr->StringOffset;
        for (loop=0 ; loop<pevlr->NumStrings ; loop++)
        {
            pStrs[loop] = pStr;
            pStr = strchr(pStr,'\0')+1;
        }
        dwFlags |= FORMAT_MESSAGE_ARGUMENT_ARRAY;
    }
    FormatMessage(dwFlags, hm, pevlr->EventID,
        MAKELANGID(LANG_ENGLISH, SUBLANG_DEFAULT),
        buffer, 1024, pStrs);
```

*(continued)*

**Listing 5-5** *continued*

```
                printf("Message: %s\n", buffer);
                FreeLibrary(hm);
            }

            dwBytesRead -= pevlr->Length;
            pevlr = (EVENTLOGRECORD *)
                ((LPBYTE) pevlr + pevlr->Length);
            ::RegCloseKey(hKey);
        }

        pevlr = (EVENTLOGRECORD *) &bBuffer;
    }

    CloseEventLog(h);
}

int main(int argc, char* argv[])
{
    printf("Hello Registry World!\n");
    DisplayEvents();
    return 0;
}
```

# CONCLUSION

One of the biggest surprises associated with server-based application development has been the disparity between the perceived complexity of performing a task and the task's actual complexity. While I expected the Service API to be terribly complex and fraught with difficulties, in general it is easy to understand and use. The opposite is true of event logging.

The examples in this chapter are not the most complex examples in the book, but neither are they the simplest. For instance, loading a library so that message resources can be read, while not taking the time or risk of failure that is possible if DLL references are resolved, is an advanced and uncommon operation. This kind of complexity seems at odds with the apparently simple requirement of reading an event log.

Along with Event Logging API's complexity, we have also seen its advanced capabilities, including the increasingly important task of allowing applications to operate globally with minimal changes required. In the end, the ability to have an operating system supported by an event logging system is worth the additional complexity of the API.

*Chapter 6*

# Remote Access Service API

Back in the old days—around 1988—I was working on a 16-bit MS-DOS application that required a consolidation of billing information from dozens of remote sites into a central location on a nightly basis. The sites were separated by hundreds of miles, many in locations so remote that physical transportation of diskettes to the central site was impractical. Furthermore, this happened long before the ubiquitous Internet and freely available e-mail. The solution back then was a polling program that called each remote site on a nightly basis and used a custom program to handle the Xmodem protocol required for binary file transfers.

Today things would be very different. While much of what I did could be handled in essentially the same way, using the Telephony API (TAPI) discussed in the next chapter, or using e-mail via the Messaging API (MAPI), which is also discussed in the next chapter, there is also a third way. Remote Access Service (RAS) allows two computers to be connected using standard phone lines. The connection does not result in a special-purpose link between the two machines, but rather in an extended wide area network (WAN). With this WAN established, all of the APIs that work on a local area network (LAN) are available, giving you the ability to simply copy files from one machine to another, though admittedly at a slower rate than a LAN connection. This ability to establish extended WAN connections allows a single code base to be used for both LAN-attached and remote sites. This flexibility allows seamless scalability from multiple remote sites, hooked only by phone wires, to massive WANs crossing the country or the globe.

The client side of RAS—where your computer dials into a server that is waiting to accept such connections—is employed whenever a user makes a phone connection to the Internet. The server can be a Microsoft Windows 2000 server or any server that can provide a connection understood by RAS, such as the commonly used Point-to-Point Protocol (PPP) or Serial Line Internet Protocol (SLIP).

Like many aspects of Windows development, the naming of components related to this technology has not helped foster a coherent image for RAS, especially in how the names differ between what the developer sees and what the Windows 2000 user sees. On my Windows NT 4 server, the RAS client is accessed through the Accessories menu as Dial-Up Networking. In Windows 2000, the feature previously known as Dial-Up Networking is available on the Settings menu (and in Control Panel) as Network And Dial-Up Connections. Thus, even if you are a programmer who regularly uses RAS to connect to remote sites or to the Internet, you might not be aware of RAS under the new name.

## RAS API Overview

There are approximately 55 RAS functions detailed in the Win32 SDK documentation. Several of these are actually callback functions, used to allow RAS to send status information asynchronously to an application or to allow third-party vendors to provide custom functionality, as with *RasCustomHangUp*. In addition, several of these functions are enumeration functions that allow an application to discover devices and connections. Finally, there is a class of RAS functions that involve the RAS user interface. With the notable exception of the callback functions used for dialing up connections, I will not be covering many of these functions here. In most server situations, the connection information is already known, not discovered during a session. Furthermore, the goal of a service application is to operate unattended, so there is no need to employ the RAS user interface.

## An Example Using *RasDial*

So what would you do with RAS? Take as an example the application I mentioned above—getting information from several remote sites to a central location. Listing 6-1 contains the code for a simple console mode application named RasDial.exe that allows a file to be copied from a local drive to a remote drive after the establishment of a RAS session. The complete project is included on the companion CD-ROM.

**RasDial.cpp**

```
// RasDial.cpp: Simple RAS dialing example...
//

#include "stdafx.h"

// Prototype for callback function...

DWORD WINAPI RasDialFunc2(
    DWORD dwCallbackId,     // User-defined value specified in
                            //  RasDial call
  DWORD dwSubEntry,         // Subentry index in multilink connection
  HRASCONN hrasconn,        // Handle to RAS connection
  UINT unMsg,               // Type of event that has occurred
  RASCONNSTATE rascs,       // Connection state about to be entered
  DWORD dwError,            // Error that may have occurred
  DWORD dwExtendedError     // Extended error information for
                            //  some errors
);

HANDLE muNotConnected;

//----------------------------------------------------------------------
// Main routine for console mode application...

int main(int argc, char* argv[])
{
    RASDIALPARAMS rdp;
    HRASCONN hrasconn=NULL;
    DWORD ret;
    FILE *in;
    FILE *out;
    char buffer[4096];

    memset((void *)&rdp, '\0', sizeof(RASDIALPARAMS));
    rdp.dwSize = sizeof(RASDIALPARAMS);
    strcpy(rdp.szEntryName, "TEST");
    strcpy(rdp.szPhoneNumber, "");
    strcpy(rdp.szCallbackNumber, "");
    strcpy(rdp.szUserName, "Dougr");
    strcpy(rdp.szPassword, "SECRET");
    strcpy(rdp.szDomain, "ACCESS");
```

**Listing 6-1** *(continued)*

**Listing 6-1** *continued*

```
// Create the mutex; don't worry about security (first NULL),
//  false (initially DO NOT own the mutex).
//  Second NULL means object not named, since it will not
//  be shared among processes...
muNotConnected = CreateMutex(NULL, false, NULL);

ret = RasDial(NULL, NULL, &rdp, 2, RasDialFunc2, &hrasconn);
if (ret)
{
    char buffer[255];
    RasGetErrorString(ret, buffer, 255);
    printf("\nGetLastError=%d %s", GetLastError(), buffer);
    return(0);
}


// This is to give the first call to RasDialFunc2
//  time to get mutex...
Sleep(1000);

// Wait a long time, 100 seconds. This is likely longer
//  than needed for the file in question but allows
//  extra time for negotiation.
switch (WaitForSingleObject(muNotConnected, 100000))
{
case WAIT_ABANDONED:
    printf(
        "\nWait abandoned...Thread terminated without giving"
            " up control!");
    break;
case WAIT_TIMEOUT:
    printf("\n100 seconds elapsed...Bailing.");
    break;
case WAIT_OBJECT_0:
    printf("\nObject acquired...All seems well");
    in = fopen("c:\\service.log", "r+t");

    // Note that the 'c' included in the mode parameter
    //  is used to force the contents to be written
    //  directly to disk when fflush is called.
    //  Obviously, the path should be modified for
    //  your server.
    out = fopen("\\\\dougr\\shared\\service.log", "w+tc");

    if (in == NULL || out==NULL)
    {
        printf("\nCannot open file...");
    }
```

```
        else
        {
            size_t bytes;
            while ((bytes = fread((void *)buffer, 1, 4096, in)))
            {
                fwrite((void *)buffer, 1, bytes, out);
            }

            fclose(in);
            fflush(out);
            fclose(out);
            printf("\nData Copied!");
        }
        break;
    }
    RasHangUp(hrasconn);
    CloseHandle(muNotConnected);
    return 0;
}

//----------------------------------------------------------------------
// Callback function...
DWORD WINAPI RasDialFunc2(
    DWORD dwCallbackId,          // User-defined value specified in
                                 //  RasDial call
    DWORD dwSubEntry,            // Subentry index in multilink
                                 //  connection
    HRASCONN hrasconn,           // Handle to RAS connection
    UINT unMsg,                  // Type of event that has occurred
    RASCONNSTATE rasconnstate,   // Connection state about to be
                                 //  entered
    DWORD dwError,               // Error that may have occurred
    DWORD dwExtendedError        // Extended error information for
                                 //  some errors
)
{

    switch(rasconnstate)
    {
    case RASCS_OpenPort:
        if (WaitForSingleObject(muNotConnected, 0) !=
            WAIT_OBJECT_0)
        {
            printf("\nShould not be here!  Can't get mutex!");
        }
```

*(continued)*

**Listing 6-1** *continued*

```
        else
        {
            printf("\nrasconnstate=RASCS_OpenPort");
        }
        break;
    case RASCS_PortOpened:
        printf("\nrasconnstate=RASCS_PortOpened");
        break;
    case RASCS_ConnectDevice:
        printf("\nrasconnstate=RASCS_ConnectDevice");
        break;
    case RASCS_DeviceConnected:
        printf("\nrasconnstate=RASCS_DeviceConnected");
        break;
    case RASCS_AllDevicesConnected:
        printf("\nrasconnstate=RASCS_AllDevicesConnected");
        break;
    case RASCS_Authenticate:
        printf("\nrasconnstate=RASCS_Authenticate");
        break;
    case RASCS_AuthNotify:
        printf("\nrasconnstate=RASCS_AuthNotify");
        break;
    case RASCS_AuthRetry:
        printf("\nrasconnstate=RASCS_AuthRetry");
        break;
    case RASCS_AuthCallback:
        printf("\nrasconnstate=RASCS_AuthCallback");
        break;
    case RASCS_AuthChangePassword:
        printf("\nrasconnstate=RASCS_AuthChangePassword");
        break;
    case RASCS_AuthProject:
        printf("\nrasconnstate=RASCS_AuthProject");
        break;
    case RASCS_AuthLinkSpeed:
        printf("\nrasconnstate=RASCS_AuthLinkSpeed");
        break;
    case RASCS_AuthAck:
        printf("\nrasconnstate=RASCS_AuthAck");
        break;
    case RASCS_ReAuthenticate:
        printf("\nrasconnstate=RASCS_ReAuthenticate");
        break;
```

```
    case RASCS_Authenticated:
        printf("\nrasconnstate=RASCS_Authenticated");
        break;
    case RASCS_PrepareForCallback:
        printf("\nrasconnstate=RASCS_PrepareForCallback");
        break;
    case RASCS_WaitForModemReset:
        printf("\nrasconnstate=RASCS_WaitForModemReset");
        break;
    case RASCS_WaitForCallback:
        printf("\nrasconnstate=RASCS_WaitForCallback");
        break;
    case RASCS_Projected:
        printf("\nrasconnstate=RASCS_Projected");
        break;
    case RASCS_SubEntryConnected:
        printf("\nrasconnstate=RASCS_SubEntryConnected");
        break;
    case RASCS_SubEntryDisconnected:
        printf("\nrasconnstate=RASCS_SubEntryDisconnected");
        break;
    case RASCS_Interactive:
        printf("\nrasconnstate=RASCS_Interactive");
        break;
    case RASCS_RetryAuthentication:
        printf("\nrasconnstate=RASCS_RetryAuthentication");
        break;
    case RASCS_CallbackSetByCaller:
        printf("\nrasconnstate=RASCS_CallbackSetByCaller");
        break;
    case RASCS_PasswordExpired:
        printf("\nrasconnstate=RASCS_PasswordExpired");
        break;
#if (WINVER >= 0x500)
    case RASCS_InvokeEapUI:
        printf("\nrasconnstate=RASCS_InvokeEapU");
        break;
#endif
    case RASCS_Connected:
        printf("\nrasconnstate=RASCS_Connected - Copy the data...");

        ReleaseMutex(muNotConnected);
        break;
```

*(continued)*

**Listing 6-1** *continued*

```
        case RASCS_Disconnected:
            printf("\nrasconnstate=RASCS_Disconnected");
            break;
        }
        if (dwError)
        {
            printf("\nGot here error=%d rasconnstate=%d",
                dwError,rasconnstate);
        }
        return 1;  // Continue getting notifications...
    }
```

Take a look at the top of the listing. The *main* routine first declares several variables used for the RAS calls and for the actual file copying that is the objective of this exercise. The RASDIALPARAMS structure, *rdp*, is initialized next. First, *dwSize* is set to the size of the structure. This entry is used by RAS to determine the version of the structure being sent. The next entry, *szEntryName*, is the name of the dial-up connection as it appears on the Settings/Network and Dial-Up Connections menu. The *szPhoneNumber* entry is the phone number to dial if it differs from the phone number stored in the connection specified by *szEntryName*. The *szCallbackNumber* entry is used to specify a number for the remote site to call back to the originator of the call.

> **NOTE** In some previous Windows versions, *szCallbackNumber* could be set to an asterisk (*) to indicate that the number stored in the registry as a callback should be used. This is not a valid option in Windows 2000 or Windows NT version 4 or later. This callback number is ignored unless the user has "Set By Caller" permission for callbacks on the remote RAS server.

The next three entries are used for authenticating the RAS connection. The user name and password are self-explanatory, but the connection might not work exactly as you think it will. For example, the user name and password are used for access to the RAS server on the other end of the connection, but this does not mean you are logged on as that user on the remote network. If the user name and password on the local machine and the remote machine are the same, this gives an appearance of simultaneously logging on to the RAS server and some of the resources on the other end of the connection. This is only an appearance. If you need to access resources under an authority different from the user name and password on the local machine, the application might need to call *LogonUser*, as described in Chapter 4.

You might or might not need to set the *szDomain* entry, depending on the identity of the server being called. If you're connecting to a Windows 2000 server, you are better off specifying a domain. Connecting to Internet servers running other operating systems, such as Unix, generally does not require a domain name to be specified. Setting an asterisk for the domain name specifies that the domain set in the phonebook entry should be used.

## Controlling Multiple Threads

The mutex *muNotConnected* is created with a call to *CreateMutex*. (See Chapter 2 for details.) The mutex is created with a NULL passed as the security descriptor to get the default security descriptor, a *false* indicating that the calling thread does not want ownership of the object, and a final NULL indicating that no name is to be used. The name is not required because this mutex will not be used across process boundaries.

The next step is to actually dial the phone, using the *RasDial* Win32 API function. The prototype for this function is as follows:

```
DWORD RasDial(
    LPRASDIALEXTENSIONS lpRasDialExtensions,
                            // Pointer to function extensions data
    LPCTSTR lpszPhonebook,  // Pointer to full path and filename of
                            //  phonebook file
    LPRASDIALPARAMS lpRasDialParams,
                            // Pointer to calling parameters data
    DWORD dwNotifierType,   // Specifies type of RasDial event handler
    LPVOID lpvNotifier,     // Specifies a handler for RasDial events
    LPHRASCONN lphRasConn   // Pointer to variable to receive
                            //  connection handle
);
```

The first parameter, *lpRasDialExtensions*, is used to set some advanced options or can be set to NULL if no options need to be set. Features you can set using this structure include the use of a dialing prefix and suffix, the modem speaker, software compression, the use of scripting options, and Windows 2000 Extensible Authentication Protocol (EAP). In the RasDial.exe sample program, *lpRasDialExtensions* is set to NULL.

The second parameter, *lpszPhonebook*, is a pointer to the name of a phonebook file if the default phonebook is not to be used. Phonebook files have a .pbk extension. Next, the address of the RASDIALPARAMS structure filled in earlier is passed as the *lpRasDialParams* parameter. The fourth parameter, *dwNotifierType*, specifies the way in which asynchronous events generated by dialing are handled. Interestingly, there are no defined constants for these values. 0xFFFFFFFF specifies that a window procedure should receive notifications and that the fifth parameter, *lpvNotifier*, should contain a window handle. This parameter is not commonly used in server-based application development. A value of 0, 1, or 2 specifies that, respectively, *lpvNotifier* should contain a pointer to a *RasDialFunc*, *RasDialFunc1*, or *RasDialFunc2* function. The RasDial.exe example uses a *dwNotifierType* of 2 and therefore specifies a callback function, *RasDialFunc2*, whose prototype is declared earlier. The name of the function could be anything; I use *RasDialFunc2* here for clarity. Alternatively, *lpvNotified* could be NULL, in which case *RasDial* operates synchronously. This is seldom an ideal choice in a server application. *RasDialFunc*, *RasDialFunc1*, and *RasDialFunc2* behave similarly, with *RasDialFunc* only accepting *uMsg*, *rasconnstate*, and *dwError* and returning no value. *RasDialFunc1* adds *hrasconn* and *dwExtendedError*. *RasDialFunc2* has the prototype above, and the value returned allows the callback to indicate if it wishes to receive further notifications. Returning 0 indicates no further notifications should be sent; a nonzero value indicates notifications should continue.

The final parameter is *lphRasConn*, a handle that is used for other RAS operations, including *RasHangUp*. If an error occurs in the call to *RasDial*, a message is displayed using another RAS API function, *RasGetErrorString*. The prototype for this function is as follows:

```
DWORD RasGetErrorString(
    UINT uErrorValue,         // Error to get string for
    LPTSTR lpszErrorString,   // Buffer to hold error string
    DWORD cBufSize            // Size, in characters, of buffer
);
```

The *uErrorValue* parameter is the value returned by one of the RAS functions. The *lpszErrorString* parameter is the buffer to receive the error string, and *cBufSize* is the size, in characters, of the buffer.

Once *RasDial* returns with a value of 0, the function waits briefly to allow the callback function to acquire the mutex *muNotConnected*. One second is allowed for this, and the mutex will be acquired on the first call to *RasDialFunc2*, when the port is opened.

> **NOTE** One unusual thing about copying files over a RAS connection became clear to me during testing of this application. Notice in *main* the unusual file open mode passed in the call to *fopen* to open the file on the remote server. The "w" indicates the file should be opened for writing, the "+" indicates the file should be created if it does not exist, and the "t" indicates this is a text mode file, not unreasonable for the data being copied. But what about that "c"? I have programmed in C and C++ since 1984, and I've never seen this. The Microsoft Visual C++ documentation indicates the "c" is used to force the waiting data to be flushed to the disk when a call to *fflush* is made. On some occasions, without this additional character in the open mode parameter, I received an error upon the termination of the RAS connection indicating that not all data had been written to the disk before the connection was terminated. So while RAS is almost like being attached via a traditional network, it is not *exactly* like it.

The *main* function next calls *WaitForSingleObject* on the *muNotConnected* mutex with a timeout of 100,000 to allow 100 seconds for the connection to take place. If *WaitForSingleObject* returns with a return value of WAIT_ABANDONED, the thread that owned the mutex (in this case the thread calling *RasDialFunc2*) has terminated without giving up ownership of the mutex. This indicates some catastrophic failure in the RAS system. If *WaitForSingleObject* returns WAIT_TIMEOUT, 100 seconds have elapsed and the application assumes that the operation has failed.

If the object is acquired, which *WaitForSingleObject* indicates by returning WAIT_OBJECT_0, the connection should be present and the file copy takes place. Finally, *RasHangUp* is called with the handle obtained during the call to *RasDial*, and the handle to the mutex object is freed.

## The *RasDialFunc2* Callback Function

*RasDialFunc2* is one of three different callback functions that can be used to make *RasDial* operate asynchronously. In the example program, *RasDialFunc2* is little more than a *switch* statement that displays messages as the dial-up process takes place. One element that is important in creating a callback such as this is that any operation must take place and quickly return to the caller so that actual work can be done. In the case of communications in which modem negotiations are taking place, any delay could cause RAS to think an error has occurred. Of course, in the event of an error, it is allowable to take some time in the function, even putting up a message box if needed. In server-based applications, however, this is not usually advisable.

The only *case* blocks that are anything beyond debugging aids are the handlers for opening the port and connecting. When the port is opened, the following code section is executed:

```
case RASCS_OpenPort:
    if (WaitForSingleObject(muNotConnected,0) != WAIT_OBJECT_0)
    {
        printf("\nShould not be here!  Can't get mutex!");
    }
    else
    {
        printf("\nrasconnstate=RASCS_OpenPort");
    }
    break;
```

This function waits for the mutex with a timeout of 0, meaning that the function should immediately return, even if the object has not been acquired. If the return is not a return value indicating the object has been acquired, a message is displayed indicating the mutex cannot be obtained. This should never occur. When the connection is made, the code shown at the top of the next page is executed.

```
case RASCS_Connected:
    printf("\nrasconnstate=RASCS_Connected - Copy the data...");
    ReleaseMutex(muNotConnected);
    break;
```

This releases the mutex, which lets the *main* routine know that the connection has been made and the copy can proceed. This is how the callback lets the rest of the program know that a connection has been established.

When the program is run, notifications are received as the dialing takes place. The specific order of the notifications cannot be counted on, though using the notification associated with opening the port and the establishment of connections seems reliable in practice.

# OTHER USES FOR RAS

There are many other uses for RAS, but few are useful for server-based applications. One exception is the set of functions associated with managing autodial connections. If a server needs to periodically connect to a remote location, and the server cannot know that a particular network resource is remote, the RAS functions allow the connection between a particular network resource and a dial-up connection to take place—the connection is handled at the operating system level. *RasSetAutodialAddress* is one of these functions. This function allows for a connection to remote resources in a reasonably transparent way, handled automatically by the operating system. The prototype for *RasSetAutodialAddress* is

```
DWORD RasSetAutodialAddress(
    LPCTSTR lpszAddress,        // Pointer to a network address
                                //  string
    DWORD dwReserved,           // Reserved; must be zero
    LPRASAUTODIALENTRY lpAutoDialEntries,
                                // Pointer to buffer containing
                                //  AutoDial entry data
    DWORD dwcbAutoDialEntries,  // Size, in bytes, of the buffer
    DWORD dwcAutoDialEntries    // Number of entries in the buffer
);
```

The *lpszAddress* parameter is a pointer to a string containing the name of a network address—either an IP dotted address ("10.10.10.0"), an Internet host name ("www.microsoft.com"), or a NetBIOS name ("DougR"). The *lpAutoDialEntries* parameter points to an array of RASAUTODIALENTRY structures. These structures contain the names of the entries in the RAS phonebook as well as TAPI-related information about the dialing location. If this entry is NULL and the value for the next parameter, *dwcbAutoDialEntries*, is 0, all information in the mapping database related to *lpszAddress* is eliminated. The *dwcbAutoDialEntries* parameter normally specifies the size, in bytes, of the buffer pointed to by *lpAutoDialEntries*. The *dwcAutoDialEntries* parameter specifies the number of RASAUTODIALENTRY structures pointed to by *lpAutoDialEntries*.

*RasSetAutodialParam* is another function for setting up autodialing using RAS.

```
DWORD RasSetAutodialParam(
    DWORD dwKey,      // Indicates the parameter to set
    LPVOID lpvValue, // Pointer to a buffer that specifies the value
    DWORD dwcbValue  // Size, in bytes, of the buffer
);
```

The *dwKey* parameter specifies the autodial parameter to be set; *lpvValue* points to the value to be set for the *dwKey* parameter. The *dwcbValue* parameter is the size, in bytes, of the buffer passed as *lpvValue*. Table 6-1 shows the values for *dwKey* and the meaning of those values.

**TABLE 6-1**
**VALUES OF *DWKEY* PARAMETER TO *RASSETAUTODIALPARAM***

| *dwKey* | *Possible Values* | *Details* |
|---|---|---|
| RASADP_DisableConnectionQuery | 0 or 1 | DWORD—the default (0)—shows a dialog box to query the user before autodialing. 1 disables that dialog box. |
| RASADP_LoginSessionDisable | 0 or 1 | DWORD—the default (0)—allows autodial connections. 1 disables autodial connections for this session. This is reset to 0 each time a user logs on. |
| RASADP_SavedAddressesLimit | Any valid DWORD | The number of addresses autodial stores in the registry. This number does not affect addresses saved using the *RasSetAutodialAddress* function, only the addresses learned by RAS after a connection is made. The default is 100. |
| RASADP_FailedConnectionTimeout | Any valid DWORD | The timeout in seconds that subsequent attempts to reach an address that previously failed must wait. This is to prevent multiple dialogs from appearing for the same failed connection. The default is 5. |
| RASADP_ConnectionQueryTimeout | Any valid DWORD | The timeout, in seconds, that an autodial dialog will wait for the user to cancel an autodial in progress. |

Some of these parameters, especially RASADP_DisableConnectionQuery and RASADP_ConnectionQueryTimeout, have obvious applicability to server-based applications, which—wherever possible—want no user interface at all, since no user will be able to respond if the service application is a Windows 2000 service.

## CONCLUSION

This admittedly brief overview of the capabilities of this relatively simple API gives you a small taste of what is possible using RAS. The next chapter will cover TAPI and MAPI; I'll show you some alternative ways of doing the same task we used RAS for. One alternative to using RAS, TAPI, or MAPI for a file transfer is using File Transfer Protocol (FTP), a topic more appropriately covered as a client-side technology. Of course, RAS can even be used to establish a connection that FTP could use to do the actual file transfer.

There are certainly advantages to the other methods of dealing with a file transfer such as this, but RAS can often be a solution when you want to do something remotely that is easy to do on a local area network. Copying files is certainly one example—but not the only example—in which RAS can be the next best thing to being there.

*Chapter 7*

# Telephony API and the Messaging API

In the previous chapter, I covered the Remote Access Server (RAS) API. That API allows an application to create a virtual wide-area network so that an application can continue as if the attached network were local. The Telephony API (TAPI) and the Messaging API (MAPI) can allow some of the same things to happen, but in a much different way.

## TAPI

TAPI interacts with the phone in some of the same ways as the RAS API. In fact, some RAS functions require information obtained from TAPI. But TAPI is very different from RAS. While RAS focuses on creating a seamless link between local and remote networks, TAPI's goal is the creation of a seamless link between the computer and the phone system. Recent additions to TAPI have included all the hooks required to support a full-fledged call center application. One of the things strangely lacking from TAPI is a reasonable facility to allow faxing. While technically MAPI covers this feature, it is not MAPI's major focus—which is enabling applications to integrate e-mail support.

## TAPI Versions

Windows 2000 supports some new versions of TAPI. TAPI 2.1 is mostly compatible with previous versions of TAPI, providing a function call API. TAPI 3, which is also new with Windows 2000, is an entirely new COM interface for TAPI. Both interfaces provide essentially the same functionality, although some of the more advanced call center features are more fully developed and easier to use in TAPI 3.

One of the downsides of TAPI 3 is that it is not optimized for a service environment. For instance, TAPI 3 requires a call to *CoInitialize*, which indirectly creates windows. Applications that create windows must have a message pump, which is something commonly required for Windows GUI applications but is not required for service applications. In addition, these same constraints require special versions of waiting functions, so rather than use something like *WaitForSingleObject* or even the simple *Sleep*, you must use the *CoWaitForMultipleHandles* function. This complication, as well as TAPI 2.1's reasonably complete functionality, favors TAPI 2.1 over TAPI 3 in a service application. Thus, the examples in this book will use TAPI 2.1.

TAPI allows the developer to specify the version of TAPI that the application will support. Just as important, the version supported can be negotiated; an application can determine the current version of TAPI supported on the system it runs and negotiate the version of the interface it will support. TAPI versions are returned to the application and sent to TAPI as a DWORD, with the high-order word containing the major version number and the low-order word containing the minor version number. For instance, 0x20001 returned as a version means TAPI 2.1.

## TAPI Devices

Another TAPI feature is the device ID. This is a number that identifies a particular device on the system, commonly a modem. Device IDs range from 0 through one less than the number of devices returned by TAPI. Under Windows NT 4, the number of devices reported seems simple and consistent: on a machine containing a single device, the number of devices returned is 1, and device ID 0 is that single device. Under Windows 2000 (as of Windows 2000 RC 1), the number of devices returned seems a bit unusual, generally seen as a number greater than 1000, with the device at device ID 1000 corresponding to the device at device ID 0 on a similarly equipped Windows NT 4.x machine.

## TAPI Errors

Unlike many Win32 APIs, TAPI errors are not reported using the *GetLastError* Win32 API function. Errors are returned directly from the TAPI functions, and the error numbers are less than zero, meaning that properly interpreting them requires a signed number. In some cases TAPI errors are returned in data elements of structures declared as DWORDs, meaning that they are unsigned. For instance, one way that information is obtained about the progress of asynchronous TAPI operations is through a function that gets a message from TAPI. To properly interpret the error code in these cases, the structure data element must be cast as a *long*.

## Getting Feedback from TAPI

Getting feedback about the success or failure of an operation is one of the most important tasks of any API. Within TAPI, many operations return a code indicating success or failure, but that code refers to the beginning of the operation, not to the success of the operation itself. For instance, one of the functions used in this chapter's example programs is *lineMakeCall*. This is an asynchronous function, meaning that it returns before the actual operation requested is complete.

> **NOTE** The capitalization of TAPI function names is a bit different than most Win32 API function naming conventions. While virtually all Win32 functions begin with an initial capital letter, none of the TAPI functions do. They are broadly grouped into functions beginning with *line* and functions beginning with *phone*. The *phone* functions are used to control a telephone handset, allowing lights to be turned on and off, the line flashed, and so on. We will focus on the *line* functions, useful for the examples in this chapter. The general structure of the *phone* functions is similar to that of the *line* functions.

There are several ways that TAPI can give feedback to an application about the progress of an asynchronous operation. They are

- completion ports
- hidden windows
- event objects

Completion ports will be discussed in Chapter 12. A hidden window is not an ideal solution for a service since this implies an operational message pump, something a service is unlikely to have. That leaves event objects, one of the kernel synchronization objects I discussed in Chapter 2.

## A TAPI Example

One of the many examples of what TAPI can be used for is allowing a service application to let someone know that the service is having a problem, using a standard numeric pager.

Listing 7-1 is the header file for the TAPI21Sample program in Listing 7-2. TAPI21Sample is a simple console mode program that demonstrates the TAPI functions required to initiate a call. TAPI21Sample simply calls a beeper service and places a beep. When you look at the code, you might very well say to yourself: Is all this necessary? The answer is yes—this is what TAPI requires.

**StdAfx.h**

```
// stdafx.h : include file for sample TAPI application.
//

#if !defined(AFX_STDAFX_H__ECF1090B_57E8_11D3_B4AA_00C04F79B510__
INCLUDED_)
#define AFX_STDAFX_H__ECF1090B_57E8_11D3_B4AA_00C04F79B510__INCLUDED_

#if _MSC_VER > 1000
#pragma once
#endif // _MSC_VER > 1000

#define WIN32_LEAN_AND_MEAN     // Exclude rarely used stuff from
                                //  Windows headers.

#include <stdio.h>
#include <windows.h>
#include <tapi.h>

// TODO: reference additional headers your program requires here.

//{{AFX_INSERT_LOCATION}}
// Microsoft Visual C++ will insert additional declarations
//  immediately before the previous line.

#endif //
 !defined(AFX_STDAFX_H__ECF1090B_57E8_11D3_B4AA_00C04F79B510__
INCLUDED_)
```

**Listing 7-1**

**TAPI21Sample.cpp**

```
// TAPI21Sample.cpp : Console application to test TAPI 2
//

#include "stdafx.h"
// Forward declaration
```

**Listing 7-2**

```
void ReportTAPIError(LONG ret, char *op);
int CallBeeper(char *beeperNumber, char *beepTo);

int main(int argc, char* argv[])
{
    // Replace these strings with your beeper access number and the
    //  number to send to the beeper.
    CallBeeper("555-5166", "555-1605");
    return 0;
}

int CallBeeper(char *beeperNumber, char *beepTo)
{
    HLINEAPP hLineApp;
    HLINE hLine;
    char szFriendlyAppName[255];
    char szAddress[255];
    DWORD dwNumDevs = 0;
    DWORD dwAPIVersion = 0x00020000;
    DWORD dwCallbackInstance = 43;  // Just a lucky number,
                                    //  NOT interpreted by TAPI
    DWORD dwStatus;
    DWORD dwDeviceID = 0;
    LONG ret;
    LINEINITIALIZEEXPARAMS LineInitializeExParams;
    LINEEXTENSIONID ExtensionID;
    LPLINEDEVCAPS DevCaps = NULL;

    strcpy(szFriendlyAppName, "TAPI Beeper Program");
    memset((void *)&LineInitializeExParams, 0,
        sizeof(LINEINITIALIZEEXPARAMS));
    LineInitializeExParams.dwTotalSize =
        sizeof(LINEINITIALIZEEXPARAMS);
    LineInitializeExParams.dwOptions =
        LINEINITIALIZEEXOPTION_USEEVENT;

    printf("TAPI Beeper Program\n");

    ret = lineInitializeEx(&hLineApp, NULL, NULL, szFriendlyAppName,
        &dwNumDevs, &dwAPIVersion, &LineInitializeExParams);
    ReportTAPIError(ret, "lineInitializeEx");
    if (ret == 0)
```

*(continued)*

**Listing 7-2** *continued*

```
    {
        // It worked!
        printf(
            "\nMAPI reports \nNumber of Devices: %d\nVersion %08x",
            dwNumDevs, dwAPIVersion);
        // Loop through available devices till we find a good one.
        for (dwDeviceID = 0; dwDeviceID < dwNumDevs; dwDeviceID++)
        {
            ret = lineNegotiateAPIVersion(
                hLineApp,
                dwDeviceID,
                0x00020000,
                0x00020001,
                &dwAPIVersion,
                &ExtensionID);
            if (ret == 0)
            {
                ret = lineOpen(hLineApp, dwDeviceID, &hLine,
                    dwAPIVersion, 0, dwCallbackInstance,
                    LINECALLPRIVILEGE_NONE, 0, 0);
                ReportTAPIError(ret, "lineOpen");
                if (ret == 0)
                {
                    break;
                }
            }
        }
        ReportTAPIError(ret, "lineNegotiateAPIVersion");
        if (ret == 0)
        {

            HCALL hCall;
            char szLineName[255];

            DevCaps = (LPLINEDEVCAPS)new char[1024];
            DevCaps->dwTotalSize = 1024;
            ret = lineGetDevCaps(hLineApp, dwDeviceID,
                dwAPIVersion, 0, DevCaps);
            ReportTAPIError(ret, "lineGetDevCaps");
            if (ret >= 0 && DevCaps->dwLineNameSize > 0)
            {
                if (DevCaps->dwLineNameSize > (254))
                {
                    strncpy (szLineName,
```

```
                (LPSTR) DevCaps +
                DevCaps->dwLineNameOffset, 254);
            szLineName[254] = '\0';
        }
        else
        {
            lstrcpy(szLineName,
                (LPSTR) DevCaps +
                DevCaps->dwLineNameOffset);
        }
        printf("\nDevice name %s ", szLineName);
    }
    delete (char *)DevCaps;

    // Set what TAPI calls the address, which is
    //  really just a phone number.
    sprintf(szAddress, "%s,,,%s#", beeperNumber, beepTo);
    ret = lineMakeCall(hLine, &hCall, szAddress, 0, 0);
    if (ret > 0)
    {
        printf("\nlineMakeCall returned %d", ret);
    }
    ReportTAPIError(ret, "lineMakeCall");

    while ((dwStatus = WaitForSingleObject(
        LineInitializeExParams.Handles.hEvent, 20000)) ==
        WAIT_OBJECT_0)
    {
        LINEMESSAGE lm;
        // TAPI's returning some information.
        if ((ret = lineGetMessage(hLineApp, &lm, 0)) != 0)
        {
            ReportTAPIError(ret, "lineGetMessage");
            return (ret);
        }
        switch (lm.dwMessageID)
        {
        case LINE_REPLY:
            if ((long)lm.dwParam2 < 0)
            {
                printf(
                    "\nError occured...Request ID %d",
                    lm.dwParam1);
            }
            break;
```

*(continued)*

**Listing 7-2** *continued*

```
                case LINE_CALLSTATE:
                    if (LINECALLSTATE_DIALTONE&lm.dwParam1)
                    {
                        printf("\nDialtone detected");
                    }
                    if (LINECALLSTATE_DIALING&lm.dwParam1)
                    {
                        printf("\nDialing");
                    }

                    if (LINECALLSTATE_RINGBACK&lm.dwParam1)
                    {
                        printf("\nRinging...");
                    }

                    if (LINECALLSTATE_BUSY&lm.dwParam1)
                    {
                        printf("\nBusy...");
                    }

                    if (LINECALLSTATE_PROCEEDING&lm.dwParam1)
                    {
                        printf("\nProceeding...");
                    }

                    if (LINECALLSTATE_CONNECTED&lm.dwParam1)
                    {
                        printf("\nConnected...");
                    }

                    if (LINECALLSTATE_DISCONNECTED&lm.dwParam1)
                    {
                        printf("\nDisconnected...");
                        lineClose(hLine);
                    }

                    if (LINECALLSTATE_IDLE&lm.dwParam1)
                    {
                        printf("\nIdle...");
                        lineClose(hLine);
                    }
                } // ...switch (lm.dwMessageID)
            } // ...while ((dwStatus = WaitForSingleObject(
        } // ...if (ret == 0)
    }
```

```
    lineShutdown(hLineApp);
    return 0;
}

void ReportTAPIError(LONG ret, char *op)
{
    switch (ret)
    {
    case LINEERR_INVALAPPNAME:
        printf("\nop=%s Ret=LINEERR_INVALAPPNAME", op);
        break;
    case LINEERR_OPERATIONFAILED:
        printf("\nop=%s Ret=LINEERR_OPERATIONFAILED", op);
        break;
    case LINEERR_INIFILECORRUPT:
        printf("\nop=%s Ret=LINEERR_INIFILECORRUPT", op);
        break;
    case LINEERR_INVALPOINTER:
        printf("\nop=%s Ret=LINEERR_INVALPOINTER", op);
        break;
    case LINEERR_REINIT:
        printf("\nop=%s Ret=LINEERR_REINIT", op);
        break;
    case LINEERR_NOMEM:
        printf("\nop=%s Ret=LINEERR_NOMEM", op);
        break;
    case LINEERR_INVALPARAM:
        printf("\nop=%s Ret=LINEERR_INVALPARAM", op);
        break;
    case LINEERR_BADDEVICEID:
        printf("\nop=%s Ret=LINEERR_BADDEVICEID", op);
        break;
    case LINEERR_NODRIVER:
        printf("\nop=%s Ret=LINEERR_NODRIVER", op);
        break;
    case LINEERR_INCOMPATIBLEAPIVERSION:
        printf("\nop=%s Ret=LINEERR_INCOMPATIBLEAPIVERSION", op);
        break;
    case LINEERR_INVALAPPHANDLE:
        printf("\nop=%s Ret=LINEERR_INVALAPPHANDLE", op);
        break;
    case LINEERR_RESOURCEUNAVAIL:
        printf("\nop=%s Ret=LINEERR_RESOURCEUNAVAIL", op);
        break;
```

*(continued)*

**Listing 7-2** *continued*

```
    case LINEERR_UNINITIALIZED:
        printf("\nop=%s Ret=LINEERR_UNINITIALIZED", op);
        break;
    case LINEERR_OPERATIONUNAVAIL:
        printf("\nop=%s Ret=LINEERR_OPERATIONUNAVAIL", op);
        break;
    case LINEERR_NODEVICE:
        printf("\nop=%s Ret=LINEERR_NODEVICE", op);
        break;
    case LINEERR_ALLOCATED:
        printf("\nop=%s Ret=LINEERR_ALLOCATED", op);
        break;
    case LINEERR_LINEMAPPERFAILED:
        printf("\nop=%s Ret=LINEERR_LINEMAPPERFAILED", op);
        break;
    case LINEERR_INCOMPATIBLEEXTVERSION:
        printf("\nop=%s Ret=LINEERR_INCOMPATIBLEEXTVERSION", op);
        break;
    case LINEERR_INVALMEDIAMODE:
        printf("\nop=%s Ret=LINEERR_INVALMEDIAMODE", op);
        break;
    case LINEERR_STRUCTURETOOSMALL:
        printf("\nop=%s Ret=LINEERR_STRUCTURETOOSMALL", op);
        break;
    case LINEERR_INVALPRIVSELECT:
        printf("\nop=%s Ret=LINEERR_INVALPRIVSELECT", op);
        break;
    case LINEERR_ADDRESSBLOCKED:
        printf("\nop=%s Ret=LINEERR_ADDRESSBLOCKED", op);
        break;
    case LINEERR_DIALBILLING:
        printf("\nop=%s Ret=LINEERR_DIALBILLING", op);
        break;
    case LINEERR_DIALDIALTONE:
        printf("\nop=%s Ret=LINEERR_DIALDIALTONE", op);
        break;
    case LINEERR_NOTOWNER:
        printf("\nop=%s Ret=LINEERR_NOTOWNER", op);
        break;
    case LINEERR_DIALPROMPT:
        printf("\nop=%s Ret=LINEERR_DIALPROMPT", op);
        break;
    case LINEERR_DIALQUIET:
        printf("\nop=%s Ret=LINEERR_DIALQUIET", op);
        break;
```

```
        case LINEERR_INVALCALLHANDLE:
            printf("\nop=%s Ret=LINEERR_INVALCALLHANDLE", op);
            break;
        case LINEERR_INVALCALLSTATE:
            printf("\nop=%s Ret=LINEERR_INVALCALLSTATE", op);
            break;
        case LINEERR_INVALCOUNTRYCODE:
            printf("\nop=%s Ret=LINEERR_INVALCOUNTRYCODE", op);
            break;
        }
}
```

**NOTE** This application could be made much more elaborate with an alphanumeric pager using the TAP protocol, but numeric pagers are simpler and more numerous than the alphanumeric kind. Information on the TAP protocol can be found at *http://www.pcia.com/.*

The *main* function in Listing 7-2 does nothing more than call the *CallBeeper* function. *CallBeeper* accepts two strings as parameters. The first, *beeperNumber*, is the beeper access number to dial to get to the beeper, and the second, *beepTo*, is the number that is sent to the beeper. *CallBeeper* places a delay between the two numbers so that the *beepTo* string is sent when the service expects it.

### Using *lineInitializeEx*

The first step in any TAPI application is a call to *lineInitializeEx*:

```
LONG WINAPI lineInitializeEx(
    LPHLINEAPP lphLineApp,
    HINSTANCE hInstance,
    LINECALLBACK lpfnCallback,
    LPCSTR lpszFriendlyAppName,
    LPDWORD lpdwNumDevs,
    LPDWORD lpdwAPIVersion,
    LPLINEINITIALIZEEXPARAMS lpLineInitializeExParams
);
```

The first parameter is the address of a handle to be filled in by *lineInitializeEx* upon a successful call. This handle is used for many of the other TAPI calls required. The second parameter is *hInstance*. In most cases, this can be set to NULL to allow TAPI to use the module handle of the root executable of the process making the call. Next is *lpfnCallback*, a callback function used when neither the event handle nor the completion port method of asynchronous notifications is selected. A pointer to the "friendly" name of the application—used by the user interface to display a user-friendly application name—is passed as the *lpszFriendlyAppName* parameter. The number of devices is placed by TAPI in the DWORD pointed to by *lpdwNumDevs*, and the API version is placed by TAPI into the DWORD pointed to by *lpdwAPIVersion*.

The final parameter, *lpLineInitializeExParams*, points to a structure of type LINEINITIALIZEEXPARAMS:

```
typedef struct lineinitializeexparams_tag {
    DWORD  dwTotalSize;
    DWORD  dwNeededSize;
    DWORD  dwUsedSize;
    DWORD  dwOptions;

    union
    {
        HANDLE  hEvent;
        HANDLE  hCompletionPort;
    } Handles;

    DWORD  dwCompletionKey;

} LINEINITIALIZEEXPARAMS;
```

Upon entry to *lineInitializeEx*, the *dwTotalSize* must be initialized to the size of the buffer allocated to this structure. The asynchronous notification type is specified in *dwOptions* and is one of the following values: LINEINITIALIZEEXOPTION_USECOMPLETIONPORT, LINEINITIALIZEEXOPTION_USEEVENT, or LINEINITIALIZEEXOPTION_USEHIDDENWINDOW. Applications using TAPI 3 and later might also use LINEINITIALIZEEXOPTION_CALLHUBTRACKING to enable call hub tracking notifications. The TAPI21Sample example in Listing 7-2 uses LINEINITIALIZEEXOPTION_USEEVENT to specify that the *hEvent* member of the *Handles* union of the structure should contain an event handle upon a successful call to *lineInitializeEx*. Note that an older initialization function, *lineInitialize*, is not supported in TAPI 2 or later.

After the call to *lineInitializeEx* is completed, TAPI21Sample calls the local *ReportTAPIError* function. Since no convenient function is provided to convert a numeric return value to a string, *ReportTAPIError* provides this functionality, in this case printing the result to the screen. *ReportTAPIError* prints the error condition and its associated constant because the error conditions returned by TAPI are large negative numbers. (While you might remember that the standard Win32 API error 2 means the file cannot be found and 5 means access is denied, it is unlikely you will remember that –2147483646 means LINEERR_BADDEVICEID.)

### Finding a TAPI device and negotiating versions

If the return value from *lineInitializeEx* is 0, we have the number of TAPI devices that the system supports as well as the TAPI version. In TAPI21Sample these devices are just displayed, but the version number in particular might be used to make decisions about what level of functionality can be supported. Simply knowing the version of TAPI returned by *lineInitializeEx* is not sufficient. When you want to use a specific device, the version of the interface must be negotiated between the application and TAPI for that device. This negotiation is performed using *lineNegotiateAPIVersion*:

```
LONG WINAPI lineNegotiateAPIVersion(
    HLINEAPP hLineApp,
    DWORD dwDeviceID,
    DWORD dwAPILowVersion,
    DWORD dwAPIHighVersion,
    LPDWORD lpdwAPIVersion,
    LPLINEEXTENSIONID lpExtensionID
);
```

The handle returned from the call to *lineInitializeEx* is passed as the first parameter to *lineNegotiateAPIVersion*. The device ID is passed as the second parameter. This is a number that must be between 0 and the number of devices minus one. The next two parameters, *dwAPILowVersion* and *dwAPIHighVersion*, are used to let the application let TAPI know what versions it is willing to support. Before TAPI 3.0, programmers commonly specified a reasonable number for *dwAPILowVersion* and a very high number for *dwAPIHighVersion*, expecting that all future TAPI versions would support essentially the same framework. This tactic is not recommended, and current applications that use this tactic can expect to break when run on a machine that tries to use TAPI 3.

The next parameter is a pointer to a DWORD that TAPI fills with the version to be used, if the call succeeds. The final parameter is *lpExtensionID*, a pointer to a LINEEXTENSIONID structure. This parameter is used to identify service provider–specific extensions. TAPI21Sample uses no service provider–specific extensions.

TAPI21Sample uses the following code segment to determine the device ID to be used. (This information is required because it is possible that multiple devices will be available, and they might not all support the service or the version you request.)

```
// Loop through available devices till we find a good one.
for (dwDeviceID = 0; dwDeviceID < dwNumDevs; dwDeviceID++)
{
    ret = lineNegotiateAPIVersion(
        hLineApp,
        dwDeviceID,
```

*(continued)*

```
            0x00020000,
            0x00020001,
            &dwAPIVersion,
            &ExtensionID);
        if (ret == 0)
        {
            ret = lineOpen(hLineApp, dwDeviceID, &hLine,
                dwAPIVersion, 0, dwCallbackInstance,
                LINECALLPRIVILEGE_NONE, 0, 0);
            ReportTAPIError(ret, "lineOpen");
            if (ret == 0)
            {
                break;
            }
        }
    }
```

This code fragment loops through the available devices and tries to negotiate a compatible version. Upon success, *lineOpen* is called. If this call succeeds, the loop is exited and the device ID in *dwDeviceID* is used for the rest of the processing. The prototype for *lineOpen* is as follows:

```
LONG WINAPI lineOpen(
    HLINEAPP hLineApp,
    DWORD dwDeviceID,
    LPHLINE lphLine,
    DWORD dwAPIVersion,
    DWORD dwExtVersion,
    DWORD dwCallbackInstance,
    DWORD dwPrivileges,
    DWORD dwMediaModes,
    LPLINECALLPARAMS const lpCallParams
);
```

The first parameter is the handle obtained from the call to *lineInitializeEx*. The device ID to open is passed as *dwDeviceID*, and *lphLine* points to the buffer where *lineOpen* will place a line handle upon success. Version information is contained in the next two parameters. The API version returned by the previous call to *lineNegotiateAPIVersion* is passed as *dwAPIVersion*, and *dwExtVersion* contains the extension version previously negotiated. In TAPI21Sample, no extensions are used so *dwExtVersion* is 0.

The sixth parameter, *dwCallbackInstance*, is a context identifier that is passed back to the application by TAPI with messages associated with this line. This number is not interpreted by TAPI, but simply passed back to the application. The privileges the application requests on the line are passed in the *dwPrivileges* parameter. Table 7-1 outlines the constants and combinations allowed for this parameter.

**NOTE** TAPI structures have some unusual properties. For instance, LINE-CALLPARAMS contains a member named *dwOrigAddressOffset*. This variable holds the offset from the beginning of the structure to the variable length value of the originating address. This differs from many other Win32 structures that contain true embedded pointers or embedded character arrays to contain strings. Another example of a structure that uses this type of variable is the LINEDEV-CAPS structure, described in the next section. You cannot simply allocate a buffer the size of the declared structure, since this will not allow the fields that are placed after the declared structure to be sent.

**TABLE 7-1**
**POSSIBLE VALUES FOR THE *DWPRIVILEGES* PARAMETER TO *LINEOPEN***

| *Privilege* | *Meaning* |
|---|---|
| LINECALLPRIVILEGE_NONE | The application can make only outgoing calls. |
| LINECALLPRIVILEGE_MONITOR | The application can monitor only incoming and outgoing calls. |
| LINECALLPRIVILEGE_OWNER | The application can own only incoming calls of the types specified by *dwMediaMode*. |
| LINECALLPRIVILEGE_MONITOR + LINECALLPRIVILEGE_OWNER | The application can be the owner of calls of the types specified by *dwMediaMode*, but it is a monitor for calls it does not own. |
| LINECALLPRIVILEGE_ SINGLEADDRESS | The application is interested only in new calls that appear on the address specified by the *dwAddressID* member of the *lpCallParams*, which must be specified. (More details are available in the TAPI documentation.) |
| LINECALLPRIVILEGE_PROXY | The application is willing to handle certain types of requests from other applications that have the line open. Requests are delivered to the application using LINE_PROXYREQUEST messages. (More details are available in the TAPI documentation.) |

Interestingly, the privilege required for the task performed by TAPI21Sample is the somewhat misnamed LINECALLPRIVILEGE_NONE because this program is only interested in making outgoing calls. Any combination not listed in Table 7-1 is not allowed and will result in an error.

TAPI can interact with many different types of calls, including but not limited to interactive voice, automated voice, data modem, G3 fax, and Telephony Devices for the Deaf. The types of calls the application is interested in are specified in the *dwMediaModes* parameter. This parameter is meaningful only if the *dwPrivileges* parameter includes LINECALLPRIVILEGE_OWNER. The final parameter is *lpCallParams*, a pointer to a buffer containing a LINECALLPARAMS structure. This structure is only used if a special value for *dwDeviceID* is used—LINEMAPPER. This special constant tells *lineOpen* to search for a matching device based upon the values in the LINECALLPARAMS structure.

### Getting the capabilities of a TAPI line

Once *lineOpen* succeeds, we try to get information about the device ID selected. This requires calling *lineGetDevCaps*:

```
LONG WINAPI lineGetDevCaps(
    HLINEAPP hLineApp,
    DWORD dwDeviceID,
    DWORD dwAPIVersion,
    DWORD dwExtVersion,
    LPLINEDEVCAPS lpLineDevCaps
);
```

The first argument is the handle returned by *lineInitializeEx*. The device ID, API version, and extension version are passed in *dwDeviceID, dwAPIVersion,* and *dwExtVersion*, respectively. These values are the ones previously determined via calls to *lineNegotiateAPIVersion*.

The final argument, *lpLineDevCaps*, is a structure that contains within it offsets that point to variable-length buffers just beyond the declared area of the buffer. To support this behavior, the first three elements of this structure are *dwTotalSize*, *dwNeededSize*, and *dwUsedSize*. The total size should be set before the call to *lineGetDevCaps*, the needed size is the size that must be allocated in order to hold all the information that could be returned, and the used size is the size of the buffer that contains useful information.

The following fragment from TAPI21Sample illustrates the method to get device capabilities from TAPI.

```
DevCaps = (LPLINEDEVCAPS)new char[1024];
DevCaps->dwTotalSize = 1024;
ret = lineGetDevCaps(hLineApp, dwDeviceID,
    dwAPIVersion, 0, DevCaps);
ReportTAPIError(ret, "lineGetDevCaps");
if (ret >= 0 && DevCaps->dwLineNameSize > 0)
{
    if (DevCaps->dwLineNameSize > (254))
    {
        strncpy (szLineName,
            (LPSTR) DevCaps +
             DevCaps->dwLineNameOffset, 254);
```

```
        szLineName[254] = '\0';
    }
    else
    {
        lstrcpy(szLineName, (LPSTR) DevCaps +
            DevCaps->dwLineNameOffset);
    }
    printf("\nDevice name %s ", szLineName);
}
delete (char *)DevCaps;
```

This code allocates a buffer and sets *dwTotalSize* to the size of the buffer before calling *lineGetDevCaps*. After the successful call to *lineGetDevCaps*, it checks *dwLineNameSize* to see whether the name of the line is present. This name is commonly the name of the modem, for instance "Sportster 28800-33600 External." The name, if present, is located *dwLineNameOffset* bytes from the beginning of the structure. TAPI21Sample prints the name, but the name might be used for logging purposes in a server-based application. In addition to the name of the device, a great deal of other information is present in *lineDevCaps*, including the types of calls the line is capable of handling.

### TAPI addresses

As is the case in many areas of Win32 programming, unfortunate TAPI naming choices have created no end of grief for developers over the years. What is an address from the TAPI perspective? It is a phone number to you and me. Of course, there is more to the story.

For instance, suppose "+1 (732) 555-2683" is the phone number given as the address to a TAPI function. What would happen if this address were dialed from my home phone, also in the 732 area code? The call would not go through because calls within an area must not include the area code in the number you dial. The solution is to translate the address using the information about the current area and country code so that the number to be dialed is correct, relative to that current area and country code. This translation from the canonical address results in a phone number that can be dialed correctly from the current location. In addition to correcting the phone number to a proper relative phone number, calling cards can be specified and call waiting can be disabled, if there is a cancel call waiting string defined for the current location. This flexibility is much more useful for mobile users. These users might dial from many different locations, and so entering canonical addresses for all contacts is worthwhile. However, even for stationary users, such as server-based applications, entering canonical addresses and doing translation in the applications can be useful in case the area code where the server is located splits, requiring calls that previously dialed using 7 digits to dial 11 digits—1 plus the area code plus the 7 digits of the phone number.

### Making the call with TAPI

The address, or phone number, in Listing 7-2 is built up using the beeper access number and the number to send to the beeper service. Commas are inserted between the numbers to allow dialing to pause between the two numbers and thus allow the beeper service to answer the call. The call is initiated through a call to *lineMakeCall*:

```
LONG WINAPI lineMakeCall(
    HLINE hLine,
    LPHCALL lphCall,
    LPCSTR lpszDestAddress,
    DWORD dwCountryCode,
    LPLINECALLPARAMS const lpCallParams
);
```

The first parameter is *hLine*, the handle to the line obtained through a call to *lineOpen*. The call is tracked after initiated using a call handle, which is returned in the buffer pointed to by the second parameter, *lphCall*. The address (phone number to you and me) is sent in the *lpszDestAddress* parameter with *dwCountryCode* set to the country code, or 0 to use the default for this dialing location.

The final parameter is *lpCallParams*. This parameter is a pointer to a structure that can be used to specify particulars such as the types of call to support, blocking of caller ID, and the originating address. This parameter can be NULL if no special treatment is required. Additional digits or all dialing for the call can be done using *lineDial*. If any address is specified in the call to *lineMakeCall*, the address should be terminated with a semicolon. The parameters are a subset of the parameters passed to *lineMakeCall*, with the exception of the *hCall*, which is not a pointer but must be the handle passed back from *lineMakeCall*.

```
LONG WINAPI lineDial(
    HCALL hCall,
    LPCSTR lpszDestAddress,
    DWORD dwCountryCode
);
```

Listing 7-2 does not use *lineDial*, but it could if we wanted to split the dialing. The call handle is not valid until a LINE_REPLY message is received from TAPI. TAPI messages are described in the next section.

### Waiting for TAPI messages

As I mentioned previously, TAPI21Sample uses an event object to receive asynchronous notifications from TAPI. One important distinction with using an event object supplied by TAPI is that the only operation that can safely be done with the object is waiting for the object, using one of the *WaitForSingleObject, WaitForMultipleObjects*, or another one of the Win32 waiting functions. *SetEvent*, *ClearEvent*, or *CloseHandle* should not be called using the returned event handle. When the event is signaled,

TAPI has a notification waiting, and a call to *lineGetMessage* gives us the actual notification.

```
LONG WINAPI lineGetMessage(
    HLINEAPP hLineApp,
    LPLINEMESSAGE lpMessage,
    DWORD dwTimeout
);
```

The first parameter is the handle returned by *lineInitializeEx*. The second parameter is a pointer to a TAPI LINEMESSAGE structure, *lpMessage*. The final parameter is *dwTimeout*, the amount of time to wait for the message. In Listing 7-2 we set this to 0 to allow the function to return immediately if a message is not waiting since we only call this function when the event handle returned by TAPI is signaled. If no message is waiting, a serious error has occurred because TAPI has just told us that a message was waiting. The LINEMESSAGE structure has the following members:

```
typedef struct linemessage_tag {
    DWORD  hDevice;
    DWORD  dwMessageID;
    DWORD  dwCallbackInstance;
    DWORD  dwParam1;
    DWORD  dwParam2;
    DWORD  dwParam3;
} LINEMESSAGE;
```

The *hDevice* member is either a handle to the line or the call, depending upon the context, as decided by *dwMessageID*. For instance, one of the messages that can be received is LINE_CALLSTATE. If *dwMessageID* is LINE_CALLSTATE, *hDevice* is a handle to the call. On the other hand, if *dwMessageID* is LINE_REPLY, *hDevice* has no meaning and should be ignored. The various message types are described in the TAPI documentation.

Listing 7-2 contains a switch statement controlled by the value of *dwMessageID*:

```
switch (lm.dwMessageID)
{
case LINE_REPLY:
    if ((long)lm.dwParam2 < 0)
    {
        printf("\nError occured...Request ID %d", lm.dwParam1);
    }
    break;
case LINE_CALLSTATE:
    if (LINECALLSTATE_DIALTONE&lm.dwParam1)
    {
        printf("\nDialtone detected");
    }
```

*(continued)*

```
        if (LINECALLSTATE_DIALING&lm.dwParam1)
        {
            printf("\nDialing");
        }
        if (LINECALLSTATE_RINGBACK&lm.dwParam1)
        {
            printf("\nRinging...");
        }
        if (LINECALLSTATE_BUSY&lm.dwParam1)
        {
            printf("\nBusy...");
        }
        if (LINECALLSTATE_PROCEEDING&lm.dwParam1)
        {
            printf("\nProceeding...");
        }
        if (LINECALLSTATE_CONNECTED&lm.dwParam1)
        {
            printf("\nConnected...");
        }
        if (LINECALLSTATE_DISCONNECTED&lm.dwParam1)
        {
            printf("\nDisconnected...");
            lineClose(hLine);
        }
        if (LINECALLSTATE_IDLE&lm.dwParam1)
        {
            printf("\nIdle...");
            lineClose(hLine);
        }
    } // ...switch (lm.dwMessageID)
```

The order or even the presence of any of these specific notifications depends upon the TAPI service provider. In Listing 7-2 the duration of the call should be brief in any event, so setting a timeout of 20 seconds allows the call to proceed, and after 20 seconds with no further TAPI notification, the call and the session are terminated using *lineShutdown*.

## What Else Can TAPI Do?

TAPI can do much more than signal a beeper. TAPI can be set to monitor the line for specific tones using *lineMonitorTones*, as well as monitor the type of call using *lineMonitorMedia*. TAPI can be used to create a full service call center, allowing parking and pickup of calls, conferencing, and many other features considered essential for an up-to-date phone system. Using the *phone* set of functions (not discussed in this book), individual phones can be controlled, allowing lights to blink as needed on the actual phone deskset.

Later in this chapter, we'll see how the ability to beep a network administrator and the ability to send e-mail will work together to create a service application that notifies responsible parties when it encounters a problem.

# MAPI

The Messaging API (MAPI) is at the heart of many of today's Internet-enabled applications. Using MAPI, both the client and the server in a client/server system can make people or even other systems aware of information needed to get the job done. Of course our emphasis will be on server-based applications using MAPI, but normally the operation of MAPI is the same for both clients and servers.

One significant difference between clients and servers is that servers need to have UI-free interactions with MAPI. Fortunately, allowances are made for interacting with MAPI without the UI, and some of the techniques can even be used for client applications that need to send a message without user intervention.

## Flavors of MAPI

MAPI comes in several flavors, which adds to the confusion, of course. What exactly do I mean when I say MAPI? When we discuss MAPI, we are talking about the following four families of client interfaces:

- **Common Messaging Calls (CMC)** A cross-platform client interface for C/C++ programs, supported in Windows and some UNIX implementations
- **Simple MAPI** A Windows-only client interface with a function-call API suitable for both C/C++ and Microsoft Visual Basic
- **MAPI** A COM Windows-only client interface for use by C/C++ programs
- **Collaboration Data Objects (CDO)** An automation client interface supporting only Windows clients

Some additional distinctions exist between the client interfaces, but they are not important for server-based applications. For instance, MAPI and CDO both support forms processing, something a server-based application does not need. We will focus on Simple MAPI and MAPI, with a special emphasis on the steps required to allow MAPI to work in a Windows 2000 server-based application. For a Windows 2000 server-based application, the multiplatform advantage offered by CMC is hardly worth using this lesser-known interface. CDO is overkill for what most server-based applications need to do. So, the choice narrows down to Simple MAPI or MAPI.

## Selecting the Correct Client Interface

Given the above descriptions, which interface is best? That requires knowing exactly what the application must do. Do you want your server-based application to send and receive e-mail? Both Simple MAPI and MAPI do that. Do you need to interact with the address book on the server? Here things become a bit more difficult. While Simple MAPI does provide some ability to interact with address book entries, doing so using MAPI might be better.

Of course, MAPI takes its own toll. As with TAPI 3, special care must be taken when using COM functions that create hidden windows that require message pumps, and special care must be taken to allow MAPI to work in a server-based application. On the other hand, some of the concern with using MAPI is reduced by explicit support in the API for use within a Windows 2000 server-based application.

> **NOTE** Of course, if your service application will be integrated with Microsoft SQL Server, you have an alternative to doing your own MAPI application. SQL Server contains extended stored procedures that allow e-mail to be sent from Transact-SQL. Chapter 13 contains an example that uses extended stored procedures to send e-mail. Of course this solution results in *really* simple MAPI.

## Simple MAPI?

The name Simple MAPI is somewhat misleading. While it certainly is the simplest of the messaging APIs, it is by no means simple. For instance, rather than calling the functions via an import library, the library is called after an explicit call to *LoadLibrary* and *GetProcAddress*. While this is not terribly difficult, it does not always seem simple.

What can Simple MAPI do? A list of the supported functions is fairly short, but does include the bulk of what many server-based applications will need. The Simple MAPI functions are

- *MAPILogon*
- *MAPILogoff*
- *MAPISendMail*
- *MAPISendDocuments*
- *MAPIFindNext*
- *MAPIReadMail*
- *MAPISaveMail*
- *MAPIDeleteMail*
- *MAPIFreeBuffer*
- *MAPIAddress*
- *MAPIDetails*
- *MAPIResolveName*

Given these 12 functions, you can send e-mail with and without file attachments, read e-mail with and without file attachments, peek at e-mail, get information on addresses, and look through a filtered list of messages. The bad news for server-based applications is that some of this functionality is clearly aimed at client applications. For instance, *MAPIAddress* and *MAPIDetails* both create dialogs suitable for a user sitting at the machine but don't expose a suitable interface for a server. A common requirement for e-mail applications is the ability to take incoming e-mail and place it in certain folders, depending upon the content of the message, rather than placing it all in the Inbox. This is not possible with Simple MAPI.

If you have bare-bones requirements, do consider Simple MAPI. While 12 Simple MAPI functions are supported, we'll use only 5 of them in the Send Mail example in the following section. For limited applications in which we know the addressees and can limit our requirements to sending and receiving e-mail, Simple MAPI can do the trick.

### Simple MAPI send/read mail example

Listings 7-3 and 7-4 contain the header file and the source, respectively, for a Simple MAPI program to send and read e-mail. It is, of course, simple.

**MAPIInit.h**

```
#define SZ_MAPILOGON "MAPILogon"
#define SZ_MAPILOGOFF "MAPILogoff"
#define SZ_MAPISENDMAIL "MAPISendMail"
#define SZ_MAPISENDDOC "MAPISendDocuments"
#define SZ_MAPIFINDNEXT "MAPIFindNext"
#define SZ_MAPIREADMAIL "MAPIReadMail"
#define SZ_MAPISAVEMAIL "MAPISaveMail"
#define SZ_MAPIDELMAIL "MAPIDeleteMail"
#define SZ_MAPIFREEBUFFER "MAPIFreeBuffer"
#define SZ_MAPIADDRESS "MAPIAddress"
#define SZ_MAPIDETAILS "MAPIDetails"
#define SZ_MAPIRESOLVENAME "MAPIResolveName"
#define MAPIDLL "MAPI32.DLL"

#define ERR_LOAD_LIB  0x02
#define ERR_LOAD_FUNC 0x04

typedef ULONG (FAR PASCAL *PFNMAPILOGON)(HWND, LPSTR, LPSTR,
    FLAGS, ULONG, LPLHANDLE);
typedef ULONG (FAR PASCAL *PFNMAPILOGOFF)(LHANDLE, HWND,
    FLAGS,ULONG);
```

**Listing 7-3** *(continued)*

**Listing 7-3** *continued*

```
typedef ULONG (FAR PASCAL *PFNMAPISENDMAIL)(LHANDLE, HWND,
    lpMapiMessage, FLAGS, ULONG);

typedef ULONG (FAR PASCAL *PFNMAPISENDDOCUMENTS)(HWND, LPSTR,
    LPSTR, LPSTR, ULONG);

typedef ULONG (FAR PASCAL *PFNMAPIFINDNEXT)(LHANDLE, HWND,
    LPSTR, LPSTR, FLAGS, ULONG, LPSTR);

typedef ULONG (FAR PASCAL *PFNMAPIREADMAIL)(LHANDLE, HWND,
    LPSTR, FLAGS, ULONG, lpMapiMessage FAR *);

typedef ULONG (FAR PASCAL *PFNMAPISAVEMAIL)(LHANDLE, HWND,
    lpMapiMessage, FLAGS, ULONG, LPSTR);

typedef ULONG (FAR PASCAL *PFNMAPIDELETEMAIL)(LHANDLE, HWND, LPSTR,
    FLAGS, ULONG);

typedef ULONG (FAR PASCAL *PFNMAPIFREEBUFFER)(LPVOID);

typedef ULONG (FAR PASCAL *PFNMAPIADDRESS)(LHANDLE, HWND, LPSTR,
    ULONG, LPSTR, ULONG, lpMapiRecipDesc, FLAGS, ULONG,
    LPULONG, lpMapiRecipDesc FAR *);

typedef ULONG (FAR PASCAL *PFNMAPIDETAILS)(LHANDLE, HWND,
    lpMapiRecipDesc, FLAGS, ULONG);

typedef ULONG (FAR PASCAL *PFNMAPIRESOLVENAME)(LHANDLE, HWND,
    LPSTR, FLAGS, ULONG, lpMapiRecipDesc FAR *);

#ifdef THE_MAIN

PFNMAPILOGON lpfnMAPILogon;
PFNMAPILOGOFF lpfnMAPILogoff;
PFNMAPISENDMAIL lpfnMAPISendMail;
PFNMAPISENDDOCUMENTS lpfnMAPISendDocuments;
PFNMAPIFINDNEXT lpfnMAPIFindNext;
PFNMAPIREADMAIL lpfnMAPIReadMail;
PFNMAPISAVEMAIL lpfnMAPISaveMail;
PFNMAPIDELETEMAIL lpfnMAPIDeleteMail;
PFNMAPIFREEBUFFER lpfnMAPIFreeBuffer;
PFNMAPIADDRESS lpfnMAPIAddress;
PFNMAPIDETAILS lpfnMAPIDetails;
PFNMAPIRESOLVENAME lpfnMAPIResolveName;
```

```
#else

extern PFNMAPILOGON lpfnMAPILogon;
extern PFNMAPILOGOFF lpfnMAPILogoff;
extern PFNMAPISENDMAIL lpfnMAPISendMail;
extern PFNMAPISENDDOCUMENTS lpfnMAPISendDocuments;
extern PFNMAPIFINDNEXT lpfnMAPIFindNext;
extern PFNMAPIREADMAIL lpfnMAPIReadMail;
extern PFNMAPISAVEMAIL lpfnMAPISaveMail;
extern PFNMAPIDELETEMAIL lpfnMAPIDeleteMail;
extern PFNMAPIFREEBUFFER lpfnMAPIFreeBuffer;
extern PFNMAPIADDRESS lpfnMAPIAddress;
extern PFNMAPIDETAILS lpfnMAPIDetails;
extern PFNMAPIRESOLVENAME lpfnMAPIResolveName;

#endif

int PASCAL InitMAPI(void);
int DeInitMAPI(void);
void FormatSimpleMAPIError(ULONG ret, char *str);
```

**SimpleMAPI.cpp**

```
// SimpleMAPI.cpp : Main routine of Simple MAPI send/read
//  mail example
//

#define THE_MAIN

#include "stdafx.h"

HMODULE hLibrary;

PFNMAPILOGON lpfnMAPILogon;
PFNMAPILOGOFF lpfnMAPILogoff;
PFNMAPISENDMAIL lpfnMAPISendMail;
PFNMAPISENDDOCUMENTS lpfnMAPISendDocuments;
PFNMAPIFINDNEXT lpfnMAPIFindNext;
PFNMAPIREADMAIL lpfnMAPIReadMail;
PFNMAPISAVEMAIL lpfnMAPISaveMail;
PFNMAPIDELETEMAIL lpfnMAPIDeleteMail;
PFNMAPIFREEBUFFER lpfnMAPIFreeBuffer;
```

**Listing 7-4** *(continued)*

**Listing 7-4** *continued*

```
PFNMAPIADDRESS lpfnMAPIAddress;
PFNMAPIDETAILS lpfnMAPIDetails;
PFNMAPIRESOLVENAME lpfnMAPIResolveName;

LHANDLE lHandle;


int main(int argc, char* argv[])
{
    MapiMessage Message;
    MapiMessage *pMessage;
    MapiRecipDesc To;
    MapiRecipDesc Originator;
    char szMessageID[512];
    ULONG ret;

    if (InitMAPI() != 0)
    {
        printf("\nCan't initialize Simple MAPI");
        return (1);
    }
    if (ret = lpfnMAPILogon(0, NULL, NULL, 0,
        0, &lHandle) != SUCCESS_SUCCESS)
    {
        char buffer[255];
        FormatSimpleMAPIError(ret, buffer);
        printf("\nMAPILogon: %s", buffer);
    }
    memset(&Message, '\0', sizeof(Message));
    memset(&To, '\0', sizeof(To));

    memset((void *)&Originator, '\0', sizeof(Originator));
    Originator.ulRecipClass = MAPI_ORIG;
    Originator.lpszName = "test";
    Originator.lpszAddress = "test";

    memset((void *)&To, '\0', sizeof(To));
    To.ulRecipClass = MAPI_TO;
    To.lpszName = "Doug Reilly";
    To.lpszAddress = "SMTP:74040.607@compuserve.com";

    memset((void *)&Message, '\0', sizeof(Message));
    Message.lpszSubject = "Test";
    Message.lpszNoteText = "This is a test";
```

```
Message.lpOriginator = &Originator;
Message.lpRecips = &To;
Message.nRecipCount = 1;
Message.nFileCount = 0;
Message.lpFiles = 0;

if (ret = lpfnMAPISendMail(lHandle, 0, &Message,
    0, 0) != SUCCESS_SUCCESS)
{
    char buffer[255];
    FormatSimpleMAPIError(ret, buffer);
    printf("\nMAPISendMail: %s", buffer);
}

// Now let's read the oldest message.
if (ret = lpfnMAPIFindNext(lHandle, 0, NULL, NULL,
    MAPI_GUARANTEE_FIFO | MAPI_LONG_MSGID, 0,
    szMessageID) != SUCCESS_SUCCESS)
{
    if (ret != MAPI_E_NO_MESSAGES)
    {
        char buffer[255];
        FormatSimpleMAPIError(ret, buffer);
        printf("\nMAPIFindNext: %s", buffer);
    }
}
else
{
    // Loop until we find an attachment.
    bool foundFile = false;
    do {
        if (ret = lpfnMAPIReadMail(lHandle, 0, szMessageID,
            0,0,&pMessage) != SUCCESS_SUCCESS)
        {
            char buffer[255];
            FormatSimpleMAPIError(ret, buffer);
            printf("\nMAPIFindNext: %s", buffer);
        }
        else
        {
            printf("\nOriginator: %s", pMessage->lpOriginator);
            printf("\nReceived: %s ",
                pMessage->lpszDateReceived);
```

*(continued)*

**Listing 7-4** *continued*

```
                printf("\nSubject: %s ", pMessage->lpszSubject);
                if (pMessage->nFileCount>0)
                {
                    printf("\nAttachment in %s",
                        pMessage->lpFiles->lpszPathName);
                    foundFile = true;
                }
                lpfnMAPIFreeBuffer(pMessage);
            }
        } while (!(foundFile) &&
            (ret = lpfnMAPIFindNext(lHandle, 0, NULL, szMessageID,
            MAPI_GUARANTEE_FIFO  |MAPI_LONG_MSGID, 0,
            szMessageID)) == SUCCESS_SUCCESS);
    }

    if (ret = lpfnMAPILogoff(lHandle, 0, 0, 0) != SUCCESS_SUCCESS)
    {
        char buffer[255];
        FormatSimpleMAPIError(ret, buffer);
        printf("\nMAPISendMail: %s", buffer);
    }
    DeInitMAPI();
    return 0;
}

void FormatSimpleMAPIError(ULONG ret,char *str)
{
        switch (ret)
        {
        case MAPI_USER_ABORT:
            sprintf(str, "MAPI_USER_ABORT");
            break;
        case MAPI_E_FAILURE:
            sprintf(str, "MAPI_E_FAILURE");
            break;
        case MAPI_E_LOGIN_FAILURE:
            sprintf(str, "MAPI_E_LOGIN_FAILURE");
            break;
        case MAPI_E_DISK_FULL:
            sprintf(str, "MAPI_E_DISK_FULL");
            break;
        case MAPI_E_INSUFFICIENT_MEMORY:
            sprintf(str, "MAPI_E_INSUFFICIENT_MEMORY");
            break;
```

```
    case MAPI_E_ACCESS_DENIED:
        sprintf(str, "MAPI_E_ACCESS_DENIED");
        break;
    case MAPI_E_TOO_MANY_SESSIONS:
        sprintf(str, "MAPI_E_TOO_MANY_SESSIONS");
        break;
    case MAPI_E_TOO_MANY_FILES:
        sprintf(str, "MAPI_E_TOO_MANY_FILES");
        break;
    case MAPI_E_TOO_MANY_RECIPIENTS:
        sprintf(str, "MAPI_E_TOO_MANY_RECIPIENTS");
        break;
    case MAPI_E_ATTACHMENT_NOT_FOUND:
        sprintf(str, "MAPI_E_ATTACHMENT_NOT_FOUND");
        break;
    case MAPI_E_ATTACHMENT_OPEN_FAILURE:
        sprintf(str, "MAPI_E_ATTACHMENT_OPEN_FAILURE");
        break;
    case MAPI_E_ATTACHMENT_WRITE_FAILURE:
        sprintf(str, "MAPI_E_ATTACHMENT_WRITE_FAILURE");
        break;
    case MAPI_E_UNKNOWN_RECIPIENT:
        sprintf(str, "MAPI_E_UNKNOWN_RECIPIENT");
        break;
    case MAPI_E_BAD_RECIPTYPE:
        sprintf(str, "MAPI_E_BAD_RECIPTYPE");
        break;
    case MAPI_E_NO_MESSAGES:
        sprintf(str, "MAPI_E_NO_MESSAGES");
        break;
    case MAPI_E_INVALID_MESSAGE:
        sprintf(str, "MAPI_E_INVALID_MESSAGE");
        break;
    case MAPI_E_TEXT_TOO_LARGE:
        sprintf(str, "MAPI_E_TEXT_TOO_LARGE");
        break;
    case MAPI_E_INVALID_SESSION:
        sprintf(str, "MAPI_E_INVALID_SESSION");
        break;
    case MAPI_E_TYPE_NOT_SUPPORTED:
        sprintf(str, "MAPI_E_TYPE_NOT_SUPPORTED");
        break;
    case MAPI_E_AMBIGUOUS_RECIPIENT:
        sprintf(str, "MAPI_E_AMBIGUOUS_RECIPIENT");
        break;
```

*(continued)*

**Listing 7-4** *continued*

```
        case MAPI_E_MESSAGE_IN_USE:
            sprintf(str, "MAPI_E_MESSAGE_IN_USE");
            break;
        case MAPI_E_NETWORK_FAILURE:
            sprintf(str, "MAPI_E_NETWORK_FAILURE");
            break;
        case MAPI_E_INVALID_EDITFIELDS:
            sprintf(str, "MAPI_E_INVALID_EDITFIELDS");
            break;
        case MAPI_E_INVALID_RECIPS:
            sprintf(str, "MAPI_E_INVALID_RECIPS");
            break;
        case MAPI_E_NOT_SUPPORTED:
            sprintf(str, "MAPI_E_NOT_SUPPORTED");
            break;
        }
}

int PASCAL InitMAPI()
{
    if ((hLibrary = LoadLibrary(MAPIDLL)) < (HANDLE)32)
    {
        return (ERR_LOAD_LIB);
    }

    if ((lpfnMAPILogon = (PFNMAPILOGON)GetProcAddress(
        hLibrary, SZ_MAPILOGON)) == NULL)
    {
        return (ERR_LOAD_FUNC);
    }

    if ((lpfnMAPILogoff = (PFNMAPILOGOFF)GetProcAddress(
        hLibrary, SZ_MAPILOGOFF)) == NULL)
    {
        return (ERR_LOAD_FUNC);
    }

    if ((lpfnMAPISendMail = (PFNMAPISENDMAIL)GetProcAddress(
        hLibrary, SZ_MAPISENDMAIL)) == NULL)
    {
        return (ERR_LOAD_FUNC);
    }
```

```
if ((lpfnMAPISendDocuments =
    (PFNMAPISENDDOCUMENTS)GetProcAddress(
    hLibrary, SZ_MAPISENDDOC)) == NULL)
{
    return (ERR_LOAD_FUNC);
}

if ((lpfnMAPIFindNext = (PFNMAPIFINDNEXT)GetProcAddress(
    hLibrary, SZ_MAPIFINDNEXT)) == NULL)
{
    return (ERR_LOAD_FUNC);
}

if ((lpfnMAPIReadMail = (PFNMAPIREADMAIL)GetProcAddress(
    hLibrary, SZ_MAPIREADMAIL)) == NULL)
{
    return (ERR_LOAD_FUNC);
}

if ((lpfnMAPISaveMail = (PFNMAPISAVEMAIL)GetProcAddress(
    hLibrary, SZ_MAPISAVEMAIL)) == NULL)
{
    return (ERR_LOAD_FUNC);
}

if ((lpfnMAPIDeleteMail = (PFNMAPIDELETEMAIL)GetProcAddress(
    hLibrary, SZ_MAPIDELMAIL)) == NULL)
{
    return (ERR_LOAD_FUNC);
}

if ((lpfnMAPIFreeBuffer = (PFNMAPIFREEBUFFER)GetProcAddress(
    hLibrary, SZ_MAPIFREEBUFFER)) == NULL)
{
    return (ERR_LOAD_FUNC);
}

if ((lpfnMAPIAddress = (PFNMAPIADDRESS)GetProcAddress(
    hLibrary, SZ_MAPIADDRESS)) == NULL)
{
    return (ERR_LOAD_FUNC);
}
```

*(continued)*

**Listing 7-4** *continued*

```
    if ((lpfnMAPIDetails = (PFNMAPIDETAILS)GetProcAddress(
        hLibrary, SZ_MAPIDETAILS)) == NULL)
    {
        return (ERR_LOAD_FUNC);
    }

    if ((lpfnMAPIResolveName = (PFNMAPIRESOLVENAME)GetProcAddress(
        hLibrary, SZ_MAPIRESOLVENAME)) == NULL)
    {
        return (ERR_LOAD_FUNC);
    }

    return (0);
}

int PASCAL DeInitMAPI()
{
    lpfnMAPILogon          = NULL;
    lpfnMAPILogoff         = NULL;
    lpfnMAPISendMail       = NULL;
    lpfnMAPISendDocuments = NULL;
    lpfnMAPIFindNext       = NULL;
    lpfnMAPIReadMail       = NULL;
    lpfnMAPISaveMail       = NULL;
    lpfnMAPIDeleteMail     = NULL;
    lpfnMAPIFreeBuffer     = NULL;
    lpfnMAPIAddress        = NULL;
    lpfnMAPIDetails        = NULL;
    lpfnMAPIResolveName    = NULL;
    FreeLibrary(hLibrary);
    return (0);
}
```

Listing 7-3 is MAPIInit.h, a header file containing function type declarations and manifest constant declarations required to dynamically load the Simple MAPI functions. The first group of *#define* statements is used to create constants for the literal names of the Simple MAPI functions. These are used later for getting the address of a function in the loaded DLL. Following the *#define* statements are some constant declarations used to signal particular types of errors.

Next comes a series of type definitions for the function pointers, required when dynamically loading DLLs and obtaining pointers to exported functions. Finally variables of the function types just created with the typedefs are declared.

Listing 7-4 is the source for SimpleMAPI.cpp. The *main* function first calls *InitMAPI*, a function defined later in the module. *InitMAPI* loads MAPI32.dll using *LoadLibrary* and then calls the Win32 API function *GetProcAddress* to obtain the address of each of the Simple MAPI functions. If this operation succeeds, *MAPILogon* is called through the *lpfnMAPILogon* function pointer. Like the functions they point to, all function pointers are named with an *lpfn* prefix. The prototype for *MAPILogon* is as follows:

```
ULONG FAR PASCAL MAPILogon(
    ULONG ulUIParam,
    LPTSTR lpszProfileName,
    LPTSTR lpszPassword,
    FLAGS flFlags,
    ULONG ulReserved,
    LPLHANDLE lplhSession
)
```

The first parameter is the parent window handle, or 0. For service applications, 0 is always appropriate since the goal is not to use the user interface Simple MAPI provides. This parameter is included in many of the Simple MAPI calls, and we will always pass 0 as the parameter.

The profile is the key to MAPI of any flavor. A profile is used to store information about the service providers and message services that are available. Whenever a user logs on to MAPI, she must specify a profile or use the default. The *lpszProfileName* parameter can point to a string containing the name of the profile to use, point to an empty string, or point to NULL. MAPI service providers can require a password, and *lpszPassword* should be set to the password if one is required. It is important to set this if needed, but if it is set to NULL or an empty string, MAPI will not present a dialog if *flFlags* does not contain the MAPI_LOGON_UI bit flag. MAPI_PASSWORD_UI is another bit flag that can be set to force the entry of only a password, while not allowing the user to change the profile name. These two flags are mutually exclusive.

MAPI_FORCE_DOWNLOAD tells *MAPILogon* to attempt to download messages before the function returns. If this flag is not set, messages can be downloaded in the background after the return from the function call. MAPI_NEW_SESSION causes *MAPILogon* to attempt to create a new session rather than to acquire the environment's shared session. The fifth parameter is reserved and must be 0. The final parameter is a pointer to a Simple MAPI session handle that will be set upon a successful call. If the call is not successful, the return code indicates which error has occurred. This error code, along with a pointer to a string, is passed to *FormatSimpleMAPIError*, a function defined later in the module that is a simple switch statement controlled by the return value from a Simple MAPI function.

To send a message with Simple MAPI, a *MapiMessage* structure must be filled in:

```
typedef struct {
    ULONG ulReserved;
    LPTSTR lpszSubject;
```

*(continued)*

```
    LPTSTR lpszNoteText;
    LPTSTR lpszMessageType;
    LPTSTR lpszDateReceived;
    LPTSTR lpszConversationID;
    FLAGS flFlags;
    lpMapiRecipDesc lpOriginator;
    ULONG nRecipCount;
    lpMapiRecipDesc lpRecips;
    ULONG nFileCount;
    lpMapiFileDesc lpFiles;
} MapiMessage;
```

The first data element of the *MapiMessage* structure is reserved and must be set to 0. The subject and text of the message are passed in the next two parameters, *lpszSubject* and *lpszNoteText*. The message type can be passed in the *lpszMessageType* element of the structure. A NULL is commonly passed for this parameter. The default message type is interpersonal messages (IPM), and if the client does not support any type but interpersonal messages, the parameter is ignored. Another type of message supported by some clients is interprocess communications (IPC). The fifth and sixth members of the structure, *lpszDateReceived* and *lpszConversationID*, are pointers to buffers to accept the date received and a conversation identifier, respectively. The date received is in the format YYYY-MM-DD HH:MM—for example, 1999-08-25 10:08. The conversation ID can point to a string identifying the thread to which the message belongs. Some messaging systems ignore this member.

The next element of the *MapiMessage* structure is *flFlags*. The defined flags for this bit flag are MAPI_RECEIPT_REQUESTED to request a receipt (set when sending a message), MAPI_SENT to indicate the message has been sent, and MAPI_UNREAD to indicate that the message has not been read. Note that when we go to read a MAPI message, we can peek at the message without setting this bit.

There are two instances of an embedded *MapiRecipDesc* structure within the *MapiMessage* structure. The originator is described in *lpOriginator*, and the recipients are described in *lpRecips*. The count of the number of *MapiRecipDesc* structures pointed to by *lpRecips* is contained in *nRecipCount*. The prototype for the *MapiRecipDesc* structure is as follows:

```
typedef struct {
    ULONG ulReserved;
    ULONG ulRecipClass;
    LPTSTR lpszName;
    LPTSTR lpszAddress;
    ULONG ulEIDSize;
    LPVOID lpEntryID;
} MapiRecipDesc;
```

The first member is reserved and must be set to 0. The second parameter, *ulRecipClass*, is one of the following values:

- **MAPI_ORIG** The originator of the message
- **MAPI_TO** A primary message recipient
- **MAPI_CC** A receiver of a copy of the message
- **MAPI_BCC** A receiver of a blind copy of the message

The display name of the person referred to in this structure is pointed to by *lpszName*. Like TAPI, MAPI has its own concept of what an address is. The address of the person referred to in this structure is pointed to by *lpszAddress*. This address has a specific format: [AddressType]:[Address]. Valid MAPI addresses include *SMTP:74040.607@compuserve.com* and *FAX:732-555-2683*. For outbound messages, the address can also point to the name of someone in the address book rather than a custom address. The final two members of the structure, *ulEIDSize* and *lpEntryID*, identify the recipient to the messaging system service. These are not decipherable by the client application, and the *lpEntryID* should be considered a black box not to be opened.

The final two members of the *MapiMessage* structure are related to file attachments. An array of *MapiFileDesc* structures is pointed to by *lpFiles*, and *nFileCount* contains the number of file description structures.

```
typedef struct {
    ULONG ulReserved;
    ULONG flFlags;
    ULONG nPosition;
    LPTSTR lpszPathName;
    LPTSTR lpszFileName;
    LPVOID lpFileType;
} MapiFileDesc;
```

The first member of the structure is reserved and must be set to 0. The second member, *flFlags*, is a bit-mapped field that can contain one or both of the following flags:

- **MAPI_OLE** The attachment is an OLE object. If MAPI_OLE_STATIC is also set, the attachment is a static OLE object. Otherwise the attachment is an embedded OLE object.
- **MAPI_OLE_STATIC** The attachment is a static OLE object.

The position of the file within the note text is returned in *nPosition*. This positioning allows the e-mail client to properly position an icon or other visual cue for the placement of the file in the note text. Server-based applications commonly do not display the note text, so this member is generally ignored. The full path of the attached file and the filename are placed in *lpszPathName* and *lpszFileName*, respectively. The path name is a fully qualified path name with drive and directory. The filename is the name as seen by the recipient and generally can be ignored by server-based applications. The type of the file is pointed to by the *lpFileType* member, which can point to a structure of type *MapiFileTagExt*. This structure contains information about the name of the file type (*lpTag*) as well as the encoding scheme used (*lpEncoding*), for example *MacBinary*, *UUENCODE*, or *binary*.

```
typedef struct {
    ULONG ulReserved;
    ULONG cbTag;
    LPBYTE lpTag;
    ULONG cbEncoding;
    LPBYTE lpEncoding;
} MapiFileTagExt;
```

Once the *MapiMessage* structure is filled in, we call *MapiSendMail* to actually send the message. There is also a *MapiSendDocuments* function that, while less flexible, is significantly less complex. *MapiSendMail*, which has the following prototype, is virtually always worth the additional effort.

```
ULONG FAR PASCAL MAPISendMail(
    LHANDLE lhSession,
    ULONG ulUIParam,
    lpMapiMessage lpMessage,
    FLAGS flFlags,
    ULONG ulReserved
)
```

The first parameter, *lhSession*, is the session handle returned from the call to *MAPILogon*, and *ulUIParam* is the parent window handle, or 0. Once again, 0 is used in this example because we do not expect to generate any UI. The address of the message structure just described is sent as *lpMessage*. The bit flag parameter, *flFlags*, can include:

- **MAPI_DIALOG** Used to cause a dialog to appear to allow the user to select recipients—something our server-based applications will never want to do.
- **MAPI_LOGON_UI** Used to cause a logon dialog to appear if needed—another option that server-based applications will not use.
- **MAPI_NEW_SESSION** Used to request that a new MAPI session be started. If this flag is not set, the function uses an existing session. No examples presented in this chapter use this flag.

The final parameter to *MapiSendMail*—*ulReserved*—must be 0. As with all the Simple MAPI functions, a return code other than SUCCESS_SUCCESS indicates an error, and the SimpleMAPI example application in Listing 7-4 will call a routine to create an error string describing the problem and then display the string. Depending upon the state of the current connection, the message will either be immediately sent, or in the case of a machine connected through a dial-up Internet connection, the message will be placed in the Outbox and sent when a connection is established.

### A Simple MAPI read mail example

Once we have sent e-mail, we might want to read e-mail. For example, if we had requested a return receipt in the previous portion of Listing 7-4, we might want the server application to next await a reply indicating that the remote user or system has received the e-mail. Doing this with Simple MAPI is a two-step operation. First we must find the message, and then we can read it.

*MapiFindNext* is the somewhat misnamed function used to find a message so that it can be read. While many APIs have *FindFirst* and *FindNext* pairs of functions, Simple MAPI uses *MapiFindNext* to do both:

```
ULONG FAR PASCAL MAPIFindNext(
    LHANDLE lhSession,
    ULONG ulUIParam,
    LPTSTR lpszMessageType,
    LPTSTR lpszSeedMessageID,
    FLAGS flFlags,
    ULONG ulReserved,
    LPTSTR lpszMessageID
)
```

The first two parameters, *lhSession* and *ulUIParam*, are used exactly as previous Simple MAPI functions. The next parameter, *lpszMessageType*, is used the same way as the member of the same name in the *MapiMessage* structure, with NULL passed for IPM messages. The fourth parameter, *lpszSeedMessageID*, is used to find a specific message. If this is NULL or points to an empty string, the first message that matches the type specified is returned.

The three flags that can be sent in *flFlags* are

- **MAPI_GUARANTEE_FIFO** Messages should be returned in the order they were received.
- **MAPI_LONG_MSGID** The returned message ID (pointed to by *lpszMessageID*) can be as long as 512 characters. If you don't set this flag, operations that attempt to read messages with longer message IDs might fail. Early versions of MAPI only supported 64-character message IDs.
- **MAPI_UNREAD_ONLY** Only unread messages should be read.

The next parameter to *MapiFindNext*—*ulReserved*—must be 0. The last parameter is *lpszMessageID*. This should point to a buffer allocated by the application at least 64 bytes in size unless MAPI_LONG_MESID is specified in *flFlags*, in which case it must be 512 bytes.

In Listing 7-4, *MapiFindNext* is first called with NULL passed for the *lpszMessageType* and *lpszSeedMessageID*, MAPI_GUARANTEE_FIFO, and MAPI_LONG_MSGID in *flFlags*. A second call to *MapiFindNext* is made in a loop with *lpszSeedMessageID* set to the message ID of the previously read message.

If *MapiFindNext* succeeds, *MapiReadMail* is called to actually read the message.

```
ULONG FAR PASCAL MAPIReadMail(
    LHANDLE lhSession,
    ULONG ulUIParam,
    LPTSTR lpszMessageID,
    FLAGS flFlags,
    ULONG ulReserved,
    lpMapiMessage FAR * lppMessage
)
```

The first two parameters, *lhSession* and *ulUIParam*, are used exactly as we've used in previous Simple MAPI functions. The *lpszMessageID* points to a message ID, which is generally discovered through an earlier call to *MapiFindNext*. Four values can be sent in the *flFlags* parameter:

- **MAPI_BODY_AS_FILE** *MapiReadMail* should save the note text of the message to a file and save it as the first attachment.
- **MAPI_ENVELOPE_ONLY** *MapiReadMail* should only read the header. This can significantly improve performance.
- **MAPI_PEEK** If the messaging system supports it, the message is read, but the message is not marked as read. If the messaging system does not support this flag, it marks the message as read.
- **MAPI_SUPPRESS_ATTACH** *MapiReadMail* should not copy attachments to temporary files—thus enhancing performance.

The final parameter to *MapiReadMessage* is a pointer to a pointer to contain a *MapiMessage* structure. This structure is allocated by MAPI and must be freed later with a call to *MapiFreeBuffer*. This function takes as its sole parameter the pointer to the *MapiMessage* structure.

Listing 7-4 contains this code fragment to loop through messages, reporting on the subject and date. If an attachment is found, information on that is displayed. The loop continues until it finds a file with an attachment and then exits the loop.

```
// Loop until we find an attachment.
bool foundFile = false;
do {
    if (ret = lpfnMAPIReadMail(lHandle, 0, szMessageID,
        0,0,&pMessage) != SUCCESS_SUCCESS)
    {
        char buffer[255];
        FormatSimpleMAPIError(ret, buffer);
        printf("\nMAPIFindNext: %s", buffer);
    }
    else
    {
        printf("\nOriginator: %s", pMessage->lpOriginator);
        printf("\nReceived: %s ", pMessage->lpszDateReceived);
        printf("\nSubject: %s ", pMessage->lpszSubject);
        if (pMessage->nFileCount > 0)
        {
            printf("\nAttachment in %s",
                pMessage->lpFiles->lpszPathName);
            foundFile = true;
        }
        lpfnMAPIFreeBuffer(pMessage);
    }
} while (!(foundFile) &&
    (ret = lpfnMAPIFindNext(lHandle, 0, NULL,szMessageID,
    MAPI_GUARANTEE_FIFO | MAPI_LONG_MSGID, 0,
    szMessageID)) == SUCCESS_SUCCESS);
```

The significant part of this code is that the second call to *MapiFindNext* is made with the message ID from the previous read. Failing to do this will cause the program to simply loop, displaying information about the same message over and over again.

## Closing Out MAPI

The last MAPI function used in Listing 7-4 is *MapiLogoff*.

```
ULONG FAR PASCAL MAPILogoff (
    LHANDLE lhSession,
    ULONG ulUIParam,
    FLAGS flFlags,
    ULONG ulReserved
)
```

The only parameter that is significant is *lhSession*, which is the session handle obtained through a call to *MapiLogon*. After *MapiLogoff* is called, the *DeInitMapi* function is called, which sets all the function pointers to NULL and frees the MAPI library.

## Full MAPI

Now that you've had a thorough introduction to Simple MAPI, what more should you know to use full MAPI? You'll recognize many of the full MAPI functions. The way that the functions are called—through function pointers obtained by a call to *LoadLibrary* and *GetProcAddress*—is also similar. In fact, some of the initial calls in a full MAPI application (which I'll call MAPI for the balance of the book) look similar to the calls used in Simple MAPI.

The differences, however, are quite striking when you begin to manipulate messages. Rather than calling a function such as *MAPISendMail,* you create a message in the Outbox using a COM interface. This can be quite a complicated process, involving several interfaces and lots of structures, but it also offers flexibility that can be important for a server-based application.

For instance, suppose that you are writing a monitoring application that will send out e-mail messages in the event of problems, or perhaps messages at scheduled intervals to let you know the application is still running. Just as if you were entering the text of the message in Microsoft Outlook, when you create a message using Simple MAPI the message briefly appears in the Outbox and then moves to the Sent Items folder. For messages created manually, this might not be a problem. In fact, this is a feature that allows you to retain copies of messages you have sent and thus decide when these messages should be purged. The situation might be different for messages automatically created. Rather than a couple dozen messages a week, a server-based application operating robotically might create hundreds or even thousands of messages per week. OK, you say, I'll just have the program delete them periodically. *MAPIDeleteMessage* sounds like it might do the trick; however, it only deletes messages in the Inbox. But you need a MAPI program at least for the deletion of sent messages. MAPI allows you to go one step farther, eliminating the messages from the Outbox and not sending them to the Sent Items folder. If the details of the sent messages are not important, or if those details are stored elsewhere in the application, this might be an even better solution.

A server-based application might also want to read incoming messages and sort them according to criteria such as the sender, the message, or the existence of attachments. Doing this requires MAPI. Simple MAPI does not provide the ability to enumerate folders, let alone move messages from the Inbox to other folders.

MAPI's flexibility comes at the cost of added complexity in a normal application. This complexity increases even more for services. As I've mentioned, the application will need to have a message pump operational for messages MAPI will send to the hidden window it will create. Furthermore, other special settings must be present for a MAPI application to run within a service.

### Full MAPI example

Let's take a look at a basic MAPI application that enumerates all folders and then places a message in the Outbox. Listing 7-5 shows the headers for this application (MAPIInit.h and StdAfx.h) and Listing 7-6 shows the code for the program itself, FullMAPI.cpp.

**MAPIInit.h**

```
#define SZ_MAPIINITIALIZE          "MAPIInitialize"
#define SZ_MAPIUNINITIALIZE        "MAPIUninitialize"
#define SZ_MAPILOGONEX             "MAPILogonEx"
#define SZ_MAPIFREEBUFFER          "MAPIFreeBuffer"
#define SZ_MAPIALLOCATEBUFFER      "MAPIAllocateBuffer"
#define SZ_HRGETONEPROP            "HrGetOneProp@12"
#define SZ_HRQUERYALLROWS          "HrQueryAllRows@24"
#define SZ_FREEPROWS               "FreeProws@4"
#define SZ_FREEPADRLIST            "FreePadrlist@4"

#define MAPIDLL "MAPI32.DLL"
#define ERR_LOAD_LIB  0x02
#define ERR_LOAD_FUNC 0x04

typedef VOID    (FAR PASCAL *PFNFREEPADRLIST        )
    (LPADRLIST pAdrList);
typedef VOID    (FAR PASCAL *PFNFREEPROWS           )
    (LPSRowSet prows);
typedef HRESULT (FAR PASCAL *PFNHRGETONEPROP        )(LPMAPIPROP,
    ULONG, LPSPropValue FAR *);
typedef HRESULT (FAR PASCAL *PFNMAPIINITIALIZE      )(LPVOID);
typedef HRESULT (FAR PASCAL *PFNHRQUERYALLROWS      )(LPMAPITABLE,
    LPSPropTagArray, LPSRestriction, LPSSortOrderSet, LONG,
    LPSRowSet FAR *);
typedef VOID    (FAR PASCAL *PFNMAPIUNINITIALIZE    )(void);
typedef HRESULT (FAR PASCAL *PFNMAPILOGONEX         )(ULONG,
    LPTSTR, LPTSTR, FLAGS, LPMAPISESSION FAR *);
typedef ULONG   (FAR PASCAL *PFNMAPIFREEBUFFER      )(LPVOID);
typedef SCODE   (FAR PASCAL *PFNMAPIALLOCATEBUFFER)(ULONG,
    LPVOID FAR *);

int PASCAL InitMAPI(void);
int PASCAL DeInitMAPI(void);
```

**Listing 7-5** *(continued)*

**Listing 7-5** *continued*

### StdAfx.h

```
// stdafx.h : include file for standard system include files,
//  or project-specific include files that are used frequently but
//  are changed infrequently
//

#if !defined(AFX_STDAFX_H__289B1463_5BB0_11D3_B4AD_00C04F79B510__
INCLUDED_)
#define AFX_STDAFX_H__289B1463_5BB0_11D3_B4AD_00C04F79B510__INCLUDED_

#if _MSC_VER > 1000
#pragma once
#endif // _MSC_VER > 1000

#define WIN32_LEAN_AND_MEAN

#include <stdio.h>
#include <windows.h>
#include <mapi.h>
#include <mapix.h>
#include "mapiinit.h"
#include <initguid.h>
#include <mapitags.h>

//{{AFX_INSERT_LOCATION}}
// Microsoft Visual C++ will insert additional declarations
//  immediately before the previous line.

#endif //!defined(AFX_STDAFX_H__289B1463_5BB0_11D3_B4AD_00C04F79B510__
INCLUDED_)
```

### FullMAPI.cpp

```
// FullMAPI.cpp: Defines the entry point for the console application.
//

#include "stdafx.h"
#include <mapiguid.h>

PFNHRQUERYALLROWS      lpfnHrQueryAllRows;
PFNHRGETONEPROP        lpfnHrGetOneProp;
```

**Listing 7-6**

```
PFNMAPIALLOCATEBUFFER lpfnMAPIAllocateBuffer;
PFNMAPIFREEBUFFER     lpfnMAPIFreeBuffer;
PFNMAPIINITIALIZE     lpfnMAPIInitialize;
PFNMAPIUNINITIALIZE   lpfnMAPIUninitialize;
PFNMAPILOGONEX        lpfnMAPILogonEx;
PFNFREEPROWS          lpfnFreeProws;
PFNFREEPADRLIST       lpfnFreePadrlist;

HMODULE hLibrary;

IMsgStore      *pmdb           = NULL;
IMAPISession   *psess          = NULL;
IMAPIFolder    *prootfolder    = NULL;
IAddrBook      *pAddrBook      = NULL;
ULONG nfolders = 0;

typedef struct {
    short int k;
    char        *name;
    short int    depth;
    SBinary     *pbv;
    SRowSet     *prs;
    IMAPIFolder *pfolder;
    IMAPITable  *pcontentstable;
} FOLDER;
FOLDER folder[200];

int inboxidx   =-1;
int deletedidx =-1;
int sentidx    =-1;
int outboxidx  =-1;

char *pInboxName     = "Inbox";
char *pDeletedName   = "Deleted Items";
char *pSentItemsName = "Sent Items";
char *pOutboxName    = "Outbox";

char ename[512];

bool GetRootFolder(void);
bool GetFoldersHierarchy(char *name, IMAPIFolder *pfolder,
    short int depth);
bool AssignInOutSentDel();
```

*(continued)*

**Listing 7-6** *continued*

```
#define FREEBUFFS if (pMessage) pMessage->Release(); \
                  if (lpPropProblems)
                      (lpfnMAPIFreeBuffer)(lpPropProblems); \
                  if (pr) (lpfnMAPIFreeBuffer)(pr); \
                  if (pAdrList) (lpfnFreePadrlist)(pAdrList);


int main(int argc, char* argv[])
{
    MAPIINIT_0          MapiInitInfo;
    LPSPropValue        pr = NULL;
    LPADRLIST           pAdrList = NULL;
    LPSPropProblemArray lpPropProblems = 0;
    IMessage            *pMessage = NULL;
    FLAGS flags = MAPI_EXTENDED | MAPI_NEW_SESSION |
        MAPI_USE_DEFAULT;

    InitMAPI();
    MapiInitInfo.ulFlags = MAPI_MULTITHREAD_NOTIFICATIONS;
    MapiInitInfo.ulVersion = 0;
    lpfnMAPIInitialize(&MapiInitInfo);

    HRESULT hr = lpfnMAPILogonEx(0, NULL, NULL, flags, &psess);
    if (FAILED(hr))
    {
        DWORD dRet = GetLastError();
        return (-1);
    }

    if ((GetRootFolder()) == false)
    {
        return (-1);
    }
    if ((GetFoldersHierarchy(ename, prootfolder, 0)) == false)
    {
        return (-1);
    }
    AssignInOutSentDel();

    for (unsigned loop = 0; loop < nfolders; loop++)
    {
        printf("Folder %d \t%s\n", loop, folder[loop].name);
    }
```

```
hr = psess->OpenAddressBook(0, NULL, AB_NO_DIALOG, &pAddrBook);
if (FAILED(hr))
{
    printf("Open Address Book");
    FREEBUFFS;
    return (-1);
}

hr = lpfnMAPIAllocateBuffer(CbNewADRLIST(1),
    (LPVOID*)&pAdrList);
if (FAILED(hr))
{
    printf("Alloc AdrList");
    FREEBUFFS;
    return (-1);
}
ZeroMemory(pAdrList, CbNewADRLIST(1));

hr = lpfnMAPIAllocateBuffer(sizeof(SPropValue)*3,
    (LPVOID*)&(pAdrList->aEntries[0].rgPropVals));
if (FAILED(hr))
{
    printf("Alloc SPropValue 2");
    FREEBUFFS;
    return (-1);
}
ZeroMemory(pAdrList->aEntries[0].rgPropVals,
    sizeof(SPropValue)*2);

pAdrList->cEntries = 1;
pAdrList->aEntries[0].cValues = 2;
pAdrList->aEntries[0].rgPropVals[0].ulPropTag     =
    PR_DISPLAY_NAME;
pAdrList->aEntries[0].rgPropVals[0].Value.lpszA  =
    "Douglas Reilly";
pAdrList->aEntries[0].rgPropVals[1].ulPropTag     =
    PR_RECIPIENT_TYPE;
pAdrList->aEntries[0].rgPropVals[1].Value.l       =
    MAPI_TO;
hr = pAddrBook->ResolveName(NULL, 0, NULL, pAdrList);
if (FAILED(hr))
{
    printf("Resolve Name");
    FREEBUFFS;
    return (-1);
}
```

*(continued)*

**Listing 7-6** *continued*

```
    hr = lpfnMAPIAllocateBuffer(sizeof(SPropValue)*5, (LPVOID*)&pr);
    if (FAILED(hr))
    {
        printf("Alloc SPropValue 5");
        FREEBUFFS;
        return (-1);
    }
    ZeroMemory(pr, sizeof(SPropValue)*5);
    char *pStamp = "Messsage Subject ";

    pr[0].ulPropTag    = PR_PRIORITY;
    pr[0].Value.ul     = PRIO_NORMAL;
    pr[1].ulPropTag    = PR_ORIGINATOR_DELIVERY_REPORT_REQUESTED;
    pr[1].Value.b      = TRUE;
    pr[2].ulPropTag    = PR_SUBJECT;
    pr[2].Value.lpszA = pStamp;
    pr[3].ulPropTag    = PR_BODY;
    pr[3].Value.lpszA = "This the body of the message.";
    pr[4].ulPropTag    = PR_DELETE_AFTER_SUBMIT;
    pr[4].Value.b      = TRUE;

    hr = folder[outboxidx].pfolder->CreateMessage(NULL, 0,
        &pMessage);
    if (FAILED(hr))
    {
        printf("SetProps");
        FREEBUFFS;
        return (-1);
    }

    hr = pMessage->ModifyRecipients(MODRECIP_ADD, pAdrList);
    if (FAILED(hr))
    {
        printf("ModifyRecipients");
        FREEBUFFS;
        return (-1);
    }

    hr = pMessage->SetProps(5, pr, &lpPropProblems);
    if (FAILED(hr))
    {
        printf("SetProps");
        FREEBUFFS;
        return (-1);
    }
```

```
    hr = pMessage->SubmitMessage(0);
    if (FAILED(hr))
    {
        printf("SubmitMessage %d ", hr);
        FREEBUFFS;
        return (-1);
    }

    FREEBUFFS;

    psess->Logoff(0,0,0);
    psess->Release();
    psess = NULL;
    pAddrBook->Release();
    pAddrBook = NULL;
    lpfnMAPIUninitialize();
    DeInitMAPI();
    return 0;
}

bool AssignInOutSentDel()
{
    for (int i = 0; i < (int)nfolders; i++)
    {
        if (strcmp(folder[i].name, pInboxName     ) == 0 )
            inboxidx       = i;
        if (strcmp(folder[i].name, pDeletedName   ) == 0)
            deletedidx     = i;
        if (strcmp(folder[i].name, pSentItemsName) == 0)
            sentidx        = i;
        if (strcmp(folder[i].name, pOutboxName    ) == 0)
            outboxidx      = i;
    }
    return true;
}

bool GetFoldersHierarchy(char *name, IMAPIFolder *pfolder,
    short int depth)
{
    IMAPITable *ptable = NULL;
    ULONG   ulRowCount = 0;
    HRESULT hr;
    SPropTagArray *ptag = NULL;
    hr = pfolder->GetHierarchyTable(0, &ptable);
```

*(continued)*

```
    if (FAILED(hr))
    {
        return false;
    }
    hr = ptable->GetRowCount(0, &ulRowCount);
    if (ulRowCount)
    {
        hr = ptable->QueryColumns(TBL_ALL_COLUMNS, &ptag);
        hr = ptable->SetColumns(ptag, 0);
        hr = ptable->SeekRow(BOOKMARK_BEGINNING, 0, NULL);
        for (unsigned i = 0; i < ulRowCount; i++)
        {
            ++nfolders;
            hr = ptable->QueryRows(1, 0, &folder[nfolders-1].prs);
            if (FAILED(hr))
            {
                return false;
            }
            SPropValue* p = folder[nfolders-1].prs->aRow->lpProps;

            folder[nfolders-1].depth = depth;
            for (int j = 0;j < (int)ptag->cValues;j++)
            {
                if (p[j].ulPropTag == PR_DISPLAY_NAME)
                    folder[nfolders-1].name = p[j].Value.lpszA;
                if (p[j].ulPropTag == PR_ENTRYID)
                    folder[nfolders-1].pbv = &p[j].Value.bin;
            }
            ULONG ul;
            hr = pmdb->OpenEntry(folder[nfolders-1].pbv->cb,
                (LPENTRYID)folder[nfolders-1].pbv->lpb,
                (LPCIID)&IID_IMAPIFolder,
                MAPI_MODIFY|MAPI_BEST_ACCESS, &ul,
                (IUnknown**)&folder[nfolders-1].pfolder);
            if (hr == S_OK)
                GetFoldersHierarchy(
                    folder[nfolders-1].name,
                    folder[nfolders-1].pfolder, depth+1);
        }
    }
    lpfnMAPIFreeBuffer(ptag);
    ptable->Release();
    return true;
}
```

```
bool GetRootFolder(void)
{
    ULONG   ulRowCount;
    HRESULT hr;
    IMAPITable *ptable = NULL;
    hr = psess->GetMsgStoresTable(0L, &ptable);

    SPropTagArray *ptag = NULL;
    hr = ptable->GetRowCount(0, &ulRowCount);
    hr = ptable->QueryColumns(TBL_ALL_COLUMNS, &ptag);
    hr = ptable->SetColumns(ptag, 0);

    for (unsigned i = 0; i < ulRowCount; i++)
    {
        char *provname = "", *storname = "";
        SRowSet *prs = NULL;
        hr = ptable->SeekRow(BOOKMARK_BEGINNING, i, NULL);
        hr = ptable->QueryRows(1, TBL_NOADVANCE, &prs);
        SPropValue* p = prs->aRow->lpProps;
        SBinary bv;

        for (int k = 0; k < (int)ptag->cValues; k++)
        {
            if (p[k].ulPropTag == PR_DEFAULT_STORE &&
                p[k].Value.b == 1)
            {
                for (int j = 0; j < (int)ptag->cValues; j++)
                {
                    if (p[j].ulPropTag == PR_DISPLAY_NAME)
                        storname =  p[j].Value.lpszA;
                    if (p[j].ulPropTag == PR_PROVIDER_DISPLAY)
                        provname =  p[j].Value.lpszA;
                    if (p[j].ulPropTag == PR_ENTRYID)
                        memcpy(&bv, &p[j].Value.bin,
                            sizeof(SBinary));
                }
                hr = psess->OpenMsgStore(0,bv.cb,
                        (LPENTRYID)bv.lpb, NULL,
                        MAPI_BEST_ACCESS | MDB_NO_DIALOG, &pmdb);
                lpfnMAPIFreeBuffer(prs);
                if (FAILED(hr))
                {
                    printf("\nError when opening "
                        "default message store.");
```

*(continued)*

```
                    return false;
                }

                ULONG ulObjType;
                hr = pmdb->OpenEntry(0, NULL,
                    /*(LPCIID)&IID_IMAPIFolder,*/ NULL,
                    MAPI_MODIFY | MAPI_BEST_ACCESS,
                    &ulObjType,
                    (IUnknown**)&prootfolder);
                if (FAILED(hr))
                {
                    return false;
                }
                strcpy(ename, storname);
                break;
            }
        }
        lpfnMAPIFreeBuffer(prs);
        if (prootfolder)
            break;
    }
    lpfnMAPIFreeBuffer(ptag);
    ptable->Release();
    if (!pmdb)
    {
        printf("Unable to find default message store record.");
        return false;
    }
    return true;
}

int PASCAL InitMAPI()
{

    if ((hLibrary = LoadLibrary(MAPIDLL)) < (HANDLE)32)
    {
        return (ERR_LOAD_LIB);
    }

    if ((lpfnHrQueryAllRows =
        (PFNHRQUERYALLROWS)GetProcAddress(hLibrary,
        SZ_HRQUERYALLROWS)) == NULL)
    {
        return (ERR_LOAD_FUNC);
    }
```

```
if ((lpfnHrGetOneProp =
    (PFNHRGETONEPROP)GetProcAddress(hLibrary,
    SZ_HRGETONEPROP)) == NULL)
{
    return (ERR_LOAD_FUNC);
}

if ((lpfnMAPIAllocateBuffer =
    (PFNMAPIALLOCATEBUFFER)GetProcAddress(hLibrary,
    SZ_MAPIALLOCATEBUFFER)) == NULL)
{
    return (ERR_LOAD_FUNC);
}

if ((lpfnMAPIFreeBuffer =
    (PFNMAPIFREEBUFFER)GetProcAddress(hLibrary,
    SZ_MAPIFREEBUFFER)) == NULL)
{
    return (ERR_LOAD_FUNC);
}

if ((lpfnMAPIInitialize =
    (PFNMAPIINITIALIZE)GetProcAddress(hLibrary,
    SZ_MAPIINITIALIZE)) == NULL)
{
    return (ERR_LOAD_FUNC);
}

if ((lpfnMAPIUninitialize =
    (PFNMAPIUNINITIALIZE)GetProcAddress(hLibrary,
    SZ_MAPIUNINITIALIZE)) == NULL)
{
    return (ERR_LOAD_FUNC);
}

if ((lpfnMAPILogonEx =
    (PFNMAPILOGONEX)GetProcAddress(hLibrary,
    SZ_MAPILOGONEX)) == NULL)
{
    return (ERR_LOAD_FUNC);
}

if ((lpfnFreeProws =
    (PFNFREEPROWS)GetProcAddress(hLibrary,
    SZ_FREEPROWS)) == NULL)
```

*(continued)*

**Listing 7-6** *continued*

```
        {
            return (ERR_LOAD_FUNC);
        }

        if ((lpfnFreePadrlist =
            (PFNFREEPADRLIST)GetProcAddress(hLibrary,
            SZ_FREEPADRLIST)) == NULL)
        {
            return (ERR_LOAD_FUNC);
        }
        return (0);
    }

    int PASCAL DeInitMAPI()
    {
        lpfnHrQueryAllRows = NULL;
        lpfnHrGetOneProp = NULL;
        lpfnMAPIAllocateBuffer = NULL;
        lpfnMAPIFreeBuffer = NULL;
        lpfnMAPIInitialize = NULL;
        lpfnMAPIUninitialize = NULL;
        lpfnMAPILogonEx = NULL;
        lpfnFreeProws = NULL;
        lpfnFreePadrlist = NULL;
        FreeLibrary(hLibrary);
        return (0);
    }
```

MAPIInit.h is similar to the Simple MAPI header of the same name, but the function pointers declared are slightly different. There are also fewer function pointers; in fact, only six of the nine function pointers are actually used in this example. One thing that is important about StdAfx.h is the *#include* statement for Mapix.h in addition to Mapi.h. There are several other files included to support the COM side of MAPI.

FullMAPI.cpp first declares the function pointers defined in FullMAPI.h. Next you'll see some other declarations, including a structure used to store information about folders. This structure has a couple of members that are important to understand:

```
typedef struct {
    short int k;
    char        *name;
    short int    depth;
    SBinary     *pbv;
    SRowSet     *prs;
    IMAPIFolder *pfolder;
    IMAPITable  *pcontentstable;
} FOLDER;
```

The *name* member holds the actual name of the folder, such as Inbox or Sent. The interface pointer, *pfolder*, is used to create a message using the *CreateMessage* method of the *IMAPIFolder* interface. Following the definition of the *FOLDER* structure, there are declarations to give special support to the four common folders: Inbox, Outbox, Sent Items, and Deleted Items. Next comes some function declarations, and the *#define* statement that defines a FREEBUFFS macro used to clean up memory allocations.

After a call to *MapiInit*, which is similar to the call to *MapiInit* in the Simple MAPI example, *MAPIInitialize* is called through a pointer, *lpfnMAPIInitialize*. (All function pointers are named like the functions they point to, with an *lpfn* prefix.) *MAPIInitialize* takes as its single parameter a pointer to a *MAPIINIT_0* structure.

```
typedef struct
{
     ULONG ulVersion;
     ULONG ulFlags;
} MAPIINIT_0;
```

The only member that needs to be set is *ulFlags*. This bit flag has two possible values:

- **MAPI_MULTITHREAD_NOTIFICATIONS** MAPI should generate notifications using a thread dedicated to notification handling, rather than the first thread that calls *MAPIInitialize*.
- **MAPI_NT_SERVICE** This must be set for Windows 2000 and Windows NT service applications and must not be set for nonservice applications.

*MAPILogonEx* is similar in function to *MAPILogon* (which we used with Simple MAPI), but it acts as the gateway to MAPI's COM interface by returning an *IMAPISession* interface.

```
HRESULT MAPILogonEx(
    ULONG ulUIParam,
    LPTSTR lpszProfileName,
    LPTSTR lpszPassword,
    FLAGS flFlags,
    LPMAPISESSION FAR * lppSession
);
```

The first three parameters are similar to the same parameters in *MAPILogon*. The *flFlags* parameter accepts 13 different values. Several of the important ones for server-based applications are

- **MAPI_EXTENDED** Not an option—this must be set.
- **MAPI_FORCE_DOWNLOAD** Forces a synchronous download of all messages for the user.

- **MAPI_NEW_SESSION** MAPI tries to create a new session rather than sharing an existing session.
- **MAPI_NT_SERVICE** Must be set for services and must not be set for other applications.
- **MAPI_TIMEOUT_SHORT** Logon should fail if blocked for more than a few seconds.
- **MAPI_USE_DEFAULT** MAPI default profile should be used. This is not likely to work in a service if the service is operating under the System account.

The final parameter is a pointer to a pointer to an *IMAPISession* interface. The return from *MAPILogon* can be checked using the FAILED macro. This interface is used extensively, and in this example it is declared as a global variable.

**Getting the root folder** If the logon succeeds, three functions defined within FullMAPI.cpp are called. *GetRootFolder* gets the root folder that allows other folders to be found. *GetRootFolder* first obtains an *IMAPITable* interface by calling *GetMsgStoresTable* to access the message stores table. Using *pTable*, the interface returned by *GetMsgStoresTable*, the rows and columns of the message stores table are gathered. Next it loops through the rows checking properties until it finds the default store. Properties have tags and values. The tag identifies the type of property; for instance, PR_DISPLAY_NAME is the display name. The value of the display name of a message store provider might be "Personal Message Store". Looping through the tags and values of a row is handled in the following code fragment from *GetRootFolder* in FullMAPI.cpp.

```
for (int j = 0;j < (int)ptag->cValues;j++)
{
    if (p[j].ulPropTag == PR_DISPLAY_NAME)
        storname =  p[j].Value.lpszA;
    if (p[j].ulPropTag == PR_PROVIDER_DISPLAY)
        provname =  p[j].Value.lpszA;
    if (p[j].ulPropTag == PR_ENTRYID)
        memcpy(&bv,&p[j].Value.bin,sizeof(SBinary));
}
```

This example might include any number of properties, but our interest is only in the display name, the display name of the service provider, and the entry ID. The entry ID is then used to open the appropriate message store, getting an *IMsgStore* interface pointer through a call to the *OpenMsgStore* method of the *IMAPISession* interface.

```
HRESULT OpenMsgStore (
    ULONG ulUIParam,
    ULONG cbEntryID,
    LPENTRYID lpEntryID,
    LPCIID lpInterface,
    ULONG ulFlags,
    LPMDB FAR * lppMDB
);
```

The values for these parameters are documented in the MAPI documentation, but server-based applications should always include the MDB_NO_DIALOG flag in *ulFlags*. Generally, all bit flags in MAPI also accept the MAPI_BEST_ACCESS flag. This flag tries to get the best possible access to the object being returned, given the rights of the client. The default interface can be selected by passing NULL to *lpInterface*. The interface pointer returned in *lppMDB* is then used to call the *OpenEntry* method of the *IMsgStore* interface:

```
HRESULT OpenEntry (
    ULONG cbEntryID,
    LPENTRYID lpEntryID,
    LPCIID lpInterface,
    ULONG ulFlags,
    ULONG FAR * lpulObjType,
    LPUNKNOWN FAR * lppUnk
)
```

*OpenEntry* returns the root folder in *lppUnk*. NULL passed as the *lpInterface* means that the default interface will be returned, in this case *IMAPIFolder*.

**Getting the folder hierarchy** Once we have the root folder, *GetFoldersHierarchy* is called with the name of the root folder and a pointer to the *IMAPIFolder* interface pointing to the root. *GetFoldersHierarchy* operates like *GetRootFolder* in that it obtains an *IMAPITable* interface pointer by calling the *GetHierarchyTable* method of the *IMAPIContainer* interface pointer, using the root folder interface pointer passed as a parameter.

```
HRESULT GetHierarchyTable(
    ULONG ulFlags,
    LPMAPITABLE FAR * lppTable
);
```

One value that can be included in *ulFlags* worth noting is MAPI_DEFERRED_ERRORS. This should never be called in a server-based application because the method can return—indicating success quickly—but in fact might fail.

If this happens, making subsequent calls using the interface pointer returned will result in an error. This is another case in which the possibility of errors occurring that no one will see outweighs any possible optimization advantage. This flag is available in many areas of MAPI, but I don't use it in any of this book's examples.

Once the interface pointer to the hierarchy table is obtained, the balance of the logic is similar, though in this case rather than looking for a particular entry, the program writes all entries into the FOLDERS structure array, which makes them available elsewhere in the program.

**Assigning common folders** Once the FOLDERS structure array is filled, some offsets in the array are set as pointers to the special folders used most often: Inbox, Outbox, Sent Items, and Deleted Items. *AssignInOutSentDel* is a straightforward function:

```
void AssignInOutSentDel()
{
    for (int i = 0; i < (int)nfolders; i++)
    {
        if (strcmp(folder[i].name, pInboxName     ) == 0)
            inboxidx     = i;
        if (strcmp(folder[i].name, pDeletedName   ) == 0)
            deletedidx   = i;
        if (strcmp(folder[i].name, pSentItemsName) == 0)
            sentidx      = i;
        if (strcmp(folder[i].name, pOutboxName    ) == 0)
            outboxidx    = i;
    }
}
```

After we get the folders, we simply print a list of them. In real-world applications, other activities are performed using the folder information. We use the Outbox folder next to send a message.

**Sending a message** In MAPI, sending a message requires that we create a message and place it in the Outbox. One of the other advantages of MAPI over Simple MAPI is the ability to easily resolve addresses using the address book. To do so, the address book must be accessed through an *IaddrBook* interface pointer obtained by calling the *OpenAddressBook* method of the *IMAPISession* interface.

```
HRESULT OpenAddressBook(
    ULONG ulUIParam,
    LPCIID lpInterface,
    ULONG ulFlags,
    LPADRBOOK FAR * lppAdrBook
);
```

Again, *ulUIParam* is set to 0 because our goal is to not use any user interface. We want the default interface, so *lpInterface* can be passed as NULL. The only value defined for the *ulFlags* bit flag is AB_NO_DIALOG, which suppresses the display of dialogs, a feature that server-based applications require.

Next, several buffers are allocated using *MAPIAllocateBuffer*, a simple function that takes the size of the buffer and the pointer to a pointer to the allocated memory. An address list for a single address and an array of three property values are allocated in separate calls.

Setting the recipients is a bit different than in the Simple MAPI example but similar in principal. With MAPI, a number of properties can be set. In FullMAPI.cpp, two are set.

```
pAdrList->cEntries = 1;
pAdrList->aEntries[0].cValues = 2;
pAdrList->aEntries[0].rgPropVals[0].ulPropTag   =
    PR_DISPLAY_NAME;
pAdrList->aEntries[0].rgPropVals[0].Value.lpszA =
    "Douglas Reilly";
pAdrList->aEntries[0].rgPropVals[1].ulPropTag   =
    PR_RECIPIENT_TYPE;
pAdrList->aEntries[0].rgPropVals[1].Value.l     =
    MAPI_TO;
hr = pAddrBook->ResolveName(0, 0, NULL, pAdrList);
```

Once again we have property tags and values. First the display name of the recipient is set, and the recipient is identified as a MAPI_TO recipient. Finally, since we have set only a display name, we need to call the *ResolveName* method of the *IMAPIAddrBook* interface to properly identify this recipient.

```
HRESULT ResolveName(
    ULONG ulUIParam,
    ULONG ulFlags,
    LPTSTR lpszNewEntryTitle,
    LPADRLIST lpAdrList
);
```

The first two parameters are passed as 0, and *lpszNewEntryTitle* is passed as NULL, since this parameter, used as a caption for a dialog box, should not be used. The parameter *lpAdrList* is an in-out pointer, and in FullMAPI.cpp we pass *pAddrList* as this parameter, allowing it to be modified to contain the proper address.

Next we allocate a buffer for five property values to be used for properties of the message. The properties are set as follows:

```
pr[0].ulPropTag    = PR_PRIORITY;
pr[0].Value.ul     = PRIO_NORMAL;
pr[1].ulPropTag    = PR_ORIGINATOR_DELIVERY_REPORT_REQUESTED;
pr[1].Value.b      = TRUE;
pr[2].ulPropTag    = PR_SUBJECT;
```

*(continued)*

```
pr[2].Value.lpszA = pStamp;
pr[3].ulPropTag   = PR_BODY;
pr[3].Value.lpszA = "This the body of the message.";
pr[4].ulPropTag   = PR_DELETE_AFTER_SUBMIT;
pr[4].Value.b     = TRUE;
```

We set the priority to normal, request delivery status reports, set the subject and the body, and request that the message is deleted after submission. The details of what is happening in MAPI are hidden from normal users because MAPI is virtually always accessed through a UI with behaviors such as moving messages from the Outbox to Sent Items when the message is sent. This is not native MAPI behavior, and if we don't specify that the message should be deleted after delivery, the message will remain in the Outbox after being sent.

Finally we call four methods of the *IMAPISession* interface to create the message, add the recipient, set the properties that have just been filled in, and actually submit the message. You can see this set of actions in the following code fragment from FullMAPI.cpp:

```
hr = folder[outboxidx].pfolder->CreateMessage(
    NULL, 0, &pMessage);
if (FAILED(hr))
{
    printf("Create Message");
    FREEBUFFS;
    return (-1);
}

hr = pMessage->ModifyRecipients(MODRECIP_ADD, pAdrList);
if (FAILED(hr))
{
    printf("ModifyRecipients");
    FREEBUFFS;
    return (-1);
}

hr = pMessage->SetProps(5, pr, &lpPropProblems);
if (FAILED(hr))
{
    printf("SetProps");
    FREEBUFFS;
    return (-1);
}

hr = pMessage->SubmitMessage(0);
if (FAILED(hr))
{
    printf("SubmitMessage %d ", hr);
    FREEBUFFS;
    return (-1);
}
```

First we create the message in the Outbox (to indicate it should be sent) by calling the *CreateMessage* method of the *IMAPIFolder* interface. We pass NULL for the first parameter to accept the default interface type, 0 for the second parameter, *ulFlags*, because there aren't any appropriate flags to set, and the address of our *IMAPIMessage* interface pointer, *pMessage*, as the final parameter. Next we call the *ModifyRecipients* method of the *IMAPIMessage* interface, adding the address list previously filled in. We set the properties using the *SetProperties* method of the *IMAPIMessage* interface, to which we pass the number of properties, the pointer to the properties, and a pointer to an *LPSPropProblemArray*. In FullMAPI.cpp, the pointer is set to NULL on entry and so is not updated. If the pointer were non-null, detailed information about setting properties would be filled in. At this point the message does not exist except in the memory system running this program. The message is actually sent when we call the *SubmitMessage* method of the *IMAPIMessage* interface.

**Cleaning up** When the session is done, we call the *Logoff* method of the *IMAPISession* interface:

```
HRESULT Logoff(
    ULONG ulUIParam,
    ULONG ulFlags,
    ULONG ulReserved
);
```

We pass all zeros as the parameters in this example because the UI should not appear, no appropriate flags are available, and the last parameter is reserved and must be 0. After we have logged off the session, we call *Release* on the session interface and set the pointer to the interface to NULL. We repeat this process for the address book, and then we call *MAPIUninitialize*. Once all MAPI operations are completed, we call *DeInitMAPI* to unload the MAPI DLL.

## Putting It All Together: Using MAPI and TAPI in a Service

You might want to put both TAPI and MAPI together in a Windows 2000 service. If the server encounters a problem, sending an e-mail first with a follow-up beep if the problem is not resolved can allow the server to run without constant monitoring. There are several areas to consider when adding support for TAPI and MAPI. MAPI requires a change to the C++ Windows 2000 *CPPService* class first introduced in Chapter 3 and updated for event logging in Chapter 5. Changes have been made to support MAPI in particular and COM in general. Listing 7-7 contains the updated CPPService.h. Listing 7-8 contains the updated CPPService.cpp. In both cases, I've noted changes to the code in the comments.

**CPPService.h**

```
#define SERVICE_CONTROL_USER 128

VOID StartThisService(char *serviceName);
class CPPService {
public:
    // Added for Chapter 7
    static unsigned long _stdcall MessagePumpThread(
    void *StillRunning);
    // Added for Chapter 5
    BOOL LogEvent(WORD wType, DWORD dwEventID, const char *ps1 = 0,
                            const char *ps2 = 0,
                            const char *ps3 = 0,
                            const char *ps4 = 0,
                            const char *ps5 = 0);
    // CreateMsgPump Added for Chapter 7
    CPPService(char *tsvcName, char *tdispName,
        DWORD tsvcStart = SERVICE_DEMAND_START,
        bool CreateMsgPump = false);
    virtual ~CPPService();
    BOOL IsInstalled();
    BOOL Install();
    BOOL UnInstall();
    BOOL StartService();
    void SetStatus(DWORD dwControl);
    BOOL Initialize();
    BOOL ParseArguments(int argc, char *argv[]);
    char *ServiceName()
    {
        return serviceName;
    }
    void SetUserAndPassword(char *user = NULL, char *pwd = NULL);
    virtual void OnInstall();
    virtual void OnUninstall();
    virtual BOOL OnInit(DWORD *status);
    virtual void Run();
    virtual void OnStop();
    virtual void OnPause();
    virtual void OnContinue();
    virtual BOOL OnUserControl(DWORD dwControl);
    virtual void OnParamChange();
    virtual void OnNetBindAdd();
    virtual void OnNetBindRemove();
    virtual void OnNetBindEnable();
    virtual void OnNetBindDisable();
```

**Listing 7-7**

```
#ifdef _WIN2K_COMPAT
    virtual void OnDeviceEvent(DWORD dwEventType, LPVOID pvEventData);
    virtual void OnPowerEvent(DWORD dwEventType, LPVOID pvEventData);
    virtual void OnHardwareProfileChange(DWORD dwEventType);
#endif
protected:
    SC_HANDLE m_scmHandle;
    SC_HANDLE m_scHandle;
    // Added for Chapter 5
    HANDLE m_EventHandle;

    SERVICE_STATUS ServiceStatus;
    SERVICE_STATUS_HANDLE ServiceStatusHandle;
    static CPPService *m_this;
    char serviceName[128];
    char serviceDisplayName[128];
    VOID logError(char *msg);
    FILE *log;
    char m_diag[255];
    DWORD m_svcStartType;
    DWORD m_status;
    BOOL m_isRunning;
    BOOL m_isPaused;
    // Added for Chapter 7
    BOOL m_CreateMsgPump;
#ifdef _WIN2K_COMPAT
    static DWORD WINAPI HandlerEx(DWORD dwControl, DWORD dwEventType,
        LPVOID lpEventData, LPVOID lpContext);
#else
    static VOID WINAPI Handler(DWORD dwControl);
#endif
    static VOID WINAPI ServiceMain(DWORD dwArgc, LPTSTR *lpszArgv);

};
```

**CPPService.cpp**

```
#include "Stdafx.h"
CPPService* CPPService::m_this = NULL;

VOID StartThisService(char *serviceName)
{
    SERVICE_STATUS ssStatus;
    DWORD dwOldCheckPoint;
```

**Listing 7-8** *(continued)*

**Listing 7-8** *continued*

```
SC_HANDLE schSCManager =
    OpenSCManager(NULL,      // Local machine
    NULL, // ServicesActive database
    SC_MANAGER_ALL_ACCESS); // Full access

printf("\nStarting Service...\n");
SC_HANDLE schService =
    OpenService(
    schSCManager,          // SCM database
    TEXT(serviceName),     // Service name
    SERVICE_ALL_ACCESS);
if (schService == NULL)
{
    printf("\nCan't Open Service...Last Error =%d",
        GetLastError());
    return;
}
if (!StartService(
    schService,  // Handle to service
    0,           // Number of arguments
    NULL))       // No arguments
{
    printf("\nStart Service failure...");
    return;
}
else
{
    printf("Service start pending\n");
}
// Check the status until the service is no longer start pending.
if (!QueryServiceStatus(
    schService,   // Handle to service
    &ssStatus))   // Address of status information
{
    printf("\nError in Query Service Status");
    return;
}

// Some services take a long time to start, so there is
//  an elaborate mechanism to handle that. This is not
//  very useful with the example services provided but
//  could be more so for more complex services.
while (ssStatus.dwCurrentState == SERVICE_START_PENDING)
```

```
    {
        // Save the current checkpoint.
        dwOldCheckPoint = ssStatus.dwCheckPoint;
        // Wait for the specified interval.
        Sleep(ssStatus.dwWaitHint);        // Check the status again.
        if (!QueryServiceStatus(
            schService,   // Handle to service
            &ssStatus))   // Address of status information
        {
            break;
        }
        // Break if the checkpoint has not been incremented.
        if (dwOldCheckPoint >= ssStatus.dwCheckPoint)
        {
            break;
        }
    }
    if (ssStatus.dwCurrentState == SERVICE_RUNNING)
    {
        printf("\nService Started\n");
    }
    else
    {
        printf("  Current State: %d\n",
            ssStatus.dwCurrentState);
        printf("  Exit Code: %d\n", ssStatus.dwWin32ExitCode);
        printf("  Service Specific Exit Code: %d\n",
            ssStatus.dwServiceSpecificExitCode);
        printf("  Check Point: %d\n", ssStatus.dwCheckPoint);
        printf("  Wait Hint: %d\n", ssStatus.dwWaitHint);
    }
    CloseServiceHandle(schService);
    CloseServiceHandle(schSCManager);
}

// CreateMsgPump Added for Chapter 7
CPPService::CPPService(char *tsvcName, char *tdispName,
                       DWORD tsvcStartType,
                       bool CreateMsgPump)
{
    strncpy(serviceName, tsvcName,128);
    strncpy(serviceDisplayName, tdispName,128);
    m_svcStartType = tsvcStartType;
    m_scmHandle = OpenSCManager(NULL,
```

*(continued)*

**Listing 7-8** *continued*

```
        SERVICES_ACTIVE_DATABASE,
        SC_MANAGER_ALL_ACCESS);
    if (m_scmHandle == NULL)
    {
        printf("\n OpenSCManager error %d ",
            GetLastError());
    }
    m_scHandle = 0;
    m_this = this;
    m_isRunning = false;
    m_isPaused = false;
    // Added for Chapter 5
    m_EventHandle = 0;
    // Added for Chapter 7
    m_CreateMsgPump = CreateMsgPump;

    ServiceStatus.dwServiceType        = SERVICE_WIN32_OWN_PROCESS;
    ServiceStatus.dwCurrentState       = SERVICE_START_PENDING;
    ServiceStatus.dwControlsAccepted   =
        SERVICE_ACCEPT_STOP | SERVICE_ACCEPT_PAUSE_CONTINUE;
    ServiceStatus.dwWin32ExitCode      = 0;
    ServiceStatus.dwServiceSpecificExitCode = 0;
    ServiceStatus.dwCheckPoint         = 0;
    ServiceStatus.dwWaitHint           = 0;
}

CPPService::~CPPService()
{
    if (m_scmHandle != 0)
    {
        ::CloseHandle(m_scmHandle);
    }
    if (m_scHandle != 0)
    {
        ::CloseHandle(m_scHandle);
    }
}

BOOL CPPService::ParseArguments(int argc, char **argv)
{
    BOOL result = false;
    if (argc > 1 && !(_strnicmp(argv[1], "-i", 2)))
    {
        if ((Install()))
        {
            printf("\n%s installed!", ServiceName());
        }
```

```
        else
        {
            printf("\n%s NOT installed!  Last error %d",
                ServiceName(), GetLastError());
        }
        result = true;
    }
    else if (argc > 1 && !(_strnicmp(argv[1], "-u", 2)))
    {
        if ((UnInstall()))
        {
            printf("\n%s uninstalled!", ServiceName());
        }
        else
        {
            printf("\n%s NOT uninstalled!  Last error %d",
                ServiceName(), GetLastError());
        }
        result = true;
    }
    return result;
}

VOID CPPService::logError(char *text)
{
    // Added for Chapter 5
    LogEvent(EVENTLOG_INFORMATION_TYPE,EVMSG_DEBUG,
        (const char *)text);
    // Removed for Chapter 5
//    log = fopen("c:\\service.log", "a+t");
//    if (log)
//    {
//        fprintf(log, "%s\n", text);
//        fclose(log);
//    }
    return;
}

BOOL CPPService::Install()
{
    char szPath[MAX_PATH];
    char szBuffer[MAX_PATH+2];

    // Added for Chapter 5
    char szKey[256];
```

*(continued)*

**Listing 7-8** *continued*

```
    HKEY hKey = NULL;
    // End Added for Chapter 5

    BOOL result = true;  // Default to success

    GetModuleFileName(GetModuleHandle(NULL), szPath, MAX_PATH);
    // Why do we do this? The path might contain spaces.
    //  If it does, the path must be quoted.
    strcpy(szBuffer, "\"");
    strcat(szBuffer, szPath);
    strcat(szBuffer, "\"");
    printf("\nInstalling service %s", szPath);

    m_scHandle = CreateService (m_scmHandle, serviceName,
        serviceDisplayName, SERVICE_ALL_ACCESS,
        SERVICE_WIN32_OWN_PROCESS,
        m_svcStartType,
        SERVICE_ERROR_NORMAL, szBuffer,
        NULL, NULL, NULL, NULL, NULL);

    if (m_scHandle == NULL) // process error
    {
        DWORD lastError;
        lastError = GetLastError();
        if (lastError == 1073) // Service already installed
        {
            wsprintf(m_diag, " CreateService error = "
                "Service Already Installed (1073)\n");
        }
        else
        {
            wsprintf(m_diag, " CreateService error = %d\n",
                lastError);
        }
        printf("%s\n", m_diag);
        logError(m_diag);
        result = false;
    }

    // Added for Chapter 5
    strcpy(szKey, "SYSTEM\\CurrentControlSet\\Services\\"
        "EventLog\\Application\\");
    strcat(szKey, ServiceName());
    if (::RegCreateKey(HKEY_LOCAL_MACHINE,
        szKey, &hKey) != ERROR_SUCCESS)
```

```
    {
        return FALSE;
    }

    // Add the Event ID Message file (in this case, the .EXE file).
    ::RegSetValueEx(hKey,
        "EventMessageFile",
        0,
        REG_EXPAND_SZ,
        (CONST BYTE*)szPath,
        strlen(szPath) + 1);

    // Set the supported types flags.
    DWORD dwData = EVENTLOG_ERROR_TYPE | EVENTLOG_WARNING_TYPE |
        EVENTLOG_INFORMATION_TYPE;

    ::RegSetValueEx(hKey,
        "TypesSupported",
        0,
        REG_DWORD,
        (CONST BYTE*)&dwData,
        sizeof(DWORD));
    ::RegCloseKey(hKey);
    // End Added for Chapter 5

    OnInstall();
    return result;
}

BOOL CPPService::StartService()
{
    SERVICE_TABLE_ENTRY DispatchTable[] = {
        {serviceName, CPPService::ServiceMain},
        {NULL, NULL}
    };

    BOOL b = ::StartServiceCtrlDispatcher(DispatchTable);
    // Added for Chapter 5
    if (b)
    {
        // No strings needed for this message.
        LogEvent(EVENTLOG_INFORMATION_TYPE, EVMSG_STARTED);
    }
    // End Added for Chapter 5
    return b;
}
```

*(continued)*

**Listing 7-8** *continued*

```
BOOL CPPService::UnInstall()
{
    m_scHandle = OpenService(m_scmHandle, serviceName,
        SERVICE_ALL_ACCESS);
    if (m_scHandle != NULL)
    {
        DeleteService(m_scHandle);
        printf("\n%s uninstalled...", serviceName);
//        CloseHandle(m_scHandle);
        m_scHandle = 0;
        // Added for Chapter 5
        LogEvent(EVENTLOG_INFORMATION_TYPE,
            EVMSG_REMOVED, ServiceName());
        // End Added for Chapter 5
        OnUninstall();
        return (true);
    }
    printf("\nOpen Service error: %d ", GetLastError());
    return (false);
}

void CPPService::SetStatus(DWORD dwControl)
{
    ServiceStatus.dwCurrentState        = dwControl;
    ServiceStatus.dwCheckPoint          = 0;
    ServiceStatus.dwWaitHint            = 0;

    if (!SetServiceStatus (ServiceStatusHandle, &ServiceStatus))
    {
        m_status = GetLastError();
        wsprintf(m_diag,
            " %s SetServiceStatus error %ld dwControl =%d\n",
            serviceName, m_status, dwControl);
        logError(m_diag);
    }
}

VOID WINAPI CPPService::ServiceMain(DWORD argc, LPTSTR *argv)
{
    BOOL initStat;
    DWORD specificError;
    CPPService *thisPtr;

    thisPtr = m_this;
```

```
#ifdef _WIN2K_COMPAT
    char szContext[255];
    strcpy(szContext, thisPtr->ServiceName());
    thisPtr->ServiceStatusHandle = RegisterServiceCtrlHandlerEx(
        thisPtr->ServiceName,
        HandlerEx,
        &szContext);
#else
    thisPtr->ServiceStatusHandle = RegisterServiceCtrlHandler(
        thisPtr->serviceName,
        Handler);
#endif
    if (thisPtr->ServiceStatusHandle == (SERVICE_STATUS_HANDLE)0)
    {
        wsprintf(thisPtr->m_diag,
            " RegisterServiceCtrlHandler failed %d",
            GetLastError());
        thisPtr->logError(thisPtr->m_diag);
        return;
    }

    thisPtr->SetStatus(SERVICE_START_PENDING);
    // Initialization code goes here.

    initStat = thisPtr->OnInit(&specificError);

    // Handle error condition
    if (initStat == false)
    {
        thisPtr->SetStatus(SERVICE_STOPPED);
        wsprintf(thisPtr->m_diag,
            "OnInit failed initStat =%d...", initStat);
        thisPtr->logError(thisPtr->m_diag);
        return;
    }

    thisPtr->SetStatus(SERVICE_RUNNING);
    thisPtr->m_isRunning = true;

    // Added for Chapter 7
    if (thisPtr->m_CreateMsgPump)
    {
         wsprintf(thisPtr->m_diag, "Starting Message Pump"
             " Thread...\n");
         DWORD dwCreationFlags = 0;
```

*(continued)*

**Listing 7-8** *continued*

```
        DWORD dwThreadID = 0;
        CreateThread(NULL, 0, MessagePumpThread,
            &thisPtr->m_isRunning,
            dwCreationFlags,
            &dwThreadID);
    }

    wsprintf(thisPtr->m_diag, "Just before processing loop...\n");
    thisPtr->logError(thisPtr->m_diag);
    // This is where the service does its work.

    thisPtr->Run();

    // Send current status.
    thisPtr->SetStatus(SERVICE_STOPPED);

    return;
}

#ifdef _WIN2K_COMPAT
DWORD WINAPI CPPService::HandlerEx(DWORD dwControl, DWORD dwEventType,
    LPVOID lpEventData, LPVOID lpContext)
{
    DWORD status = SERVICE_RUNNING;
    CPPService *thisPtr;

    thisPtr = m_this;

    wsprintf(thisPtr->m_diag, "IN to service Control...\n");
    thisPtr->logError(thisPtr->m_diag);
    switch(dwControl)
    {
        case SERVICE_CONTROL_PAUSE:
        // Do whatever it takes to pause here.
            wsprintf(thisPtr->m_diag, "Pausing...\n");
            thisPtr->logError(thisPtr->m_diag);
            if (!(thisPtr->m_isPaused))
            {
                thisPtr->m_isPaused = true;
                thisPtr->OnPause();
                status = SERVICE_PAUSED;
            }
            break;
```

```
case SERVICE_CONTROL_CONTINUE:
// Do whatever it takes to continue here.
    sprintf(thisPtr->m_diag, "Continuing...\n");
    thisPtr->logError(thisPtr->m_diag);
    if (thisPtr->m_isPaused)
    {
        thisPtr->OnContinue();
        thisPtr->m_isPaused = false;
        status = SERVICE_RUNNING;
    }
    break;

case SERVICE_CONTROL_STOP:
// Do whatever it takes to stop here.
    wsprintf(thisPtr->m_diag, "Stopping...\n");
    thisPtr->logError(thisPtr->m_diag);
    if (thisPtr->m_isRunning)
    {
        thisPtr->OnStop();
        status = SERVICE_STOP_PENDING;
        thisPtr->m_isRunning = false;
    }

    thisPtr->SetStatus (status);
    wsprintf(thisPtr->m_diag,
        " Service Leaving Handler \n", 0);
    thisPtr->logError(thisPtr->m_diag);
    return;

case SERVICE_CONTROL_PARAMCHANGE:
    thisPtr->OnParamChange();
    break;

case SERVICE_CONTROL_NETBINDADD:
    thisPtr->OnNetBindAdd();
    break;

case SERVICE_CONTROL_NETBINDDELETE:
    thisPtr->OnNetBindDelete();
    break;

case SERVICE_CONTROL_NETBINDREMOVE:
    thisPtr->OnNetBindRemove();
    break;
```

*(continued)*

**Listing 7-8** *continued*

```
        case SERVICE_CONTROL_NETBINDENABLE:
            thisPtr->OnNetBindEnable();
            break;

        case SERVICE_CONTROL_NETBINDDISABLE:
            thisPtr->OnNetBindDisable();
            break;

        case SERVICE_CONTROL_DEVICEEVENT:
            thisPtr->OnDeviceEvent(dwEventType, lpEventData);
            break;

        case SERVICE_CONTROL_POWEREVENT:
            thisPtr->OnPowerEvent(dwEventType, lpEventData);
            break;

        case SERVICE_CONTROL_HARDWAREPROFILECHANGE:
            thisPtr->OnHardwareProfileChange(dwEventType);
            break;

        case SERVICE_CONTROL_INTERROGATE:
        // Fall through to send current status.
            break;

        default:
            if (dwControl >= SERVICE_CONTROL_USER)
            {
                if (!thisPtr->OnUserControl(dwControl))
                {
                    wsprintf(thisPtr->m_diag,
                        " %s Unhandled control code %ld\n",
                        thisPtr->ServiceName(),
                        dwControl);
                    thisPtr->logError(thisPtr->m_diag);
                }
            }
            else
            {
                wsprintf(thisPtr->m_diag,
                    " %s Unrecognized control code %ld\n",
                    thisPtr->ServiceName(),
                    dwControl);
                thisPtr->logError(thisPtr->m_diag);
            }
            break;
    }
```

```
    // Send current status.
    thisPtr->SetStatus (status);
    return 0;
}
#else
VOID WINAPI CPPService::Handler(DWORD dwControl)
{
    DWORD status = SERVICE_RUNNING;
    CPPService *thisPtr;

    thisPtr = m_this;

    wsprintf(thisPtr->m_diag, "IN to service Control...\n");
    thisPtr->logError(thisPtr->m_diag);
    switch(dwControl)
    {
        case SERVICE_CONTROL_PAUSE:
        // Do whatever it takes to pause here.
            wsprintf(thisPtr->m_diag, "Pausing...\n");
            thisPtr->logError(thisPtr->m_diag);
            if (!(thisPtr->m_isPaused))
            {
                thisPtr->m_isPaused = true;
                thisPtr->OnPause();
                status = SERVICE_PAUSED;
            }
            break;

        case SERVICE_CONTROL_CONTINUE:
        // Do whatever it takes to continue here.
            wsprintf(thisPtr->m_diag, "Continuing...\n");
            thisPtr->logError(thisPtr->m_diag);
            if (thisPtr->m_isPaused)
            {
                thisPtr->OnContinue();
                thisPtr->m_isPaused = false;
                status = SERVICE_RUNNING;
            }
            break;

        case SERVICE_CONTROL_STOP:
        // Do whatever it takes to stop here.
            // Removed for Chapter 5
//            wsprintf(thisPtr->m_diag, "Stopping...\n");
//            thisPtr->logError(thisPtr->m_diag);
            if (thisPtr->m_isRunning)
```

*(continued)*

**Listing 7-8** *continued*

```
        {
            thisPtr->OnStop();
            // Added for Chapter 5
            thisPtr->LogEvent(
                EVENTLOG_INFORMATION_TYPE,
                EVMSG_STOPPED,
                thisPtr->ServiceName());
            // End Added for Chapter 5
            status = SERVICE_STOP_PENDING;
            thisPtr->m_isRunning = false;
        }

            thisPtr->SetStatus (status);
            wsprintf(thisPtr->m_diag,
                " BeeperService Leaving Handler \n",0);
            thisPtr->logError(thisPtr->m_diag);
            return;

    case SERVICE_CONTROL_PARAMCHANGE:
        thisPtr->OnParamChange();
        break;

    case SERVICE_CONTROL_NETBINDADD:
        thisPtr->OnNetBindAdd();
        break;

    case SERVICE_CONTROL_NETBINDDISABLE:
        thisPtr->OnNetBindDisable();
        break;

    case SERVICE_CONTROL_NETBINDREMOVE:
        thisPtr->OnNetBindRemove();
        break;

    case SERVICE_CONTROL_NETBINDENABLE:
        thisPtr->OnNetBindEnable();
        break;

    case SERVICE_CONTROL_INTERROGATE:
    // Fall through to send current status.
        break;

    default:
        if (dwControl >= SERVICE_CONTROL_USER)
        {
```

```
                if (!thisPtr->OnUserControl(dwControl))
                {
                    wsprintf(thisPtr->m_diag,
                        " %s Unhandled control code %ld\n",
                        thisPtr->ServiceName(),
                        dwControl);
                    thisPtr->logError(thisPtr->m_diag);
                }
            }
            else
            {
                wsprintf(thisPtr->m_diag,
                    " %s Unrecognized control code %ld\n",
                    thisPtr->ServiceName(),
                    dwControl);
                thisPtr->logError(thisPtr->m_diag);
            }
            break;
    }

    // Send current status.
    thisPtr->SetStatus (status);
    return;
}
#endif

// Virtual functions, generally overridden if needed.
BOOL CPPService::OnUserControl(DWORD dwControl)
{
    LogEvent(EVENTLOG_INFORMATION_TYPE, EVMSG_DEBUG, "OnContinue");
    return false;
}

void CPPService::OnContinue()
{
    LogEvent(EVENTLOG_INFORMATION_TYPE, EVMSG_DEBUG, "OnContinue");
    return;
}

void CPPService::OnPause()
{
    LogEvent(EVENTLOG_INFORMATION_TYPE, EVMSG_DEBUG, "OnPause");
    return;
}
```

*(continued)*

**Listing 7-8** *continued*

```
void CPPService::OnStop()
{
    LogEvent(EVENTLOG_INFORMATION_TYPE, EVMSG_DEBUG, "OnStop");
    return;
}

void CPPService::OnInstall()
{
    LogEvent(EVENTLOG_INFORMATION_TYPE, EVMSG_DEBUG, "OnInstall");
    return;
}

void CPPService::OnUninstall()
{
    LogEvent(EVENTLOG_INFORMATION_TYPE, EVMSG_DEBUG, "OnUninstall");
    return;
}

BOOL CPPService::OnInit(DWORD *status)
{
    LogEvent(EVENTLOG_INFORMATION_TYPE, EVMSG_DEBUG, "OnInit");
    *status = 0;
    return true;
}

void CPPService::OnParamChange()
{
    LogEvent(EVENTLOG_INFORMATION_TYPE, EVMSG_DEBUG, "OnParamChange");
    return;
}

void CPPService::OnNetBindAdd()
{
    LogEvent(EVENTLOG_INFORMATION_TYPE, EVMSG_DEBUG, "OnNetBindAdd");
    return;
}

void CPPService::OnNetBindRemove()
{
    LogEvent(EVENTLOG_INFORMATION_TYPE, EVMSG_DEBUG,
        "OnNetBindRemove");
    return;
}
```

```
void CPPService::OnNetBindEnable()
{
    LogEvent(EVENTLOG_INFORMATION_TYPE, EVMSG_DEBUG,
        "OnNetBindEnable");
    return;
}

void CPPService::OnNetBindDisable()
{
    LogEvent(EVENTLOG_INFORMATION_TYPE, EVMSG_DEBUG,
        "OnNetBindDisable");
    return;
}

void CPPService::Run()
{
    while (m_isRunning)
    {
        Sleep(1000);
    }
    return;
}

#ifdef _WIN2K_COMPAT

void OnDeviceEvent(DWORD dwEventType,LPVOID pvEventData)
{
    LogEvent(EVENTLOG_INFORMATION_TYPE, EVMSG_DEBUG,
        "OnDeviceEvent");
    return;
}

void OnPowerEvent(DWORD dwEventType,LPVOID pvEventData)
{
    LogEvent(EVENTLOG_INFORMATION_TYPE, EVMSG_DEBUG, "OnPowerEvent");
    return;
}

void OnHardwareProfileChange(DWORD dwEventType)
{
    LogEvent(EVENTLOG_INFORMATION_TYPE, EVMSG_DEBUG,
        "OnHardwareProfileChange");
    return;
}
```

*(continued)*

**Listing 7-8** *continued*

```
#endif

// Added for Chapter Five
BOOL CPPService::LogEvent(WORD wType, DWORD dwEventID,
                const char *ps1,
                const char *ps2,
                const char *ps3,
                const char *ps4,
                const char *ps5)
{
    WORD wNumStrings;
    const char *pStrings[5];

    if (m_EventHandle == 0)
    {
        m_EventHandle = ::RegisterEventSource(NULL, ServiceName());
    }
    if (m_EventHandle != 0)
    {
        wNumStrings = 0;
        if (ps1 != 0)
        {
            pStrings[wNumStrings] = ps1;
            wNumStrings++;
            if (ps2 != 0)
            {
                pStrings[wNumStrings] = ps2;
                wNumStrings++;
                if (ps3 != 0)
                {
                    pStrings[wNumStrings] = ps3;
                    wNumStrings++;
                    if (ps4 != 0)
                    {
                        pStrings[wNumStrings] = ps4;
                        wNumStrings++;
                        if (ps5 != 0)
                        {
                            pStrings[wNumStrings] = ps5;
                            wNumStrings++;
                        }
                    }
                }
            }
        }
```

```
        ::ReportEvent(m_EventHandle, wType, 0, dwEventID, NULL,
            wNumStrings, 0, pStrings, NULL);

        return true;
    }
    return false;
}
// End added for Chapter 5

// Added for Chapter 7
unsigned long _stdcall CPPService::MessagePumpThread(
    void *StillRunning)
{

    MSG msg;
    HACCEL hAccelTable = 0;
    CPPService *thisPtr;

    thisPtr = m_this;

    while (GetMessage(&msg, NULL, 0, 0) && thisPtr->m_isRunning)
    {
        if (!TranslateAccelerator(msg.hwnd, hAccelTable, &msg))
        {
            TranslateMessage(&msg);
            DispatchMessage(&msg);
        }
    }
    return (0);
}
// End Added for Chapter 7
```

All the changes to *CPPService* are related to adding support for a message pump, which is required for MAPI. The message pump is placed in a separate thread, and the thread monitors the *m_isRunning* flag. I added a flag to the *CPPService* constructor to determine whether a message pump should be created. The default value for the flag is *false*. If this flag is *true*, the following code is executed during the *ServiceMain* method:

```
// Added for Chapter 7
if (thisPtr->m_CreateMsgPump)
{
    wsprintf(thisPtr->m_diag,"Starting Message Pump Thread...\n");
    DWORD dwCreationFlags = 0;
    DWORD dwThreadID = 0;
```

*(continued)*

```
        CreateThread(NULL, 0, MessagePumpThread,
            &thisPtr->m_isRunning,
            dwCreationFlags,
            &dwThreadID);
}
```

A message is written to the event log if the flag is set as an aid to diagnostics. The thread function *MessagePumpThread* is a static member function declared as *stdcall*. The pointer to the *m_isRunning* member variable is sent as the argument to the thread function. *MessagePumpThread* is a simple message pump—it calls *GetMessage*, checks the value of *m_isRunning*, and breaks when *GetMessage* returns 0 or *m_isRunning* is *false*.

### CTAPIMAPIService

Inheriting from *CPPService,* I created a new class, *CTAPIMAPIService*. This class adds functions based upon the TAPI and MAPI code from Listings 7-2 and 7-6, respectively. I modified most of the code from these previous examples simply to change from displaying messages on the screen to writing the messages to the event log. Using the code from the previous examples, the *CallBeeper* method is called during the *Run* method, and a new function based upon the main function in Listing 7-6, named *SendMapiMessage*, is called. Obviously the phone numbers and names used for the e-mail should be modified for your applications. A more useful example in Chapter 14 will call a beeper or send e-mail as the result of a specific event.

Listing 7-9 contains the headers for *CTAPIMAPIService* and Listing 7-10 contains the source.

**MapiInit.h**

```
#define SZ_MAPIINITIALIZE           "MAPIInitialize"
#define SZ_MAPIUNINITIALIZE         "MAPIUninitialize"
#define SZ_MAPILOGONEX              "MAPILogonEx"
#define SZ_MAPIFREEBUFFER           "MAPIFreeBuffer"
#define SZ_MAPIALLOCATEBUFFER       "MAPIAllocateBuffer"
#define SZ_HRGETONEPROP             "HrGetOneProp@12"
#define SZ_HRQUERYALLROWS           "HrQueryAllRows@24"
#define SZ_FREEPROWS                "FreeProws@4"
#define SZ_FREEPADRLIST             "FreePadrlist@4"

#define MAPIDLL "MAPI32.DLL"
#define ERR_LOAD_LIB  0x02
#define ERR_LOAD_FUNC 0x04

typedef VOID    (FAR PASCAL *PFNFREEPADRLIST       )
    (LPADRLIST pAdrList);
```

**Listing 7-9**

```
typedef VOID    (FAR PASCAL *PFNFREEPROWS          )(LPSRowSet prows);
typedef HRESULT (FAR PASCAL *PFNHRGETONEPROP       )(LPMAPIPROP,
    ULONG, LPSPropValue FAR *);
typedef HRESULT (FAR PASCAL *PFNMAPIINITIALIZE     )(LPVOID);
typedef HRESULT (FAR PASCAL *PFNHRQUERYALLROWS     )(LPMAPITABLE,
    LPSPropTagArray, LPSRestriction, LPSSortOrderSet, LONG,
    LPSRowSet FAR *);
typedef VOID    (FAR PASCAL *PFNMAPIUNINITIALIZE  )(void);
typedef HRESULT (FAR PASCAL *PFNMAPILOGONEX        )
    (ULONG, LPTSTR, LPTSTR, FLAGS, LPMAPISESSION FAR *);
typedef ULONG   (FAR PASCAL *PFNMAPIFREEBUFFER     )
    (LPVOID);
typedef SCODE   (FAR PASCAL *PFNMAPIALLOCATEBUFFER)
    (ULONG, LPVOID FAR *);

int PASCAL InitMAPI(void);
int PASCAL DeInitMAPI(void);
```

**StdAfx.h**

```
// stdafx.h : include file for standard system include files,
//  or project-specific include files that are used frequently but
//  are changed infrequently.
//

#if !defined(AFX_STDAFX_H__9B829C11_5BC2_11D3_B4AE_00C04F79B510__
INCLUDED_)
#define AFX_STDAFX_H__9B829C11_5BC2_11D3_B4AE_00C04F79B510__INCLUDED_

#if _MSC_VER > 1000
#pragma once
#endif // _MSC_VER > 1000

#define WIN32_LEAN_AND_MEAN         // Exclude rarely used stuff from
                                    //  Windows headers

#include <stdio.h>
#include <windows.h>
#include <stdlib.h>
extern "C" {
#include <process.h>
}
#include <tapi.h>
#include <stdio.h>
```

*(continued)*

**Listing 7-9** *continued*

```
#include <mapi.h>
#include <mapix.h>
#include "mapiinit.h"
#include <initguid.h>
#include <mapitags.h>
#include "cppservice.h"
#include "cppsvcmsg.h"
#include "CTapiMapiService.h"

// TODO: reference additional headers your program requires here

//{{AFX_INSERT_LOCATION}}
// Microsoft Visual C++ will insert additional
//  declarations immediately before the previous line.

#endif
// !defined(AFX_STDAFX_H__9B829C11_5BC2_11D3_B4AE_00C04F79B510__
INCLUDED_)
```

**CTAPIMAPIService.h**

```
class CTAPIMAPIService : public CPPService
{
public:
    CTAPIMAPIService(char *tsvcName, char *tdispName,
        DWORD tsvcStart = SERVICE_DEMAND_START,
        bool CreateMsgPump = true);
    virtual BOOL OnInit(DWORD *status);
    virtual void Run();
    virtual void OnInstall();
    void ReportTAPIError(LONG ret, char *op);
    int CallBeeper(char *beeperNumber, char *beepTo);
    int SendMapiMessage(char *szTo,
        char *szMessage, char *szNote);
    void GetFoldersHierarchy(char *name,
        IMAPIFolder *pfolder,
        short int depth);
    void GetRootFolder(void);
};
```

**CTAPIMAPIService.cpp**

```
// CTAPIMAPIService.cpp : Defines the entry point for the console
//  application
```

**Listing 7-10**

```
#include "stdafx.h"

// These are MAPI items.
#include <mapiguid.h>

PFNHRQUERYALLROWS      lpfnHrQueryAllRows;
PFNHRGETONEPROP        lpfnHrGetOneProp;
PFNMAPIALLOCATEBUFFER lpfnMAPIAllocateBuffer;
PFNMAPIFREEBUFFER      lpfnMAPIFreeBuffer;
PFNMAPIINITIALIZE      lpfnMAPIInitialize;
PFNMAPIUNINITIALIZE    lpfnMAPIUninitialize;
PFNMAPILOGONEX         lpfnMAPILogonEx;
PFNFREEPROWS           lpfnFreeProws;
PFNFREEPADRLIST        lpfnFreePadrlist;

HMODULE hLibrary;

IMsgStore      *pmdb        = NULL;
IMAPISession   *psess       = NULL;
IMAPIFolder    *prootfolder = NULL;
IAddrBook      *pAddrBook   = NULL;
ULONG nfolders = 0;

typedef struct {
    short int k;
    char        *name;
    short int    depth;
    SBinary     *pbv;
    SRowSet     *prs;
    IMAPIFolder *pfolder;
    IMAPITable  *pcontentstable;
} FOLDER;
FOLDER folder[200];

int inboxidx   = -1;
int deletedidx = -1;
int sentidx    = -1;
int outboxidx  = -1;

char *pInboxName     = "Inbox";
char *pDeletedName   = "Deleted Items";
char *pSentItemsName = "Sent Items";
char *pOutboxName    = "Outbox";

char ename[512];
```

*(continued)*

**Listing 7-10** *continued*

```
void GetFoldersHierarchy(char *name, IMAPIFolder *pfolder,
    short int depth);
void AssignInOutSentDel();
#define FREEBUFFS if (pMessage) pMessage->Release(); \
    if (lpPropProblems) \
        (lpfnMAPIFreeBuffer)(lpPropProblems); \
    if (pr) (lpfnMAPIFreeBuffer)(pr); \
    if (pAdrList) (lpfnFreePadrlist)(pAdrList);

CTAPIMAPIService::CTAPIMAPIService(char *tsvcName,
    char *tdispName, DWORD tsvcStart, bool CreateMsgPump)
: CPPService(tsvcName, tdispName, tsvcStart, CreateMsgPump)
{
    ;
}

BOOL CTAPIMAPIService::OnInit(DWORD *status)
{
    logError("OnInit");
    *status = 0;
    return true;
}

void CTAPIMAPIService::Run()
{
    bool sentBeep = false;
    // A do-nothing loop
    while (m_isRunning)
    {
        if (m_isPaused == false)
        {
            Beep(2000, 200);
        }
        if (!(sentBeep))
        {
            CallBeeper("555-5166", "555-1605");
            SendMapiMessage("Douglas Reilly", "Message From Service",
                "This is the text of the message from the service.\n"
                "This could contain anything from an alert to"
                " information on system status");
            sentBeep = true;
        }
        Sleep(1000);
    }
    return;
}
```

```
void CTAPIMAPIService::OnInstall()
{
//    printf("\nAbout to start service...");
    ::StartThisService(ServiceName());
}

int CTAPIMAPIService::CallBeeper(char *beeperNumber, char *beepTo)
{
    HLINEAPP hLineApp;
    HLINE hLine;
    char szFriendlyAppName[255];
    char szAddress[255];
    DWORD dwNumDevs = 0;
    DWORD dwAPIVersion = 0x00020000;
    // Just a lucky number, NOT interpreted by TAPI
    DWORD dwCallbackInstance = 43;
    DWORD dwStatus;
    DWORD dwDeviceID = 0;
    LONG ret;
    LINEINITIALIZEEXPARAMS LineInitializeExParams;
    LINEEXTENSIONID ExtensionID;
    LPLINEDEVCAPS DevCaps = NULL;

    strcpy(szFriendlyAppName, "TAPI Beeper Program");
    memset((void *)&LineInitializeExParams, 0,
        sizeof(LINEINITIALIZEEXPARAMS));
    LineInitializeExParams.dwTotalSize =
        sizeof(LINEINITIALIZEEXPARAMS);
    LineInitializeExParams.dwOptions =
        LINEINITIALIZEEXOPTION_USEEVENT;

    ret = lineInitializeEx(&hLineApp, NULL, NULL, szFriendlyAppName,
        &dwNumDevs,&dwAPIVersion, &LineInitializeExParams);
    ReportTAPIError(ret, "lineInitializeEx");
    if (ret == 0)
    {
        // It worked!
        // Loop through available devices until we find a good one
        for (dwDeviceID = 0; dwDeviceID < dwNumDevs; dwDeviceID++)
        {
            ret = lineNegotiateAPIVersion(
                hLineApp,
                dwDeviceID,
                0x00020000,
                0x00020001,
                &dwAPIVersion,
                &ExtensionID);
```

*(continued)*

**Listing 7-10** *continued*

```
        if (ret == 0)
        {
            ret = lineOpen(hLineApp, dwDeviceID, &hLine,
                dwAPIVersion, 0, dwCallbackInstance,
                LINECALLPRIVILEGE_NONE, 0, 0);
            ReportTAPIError(ret, "lineOpen");
            if (ret == 0)
            {
                break;
            }
        }
    }
    ReportTAPIError(ret, "lineNegotiateAPIVersion");
    if (ret == 0)
    {

        HCALL hCall;
        char szLineName[255];

        DevCaps = (LPLINEDEVCAPS)new char[1024];
        DevCaps->dwTotalSize = 1024;
        ret = lineGetDevCaps(hLineApp,
            dwDeviceID,
            dwAPIVersion,0,DevCaps);
        ReportTAPIError(ret, "lineGetDevCaps");
        if (ret >= 0 && DevCaps->dwLineNameSize > 0)
        {
            char buffer[255];
            if (DevCaps->dwLineNameSize > (254))
            {
                strncpy (szLineName,
                    (LPSTR) DevCaps +
                    DevCaps->dwLineNameOffset,254);
                szLineName[ 254 ] = '\0';
            }
            else
            {
                lstrcpy(szLineName, (LPSTR) DevCaps +
                    DevCaps->dwLineNameOffset);
            }
            wsprintf(buffer, "Line name is %s", szLineName);
            LogEvent(EVENTLOG_INFORMATION_TYPE,
                EVMSG_DEBUG, (const char *)buffer);
        }
```

```
delete (char *)DevCaps;

// Set the MAPI address, which is really a phone number.
wsprintf(szAddress, "%s,,,%s#", beeperNumber, beepTo);
ret = lineMakeCall(hLine, &hCall, szAddress, 0, 0);
if (ret > 0)
{
    char buffer[255];
    wsprintf(buffer, "lineMakeCall returned %d", ret);
    LogEvent(EVENTLOG_INFORMATION_TYPE,
        EVMSG_DEBUG, (const char *)buffer);
}
ReportTAPIError(ret, "lineMakeCall");

while ((dwStatus = WaitForSingleObject(
    LineInitializeExParams.Handles.hEvent,
    20000)) == WAIT_OBJECT_0)
{
    LINEMESSAGE lm;
    // TAPI's returning some information.
    if ((ret = lineGetMessage(hLineApp, &lm, 0)) != 0)
        {
        ReportTAPIError(ret, "lineGetMessage");
            return (ret);
    }
    switch (lm.dwMessageID)
    {
    case LINE_REPLY:
        if ((long)lm.dwParam2 < 0)
        {
            char buffer[255];
            wsprintf(buffer,
                "Error occured...Request ID %d",
                lm.dwParam1);
            LogEvent(EVENTLOG_INFORMATION_TYPE,
                EVMSG_DEBUG,
                (const char *)buffer);
        }
        break;
    case LINE_CALLSTATE:
        if (LINECALLSTATE_DIALTONE&lm.dwParam1)
        {
            char buffer[255];
            wsprintf(buffer, "Dialtone Detected");
```

*(continued)*

**Listing 7-10** *continued*

```
                LogEvent(EVENTLOG_INFORMATION_TYPE,
                    EVMSG_DEBUG,
                    (const char *)buffer);
            }
            if (LINECALLSTATE_DIALING&lm.dwParam1)
            {
                char buffer[255];
                wsprintf(buffer, "Dialing");
                LogEvent(EVENTLOG_INFORMATION_TYPE,
                    EVMSG_DEBUG,
                    (const char *)buffer);
            }

            if (LINECALLSTATE_RINGBACK&lm.dwParam1)
            {
                char buffer[255];
                wsprintf(buffer, "Ringing");
                LogEvent(EVENTLOG_INFORMATION_TYPE,
                    EVMSG_DEBUG,
                    (const char *)buffer);
            }

            if (LINECALLSTATE_BUSY&lm.dwParam1)
            {
                char buffer[255];
                wsprintf(buffer, "Busy");
                LogEvent(EVENTLOG_INFORMATION_TYPE,
                    EVMSG_DEBUG,
                    (const char *)buffer);
            }

            if (LINECALLSTATE_PROCEEDING&lm.dwParam1)
            {
                char buffer[255];
                wsprintf(buffer, "Proceeding");
                LogEvent(EVENTLOG_INFORMATION_TYPE,
                    EVMSG_DEBUG,
                    (const char *)buffer);
            }

            if (LINECALLSTATE_CONNECTED&lm.dwParam1)
            {
                char buffer[255];
                wsprintf(buffer, "Connecting");
```

```
                    LogEvent(EVENTLOG_INFORMATION_TYPE,
                        EVMSG_DEBUG,
                        (const char *)buffer);
                }

                if (LINECALLSTATE_DISCONNECTED&lm.dwParam1)
                {
                    char buffer[255];
                    wsprintf(buffer, "Disconnected");
                    LogEvent(EVENTLOG_INFORMATION_TYPE,
                        EVMSG_DEBUG,
                        (const char *)buffer);
                    lineClose(hLine);
                }

                if (LINECALLSTATE_IDLE&lm.dwParam1)
                {
                    char buffer[255];
                    wsprintf(buffer, "Idle");
                    LogEvent(EVENTLOG_INFORMATION_TYPE,
                        EVMSG_DEBUG,
                        (const char *)buffer);
                    lineClose(hLine);
                }
            } //...switch (lm.dwMessageID)
        } //...while ((dwStatus = WaitForSingleObject(
    } //...if (ret == 0)
    }
    lineShutdown(hLineApp);
    return 0;
}

void CTAPIMAPIService::ReportTAPIError(LONG ret, char *op)
{
    char buffer[255];
    switch (ret)
    {
    case LINEERR_INVALAPPNAME:
        wsprintf(buffer, "op=%s Ret=LINEERR_INVALAPPNAME",  op);
        LogEvent(EVENTLOG_ERROR_TYPE, EVMSG_DEBUG,
                    (const char *)buffer);
        break;
    case LINEERR_OPERATIONFAILED:
        wsprintf(buffer,"op=%s Ret=LINEERR_OPERATIONFAILED", op);
```

*(continued)*

**Listing 7-10** *continued*

```
            LogEvent(EVENTLOG_ERROR_TYPE, EVMSG_DEBUG,
                        (const char *)buffer);
            break;
        case LINEERR_INIFILECORRUPT:
            wsprintf(buffer,"op=%s Ret=LINEERR_INIFILECORRUPT", op);
            LogEvent(EVENTLOG_ERROR_TYPE, EVMSG_DEBUG,
                        (const char *)buffer);
            break;
        case LINEERR_INVALPOINTER:
            wsprintf(buffer,"op=%s Ret=LINEERR_INVALPOINTER", op);
            LogEvent(EVENTLOG_ERROR_TYPE, EVMSG_DEBUG,
                        (const char *)buffer);
            break;
        case LINEERR_REINIT:
            wsprintf(buffer,"op=%s Ret=LINEERR_REINIT", op);
            LogEvent(EVENTLOG_ERROR_TYPE, EVMSG_DEBUG,
                        (const char *)buffer);
            break;
        case LINEERR_NOMEM:
            wsprintf(buffer,"op=%s Ret=LINEERR_NOMEM", op);
            LogEvent(EVENTLOG_ERROR_TYPE, EVMSG_DEBUG,
                        (const char *)buffer);
            break;
        case LINEERR_INVALPARAM:
            wsprintf(buffer,"op=%s Ret=LINEERR_INVALPARAM", op);
            LogEvent(EVENTLOG_ERROR_TYPE, EVMSG_DEBUG,
                        (const char *)buffer);
            break;
        case LINEERR_BADDEVICEID:
            wsprintf(buffer,"op=%s Ret=LINEERR_BADDEVICEID", op);
            LogEvent(EVENTLOG_ERROR_TYPE, EVMSG_DEBUG,
                        (const char *)buffer);
            break;
        case LINEERR_NODRIVER:
            wsprintf(buffer,"op=%s Ret=LINEERR_NODRIVER", op);
            LogEvent(EVENTLOG_ERROR_TYPE, EVMSG_DEBUG,
                        (const char *)buffer);
            break;
        case LINEERR_INCOMPATIBLEAPIVERSION:
            wsprintf(buffer,"op=%s Ret=LINEERR_INCOMPATIBLEAPIVERSION",
                op);
            LogEvent(EVENTLOG_ERROR_TYPE, EVMSG_DEBUG,
                        (const char *)buffer);
            break;
```

```
case LINEERR_INVALAPPHANDLE:
    wsprintf(buffer,"op=%s Ret=LINEERR_INVALAPPHANDLE", op);
    LogEvent(EVENTLOG_ERROR_TYPE, EVMSG_DEBUG,
                (const char *)buffer);
    break;
case LINEERR_RESOURCEUNAVAIL:
    wsprintf(buffer,"op=%s Ret=LINEERR_RESOURCEUNAVAIL", op);
    LogEvent(EVENTLOG_ERROR_TYPE, EVMSG_DEBUG,
                (const char *)buffer);
    break;
case LINEERR_UNINITIALIZED:
    wsprintf(buffer,"op=%s Ret=LINEERR_UNINITIALIZED", op);
    LogEvent(EVENTLOG_ERROR_TYPE, EVMSG_DEBUG,
                (const char *)buffer);
    break;
case LINEERR_OPERATIONUNAVAIL:
    wsprintf(buffer,"op=%s Ret=LINEERR_OPERATIONUNAVAIL", op);
    LogEvent(EVENTLOG_ERROR_TYPE, EVMSG_DEBUG,
                (const char *)buffer);
    break;
case LINEERR_NODEVICE:
    wsprintf(buffer,"op=%s Ret=LINEERR_NODEVICE", op);
    LogEvent(EVENTLOG_ERROR_TYPE, EVMSG_DEBUG,
                (const char *)buffer);
    break;
case LINEERR_ALLOCATED:
    wsprintf(buffer,"op=%s Ret=LINEERR_ALLOCATED", op);
    LogEvent(EVENTLOG_ERROR_TYPE, EVMSG_DEBUG,
                (const char *)buffer);
    break;
case LINEERR_LINEMAPPERFAILED:
    wsprintf(buffer,"op=%s Ret=LINEERR_LINEMAPPERFAILED", op);
    LogEvent(EVENTLOG_ERROR_TYPE, EVMSG_DEBUG,
                (const char *)buffer);
    break;
case LINEERR_INCOMPATIBLEEXTVERSION:
    wsprintf(buffer,"op=%s Ret=LINEERR_INCOMPATIBLEEXTVERSION",
        op);
    LogEvent(EVENTLOG_ERROR_TYPE, EVMSG_DEBUG,
                (const char *)buffer);
    break;
case LINEERR_INVALMEDIAMODE:
    wsprintf(buffer,"op=%s Ret=LINEERR_INVALMEDIAMODE", op);
    LogEvent(EVENTLOG_ERROR_TYPE, EVMSG_DEBUG,
                (const char *)buffer);
    break;
```

*(continued)*

**Listing 7-10** *continued*

```
    case LINEERR_STRUCTURETOOSMALL:
        wsprintf(buffer,"op=%s Ret=LINEERR_STRUCTURETOOSMALL", op);
        LogEvent(EVENTLOG_ERROR_TYPE, EVMSG_DEBUG,
                    (const char *)buffer);
        break;
    case LINEERR_INVALPRIVSELECT:
        wsprintf(buffer,"op=%s Ret=LINEERR_INVALPRIVSELECT", op);
        LogEvent(EVENTLOG_ERROR_TYPE, EVMSG_DEBUG,
                    (const char *)buffer);
        break;
    case LINEERR_ADDRESSBLOCKED:
        wsprintf(buffer,"op=%s Ret=LINEERR_ADDRESSBLOCKED", op);
        LogEvent(EVENTLOG_ERROR_TYPE, EVMSG_DEBUG,
                    (const char *)buffer);
        break;
    case LINEERR_DIALBILLING:
        wsprintf(buffer,"op=%s Ret=LINEERR_DIALBILLING", op);
        LogEvent(EVENTLOG_ERROR_TYPE, EVMSG_DEBUG,
                    (const char *)buffer);
        break;
    case LINEERR_DIALDIALTONE:
        wsprintf(buffer,"op=%s Ret=LINEERR_DIALDIALTONE", op);
        LogEvent(EVENTLOG_ERROR_TYPE, EVMSG_DEBUG,
                    (const char *)buffer);
        break;
    case LINEERR_NOTOWNER:
        wsprintf(buffer,"op=%s Ret=LINEERR_NOTOWNER", op);
        LogEvent(EVENTLOG_ERROR_TYPE, EVMSG_DEBUG,
                    (const char *)buffer);
        break;
    case LINEERR_DIALPROMPT:
        wsprintf(buffer,"op=%s Ret=LINEERR_DIALPROMPT", op);
        LogEvent(EVENTLOG_ERROR_TYPE, EVMSG_DEBUG,
                    (const char *)buffer);
        break;
    case LINEERR_DIALQUIET:
        wsprintf(buffer,"op=%s Ret=LINEERR_DIALQUIET", op);
        LogEvent(EVENTLOG_ERROR_TYPE, EVMSG_DEBUG,
                    (const char *)buffer);
        break;
    case LINEERR_INVALCALLHANDLE:
        wsprintf(buffer,"op=%s Ret=LINEERR_INVALCALLHANDLE", op);
        LogEvent(EVENTLOG_ERROR_TYPE, EVMSG_DEBUG,
                    (const char *)buffer);
        break;
```

```
    case LINEERR_INVALCALLSTATE:
        wsprintf(buffer,
            "op=%s Ret=LINEERR_INVALCALLSTATE", op);
        LogEvent(EVENTLOG_ERROR_TYPE, EVMSG_DEBUG,
                    (const char *)buffer);
        break;
    case LINEERR_INVALCOUNTRYCODE:
        wsprintf(buffer,
            "op=%s Ret=LINEERR_INVALCOUNTRYCODE", op);
        LogEvent(EVENTLOG_ERROR_TYPE, EVMSG_DEBUG,
                    (const char *)buffer);
        break;
    }
}

int CTAPIMAPIService::SendMapiMessage(char *szTo,
char *szSubject,char *szNoteText)
{
    MAPIINIT_0            MapiInitInfo;
    LPSPropValue          pr = NULL;
    LPADRLIST             pAdrList = NULL;
    LPSPropProblemArray   lpPropProblems = 0;
    IMessage *pMessage = NULL;
    FLAGS flags         = MAPI_EXTENDED | MAPI_NEW_SESSION |
                          MAPI_USE_DEFAULT;
    char diag[255];

    InitMAPI();
    // Note the use of MAPI_NT_SERVICE
    MapiInitInfo.ulFlags =
        MAPI_MULTITHREAD_NOTIFICATIONS | MAPI_NT_SERVICE;
    MapiInitInfo.ulVersion = 0;
    lpfnMAPIInitialize(&MapiInitInfo);

    HRESULT hr = lpfnMAPILogonEx(0, NULL, NULL, flags, &psess);
    if (FAILED(hr))
    {
        DWORD dRet = GetLastError();
        return (-1);
    }

    GetRootFolder();
```

*(continued)*

**Listing 7-10** *continued*

```
GetFoldersHierarchy(ename, prootfolder, 0);
AssignInOutSentDel();

hr = psess->OpenAddressBook(0, NULL, AB_NO_DIALOG,
    &pAddrBook);
if (FAILED(hr))
{
    sprintf(diag, "Open Address Book");
    LogEvent(EVENTLOG_ERROR_TYPE, EVMSG_DEBUG,
                (const char *)diag);
    FREEBUFFS;
    return (-1);
}

hr = lpfnMAPIAllocateBuffer(CbNewADRLIST(1),
    (LPVOID*)&pAdrList);
if (FAILED(hr))
{
    sprintf(diag, "Alloc AdrList");
    LogEvent(EVENTLOG_ERROR_TYPE,EVMSG_DEBUG,
                (const char *)diag);
    FREEBUFFS;
    return (-1);
}
ZeroMemory(pAdrList, CbNewADRLIST(1));

hr = lpfnMAPIAllocateBuffer(sizeof(SPropValue)*3,
    (LPVOID*)&(pAdrList->aEntries[0].rgPropVals));
if (FAILED(hr))
{
    sprintf(diag, "Alloc PropValue");
    LogEvent(EVENTLOG_ERROR_TYPE, EVMSG_DEBUG,
        (const char *)diag);
    FREEBUFFS;
    return (-1);
}
ZeroMemory(pAdrList->aEntries[0].rgPropVals,
    sizeof(SPropValue)*2);

pAdrList->cEntries = 1;
pAdrList->aEntries[0].cValues = 2;
pAdrList->aEntries[0].rgPropVals[0].ulPropTag    = PR_DISPLAY_NAME;
pAdrList->aEntries[0].rgPropVals[0].Value.lpszA = szTo;
pAdrList >aEntries[0].rgPropVals[1].ulPropTag    =
```

```
        PR_RECIPIENT_TYPE;
    pAdrList->aEntries[0].rgPropVals[1].Value.l      = MAPI_TO;
    hr = pAddrBook->ResolveName(NULL, 0, NULL, pAdrList);
    if (FAILED(hr))
    {
        sprintf(diag, "ResolveName");
        LogEvent(EVENTLOG_ERROR_TYPE,EVMSG_DEBUG,
            (const char *)diag);
        FREEBUFFS;
        return (-1);
    }

    hr = lpfnMAPIAllocateBuffer(sizeof(SPropValue)*5, (LPVOID*)&pr);
    if (FAILED(hr))
    {
        sprintf(diag, "Alloc SPropValue 5");
        LogEvent(EVENTLOG_ERROR_TYPE, EVMSG_DEBUG,
            (const char *)diag);
        FREEBUFFS;
        return (-1);
    }
    ZeroMemory(pr, sizeof(SPropValue)*5);

    pr[0].ulPropTag    = PR_PRIORITY;
    pr[0].Value.ul     =  PRIO_NORMAL;
    pr[1].ulPropTag    = PR_ORIGINATOR_DELIVERY_REPORT_REQUESTED;
    pr[1].Value.b      =  TRUE;
    pr[2].ulPropTag    = PR_SUBJECT;
    pr[2].Value.lpszA =  szSubject;
    pr[3].ulPropTag    = PR_BODY;
    pr[3].Value.lpszA =  szNoteText;
    pr[4].ulPropTag    = PR_DELETE_AFTER_SUBMIT;
    pr[4].Value.b      =  TRUE;

    hr = folder[outboxidx].pfolder->CreateMessage(NULL, 0, &pMessage);
    if (FAILED(hr))
    {
        sprintf(diag, "SetProps");
        LogEvent(EVENTLOG_ERROR_TYPE, EVMSG_DEBUG,
            (const char *)diag);
        FREEBUFFS;
        return (-1);
    }

    hr = pMessage->ModifyRecipients(MODRECIP_ADD, pAdrList);
```

*(continued)*

**Listing 7-10** *continued*

```
    if (FAILED(hr))
    {
        sprintf(diag, "ModifyRecipients");
        LogEvent(EVENTLOG_ERROR_TYPE, EVMSG_DEBUG,
            (const char *)diag);
        FREEBUFFS;
        return (-1);
    }

    hr = pMessage->SetProps(5, pr, &lpPropProblems);
    if (FAILED(hr))
    {
        sprintf(diag, "SetProps");
        LogEvent(EVENTLOG_ERROR_TYPE, EVMSG_DEBUG,
            (const char *)diag);
        FREEBUFFS;
        return (-1);
    }

    hr = pMessage->SubmitMessage(0);
    if (FAILED(hr))
    {
        sprintf(diag, "SubmitMessage");
        LogEvent(EVENTLOG_ERROR_TYPE, EVMSG_DEBUG,
            (const char *)diag);
        FREEBUFFS;
        return (-1);
    }

    FREEBUFFS;

    psess->Logoff(0,0,0);
    psess->Release();
    psess = NULL;
    pAddrBook->Release();
    pAddrBook = NULL;
    lpfnMAPIUninitialize();
    DeInitMAPI();
    return 0;
}

void AssignInOutSentDel()
{
    for (int i = 0; i < (int)nfolders; i++)
```

```
    {
        if (strcmp(folder[i].name, pInboxName    ) == 0)
            inboxidx      = i;
        if (strcmp(folder[i].name, pDeletedName  ) == 0)
            deletedidx    = i;
        if (strcmp(folder[i].name, pSentItemsName) == 0)
            sentidx       = i;
        if (strcmp(folder[i].name, pOutboxName   ) == 0)
            outboxidx     = i;
    }
}

void GetFoldersHierarchy(char *name,
    IMAPIFolder *pfolder, short int depth)
{
    IMAPITable *ptable = NULL;
    ULONG   ulRowCount = 0;
    HRESULT hr;
    SPropTagArray *ptag = NULL;
    hr = pfolder->GetHierarchyTable(0, &ptable);
    if (FAILED(hr))
    {
        return;
    }
    hr = ptable->GetRowCount(0, &ulRowCount);
    if (ulRowCount)
    {
        hr = ptable->QueryColumns(TBL_ALL_COLUMNS, &ptag);
        hr = ptable->SetColumns(ptag, 0);
        hr = ptable->SeekRow(BOOKMARK_BEGINNING, 0,
            NULL);
        for (unsigned i = 0; i < ulRowCount; i++)
        {
            ++nfolders;
            hr = ptable->QueryRows(1, 0,
                &folder[nfolders-1].prs);
            if (FAILED(hr))
            SPropValue* p = folder[nfolders-1].prs->aRow->lpProps;
            folder[nfolders-1].depth = depth;
            for (int j = 0; j < (int)ptag->cValues; j++)
            {
                if (p[j].ulPropTag == PR_DISPLAY_NAME)
```

*(continued)*

**Listing 7-10** *continued*

```
                folder[nfolders-1].name = p[j].Value.lpszA;
            if (p[j].ulPropTag == PR_ENTRYID)
                folder[nfolders-1].pbv  = &p[j].Value.bin;
        }
        ULONG ul;
        hr = pmdb->OpenEntry(folder[nfolders-1].pbv->cb,
            (LPENTRYID)folder[nfolders-1].pbv->lpb,
            (LPCIID)&IID_IMAPIFolder,
            MAPI_MODIFY | MAPI_BEST_ACCESS, &ul,
            (IUnknown**)&folder[nfolders-1].pfolder);
        if (hr == S_OK)
            GetFoldersHierarchy(
                folder[nfolders-1].name,
                folder[nfolders-1].pfolder, depth+1);
        }
    }
    lpfnMAPIFreeBuffer(ptag);
    ptable->Release();
    return;
}

void GetRootFolder(void)
{
    ULONG   ulRowCount;
    HRESULT hr;
    IMAPITable *ptable = NULL;
    char diag[255];
    hr = psess->GetMsgStoresTable(0L, &ptable);

    SPropTagArray *ptag = NULL;
    hr = ptable->GetRowCount(0, &ulRowCount);
    hr = ptable->QueryColumns(TBL_ALL_COLUMNS, &ptag);
    hr = ptable->SetColumns(ptag, 0);

    for (unsigned i = 0; i < ulRowCount; i++)
    {
        char *provname = "", *storname = "";
        SRowSet *prs = NULL;
        hr = ptable->SeekRow(BOOKMARK_BEGINNING, i, NULL);
        hr = ptable->QueryRows(1, TBL_NOADVANCE, &prs);
        SPropValue* p = prs->aRow->lpProps;
        SBinary bv;

        for (int k = 0; k < (int)ptag->cValues; k++)
```

```
        {
            if (p[k].ulPropTag == PR_DEFAULT_STORE &&
                p[k].Value.b == 1)
            {
                for (int j = 0; j < (int)ptag->cValues; j++)
                {
                    if (p[j].ulPropTag == PR_DISPLAY_NAME)
                        storname =  p[j].Value.lpszA;
                    if (p[j].ulPropTag == PR_PROVIDER_DISPLAY)
                        provname =  p[j].Value.lpszA;
                    if (p[j].ulPropTag == PR_ENTRYID)
                        memcpy(&bv,
                            &p[j].Value.bin,
                            sizeof(SBinary));
                }
                hr = psess->OpenMsgStore(0, bv.cb,
                    (LPENTRYID)bv.lpb, NULL,
                    MAPI_BEST_ACCESS | MDB_NO_DIALOG, &pmdb);
                lpfnMAPIFreeBuffer(prs);
                if (FAILED(hr))
                {
                    sprintf(diag,
                        "Error when opening default message store.");
                    LogEvent(EVENTLOG_ERROR_TYPE, EVMSG_DEBUG,
                        (const char *)diag);
                    return;
                }

                ULONG ulObjType;
                hr = pmdb->OpenEntry(0,
                    NULL, /*(LPCIID)&IID_IMAPIFolder,*/ NULL,
                    MAPI_MODIFY | MAPI_BEST_ACCESS, &ulObjType,
                    (IUnknown**)&prootfolder);
                if (FAILED(hr))
                {
                    return;
                }
                strcpy(ename, storname);
                break;
            }
        }
        lpfnMAPIFreeBuffer(prs);
        if (prootfolder)
            break;
    }
```

*(continued)*

**Listing 7-10** *continued*

```
    lpfnMAPIFreeBuffer(ptag);
    ptable->Release();
    if (!pmdb)
    {
        sprintf(diag,
            "Unable to find default message store record.");
        LogEvent(EVENTLOG_ERROR_TYPE,EVMSG_DEBUG,
            (const char *)diag);
        return;
    }
    return;
}

int PASCAL InitMAPI()
{
    if ((hLibrary = LoadLibrary(MAPIDLL)) < (HANDLE)32)
    {
        return (ERR_LOAD_LIB);
    }

    if ((lpfnHrQueryAllRows =
        (PFNHRQUERYALLROWS)GetProcAddress(hLibrary,
        SZ_HRQUERYALLROWS)) == NULL)
    {
        return (ERR_LOAD_FUNC);
    }

    if ((lpfnHrGetOneProp =
        (PFNHRGETONEPROP)GetProcAddress(hLibrary,
        SZ_HRGETONEPROP)) == NULL)
    {
        return (ERR_LOAD_FUNC);
    }

    if ((lpfnMAPIAllocateBuffer =
        (PFNMAPIALLOCATEBUFFER)GetProcAddress(hLibrary,
        SZ_MAPIALLOCATEBUFFER)) == NULL)
    {
        return (ERR_LOAD_FUNC);
    }

    if ((lpfnMAPIFreeBuffer =
        (PFNMAPIFREEBUFFER)GetProcAddress(hLibrary,
        SZ_MAPIFREEBUFFER)) == NULL)
    {
        return (ERR_LOAD_FUNC);
    }
```

```
    if ((lpfnMAPIInitialize =
        (PFNMAPIINITIALIZE)GetProcAddress(hLibrary,
        SZ_MAPIINITIALIZE)) == NULL)
    {
        return (ERR_LOAD_FUNC);
    }

    if ((lpfnMAPIUninitialize =
        (PFNMAPIUNINITIALIZE)GetProcAddress(hLibrary,
        SZ_MAPIUNINITIALIZE)) == NULL)
    {
        return (ERR_LOAD_FUNC);
    }

    if ((lpfnMAPILogonEx =
        (PFNMAPILOGONEX)GetProcAddress(hLibrary,
        SZ_MAPILOGONEX)) == NULL)
    {
        return (ERR_LOAD_FUNC);
    }

    if ((lpfnFreeProws =
        (PFNFREEPROWS)GetProcAddress(hLibrary,
        SZ_FREEPROWS)) == NULL)
    {
        return (ERR_LOAD_FUNC);
    }

    if ((lpfnFreePadrlist =
        (PFNFREEPADRLIST)GetProcAddress(hLibrary,
        SZ_FREEPADRLIST)) == NULL)
    {
        return (ERR_LOAD_FUNC);
    }

    return (0);
}

int PASCAL DeInitMAPI()
{

    lpfnHrQueryAllRows      = NULL;
    lpfnHrGetOneProp        = NULL;
    lpfnMAPIAllocateBuffer = NULL;
    lpfnMAPIFreeBuffer      = NULL;
```

*(continued)*

**Listing 7-10** *continued*

```
    lpfnMAPIInitialize      = NULL;
    lpfnMAPIUninitialize    = NULL;
    lpfnMAPILogonEx         = NULL;
    lpfnFreeProws           = NULL;
    lpfnFreePadrlist        = NULL;

    FreeLibrary(hLibrary);

    return (0);
}

int main(int argc, char* argv[])
{
    CTAPIMAPIService MyTAPIMAPIService("CTAPIMAPIService",
        "TAPI/MAPI Service",
        SERVICE_DEMAND_START,
        true);
    // Have we handled the arguments and done
    //  an install or uninstall?
    if (MyTAPIMAPIService.ParseArguments(argc, argv) == false)
    {
        // If not, start the service running.
        MyTAPIMAPIService.StartService();
    }

    return 0;
}
```

The *Run* routine is still the same old processing loop from *CBeeperService* but has some additional calls during the first processing loop:

```
if (!(sentBeep))
{
    CallBeeper("555-5166", "555-1605");
    SendMapiMessage("Douglas Reilly", "Message From Service",
        "This is the text of the message from the service.  \n"
        "This could contain anything from an alert to info"
        " on system status");
    sentBeep = true;
}
```

The code checks the *sentBeep* flag, and if *false*, calls the *CallBeeper* function and sends a MAPI message. The only other significant difference in functionality between the TAPI- and MAPI-related class member functions and those in Listings 7-2 and 7-6 is the inclusion of the MAPI_NT_SERVICE in the *ulFlags* member of the *MapiInitInfo* structure that I pass to *MAPIInitialize*.

## CONCLUSION

No server is an island. In this chapter we have begun to allow the server to be seen and heard. Both MAPI and TAPI can be critical to the operation of a reliable and reactive server-based application. The addition of a message pump within the service broadens the ability of the *CPPService* framework to interact with the wide variety of COM APIs beginning to emerge.

Chapter 12 will enable the service framework to reach out even further, via two of the more common client/server communications methods: WinSock and named pipes.

*Chapter 8*

# The ODBC API

Prior to Open Database Connectivity (ODBC), clients who interacted with data located on a remote server had to use a proprietary API or an embedded SQL code. An example of a proprietary API is the *BTRV* function used to access data stored in Pervasive Software Btrieve. Calls to *BTRV* were identical, semantically, regardless of where the data resided, but the code would have to be recompiled for each client platform and relinked as well. Of course, getting data from other sources required other methods.

The more convenient option for accessing server data was embedded SQL code—SQL code was embedded in the source program and a precompiler was required to properly set up the SQL calls. This model was acceptable as long as most programs dealt with only a single data source. If you had to access data sources from multiple database vendors, you needed multiple versions of a program and you needed to know the name of each destination database at compile time.

In the 1980s, the proprietary API and embedded SQL models began to fail under the weight of multiple databases and the widespread availability of applications such as Lotus 1-2-3, Microsoft Excel, and Microsoft Access. Users of these PC programs needed to access information from a variety of server-based data sources, and they wanted convenient access from within their favorite productivity applications. Blending data from both PC and mainframe data sources became a necessity.

ODBC was developed to provide client workstations with the ability to attach to databases located on remote servers. Within server-based development, ODBC has recently become a significant force because of the role of Microsoft Windows NT and Windows 2000 in the network operating systems market and the emergence of Windows 2000 Server as a Web host. The reliance of most Web servers on convenient data connectivity also has placed new emphasis on ODBC. Furthermore, using ODBC is the primary way to access data from the script-based Active Server Pages provided by Microsoft Internet Information Server (included with Windows 2000 Server).

# WHAT ODBC PROVIDES

According to the *Microsoft ODBC 2.0 Programmer's Reference and SDK Guide,* ODBC provides the following:

- A library of functions that enable you to connect to a database, execute SQL code, and retrieve results
- A standard SQL syntax
- A standard set of error codes
- A standard way to connect and log on to a database
- A standard representation of data types

The first, second, and fourth provisions in the list are fairly straightforward, but the third and fifth are not. Although ODBC provides a standard way of getting to error codes, I would argue that the actual error codes are not standard. I have seen an error message that simply told me the database driver's error database could not be found and then only provided me with an error code. (See Figure 8-1.) A driver from another vendor routinely returns an error message that says, informatively, *"<<error>> Failed to connect to server"*.

**Figure 8-1** *Uninformative error dialog generated by an ODBC driver.*

Although representing data in a standard way has many benefits, it has a few drawbacks as well. The problem is that the goal is too ambitious. Before getting to examples, let's take a look at a warning in the data types appendix from the current ODBC documentation included with MSDN July 1999:

> ***Important:*** *The tables throughout this appendix are only a guideline and show commonly used names, ranges, and limits of SQL data types. A given data source may support only some of the listed data types and the characteristics of the supported data types may differ from those listed.*

From this previous information, it is unclear what data types are available and what the ranges allowed might be. How can this be problematic? Consider a program that copies date and time information from a Microsoft Access database to a Microsoft

SQL Server database. The Microsoft SQL Server SMALLDATETIME field type is not identical to the Microsoft Access DATETIME field type; the conversion from the Access type to the SQL Server type will drop seconds and milliseconds. If the date and time field is being used to generate a unique key, this data loss will likely cause problems.

Despite the previous warnings, ODBC generally works. I will provide sample code that will run on either SQL Server or Access without any change to the object code. The SQL code passed to an ODBC driver can be generated at compile time or at run time, allowing the program to work with dynamically changing data sources. ODBC will often be the only feasible option. If you want to create a data-driven Web page in Internet Information Server and you do not want to resort to a custom data interface ISAPI program, ODBC is essential.

# ODBC ALTERNATIVES

Alternatives to ODBC include ADO (which is used in the Active Server Pages examples in Chapter 9) and OLE DB. Currently, most ODBC alternatives are implemented as wrappers around ODBC. If you are creating an application accessing a database that uses direct ODBC calls, it will virtually always perform better than ADO. In a client application, this difference might not be too important because most of the time is spent waiting for the relatively slow user. In the world of server applications, however, the program will seldom have time to catch its breath, and the best performance possible is almost always best.

To test my assumptions, I ran a series of tests using Microsoft Application Performance Explorer. Usually it is not necessary to draw conclusions based on very small differences in performance, but the differences I discovered were not small. Figure 8-2 shows the result of the third test run using ADO as the data transport mechanism. It is important to note that the first test will be noticeably slower than subsequent tests due to the startup tasks associated with each protocol. In general, these differences should be ignored—especially in long-lived processes such as server applications. Figure 8-3 shows the results from the third run of the same test using the ODBC API. The difference is dramatic.

Overall calls per second for ODBC were almost twice those for ADO; client calls per second for ODBC were over twice those for ADO. The total test times were also much shorter with the direct ODBC calls. Of course, your mileage may vary. As with any benchmarks, these measurements may or may not be representative of your application.

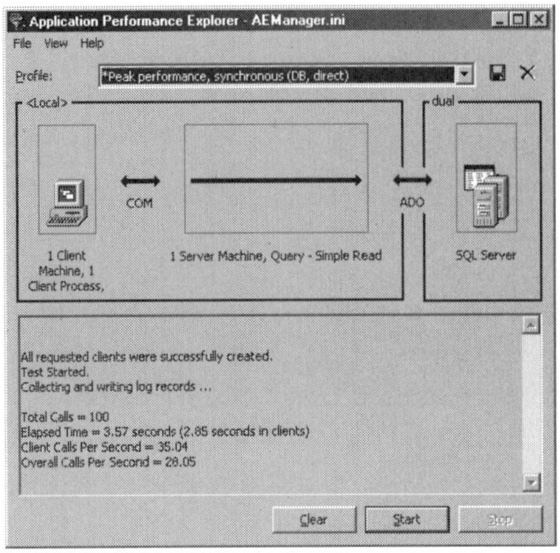


**Figure 8-2** *Microsoft Application Performance Explorer output for an ADO test.*

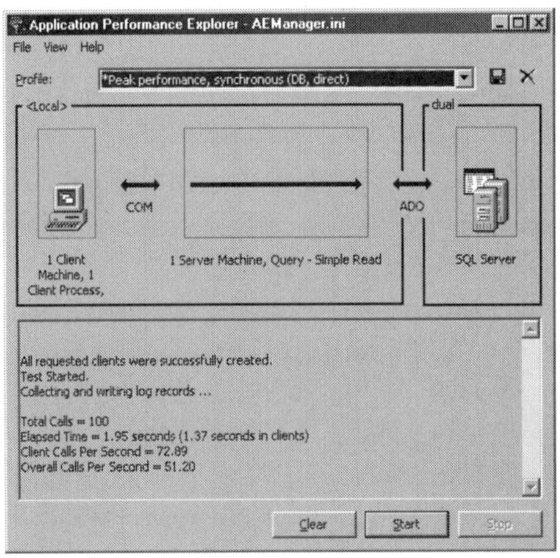


**Figure 8-3** *Application Performance Explorer output for an ODBC API test.*

The only other reasonable alternatives that provide database access are the various proprietary APIs provided by database vendors. Of course, the difficulty involved in writing applications to proprietary APIs is exactly why ODBC was invented. If you write to the proprietary API and supporting another database vendor's product becomes important, a rewrite is likely on the horizon. Additionally, database vendors are increasingly moving away from support for their proprietary APIs. SQL Server supports a proprietary API: dbLib. This API has not been changed to support all new features of SQL Server 7.0, and the presumption is that it will not be updated to fully exploit future releases.

# ODBC COMPONENTS

ODBC is composed of four components: the application, the driver manager, one or more drivers, and one or more data sources. ODBC can be difficult to work with because some of these components are supplied with the operating system, some are provided by the database vendor, and some are provided by the application vendor. When troubleshooting ODBC, pinning down exactly what part of the system is causing the problem can be difficult. Figure 8-4 shows the relationship of the four ODBC components and the network boundary that sometimes separates the driver from the data source.

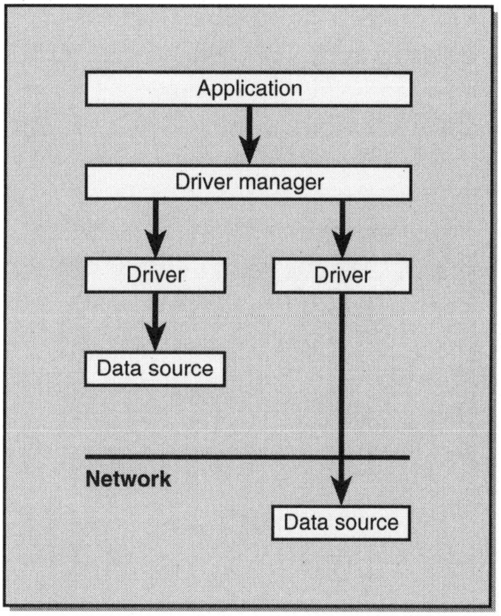


**Figure 8-4** *The relationship of the four components of ODBC.*

## The Application

The application component of ODBC is the portion of the code that resides in the application and calls the ODBC API. The code in the application is responsible for selecting the data source to be used, submitting SQL statements for execution, retrieving results, and processing errors. The application might also configure the ODBC data sources.

Using the ODBC API can be daunting, but this task can be made easier by the use of class libraries that hide the details of implementation, allow clean access to the data retrieved, and provide error-handling capabilities. MFC offers two sets of classes that provide direct and indirect access to ODBC data sources—the *CDatabase* class and the *CDAODatabase* class respectively—but neither set will be covered here. Later in this chapter we will discuss the issues associated with creating a generic wrapper around the ODBC API.

## The Driver Manager

The Driver Manager is the component of ODBC that manages communication between the application and the ODBC drivers. In the Windows environment, the Driver Manager is implemented as one or more DLLs that are provided by Microsoft; it is part of the ODBC SDK and can be freely distributed. Today virtually all corporate machines have ODBC installed. The Driver Manager component is primarily a convenience to the developer. It provides a convenient, single set of functions that are called to access the various ODBC drivers. Rather than maintaining a list of pointers for each driver in use, an application can simply use the functions in the ODBC Driver Manager for any ODBC driver. The Driver Manager also performs some parameter checking to ensure that handles passed in are not NULL pointers and that functions are called in the correct order.

Another major task of the Driver Manager is to manage the loading and unloading of drivers. The application loads and unloads only the Driver Manager. The Driver Manager then loads the proper driver (if it is not already loaded) based on its search of the data source information stored in the registry. Once the driver is loaded, the Driver Manager calls the connection function in the driver, and the connection is made. When the request to disconnect from a driver is received, the Driver Manager might delay the actual unloading of the driver because once one connection is broken, another connection that could use the loaded driver can be requested. The operating system vendor—in the case of Windows 2000, Microsoft—provides this component of ODBC.

## The Drivers

The drivers component of ODBC consists of one or more vendor-supplied DBMS-specific drivers, which are contacted by the Driver Manager on behalf of the application. Drivers have two basic architectures. The first is used by file-based DBMS systems. In this architecture, the driver retrieves the data. Examples of this kind of system include Borland dBASE and Microsoft Access. The other major driver architecture is the server-based architecture. This driver passes the requests from the application (by way of the Driver Manager) to another database engine for processing. The database engine can reside either on the machine where the request originates or on another machine.

Drivers are responsible for sending and receiving data, mapping DBMS-specific errors to ODBC SQLSTATES, connecting and disconnecting from the data sources, and checking for errors not detected by the Driver Manager.

### The Data Sources

The data sources are the final component of ODBC. A data source is specific to each DBMS. The data source can be a file (similar to a file-based DBMS such as Access) or a database on a database server. It can also be a machine data source, which is stored on a single system using a user-defined name or a file data source—the same information is stored in both a machine data source and a file data source. The file can be stored on a network-accessible drive and shared, or it can be unshared and located on a local drive pointing to a local machine data source. Each DBMS vendor provides a data source for its product.

## ODBC CLASSES

From our examination of the native ODBC API, it is clear that a great deal of boilerplate code can easily be moved off into class member functions. For instance, several types of handles are used by ODBC. To avoid leaking resources, each of these handles needs to be allocated before being used and freed before the class is destroyed. These tasks are ideal candidates for C++ class constructors and destructors.

As a brief review, constructors and destructors are special C++ class member functions that are called when a class is created and destroyed, respectively. The construction commonly takes place in one of the two following ways: a locally defined class calls its constructor when the object comes into scope as it is declared, or a class pointer can be declared and the constructor called when the *new* operator is called to dynamically create the class instance. Consider the following code fragment:

```
CODBCDatabase *Db;
Db = new CODBCDatabase(/* constructor arguments*/);
```

The destructor is called as a class goes out of scope (in the case of a locally declared class instance) or when the *delete* operator is called on a class instance. This mechanism is ideal for allocation and deallocation of resources such as handles or memory.

Considering the information previously discussed, what classes should be created to interact with ODBC data? A reasonable class represents a connection to a data source. This would create a connection that could be used to access multiple independent tables, views, or queries within the single data source. In our ODBC database access classes, which will be used throughout the rest of the book, this reasonable class is called *CODBCDatabase*. It is similar to the MFC *CDatabase* class, although it is not derived from that class nor does it implement identical functionality.

We also need classes to manage the interaction with the various tables, views, and queries. In the MFC classes, such class management would be provided by something like *CRecordset*. The *CODBCDatabase* class won't have all the functionality of the *CRecordset* class. The *CRecordset* class contains functionality that is completely appropriate and necessary for a client application, but superfluous for server-based applications. (For example, server-based applications don't need the *CRecordset* field-exchange mechanism, which allows database fields to be bound to form fields.) What server-based applications do need is a way to bind variables to values returned by queries. The *CODBCCursor* class will accomplish that.

Note that this chapter will not replace the ODBC SDK documentation. Most of my coverage of the raw ODBC API will describe function use within the *CODBCCursor* class; the *CODBCCursor* class is not representative of every possible ODBC application. For instance, the *CODBCCursor* class will use the *SQLFetch* function to get data returned by the queries executed by the class. In many cases, the function *SQLExtendedFetch* would be the better choice, allowing many rows to be returned in a single operation. The *SQLExtendedFetch* function is beyond the scope of this discussion and will not be essential for the way this class will be used in future chapters.

## An Example: ODBC Classes in Action

Listing 8-1 presents a simple console mode application that displays the fields of the *tblProblems* table of the Troubleshooter database (introduced in Chapter 9). The problem ID, the date entered, the name of the user who entered the problem, and part of the Description field are captured and displayed in the console. This is a simple application—in the real world, we'd want to scroll through entries or page the output so that all entries could be easily seen. Here the emphasis is simply on getting the data.

**ODBCTest.cpp**

```
// ODBCTest.cpp : Defines the entry point for the
//  console application.

#include "windows.h"
// Definition for our simple ODBC class
#include "odbclass.h"


// Converts date from YYYY-MM-DD format to MM/DD/YYYY format.
char *fixDate(char *tdate)
```

**Listing 8-1**

```
{
    char result[255];
    strcpy(result, "null");

    if (tdate[0]!='\0')
    {
        sprintf(result, "%2.2s/%2.2s/%4.4s", &tdate[5],
            &tdate[8], tdate);
    }
    strncpy((char *)tdate, result,
        strlen((const char *)result) + 1);
    return(tdate);
}

int main(int argc, char* argv[])
{
    WORD rc;
    WORD col = 1;
    // InitCriticalSection must be called before the first use
    //  of the CODBCDatabase class.
    CODBCDatabase::InitCriticalSection();

    // Declare and dynamically create CODBCDatabase object.
    CODBCDatabase *Db;
    Db = new CODBCDatabase("TroubleshootSQL","sa","SECRET");

    // Declare and create CODBCCursor object.
    CODBCCursor *curs;
    curs = new CODBCCursor(Db);

    // Set the table or tables.
    curs->setTables("tblProblems");

    // Bind the fields.
    curs->bindColumn(col, "ProblemID", 255);
    curs->bindColumn(col, "DateEntered", 255);
    curs->bindColumn(col, "EnteredBy", 255);
    curs->bindColumn(col, "Description", 255);

    // Set an ORDER BY clause.
    curs->setOrderBy("Description");

    // Also set WHERE clause in order to filter the data.
    curs->setRestrict("WHERE Description > ''");
```

*(continued)*

**Listing 8-1** *continued*

```
    // Select the records.  No data yet...
    curs->doSelect();

    // ...NOW we have the data.
    rc=curs->fetch();

    // Print a header.
    printf("Problem ID Date Entered   Entered By      Description\n");
    printf("==================================================");
    printf("===============\n");
    do {
        // If the fetch was successful, print the data.
        if (rc==SQL_SUCCESS)
        {
            printf("%10.10s %-14.14s %-14.14s %-32.32s\n",
                (char *)(*curs)[1],
                fixDate((char *)(*curs)[2]),
                (char *)(*curs)[3],
                (char *)(*curs)[4]);
            rc=curs->fetch();
        }
    } while (rc==SQL_SUCCESS);

    delete curs;
    delete Db;
    CODBCDatabase::DelCriticalSection();

    return 0;
}
```

The first function defined in this simple test application, *fixDate*, converts a non-NULL date from YYYY-MM-DD format to MM/DD/YYYY format. (SQL Server, the server database used, returns dates in the YYYY-MM-DD format.) Of course, a more elegant solution would take the value returned by SQL Server and convert it to the format specified in the regional settings of the user's computer.

Next is the *main* function. The presence of *main* rather than *WinMain* reminds you that this is not a GUI application but a console mode application. Console mode applications were discussed in Chapter 1 as a reasonable way to start debugging a server application. After declaring a couple of simple variables, *main* calls the *InitCriticalSection* static method of the *CODBCDatabase* class. The details of this will be discussed shortly, but recall that a critical section is one of the synchronization objects discussed in Chapter 2. In order to make these classes thread safe, the critical section object that the *CODBCDatabase* class contains must be initialized. It is not reasonable for the critical section object to be initialized within any of the non-static member functions, so it is the responsibility of the calling application to call the static initialization member function before any objects of the *CODBCDatabase* class are created.

Next, *main* declares and dynamically creates a *CODBCDatabase* object and a *CODBCCursor* object. Dynamically creating the *CODBCDatabase* object is a convenience that lets us call the *DelCriticalSection* member function to destroy the critical section object. When we examine the internals of the classes, we will see why this is important. The constructor for the *CODBCDatabase* class takes the name of the ODBC data source and optionally the user name and password. In this example, SQL Server required a user name and password. (Other databases might or might not require a password.) The *CODBCCursor* class constructor takes a pointer to the *CODBCDatabase* class that was just created.

Internally, the class simply uses its member data members and creates SQL statements to pass on to the ODBC Driver Manager. Most SQL SELECT statements used to retrieve information (such as the statements created by our test application) are similar to the following statement:

```
SELECT ProblemID, DateEntered, EnteredBy, Description
    FROM tblProblems
    ORDER BY Description
    WHERE Description > ''
```

Note that SQL keywords are all uppercase letters. The example gets the four fields listed from each record in the *tblProblems* table, sorts them by the Description field, and filters the records so that only those that contain description information are returned.

Within *main*, we first set the table, using the *setTables* method; next we bind the columns we want returned, using the *bindColumn* method; then *setOrderBy* and *setRestrict* methods are called with the appropriate arguments; and *doSelect* is called to actually pass the SQL statement to the ODBC Driver Manager. Note that at this point no data is returned and accessible to the application. Data will be returned and accessible after the call to the *fetch* method. (The *fetch* method causes the data returned to be stuffed into the buffers created during column binding.)

The output of the program is shown in Figure 8-5. After all the records have been fetched, the application destroys the *CODBCDatabase* object and the *CODBC-Cursor* object. After the objects have been destroyed, the critical section object is destroyed with the call to *DelCriticalSection*.

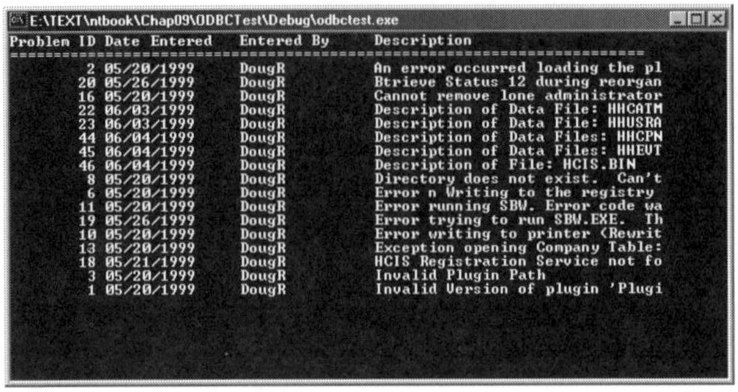


**Figure 8-5** *Output from the simple ODBC sample program.*

Simply displaying some records on a console seems like a lot of work, but what is happening is amazing. The same code could operate on data from a Microsoft Access database (with the exception of the call to *fixDate* since by default Access does not return dates in the same format as SQL Server). There are virtually no dependencies on the particular DBMS, leaving us with a comfortable level of abstraction. This abstraction is quite useful and a great deal easier than the equivalent—pure ODBC API calls. Looking at the actual class source will provide us with a better understanding of the native ODBC API and show why wrapping it is such a good idea.

## The *ODBCDatabase* Class

Some of the complications in the *ODBCDatabase* class are caused by the way ODBC works. Virtually all ODBC operations take one or more handles to do their task. The following are the three types of handles used by ODBC:

- *Environment handles.* One per application
- *Connection handles.* One per connection, although you can have more if it is convenient for the application
- *Statement handles.* Generally more than one per application

A single environment handle needs to be allocated for an application. You can allocate more than one, but the second environment handle that you allocate will hide some of the resources associated with the first handle, causing a resource leak (a very bad thing to do in a server application). The way the *CODBCDatabase* class manages this allocation is through use of a reference count. Now the critical section comes in handy. Look at the header for the ODBC classes in Listing 8-2. The first three data members of the *CODBCDatabase* class are the static reference count, critical section, and environment handle: *referenceCount*, *CriticalSection*, and *henv*, respectively. Two static methods also exist: one for initializing the critical section and one for deleting it. Additional private data members hold the data source name, user name, and password, and track both the number of tables in use and the connection status of the object. Most of the methods are simply access methods to get at the member variables. The two exceptions are *GetSQLError* and *ExecuteSQL*. Both of these exceptions will be described in detail as we look at the implementations.

**ODBClass.h**

```
#ifndef ODBCLASS_H
#define ODBCLASS_H

#include <windows.h>
#include <stdio.h>
#include <string.h>
#include <stdlib.h>
#include "SQL.H"
#include "sqlext.h"
#include <string.h>

// 512 columns should be adequate.
#define MAX_COLUMNS              512

class CODBCDatabase {
    private:
        // The referenceCount and the CriticalSection
        //  member variables must be static; there can
        //  be only one of each for all class instances.
        static     referenceCount;
        static     CRITICAL_SECTION CriticalSection;
        static     HENV   henv;
        int        numTables;
        char       dataSourceName[255];
        char       uid[255];
        char       password[255];
        int        connected;
        RETCODE    lastRetCode;
    public:
        HDBC       hdbc;
        CODBCDatabase(char *_dataSourceName,
            char *_uid=NULL,
            char *_password=NULL);
        ~CODBCDatabase();
```

**Listing 8-2** *(continued)*

**Listing 8-2** *continued*

```
        // These static functions deal with static variables.
        static void InitCriticalSection()
        {
            InitializeCriticalSection(&CriticalSection);
        }
        static void DelCriticalSection()
        {
            DeleteCriticalSection(&CriticalSection);
        }
        RETCODE GetSQLError(SQLSMALLINT HandleType,SQLHANDLE handle);
        RETCODE ExecuteSQL(char *command);
        operator HDBC()
        {
            return(hdbc);
        }
        char *getDataSourceName(char *t)
        {
            if (connected==TRUE)
            {
                strcpy(t,dataSourceName);
                return(t);
            }
            return(NULL);
        }
        int isConnected()
        {
            return(connected);
        }
        int numTablesOpen()
        {
            return(numTables);
        }
};

struct COLUMN_INFO {
    char *name;
    char *data;
    long len;
    long retLen;
    SQLSMALLINT type;
};

class CODBCCursor {
    private:
        CODBCDatabase *_database;
        HSTMT  hstmt;
```

```
    // Arbitrarily limit to 512 columns. (Increase as needed.)
    struct COLUMN_INFO *colInfo[MAX_COLUMNS];
    UWORD numCols;
    UWORD m_topN;
    RETCODE lastRetCode;
    char whereClause[512];
    char tableClause[256];
    char orderByClause[256];
    char setClause[256];
    CRITICAL_SECTION CriticalSection;
public:
    // Default to NULL for UID and Password.
    CODBCCursor(CODBCDatabase *db);
    ~CODBCCursor();
    // Allow columns to be bound to returned rows.
    RETCODE bindColumn(UWORD& colNum,char *columnName,
        SDWORD len,SWORD type=SQL_C_CHAR);
    UWORD getTopN()
    {
        return(m_topN);
    }
    void setTopN(UWORD value)
    {
        m_topN=value;
    }
    UWORD getNumCol()
    {
        return(numCols);
    }
    RETCODE GetSQLError(SQLSMALLINT handleType, SQLHANDLE handle)
    {
        return(_database->GetSQLError(handleType,handle));
    }
    void *getColData(UWORD colNum)
    {
        if (colInfo[colNum]!=0)
        {
            return((void *)colInfo[colNum]->data);
        }
        return(0);
    }
    int clearBindings()
    {
        for (int loop=1 ; colInfo[loop]!=0 ; loop++)
        {
            delete colInfo[loop]->name;
            delete colInfo[loop]->data;
```

*(continued)*

**Listing 8-2** *continued*

```
            delete colInfo[loop];
            colInfo[loop]=0;
        }
        return(loop);
    }
    void setRestrict(char *_whereClause)
    {
        strcpy(whereClause,_whereClause);
    }
    char *getRestrict(char *_whereClause)
    {
        strcpy(_whereClause,whereClause);
        return(_whereClause);
    }
    char *getTables(char *_tableClause)
    {
        strcpy(_tableClause,tableClause);
        return(_tableClause);
    }
    void setTables(char *_tableClause)
    {
        strcpy(tableClause,_tableClause);
    }
    void setOrderBy(char *_orderByClause)
    {
        strcpy(orderByClause,_orderByClause);
    }
    char *getOrderBy(char *_orderByClause)
    {
        strcpy(_orderByClause,orderByClause);
        return(_orderByClause);
    }
    char *getSet(char *_setClause)
    {
        strcpy((char *)_setClause,(char *)setClause);
        return(_setClause);
    }
    void setSet(char *_setClause)
    {
        strcpy((char *)setClause,(char *)_setClause);
    }
    int doSelect();
    int doDelete();
    int doUpdate();
    RETCODE fetch();
```

```
        UWORD assignColumn(char *fname,SDWORD len);
        void * operator [](unsigned long i)
        {
            if (colInfo[i]!=0)
            {
                return((void *)colInfo[i]->data);
            }
            return(0);
        }
        void * operator [](char *colName)
        {
            UWORD loop;
            for (loop=1;
              colInfo[loop]!=0 &&
              (stricmp((char *)colInfo[loop]->name,
              (char *)colName));)
            {
                loop++;
            }
            if (colInfo[loop]!=0)
            {
                return((void *)colInfo[loop]->data);
            }
            return(0);
        }

};

#endif
```

The COLUMN_INFO structure is used by the *CODBCCursor* class to store information about the fields bound to each object. Most of the members of the structure are self-explanatory, with the exception of the *type* member. The *type* member is designed to hold the type of the column. The constants used for this are part of the ODBC standard and represent virtually any data type you might need. See the ODBC online documentation for details about types other than those used in the example.

The *CODBCCursor* class contains a pointer to a *CODBCDatabase* object, a statement handle, an array of COLUMN_INFO structures (arbitrarily limited to 512), and several variables that hold the parts of the SQL statements used to construct the final SQL statement. Additionally, the *CODBCCursor* class has its own critical section object, used to ensure that the object is thread-safe. The *CODBCCursor* class could have used the critical section of the *CODBCDatabase* class, but that would have serialized through a single critical section access to *CODBCCursor* objects. Serialization of access is guaranteed to cause problems as the number of *CODBCCursor* objects increases within an application.

Many of the inline methods of *CODBCCursor* are self-explanatory, but two are not: the two functions that overload the [] array operators. These functions are used to allow the application to index into the *CODBCCursor* object either by the column number (assigned as the column is bound) or by the name. In Listing 8-1, the following lines would return the same value:

```
(char *)(*curs)[1];
(char *)(*curs)["ProblemID"];
```

Because ProblemID is the first column bound, and because the column variable is initialized to 1, these lines would both return void pointers to the ProblemID field. Indexing based on the column number is faster, but the ability to index based on the field name can be quite convenient and often worth the extra time required. To improve performance, it is also possible to use variables to cache the column numbers as the columns are bound and then use those variables to index using the column number.

Listing 8-3 shows the implementation of the *CODBCDatabase* class and the *CODBCCursor* class. The constructor for the *CODBCDatabase* class first enters the critical section (thus it is necessary to have this initialized before any *CODBCDatabase* object is constructed). Once safely within the critical section, the reference count is checked. If the count is 0, indicating that this database object is the first one constructed, the environment handle is allocated using the *SQLAllocHandle* ODBC API function. Next *SQLSetEnvAttr* is called. (The SQL_OV_ODBC3 parameter indicates that this will be an ODBC version 3 application.) If all that succeeds, the reference count is incremented.

**ODBClass.cpp**

```
#include <windows.h>
#include <stdio.h>
#include <string.h>
#include <stdlib.h>
#include <string.h>
#include "SQL.H"
#include "sqlext.h"
#include "odbclass.h"

#ifndef NULL
#define NULL 0
#endif
```

**Listing 8-3**

```
// Static variables need to be defined like this exactly once,
//  which is why they are defined in the CPP file rather than
//  in the H file where their class is defined.
int CODBCDatabase::referenceCount=0;
HENV CODBCDatabase::henv=0;
CRITICAL_SECTION CODBCDatabase::CriticalSection;

CODBCDatabase::CODBCDatabase(char *_dataSourceName,char *_uid,
    char *_password)
{
    RETCODE rc = SQL_SUCCESS;
    numTables = 0;

    EnterCriticalSection(&CriticalSection);
    // Allocate environment (only for first instance).
    if (referenceCount==0)
    {
        SDWORD valEnv=SQL_OV_ODBC3;
        RETCODE rc2;
        // Allocate an environment handle.
        rc = SQLAllocHandle(SQL_HANDLE_ENV, SQL_NULL_HANDLE,
            &henv);
        // Set the version information. (Without the version
        //  information, you will get sequence errors.)
        rc2 = SQLSetEnvAttr(henv, SQL_ATTR_ODBC_VERSION,
            (SQLPOINTER) SQL_OV_ODBC3, SQL_IS_INTEGER);
        if (rc2!=SQL_SUCCESS)
        {
            GetSQLError(SQL_HANDLE_ENV,henv);
        }
    }
    if (rc==SQL_SUCCESS || rc==SQL_SUCCESS_WITH_INFO)
    {
        referenceCount++;
    }
    LeaveCriticalSection(&CriticalSection);

    // Allocate a connection handle.
    rc = SQLAllocHandle(SQL_HANDLE_DBC, henv, &hdbc);
    if (rc!=SQL_SUCCESS && rc!=SQL_SUCCESS_WITH_INFO)
    {
        GetSQLError(SQL_HANDLE_ENV, henv);
        connected=FALSE;
    }
```

*(continued)*

**Listing 8-3** *continued*

```
        else
        {
            strcpy(dataSourceName, _dataSourceName);

            // Default values for these are NULL. Some ODBC
            //  drivers (notably OpenM) fail on NULL user or password.
            if (_uid!=NULL)
            {
                strcpy(uid,_uid);
            }
            else
            {
                strcpy(uid,"");
            }
            if (_password!=NULL)
            {
                strcpy(password,_password);
            }
            else
            {
                strcpy(password,"");
            }
            // Connect to the data source. The data source must be set
            //  up using the ODBC Administrator (or the
            //  32-Bit Administrator) program.
            rc = SQLConnect(hdbc, (unsigned char *)dataSourceName,
                SQL_NTS, (unsigned char *)uid, SQL_NTS,
                (unsigned char *)password, SQL_NTS);
            lastRetCode = rc;
            if (rc != SQL_SUCCESS && rc != SQL_SUCCESS_WITH_INFO)
            {
                connected=FALSE;
                this->GetSQLError(SQL_HANDLE_DBC,hdbc);
            }
            else
            {
                connected=TRUE;
            }
        }
    }

    CODBCDatabase::~CODBCDatabase()
    {
        // These three functions are paired with SQLConnect,
        //  SQLAllocConnect, and SQLAllocEnv.
```

```
    SQLDisconnect(hdbc);
    SQLFreeHandle(SQL_HANDLE_DBC,hdbc);

    EnterCriticalSection(&CriticalSection);
    referenceCount--;
    // Is the last instance being destroyed?
    if (referenceCount==0)
    {
        SQLFreeHandle(SQL_HANDLE_ENV,henv);
    }
    LeaveCriticalSection(&CriticalSection);

}

RETCODE CODBCDatabase::ExecuteSQL(char *command)
{
    HSTMT hstmt;
    RETCODE ret;
    lastRetCode = SQLAllocHandle(SQL_HANDLE_STMT, hdbc, &hstmt);
    if (lastRetCode!=SQL_SUCCESS)
    {
        GetSQLError(SQL_HANDLE_DBC, hdbc);
    }
    else
    {
        if ((lastRetCode=SQLExecDirect(hstmt,
            (unsigned char *)command, SQL_NTS))!=SQL_SUCCESS &&
            lastRetCode!=SQL_SUCCESS_WITH_INFO)
        {
            GetSQLError(SQL_HANDLE_STMT, hstmt);
        }
        ret = SQLFreeHandle(SQL_HANDLE_STMT, hstmt);
        if (ret!=SQL_SUCCESS)
        {
            GetSQLError(SQL_HANDLE_STMT, hstmt);
        }
        return(lastRetCode);
    }
    return(SQL_ERROR);
}


SQLRETURN CODBCDatabase::GetSQLError(SQLSMALLINT HandleType,
    SQLHANDLE handle)
{
    SQLRETURN rc;
    char szSqlState[256];
```

*(continued)*

**Listing 8-3** *continued*

```
    char szErrorMsg[256];
    SQLSMALLINT bufLen = 255;
    SQLSMALLINT textLen;
    SDWORD pfNativeError = 255;
    short recNum = 1;

    do{
        rc = SQLGetDiagRec(HandleType,
            handle,
            recNum++,    // Get record 1, try 2, and so on.
            (unsigned char *)szSqlState,
            &pfNativeError,
            (unsigned char *)szErrorMsg,
            bufLen,
            &textLen);

        if (rc==SQL_SUCCESS)
        {
            printf("\nSqlState=|%s| szErrorMsg=|%s| rc=%d",
                szSqlState,szErrorMsg,rc);
            printf("\nSQL_INVALID_HANDLE=%d rc=%d ",
                SQL_INVALID_HANDLE, rc);
        }
    } while (rc==SQL_SUCCESS);
    return(rc);
}

CODBCCursor::CODBCCursor(CODBCDatabase *db)
{
    int loop;
    InitializeCriticalSection(&CriticalSection);

    if (db==0 || db->isConnected()==0)
    {
        return;
    }
    _database=db;
    // Allocate a statement handle; the statement handle is used
    //  for other transactions.
    lastRetCode=SQLAllocStmt(_database->hdbc, &hstmt);
    if (lastRetCode!=SQL_SUCCESS)
    {
        GetSQLError(SQL_HANDLE_DBC, _database->hdbc);
    }
```

```
    for (loop=0 ; loop<MAX_COLUMNS ; loop++)
    {
        colInfo[loop] = 0;
    }
    tableClause[0] = '\0';
    orderByClause[0] = '\0';
    whereClause[0] = '\0';
    m_topN=0;
}

CODBCCursor::~CODBCCursor()
{
    int loop;
    SQLFreeHandle(SQL_HANDLE_STMT,hstmt);
    for (loop=1 ; loop<MAX_COLUMNS && colInfo[loop]!=0 ; loop++)
    {
        delete colInfo[loop]->name;
        delete colInfo[loop]->data;
        delete colInfo[loop];
    }
    DeleteCriticalSection(&CriticalSection);

}

RETCODE CODBCCursor::bindColumn(UWORD& col, char *columnName,
    SDWORD len, SWORD type)
{
    SDWORD retLen;
    EnterCriticalSection(&CriticalSection);
    col=assignColumn(columnName, len);
    colInfo[col]->type = type;
    LeaveCriticalSection(&CriticalSection);
    return(SQLBindCol(hstmt, col, type, colInfo[col]->data,
        len, &retLen));
}

UWORD CODBCCursor::assignColumn(char *columnName, SDWORD len)
{
    UWORD loop = 1;
    while (colInfo[loop]!=0)
    {
        loop++;
    }
    colInfo[loop] = new struct COLUMN_INFO;
```

*(continued)*

**Listing 8-3** *continued*

```
    numCols = loop;

    if (colInfo[loop]!=0)
    {
        // Allocate the space for the name and the data element.
        colInfo[loop]->name = new char[(strlen(columnName))+1];
        colInfo[loop]->data = new char[len+1];
        colInfo[loop]->len = len;
        if (colInfo[loop]->name==0 || colInfo[loop]->data==0)
        {
            delete colInfo[loop];
            colInfo[loop]=0;
        }
        strcpy(colInfo[loop]->name, columnName);
    }
    return(loop);
}

int CODBCCursor::doSelect()
{
    char select[1280];
    UWORD loop;
    UWORD col = 1;
    UWORD rc;

    memset(select, '\0', 1024);

    if (tableClause[0]!='\0')
    {
        // Construct a SELECT statement.
        if (getNumCol())
        {
            if (m_topN>0)
            {
                sprintf(select, "SELECT TOP %d ", m_topN);
            }
            else
            {
                strcpy(select, "SELECT ");
            }
            for (loop=1 ; colInfo[loop]!=0 ; loop++)
            {
                if (loop>1)
                {
                    strcat(select, ", ");
                }
```

```
                else
                {
                    strcat(select, " ");
                }
                strcat(select,colInfo[loop]->name);
            }
            strcat(select, " FROM ");
            strcat(select, tableClause);

            if (whereClause[0]!='\0')
            {
                strcat(select, " ");
                strcat(select, whereClause);
            }

            if (orderByClause[0]!='\0')
            {
                strcat(select, " ORDER BY ");
                strcat(select, orderByClause);
            }

            if ((lastRetCode = SQLExecDirect(hstmt,
                (unsigned char *)select,SQL_NTS))!=SQL_SUCCESS)
            {
                GetSQLError(SQL_HANDLE_STMT, hstmt);
            }
            return(lastRetCode);
        }
    }
    return(SQL_ERROR);
}

int CODBCCursor::doDelete()
{
    char del[1280];

    memset(del, '\0', 1024);

    if (tableClause[0]!='\0')
    {
        // Construct a DELETE statement.
        if (getNumCol())
        {
            strcpy(del, "DELETE * ");
            strcat(del, " FROM ");
            strcat(del, tableClause);
```

*(continued)*

**Listing 8-3** *continued*

```
            if (whereClause[0]!='\0')
            {
                strcat(del, " ");
                strcat(del, whereClause);
            }

            if ((lastRetCode = SQLExecDirect(hstmt,
                (unsigned char *)del,SQL_NTS))!=SQL_SUCCESS)
            {
                GetSQLError(SQL_HANDLE_STMT, hstmt);
            }
            return(lastRetCode);
        }
    }
    return(SQL_ERROR);
}

int CODBCCursor::doUpdate()
{
    char update[1280];

    memset(update, '\0', 1024);

    if (tableClause[0]!='\0' || setClause[0]!='\0')
    {
        // Construct an UPDATE statement.
        if (getNumCol())
        {
            strcpy(update, "UPDATE ");
            strcat(update, tableClause);

            strcat(update, " SET ");
            strcat(update, setClause);

            if (whereClause[0]!='\0')
            {
                strcat(update, " ");
                strcat(update, whereClause);
            }

            if ((lastRetCode=SQLExecDirect(hstmt,
                (unsigned char *)update,SQL_NTS))!=SQL_SUCCESS)
```

```
            {
                GetSQLError(SQL_HANDLE_STMT, hstmt);
            }
            return(lastRetCode);
        }
    }
    return(SQL_ERROR);
}

RETCODE CODBCCursor::fetch()
{
    int col;
    // This function retrieves the data. The function returns a
    //  single row at a time and moves the cursor one row forward.
    for (col=1 ; colInfo[col]!=0 ; col++)
    {
        memset(colInfo[col]->data, 0, colInfo[col]->len);
    }
    lastRetCode = SQLFetch(hstmt);
    if (lastRetCode!=SQL_SUCCESS)
    {
        GetSQLError(SQL_HANDLE_STMT, hstmt);
    }
    return(lastRetCode);
}
```

Once the critical section is relinquished, the class copies of the data source name, user name, and password are saved. Finally the connection to the database is made, using the ODBC API function *SQLConnect*. (Several other functions allow connection to the data source and are documented in the SDK and MSDN.) Note that the error-handling method, *GetSQLError*, does little more than get the error text and then print it to the screen. Real applications would log errors and do a better job of handling the presentation.

The destructor acts as the deallocation function for resources allocated in the constructor by closing the connection using *SQLDisconnect* and freeing the connection handle using *SQLFreeHandle*. Inside the critical section, the destructor decrements the reference count and frees the environment handle if the count has decreased to 0.

The *ExecuteSQL* method is the heart of the *CODBCDatabase* class. *ExecuteSQL* allows arbitrary SQL statements to be executed. This flexibility is useful for perfoming an action query such as an update or a delete that might not fit into the *CODBCCursor* structure. A statement handle is allocated, and if it is successful, the SQL statement is executed using *SQLExecDirect*. Finally the statement handle is freed and the method returns.

As I previously mentioned, the *GetSQLError* method collects the information about an error from an ODBC command in a reasonable fashion, but it presents the information poorly, by simply printing the error message to the screen. The underlying API for gathering error information resulting from ODBC API calls has changed dramatically in ODBC version 3. The old function that was used to gather error information, *SQLError*, had a rather odd calling convention that required passing all three types of handles to the error function or NULL values as placeholders. The *SQLGetDiagRec* function is a vast improvement. *SQLGetDiagRec* allows you to specify the handle that the error occurred with directly, and it also allows the return of as many diagnostic records as required to describe each error. The first error specified is virtually always enough to track down the cause of the problem, but the additional information could be useful in complicated error situations.

## The *CODBCCursor* Class

The *CODBCCursor* constructor allocates resources and initializes class data members; the destructor frees the resources allocated in the constructor. Each *CODBCCursor* instance has its own critical section object that can safely be initialized in the constructor because one critical section object is not shared among all instances of the class (unlike the critical section object in *CODBCDatabase*, which is declared as static).

The *bindColumn* and *assignColumn* methods work together to bind columns in data sets. The data sets are returned in the *data* member of each element in the array of COL_INFO structures. This array contains information about each column, including the name of the field being bound and the data type of the field. The *assignColumn* method is used to actually determine the first element of the COL_INFO array available for use. The *CODBCCursor*'s critical section is entered within the *bindColumn* method so the column can be assigned safely even in multithreaded applications. Finally the *SQLBindCol* ODBC API function is called to actually bind the column in the query to the *data* member of the class, and the return value of the *SQLBindCol* function becomes the return value for the *bindColumn* method.

The *doSelect*, *doDelete*, and *doUpdate* member functions all perform the same task: they create SQL statements to pass on to ODBC based on the operation that is to be performed. This is possible because of the regular structure of the SELECT, DELETE, and UPDATE SQL statements. Given the table name, field name (for the SELECT and the UPDATE statements), the field values (for the UPDATE statement), and the restriction and sorting information (for the SELECT statement), creating the required SQL code is possible. (Behind the scenes, tools such as Microsoft Visual

Studio perform exactly the same tasks when you are using two-way tools that allow the program to properly reflect changes in SQL code.) At the end of each method, the *SQLExecDirect* ODBC API function is called to execute the SQL code generated.

The *fetch* method is the final function defined in *CODBCCursor*. This method is responsible for getting the results and setting up the bound columns, and the code is quite straightforward. First the *data* member of each element of the COL_INFO structure array is initialized to NULL. This is not always necessary, but in some cases ODBC drivers do not properly set the bound field when the fields are NULL. Defensive programming dictates that when an error occurs in a module you cannot control, it is wise to try and prevent collateral damage based on that error.

> **NOTE** Changing this class to use *SQLExtendedFetch* to get more than a single record at a time would be an interesting exercise. It would require changes to the COL_INFO structure to allow it to handle the larger number of rows returned at one time, as well as changes to the *fetch* method of the class.

## ODBC TRAPS AND PITFALLS

The code presented in this chapter is designed to use the ODBC version 3–compatible functions. In theory, the applications created using this class should work even if the driver does not understand ODBC version 3, by transparently mapping ODBC version 3 functions to the ODBC version 2 functions. Mapping seems like a good idea, but in practice it is less than perfect. At least one recently released ODBC-compatible DBMS does not support the version 3 semantics and will not allow version 3 applications to run correctly. This can become a major problem, which might require you to maintain an older version of the class for use with the non-complying application—and at the same time maintain a newer version that will fully exploit the features the latest ODBC has to offer.

Additionally, the lack of data type standardization can lead to problems. Even in the simple example presented in Listing 8-1, dependencies on date formats would likely require minor application modifications before the application would work properly with other ODBC-compliant databases. The need to make changes to accommodate data type differences between ODBC data sources is not ideal, and it can cause tremendous difficulties when moving an ostensibly data-neutral ODBC application from one database to another. Number representation is another potential trouble area.

Another important task for developers of server applications is ensuring that the ODBC driver does not present a user interface and display message boxes, but rather notifies the application program of errors directly. Testing for this error notification is important if the vendor cannot or will not certify that the driver is without a UI. The problems can be subtle. For instance, one ODBC driver required for a recent project appeared to meet the criteria because errors seemed to properly generate return codes that indicated errors had occurred. Unfortunately, when the ODBC API functions were used to gather diagnostic information concerning errors that occurred, it was discovered that the driver did generate a message box.

In limited cases, some drivers might generate message boxes for only certain classes of errors. Perhaps in these situations, the developer of the driver considered it impossible to propagate the error code without showing a message box.

*Chapter 9*

# Active Server Pages

More than anything else, the advent of the Internet and intranets has fed the need for server-based applications. The primary motivation for the move to server-based applications is the limited bandwidth available between some of today's clients and servers, especially Internet clients and the servers that feed them. Traditional client/server systems have relied on relatively fat clients, as well as the relatively speedy access to the servers containing the data. When the fat clients could do much of the work of manipulating the data, there was less incentive to create truly scalable server-based applications. The Internet changes all of this.

The earliest Web pages made only modest use of the servers they ran on, merely serving up Hypertext Markup Language (HTML) pages to relatively primitive Web browsers. For a long time, this was enough. Even today, many Web sites simply provide static documents and perhaps a modest search capability—for example, sites that allow searches of archives of medical and scientific information.

As time progressed, however, Web sites began to transform into Web applications. A Web application is distinguished by the fact that the content provided is not simply a set of static Web pages, though there might be some static content included. A Web application presents dynamic content to the user and, more often than not, allows the user to interact with the database behind the dynamic content. This moves the Web application beyond animated icons and musical pages.

There are several alternatives to consider for creating Web applications. The first method, used primarily on UNIX Web servers, is Common Gateway Interface (CGI). I discussed CGI briefly in Chapter 3, so I won't dwell on it here, but in general, CGI provides a way to use existing programming tools to create applications that use the standard input of a program to get information from the user of the browser and send information back to the browser using standard output. CGI programs can therefore be written in languages that UNIX users are comfortable with, including C and scripted languages like Perl.

CGI has a dark side, however. Each time it is called, a CGI program creates a new process for each user. Process creation is a relatively expensive operation, and thus limits the scalability of these Web applications. In the Microsoft Windows NT world, these CGI applications never really caught on, primarily because of the inclusion of Microsoft Internet Information Server (IIS) with Windows NT and, later, Windows 2000. IIS offers several alternatives to CGI applications. Some of these options—which I'll discuss in later chapters—make use of the Internet Server API (ISAPI). One of the most popular alternatives offered by IIS is Active Server Pages (ASP).

# WHAT IS AN ACTIVE SERVER PAGE?

## It's like an HTML Page...

When you first see an Active Server Page, it might remind you of an HTML page. The resemblance is not accidental. First and foremost, an Active Server Page is designed to create standard HTML that is sent to the browser. One way to do this is simply to place HTML code into the Active Server Page. For instance, if you saved Listing 9-1 into an ASP file, you would create the page shown in Figure 9-1.

Of course, using ASP as a simple replacement for HTML is not its intended mission. The real use for ASP is to create applications that change and react to the user who sits at the browser. This is done by using server-side scripting. Server-side

**HelloWorld. asp**

```
<HTML>
<HEAD>
</HEAD>
<BODY>

<P><H1>Hello World!</H1></P>

</BODY>
</HTML>
```

**Listing 9-1**

scripting allows developers of Web applications to create complex applications using VBScript, a simple language related to Microsoft Visual Basic.

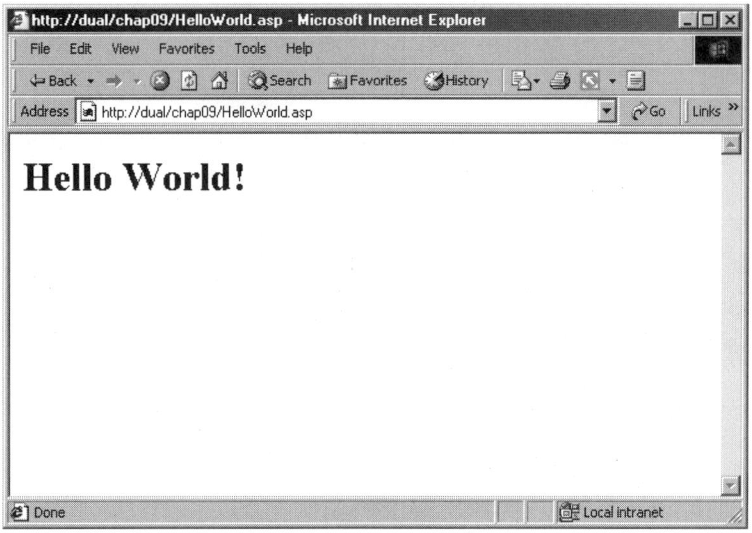


**Figure 9-1** *A simple "Hello World" Active Server Page as seen by the user at a browser.*

**NOTE** ASP pages can also contain JavaScript (or JScript, Microsoft's version of JavaScript). There are several problems with using JavaScript. First, you might think it is closely related to Java. It is not. It was named JavaScript only after the marketing success of Java. Second, virtually all Microsoft documentation on Active Server Pages deals with VBScript.

This is not as big a problem as it might seem. While your server-based scripting has limited portability, in general that limitation is not as crucial as whether your application will run on the various browsers that are out there. Here is the good news: ASP pages can create plain vanilla HTML on the browser, even when the ASP page uses VBScript on the server. Furthermore, you can even use VBScript to create JavaScript on the client browser, as I'll demonstrate in the Troubleshooter example later in this chapter. Here, use of JavaScript might be more reasonable than use of VBScript, since Netscape Navigator and most other non-Microsoft browsers support some form of JavaScript.

## ...But It's Not *Exactly* the Same as an HTML Page

Server-side scripting using VBScript is what transforms ASP pages into dynamic, living applications. While I've devoted most of this book to the creation of server-side applications using C++, I focus this chapter on the use of server-side scripting using a language many C++ programmers would prefer to avoid. Why? Because sometimes the right tool for the job is not the tool you are most familiar with.

Many of the applications that we will create using ASP can be augmented with the other technologies mentioned elsewhere in this book, as I'll explain. For many Web-based applications, ASP is the right place to start, perhaps just for prototyping the application, but possibly even for the entire life cycle of many simpler Web applications. As a working programmer, I have discovered that exploring all alternatives can't help but make a better end product.

You will like some features and hate some features of VBScript. When I give classes on ASP and ISAPI, I always include this list of pros and cons:

### Why you will hate coding in VBScript

- It is like Visual Basic—enough said.
- Variables are untyped or, rather, variant types, which could hold almost anything.
- Variables do not need to be declared before use—terrible for lousy typists.
- Debugging is not ideal.

### Why you will use VBScript anyway

- It is like Visual Basic—enough said.
- It gives reasonable performance for a scripting language.
- It can be extended with ActiveX controls.
- It is supported within Windows 2000, which can't be underestimated when planning which technology to use.
- Debugging is *ever so much* better with IIS 4 and later.

I'll elaborate on some of these pros and cons, but first let's look at some simple server-side scripting in action. Listing 9-2 illustrates some simple scripting that creates the page shown in Figure 9-2.

**FontSize.asp**

```
<%@ Language=VBScript %>
<HTML>
<HEAD>
</HEAD>
<BODY>
```

**Listing 9-2**

```
<%
dim tLoop
for tLoop=1 to 7
%>
<BASEFONT SIZE=<%=Cstr(tLoop)%>>
<P>Hello World!</P>
<%
next
%>
</BODY>
</HTML>
```

Just as important as the output on the browser screen is the actual source that the browser sees. Listing 9-3 shows the source, obtained by choosing Source from the View menu in Microsoft Internet Explorer. You can see that there is no magic involved. The loop is simply "unwound," and each change to the font and each instance of the actual text is placed inline in the resulting HTML code. This is a trivial example, but even the most exotic example—which might use a recordset returned from a database—is no different in principle than this example that uses a local variable.

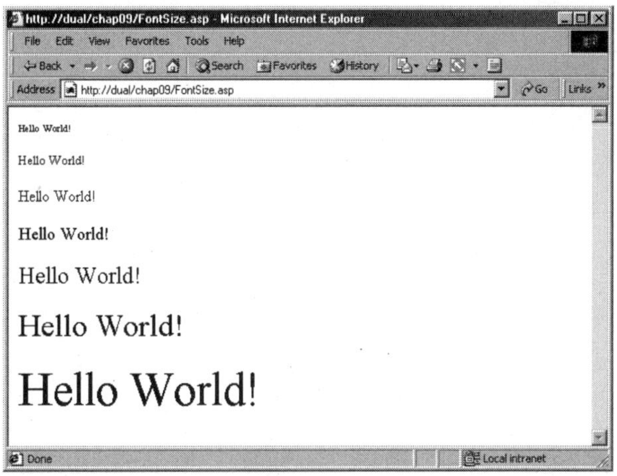


**Figure 9-2** *Browser output from simple ASP scripting that loops to increase the font size.*

**Browser's View of FontSize.asp**

```
<HTML>
<HEAD>
</HEAD>
<BODY>


<BASEFONT SIZE=1>
<P>Hello World!</P>

<BASEFONT SIZE=2>
<P>Hello World!</P>

<BASEFONT SIZE=3>
<P>Hello World!</P>

<BASEFONT SIZE=4>
<P>Hello World!</P>

<BASEFONT SIZE=5>
<P>Hello World!</P>

<BASEFONT SIZE=6>
<P>Hello World!</P>

<BASEFONT SIZE=7>
<P>Hello World!</P>

</BODY>
</HTML>
```

**Listing 9-3**

When using IIS, any file with an .asp extension is processed by default by a special DLL called ASP.DLL. Figure 9-3 shows the IIS Application Configuration dialog that allows this configuration to be set. While ASP is a standard part of IIS, it is a standard part that could be disabled or even changed if you had a different requirement for handling ASP pages. A more reasonable alternative, used by a number of Web developers, is to define a new file extension—for instance, .isp (for Internet Server Page)—and create an extension DLL that is then declared as the handler for these .isp files, just like the ASP.DLL is declared for .asp files. With this DLL in place, any file requested that has an extension of .isp will be processed by our replacement DLL. I'll discuss the realm of ISAPI extensions in more detail in Chapter 10.

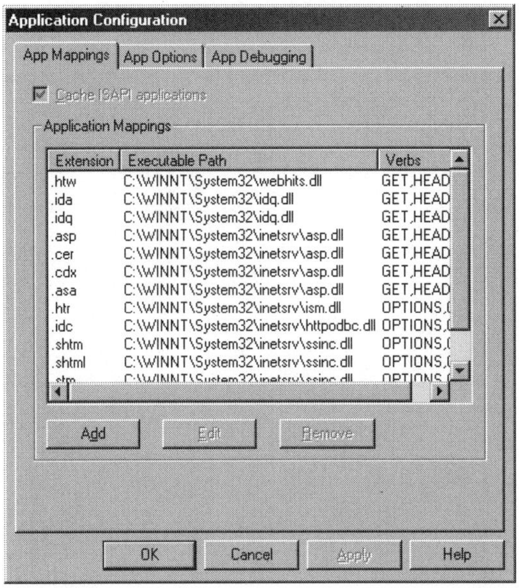


**Figure 9-3** *IIS Application Configuration dialog.*

A closer look at Listing 9-2 shows the difference between standard HTML and ASP pages. The first thing to notice is the use of delimiters to enclose the server side script. For example, <% appears just before the declaration of *tLoop*, using the *Dim* keyword. As I've mentioned, the declaration of variables in VBScript is optional but always a good idea, especially if you intend to move some of the script code into components to be compiled in Visual Basic. Next we have the start of a *for* loop, followed by the script end delimiter, %>. What comes next is some standard HTML code, followed by a special case of the script delimiter. *<%=Cstr(tLoop)%>* means that what follows is script and thus the variables currently in scope in the script are available. The "=" directly after the opening script delimiter is a special signal that the following expression should be evaluated and placed into the HTML stream going to the client. While this mixing and matching of scripting and code can be convenient, it can also lead to code that defies maintenance every bit as much as the spaghetti code of old. Alternatively, the ASP page in Listing 9-2 could have been rewritten so that it was structured like Listing 9-4, which uses the *Response* object's *Write* method. (I'll describe both shortly.) From the code, even without an understanding of the *Response* object, the intention is clear. We are looking to write out the strings of HTML code, with our variable copied into the HTML stream. I find this way of creating ASP applications much more readable, and certain optimizations can take place. For example, when you're writing a large amount of text to the browser, you might be better off concatenating strings and then at the end having a single call to *Response.Write*. Of course, the slowness of VBScript's string handling makes this less than ideal as well, but sending a single string to the browser in a single *Response.Write* statement might still be faster than sending the individual strings.

**Response.asp**

```
<%@ Language=VBScript %>
<HTML>
<HEAD>
<META NAME="GENERATOR" Content="Microsoft Visual Studio 6.0">
</HEAD>
<BODY>

<%
dim tLoop
for tLoop=1 to 7
    Response.Write("<BASEFONT SIZE="+Cstr(tLoop)+">")
    Response.Write("<P>Hello World!</P>")
next
%>

</BODY>
</HTML>
```

**Listing 9-4**

# ASP STRENGTHS

Now that you have seen a little of what ASP can do, let's examine the strengths and weaknesses of ASP in more detail. The first strength—which is also a weakness—is that VBScript is usually used for scripting ASP pages. The strength of VBScript is that it is derived from Visual Basic, and literally millions of people have at least passing familiarity with Visual Basic. VBScript takes much of its strength from the ease of use that has become the norm for many developers. The support for VBScript in Microsoft Visual InterDev (part of Microsoft Visual Studio) includes the IntelliSense code completion ability that many programmers have become accustomed to. For example, while creating the code for Listing 9-4, I only needed to type *Response* followed by a period and I was presented with a list of the methods and properties of the *Response* object. Highlight the correct method or property (either by using the arrow keys or by typing the first letter of the method or property) and press the Tab key, and the method or property appears in the code, with further help on the arguments required for any methods. This is a powerful aide in learning a new programming language.

The second strength of ASP is that the resulting application is often "fast enough." That is, you could certainly find ways to improve performance (as we will discuss), but the application might already be fast enough as written. This is especially true for intranet applications, for which you can get some idea of the likely traffic on the site when it is available. Gauging site traffic is much tougher when you're creating an Internet site. Will your site be the next Amazon.com? If so, pure ASP code will likely not be enough.

When you do hit the wall performance-wise, you just might need to tear everything out and start fresh with another technology, such as ISAPI. It is just as possible that you will be able to do spot optimizations using ActiveX components. For instance, string manipulation can be slow using Visual Basic and VBScript. If you have a page that needs to do a lot of string manipulation and that is causing a performance problem, creating an ActiveX component using the Active Template Library in Microsoft Visual C++ can have a tremendously positive impact. You will see an example of that later in this chapter.

ASP pages also are fairly well integrated into IIS, which is itself fairly well integrated into Windows 2000. This is a terrific advantage, as you can presume that Windows 2000 server machines will have IIS and thus will be able to run any ASP application you create. Documentation and support for ASP is extensive, including Microsoft's MSDN as well as third-party articles and books (some of which I've noted in the annotated bibliography).

Debugging ASP applications has become much simpler as well. In the days of IIS 3, debugging meant placing trace statements that would give you some insights into any problems running the application, or you would need to rely upon error messages that were less than user-friendly. With IIS 4 and later, debugging has reached a new height. You can debug applications on the server or client machines, and the debugger will place you at the line where the error has occurred. Variable values can be displayed as hints when the mouse cursor is placed over the variable in the source, or they can be displayed in a watch window. IIS 5, which is included with Windows 2000, introduces a new *Error* object that allows much greater control when an error occurs.

## ASP WEAKNESSES

Of course, using ASP is not all sunshine. As I mentioned, one of its strengths is also one of its weaknesses. For all its flexibility, VBScript is still fairly weak in some of the areas that would make creation of robust solutions easier. First, the structure of ASP pages can exacerbate VBScript's tendency to create applications that aren't structured the way you might want to structure them. For instance, programmers commonly use subroutines located in libraries linked in at compile time or DLLs linked in at run time to place commonly used routines in a single area. It is not as easy to do this in VBScript, though recent changes to ASP in IIS 5 have made it easier than before by introducing scripted objects that can be created at run time.

Variables present another problem for the VBScript programmer, especially the VBScript programmer who is a poor typist. While most languages will catch you if you call a variable *szFirstName* in one spot and *szFristName* in another, VBScript will happily create a second variable named *szFristName*, initialized to nothing. This can drive you crazy. Second, all VBScript variables are variants. Variants are variables that can be one of any number of types, and at run time you can place whatever you want into the variable. For instance, in a single module, you could say *szFirstName="Fred"* and several lines later say *szFirstName=72*. In this example, the second assignment obviously defies the implied intention for use of the variable, since 72 is clearly not a first name, and our use of "sz" as a prefix implies that we are looking to place a string in the variable. Real-world cases are often much less obvious. A consequence using variants is that if you decide to move some of the code into an object that will be created in Visual Basic and used by the VBScript in an ASP application, you will have some work to do declaring the variables with types and then tracking down the places where you inadvertently do things that are not type-safe.

While ASP applications are much easier to debug than they once were, they are still not as easy to debug as a traditional Visual Basic or C++ application. In many scenarios, the debugger will show you the problem and allow you to check the value of variables. The view of the actual source will still be read-only, meaning that you can determine the problem and then fix it using another tool.

Another ASP weakness—especially if you intend to distribute the application—is the fact that the actual script code, not some compiled version, must be distributed. If you are creating an application for resale, this is a serious problem because a user might inadvertently modify the code and any trade secrets embedded in the script will be visible. This can be mitigated somewhat by placing key code in ActiveX components, but undoubtedly, much of the code will be exposed to your customers.

## OBJECTS AVAILABLE IN ASP APPLICATIONS

In order to do any nontrivial task with ASP, and indeed, even to do some trivial tasks in a clean way (see Listing 9-4), you need to understand the native objects available in ASP applications. There are six major objects available to ASP applications:

- *Application* object—one per application
- *Session* object—one per session
- *Server* object—server-related methods
- *Request* object—information coming in

- *Response* object—information going out
- *ObjectContext* object—transaction support.

Some objects you will virtually always use, such as the *Response* and *Session* objects, and some you will seldom use, such as the *ObjectContext* object. The next several sections describe each object in detail. You'll also find tables with their commonly used methods, properties, and events. You'll find more information about these objects in the MSDN documentation.

## The *Application* Object

The *Application* object is used to share information among sessions using a single application. The *Application* object also exposes two events that allow setup and shutdown operations to take place for the application. Table 9-1 details the *Application* object's major properties and methods.

**TABLE 9-1**
***APPLICATION* OBJECT COLLECTIONS, METHODS, AND EVENTS**

| *Name* | *Description* |
|---|---|
| *Contents* | A collection that contains all items added to the application object through scripting |
| *StaticObjects* | A collection that contains objects added to the application through the <OBJECT> tag |
| *Lock* | A method to lock the application, serializing access to the application object (required because more than one user can be interacting with the application object at one time) |
| *Unlock* | A method to unlock the application after it has been locked using the *Lock* method |
| *Application_OnEnd* | An event fired when the application ends; used for cleanup of anything created in the *Application_OnStart* event |
| *Application_OnStart* | An event fired when an application starts; used to set up any application-level information that is required, fired once in the life of the application |

To fully understand the *Application* object, you must understand the structure of an ASP application. Separate applications are set up in separate virtual directories. (See Appendix A for information on setting up virtual directories in IIS 5.) When an application is run (specifically, when the first ASP document is requested), IIS looks in the root directory of the application's virtual directory for a file named Global.asa. Listing 9-5 shows a simple example of a Global.asa file.

**NOTE** One thing that you will notice about ASP VBScript code is that it often uses shortcuts to get at some member variables. For instance, look at the following line of code from Listing 9-5:

Application("SQLLOGIN")="UID=sa;PWD=PASSWORD;DSN=EXCEPTIONS"

The expression on the left of the equal sign is a shortcut to the actual variable, *Application.Contents("SQLLOGIN"). Contents* is the default property for the application object, and thus can be eliminated in expressions that would otherwise require it.

This type of shortcut is common, and virtually all of the objects have default properties that allow you to essentially subscript the object itself to access elements within it. Some of the objects have more complex behaviors than a default property.

**Global.asa**

```
<SCRIPT LANGUAGE="VBScript" RUNAT="Server">

'You can add special event handlers in this file that will get run
' automatically when special Active Server Pages events occur.  To
' create these handlers, just create a subroutine with a name from
' the list below that corresponds to the event you want to use.

sub Application_OnStart 'Runs once when the first page of your
                        ' application is run for the first time by
                        ' any user.
    Application("SQLLOGIN")="UID=sa;PWD=PASSWORD;DSN=EXCEPTIONS"
end sub

'sub Application_OnEnd   ' Runs once when the Web server shuts down.
'end sub

Sub Session_OnStart
    session("User")=""
    session("UserCode")=0
    session("UserLevel")=0
    session("UserFirstName")=""
    response.redirect "login.asp"
End Sub

Sub Session_OnEnd
    session("UserCode")=0
End Sub

</SCRIPT>
```

**Listing 9-5**

The .asa extension stands for Active Server Application. Within this file, IIS executes the *Application_OnStart* event handler if it exists. In Listing 9-5, the application variable *SQLLOGIN* is set. The other bookend for *Application_OnStart* is *Application_OnEnd*. In Listing 9-5, the *Application_OnEnd* event handler is commented out. It is faster not to have one of these handlers present if no code needs to be run. In Listing 9-5, no resources are allocated in *Application_OnStart*, so *Application_OnEnd* is not needed.

Two other points are worth noting about this file. An application-level variable is set within *Application_OnStart*, and there is no synchronization of the variable using *Application.Lock* and *Application.Unlock*. Synchronization is not necessary here because this event will be called exactly once and no other application-level code can execute until *Application_OnStart* returns. The second notable feature of this file is that while the *Application_OnEnd* event is supported, it is not a good idea to actually place any critical resource deinitialization operations in this event handler, because in certain cases it might not be called reliably. I'll discuss similar concerns about the *Session_OnEnd* event shortly. The *Application_OnEnd* handler is especially prone not to get called—for instance, if the server just goes down rather than properly shutting down. In many cases, the resource leak won't matter because if the server drops, the disposition of the resources is not a major concern. However, in situations in which a resource is owned on behalf of the server by another server, a resource leak can be a concern.

Because access to application scope variables must be gated with calls to *Application.Lock* and *Application.Unlock*, avoid using application-level variables. Using application-level variables thus can cause the application to have a choke point—a point through which the application is serialized. In Listing 9-5, the application-level variable that is set is treated as a read-only variable, and so its use will not cause a problem.

> **NOTE** One concern when using ASP script files is the possibility that the script might become visible or readable by clients. This is not entirely unfounded, as IIS 3 did have a bug that caused a fully qualified URL, including a file name entered with a trailing period (for instance, *http://pro/default.asp.*), to display the contents of the ASP file rather than the pure HTML code that would be generated if the script was properly processed. Though this bug has been corrected in subsequent versions of IIS, its recurrence is still a concern. One precaution I take is never to place anything that I would not like displayed to end users (such as the user name and password for access to the SQL Server database) in an ASP file. Therefore, I set an application variable in the Global.asa file that will allow all ASP files to get at the information indirectly.

## The *Session* Object

The *Session* object contains per-session information and allows an application to track the state of a single user's session. The *Session* object is similar to the *Application* object in that it exposes events that are placed in the Global.asa file. In the *Session_OnStart* event handler in Listing 9-5, session variables are initialized and the user is then redirected to a specific page—Login.asp—using the *Response* object, which I'll discuss shortly. Table 9-2 details the *Session* object's major properties and methods.

> **NOTE** Since an application can have a default page, why is it important to redirect a user to a page here? Suppose that the default page in the ASP application is Default.asp. Now suppose that the end user happens to know that there was a page in the application called TopSecret.asp. If rather than entering only the virtual directory name (for instance *http://pro/*), the user entered the virtual directory name with the other ASP file name appended (for instance *http://pro/topsecret.asp*), he could bypass the default start page for the site. By redirecting the user in the *Session_OnStart* event handler, we force the user to pass through the initial page that we specify.

**TABLE 9-2**
***SESSION* OBJECT COLLECTIONS, METHODS, AND EVENTS**

| *Name* | *Description* |
|---|---|
| *Contents* | A collection that contains all items added to the *Session* object through scripting |
| *StaticObjects* | A collection that contains objects added to the *Session* object through the <OBJECT> tag and given session scope |
| *CodePage* | A code page used for symbol mapping |
| *LCID* | A locale identifier |
| *SessionID* | Returns the session identification for this user. The *SessionID* property is a LONG value and should *not* be used for generation of database keys or for any other persistent data store. *SessionID* values are reused when the server is restarted. |
| *Timeout* | The timeout period, in minutes, for this session state. This property determines how long the session needs to be inactive before it will be terminated. |
| *Abandon* | This method destroys a *Session* object and frees the contents. The actual destruction of the *Session* object is delayed until the current page has exited. |
| *Session_OnEnd* | An event fired when the session ends. Used for cleanup of anything created in the *Session_OnStart* event. |
| *Session_OnStart* | An event fired when a user's session starts. Used to set up any session-level information that is required. This event is fired once for each session. |

Most of the *Session* object's collections, methods, and events are either similar to those of the *Application* object, self-explanatory, or not that significant. One exception is the *Timeout* property, which determines the amount of time a session needs to be inactive before the session is killed. This can be useful in situations where the system should time out if inactive—for example, a clinical system in a hospital. Often healthcare workers are called away in the middle of using the system, and these systems might be located in semi-public places. In such cases, you might set a shorter inactivity timeout. Very busy sites might also set a shorter timeout to free resources sooner from inactive users. When the timeout expires, the *Session_OnEnd* event handler will be called.

## The *Server* Object

The *Server* object is a utility object that provides access to methods and properties on the server. Unlike the *Application* and *Session* objects, the *Server* object has no collections associated with it. Table 9-3 provides an overview of the important properties and methods of the *Server* object.

### HYPERTEXT TRANSFER PROTOCOL

Hypertext Transfer Protocol (HTTP) is a stateless protocol. This means that the server sees each request and response as a new event—not tied to previous requests. How then does the *Session* object establish sessions and keep track of session-level variables and inactivity timeouts? The answer is through the use of cookies. Cookies are files stored on the local hard drive by browsers that accept cookies. These cookies have been the cause of some privacy concerns, and there certainly are abuses of cookies. For example, seemingly unrelated sites share information about cookies so that when you visit one site, the second site will change behavior based upon your visit to the first site. Most modern browsers let you turn off cookies, but doing so will most likely deprive you of some of their benefits such as persistence of user preferences.

Are there alternatives to cookies for maintaining state? If you wish to step outside specific support within IIS, you can certainly manage your own concept of state by using hidden text entry fields on each form that will contain information, allowing your application to know who your users are and where in the application they have been. This seems like an awful lot of work and is probably only worth pursuing if you need to communicate with users over the Internet and you don't want to do anything that might discourage users from using your site.

**TABLE 9-3**
**SERVER OBJECT METHODS AND PROPERTIES**

| *Name* | *Description* |
|---|---|
| *ScriptTimeout* | A property that specifies the amount of time a script can run before being terminated. This timeout value does not apply while a server component is running. Additionally, this value cannot be less than the value set in the IIS metabase.* |
| *CreateObject* | A method used to create an instance of a server component. The method takes a single argument—a string representing the program ID (for instance, *ADODB.Recordset*). There is no *DestroyObject* method. Objects are destroyed by setting them equal to the VBScript keyword *Nothing*. |
| *Execute* | *Execute* is a new method in IIS 5. It executes the ASP file specified as the argument as if it were part of the current ASP file. This method is intended to act like procedure calls in other languages, allowing applications to be structured neatly and providing for reuse. |
| *GetLastError* | This is another new method in IIS 5. It might sound familiar to Win32 programmers; its function is similar to the Win32 function. It returns an *ASPErrorObject* that gives more complete error information than previous error handling provided. |
| *HTMLEncode* | This method encodes HTML so that the code itself can be displayed rather than being rendered as HTML. |
| *MapPath* | This method maps a virtual path to a physical path. For instance, if you passed in a virtual path of *\troubleshoot\default.asp*, this method might return something like *d:\inetpub\wwwroot\troubleshoot\default.asp* |
| *Transfer* | This method is new for IIS 5. It sends all of the current state information to another ASP for processing. Even if the ASP specified is in another virtual path, the variables defined within the current application will be available in the called ASP. |
| *URLEncode* | This method encodes a Uniform Resource Locator (URL) so that it can be displayed directly. |

* The IIS metabase is the repository for most IIS configuration information. In versions of IIS prior to version 5, a large amount of this configuration information was stored in the registry. IIS 5 uses virtually no registry entries for configuration information.

The *CreateObject* method is the one element of the *Server* object that virtually all applications will use. This is the great escape clause that allows ASP applications to move beyond scripts and leverage existing code—at least existing code that can be modified to work within an ActiveX component. The *Execute* and *Transfer* methods are the most important new additions to IIS 5. While much of the functionality provided by these two methods can also be provided using the *Response.Redirect* method, *Execute* and *Transfer* offer the following advantages.

- No round-trip to the client machine is required. The transfer takes place entirely on the server.
- The state of the session is available even in the case of a transfer to another application.
- There is no chance that the user of the browser will get a message about the page moving. This is in contrast to what happens on some browsers when a *Response.Redirect* is performed on the server.

The *GetLastError* method returns an *ASPError* object that provides the following information about the most recent error:

- *ASPCode* Returns the ASP error code.
- *Number* Returns the COM error code.
- *Source* A string indicating whether the error was internal to ASP, to the scripting language, or to an object.
- *FileName* The name of the file where the error occurred.
- *LineNumber* The line number within the file where the error occurred.
- *Description* Returns a short description of the error. This could be something like the OLE DB error message.

This information is a significant improvement over previously available error information.

## The *Request* Object

The *Request* object is the object that allows the user of a browser to provide information to the server to process the user's request. The information in the *Request* object is generally what drives the progress of the application. Table 9-4 provides an overview of the collections, properties, and methods of the *Request* object.

Of the members of the *Request* object, *TotalBytes* and *BinaryRead* are outside the scope of this discussion. The collections operate in a somewhat peculiar way. For instance, if we were to try and send to the browser *Request("MY_VAR")*, not a single default collection would be searched. Each of the collections will be searched in the order shown on the following page.

1. *QueryString*
2. *Form*
3. *Cookies*
4. *ClientCertificates*
5. *ServerVariables*

TABLE 9-4
***REQUEST* OBJECT COLLECTIONS, PROPERTIES, AND METHODS**

| *Name* | *Description* |
|---|---|
| *ClientCertificate* | This collection contains the certification fields (as specified in the X.509 standard) from a request issued by the Web browser. These certificates are generally available only when connecting to a server using a URL beginning in *https://* rather than *http://*. The Web server must request the client certificates. |
| *Cookies* | This collection contains the values sent to the server from the client browser during a request. Cookies are used, among other things, to establish session state. |
| *Forms* | This collection contains the values of form elements in the HTTP request. This can be used to retrieve values entered on forms. The values can be from text boxes, list boxes, or any of the other supported HTTP controls. |
| *QueryString* | This collection contains the values passed as part of the URL. For instance, given the URL *http://dual/default.asp?N=Doug*, *Request.QueryString("N")* would be equal to "Doug". |
| *ServerVariables* | This collection contains the values of a set of predetermined environment variables. These variables are further explained in the MSDN documentation and will be displayed by the Server-Variables.asp example ASP page presented in this section. |
| *TotalBytes* | This read-only property contains the number of bytes the client is sending in the request. |
| *BinaryRead* | This method reads the number of bytes specified by its single argument and returns a safe array with those bytes. *BinaryRead* is generally used in conjunction with the *TotalBytes* property and only if specialized access to the request is required. Once *BinaryRead* is called, trying to access *Request.Form* will generate an error, and calling *BinaryRead* after *Request.Form* has been accessed will also generate an error. |

This can lead to some interesting problems and some useful optimizations. If you had two variables named *MY_VAR*, one in the *QueryString* collection, and another in the *Forms* collection, you would get the copy in *QueryString* unless you fully qualified the variable—for instance, *Request.Form("MY_VAR")*. In a complex application, and especially when searching the *ServerVariables* collection, it is much more efficient to specifically look for the variable in the collection it is in.

The *ServerVariables* collection contains many details about the current session. Listing 9-6 contains code that prints out all of the server variable names and values. Listing 9-7 contains the results of running this code on my machine, detailing all of the server variables available.

**ServerVariables.asp**

```
<%@ Language=VBScript %>
<HTML>
<HEAD>
<META NAME="GENERATOR" Content="Microsoft Visual Studio 6.0">
</HEAD>
<BODY>

<%
dim iLoop

Response.Write("<H1>Server Variables</H1><P>")

for iLoop=1 to Request.ServerVariables.Count
    Response.Write(Request.ServerVariables.Key(iLoop)&" - ")
    Response.Write(Request.ServerVariables.Item(iLoop)&"<es>")
next

%>
<P> </P>

</BODY>
</HTML>
```

**Listing 9-6**

**Output from ServerVariables.asp**

```
ALL_HTTP - HTTP_ACCEPT:*/* HTTP_ACCEPT_LANGUAGE:en-us
⋮
APPL_MD_PATH - /LM/W3SVC/1/Root/Chap09
APPL_PHYSICAL_PATH - \\PRO\e\TEXT\ntbook\Chap09\
AUTH_PASSWORD -
AUTH_TYPE - NTLM
AUTH_USER - DUAL\Administrator
```

**Listing 9-7** *(continued)*

**Listing 9-7** *continued*

```
CERT_COOKIE -
CERT_FLAGS -
CERT_ISSUER -
CERT_KEYSIZE -
CERT_SECRETKEYSIZE -
CERT_SERIALNUMBER -
CERT_SERVER_ISSUER -
CERT_SERVER_SUBJECT -
CERT_SUBJECT -
CONTENT_LENGTH - 0
CONTENT_TYPE -
GATEWAY_INTERFACE - CGI/1.1
HTTPS - off
HTTPS_KEYSIZE -
HTTPS_SECRETKEYSIZE -
HTTPS_SERVER_ISSUER -
HTTPS_SERVER_SUBJECT -
INSTANCE_ID - 1
INSTANCE_META_PATH - /LM/W3SVC/1
LOCAL_ADDR - 127.0.0.1
LOGON_USER - DUAL\Administrator
PATH_INFO - /chap09/ServerVariables.asp
PATH_TRANSLATED - \\PRO\e\TEXT\ntbook\Chap09\ServerVariables.asp
QUERY_STRING -
REMOTE_ADDR - 127.0.0.1
REMOTE_HOST - 127.0.0.1
REMOTE_USER - DUAL\Administrator
REQUEST_METHOD - GET
SCRIPT_NAME - /chap09/ServerVariables.asp
SERVER_NAME - localhost
SERVER_PORT - 80
SERVER_PORT_SECURE - 0
SERVER_PROTOCOL - HTTP/1.1
SERVER_SOFTWARE - Microsoft-IIS/4.0
URL - /chap09/ServerVariables.asp
HTTP_ACCEPT - */*
HTTP_ACCEPT_LANGUAGE - en-us
HTTP_CONNECTION - Keep-Alive
HTTP_HOST - localhost
HTTP_USER_AGENT - Mozilla/4.0 (compatible; MSIE 5.0; Windows NT;
 DigExt)
HTTP_COOKIE - ASPSESSIONIDQQQQQQCG=ONMLKIEDDAEFEHOAHOFHIBIL
HTTP_AUTHORIZATION - NTLM TlRMTVNTUAADAAAAAAAAAEAAAAAAAAAAQAAAAAAAA
BAAAAAAAAAAEAAAAAAAAAAQAAAAAAAAABAAAAABcIBAA==
HTTP_ACCEPT_ENCODING - gzip, deflate
HTTP_EXTENSION - Security/Remote-Passphrase
```

The code in Listing 9-6 uses a variable to loop through *Request.ServerVariables-.Count* variables, printing the "Key" (actually the name of the variable) and the "Item" (the value itself). A couple of the results related to security require some explanation. Notice that AUTH_USER is DUAL/Administrator, as I am logged in as administrator on the machine DUAL. This page is using Windows NT Challenge/Response as the authentication, so the AUTH_TYPE reports itself as NTLM, for NT LAN Manager. AUTH_PASSWORD is blank because NTLM authentication does not store the actual password. If the page were set up to allow Basic authentication, the AUTH_TYPE would be BASIC, and AUTH_PASSWORD would contain the password as entered. This is not an ideal authentication method, since the user name and password are sent using only simple Base64 encoding—essentially equivalent to sending it as clear text.

Notice also that the APPL_PHYSICAL_PATH shows that the virtual directory is actually on another machine—in this case, on the server PRO—since the path is \\PRO\e\TEXT\ntbook\Chap09\. Some of the other information would be more interesting when the page is not run from the workstation where IIS is loaded—for instance, the REMOTE_ADDR and LOCAL_ADDR, which here are set to the loop back address 127.0.0.1. If you were creating an application on an intranet that used static IP addresses, the addresses could be used to provide additional security, allowing the application to grant or deny access to a given page based upon the user as well as the address of the request.

## The *Response* Object

The *Response* object is used to send output to the client. Some of the methods in the *Response* object will be used constantly in any real-world application. An example of this is *Response.Write*. If you elect not to use nonscripted HTML to send output to the browser, *Response.Write* is commonly how you would send output. Other methods, such as *Response.BinaryWrite*, are much less common in the real world. Table 9-5 lists the collections, properties, and methods of the *Response* object.

Of the six native IIS objects, the *Response* object contains the most members. Since the goal of any Web application is to present information to the user, this should not be surprising. Output can be sent to users using ASP pages in many ways, and subtle differences in the method used to present the information can make dramatic differences in performance, and more importantly in perceived performance.

The *Buffer* property is the key to some performance improvements. When all output is saved and sent together after all processing is done, performance is enhanced. Of course, there is one problem. The user's perception of speed might be based upon seeing some immediate activity on the browser. Buffering prevents this from happening. The page will be blank until the output is flushed. Unfortunately, either all or none of the output to the browser can be buffered. In addition, HTML's way of handling some kinds of output can complicate matters. IIS does not send tables to the browser, regardless of the setting of the *Response.Buffer* property, until the entire table has been output. So, if you are outputting a page that is primarily a table, setting *Response.Buffer* to True might not make any real difference in how quickly the user sees the information because the table will be buffered in any event.

**TABLE 9-5**
**RESPONSE OBJECT COLLECTIONS, PROPERTIES, AND METHODS**

| *Name* | *Description* |
|---|---|
| *Cookies* | This collection allows you to set the value of each cookie. If the cookie does not exist, IIS creates it. |
| *Buffer* | This property specifies whether the output is buffered. (The behavior of this property has changed in IIS and will be discussed later in this section.) |
| *CacheControl* | This property determines whether the proxy server can cache the output of ASP pages. Generally this will not help performance on ASP pages that generate custom HTML for every request. |
| *CharSet* | This property appends a string to the content-type header in the response object. While it is expected that this will be a valid character set, such as ISO-LATIN-7, no checking is done. |
| *ContentType* | This property changes the content type from the default of text/HTML. |
| *Expires* | This property specifies the length of time before a page cached on the browser expires. This will affect what happens when a browser requests a page more than once. Setting *Expires* to a value less than 0 immediately expires the page. |
| *ExpiresAbsolute* | This property specifies a date and time when the page expires. |
| *IsClientConnected* | This is a read-only property that indicates whether the client is still connected. This can be useful when processing a client's request takes a long time and uses lots of resources. It might be worthwhile to check periodically to see if the client is still connected while processing the request. |
| *PICS* | This property adds a value to the pics-label field of the response header. |
| *Status* | This property modifies the status line returned by the server. This should be a 3-digit number followed by an explanation—for instance, *401 Unauthorized*. |
| *AddHeader* | This advanced method allows you to add a header with a specified value to the response. You can find further details on *AddHeader* in the MSDN documentation. |

| *Name* | *Description* |
|---|---|
| *AppendToLog* | This method appends a message to the end of the server log entry for this request. |
| *BinaryWrite* | This method allows you to write information to the response without character conversion. This could be used to send nonstring information to the browser. |
| *Clear* | This method clears buffered HTML output. An error occurs if this is called when nonbuffered output has already been sent. |
| *End* | This method stops processing and returns the current content. The balance of the output specified is skipped. |
| *Flush* | This method sends buffered output to the browser immediately. |
| *Redirect* | This method causes the browser to try to redirect to the URL specified as the argument to this method. Compare this to the behavior of *Server.Execute* and *Server.Transfer*, where no client involvement is needed. |
| *Write* | The *Write* method is the workhorse of the *Response* object. The string passed as the single argument to this method is either buffered for output to the server or is immediately sent to the server, based upon the setting of the *Buffer* property. |

To further complicate matters, IIS 5 changes the default value of *Response.Buffer*. This property had defaulted to False, but now will default to True. An additional twist is that in an attempt not to break existing applications, upgraded servers will continue to use False as the default value for *Response.Buffer*.

The remaining members of the *Response* object are either obscure (such as PICS) or self-explanatory. The sample application presented at the end of this chapter makes extensive use of the *Response* object.

## The *ObjectContext* Object

The *ObjectContext* object is perhaps the most misunderstood of the native objects. The *ObjectContext* object is used to manage transactions managed by Component Services in Windows 2000 (or Microsoft Transaction Server in Windows NT 4). Often when creating Web applications, you are required to perform a series of operations in multiple steps. Sometimes it is crucial that the actions should be completed in an all-or-nothing fashion. The @TRANSACTION directive within ASP pages is designed for those situations. Pages that use the @TRANSACTION directive are transactional, and either succeed completely or fail. The @TRANSACTION directive must be the first line in the ASP file, and @TRANSACTION must be set to one of the choices shown on the following page.

- *Required*
- *Requires_New*
- *Supported*
- *Not_Supported*

Transactions are one area in which the new *Server.Execute* and *Server.Transfer* are required. If you have two pages—one called by another—and you want them both to be part of a single transaction, *Response.Redirect* will not work, but either of the *Server* object methods will. Table 9-6 presents the *ObjectContext* methods and events.

**TABLE 9-6**
***OBJECTCONTEXT* OBJECT METHODS AND EVENTS**

| *Name* | *Description* |
|---|---|
| *SetComplete* | This method declares that the script knows of no reason why the transaction should not complete. If all components involved in the transaction also call *SetComplete*, the transaction will be committed. |
| *SetAbort* | This method declares that the transaction initiated by the script has not completed, and the resources involved should not be changed. |
| *OnTransactionCommit* | This event handler is called after a transaction commits and is found on the page where the transaction is located. |
| *OnTransactionAbort* | This event handler is called if the transaction is aborted and is found on the page where the transaction is located. |

Not every action taken by a script will be rolled back when a transaction aborts. For example, if you are writing to a file on the server that is not part of a database, that write to the file will not roll back. Components used by the transactional page must also be MTS-aware if the actions taken are to be all-or-nothing.

## ACTIVE SERVER PAGE EXAMPLES

One of the toughest things about getting started with Active Server Pages is just that—getting started. When I became interested in ASP, I looked around to see if I could find one area for a first attempt that met the following criteria:

- The application should be required by a fair number of people, making a compelling argument for the ease of deployment possible with ASP applications.

- The application should be a modest user of database resources—ideally a read-only application.
- The application should be modest in scope.

## A Simple Phone Directory

The first application that met these criteria was a phone directory. While a phone directory could be created as a simple static set of HTML pages, that solution was awkward and didn't allow the kind of clever searching I wanted. For instance, I might want to find all the folks in a particular department, or I might be looking for "Joe" without knowing Joe's last name. The client that was to use this application had tried several approaches to this problem. First they tried Microsoft Word documents and Microsoft Excel spreadsheets. These items were distributed to those who requested them, but they were often outdated before reaching their intended users. Additionally, changes to document formats created support nightmares for the help desk. The same was true for Help files. Paper lists were even worse with regard to timeliness, but at least they did not cause support calls. An ASP application seemed like the perfect solution.

The number of names in the address book was not large (under 1000), so I created a lookup that would search for the entered text anywhere in the record. The record had fields for last name, first name, department, and facility. Thus, if I wanted to see the numbers for all the M.I.S. staff, I could just enter M.I.S. in the query field and get the results. Figure 9-4 shows the screen that allows the user to search for phone numbers, and Figure 9-5 shows the results screen. The complete code, along with a sample database, is included on the companion CD-ROM.

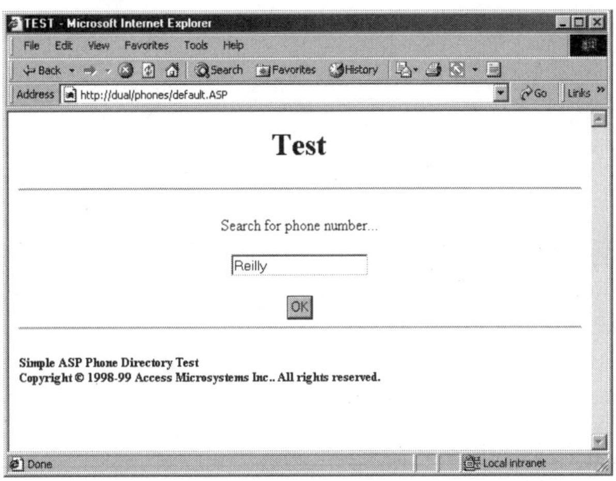


**Figure 9-4** *The simple entry screen for the phone lookup.*

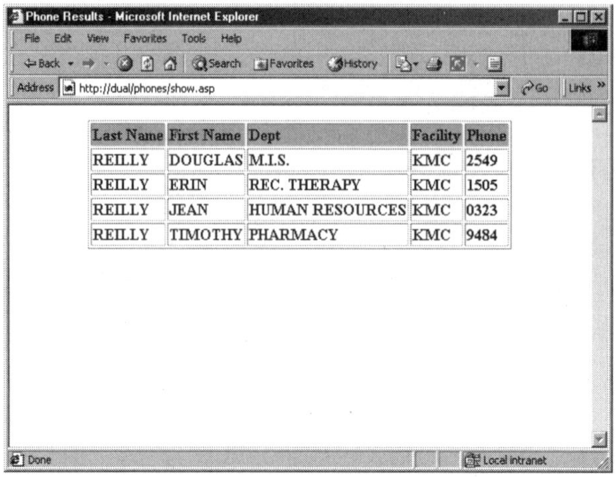


**Figure 9-5** *The results screen for the phone lookup.*

The entry screen in Figure 9-4 contains two simple HTML controls: a text entry box and a submit button. The ASP code in Listing 9-8 generates this screen, which is actually pure HTML. It makes sense to keep this as an ASP page rather than an HTML page. With IIS 5, the overhead associated with processing the file as an ASP rather than an HTML file is minimal, and if future enhancements require ASP code (for instance, to display the current date or time), no references to the page will need to change. The HTML form described in this ASP has as its action Show.asp, the ASP file in Listing 9-9. When the submit button is clicked, control is transferred to Show.asp.

**PhoneBook.asp**

```
<html>

<head>
<title>TEST</title>
<meta NAME="FORMATTER" CONTENT="Microsoft Visual InterDev 1.0">

</head>

<body>
<CENTER>
<h1><a NAME="top">Test</a></h1>

<hr>
<FORM method=POST action=show.asp>
<p>
Search for phone number...
<p><p>
```

**Listing 9-8**

```
<INPUT TYPE=text NAME=showit>
<p>
<INPUT type=submit VALUE="OK">
</CENTER>

<hr>

<h5>Simple ASP Phone Directory Test<br>
Copyright © 1998-99 Access Microsystems Inc.. All rights
 reserved.<br>
</h5>
</body>
</html>
```

Figure 9-5 shows the table that results from the search for entries with "Reilly" anywhere in the record. Take a look at the code in Listing 9-9. The first line is a scripting directive letting ASP know that the file is using VBScript. Next is an *include* statement that defines many symbolic constants that make using ADO easier. This is followed by some fairly straightforward HTML code that sets up some metatags and the title, as well as the start of the body of the HTML page that will be generated. The "<%" is the beginning of the script on this page.

**Show.asp**

```
<%@ LANGUAGE="VBSCRIPT" %>
<!--#include file="adovbs.inc"-->

<HTML>
<HEAD>
<META NAME="GENERATOR" Content="Microsoft Visual InterDev 1.0">
<META HTTP-EQUIV="Content-Type" content="text/html;
 charset=iso-8859-1">
<TITLE>Phone Results</TITLE>
</HEAD>
<BODY>

<%
dim rstPhones
dim db
dim strSQL
dim lookFor

    lookFor = Request.Form("ShowIt")
    set db = Session("db")
    set rstPhones = Server.CreateObject("ADODB.Recordset")
```

**Listing 9-9** *(continued)*

**Listing 9-9** *continued*

```
    ' Construct SQL statement.
    strSQL="Select LName, FName, Dept, Facility, Phone from tblPhone "
    strSQL=strSQL & "WHERE SearchString like '%" & lookFor
    strSQL=strSQL & "%' ORDER BY lName, fName, Dept "
    ' Open recordset based on the SQL statement.
    rstPhones.Open strSQL, db, adOpenDynamic, adLockReadOnly

    ' Check record count, and let them know if nothing found.
    if rstPhones.RecordCount = 0 then
        Response.Write("<CENTER><H2>Sorry! " & _
            " No match found!</H2></CENTER><es>")
    else
        ' Records found?  Move to first record.
        rstPhones.MoveFirst
        ' Write table header.
        Response.Write("<CENTER>")
        Response.Write("<P><TABLE BORDER=1 ><TR>")
        Response.Write("<TD BGCOLOR=aqua><B>Last Name</B></TD>")
        Response.Write("<TD BGCOLOR=aqua><B>First Name</B></TD>")
        Response.Write("<TD BGCOLOR=aqua><B>Dept</B></TD>")
        Response.Write("<TD BGCOLOR=aqua><B>Facility</B></TD>")
        Response.Write("<TD BGCOLOR=aqua><B>Phone</B></TD>")
        Response.Write("</TR>")

        Response.Write("<H3>")
        ' Loop through results to write table details.
        Do While Not rstPhones.EOF
            Response.Write("<TR BGCOLOR=WHITE>")
            Response.Write("<TD BGCOLOR=white><B>" & _
                rstPhones("LName") & "</B></TD>")
            Response.Write("<TD BGCOLOR=white><B>" & _
                rstPhones("FName") & "</B></TD>")
            Response.Write("<TD BGCOLOR=white><B>" & _
                rstPhones("DEPT") & "</B></TD>")
            Response.Write("<TD BGCOLOR=white><B>" & _
                rstPhones("Facility") & "</B></TD>")
            Response.Write("<TD BGCOLOR=white><B>" & _
                rstPhones("Phone") & "</B></TD>")
            Response.Write("</TR>")
            RstPhones.MoveNext
        loop
        Response.Write("</H3>")
        Response.Write("</CENTER)")
    end if
    RstPhones.Close
    ' Free resources associated with the record set.
    set RstPhones = nothing
%>
</BODY>
</HTML>
```

The first thing the script does is use *dim* statements to declare the variables to be used. This is not required, and the *dim* statements are a little different from standard Visual Basic or even Visual Basic for Applications (VBA) in that no type is declared. A local variable, *lookfor*, is set to the *ShowIt* element of the form (which is the text box from the initial screen), explicitly using the *Forms* collection of the *Request* object.

After the script creates an *ADODB.Recordset* object, it constructs a standard SQL SELECT statement and opens the recordset. The count of the recordset is checked, and then based upon whether any records were returned, the code either tells the user that no records were found or creates the table that will contain the results. The bulk of the work is done simply using the *Response.Write* method to write standard HTML to the client browser. Once all the records are written to the browser, the recordset is closed and then set to nothing, destroying the object.

The next step is not a suggested technique, but is here for illustrative purposes. The Global.asa for this application (shown in Listing 9-10) actually creates an *ADODB.Connection* object and saves it in the *Session* object. This is not ideal and will hurt the ability to use the IIS's build in connection pooling. This is not a great loss in this case, as the database for this simple example is a Microsoft Access database, and the Access ODBC driver is not thread-safe and therefore should be operated with IIS's thread pooling turned off. The Global.asa file also redirects the user to the Default.asp file.

**Global.asa**

```
<SCRIPT LANGUAGE="VBScript" RUNAT="Server">

' You can add special event handlers in this file that will get run
'  automatically when special Active Server Pages events occur. To
'  create these handlers, just create a subroutine with a name from
'  the list below that corresponds to the event you want to use.
'  For example, to create an event handler for Session_OnStart, you
'  would put the following code into this file (without the
'  comments):
Sub Session_OnStart
    Dim db

    ' This is just an example. It would be MUCH better to use
    '  connection pooling, creating and destroying
    '  connections as needed.
    Set db=Server.CreateObject("ADODB.Connection")
    db.Open("UID=;PWD=;DSN=PHONES")
```

**Listing 9-10** *(continued)*

**Listing 9-10** *continued*

```
        set session("db")=db
        response.redirect "default.ASP"
    End Sub

    Sub Session_OnEnd
        Dim db
        set db=session("db")
        if isObject(db) then
            set db=nothing
        end if
    End Sub

    'Application_OnStart ' Runs once when the first page of your
                         '  application is run for the first time
                         '  by any user.
    'Application_OnEnd   ' Runs once when the Web server shuts down.

    </SCRIPT>
```

## A More Complex ASP Example: Troubleshooter

While the preceding example was a useful exercise, it was a bit too simple. In the real world, the structure of the data we must use is often more complex than a single, simple table. In addition, we often need to write the date as well as read it. And we sometimes need to move beyond scripting. The following example will allow us to do that.

In the life of a project, there is often a time when the specialized knowledge of a few people needs to be shared with many. So it was recently when I became involved in the rollout of a fairly significant update of a company's major product. This was the company's first significant 32-bit Windows product. It was designed to replace an MS-DOS product, but it needed to coexist with the MS-DOS product, as not all users at all customer sites were ready for a 32-bit Windows program. This led to added complexity in the final product and required that the specialized knowledge of the MS-DOS programmers and the Windows programmers be available to the support staff.

There are many ways to do this, but creating a Web application knowledge base was the option we selected. This choice circumvented the problems with using an application like Microsoft Access. (Not all users had Access installed, and there were at least four different versions of Access running on the support staff's machines in support of end users.) In addition, field installers could dial into the network and gain access to the latest product notes and suggestions from the road. This type of remote access was a key advantage for this rapidly evolving product: since the product was a bit overdue, the installers might be on the road for weeks at a time, making physical distribution of updated databases awkward.

The solution created to meet these requirements is the application shown in Figure 9-6. The first screen is much like the first screen in the phone search application—it is only used to enter criteria for a search. This screen is a bit more complex because it has three controls for entry: a text box, a check box, and a combo box. In addition, the combo box is populated from a table—in this case, a table stored in a Microsoft Database Engine (MSDE) database. The MSDE is a freely distributable data engine, fully compatible with SQL Server 7.0, used to build desktop and shared applications. It is available on the Microsoft Web site at *http://msdn.microsoft.com/vstudio/msde/download.asp*.

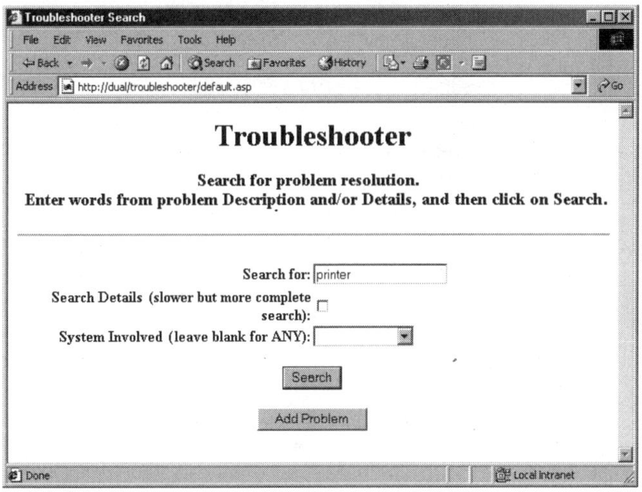


**Figure 9-6** *The search screen for the Troubleshooter system.*

Depending upon the criteria entered, when the Search button is clicked, you will see either a screen telling you that no records met the criteria or a screen with one or more records displayed. Figure 9-7 is an example of the latter screen. From this screen, you can either return to the search screen or click one of the hyperlinks in the Problem Description field and be brought to a screen that shows all the details of the problem. Alternatively, you can go directly from the search screen to an Add New Problem screen. In the real world, the problems added through this screen are placed in a pending status, but the working example on the companion CD-ROM writes out new records with a ready status that will therefore be displayed immediately. The search screens are fairly self-explanatory, but I will discuss some of the finer points of the results screen shortly.

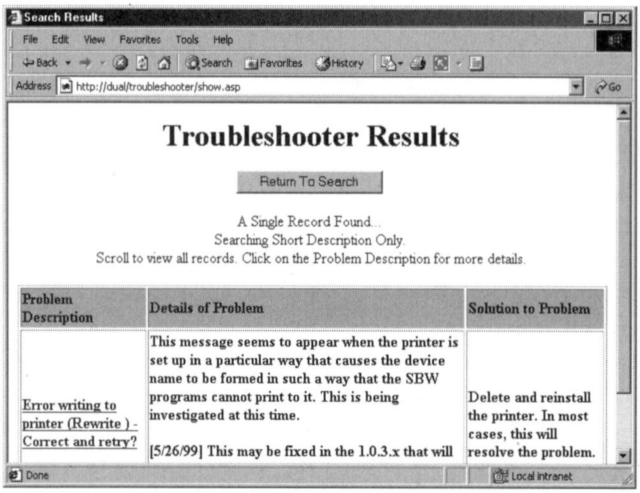


**Figure 9-7** *The results screen for the Troubleshooter system.*

## Integrating ActiveX components

One significant problem existed with the initial implementation. When records from the SQL database were first displayed, it was apparent that the formatting of the entered memo fields was lost in the HTML presentation. Of course, the reason is obvious in retrospect: HTML does not rely upon actual CR/LF pairs to determine where line breaks exist, but rather ignores literal CR/LF pairs and formats line breaks only when "<es>" literals are seen. The solution seemed clear: create a function that will add literal "<es>" strings within the memo fields. The VBScript code fragment below does the trick.

```
function AddBreaks(strIn)
dim tloop
dim strInLen
dim strRet
dim ch
strInLen = len(strIn)
for tloop = 1 to strInLen
    ch = mid(strIn,tloop,1)
    if ch = chr(10) then
        strRet = strRet&"<es>"
    else
        strRet = strRet&ch
    end if
next
addBreaks = strRet
end function
```

While this did solve the problem of line breaks not really appearing in the formatted output, it was not an ideal solution because of the time it took to format the text for some of the longer descriptions. If I entered a query that would return 20 or so records, displaying the results might take between four and six seconds. This lag was due in part to the performance of scripting languages in general and VBScript's string handling in particular.

The solution was to create a simple Active Template Library (ATL) object in Visual C++ that would handle this particular task, as well as any others that might appear. ATL is a library that is ideally suited for creating ASP components. ATL is not as suitable for creating user-interface types of components, but this is not a problem. Wizards for creating objects within the ATL DLL make the task reasonably easy.

The first step is to create a new ATL project using the ATL COM AppWizard. Figure 9-8 shows the wizard's one and only step. Select Dynamic Link Library for the Server Type to create an in-proc server. Check the Support MTS box so if needed the component can be managed by Microsoft Transaction Server (or Component Services in Windows 2000). Click Finish, and then click OK on the confirmation dialog, and the wizard creates the project.

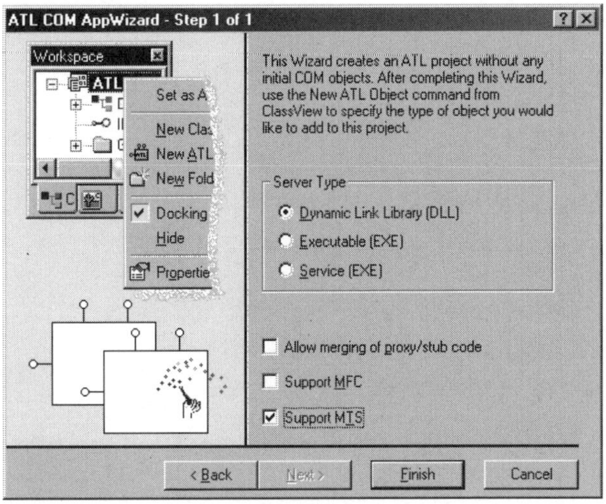


**Figure 9-8** *The Visual C++ ATL COM AppWizard.*

The next step is to create a new ATL object. From the Insert menu, select New ATL COM Object. This brings up the dialog in Figure 9-9. Select the ActiveX Server Component from the Objects category, and click the Next button. This results in the dialog shown in Figure 9-10. As you enter a name in the Short Name field in the C++ panel, the balance of the names are filled in with default values based upon the short name. Select the name carefully because it will be used as part of the ProgID, which will be used to create the object within scripting languages, such as ASP. The ProgID is created in the form of FILENAME.OBJNAME, so if we create the ASP project as *HTMLUtil* and insert an ATL object named *TextUtil*, the ProgID will be *HTMLUtil-.TextUtil*, optionally with a dot and a version number appended.

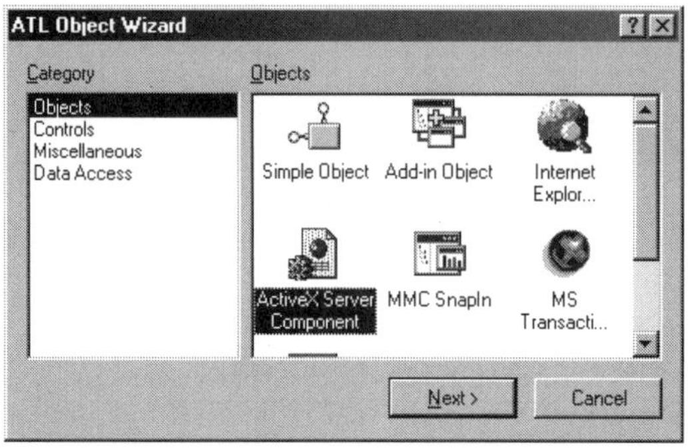


**Figure 9-9** *The Visual C++ ATL Object Wizard.*

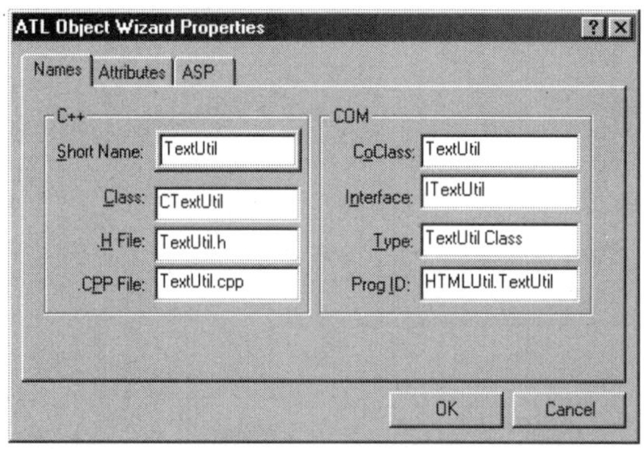


**Figure 9-10** *The Visual C++ ATL Object Wizard Properties.*

The other two tabs allow you to customize the object to be inserted. The Attributes tab allows you to select the threading model and several other minor options. Change the threading model to "Both" because the component we're building will not contain any state information and will be reentrant. The wizard does not allow you to change the interface from Dual to Custom because ASP requires a Dual interface. The ASP tab allows you to set some ASP-specific options. The component can get *OnStartPage* and *OnEndPage* notifications, and can have access to five of the native objects discussed in this chapter (all but the *ObjectContext* object). Select all the options on this page (more for educational purposes than any real necessity).

Once the object is added, right-click on the interface in the ClassView. (The interface will have the standard COM lollipop image.) Select Add Method from the context menu, and the dialog pictured in Figure 9-11 appears. Fill it in as it appears in Figure 9-11. The references in the square brackets are used to describe the interface, with the first parameter an *in* parameter and the second an *out* parameter. The *retval* means that the second parameter is what will be returned by the function. Both of the strings are BSTR types, meaning that they are Visual Basic–compatible strings. Clicking the Attributes button allows you to change the ID or help string value. Click OK, and a method will be added to the interface. You can then expand the interface tree in the *CTextUtil* class and double click on the *AddBreaks* method. The default code is a bare implementation that returns S_OK with the standard Wizard generated TODO comments.

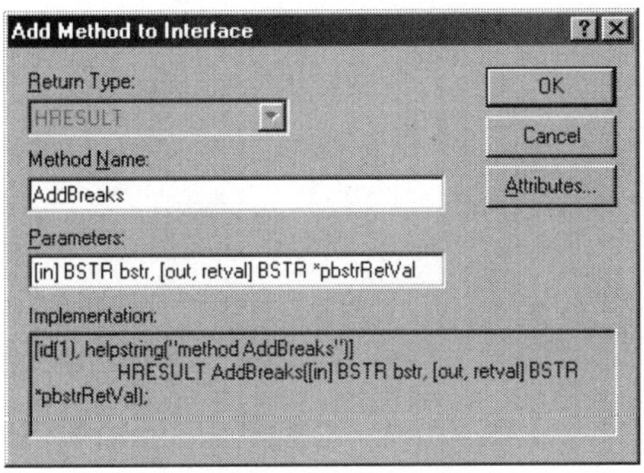


**Figure 9-11** *The Add Method To Interface dialog.*

Listing 9-11 contains the final *AddBreaks* method. The source for the entire object is on the companion CD-ROM. The actual code is mostly self-explanatory, with a couple of exceptions. First, the BSTR type is used throughout, but internally we use *wchar_t* buffers to do the actual manipulation of the elements of the array. Second, when dealing with BSTRs, you'll generally use the *CComBSTR* class. This utility class makes many of the operations a bit easier—for instance, providing methods for the length of the underlying BSTR, as well as ways to get the BSTR into the BSTR pointer that is returned.

**TextUtil.cpp**

```
STDMETHODIMP CTextUtil::AddBreaks(BSTR bstr, BSTR *pbstrRetval)
{
    int tloop;
    // Use wchar_t type because BSTRs use wide characters.
    wchar_t *ptr;
    wchar_t *dst;
    wchar_t temp[255];
```

**Listing 9-11** *(continued)*

**Listing 9-11** *continued*

```
    // Just return if the pointers are not valid.
    if (bstr == NULL || pbstrRetval == NULL)
    {
        return E_POINTER;
    }

    // Create a temporary CComBSTR that provides for better
    //  manipulation of BSTRs.
    CComBSTR bstrTemp(bstr);
    if (!(bstrTemp))
    {
        return E_OUTOFMEMORY;
    }

    // Create buffers to manipulate more easily than the BSTRs.
    ptr = new wchar_t[bstrTemp.Length()+2];
    dst = new wchar_t[bstrTemp.Length()+1024];

    wcscpy(ptr,bstrTemp);
    dst[0] = 0;
    for (tloop=0 ; ptr[tloop] ; tloop++)
    {
        temp[0] = 0;
        if (ptr[tloop] == L'\n')
        {
            wcscpy(temp, L"<es>");
        }
        else
        {
            temp[0] = ptr[tloop];
            temp[1] = 0;
        }
        wcscat(dst, temp);
    }

    CComBSTR Result(dst);
    if (!(Result))
    {
        return E_OUTOFMEMORY;
    }

    *pbstrRetval = Result.Detach();

    delete ptr;
    delete dst;

    return S_OK;
}
```

The adjustment necessary to use the *HTMLUtil* object's *AddBreaks* method was minimal. I simply created the object, used it instead of calling the VBScript function listed on page 334, and then destroyed the object by setting it equal to nothing. The improvement in performance was dramatic. What had previously taken up to six seconds was now virtually instantaneous. While implementing this component in Visual Basic might have been somewhat easier, I expect the speed improvement would have been less dramatic, as C's string handling tends to be quicker than Visual Basic's. Using the ATL COM wizards made this a reasonably easy task, even with the complexity of dealing with the BSTR type.

### The rest of the application

Listings 9-12, 9-13, and 9-14 contain Global.asa, Default.asp, and Show.asp, respectively.

**Global.asa**

```
<SCRIPT LANGUAGE="VBScript" RUNAT="Server">

' You can add special event handlers in this file that will get run
'  automatically when special Active Server Pages events occur.
'  To create these handlers, just create a subroutine with a name
'  from the list below that corresponds to the event you want to
'  use. For example, to create an event handler for Session_OnStart,
'  you would put the following code into this file (without the
'  comments):
Sub Session_OnStart
    session("TroubleDSN")="UID=sa;PWD=;DSN=TroubleshootSQL"
End Sub

'Sub Session_OnEnd
'End Sub

'Application_OnStart ' Runs once when the first page of your application
                     '    is run for the first time by any user.
'Application_OnEnd   ' Runs once when the Web server shuts down.

</SCRIPT>
```

**Listing 9-12**

**Default.asp**

```
<!--#include file="client.inc"-->
<%
Response.Buffer=true
```

**Listing 9-13** *(continued)*

**Listing 9-13** *continued*

```
%>
<html>

<head>
<title>Troubleshooter Search</title>
<meta NAME="FORMATTER" CONTENT="Microsoft Visual InterDev 1.0">

</head>
<BODY>
<CENTER>
<h1><a NAME="top">Troubleshooter</a></h1>

<%
dim cbStr
dim rstSystems
dim db
dim strSQL

    Response.Write("<H3>Search for problem resolution. ")
    Response.Write("<br>Enter words from problem Description")
    Response.Write(" and/or Details, and then click on Search.</H3><p>")
    Response.Write("<hr><FORM method=POST action=show.asp ")
    Response.Write("id=form1 name=form1><p>")
    Response.Write("<P><TABLE BORDER=0 cellspacing=0><TR>")
    Response.Write("<TD  width=""50%%""><B></B></TD>")
    Response.Write("<TD ><B></B></TD>")
    Response.Write("</TR>")
    Response.Write("<TR BGCOLOR=WHITE>")

    Response.Write("<TD align=right width=""50%%"">")
    Response.Write("<B>Search for:</B></TD>")
    Response.Write("<TD><B><INPUT TYPE=text ")
    Response.Write("<TD><B><INPUT TYPE=text NAME=Description>" + _
        "</B></TD></TR><TR BGCOLOR=WHITE>")

    Response.Write("<TD align=right width=""50%%"">")
    Response.Write("<B>Search Details (slower but more ")
    Response.Write("complete search):</B></TD>")
    Response.Write("<TD><B><INPUT TYPE=""checkbox"" ")
    Response.Write("id=SearchDetails name=SearchDetails ")
    Response.Write("value=SearchDetails></B></TD></TR>")
    Response.Write("<TR BGCOLOR=WHITE>")

    Response.Write("<TD align=right width=""50%%"">")
    Response.Write("<B>System Involved (leave blank for ANY):" + _
        "</B></TD>")
    cbStr="<SELECT id=cbSystem name=cbSystem>"
```

```
    Set db=Server.CreateObject("ADODB.Connection")
    db.Open(session("TroubleDSN"))
    set rstSystems = Server.CreateObject("ADODB.Recordset")
    strSQL="SELECT SystemName, SystemID FROM tblSystems "
    strSQL=strSQL & "ORDER BY SystemName"
    rstsystems.open strSQL,db,1,4
    cbStr=cbStr+"<OPTION value=0></OPTION>"
    while rstSystems.EOF<>true
        cbStr=cbStr+"<OPTION VALUE="+CStr(rstSystems("SystemID"))+">"+_
            rstSystems("SystemName")
        rstSystems.MoveNext
    wend
    cbStr=cbStr+"</SELECT>"
    set rstSystems=nothing
    set db=nothing
    Response.Write("<TD><B>"+cbStr+"</B></TD>")

    Response.Write("</TR></TABLE><es>")
    Response.Flush

%>
<Center><INPUT type=submit VALUE="Search" id=submit1 name=submit1>
</Center>
</CENTER>
</FORM>

<FORM action="EnterAdd.Asp" method=POST id=frmAdd name=frmAdd>
<Center><INPUT type=submit VALUE="Add Problem" id=Add name=Add>
</Center>

</FORM>
</body>
</html>
```

**Show.asp**

```
<%@ LANGUAGE="VBSCRIPT" %>
<!--#include file="adovbs.inc"-->
<%
Response.Buffer=true

%>
<HTML>
<HEAD>
<META NAME="GENERATOR" Content="Microsoft Visual InterDev 1.0">
```

**Listing 9-14** *(continued)*

**Listing 9-14** *continued*

```
<META HTTP-EQUIV="Content-Type"
 content="text/html; charset=iso-8859-1">
<TITLE>Search Results</TITLE>
</HEAD>
<body>
<CENTER>
<h1><a NAME="top">Troubleshooter Results</a></h1>

<FORM action="default.asp" method=POST id=form1 name=form1>
<CENTER>
<INPUT type=submit VALUE="Return To Search" id=Close name=Close>
<es>
</CENTER>
</FORM>
<%
dim showDescription
dim showDetails

showDescription=Request.Form("Description")
showDetails=Request.Form("Details")

dim rstProblems
dim db
dim strSQL
dim finalDescription
dim finalDetails
dim lookFor
dim tloop
dim whereAdded
dim title
dim SearchDetails
dim tstr
dim htmlUtil

whereAdded=0
for tloop=1 to len(showDescription)
    if mid(showDescription,tloop,1)="'" then
        finalDescription=finalDescription&"''"
    else
        finalDescription=finalDescription&mid(showDescription,tloop,1)
    end if
next

Set db=Server.CreateObject("ADODB.Connection")
db.Open(session("TroubleDSN"))
set rstProblems = Server.CreateObject("ADODB.Recordset")
```

```
strSQL="Select * from [QryProblemsReady] "
if Request.Form("SearchDetails")<>"SearchDetails" then
    if finalDescription<>"" then
        strSQL = strSQL &
            " WHERE ([Description] like '%" & _
            finalDescription & "%') "
        whereAdded=1
    end if
    SearchDetails=False
else
    if finalDescription<>"" then
        strSQL = strSQL &
            " WHERE ([Description] like '%" & finalDescription & _
            "%' OR [details] like '%" & finalDescription& "%') "
        whereAdded=1
    end if
    SearchDetails=True
end if

if CInt(Request.Form("cbSystem"))<>0 then
    if whereAdded=0 then
        strSQL=strSQL&" WHERE "
        whereAdded=1
    else
        strSQL=strSQL&" AND "
    end if
    strSQL=strSQL&" SystemID="&Cstr(Request.Form("cbSystem"))
end if

strSQL=strSQL&" ORDER BY [DateEntered] DESC"

rstProblems.Open strSQL,db,adOpenStatic,adLockReadOnly

if rstProblems.recordCount=0 then
    Response.Write("<CENTER><H2>Sorry! " & _
        " No match found!</H2></CENTER><es>")
else

    if rstProblems.RecordCount>1 then
        Response.Write(CStr(rstProblems.RecordCount) + & _
            " Records Found...<es>")
    else
        Response.Write("A Single Record Found...<es>")
    end if
    if SearchDetails=false then
         Response.Write("Searching Short Description Only.")
```

*(continued)*

**Listing 9-14** *continued*

```
        else
            Response.Write("Searching Short Description " & _
                "<b>and</B> Details")
        end if
        Response.Write("<es>Scroll to view all records. " & _
            " Click on the Problem Description for more details.<es>")

        set htmlutil=server.CreateObject("asp.htmlutil")
        rstProblems.MoveFirst
        Response.Write("<BODY>")
        Response.Write("<CENTER>")
        Response.Write("<P><TABLE BORDER=1><TR bgcolor=cyan>")
        Response.Write("<TD><B>Problem Description</B></TD>")
        Response.Write("<TD><B>Details of Problem</B></TD>")
        Response.Write("<TD><B>Solution to Problem</B></TD>")
        Response.Write("</TR>")

        Response.Write("<H3>")
        Do While Not rstProblems.EOF
            Response.Write("<TR>")
            title="details.ASP?ID=" & rstProblems("ProblemID")
            Response.Write("<TD><B><A HREF=" & title & ">" & _
                rstProblems("Description")&"</A></B></TD>")

            Response.Write("<TD><B>" & htmlUtil.AddBreaks(
                rstProblems("Details")) & "</B></TD>")
            Response.Write("<TD><B>" & htmlUtil.AddBreaks(
                rstProblems("Solution")) & "</B></TD>")
            Response.Write("</TR>")
            rstProblems.MoveNext
        loop
        Response.Write("</H3>")
        Response.Write("</CENTER)")
    end if
    rstProblems.Close
    set rstProblems=nothing
    Response.Flush

    %>

    </BODY>
    </HTML>
```

Global.asp has a single event handler, *Application_OnStart*, which simply sets an application-level variable to hold the DSN that the entire application will use. Default.asp exhibits an interesting technique for aligning controls that is useful in HTML as well as in ASP applications. HTML is not designed as a page description language. One of the consequences of this is that precise placement of text or controls on a page is not possible. Dynamic HTML allows for greater precision but is implemented in ways that do not allow cross-browser support.

The solution to this problem that is used in Default.asp is the placement of controls and labels by using a table. Hiding the borders and using alignment properties of the table cells can align the controls to look as if they were placed using a grid, as in Visual Basic. In addition, Default.asp contains code to load the systems available for troubleshooting into a combo box.

Show.asp creates a table similar to the phone application's table, with a significant difference. Each problem description is added to the table as a hyperlink, with the ProblemID used as an argument to the Details.asp script shown in Listing 9-15. Details.asp uses a SQL Server view to display all details of the problem without requiring the logic to convert the various IDs to the text representations. This is done on the server through joins from the Problems table to the Systems and Server OS tables.

**Details.asp**

```
<!--#include file="adovbs.inc"-->

<HTML>
<HEAD>
<META NAME="GENERATOR"
Content="Microsoft Visual InterDev 1.0">
<META HTTP-EQUIV="Content-Type"
content="text/html; charset=iso-8859-1">
<TITLE>Search Results</TITLE>
</HEAD>
<body>
<CENTER>
<h1><a NAME="top">Troubleshooter Search Details</a></h1>

<FORM action="default.asp"
method=POST id=form1 name=form1>
<INPUT type=submit VALUE="Return to Search"
id=Close name=Close>
</FORM>
</CENTER>
<%

dim rstProblems
dim rstComments
dim db
```

**Listing 9-15** *(continued)*

**Listing 9-15** *continued*

```
dim strSQL
dim finalTitle
dim finalSynopsis
dim lookFor
dim tloop
dim whereAdded
dim title
dim retStr
dim htmlUtil

    session("ID") = request("ID")
    Set db = Server.CreateObject("ADODB.Connection")
    db.Open(session("TroubleDSN"))
    set rstProblems = Server.CreateObject("ADODB.Recordset")

    strSQL="Select * FROM [QryProblemSysOSJoin] "
    strSQL=strSQL & "WHERE ProblemID="&request("ID")

    rstProblems.Open strSQL, db, adOpenDynamic, adLockOptimistic

    if rstProblems.RecordCount=0 then
        Response.Write("<CENTER><H2>Sorry!  ")
        Response.Write("No match found!</H2></CENTER><es>")
    else
        Response.Write("<CENTER>")
        Response.Write("<TABLE width=""80%"" border=1 cellpadding=1")
        Response.Write(" BGCOLOR=darkslateblue>")
        Response.Write("<TR><TD><CENTER><H2>Problem ID: ")
        Response.Write(Cstr(rstProblems("ProblemID")))
        Response.Write("<es></H2></TD></TR>")
        Response.Write("<TR><TD><H3>Entered By ")
        Response.Write(Cstr(rstProblems("EnteredBy"))&" On ")
        Response.Write(Cstr(rstProblems("DateEntered")))
        Response.Write("</H3>"&"</TD></TR>")
        if isDate(rstProblems("DateModified"))<>false then
            Response.Write("<TR><TD><H3>Modified By ")
            Response.Write(Cstr(rstProblems("ModifiedBy"))&" On ")
            Response.Write(Cstr(rstProblems("DateModified")))
            Response.Write("</H3>"&"</TD></TR>")
        end if
        Response.Write("<TR><TD><H3>System: ")
        Response.Write(rstProblems("SystemName"))
        Response.Write(" Version "&rstProblems("VersionInfo"))
        Response.Write("</H3></CENTER>"&"</TD></TR>")
        Response.Write("<TR><TD><H3>Server OS: ")
        Response.Write(rstProblems("ServerOS"))
        Response.Write("</H3></CENTER>"&"</TD></TR>")
```

```
        Response.Write("<TR><TD><H3>Description: ")
        Response.Write(rstProblems("Description"))
        Response.Write("</H3></CENTER>"&"</TD></TR>")
        Response.Write("<p>")

        ' Just in time creation...
        set htmlutil=server.CreateObject("htmlutil.textutil")

        Response.Write("<TR><TD><CENTER><H2>Details</H2></CENTER><P>")
        Response.Write(htmlUtil.AddBreaks(rstProblems("Details")))
        Response.Write("</TD></TR><p>")
        Response.Write("<TR><TD><CENTER><H2>Solution")
        Response.Write("</H2></CENTER><P><P>")
        Response.Write(htmlUtil.AddBreaks(rstProblems("Solution")))
        Response.Write("</TD></TR><p>")
        Response.Write("</TABLE>")
        Response.Write("</CENTER>")

        ' Free the component
        set htmlUtil = nothing
    end if
%>
<es>

</BODY>
```

One more ASP page is used by this simple system. This is the screen that allows entry of new problems into the system. Listing 9-16 shows the EnterAdd.asp script. Some of the same code used to fill in the System combo box on the search screen is used (an ideal candidate for becoming a callable function). Additionally, a file called Client.inc is included in this script. This is an *include* that implements a client-side JavaScript that ensures fields are properly filled in. Why JavaScript? Unlike the rest of the script code presented, this needs to operate on the client browser. While support for JavaScript is not perfect, it is far more universal than browser support for VBScript.

**EnterAdd.asp**

```
<%@ Language=VBScript %>
<!--#include file="adovbs.inc"-->
<!--#include file="client.inc"-->
<%
    ' Write out the validation code, from client.inc
    writeValidate()
```

**Listing 9-16** *(continued)*

**Listing 9-16** *continued*

```
%>
<HTML>
<HEAD>
<META NAME="GENERATOR" Content="Microsoft Visual InterDev 1.0">
<META HTTP-EQUIV="Content-Type"
    content="text/html; charset=iso-8859-1">
<TITLE>Troubleshooter Problem Entry</TITLE>
</HEAD>
<body>
<CENTER>
<H1><a NAME="top">Troubleshooter Problem Entry</a></H1><P>
<H3>Please enter the requested information and click
<I>'OK'</I> below.  The problem will be reviewed and made
active as soon as possible.  Click <I>'Cancel'</I>
to abandon the addition of this record.
</H3>
<FORM action="Process.ASP?Action=ADD" method=POST
id=AddForm name=AddForm onSubmit="return validate(this);">

<H1>
<TABLE border=0 cellPadding=0 cellSpacing=0 width="75%">

<TR>
<TD align=right width="50%"><H4>Entered By:</B></TD>
<TD><INPUT id=EnteredBy name=EnteredBy ></TD></TR></TABLE></H1>
<H4>
<TABLE border=0 cellPadding=0 cellSpacing=0 width="75%">

<TR>
<TD width="50%" align=Right><B>System:</B></TD>
<%
dim cbStr
dim db
dim rstSystems
dim rstServerOS

    cbStr="<SELECT id=cbSystem name=cbSystem>"
    set db=Server.CreateObject("ADODB.Connection")
    db.Open(session("TroubleDSN"))
    set rstSystems = Server.CreateObject("ADODB.Recordset")
    strSQL="SELECT SystemName, SystemID FROM tblSystems "
    strSQL=strSQL & "ORDER BY SystemName"
    rstsystems.open strSQL,db,1,4
    cbStr=cbStr+"<OPTION value=0>ANY</OPTION>"
```

```
    while rstSystems.EOF<>true
        cbStr=cbStr+"<OPTION VALUE="+CStr(rstSystems("SystemID"))+">"+_
            rstSystems("SystemName")
        rstSystems.MoveNext
    wend
    cbStr=cbStr+"</SELECT>"
    set rstSystems=nothing

    Response.Write("<TD><B>"+cbStr+"</B></TD>")
    Response.Write("</TR></TABLE></H4>")
    Response.Write("<TABLE border=0 cellPadding=0 ")
    Response.Write("cellSpacing=0 width=""75%"">")
    Response.Write("<TR><TD width=""50%"" align=Right>"
    Response.Write("<B>Server OS:</B></TD>")
    cbStr="<SELECT id=cbServerOS name=cbServerOS>"

    set rstServerOS = Server.CreateObject("ADODB.Recordset")
    strSQL="SELECT ServerOS, ServerOSID FROM tblServerOS "
    strSQL="ORDER BY ServerOS"
    rstServerOS.open strSQL,db,1,4

    while rstServerOS.EOF<>true
        cbStr=cbStr+"<OPTION VALUE="+_
            CStr(rstServerOS("ServerOSID"))+">"+_
            rstServerOS("ServerOS")
        rstServerOS.MoveNext
    wend
    cbStr=cbStr+"</SELECT>"
    set rstServerOS=nothing
    set db=nothing
    Response.Write("<TD><B>"+cbStr+"</B></TD>")
    ' The balance is native HTML as a convenience.  I used
    '  Visual Studio to help format the text areas.
%>
</TR></TABLE></H4>
<H4>Description:</H4>
<TEXTAREA id=Description name=Description
style="HEIGHT: 48px; WIDTH: 434px"></TEXTAREA>
<H4>Details:</H4>
<TEXTAREA id=Details name=Details
style="HEIGHT: 105px; WIDTH: 434px"></TEXTAREA>
<H4>Solution:</H4>
<TEXTAREA id=Solution name=Solution
style="HEIGHT: 119px; WIDTH: 434px"></TEXTAREA>
```

*(continued)*

**Listing 9-16** *continued*

```
<H1><INPUT type=submit VALUE="OK" id=OK name=OK>
</CENTER>
</FORM>
<FORM id=form1 name=form1 action=DEFAULT.ASP>
<CENTER>
<INPUT type=submit VALUE="Cancel" id=Cancel name=Cancel> </H1>
</FORM>
</CENTER>
</body></HTML>
```

The *WriteValidate* function does the actual work, concatenating a string containing all of the JavaScript code to sense if fields are properly filled in. The major function is *Validate*. This text is then sent to the browser by a single *Response.Write* call. This code is visible on the browser (use the View/Source Code menu option in Microsoft Internet Explorer), but it has the advantage of saving a round-trip to the server for obviously invalid entries. The resulting code as seen by the browser is shown in Listing 9-17. *Validate* could be expanded to allow detection of other kinds of problems that could be detected on the client side. The *OnSubmit* handler of the form is set to *Validate(this)*, meaning that *Validate* should be called with *this* as a parameter. If the form is submitted with any of the TEXT or TEXTAREA fields blank, an error dialog is presented. This dialog comes from the browser and was generated without the form actually being posted to the server, thus cutting out one round-trip to the server.

**Output.htm**

```
<SCRIPT LANGUAGE="JavaScript1.1">
// All blanks?
function allblanks(s)
{
    for(var loop = 0; loop < s.length; loop++) {
        var ch = s.charAt(loop);
        if ((ch != ' ') && (ch != '\n') && (ch != '\t'))
            return false;
    }
    return true;
}
// Validate entry.
function validate(f)
{
    var msg;
    var missing = "";
```

**Listing 9-17**

```
    for(var loop = 0; loop < f.length; loop++) {
        var comp = f.elements[loop];
        if (((comp.type == "text") || (comp.type == "textarea")) &&
            (comp.optional!=true)) {
            // first check if the field is empty
            if ((comp.value == null) || (comp.value == "") ||
                allblanks(comp.value)) {
                missing += "\n          " + comp.name;
                continue;
            }
        }
    }
    if (!missing) return true;
    msg  = "____________________________________________________\n\n"
    msg += "Fields listed below were missing.\n";
    msg += "____________________________________________________\n\n"
    if (missing) {
        msg += "- The following required field(s) are not filled in:"
            + missing + "\n";
    }
    alert(msg);
    return false;
}
</SCRIPT>

<HTML>
<HEAD>
<META NAME="GENERATOR" Content="Microsoft Visual InterDev 1.0">
<META HTTP-EQUIV="Content-Type" content="text/html;
 charset=iso-8859-1">
<TITLE>Troubleshooter Problem Entry</TITLE>
</HEAD>
<body>
<CENTER>
<H1><a NAME="top">Troubleshooter Problem Entry</a></H1><P>
<H3>Please enter the requested information and click <I>'OK'</
I> below.
 The problem will be reviewed and made active as soon as possible.
 Click <I>'Cancel'</I> to abandon the addition of this record.
</H3>
<FORM action="Process.ASP?Action=ADD" method=POST
id=AddForm name=AddForm onSubmit="return validate(this);">

<H1>
<TABLE border=0 cellPadding=0 cellSpacing=0 width="75%">
```

*(continued)*

**Listing 9-17** *continued*

```
  <TR>
    <TD align=right width="50%"><H4>Entered By:</B></TD>
    <TD><INPUT id=EnteredBy name=EnteredBy ></TD></TR></TABLE></H1>
      <H4>
<TABLE border=0 cellPadding=0 cellSpacing=0 width="75%">

  <TR>
    <TD width="50%" align=Right><B>System:</B></TD>
<TD><B><SELECT id=cbSystem name=cbSystem><OPTION value=0>ANY</OPTION>
<OPTION VALUE=5>DosAPGL<OPTION VALUE=8>DosEBill
<OPTION VALUE=4>DosPayroll<OPTION VALUE=3>DosRX
<OPTION VALUE=2>DosSkilled<OPTION VALUE=6>Vscheduling
<OPTION VALUE=1>Vskilled<OPTION VALUE=7>WindowsEBill
</SELECT></B></TD></TR></TABLE></H4>
<TABLE border=0 cellPadding=0 cellSpacing=0 width="75%"><TR>
<TD width="50%" align=Right>
<B>Server OS:</B></TD><TD><B>
<SELECT id=cbServerOS name=cbServerOS>
<OPTION VALUE=1>ANY<OPTION VALUE=3>Citrix 1.7
<OPTION VALUE=4>Citrix 1.8
<OPTION VALUE=5>NetWare 3.x<OPTION VALUE=6>NetWare 4.x
<OPTION VALUE=7>NetWare 5.x
<OPTION VALUE=2>NT 4.x<OPTION VALUE=8>Windows 2000 Server</SELECT>
</B></TD>
</TR></TABLE></H4>
<H4>Description:</H4>
<TEXTAREA id=Description name=Description
style="HEIGHT: 48px; WIDTH: 434px">
</TEXTAREA>
<H4>Details:</H4>
<TEXTAREA id=Details name=Details
style="HEIGHT: 105px; WIDTH: 434px"></TEXTAREA>
<H4>Solution:</H4>
<TEXTAREA id=Solution name=Solution
style="HEIGHT: 119px; WIDTH: 434px"></TEXTAREA>
<H1><INPUT type=submit VALUE="OK" id=OK name=OK>
</CENTER>
</FORM>
<FORM id=form1 name=form1 action=DEFAULT.ASP>
<CENTER>
<INPUT type=submit VALUE="Cancel" id=Cancel name=Cancel> </H1>
</FORM>
</CENTER>
</body></HTML>
```

The most significant code in the application is the code used on the Process.asp page, shown in Listing 9-18, that actually adds the records to the database. While it is sometimes convenient to simply create SQL UPDATE statements on the fly, doing so here is problematic, since the memo fields often contain embedded line breaks. Instead, the code uses the *AddNew* method of the *ADODB.Recordset*, sets the various fields, and then calls the *Update* method of the recordset.

**Process.asp**

```
<%@ Language=VBScript %>
<!--#include file="adovbs.inc"-->
<%
Response.Buffer=true
%>
<HTML>
<HEAD>
<META NAME="GENERATOR" Content="Microsoft Visual Studio 6.0">
</HEAD>
<body>
<%
dim db
dim rstProblems
dim rstCheckout
dim strSQL
dim OBJdbConnection
dim finalTitle

    if request("Cancel")="Cancel" then
        Response.Redirect("Default.ASP")
    end if

    set db=Server.CreateObject("ADODB.Connection")
    db.Open(session("TroubleDSN"))

    set rstProblems=server.CreateObject("ADODB.Recordset")
    rstProblems.CursorType=adOpenKeyset
    rstProblems.Open "tblProblems",db,adOpenDynamic,adLockOptimistic
    if request("Action")="ADD" then
        rstProblems.AddNew
        rstProblems("StatusID")=2
        if request("cbSystem")<>0 then
            rstProblems("SystemID")=request("cbSystem")
        end if
        if request("cbServerOS")<>0 then
            rstProblems("ServerOSID")=request("cbServerOS")
```

**Listing 9-18** *(continued)*

**Listing 9-18** *continued*

```
        end if
        rstProblems("VersionInfo")="ANY"
        rstProblems("EnteredBy")=request("EnteredBy")
        rstProblems("Description")=request("Description")
        rstProblems("Details")=request("Details")
        rstProblems("Solution")=request("Solution")
        rstProblems.Update
        Response.Write("<h2><Center>Problem entered ")
            Response.Write("into database as 'Pending' Will be added")
        Response.Write(" to active database ASAP</Center></H2>")
    end if

    Response.Write("<CENTER><h2>")
    Response.Write("<FORM action=""DEFAULT.ASP"" method=POST")
        Response.Write(" id=form1 name=form1>")
    Response.Write("<INPUT type=""submit"" value=""Return ")
        Response.Write("to Search"" id=button1 name=button1>")
    Response.Write("</H2></FORM></CENTER></BODY></HTML>")
%>
```

Of course, improvements could be made to this system. Obviously, it might be useful to allow comments on problems to be entered and then perhaps searched and displayed. Editing existing entries might also be useful as well, though obviously this would require authentication to ensure that only authorized users could edit the database.

# CONCLUSION

You can see that ASP is a viable alternative for developing robust Web applications. You have also seen some of the limitations that might cause problems, namely the problem of speed when, for instance, you are manipulating large amounts of text. You have also seen how easy it is to overcome this problem by using ActiveX Server components. The most important lesson is that the sum of ASP's parts is more powerful than its individual elements.

An interesting exercise will be to duplicate these simple applications using ISAPI, the other major way of serving Web applications using IIS. And of course, we will also find that neither ASP nor ISAPI is the perfect tool for all Web applications. Together, however, ASP and ISAPI provide the tools to build whatever we can dream up.

*Chapter 10*

# Internet Server API (ISAPI)

From the standpoint of developers working on server applications, the inclusion in Microsoft Windows NT 4 of the Internet Information Server (IIS) is one of the single biggest improvements over previous versions of the Windows NT operating system. The inclusion in Microsoft Windows 2000 of IIS 5 adds many improvements for server-side developers. In addition to Active Server Pages (ASP) (covered in Chapter 9), the Internet Server API (ISAPI) offers tremendous opportunities for developers who need to exploit the benefits of server-based systems.

Interestingly, ASP itself is implemented as an ISAPI DLL named ASP.DLL. Recall from Chapter 9 the configuration screen for IIS 5—shown in Figure 10-1—that allows the association between file extensions and the ISAPI DLLs that IIS calls when a program requests a file with that extension. This ability to change the behavior of IIS by selecting the DLL to be called is a powerful way to customize its operation. All of the DLLs listed in Figure 10-1 are ISAPI Extension DLLs.

If we need any proof that ASP.DLL is an ISAPI extension, we need only load the DLL into the Microsoft Visual C++ Dependency Walker to see the DLL's list of

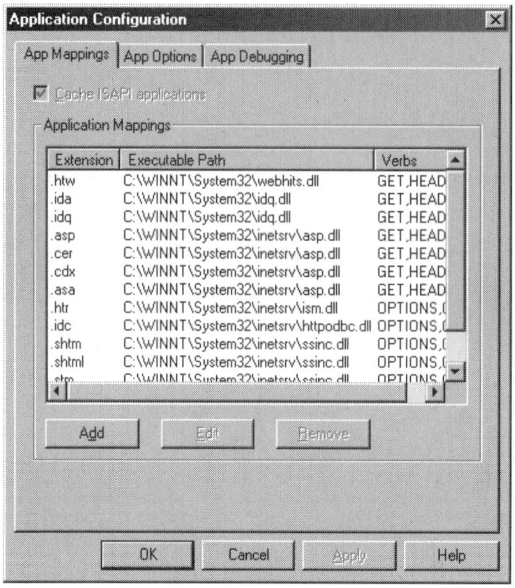


**Figure 10-1** *IIS configuration screen.*

imported and exported functions. Figure 10-2 shows some of the functions exported from the Windows 2000 ASP.DLL. The most significant of these functions are *GetExtensionVersion* and *HttpExtensionProc*. As we will see, these are the functions that must be supported by any ISAPI Extension DLL.

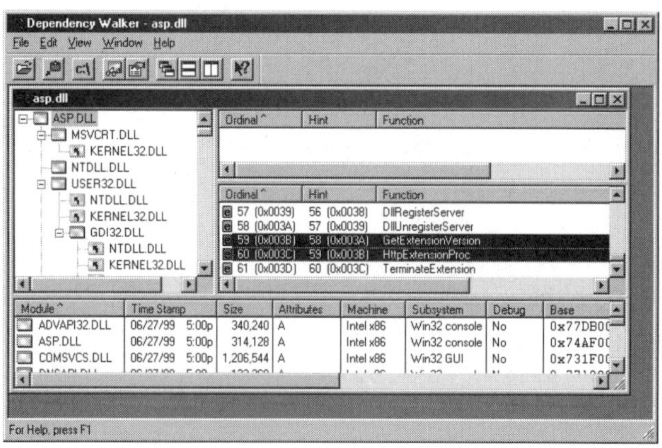


**Figure 10-2** *Dependency Walker showing some of ASP.DLL's exported functions.*

# DLL REVIEW

Before we get too deeply involved in ISAPI specifics, a brief review of dynamic-link libraries (DLLs) might be helpful. Understanding DLLs is critical to understanding ISAPI DLLs.

Years ago, before Windows became popular with programmers who needed to expose some functionality to other programmers, the only option was to send object files (files with an .obj extension) or library files (files with an .lib extension). This was not an ideal solution because the functionality was then locked in at link time. If a new version of the object or library files became available, the only option was to relink the application program with the new files. In addition, if many programs required the same functionality (a common occurrence), the object code needed to be linked into each program. And when a new version became available, each program needed to be relinked. To further add to these limitations, the code linked into each and every program added to the size of each executable.

DLLs were an improvement on this method of functionality sharing. These files with a .dll extension contain functions that are made available, or exported, in a way that allows other programs to get to them. If you have a program that links to a DLL and a new version of the DLL becomes available, dropping in the new DLL is easy, and the new functionality will be available—presuming there is a way for the application program to access that functionality. This is the ideal solution; in the real world, there are many ways this can go awry. See Appendix A for some examples of possible problems.

In addition to the DLL files, vendors commonly send library files to developers. These files are linked into the application in the same way the old-fashioned MS-DOS library files were linked in but with an important difference. Library files do not contain the actual functionality but rather the code needed—at load time—to dynamically link in the code from the DLL. These libraries are called import libraries.

> **NOTE** Microsoft Visual C++ has new options that allow for delayed loading of DLLs, making some of the following discussion less critical. Nonetheless, it is important to understand these concepts, even if it is just to get the delayed loading allowed by the compiler to work.

This DLL model was a vast improvement over the old MS-DOS model of distributing object code that needed to be linked into an application. Now bug fixes and some types of enhancements could be added to a system without requiring changes to the executable programs. Multiple executable files could also share the same DLL, thus cutting down on the amount of code lying around on the hard disk. One problem remained: if a DLL referenced in the import library that linked into the application was not present, the application would fail to load, returning a message like the one in Figure 10-3.

The solution to this problem is the use of two function calls: *LoadLibrary* and *GetProcAddress*. These functions allow an application to explicitly request that a DLL be loaded at run time and to get a function pointer from the loaded DLL, respectively. *LoadLibrary* takes a single parameter, a pointer to a string containing the name of the DLL, optionally with a full or relative path name. Simply calling *LoadLibrary* with the name of the DLL will cause Windows 2000 to search for the DLL according to the rules spelled out in the Windows SDK documentation. If *LoadLibrary* fails, it returns NULL, and the reason for the failure can be retrieved using *GetLastError*.

*GetProcAddress* takes two parameters: the handle returned by a successful call to *LoadLibrary* and a pointer to a string containing the name of the function whose pointer should be returned. If *GetProcAddress* cannot find the function, it returns NULL. The name of the function is case-sensitive and must exactly match the name that is exported by the DLL. Note that in general, the name must be a standard, "undecorated" name. In a C++ program, function names are commonly decorated, or exported with prefixes or suffixes used by the linker to handle problems such as function overloading. This function decoration makes it difficult, though not impossible, to properly load these functions. All functions exported by the examples in this book are declared using an external "C" declaration, meaning the name is not altered when exported.

This run-time linking allows several additional benefits over compile-time linking using standard .lib files and load-time linking using import libraries and DLLs. The first benefit is that if the function involved is not present, an application can degrade gracefully. Thus, rather than receiving a message like the one in Figure 10-3, the user can be presented with the options available, perhaps including the option to continue to run the application in a degraded state. A second benefit is that a program using *LoadLibrary* can even specify exactly where the DLL should be loaded from, eliminating some of the craziness that can occur when two programs load different

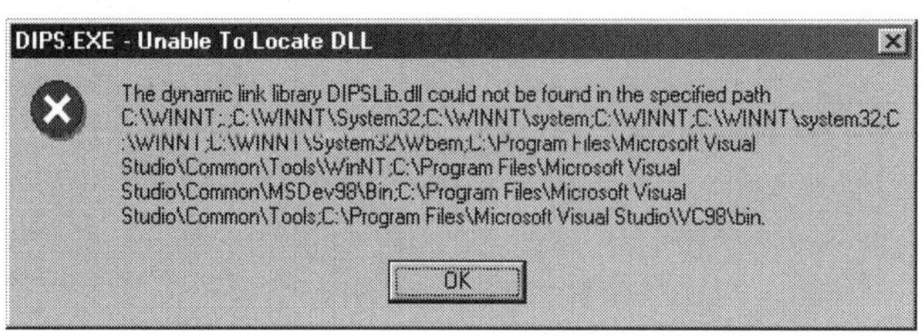


**Figure 10-3** *The error message that appears when the required DLL is not present.*

library files with the same name but with different functionality. Finally, as in IIS, the behavior of the application can be modified at run time, with the application deciding—based on values in a configuration file or the registry—exactly what DLL to load for a given bit of functionality and possibly (though not in IIS) what function should be called.

# ISAPI OVERVIEW

ISAPI defines two distinct classes of functionality. The first is the ISAPI filter. This is a DLL that is registered with IIS. From that point on, IIS will call an entry point in the DLL whenever certain actions take place. The actions that will trigger the filter are configurable by the filter's developer. The filter is never called directly. I'll cover ISAPI filters in detail in the next chapter.

The other class of functionality that ISAPI allows is the ISAPI extension. An ISAPI extension is a DLL that exports a couple of functions with a predetermined name and argument signature. In general, this is all that is required to make a DLL an ISAPI extension, though as usual, the devil is in the details. The first step is to create a DLL exactly the same way you would create any DLL. In the examples that follow, we will create the DLL using the application wizard in Visual C++ 6. Note that for this first example, we will not be using the ISAPI Extension wizard, but rather the standard Win32 Dynamic-Link Library wizard. Figure 10-4 shows the New application dialog with the wizard selected and the name of the project (ISAPI1) filled in.

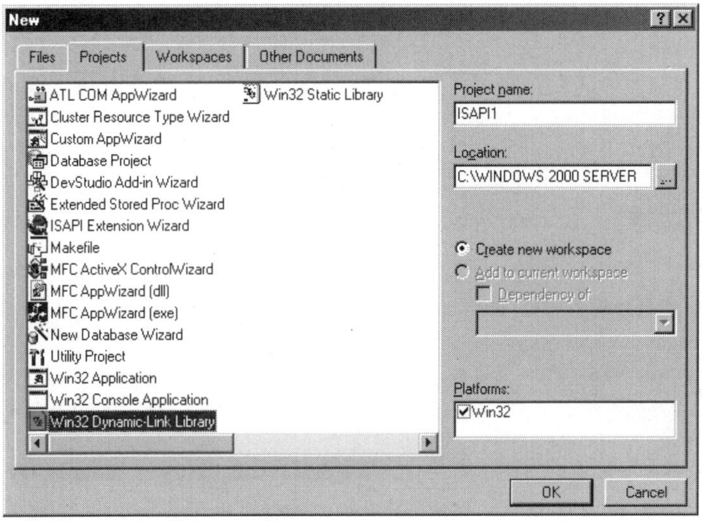


**Figure 10-4** *The New application dialog with selections to create the first example ISAPI extension.*

Click on OK, and the single dialog of the DLL wizard appears. Select A Simple DLL Project (as shown in Figure 10-5), and click on Finish. Click on OK, and the project's initial files will be created. These include ISAPI1.cpp, StdAfx.cpp, and StdAfx.h. The StdAfx files are used to include standard header files and declare any variables needed. The only modification to these files for this project is the addition to StdAfx.h of an *include* statement for httpext.h, a header that declares structure definitions and prototypes needed for ISAPI extensions.

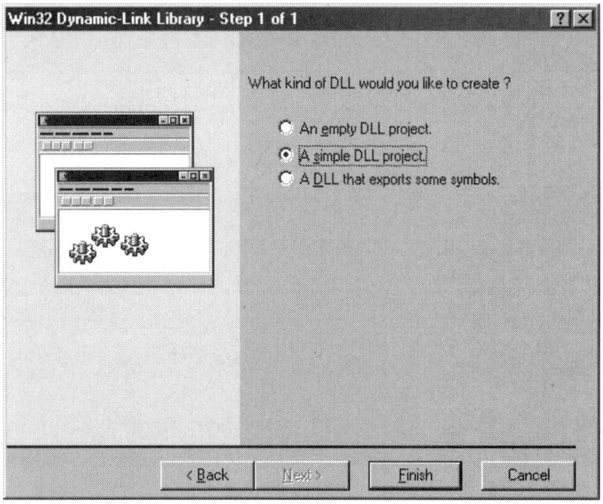


**Figure 10-5** *The Visual C++ 6 Win32 Dynamic-Link Library wizard.*

**NOTE** To run an ISAPI extension, IIS must be set to allow execution of scripts and executables from the directory in question. Without this permission, when the DLL is included on a URL, the user might be offered the option of downloading the DLL—certainly not something you would want the user to do.

## Benefits of ISAPI over CGI

What makes ISAPI a better option than CGI? Several issues differentiate ISAPI from CGI. The first is that ISAPI results in a compiled solution, while many CGI solutions use scripting tools. This can also be a disadvantage, as even minor changes require an edit-compile-test cycle. However, for many applications—especially applications that need to be sold and thus have their source protected—a compiled application can be an advantage.

Another difference between ISAPI and CGI is increased speed. Even if a CGI application is written using a compiled language, it is unlikely to perform as well as an ISAPI application. Why is this? CGI applications create a separate process for each client request. This creation and destruction of processes can be a huge drain on a Web server. ISAPI applications are commonly loaded into the server's memory space once when first called and are virtually never removed until IIS is stopped. Creating individual threads costs much less than creating processes does.

Another advantage for Windows 2000 developers is that the tools used to develop these ISAPI applications can be the exact same tools used to create client applications. I can't overstate how convenient it is to use a single tool set across the spectrum from client to server applications.

### Benefits of ISAPI over ASP

ASP applications are a reasonable alternative for a first Web application, and for many situations, ASP might even be acceptable for the entire life cycle of a Web application. However, ASP applications do have a couple of potential problems:

- ASP scripts can be read by anyone with the proper authority. For a commercial application, this can be a big problem. Even for applications designed for internal use, there is always the risk that the source could be exposed, possibly revealing information that should remain secret.
- ASP scripts might not be fast enough for extremely high volume applications. This can be mitigated by the use of compiled ActiveX components for areas of code that are bottlenecks, as in the Chapter 9 example in which string handling was the bottleneck.

Given the potential problems with the alternatives, ISAPI provides the kind of flexibility required for high-performance or commercial applications. ISAPI also provides useful alternatives for access to data that is not easily accessed using ODBC. ASP applications essentially require ODBC access to data, unless you are prepared to create ActiveX components on your own to handle data access.

## A SIMPLE ISAPI EXTENSION

The ISAPI1.cpp generated by the compiler contains just a stub *DllMain* function. This function can remain untouched for this example but would often be used to allocate and deallocate resources, as needed. To be used as an ISAPI extension, the DLL must export the two functions mentioned previously, *GetExtensionVersion* and *HttpExtensionProc*. The finished program is shown in Listing 10-1.

**ISAPI1.cpp**

```
// ISAPI1.cpp : Defines the entry point for the DLL application.
//

#include "stdafx.h"
#include "time.h"
#include "string.h"
#include "stdio.h"

BOOL APIENTRY DllMain(HANDLE hModule,
                      DWORD  ul_reason_for_call,
                      LPVOID lpReserved
                      )
{
    // This function would normally be used to initialize
    //  and allocate resources required for the extension to
    //  function.
    return TRUE;
}

BOOL WINAPI GetExtensionVersion(HSE_VERSION_INFO *pVer)
{
    pVer->dwExtensionVersion = 1;
    strcpy(pVer->lpszExtensionDesc,
        "ISAPI1 Test for Inside Windows Server Development");
    return(TRUE);
}

DWORD WINAPI HttpExtensionProc(EXTENSION_CONTROL_BLOCK *lpECB)
{
    DWORD cBuf;
    char szMessage[1024];


    HSE_SEND_HEADER_EX_INFO HeaderExInfo;


    // Prepare a header...
    HeaderExInfo.pszStatus = "200 OK";
    HeaderExInfo.cchStatus = strlen(HeaderExInfo.pszStatus);
    HeaderExInfo.pszHeader = "Content-type: text/html\r\n\r\n";
    HeaderExInfo.cchHeader = strlen(HeaderExInfo.pszHeader);
    HeaderExInfo.fKeepConn = FALSE;
```

**Listing 10-1**

```
    // Send headers using IIS-provided callback.
    // These functions are used quite a bit in ISAPI programming.
    lpECB->ServerSupportFunction(
        lpECB->ConnID,
        HSE_REQ_SEND_RESPONSE_HEADER_EX,
        &HeaderExInfo,
        NULL,
        NULL
       );


    if (!(strnicmp(lpECB->lpszQueryString, "TIME", 4)))
    {
        char szTemp[255];
        char szTime[255];

        strcpy(szMessage, "<HTML><HEAD><TITLE>");
        strcat(szMessage, " ISAPI Test </TITLE></HEAD>\r\n");
        strcat(szMessage, "<BODY><H1><CENTER><P>"
            "Hello ISAPI World!<BR>");
        _strtime(szTime);
        sprintf(szTemp, "The time on the server is %s<BR>", szTime);
        strcat(szMessage, szTemp);
        strcat(szMessage, "</P>\r\n</CENTER></H1>");
        strcat(szMessage, "</BODY></HTML>\r\n\r\n");
    }
    else  // Default behavior...
    {
        strcpy(szMessage,"<HTML><HEAD><TITLE>");
        strcat(szMessage, " ISAPI Test </TITLE></HEAD>\r\n");
        strcat(szMessage, "<BODY><H1><CENTER><P>"
            "Hello ISAPI World!");
        strcat(szMessage, "</P>\r\n</CENTER></H1>");
        strcat(szMessage, "</BODY></HTML>\r\n\r\n");
    }
    // Set the length of the buffer being written...
    cBuf = strlen(szMessage);

    // Use another of the functions provided by IIS to write content
    //  to the browser.
    lpECB->WriteClient(lpECB->ConnID, szMessage, &cBuf, HSE_IO_SYNC);
    return HSE_STATUS_SUCCESS;
}
```

*GetExtensionVersion* is a simple function. It sets the extension version and description elements of the HSE_VERSION_INFO structure and then returns. This function is never called directly, and the values set are of little practical value except that some administrative tools might use the description for display purposes.

Many of the elements of the structure are self-explanatory and can be explored more fully using the MSDN documentation, but several merit further explanation. The *connID* parameter is a number, assigned by the server, that must not be modified. This number should not be used for any purpose other than when passed to a function

## DEBUGGING ISAPI EXTENSIONS

Although debugging traditional DLLs can be daunting, debugging ISAPI extensions can be truly maddening. The first step toward being able to even develop ISAPI extensions is to disable Internet Information Server's caching of ISAPI extensions. By default, when an ISAPI extension is first used it is loaded, and it stays loaded, usually until IIS stops. This is great for performance, but can make the normal edit-compile-test cycle difficult. Fortunately, there is a solution. For IIS 4 and later, go to the Home Directory tab on the Web Site properties dialog. On that tab, click on Configuration. On the App Manager tab of the resulting dialog, uncheck Cache ISAPI Applications. This is a good first step toward at least being able to replace the DLL after a change.

To actually debug the application, MSDN has complete instructions for Visual C++ and other debugging tools. The Microsoft Knowlege Base article Q152054 gives details on debugging ISAPI DLLs. One caveat regarding that article: It mentions a registry entry to disable ISAPI Application Caching. For IIS 4 and later, it is far better to use the method I've described here, since the registry entry seems to be absent for IIS 5, included with Windows 2000.

Finally, after all the testing with caching of ISAPI Applications disabled, the application must be tested with caching enabled. With caching disabled, you can build an application that is dependent upon an initial state to operate. Enabling caching will help flush out such problems.

*HttpExtensionProc* is much more important than *GetExtensionVersion*—it is the heart of any ISAPI extension. This function is called with a pointer to an EXTENSION_CONTROL_BLOCK structure. The structure declaration is shown in Listing 10-2. Many of the elements of this structure expose variables that are also available to ASP scripts. For instance, the *lpszQueryString* contains all of the string of the URL after the question mark. For example, in the URL *http://dual/isapi1.dll?time*, *lpszQueryString* points to the string *time*.

that expects a connection ID. In addition to data members, the structure contains four function pointers. This is how the extension interacts with the server, allowing data to be read from the client and sent to the client, as well as allowing the server to be modified.

```
typedef struct _EXTENSION_CONTROL_BLOCK  {
    DWORD  cbSize;       // Size of this struct
    DWORD  dwVersion;    // Version info of this spec
    HCONN  ConnID;       // Context number not to be modified!
    DWORD  dwHttpStatusCode;                 // HTTP Status code
    CHAR   lpszLogData[HSE_LOG_BUFFER_LEN]; // NULL-terminated
                                             //  log info
    LPSTR  lpszMethod;          // REQUEST_METHOD
    LPSTR  lpszQueryString;     // QUERY_STRING
    LPSTR  lpszPathInfo;        // PATH_INFO
    LPSTR  lpszPathTranslated; // PATH_TRANSLATED
    DWORD  cbTotalBytes;        // Total bytes indicated from client
    DWORD  cbAvailable;         // Available number of bytes
    LPBYTE lpbData;             // Pointer to cbAvailable bytes
    LPSTR  lpszContentType;     // Content type of client data
    BOOL  (WINAPI * GetServerVariable);
    BOOL  (WINAPI * WriteClient);
    BOOL  (WINAPI * ReadClient);
    BOOL  (WINAPI * ServerSupportFunction);
}   EXTENSION_CONTROL_BLOCK;
```

**Listing 10-2**

*GetServerVariable* is a function that allows ISAPI extensions to access the same set of server variables that are available as part of the ASP *ServerVariables* collection of the *Request* object. As with all of the functions pointed to by the EXTENSION_CONTROL_BLOCK structure, this function accepts *connID* as a parameter. The function also accepts parameters specifying the name of the variable to retrieve, a pointer to a buffer to accept the value, and the length of the buffer.

*ReadClient* and *WriteClient* are used to receive data from and send data to the client. These functions contain a *dwSync* parameter that specifies whether the call should be synchronous or asynchronous. If the operation is to be done asynchronously, the extension should have already set up an I/O completion function using the *ServerSupportFunction*, which I'll describe shortly. If it has, the read or write function will return immediately and the I/O completion function will be called when the operation is complete. The I/O completion function is passed some context information provided by the extension when the callback is registered, as well as being passed an EXTENSION_CONTROL_BLOCK and the number of bytes read or written.

**NOTE** Asynchronous I/O is often used to allow applications to continue functioning while relatively slow I/O operations take place. This is often appropriate, especially if the number of clients is expected to be high and the duration of the I/O operations is expected to be long. Well, then, why not always use asynchronous I/O? Generally, using asynchronous I/O results in a more complex program than would result from using synchronous I/O using multiple threads. I'll discuss asynchronous I/O in more detail in Chapter 13.

*ServerSupportFunction* is a jack-of-all-trades function that we call with one of 17 possible operation codes. The possible operations run the gamut from getting certificate or impersonation information to retrieving path names from URLs or redirecting the client to a new URL. The meanings of parameters passed into *ServerSupportFunction* depend upon the operation code being used. *ServerSupportFunction*'s general form is shown in the following function prototype:

```
BOOL ServerSupportFunction(
    HCONN ConnID,            // Connection ID
    DWORD dwHSERRequest,     // Operation Code
    LPVOID lpvBuffer,        // Buffer
    LPDWORD lpdwSize,        // Size, where appropriate
    LPDWORD lpdwDataType     // Data Type, where appropriate
);
```

The *HttpExtensionProc* in the ISAPI1 example program does nothing more than display a message on the browser ("Hello ISAPI World!") and, optionally, display the time on the server. Figure 10-6 shows the results of calling this sample ISAPI extension using the URL that points to the DLL with *?time* appended. Calling the extension without *?time* (or with any value except the string *?time*) results in the same screen without the time reported.

The *HttpExtensionProc* function for this simple application illustrates the tasks associated with virtually any ISAPI extension application. The first step is to prepare a header, as shown in the following code:

```
// Prepare a header.
HeaderExInfo.pszStatus = "200 OK";
HeaderExInfo.cchStatus = strlen(HeaderExInfo.pszStatus);
HeaderExInfo.pszHeader = "Content-type: text/html\r\n\r\n";
HeaderExInfo.cchHeader = strlen(HeaderExInfo.pszHeader);
HeaderExInfo.fKeepConn = FALSE;
```

All HTTP messages have a status associated with them, indicated with a number followed by a text explanation. For instance, in this example "200 OK" is the message that tells the browser that the request has resulted in a good response. Table 10-1 shows the general classes of status messages that can be returned. Notice that when you use

IIS 4 or greater, the URL or file to be displayed in the event of an error can be custom-configured for each error message.

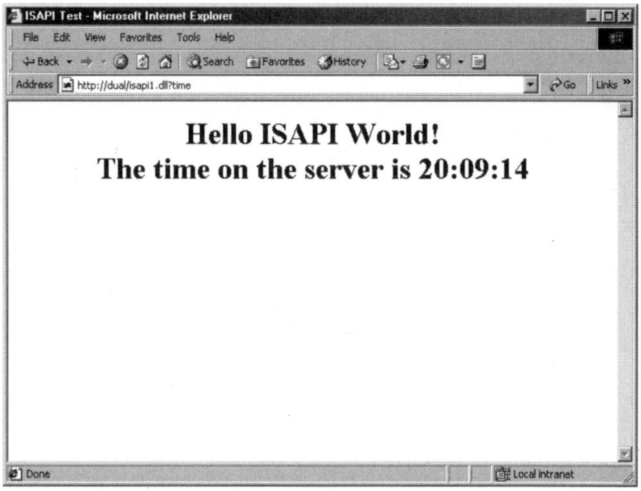


**Figure 10-6** *A simple ISAPI application as seen by the client browser.*

**TABLE 10-1**
**CLASSES OF HTTP STATUS MESSAGES**

| *HTTP Status* | *Category* | *Description* |
|---|---|---|
| 1xx | Informational | Not used, but reserved for future use. |
| 2xx | Success | The action was successfully received, understood, and accepted. |
| 3xx | Redirection | Further action is required to complete the request. |
| 4xx | Client Error | The request contains incorrect syntax and cannot be processed. |
| 5xx | Server Error | The server failed to service the apparently valid request. |

Once the header is created, you must send it. The header information here is appended to the header information already created by the IIS server. Rather than use the *WriteClient* function, we use the *ServerSupportFunction* to send the header. The call to *ServerSupportFunction* sends the connection ID, the operation code for sending a header, and a pointer to the header information structure, as in the code fragment shown at the top of the following page.

```
// Send headers using IIS-provided callback.
// These functions are used quite a bit in ISAPI programming.
lpECB->ServerSupportFunction(
    lpECB->ConnID,
    HSE_REQ_SEND_RESPONSE_HEADER_EX,
    &HeaderExInfo,
    NULL,
    NULL
    );
```

Notice that we are using the HSE_REQ_SEND_RESPONSE_HEADER_EX operation code rather than the HSE_REQ_SEND_RESPONSE_HEADER operation code; the latter has been deprecated, and its use is not recommended. The HSE_REQ_SEND_RESPONSE_HEADER_EX operation code also allows the program to specify whether the connection should be kept open.

While all of the possible operation codes are detailed in the MSDN documentation, several deserve special mention.

- HSE_REQ_GET_IMPERSONATION_TOKEN is used to retrieve a handle to the impersonation token used by the request. This operation code can be used when your ISAPI extension is attempting to use a resource like a file or registry key. The returned token can be used by the *ImpersonateLoggedOnUser* or *SetThreadToken* Win32 functions. Unlike most handles your program will use, this handle should not be closed when you are through with it; the handle will be closed when the request's EXTENSION_CONTROL_BLOCK is destroyed.
- The HSE_REQ_SEND_URL and HSE_REQ_SEND_URL_REDIRECT_RESP operation codes perform the same operation. They redirect the current connection to the absolute URL passed in the *lpvBuffer* parameter. While some browsers support relative URLs (such as *default.asp*), most require an absolute path (such as *www.microsoft.com/default.asp*). The HTTP 1.1 standard specifically requires absolute paths.
- The HSE_REQ_TRANSMIT_FILE operation code allows an ISAPI extension to send a file to the client browser using the Win32 API *TransmitFile* function. The file transmission is carried out asynchronously. What this means to your application is that you must set an asynchronous callback function, either through the HSE_REQ_IO_COMPLETION operation code or by setting the callback function in the HSE_TF_INFO structure passed in as the *lpvBuffer* parameter. Once the file transmission is started, the extension should return the HSE_STATUS_PENDING status code.

The code in Listing 10-1 next checks the value of the query string, available as the *lpszQueryString* element of the extension control block passed into *HttpExtensionProc*. Recall that the query string contains the text entered as the URL immediately past the first question mark that indicates the beginning of arguments being passed. In the ISAPI1 example, we simply check the query string to see whether it is the literal "time". We check using a case-insensitive string compare, shown in this code fragment:

```
if (!(strnicmp(lpECB->lpszQueryString, "TIME", 4)))
```

In the example shown in Figure 10-6, the query string is *http://dual/isapi1.dll?time*. Thus, this URL will meet the test and the code within the *if* block will be executed. The block of code copies normal HTML code into the *szMessage* character array and inserts the time into the string because the user requested it. Returning the time is specific to this ISAPI extension and is done solely because we programmed it this way. The HTML code copied into the *szMessage* buffer is the same code you would type to create the same simple page manually.

If "time" is not passed as an argument in the URL, the *else* clause is executed. In a real-world example, there would likely be several different functions that would be supported, each with its own set of code in the *HttpExtensionProc* function. Finally the extension procedure uses the *WriteClient* callback passed in as part of the extension control block.

## MFC—A Better Way to Create an ISAPI Extension

One thing that should be clear from the ISAPI1 example: a lot of code is essentially boilerplate. There ought to be a better way, and there is. Unlike the solution to the boilerplate associated with ODBC in Chapter 8, the ISAPI boilerplate problem has a solution within the Microsoft Foundation Classes (MFC).

Recall that in Chapter 8 I said that the database classes of MFC would not be covered primarily because using MFC for a service is often not the best approach. Why the change of heart? Nothing really has changed. I do feel that MFC, although entirely appropriate for client applications, is too much for most server applications. ISAPI is the one great exception to this.

There are several reasons why this is true. First and foremost, the MFC ISAPI classes are a work of art. While many of MFC's details require entire chapters to explain fully (and even then the explanations might not be completely satisfying), the ISAPI extension classes (and the ISAPI filter classes covered in the next chapter) are concise and easily covered, even if you have little or no experience with MFC.

The second and perhaps most important reason for using the MFC ISAPI classes is that you can do so and use only the part of MFC required for ISAPI development.

This eliminates any concern about adding too much superfluous code to your application. For instance, I created an MFC version of the simple ISAPI1.dll created in the previous section. I used the ISAPI Extension Wizard (described shortly) with the MFC components statically linked, with some modifications to ensure that only the ISAPI extension portions of MFC were linked into the resulting DLL. While the resulting MFC-based ISAPI DLL was twice the size of the hand-crafted ISAPI extension, at approximately 72 KB it was still quite small. More important, the MFC ISAPI extension DLL offered some convenient features not found in the hand-crafted ISAPI extension DLL, and the future growth in size as functionality is added is likely to be equivalent for both versions. The 36 KB penalty for using MFC in this case is a penalty I am more than willing to pay for the convenience offered.

### Step 1: Using the MFC ISAPI Extension Wizard

The first step required to use the MFC ISAPI extensions is to select New from the File menu, select the ISAPI Extension Wizard from the list of project types, and enter the base path and project name, as shown in Figure 10-7. Technically you could begin creating an ISAPI application by simply creating a basic DLL project and manually adding all the MFC ISAPI support, but using the wizard is much simpler.

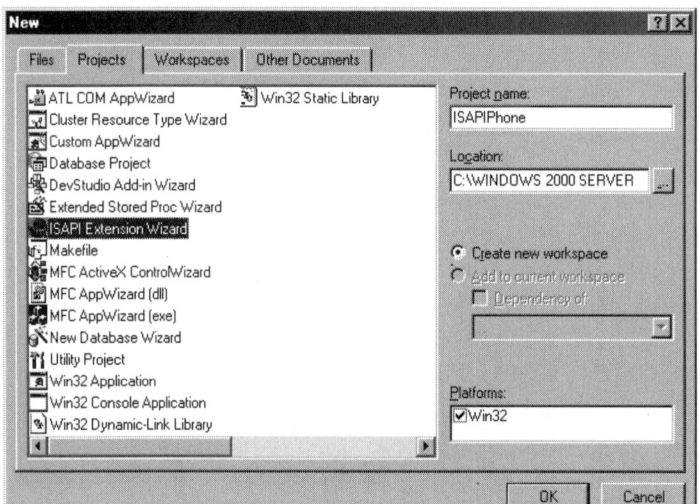


**Figure 10-7** *Selecting the ISAPI Extension Wizard from the New dialog in Visual C++ 6.*

The ISAPI Extension Wizard, shown in Figure 10-8, consists of a single dialog that allows you to select the type of server object you would like to create. For this exercise, most of the default values are fine. Leave Generate A Filter Object unchecked; I'll cover ISAPI filters in the next chapter. The default Extension Class Name and Description boxes are fine, but I generally use the MFC library as a statically linked library. In this case, the size of the MFC library that is being linked in is quite small. Click on Finish, and a confirmation dialog summarizing your selections will appear.

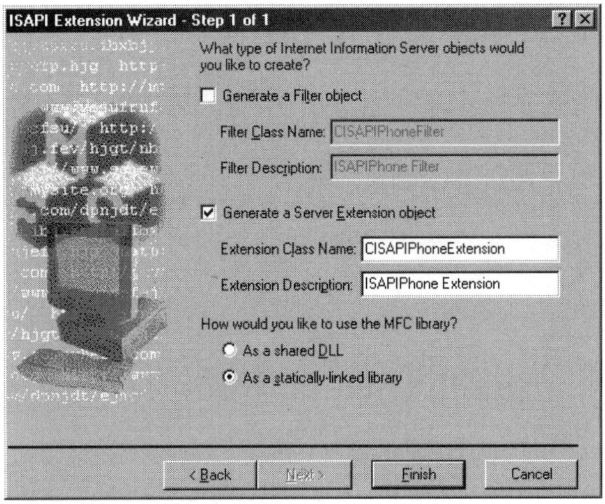


**Figure 10-8** *The ISAPI Extension Wizard dialog in Visual C++ 6.*

The resulting application is a straightforward ISAPI extension that simply sends out a message when it is called, without regard to the query string that is passed in. One of the first things that we need to do to this application is remove the vast majority of MFC code that is not needed by an ISAPI extension. Let's walk through the steps required to remove support for MFC.

First take a look at Listing 10-3, which is the main file for the wizard-generated application. Notice especially the code that is commented out at the bottom of the listing. Just above the commented code is a comment that explains the need to include this code if the extension will not use MFC. If you simply follow the instructions and compile the extension, uncommenting the commented section of code, the code will link. You need to take two additional steps, which I explain in the next section of this chapter.

**ISAPIPhone.cpp**

```
// ISAPIPHONE.CPP - Implementation file for your Internet Server
//  ISAPIPhone Extension

#include "stdafx.h"
#include "ISAPIPhone.h"
```

**Listing 10-3** *(continued)*

**Listing 10-3** *continued*

```
///////////////////////////////////////////////////////////////////////
// command-parsing map

BEGIN_PARSE_MAP(CISAPIPhoneExtension, CHttpServer)
    // TODO: insert your ON_PARSE_COMMAND() and
    //  ON_PARSE_COMMAND_PARAMS() here to hook up your commands.
    // For example:

    ON_PARSE_COMMAND(Default, CISAPIPhoneExtension, ITS_EMPTY)
    DEFAULT_PARSE_COMMAND(Default, CISAPIPhoneExtension)
END_PARSE_MAP(CISAPIPhoneExtension)


///////////////////////////////////////////////////////////////////////
// The one and only CISAPIPhoneExtension object

CISAPIPhoneExtension theExtension;


///////////////////////////////////////////////////////////////////////
// CISAPIPhoneExtension implementation

CISAPIPhoneExtension::CISAPIPhoneExtension()
{
}

CISAPIPhoneExtension::~CISAPIPhoneExtension()
{
}

BOOL CISAPIPhoneExtension::GetExtensionVersion(
    HSE_VERSION_INFO* pVer)
{
    // Call default implementation for initialization.
    CHttpServer::GetExtensionVersion(pVer);

    // Load description string.
    TCHAR sz[HSE_MAX_EXT_DLL_NAME_LEN+1];
    ISAPIVERIFY(::LoadString(AfxGetResourceHandle(),
            IDS_SERVER, sz, HSE_MAX_EXT_DLL_NAME_LEN));
    _tcscpy(pVer->lpszExtensionDesc, sz);
    return TRUE;
}
```

```
BOOL CISAPIPhoneExtension::TerminateExtension(DWORD dwFlags)
{
    // Extension is being terminated.
    // TODO: Clean up any per-instance resources.
    return TRUE;
}

///////////////////////////////////////////////////////////////////////
// CISAPIPhoneExtension command handlers

void CISAPIPhoneExtension::Default(CHttpServerContext* pCtxt)
{
    StartContent(pCtxt);
    WriteTitle(pCtxt);

    *pCtxt << _T("This default message was produced by the ");
    *pCtxt << _T("Internet Server DLL Wizard. Edit your "
        "CISAPIPhoneExtension::Default()");
    *pCtxt << _T(" implementation to change it.\r\n");

    EndContent(pCtxt);
}

// Do not edit the following lines, which are needed by ClassWizard.
#if 0
BEGIN_MESSAGE_MAP(CISAPIPhoneExtension, CHttpServer)
    //{{AFX_MSG_MAP(CISAPIPhoneExtension)
    //}}AFX_MSG_MAP
END_MESSAGE_MAP()
#endif    // 0


///////////////////////////////////////////////////////////////////////
// If your extension will not use MFC, you'll need this code to
//  ensure the extension objects can find the resource handle for the
//  module. If you want your extension to be independent of MFC,
//  remove the comments around the following AfxGetResourceHandle()
//  and DllMain() functions, and remove the g_hInstance global
//  variable.

/****

static HINSTANCE g_hInstance;
```

*(continued)*

**Listing 10-3** *continued*

```
HINSTANCE AFXISAPI AfxGetResourceHandle()
{
    return g_hInstance;
}

BOOL WINAPI DllMain(HINSTANCE hInst, ULONG ulReason,
                    LPVOID lpReserved)
{
    if (ulReason == DLL_PROCESS_ATTACH)
    {
        g_hInstance = hInst;
    }

    return TRUE;
}

****/
```

Now take a look at Listing 10-4, which contains the StdAfx.h file generated by the wizard. You'll notice a series of include statements. In order to remove reliance upon MFC, all but the line including afxisapi.h should be commented out or removed. Finally select the Project/Settings menu option, and on the General tab, change the Microsoft Foundation Classes setting to Not Using MFC, as shown in Figure 10-9. Once you've done this, the ISAPI extension can be compiled and used.

```
#if !defined(AFX_STDAFX_H__BB9DC598_3253_11D3_864F_00105A1177A2__INCLUDED_)
#define AFX_STDAFX_H__BB9DC598_3253_11D3_864F_00105A1177A2__INCLUDED_

// stdafx.h : include file for standard system include files
//  or project-specific include files that are used frequently
//  but are changed infrequently.
//

#include <afx.h>
#include <afxwin.h>
#include <afxmt.h>          // for synchronization objects
#include <afxext.h>
#include <afxisapi.h>

//{{AFX_INSERT_LOCATION}}
// Microsoft Visual C++ will insert additional declarations
//  immediately before the previous line.

#endif //
 !defined(AFX_STDAFX_H__BB9DC598_3253_11D3_864F_00105A1177A2__INCLUDED)
```

**Listing 10-4**

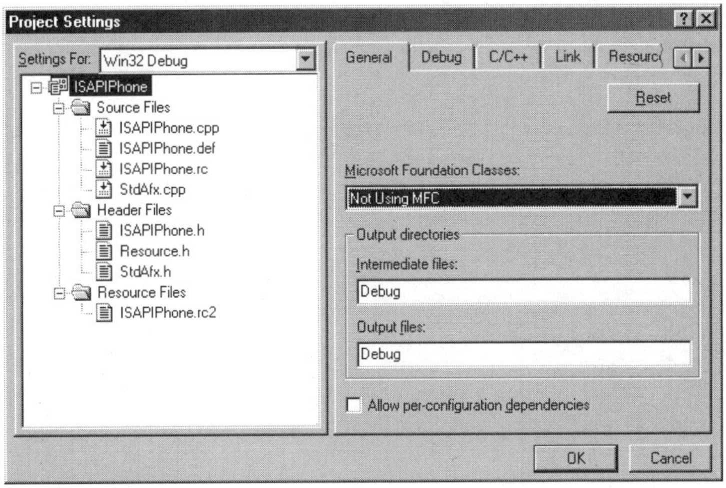


**Figure 10-9** *The Project Settings dialog in Visual C++ 6.*

### Step 2: Modify the application to suit

The next step is to take the admittedly simple application created by the wizard and to modify it to respond as required. Before doing so, however, let's examine several aspects of the MFC ISAPI classes that will allow an application to be created with greater ease and flexibility. First take a look at the function that performs the default behavior when the wizard-created extension is run:

```
void CISAPIPhoneExtension::Default(CHttpServerContext* pCtxt)
{
    StartContent(pCtxt);
    WriteTitle(pCtxt);

    *pCtxt << _T("This default message was produced by the ");
    *pCtxt << _T("Internet Server DLL Wizard. Edit your "
        "CISAPIPhoneExtension::Default()");
    *pCtxt << _T(" implementation to change it.\r\n");

    EndContent(pCtxt);
}
```

The first thing that you'll notice is that there is none of the actual HTML code that was in Listing 10-1. The next thing to notice is that rather than creating a string and then calling an API function to write the string, the text is streamed to the *CHttpServerContext* function pointed to by the single parameter passed into the *Default* function. The _T macro is used to properly handle text that can be standard ANSI or multibyte character text. Finally notice the methods that are called to begin content, write a title, and finally end content.

Since there is no obvious HTML code explicitly located in the *Default* function, what is sent to the browser? Running the default application results in the following HTML code, captured from the Microsoft Internet Explorer View/Source menu option:

```
<html><head><title>Default MFC Web Server Extension</title></head>
<body>This default message was produced by the Internet Server DLL
 Wizard. Edit your CIsapilmfcExtension::Default() implementation to
 change it.
</body></html>
```

In any good abstraction, the details that are not central to the task at hand are often just boilerplate. As such, the MFC ISAPI classes hide the details of how the HTML code is emitted. Obviously, the functions to start content, end content, and write the title are doing the job. What's also significant is that these methods can be overridden to allow customization that permits an entire application to be tied together.

The *CHttpServer* class is the base class for the major derived class in this application, *CISAPIPhoneExtension*. The *CHttpServer* class handles the bulk of the interaction with the IIS. This class takes the information passed in HTTP format and breaks it down so that it is readily available. This behavior can make the function handler code of an ISAPI application look more like a traditional function without requiring your own custom code to parse command lines, route commands, and so on.

Table 10-2 lists the significant methods of *CHttpServer* with explanations of their default functions and why they might be overridden. Several of these methods will be overridden in the example presented shortly.

While the ISAPI classes differ in many ways from the balance of the MFC classes—primarily because ISAPI classes have no direct user interface—they also share several features with many of the MFC classes. One significant feature these classes have in common is the use of some fairly exotic macros that allow class member functions to be mapped to the proper functionality. If you have done any serious MFC programming, the parse mapping macros should look familiar to you. The following code snippet is the parse map for the ISAPIPhone application:

```
BEGIN_PARSE_MAP(CISAPIPhoneExtension, CHttpServer)
    // TODO: insert your ON_PARSE_COMMAND() and
    //  ON_PARSE_COMMAND_PARAMS() here to hook up your commands.
    // For example:

    ON_PARSE_COMMAND(Default, CISAPIPhoneExtension, ITS_EMPTY)
    DEFAULT_PARSE_COMMAND(Default, CISAPIPhoneExtension)
END_PARSE_MAP(CISAPIPhoneExtension)
```

**TABLE 10-2**
**THE METHODS OF *CHTTPSERVER* THAT CAN BE OVERRIDDEN**

| CHttpServer *Method* | *Description* | *Why Override?* |
|---|---|---|
| *CallFunction* | Finds and executes the function associated with the command in the URL | Generally *CallFunction* is not overridden since it is at the core of the class, but it might need to be overridden if your form requires multiselect list boxes. (See the Microsoft Knowledge Base article Q169109.) |
| *OnParseError* | Constructs an error message to be presented to the client | Override *OnParseError* to create custom messages when parse errors occur. (See Table 10-4 for a listing of possible parse errors.) |
| *OnWriteBody* | Writes data back to the client | Override *OnWriteBody* if you need to modify the body before it is written to the client. |
| *HttpExtensionProc* | Called by the framework for each request to the ISAPI extension | Overriding *HttpExtensionProc* is not recommended. |
| *GetExtensionVersion* | Called by the framework when the ISAPI extension is loaded | Call the default version, and then override to replace the default text string with your version. |
| *ConstructStream* | Constructs a *CHtmlStream* object | Override *ConstructStream* to create your own descendant of *CHtmlStream*. This might be useful if you want to optimize the performance of your *CHtmlStream* descendant for your application. |
| *TerminateExtension* | Provides a safe way to clean up threads and complete other shutdown tasks | If the unload is of type HSE_TERM_ADVISORY_UNLOAD, the override function can return FALSE to indicate the extension is not ready to shut down. |

Every MFC ISAPI application will have the BEGIN_PARSE_MAP and END_PARSE_MAP macros. BEGIN_PARSE_MAP takes the name of the derived class—in this case *CISAPIPhoneExtension*—and the class it is based upon—in this case *CHttpServer*. At minimum, an application will have a single ON_PARSE_COMMAND macro. This macro accepts as arguments the name of the member function, the name of the class where the member function is declared, and an argument list. *Default* is the member function used here, and it is passed in along with the class name and the ITS_EMPTY, indicating that no arguments are expected with this command. Commonly, one other macro will be used, DEFAULT_PARSE_COMMAND. This macro specifies the name of a default function to be called and the class name to map the function to. The possible types that can be passed to the parse map macros are outlined in Table 10-3.

**TABLE 10-3**
**SYMBOLS AND THE RELATED TYPES FOR USE IN PARSE MAPPING OF PARAMETERS**

| *Symbol* | *Meaning* |
|---|---|
| ITS_EMPTY | Used for no arguments. (Arguments cannot simply be blank.) |
| ITS_PSTR | A pointer to a string. |
| ITS_RAW | The exact raw data is sent to the ISAPI extension. Cannot be used in conjunction with other parameter types. |
| ITS_I2 | A 2-byte integer (a short). |
| ITS_I4 | A 4-byte integer (a long). |
| ITS_R4 | A 4-byte floating-point number (a float). |
| ITS_R8 | An 8-byte floating-point number (a double). |

These powerful macros are in some ways the real magic behind the *CHttpServer* class. Imagine a native ISAPI extension like the one in Listing 10-1. Rather than supporting two functions, imagine that it supported 50 different functions. This would require pages of comparisons between the function name passed in and the functions that would be executed for each of those 50 functions. Each of those 50 functions would have to be declared and accessible somehow to the *HttpExtensionProc* function.

Now imagine a similarly complex ISAPI application using the framework provided by the *CHttpServer* class. Rather than pages of *if* and *stricmp* statements, the functions are mapped using the parse map macros. Additionally, the functions are not stand-alone functions but rather member functions of the *CHttpServer*-derived class. This is a much cleaner way to implement complex functionality.

Let's suppose that we wanted to add another function, such as a search function, to this *CISAPIPhoneExtension* class. The steps involved are as follows:

- Add a member function to *CISAPIPhoneExtension* using the Class Wizard. The return type is void, and it needs to accept a *CHttpServerContext* pointer and a string pointer, as in Figure 10-10. Note that the *CHttpServerContext* pointer is mandatory for all handlers that will be mapped using the parse map, and the string pointer is used to contain the text that will be searched.

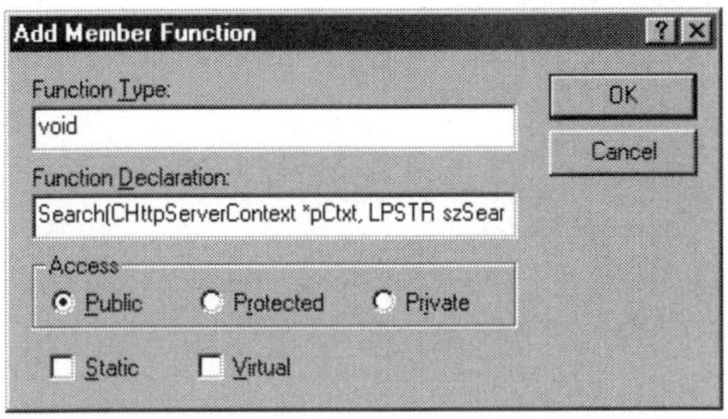


**Figure 10-10** *Adding a* Search *member function to the* CISAPIPhoneExtension *class in Visual C++ 6.*

- Add a line to the parse map: ON_PARSE_COMMAND(Search, CISAPIPhoneExtension, ITS_PSTR). This line directs all URL search requests to the *Search* function just created. ITS_PSTR indicates that the function takes a single string parameter.

  **NOTE** ON_PARSE_COMMAND looks like a traditional function call, but of course it is not. One of the significant differences is the way the macro handles multiple arguments. Suppose we had a function that allowed a more specialized search—for example, one that allowed us to specify last name and first name separately. The function prototype for such a function might look like this:

```
void CISAPIPhoneExtension::SearchName(CHttpServerContext* pCtxt,
    LPSTR szLName, LPSTR szFName)
```

  Many programmers would enter a parse map entry for this function like this:

```
ON_PARSE_COMMAND(SearchName, CISAPIPhoneExtension,
    ITS_PSTR, ITS_PSTR)
```

  This is a plausible-looking entry, but it will not pass muster. The two ITS_PSTR entries are *not* two separate arguments—they need to be a single argument, resulting in an entry that looks like this:

```
ON_PARSE_COMMAND(SearchName, CISAPIPhoneExtension,
    ITS_PSTR ITS_PSTR)
```

  Note the lack of a comma between the two ITS_PSTR argument type symbols.

The resulting code has no code between the opening and closing brackets of the *Search* method. For testing purposes, copy the default actions from the *Default* method into *Search*, changing references to the *Default* method as appropriate. Next add one line to the code, a line that simply echoes the value of the *szSearchFor*. The resulting method definition should look like the following code fragment:

```
void CISAPIPhoneExtension::Search(CHttpServerContext* pCtxt,
    LPSTR szSearchFor)
{
    StartContent(pCtxt);
    WriteTitle(pCtxt);

    *pCtxt << _T("This Search message was produced by the ");
    *pCtxt << _T("Internet Server DLL Wizard. ");
    *pCtxt << _T("Edit your CISAPIPhoneExtension::Search()");
    *pCtxt << _T(" implementation to change it.\r\n");
    *pCtxt << _T("Looking for ") << _T(szSearchFor);

    EndContent(pCtxt);
}
```

The next step is to actually get a query string to this method. While it is certainly possible to do so by simply typing a URL at the browser's address line, a more useful approach is to create a form that calls this function. This will enable us to see exactly how the information will come back from the browser. One way to do this would be to generate an ASP or HTML file similar to the file used to gather the search criteria for the ASP phone directory lookup example in Chapter 9. There is also another solution.

The *Default* method can be changed to do what the default.asp script did in the ASP phone directory lookup example. Not all of the code that was required for the ASP example—notably the <HTML>, <BODY>, and <TITLE> sections—needs to be present because the *CHttpServer* methods that start and end content and write the title will take care of that. In addition, the exact same objects and methods are not present in this ISAPI application, so it is not possible to use the same *Response.Write* syntax to emit the HTML to the client. The resulting code that writes out the HTML for a form when the default function of this ISAPI application is called is shown in the following code fragment:

```
void CISAPIPhoneExtension::Default(CHttpServerContext* pCtxt)
{
    StartContent(pCtxt);
    WriteTitle(pCtxt);

    *pCtxt << _T("<CENTER>");
    *pCtxt << _T("<h1><a NAME = ""top"">Test</a></h1>");
```

```
    *pCtxt << _T("<hr>");
    *pCtxt << _T("<FORM method=POST action=ISAPIPhone.dll?search>");
    *pCtxt << _T("<p>");
    *pCtxt << _T("Search for phone number...");
    *pCtxt << _T("<p><p>");

    *pCtxt << _T("<INPUT TYPE=text NAME=lookFor>");
    *pCtxt << _T("<p>");
    *pCtxt << _T("<INPUT type=submit VALUE=""OK"">");
    *pCtxt << _T("</CENTER>");

    *pCtxt << _T("<hr>");

    *pCtxt << _T("<h5>Simple ISAPI Phone Directory Test<br>");

    *pCtxt << _T("</h5>");

    EndContent(pCtxt);
}
```

This code uses the *CHttpServerContext* pointer that is passed in to stream out text to the client. In this case, most of the text is identical to the ASP example, with two exceptions. First the action of the form is no longer an ASP page, but rather a call to this same ISAPI extension's *Search* method. Second the description of the page has changed to reflect that this is an ISAPI application. The default screen generated by the modified version of *Default* is shown in Figure 10-11.

When example criteria are entered on this screen, for instance "Reilly", the query string is parsed such that *szSearchFor* will contain "lookFor=Reilly". This is a good

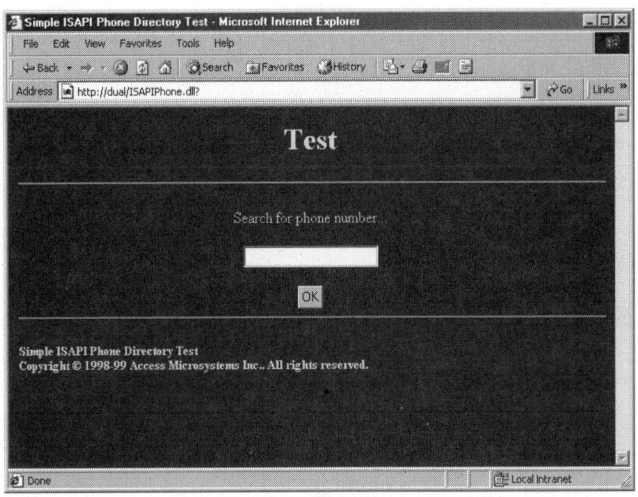


**Figure 10-11** *The ISAPIPhone.dll default screen.*

first step and would be completely acceptable if there were not more that the framework could do for you. In fact, there *is* one more step that can be taken that will result in the string entered into the criteria field being returned by the MFC framework directly to your application, with no further parsing required.

The addition of the parse map line for the *Search* method results in a parse map that contains the following lines:

```
BEGIN_PARSE_MAP(CISAPIPhoneExtension, CHttpServer)
    ON_PARSE_COMMAND(Search, CISAPIPhoneExtension, ITS_PSTR)
    ON_PARSE_COMMAND(Default, CISAPIPhoneExtension, ITS_EMPTY)
    DEFAULT_PARSE_COMMAND(Default, CISAPIPhoneExtension)
END_PARSE_MAP(CISAPIPhoneExtension)
```

These lines allow both the *Search* and *Default* methods to be called, either directly or—by not specifying another valid function—implicitly. There is one additional line that can be part of a parse map that will move us one step closer to the optimal level of parsing done by the framework. That line uses the ON_PARSE_COMMAND_PARAMS macro. Adding the following line just after the first ON_PARSE_COMMAND macro line allows the framework to parse the command line and place the value of "lookFor" into the single string parameter to *Search*:

```
ON_PARSE_COMMAND_PARAMS("lookFor")
```

The ON_PARSE_COMMAND_PARAMS macro is even more powerful than this. If required, a default argument can be specified, and since the parameters are named, they can appear in different orders or can even be absent. For instance, if the default value for "lookFor" were to be "Dave Jones", the parse map would be modified as follows:

```
ON_PARSE_COMMAND_PARAMS("lookFor='Dave Jones'")
```

Note that in this case the default value for this string argument contains a space. This space is enclosed in single quotes to signal that the entire string, including quotes, is the default. The completed parse map for the ISAPI Phone Directory Lookup example should be as follows:

```
BEGIN_PARSE_MAP(CISAPIPhoneExtension, CHttpServer)
    ON_PARSE_COMMAND(Search, CISAPIPhoneExtension, ITS_PSTR)
    ON_PARSE_COMMAND_PARAMS("lookFor")
    ON_PARSE_COMMAND(Default, CISAPIPhoneExtension, ITS_EMPTY)
    DEFAULT_PARSE_COMMAND(Default, CISAPIPhoneExtension)
END_PARSE_MAP(CISAPIPhoneExtension)
```

Given the above parse map, a URL such as *http://server/path/ISAPIPhone.dll?* will send only the contents of the *lookFor* text control on the form as the *szSearchFor* argument to the *Search* method.

The parser can encounter a number of problems, which are indicated by the values returned by the *CallFunction* method. Table 10-4 lists the *enum* values for the parse errors that might be returned by *CallFunction*. These errors can be more fully described to the user by overriding the *OnParseError* method.

**TABLE 10-4**
**RETURN CODES FROM THE *CALLFUNCTION* METHOD**

| *Enum Value* | *Description* |
|---|---|
| *callOK* | The function call was successful. |
| *callParamRequired* | A required parameter was missing. |
| *callBadParamCount* | Too many or too few parameters. |
| *callBadCommand* | The command name was not found. |
| *callNoStackSpace* | No stack space was available. |
| *callNoStream* | No *CHtmlStream* was available. |
| *callMissingQuote* | A parameter was not properly formatted. |
| *callMissingParams* | No parameters were available. |
| *callBadParam* | A parameter was not correctly formed, for example, missing a quote. |

### The final step: Searching for a number

Once we've handled the details of communicating between the initial form and the function that will eventually display the results, the next step is to have the *Search* method actually get the results. Failing that, we report either the error or that no numbers were found matching the criteria. Listing 10-5 is the final version of this example program. Listing 10-6 is the final version of the StdAfx.h file required to compile the final program.

**ISAPIPhone.cpp**

```
// ISAPIPHONE.CPP - Implementation file for your Internet Server
//  ISAPIPhone Extension

#include "stdafx.h"
#include "ISAPIPhone.h"

///////////////////////////////////////////////////////////////////////////
// command-parsing map
```

**Listing 10-5** *(continued)*

**Listing 10-5** *continued*

```
BEGIN_PARSE_MAP(CISAPIPhoneExtension, CHttpServer)
    // TODO: insert your ON_PARSE_COMMAND() and
    //  ON_PARSE_COMMAND_PARAMS() here to hook up your commands.
    // For example:

    ON_PARSE_COMMAND(Search, CISAPIPhoneExtension, ITS_PSTR)
    ON_PARSE_COMMAND_PARAMS("lookFor")
    ON_PARSE_COMMAND(Default, CISAPIPhoneExtension, ITS_EMPTY)
    DEFAULT_PARSE_COMMAND(Default, CISAPIPhoneExtension)
END_PARSE_MAP(CISAPIPhoneExtension)


///////////////////////////////////////////////////////////////////////
// The one and only CISAPIPhoneExtension object

CISAPIPhoneExtension theExtension;


///////////////////////////////////////////////////////////////////////
// CISAPIPhoneExtension implementation

CISAPIPhoneExtension::CISAPIPhoneExtension()
{
}

CISAPIPhoneExtension::~CISAPIPhoneExtension()
{
}

BOOL CISAPIPhoneExtension::GetExtensionVersion(
    HSE_VERSION_INFO* pVer)
{
    // Call default implementation for initialization.
    CHttpServer::GetExtensionVersion(pVer);

    // Load description string.
    TCHAR sz[HSE_MAX_EXT_DLL_NAME_LEN+1];
    ISAPIVERIFY(::LoadString(AfxGetResourceHandle(),
            IDS_SERVER, sz, HSE_MAX_EXT_DLL_NAME_LEN));
    _tcscpy(pVer->lpszExtensionDesc, sz);
    return TRUE;
}

BOOL CISAPIPhoneExtension::TerminateExtension(DWORD dwFlags)
```

```
{
    // Extension is being terminated.
    // TODO: Clean up any per-instance resources.
    return TRUE;
}

///////////////////////////////////////////////////////////////////////
// CISAPIPhoneExtension command handlers

void CISAPIPhoneExtension::Default(CHttpServerContext* pCtxt)
{
    StartContent(pCtxt);
    WriteTitle(pCtxt);

    *pCtxt << _T("<CENTER>");
    *pCtxt << _T("<h1><a NAME=""top"">Test</a></h1>");

    *pCtxt << _T("<hr>");
    *pCtxt << _T("<FORM method=POST action=ISAPIPhone.dll?search>");
    *pCtxt << _T("<p>");
    *pCtxt << _T("Search for phone number...");
    *pCtxt << _T("<p><p>");

    *pCtxt << _T("<INPUT TYPE=text NAME=lookFor>");
    *pCtxt << _T("<p>");
    *pCtxt << _T("<INPUT type=submit VALUE=""OK"">");
    *pCtxt << _T("</CENTER>");

    *pCtxt << _T("<hr>");

    *pCtxt << _T("<h5>Simple ISAPI Phone Directory Test<br>");


    EndContent(pCtxt);
}

void CISAPIPhoneExtension::Search(CHttpServerContext* pCtxt,
    LPSTR szSearchFor)
{
    char strSQL[255];
    UWORD col = 1;
    UWORD rc;
    CODBCDatabase *db;
    CODBCCursor *curs;
```

*(continued)*

**Listing 10-5** *continued*

```
    StartContent(pCtxt);
    WriteTitle(pCtxt);

    *pCtxt << _T("<CENTER><FORM method=POST "
        "action=ISAPIPhone.dll?>");
    *pCtxt << _T("<INPUT type=submit "
        "VALUE=""Return""></FORM></CENTER>");

try
{
    // Set up the ODBC stuff...
    db = new CODBCDatabase("Phones"); // User ID and Password
                                      //  not needed.
    if (db->isConnected())
    {
        curs = new CODBCCursor(db);

        // Pick the table.
        curs->setTables("tblPhone");

        // Bind the columns.
        curs->bindColumn(col,"LName", 255);
        curs->bindColumn(col,"FName", 255);
        curs->bindColumn(col,"Dept", 255);
        curs->bindColumn(col,"Facility", 255);
        curs->bindColumn(col,"Phone", 255);

        curs->setOrderBy(" LName,FName,Dept ");

        // Because we have used the ON_PARSE_COMMAND_PARAMS macro
        //  above, the argument to this function will be completely
        //  parsed for us. Thus, rather than szSearchFor being
        //  "lookFor=enteredValue" it will just be equal to
        //  "enteredValue".
        strcpy(strSQL, " WHERE SearchString like '%");
        strcat(strSQL, szSearchFor);
        strcat(strSQL, "%'");
        curs->setRestrict(strSQL);

        curs->doSelect();

        if (rc = curs->fetch() == SQL_SUCCESS)
        {
            // Build the table header....
            *pCtxt << _T("<CENTER>");
```

```
        *pCtxt << _T("<P><TABLE BORDER=1 ><TR>");
        *pCtxt << _T("<TD BGCOLOR=darkcyan><B>Last Name"
            "</B></TD>");
        *pCtxt << _T("<TD BGCOLOR=darkcyan><B>First Name"
            "</B></TD>");
        *pCtxt << _T("<TD BGCOLOR=darkcyan><B>Dept"
            "</B></TD>");
        *pCtxt << _T("<TD BGCOLOR=darkcyan><B>Facility"
            "</B></TD>");
        *pCtxt << _T("<TD BGCOLOR=darkcyan><B>Phone"
            "</B></TD>");
        *pCtxt << _T("</TR><H3>");

        do {
            *pCtxt << _T("<TR BGCOLOR=WHITE>");
            *pCtxt << _T("<TD BGCOLOR=blue><B>" <<
                (char *)(*curs)["LName"] << "</B></TD>");
            *pCtxt << _T("<TD BGCOLOR=blue><B>" <<
                (char *)(*curs)["FName"] << "</B></TD>");
            *pCtxt << _T("<TD BGCOLOR=blue><B>" <<
                (char *)(*curs)["DEPT"] << "</B></TD>");
            *pCtxt << _T("<TD BGCOLOR=blue><B>" <<
                (char *)(*curs)["Facility"] << "</B></TD>");
            *pCtxt << _T("<TD BGCOLOR=blue><B>" <<
                (char *)(*curs)["Phone"] << "</B></TD>");
            *pCtxt << _T("</TR>");
        } while ((rc = curs->fetch()) == SQL_SUCCESS);
        *pCtxt << _T("</H3>");
        *pCtxt << _T("</CENTER)");
    }
    else
    {
        *pCtxt << _T("<CENTER><H2>Sorry!  No match"
            " found!</H2></CENTER><BR>");
    }
    delete curs;
}
else
{
    *pCtxt << _T("<CENTER><H2>Sorry!  Can't connect"
        " to database!</H2></CENTER><BR>");
}
delete db;
}
```

*(continued)*

**Listing 10-5** *continued*

```
catch (char *str)
{
    *pCtxt << _T("<CENTER><H2>Exception thrown by"
        " database!</H2></CENTER><BR>");
    *pCtxt << _T(str);
}
    EndContent(pCtxt);

}

// Do not edit the following lines, which are needed by ClassWizard.
#if 0
BEGIN_MESSAGE_MAP(CISAPIPhoneExtension, CHttpServer)
    //{{AFX_MSG_MAP(CISAPIPhoneExtension)
    //}}AFX_MSG_MAP
END_MESSAGE_MAP()
#endif    // 0


///////////////////////////////////////////////////////////////////////
// If your extension will not use MFC, you'll need this code to
//  ensure the extension objects can find the resource handle for the
//  module. If you convert your extension to be independent of MFC,
//  remove the comments around the following AfxGetResourceHandle()
//  and DllMain() functions, as well as the g_hInstance global
//  variable.

/****/

static HINSTANCE g_hInstance;

HINSTANCE AFXISAPI AfxGetResourceHandle()
{
    return g_hInstance;
}

BOOL WINAPI DllMain(HINSTANCE hInst, ULONG ulReason,
                    LPVOID lpReserved)
{
    if (ulReason == DLL_PROCESS_ATTACH)
    {
        CODBCDatabase::InitCriticalSection();
        g_hInstance = hInst;
    }
```

```
    else if (ulReason == DLL_PROCESS_DETACH)
    {
        CODBCDatabase::DelCriticalSection();
    }

    return TRUE;
}

/****/

void CISAPIPhoneExtension::StartContent(
    CHttpServerContext* pCtxt) const
{
    // TODO: Add your specialized code here and/or call
    //  the base class.
    *pCtxt << _T("<HTML><BODY bgColor=Blue Text=yellow>");
//  CHttpServer::StartContent(pCtxt);
}

LPCTSTR CISAPIPhoneExtension::GetTitle() const
{
    // TODO: Add your specialized code here and/or call
    //  the base class.
    return "Simple ISAPI Phone Directory Test";
//  return CHttpServer::GetTitle();
}
```

**StdAfx.h**

```
#if !defined(AFX_STDAFX_H__4EDA42D8_31AE_11D3_864E_00105A1177A2__INCLUDED_)
#define AFX_STDAFX_H__4EDA42D8_31AE_11D3_864E_00105A1177A2__INCLUDED_

// stdafx.h : include file for standard system include files
//  or project-specific include files that are used frequently but
//  are changed infrequently
//


// The wizard places these here. Comment out so
//  the rest of the MFC stuff is not linked in.
//#include <afx.h>
//#include <afxwin.h>
```

**Listing 10-6** *(continued)*

**Listing 10-5** *continued*

```
//#include <afxmt.h>         // for synchronization objects
//#include <afxext.h>
#include <afxisapi.h>
#include "SQL.H"
#include "sqlext.h"
#include "odbclass.h"

// {{AFX_INSERT_LOCATION}}
// Microsoft Visual C++ will insert additional declarations
//  immediately before the previous line.

#endif // !defined(AFX_STDAFX_H__4EDA42D8_31AE_11D3_864E_
00105A1177A2__INCLUDED)
```

The most important parts of Listing 10-5 are the modifications to *Search*. In order to retrieve the records that meet the criteria entered by the user, the ODBC classes described in Chapter 8 will be used. Most of the modifications to the project required to do the data retrieval are straightforward, using methods as outlined in Chapter 8's explanation of the ODBC classes. Listing 10-6 shows the additional header files that need to be included for support of the ODBC classes: standard header files SQL.h and SQLExt.h and the ODBClass.h file from Chapter 8. ODBClass.cpp is added to the project as well.

One of the requirements of the *CODBCDatabase* class is that a static critical section be initialized and then deleted after the last instance of the class is destroyed. DLLs have a function that is roughly equivalent to the *main* function used by console mode programs and the *WinMain* function used by GUI Windows programs. This function is called *DllMain*, and the default version created by the ISAPI Extension Wizard does nothing but set a single variable, *g_hInstance*, when the DLL_PROCESS_ATTACH message is received. This function is modified in the final version to allow the *CODBCDatabase*'s critical section to be initialized as the process attaches to the ISAPI Extension and destroyed as the process detaches. This is done with simple if-then-else logic. If thread attach and detach messages had to be handled as well, a case statement might be in order.

The *Search* method first creates the required objects for the *CODBCDatabase* and *CODBCCursor* classes. If the connection to the database cannot take place, for instance, if the data source name is incorrect or if an invalid user name or password is used, the method sends a message indicating a failure to connect to the database. Once we've constructed all the objects, we set the table name, bind the columns, and set the restrictions and order by clauses. We then perform the select and fetch the data.

The *Search* method sends the actual HTML source to the client browser. Alternatives exist for this behavior. If there were lots of tables to create, we could create objects to handle the start and finish of rows and cells of tables. For this small example, we can easily hand-code these bits of HTML.

If you look back at Figure 10-11, you'll notice that the background color and the text color are different from the colors used in the ASP version of this program. All screens in this ISAPI extension use the same color scheme, and overriding one of the overridable functions mentioned in Table 10-2 sets those colors. The *StartContent* virtual method of the *CHttpServer* class is overridden to set the properties

## ISAPI ERROR HANDLING

One change was required to make the database classes from Chapter 8 safe for inclusion in an ISAPI extension. In the version of these classes we used in the console mode example programs in Chapter 8, the error handling was quite simple: just print the error to the screen using *printf*. This is obviously not adequate for an ISAPI extension.

The problem with error handling in any class that is likely to be used in many different contexts is how the error is to be presented to the user. For instance, a message box would have been a more Windows-like solution to presenting error information, but this too would fail for ISAPI applications in particular and server applications in general.

The solution used in this example is C++'s exception handling. Using three new keywords—*try*, *catch*, and *throw*—classes such as the ODBC classes used here can format a message that conveys the meaning of the error and throw that exception, with the message, to whatever level above that exists to catch the exception. Thus the presentation of the exception is kept separate from the generation of the exception, allowing the consumer application to make the user aware that an exception has occurred.

More complex exception handling is also possible. In this simple example, a character pointer is what is thrown by the ODBC classes error handling function, and the code within the *Search* function catches exceptions of type char *. In real-world examples, there will likely be more information available about the error, and simply placing that information into a string is not the best solution. For this sort of situation, a data structure can be defined that captures all of the exception information, and that structure can be thrown. It is important that the calling program be aware of the type of exception that might be thrown, because a program can best handle exceptions that it is prepared to properly handle and display.

used for the body of each HTML page generated by the extension. To add the override function, right-click *CISAPIPhoneExtension* in the ClassView of the project and select Add Virtual Function from the context menu. A list of new overridable functions as well as currently overridden functions will appear. Select StartContent from this menu, and a new member function will be added to the class. The default implementation does nothing more than call the base class:

```
void CISAPIPhoneExtension::StartContent(
    CHttpServerContext* pCtxt) const
{
    // TODO: Add your specialized code here and/or
    //  call the base class.
    CHttpServer::StartContent(pCtxt);
}
```

In some cases, it is appropriate to call the base class and take some other action. Here it is sufficient to replace the base class's functionality by adding a line similar to the following:

```
*pCtxt << _T("<HTML><BODY bgColor=Blue Text=yellow>");
```

That simple replacement makes all pages use the specified color background and text. Of course, you can get more adventurous by creating a stock scheme for all pages that includes background images and even page headings. This is a simple way to ensure uniformity within the application created by this ISAPI extension.

Another simple customization that can be done by overriding a virtual function is setting a custom title. This can be accomplished in one of two ways. In the example ISAPI extension, *GetTitle* is overridden, with a static title returned when requested. *WriteTitle*, the virtual function actually used to write out the HTML that generates the title, can also be overridden. The effect is the same in either case. A real-world example might create titles based upon the application's special knowledge of the current state of the application.

## ANOTHER USE FOR AN ISAPI EXTENSION

In the Chapter 9 discussion of ASP, our examination of how ASP was implemented on IIS led to the discovery that the ASP.dll responsible for implementing ASP is in fact an ISAPI DLL, exporting the functions required of any ISAPI extension. This discovery gives developers a powerful tool if they should require special scripting support not possible with the standard ASP scripting. Why might this be useful?

- Some development teams might have special knowledge or history of using a particular language for development. Implementing this language as a script language on IIS might offer the ability to leverage existing code and programmer skills for Web development.

- Special scripting support allows scripted access to databases that are not, for practical purposes, accessible through an ODBC data source. For instance, until recently, Pervasive Software's Pervasive.SQL was not known for speedy ODBC access. Furthermore, if the files to be accessed did not have data definition files, they could be valid Pervasive.SQL files, but they could not be accessed via ODBC.
- Imagine that you wanted the ease of a scripted application, but you needed the security of source code not offered by tools such as ASP. One possibility would be the creation of a scripting DLL that would accept encrypted script. Given an editor that allowed developers to work easily on the encrypted script, you could freely distribute the script without fear of compromising trade secrets embedded within it.

Of these three reasons, the first seems to be the most prevalent among people who have approached me on the subject. On several occasions, Perl and Python advocates have approached me after one of my talks on ISAPI. While implementing a scripting language is not for the squeamish and is fraught with manifold difficulties, it is not an overwhelming task.

For demonstration purposes, I created a simple ISAPI extension using MFC. The complete IspMFC_NG project is on the companion CD, though it is there merely as an example of what ended up not working. I set up the extension to translate any file with an extension of .isp (Internet scripting program). One of the first things I needed to do was to get the full path of the current script being executed so that my program could read and translate, as needed, the script I requested. This led to a default function similar to the following function that as yet contained no actual translation code:

```
void CIspExtension::Default(CHttpServerContext* pCtxt)
{
    char path[255];
    char script[255];
    DWORD cBytes = 255;
    StartContent(pCtxt);
    WriteTitle(pCtxt);

    *pCtxt << _T("Path information <BR>");

    pCtxt->GetServerVariable("PATH_TRANSLATED",path,&cBytes);
    *pCtxt << path << "<BR>\r\n";

    pCtxt->GetServerVariable("SCRIPT_NAME",script,&cBytes);
    *pCtxt << script << "<BR>\r\n";
```

*(continued)*

```
    strcat(path,"\\");
    strcat(path,&script[1]);
    *pCtxt << path << "<BR>\r\n";

    EndContent(pCtxt);
}
```

When called directly as a normal ISAPI extension (*http://server/path/isp.dll?*), the extension worked as expected, giving me the proper path for the "script" being executed, in my example, c:\inetpub\wwwroot\isp.dll. Next I used the IIS configuration screen shown in Figure 10-1 and associated the .isp extension with this ISP.dll. I created a simple file with an .isp extension and used a URL that specified the name of the script file (*http://server/path/test.isp*), and the path came back as expected, c:\inetpub\wwwroot\test.isp.

Finally I tried adding a query string to the end of the URL. Here is where the intelligence of the MFC ISAPI classes got in my way. I received a status 400 in the browser when the URL with the query string was called. This made sense. The framework could not parse my query and find an appropriate function. Of course, it was possible to override the *CallFunction* method, but this seemed like overkill for the fairly simple requirement to funnel all requests to a single function to interpret a script.

At this point I was at a crossroads, one familiar to folks who use frameworks like MFC. I had two choices. First I could dig farther into the framework and override the functionality at the core of the *CHttpServer* class. This was in some ways an attractive solution because the ISAPI classes are interesting to investigate and the convenience of using the classes was clear. Comparing the code for the initial simple raw ISAPI example to the MFC examples reminded me of this convenience.

On the other hand, what was my goal? Was I looking to become an expert at the MFC ISAPI classes, or was I looking to get a scripting DLL done? I knew how much work I had to do to get the raw ISAPI scripting DLL done. Was I comfortable enough with the MFC classes to be sure I was not buying into a lot more work than I wanted? Would my customizations to the *CallFunction* method come back to haunt me? Were the MFC parsing features overkill when all scripting requests would be funneled into a single function in any event?

All these concerns led me to create a raw ISAPI scripting DLL. Given that the basic framework was in place already, I took the code from the original raw ISAPI extension and converted it for use as a scripting DLL. The scripting being done in this simple example was as follows. Wherever I saw the string "!date", I replaced it with the date. I replaced "!time" with the time, and I replaced "!name" with "Doug Reilly". The resulting source is presented in Listing 10-7.

**ISPRaw.cpp**

```
// ISPRaw.cpp : Defines the entry point for the DLL application.
//

#include "stdafx.h"

BOOL APIENTRY DllMain(HANDLE hModule,
                      DWORD  ul_reason_for_call,
                      LPVOID lpReserved
                     )
{
    return TRUE;
}

BOOL WINAPI GetExtensionVersion(HSE_VERSION_INFO *pVer)
{
    pVer->dwExtensionVersion = 1;
    strcpy(pVer->lpszExtensionDesc,
        "ISAPI1 Test for Inside Windows Server Development");
    return(TRUE);
}

DWORD WINAPI HttpExtensionProc(EXTENSION_CONTROL_BLOCK *lpECB)
{
    DWORD cBuf;
    DWORD cBytes;
    char szMessage[1024];
    char path[255];
    char query[255];
    FILE *in;


    HSE_SEND_HEADER_EX_INFO HeaderExInfo;


    // Prepare a header....
    HeaderExInfo.pszStatus = "200 OK";
    HeaderExInfo.cchStatus = strlen(HeaderExInfo.pszStatus);
    HeaderExInfo.pszHeader = "Content-type: text/html\r\n\r\n";
    HeaderExInfo.cchHeader = strlen(HeaderExInfo.pszHeader);
    HeaderExInfo.fKeepConn = FALSE;


    // Send headers using IIS-provided callback.
    // These functions are used quite a bit in ISAPI programming.
```

**Listing 10-7** *(continued)*

**Listing 10-7** *continued*

```
    lpECB->ServerSupportFunction(
        lpECB->ConnID,
        HSE_REQ_SEND_RESPONSE_HEADER_EX,
        &HeaderExInfo,
        NULL,
        NULL
       );


    // Get the path that was passed in for this script, translated
    //  to a format appropriate for file reading....
    lpECB->GetServerVariable(lpECB->ConnID,
        "PATH_TRANSLATED", path,&cBytes);

    // In the real world, we would make the query string available
    //  to the script as well.
    cBytes = 255;
    lpECB->GetServerVariable(lpECB->ConnID,
        "QUERY_STRING", query,&cBytes);

    in = fopen(path, "rt");

    if (in != 0)
    {
        int ch;
        char szTemp[100];
        szMessage[0] = '\0';
        // Read through the script...
        while ((ch = fgetc(in)) != EOF)
        {
            // ...until we see our special signal character.
            if (ch != '!')
            {
                // Just pass along the text.
                szTemp[0] = ch;
                szTemp[1] = '\0';
                strcat(szMessage, szTemp);
            }
            else
            {
                // Get the 4 characters after the '!'.
                szTemp[0] = fgetc(in);
                szTemp[1] = fgetc(in);
                szTemp[2] = fgetc(in);
                szTemp[3] = fgetc(in);
                szTemp[4] = '\0';
```

```
                // Copy in the time in place of '!time'.
                if (!(strnicmp(szTemp, "time",4)))
                {
                    char szTime[255];
                    _strtime(szTime);
                    strcat(szMessage, szTime);
                }
                // Copy in the date in place of '!date'.
                else if (!(strnicmp(szTemp, "date", 4)))
                {
                    char szDate[255];
                    _strdate(szDate);
                    strcat(szMessage, szDate);
                }
                // Copy in my name in place of '!name'.
                else if (!(strnicmp(szTemp, "name", 4)))
                {
                    strcat(szMessage, "Douglas Reilly");
                }
                else
                {
                    strcat(szMessage, "!");
                    strcat(szMessage, szTemp);
                }
            }
        }
    }

    // Set the length of the buffer being written.
    cBuf = strlen(szMessage);

    // Use another of the functions provided by IIS to write content
    //  to the browser.
    lpECB->WriteClient(lpECB->ConnID,
        szMessage, &cBuf, HSE_IO_SYNC);
    return HSE_STATUS_SUCCESS;
}
```

The most significant part of the listing is within *HttpExtensionProc*. The header is sent as in the initial ISAPI example. Next the translated path is retrieved, using the *GetServerVariable* callback embedded in the EXTENSION_CONTROL_BLOCK pointer. The PATH_TRANSLATED server variable handles converting the virtual path into a path appropriate for use with the C standard file I/O functions. The *fopen* function is used to open the file, and characters are read in one at a time and appended to the *szMessage* character buffer that will be used to send information back to the browser.

While reading in characters from the script file, the character stream is monitored, and when the program sees an exclamation point (!), it checks the next four characters for the literal "time", "date", or "name". If the program finds a match, it replaces all five characters of the metatag with the time, date, or name. If the four characters after the ! character are not one of the strings to be substituted, the program appends the ! and the following four characters to the *szMessage* buffer.

Figure 10-12 shows the screen that results on a client browser when ISPRaw.dll processes the simple script shown in Listing 10-8. The result that ISPRaw.dll sends to the browser is standard HTML code.

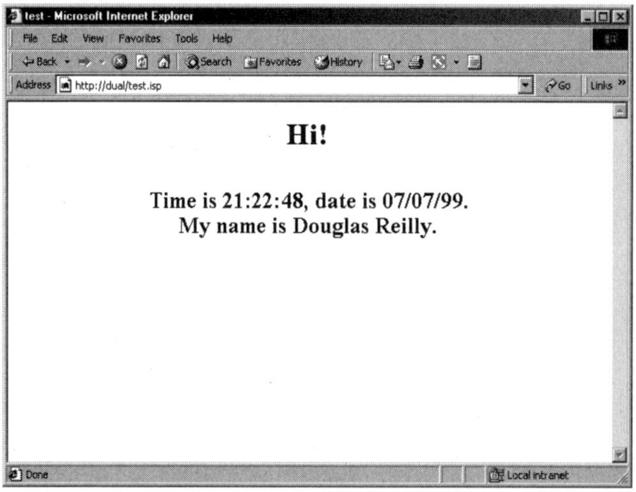


**Figure 10-12** *The result of calling a simple ISP script processed by ISPRaw.dll.*

```
<HTML>
<Title>test</TITLE>
<BODY>
<Center><H1>Hi!</H1>
<br><H2>
Time is !Time, date is !date.  <BR>
My name is !Name. </H2>
</CENTER>
</BODY>
</HTML>
```

**Listing 10-8**

# CONCLUSION

This introduction to ISAPI extensions has opened up the world of high-performance, compiled solutions for Web applications. While none of these examples seriously strained the abilities of IIS and I have not done any rigorous benchmarking, the performance of the samples is outstanding. ISAPI also allows developers to take total control of the server with the ability to do virtually anything that the Win32 API allows.

The ability to enhance the performance of IIS using ISAPI to create new scripting components takes ISAPI extensions to a different level than most other tools for Web development. Creating a scripting environment so tightly integrated with the Web server in virtually any other environment is practically impossible.

Chapter 15 will use the capability of ISAPI to bring Web integration to traditional server-based applications. The ability to interact with browser clients while at the same time using all the abilities of Win32 allows ISAPI developers to perform operations and allow integration with other applications not easily possible with other tools.

Yet even with all this capability, there is another side to ISAPI—ISAPI filters—which I'll cover in the next chapter. ISAPI extensions and ISAPI filters together provide a set of tools that allows you to create the most complex Web applications. Combined with ASP, the net result is the capacity to create the entire gamut of applications, from those that will scale for a lazy intranet site to world-class Internet sites ready to take on the world.

*Chapter 11*

# ISAPI Filters

In Chapters 9 and 10, we explored several ways of creating dynamic content for Internet and intranet applications. In Chapter 9, we created applications using Active Server Pages, both with and without Microsoft ActiveX controls. In Chapter 10, we used the Internet Server API to create ISAPI extensions. Active Server Pages and ISAPI extensions cover most of what you'll ever need to develop interactive Web-based applications. However, some occasions require just a little more power. ISAPI filters are designed for those occasions.

## ISAPI Filter Overview

As I mentioned last chapter, ISAPI extensions and ISAPI filters are similar in structure but quite different in operation. ISAPI extensions are called by the client browser and return HTML. ISAPI filters, on the other hand, are never called directly—that is part of their utility: They can transparently make existing applications behave in a different way. For instance, if you need to implement custom authentication or logging, ISAPI filters might be your only option.

An ISAPI filter is just a DLL that exports two or three specific functions that can then be called by IIS. The filter is loaded on the server. It can be installed so that all requests for all applications on the server are monitored or only requests for a single application are monitored. The filter is loaded once when IIS is loaded and remains loaded under virtually all circumstances until IIS is stopped.

An ISAPI filter sits between the client browser and IIS, as illustrated in Figure 11-1.

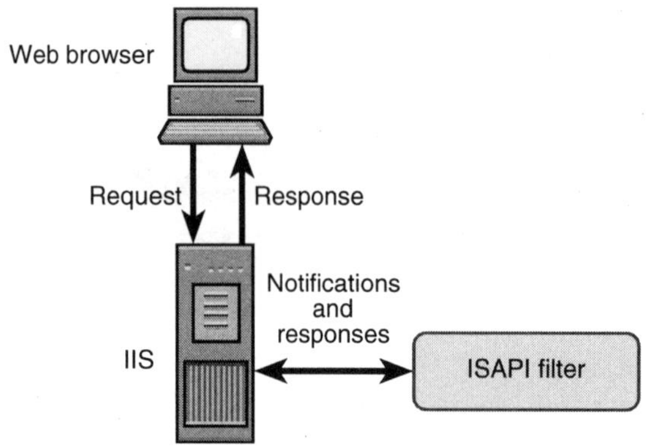


**Figure 11-1** *The relationship between a client browser, IIS, and an ISAPI filter.*

The filter will see every request that meets the criteria that you specify when you design and install the filter. One of the implications of this structure is that whatever your filter does, it must do quickly. There are several ways to ensure that an ISAPI filter does not become a roadblock to a responsive Web site:

- Request only the notifications that you absolutely need to see. Every notification you see takes some time. Within a given notification type, you cannot select some of those notification types and not others—your filter will get them all.
- If you will not be processing the notification, quickly return.
- If you need to monitor only a single application, try to have the filter installed so that it only sees requests for that one site.
- ISAPI filters can register priorities. Use the lowest priority possible.

You will encounter challenges on the road to designing a successful ISAPI filter. One of the first is debugging the filter, which for several reasons is much more difficult than it might initially appear. First, there is often no easy way to tell whether the filter is working. Some of the filter's operations are subtle, such as changing the headers sent to the client browser. Second, building the ISAPI filter DLL and getting it installed on IIS can require starting and stopping the IIS services. Finally, while you can use modern debugging tools such as Microsoft Visual Studio to debug ISAPI filters, the task is still difficult.

## Functions Exported by ISAPI Filter DLLs

ISAPI filters must export two functions—*GetFilterVersion* and *HttpFilterProc*. They can export one additional function, *TerminateFilter*. *GetFilterVersion* tells IIS which version number the filter uses and what notifications the filter wants. *HttpFilterProc* handles the basic operation of the filter. IIS calls the optional function, *TerminateFilter,* upon termination of the filter, allowing the filter to clean up any resources allocated during processing.

### *GetFilterVersion*

*GetFilterVersion*, shown in the next code fragment, is the first function an ISAPI filter must implement. This version is called once when the filter is loaded and is not called again.

```
BOOL WINAPI GetFilterVersion(
    PHTTP_FILTER_VERSION pVer
);
```

The *pVer* parameter is a pointer to an HTTP_FILTER_VERSION structure. The job of *GetFilterVersion* is to fill in this structure.

```
typedef struct _HTTP_FILTER_VERSION {
    DWORD  dwServerFilterVersion;
    DWORD  dwFilterVersion;
    CHAR   lpszFilterDesc[SF_MAX_FILTER_DESC_LEN];
    DWORD  dwFlags;
} HTTP_FILTER_VERSION;
```

The ISAPI version supported by the Web server is returned in the *dwServerFilterVersion* member. The second member of the structure, *dwFilterVersion*, should be set to the ISAPI version of the filter DLL. Some UI elements of IIS use a longer name for the ISAPI filter. This name must be placed in *lpszFilterDesc*. The final data member, *dwFlags,* can contain any of the values listed in Table 11-1. The values are broadly grouped into three areas:

- Requests for notifications
- Filter priority settings
- Port security settings

*GetFilterVersion* must return *true* for the filter to be activated. If the function returns *false*, an error event will be logged recording the failure loading the filter. If you do not want the failure to be logged, you must call *SetLastError* with a value of NO_ERROR. Otherwise, call *SetLastError* with an appropriate Win32 error code; that code will be used when recording the failure to load.

TABLE 11-1
**ISAPI FILTER FLAGS**

| *Notification Constant* | *Description* |
|---|---|
| SF_NOTIFY_READ_RAW_DATA | Indicates the filter should receive notification when data is being read from the client (This can occur more than once per request.) |
| SF_NOTIFY_PREPROC_HEADERS | Indicates the filter should receive notification just after preprocessing headers but before any processing of content |
| SF_NOTIFY_URL_MAP | Indicates the filter should receive notification after the server has converted a URL to a physical path |
| SF_NOTIFY_AUTHENTICATION | Indicates the filter should receive notification just before the server authenticates the client |
| SF_NOTIFY_ACCESS_DENIED | Indicates the filter should receive notification just after the server has determined that the client will be denied access but before notification of the client |
| SF_NOTIFY_SEND_RESPONSE | Indicates the filter should receive notification after the server has processed the request but before any headers are sent to the client |
| SF_NOTIFY_SEND_RAW_DATA | Indicates the filter should receive notification as the server sends raw data back to the client (This can occur more than once per request.) |
| SF_NOTIFY_END_OF_REQUEST | Indicates the filter should receive notification at the end of the request |
| SF_NOTIFY_LOG | Indicates the filter should receive notification at the end of the request, just before the server writes the log for the transaction |
| SF_NOTIFY_NET_END_OF_SESSION | Indicates the filter should receive notification when the network session with the client is ending |
| SF_NOTIFY_ORDER_DEFAULT | Indicates the filter should use the default priority level (low priority) |
| SF_NOTIFY_ORDER_LOW | Indicates the filter should use a low priority level |
| SF_NOTIFY_ORDER_MEDIUM | Indicates the filter should use a medium priority level |
| SF_NOTIFY_ORDER_HIGH | Indicates the filter should use a high priority level |
| SF_NOTIFY_SECURE_PORT | Indicates the filter should receive notifications for requests on a secure port (https) |
| SF_NOTIFY_NONSECURE_PORT | Indicates the filter should receive notifications for requests on a nonsecure port |

### *HttpFilterProc*

*HttpFilterProc* performs most of the work in an ISAPI filter. This is the function that IIS calls whenever one of the notifications requested by *GetFilterVersion* occurs.

```
DWORD WINAPI HttpFilterProc(
    PHTTP_FILTER_CONTEXT pfc,
    DWORD notificationType,
    LPVOID pvNotification
);
```

The first parameter, *pfc*, is a pointer to a filter context structure. This structure is the key to accessing information from the server because, in addition to several data members, it contains five callback functions used to interact with the server and the client.

```
typedef struct _HTTP_FILTER_CONTEXT {
    DWORD cbSize;
    DWORD Revision;
    PVOID ServerContext;
    DWORD ulReserved;
    BOOL  fIsSecurePort;
    PVOID pFilterContext;
    BOOL (WINAPI * GetServerVariable);
    BOOL (WINAPI * AddResponseHeaders);
    BOOL (WINAPI * WriteClient);
    VOID * (WINAPI * AllocMem);
    BOOL (WINAPI * ServerSupportFunction);
} HTTP_FILTER_CONTEXT;
```

The first member, *cbBytes*, contains the size of the structure in bytes. The *Revision* member provides the revision level of this structure. *ServerContext* and *ulReserved* are used by the server and should not be touched. Client requests can come from a secure port or a nonsecure port, and *fIsSecurePort* is a Boolean value that is *true* if this request is coming over a secure port. Of course, by using *GetFilterVersion,* you can request either or both types of requests. Therefore, if you have requested notifications for only secure port requests, this value will always be *true*. If the filter has any information it wants to associate with this request, it can allocate memory and have *pFilterContext* point to that buffer. The memory allocated is automatically freed during the SF_NOTIFY_END_OF_SESSION notification.

The next five members of HTTP_FILTER_CONTEXT are callback functions supplied by the server to allow the filter to gather information and interact with the client. *GetServerVariable* points to a function that allows the filter to get all server variables. Recall that the ISPRaw program (Listing 10-7) displays all server variables generated from an Active Server Pages script. The same variables are available to the filter through *GetServerVariable*, whose prototype is shown on the following page.

```
BOOL WINAPI * GetServerVariable(
    PHTTP_FILTER_CONTEXT pfc,
    LPSTR lpszVariableName,
    LPVOID lpvBuffer,
    LPDWORD lpdwSize
)
```

As with all the callback functions in *pfc*, *GetServerVariable* accepts as its first parameter a pointer to the HTTP_FILTER_CONTEXT sent as the first parameter to *HttpFilterProc*. The second parameter is a pointer to the variable name—for instance, SERVER_NAME for the name of the server and AUTH_USER for an authenticated user name. The final two parameters are a pointer to a buffer and the size of the buffer, respectively.

*AddResponseHeaders* points to a function that allows the filter to add headers to the HTTP response:

```
BOOL WINAPI * AddResponseHeaders(
    PHTTP_FILTER_CONTEXT pfc,
    LPSTR lpszHeaders,
    LPSTR dwReserved
);
```

Once again, the filter context is passed as the first parameter. The second parameter, *lpszHeaders*, should point to a string that contains the headers to send. The headers must be in the format "header:value\r\n". The last parameter is reserved.

*WriteClient* points to a function that allows the filter to write raw data back to the client:

```
BOOL WINAPI * WriteClient(
    PHTTP_FILTER_CONTEXT pfc,
    LPVOID buffer,
    LPDWORD lpdwBytes,
    DWORD dwReserved
);
```

After the first parameter, which should be set to point to the filter context passed into *HttpFilterProc*, the second and third parameters point to the buffer to be written and a pointer to a DWORD containing the size in bytes of the buffer. The final parameter is reserved.

*AllocMem* points to a function that allocates memory. Memory allocated with this function is automatically freed when the session ends.

```
VOID * WINAPI * AllocMem(
    PHTTP_FILTER_CONTEXT pfc,
    DWORD cbSize,
    DWORD dwReserved
);
```

This function returns the buffer upon success. The filter context is passed as the first parameter, and the size, in bytes, is passed as the second parameter, *cbSize*. The final parameter is reserved.

*ServerSupportFunction* points to a function that allows the filter to perform miscellaneous functions:

```
BOOL WINAPI * ServerSupportFunction(
    PHTTP_FILTER_CONTEXT pfc,
    enum SF_REQ_TYPE sfReq,
    PVOID pData,
    DWORD ul1,
    DWORD ul2
);
```

The first parameter is the pointer to the filter context passed to *HttpFilterProc*. The code that specifies which function should be called is *sfReq*. Table 11-2 lists the possible values for this parameter.

**TABLE 11-2**
**OPERATION CODES FOR *SERVERSUPPORTFUNCTION***

| **ServerSupportFunction *Value*** | ***Description*** |
|---|---|
| SF_REQ_ADD_HEADERS_ON_DENIAL | Adds headers to a server error response |
| SF_REQ_GET_CONNID | Not supported in IIS 4 and later |
| SF_REQ_NORMALIZE_URL | Decodes hex codes, removes illegal characters, and so on |
| SF_REQ_SET_NEXT_READ_SIZE | Sets the number of bytes read during the next raw read |
| SF_REQ_DISABLE_NOTIFICATIONS | Disables specific notifications for the balance of the request |
| SF_REQ_GET_PROPERTY | Can be used to get SF_PROPERTY_INSTANCE_NUM_ID (This can be used to get information out of the metabase—the store where IIS keeps configuration information.) |
| SF_REQ_SEND_RESPONSE_HEADER | Sends a complete HTTP response header to the client |
| SF_REQ_SET_PROXY_INFO | Indicates if the current request is an HTTP Proxy request |

The last three parameters to *ServerSupportFunction* depend on the operation being performed and should be set to 0 or NULL as appropriate when they are not used for a given operation. The use of these parameters is detailed in the MSDN documentation.

The second parameter to *HttpFilterProc* is *notificationType*. This is one of the notification types that can be set in *GetFilterVersion*, listed earlier in Table 11-1. The final parameter is *pvNotification*, a pointer to a notification-specific structure. Thus, if the notification is SF_NOTIFY_SEND_RAW_DATA, the structure pointed to is HTTP_FILTER_RAW_DATA. MSDN contains details of the structures for all of the notifications.

### *TerminateFilter*

The optional exported function for ISAPI filters is *TerminateFilter*.

```
BOOL WINAPI TerminateFilter(
    DWORD dwFlags
);
```

IIS calls this function to indicate that your filter is going to be unloaded. The single parameter, *dwFlags*, is reserved. *TerminateFilter* should be used to release any system resources that the filter has acquired.

## A SAMPLE ISAPI FILTER

What can we do with the power of ISAPI filters? One use for an ISAPI filter is to modify content on its way to the client. While the same effect can be achieved with brute force editing, sometimes an ISAPI filter can be a cleaner solution. Suppose you have hundreds of pages, each with its own concept of what a Web page should look like. The HTML <BODY> tag alone has at least 20 attributes that can be set. If this was a growing ad hoc collection of HTML files rather than a static set of HTML files, one way to create consistency among the files would be to have an ISAPI filter modify the styles that go to the client.

The following example will take the HTML code to be sent to the client in Listing 11-1 and change it to the code in Listing 11-2. Notice that the original code has a plain <BODY> tag, whereas the modified code specifies a background color and a text color.

```
<html>

<head>
<title>ISAPI Filter Test</title>
<meta NAME="FORMATTER" CONTENT="Microsoft Visual InterDev 1.0">

</head>

<body>
<CENTER>
```

```
<H1>
This is my test. This page originally had no options in the BODY
tag, but it has been modified by the ISAPI filter FilterRaw to
have blue background and yellow text.
</H1>

</body>
</html>
```

**Listing 11-1**

```
<html>

<head>
<title>ISAPI Filter Test</title>
<meta NAME="FORMATTER" CONTENT="Microsoft Visual InterDev 1.0">

</head>

<BODY BGCOLOR=BLUE TEXT=YELLOW>
<CENTER>

<H1>
This is my test. This page originally had no options in the BODY
tag, but it has been modified by the ISAPI filter FilterRaw to
have blue background and yellow text.
</H1>

</body>
</html>
```

**Listing 11-2**

Making this change is not quite as straightforward as it might appear. We obviously need to request the SF_NOTIFY_SEND_RAW_DATA notification to get to the raw data before it is sent to the client. What is less obvious is that we need to also request the SF_NOTIFY_URL_MAP to ensure that we know when the first block is received.

When the SF_NOTIFY_URL_MAP notification is received, we simply set the *pFilterContext* member of the filter notification to 1. This is so that the first request to send data to the client is recognized and treated specially. We need to ensure that we do not modify this portion of the output to the client. When the first SF_NOTIFY_SEND_RAW_DATA notification arrives (signaled by the value in *pFilterContext*) we make sure the headers are skipped. We then set *pFilterContext* to 2 so that we know future notifications do not require any special handling.

When the SF_NOTIFY_SEND_RAW_DATA notification arrives, the *pvNotification* parameter to *HttpFilterProc* points to an HTTP_FILTER_RAW_DATA structure:

```
typedef struct _HTTP_FILTER_RAW_DATA {
    PVOID pvInData;
    DWORD cbInData;
    DWORD cbInBuffer;
    DWORD dwReserved;
} HTTP_FILTER_RAW_DATA;
```

The actual raw data is pointed to by *pvInData*. The next two parameters, *cbInData* and *cbInBuffer*, hold the amount of useful data in *pvInData* and the size of the buffer allocated, respectively. The last member is reserved and should be ignored. While in some cases you can modify *pvInData* in place, this is not always possible. If you attempt to modify the data in place, you should use exception handling. If an exception occurs, allocate space and modify the allocated buffer. The new buffer must remain valid until the end of the request. This is best handled by using *AllocMem*, one of the callback functions in the filter context structure. This is the approach I take in the example in the FilterRaw program, shown in Listing 11-3, and it is especially prudent in light of the fact that we will likely change the length of the data.

**FilterRaw.cpp**

```
// FilterRaw.cpp : Raw ISAPI filter application.
//

#include "stdafx.h"

BOOL APIENTRY DllMain(HANDLE hModule,
                      DWORD  ul_reason_for_call,
                      LPVOID lpReserved)
{
    return TRUE;
}

BOOL WINAPI GetFilterVersion(
  PHTTP_FILTER_VERSION pVer
)
{
    pVer->dwFlags = SF_NOTIFY_SECURE_PORT |
        SF_NOTIFY_NONSECURE_PORT |
        SF_NOTIFY_URL_MAP |
        SF_NOTIFY_ORDER_DEFAULT |
        SF_NOTIFY_SEND_RAW_DATA;
```

**Listing 11-3**

```
    strcpy(pVer->lpszFilterDesc, "Test Filter to turn pages blue");
    return TRUE;
}

DWORD WINAPI HttpFilterProc(
    PHTTP_FILTER_CONTEXT pfc,
    DWORD notificationType,
    LPVOID pvNotification)
{
    DWORD ret;
    DWORD loop = 0, dloop = 0, bodylen;
    char *ptr;
    char *ptrIn;
    char *szNewBody = "<BODY BGCOLOR=BLUE TEXT=YELLOW>";
    bool changed = false;
    PHTTP_FILTER_RAW_DATA filterRaw;

    switch (notificationType)
    {
    case SF_NOTIFY_URL_MAP:
        pfc->pFilterContext = (VOID *)1;
        ret = SF_STATUS_REQ_NEXT_NOTIFICATION;
        break;

    case SF_NOTIFY_SEND_RAW_DATA:
        filterRaw = (PHTTP_FILTER_RAW_DATA)pvNotification;
        ptr = (char *)pfc->AllocMem(pfc,
            filterRaw->cbInBuffer+100, 0);
        memset(ptr, 0, filterRaw->cbInBuffer+100);
        ptrIn = (char *) filterRaw->pvInData;

        // First block?
        if (pfc->pFilterContext == (VOID *)1)
        {
            // Skip the header.
            while (loop < filterRaw->cbInData)
            {
                if (ptrIn[loop] == '\n' &&
                    ptrIn[loop] == '\n')
                {
                    loop += 3;
                    dloop += 3;
                    break;
```

*(continued)*

**Listing 11-3** *continued*

```
                }
                loop++;
                dloop++;
            }
            pfc->pFilterContext = (VOID *)2;
        }


        ptrIn = (char *)filterRaw->pvInData;

        while (loop<filterRaw->cbInData)
        {
            if (*(ptrIn+loop) == '<' &&
                !(strnicmp((ptrIn+loop+1), "BODY", 4)))
            {
                bodylen = 0;
                while (*(ptrIn+loop) != '>')
                {
                    loop++;
                    bodylen++;
                }
                loop++;
                strcat(ptr, szNewBody);
                dloop += strlen(szNewBody);
                changed = true;
            }
            else
            {
                *(ptr+dloop) = *(ptrIn+loop);
                loop++;
                dloop++;
            }
        }
        if (changed)
        {
            filterRaw->pvInData = (void *)ptr;
            filterRaw->cbInBuffer += 100;
            filterRaw->cbInData = dloop;
        }
        ret = SF_STATUS_REQ_NEXT_NOTIFICATION;

        break;
    }
    return(ret);
}
```

The *GetFilterVersion* function in Listing 11-3 is simple but representative of what is present in most ISAPI filters. It simply sets the requested notifications, sets the priority and secure port status flags in the *dwFlags* member of the HTTP_FILTER_VERSION structure pointed to by *pVer,* and copies a name into *lpszFilterDesc.*

*HttpFilterProc* behaves in a similarly reasonable way, using a case statement to react to the two notifications it will receive and setting the return value to SF_STATUS_REQ_NEXT_NOTIFICATION. *HttpFilterProc* has several other possible return values. Table 11-3 summarizes the constants and their meanings.

The FilterRaw example in Listing 11-3 is less than complete. For example, in the real world it is ill-advised to simply chop out one <BODY> tag and replace it with another. A more intelligent analysis should be used so that other attributes of the tag command can be properly modified and the end result can be more reasonable. A more real-world—though much more complex—example would be a filter that would create a frameset to place a navigation bar on one side and the original HTML on the other.

**TABLE 11-3**
**RETURN CODES FROM *HTTPFILTERPROC***

| **HttpFilterProc *Return Value*** | ***Description*** |
|---|---|
| SF_STATUS_REQ_FINISHED | The filter has finished this HTTP request and the session should be disconnected. |
| SF_STATUS_REQ_FINISHED_KEEP_CONN | This value is the same as SF_STATUS_REQ_FINISHED, but the TCP/IP session should be kept open if keep-alive is enabled. |
| SF_STATUS_REQ_NEXT_NOTIFICATION | The next filter in the chain should be called. This is the most common return value. |
| SF_STATUS_REQ_HANDLED_NOTIFICATION | The filter has handled the request. No other filters for this notification should be called. |
| SF_STATUS_REQ_ERROR | An error has occurred. Generally the request should be aborted. The filter should call *SetLastError* with an appropriate error code. |
| SF_STATUS_REQ_READ_NEXT | This is valid only for raw read notifications and is designed for encryption and other operations that could be described as opaque stream filters. See MSDN for details. |

Once you've created the filter, it is time to install it. Figure 11-2 shows the Default Web Site Properties dialog in Windows 2000 with the ISAPI Filters tab selected. To add a new filter, click on Add. The Filter Properties dialog appears, as shown in Figure 11-3. Simply enter the filter name and the filter filename and click OK. Click on Apply in the Default Web Site Properties dialog. The filter is now in place. The status column shown in Figure 11-2 will contain either a green up-arrow or a red down-arrow, giving a virtual thumbs-up or thumbs-down to your filter.

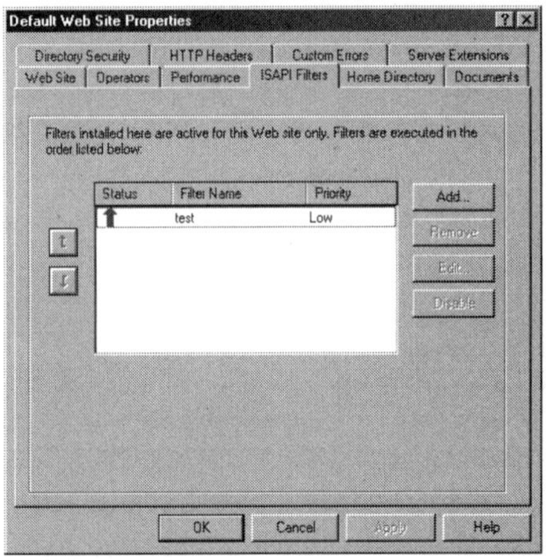


**Figure 11-2** *The Default Web Site Properties dialog in Windows 2000.*

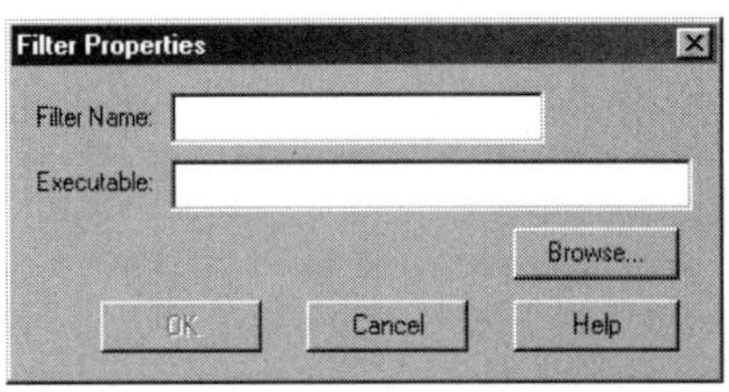


**Figure 11-3** *Adding an ISAPI filter.*

# MFC ISAPI FILTERS

As I mentioned in Chapter 10, the Microsoft Foundation Classes (MFC) have good support for ISAPI. Better yet, the ISAPI extension or filter can use only the ISAPI support within MFC, making for a leaner ISAPI application than might otherwise be possible.

The first step in creating an ISAPI filter is to select New from the File menu in Visual C++. The screen shown in Figure 11-4 will appear. Select ISAPI Extension Wizard and enter the name of the project.

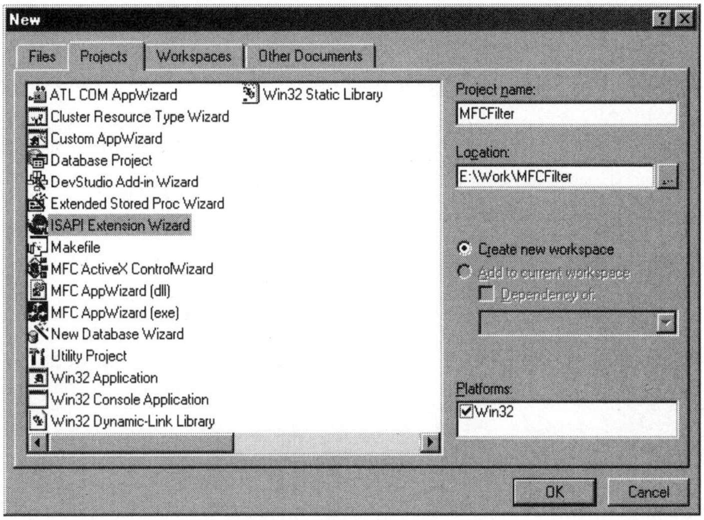

**Figure 11-4** *Visual C++ New dialog.*

Figure 11-5 shows screen 1 of 2 of the ISAPI Extension Wizard. I have changed the default settings so that Generate A Filter Object is checked and Generate A Server Extension Object is unchecked. If you check both settings, a single DLL can contain both an extension and a filter. Unless a great deal of functionality is shared between an extension and a filter and it is not necessary to expose that functionality in a DLL that can be shared, I recommend that you always create the objects in separate DLLs.

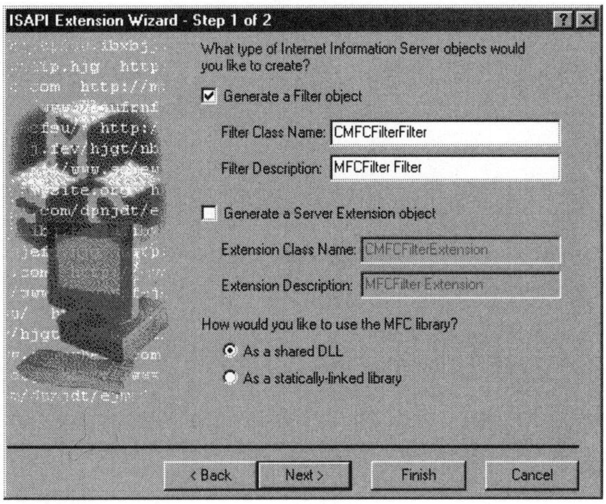

**Figure 11-5** *Step 1 of 2 in the Visual C++ ISAPI Extension Wizard.*

Figure 11-6 shows the final step of the ISAPI Extension Wizard. The same notifications used by the basic C++ ISAPI filter in Listing 11-3 are selected in this example. We can add a required notification after the fact. However, it is not as simple as adding a value to a bit flag in *GetFilterVersion* or a case statement in *HttpFilterProc*. As with much of MFC, mapping macros are used to route notifications to the correct mEember function. Unlike other areas of MFC, there is no wizard support for modifying existing ISAPI filters.

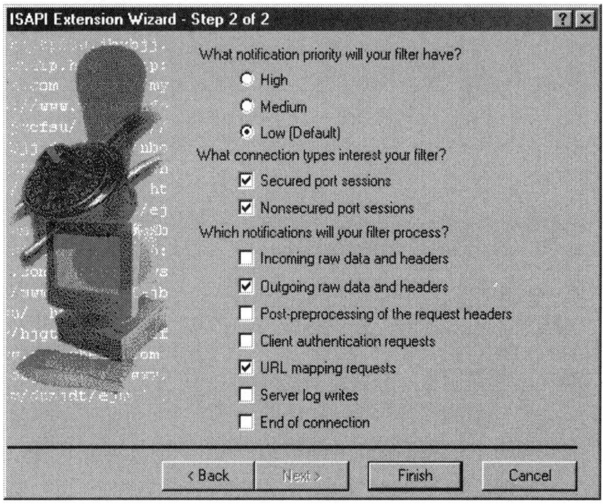


**Figure 11-6** *Step 2 of 2 in the Visual C++ ISAPI Extension Wizard.*

# CONCLUSION

ISAPI filters are used much less frequently than ISAPI extensions, and with good reason. Filters are more difficult to create, maddening to debug, and a potential drain on performance. Indiscriminate use of filters can cause a previously speedy application to become slow, and developers of other parts of the application need to be conscious of any modifications your filter will make to data destined for the browser client. Even with these limitations, they have their place in the toolbox of any Web developer.

If you need to create a Web application that must use custom authentication or automatically modify the appearance of lots of content in the Web application, filters can't be beat. In fact, filters are just about the only way to do these things.

In the next chapter we will shift gears and look at some of the problems with creating a Windows 2000 server-based application that must communicate with multiple clients and still offer reasonable performance. Chapter 13 will delve into some of the issues involved in leveraging the server-side capabilities of Microsoft SQL Server from your server-based application.

*Chapter 12*

# Client/Server Communication APIs

Just as no person is an island, virtually no server is an island. Of course, you might come across the occasional server that requires no interaction with other computers, but this is by far the exception, not the rule. Even if a server does not provide a service to client machines, the ability to remotely configure the server can make or break a server-based application.

Think about where servers are located these days. In most businesses, the servers are situated some distance away from the people who might need to monitor them. Even on my home network, the server is in another room, and it has no attached monitor. Thankfully, I can accomplish virtually everything I need to do with the server by using a server-based application that allows configuration from a remote workstation.

# CAN WE TALK? HOW CLIENTS AND SERVERS COMMUNICATE

In addition to configuration, in most cases actually using a service requires communication between the client and the server. Clients and servers talk in a number of ways. Some of these ways are fairly complex and probably deserve a book all their own. I've listed several books in the annotated bibliography that cover Distributed COM (DCOM) and Remote Procedure Calls (RPC). A book that I wrote several years ago, *Win32 Client/Server Developer's Guide* (Addison-Wesley Publishing, 1996), still has reasonable coverage of RPC. Client/server interaction is not this book's main topic, but in this chapter I provide an overview of two of the simpler, most common protocols.

## TCP/IP (WinSock)

Transmission Control Protocol/Internet Protocol (TCP/IP) is one of the most commonly used protocols today. Of course, TCP/IP is the protocol that fuels the Internet. Anyone reading this book is likely to use TCP/IP every day—checking e-mail, browsing Web pages, or chatting by using one of the many competing chat programs. Much of this interaction takes place transparently to us as users of the software. We load the browser, it establishes a connection, either through a LAN or a dial-up connection probably using RAS, and we do what we need to do.

Behind the scenes, however, a lot more goes on. When Microsoft Windows programmers talk about TCP/IP, they probably mean Windows Sockets, or WinSock. WinSock is a Windows-specific extension to Berkeley Sockets, developed in the early 1980s on the UNIX operating system. The idea behind sockets is simple: There are two endpoints, or sockets. One socket is the server, which is presumed to be always available. The other socket is the client, which intermittently transfers data to and from the server. Of course, the model is not always this simple. For instance, Hospital Level 7 (HL-7) is a common high-level, industry-specific protocol that uses TCP/IP as its underlying protocol. HL-7 is used in the healthcare industry to transfer standardized ASCII records from one system to another. Strictly speaking, it often appears that one of the systems is the client and the other is the server. In reality, each party to an HL-7 interaction is—from a TCP/IP standpoint—both client and server.

In the early 16-bit Windows days, WinSock was not part of the operating system. Competing TCP/IP "stacks" were used to allow Windows 3.x clients and MS-DOS clients to participate with the primarily UNIX computers that used TCP/IP sockets. In the early 1990s, several organizations got together to set the standards for what eventually became WinSock. Their goal was to create a standard that would allow applications written to the WinSock specifications to work on all WinSock implementations. They specified a binary standard that allowed any WinSock application to work with any WinSock implementation.

Extensions to the standard sockets interface in early versions of WinSock were primarily designed to address the weaknesses in the 16-bit Windows multitasking model. As I said in Chapter 2, 16-bit Windows used a cooperative multitasking model. This meant that applications had to agree to give up control periodically to allow the operating system to run other applications. Many sockets operations are typically blocking, meaning that they will wait for an operation to complete or time out. Blocking was not acceptable within a cooperative multitasking model. This gave rise to many asynchronous functions in WinSock: the function calls would return before the actual operation requested completed. In general, these asynchronous functions are much less important within the Win32 preemptive multitasking model.

Once it has the name of a server, how does a program connect to the right service? Every server that supports TCP/IP has a large number of socket numbers available. For instance, socket 80 is used for HTTP communication. Socket 80 is an example of what we call a well-known service. If a Web browser is looking to connect to a Web server, the browser knows to use socket 80. Similarly, a Telnet client will use socket 23. All socket numbers below 1024 are reserved for well-known services.

> **NOTE** Port numbers are one of the elements that can require byte-order swapping. Byte swapping is required because internally, some computers place the bytes that make up a number in different orders. Several WinSock functions support byte swapping. These include *htons* and *htonl,* which convert a short number and a long number, respectively, from host order to network order. To convert a short and a long from network to host order you would use *ntohs* and *ntohl.* Because we will be working with Windows Intel clients and servers, we won't need to do byte swapping. If we needed to support other clients who needed to do byte swapping, both client and server would be required to use these conversion functions.

## Named Pipes

The other major contender in the client/server communication arena is named pipes. Named pipes also has a long history. It is sometimes known as FIFOs because of its first in, first out nature. Anonymous pipes are lighter weight but somewhat less useful pipes that rely on the passing of a handle to a child process. One limitation of named pipes is that the server must be a Windows 2000 or a Windows NT machine. A Windows 9x machine can act as a named pipes client but cannot act as a named pipes server.

Once created, a named pipe handle can be passed to most functions that expect a file handle, such as *WriteFile* and *ReadFile*. Named pipes instances are named in a specific format, \\Server\Pipes\PipeName. A named pipe named *TEST* on my machine, which is named *DUAL*, would be known as \\DUAL\Pipes\TEST. The name is used to identify the pipe on the network. This combination of server name and pipe name performs the same function as the server name and socket number in TCP/IP.

There are two important things to remember about named pipes. First, named pipes can work with the client and server on the same machine—just like TCP/IP. Unlike TCP/IP, named pipes communication on the same machine seems to have some speed advantages. Second, there is a security-related problem using named pipes within services running under the System account. Named pipes is an authenticated protocol, so Windows 2000 and Windows NT by default do not allow named pipes to connect to a service running under the System account. There are several Knowledge Base articles about this issue. Later in this chapter we will add the required registry changes to the service framework first introduced in Chapter 3.

## WinSock or Named Pipes?

The choice of communication protocol depends upon the type of organization that will use the application. For instance, I have created applications for large organizations with extensive investment in TCP/IP-based networks. Each organization has a naming service in place, such as Windows Internet Naming Service (WINS) or Domain Name System (DNS). For all practical purposes, this naming service is a requirement of implementing a TCP/IP solution. These organizations are ideal candidates for a WinSock-based system.

On the other hand, I have recently been working on an application whose primary customers are mom-and-pop home healthcare companies. For this sort of environment, a named pipes solution is easier to implement. It requires nothing beyond whatever protocols are currently running on the network. In the best of all worlds, it would be useful to conveniently postpone the decision of whether to support WinSock or named pipes so the customer can decide. Later in this chapter I will discuss several alternatives to make protocol independent communication happen on the client side.

These two protocols have a couple more characteristics that can drive your decision. Named pipes let you set the number of connections that will be allowed. This can be useful in maintaining a level of service for the allowed number of active clients, although you end up with clients that cannot connect when the server is busy. Also, it is relatively easy to impersonate the client on the other end of the named pipe, allowing a server-based application to easily control a client's access to server resources.

On the other hand, WinSock will more easily allow a server-based application to interact with all types of clients. Any significant platform will allow a connection using TCP/IP, the default underlying protocol for WinSock.

# DISPATCHING COMMUNICATION REQUESTS

One decision you will need to make at the outset of any server-based development is what sort of dispatching mechanism you intend to use to handle client requests. This decision affects everything that you do. One method is to assign a single thread to handle each request, cradle to grave. This option has the advantage of not requiring any artificial state management. Your service will always know which client it is talking to for the life of the request. This is a good strategy in the following situations:

- The length of time from the beginning to the end of the request is short. In this case, the overhead of managing the state so the task can be parceled out to worker threads is simply not worth the effort.
- The number of simultaneous clients is known and relatively small. In this case, creating enough threads is not likely to be a problem. Of course, there is a limit to the number of threads that the operating system can reasonably support, but this number is not fixed and is likely to be higher than you think.

In other situations, you might be better off allowing each individual request for a given session to be handled by whatever thread happens to be available.

## Managing Client State

One of the complications of assigning one thread per request is the need to keep track of state information apart from any single thread. When a single thread manages the entire client/server interaction, state information can be stored in stack variables within the thread. Sometimes, however, this is not possible.

One way to manage the state of each client is to encapsulate every transmission of data into a structure that contains what I call a server handle. You can use a server handle to associate any particular request with state information stored in the server. A common structure I use looks like this:

```
typedef struct _DATA_PACKET {
    WORD ServerHandle;
    WORD ServiceCode;
    WORD ReturnCode;
    DWORD DataLen;
    DWORD BufLen;
    char Buffer[MAX_DATA_SIZE];
} DATA_PACKET;
```

The client initially sets the *ServerHandle* member to 0. Upon receiving a packet with a *ServerHandle* of 0, the server initiates a new session. The handle can then be used as an offset into whatever state information the server needs to maintain. The next member, *ServiceCode*, is set by the client to tell the server exactly what service is required. For instance, in one server-based application I recently completed, one service code requested verification of serial number information and another requested version information.

*ReturnCode* is set by the server to indicate success or failure. The specifics of the return code system are unimportant as long as client and server agree. Both the client and the server set *DataLen*, indicating the useful length of the *Buffer* member. The client sets *BufLen* to the number of bytes allocated for *Buffer*.

When you talk with another person, extended silences that are not mutually agreed upon can indicate trouble. So it is with client/server communication. In addition to agreement on the data packet sent back and forth, both the client and the server must agree on the sequence of sending and receiving data. They must understand when to "speak" and when to "listen." Client and server must also agree on how long to wait for responses before presuming an error occurred.

## Managing Failures

When applications run on a single machine, there is relatively little chance that two components on the machine will fail to communicate with each other. For instance, if someone reboots the machine, both components stop functioning. When the system is extended to multiple machines, there is a much greater chance of a failure that directly affects only one party. For instance, if the purpose of a client/server interaction is to update a record into a database, the following scenarios are possible:

- The client submits the record. The server fails before performing the update or responding to the client.
- The client submits the record. The server successfully performs the update but then fails before responding to the client.

In both cases, the client has initiated the operation but does not hear back. What choices does the client have? It could resend the update, hoping that it will work the second time, or it could simply log the error. Neither option is perfect. The correct solution probably depends upon the application. *Modern Operating Systems* by Andrew S. Tanenbaum (Prentice Hall, 1992) has a good discussion about the semantics of failure. Easy to implement are "at most once" semantics, meaning that an operation will be performed 0 times or 1 time. "At least once" semantics—meaning an operation will be performed 1 or more times—are also easy to implement. The preferred "exactly once" semantics—an operation will be performed exactly once—are much more difficult to implement and will depend on the specifics of the system.

## Dispatching Requests

One problem that is present regardless of the protocol used between client and server is dispatching requests from clients.

### Scenario 1: Using Events

Event objects, which I discussed in Chapter 2, can have multiple threads waiting for the event object to be signaled. When set properly, with multiple threads waiting for the event object, one thread will be notified of the signaled event and the other threads will continue waiting. This can be used to our advantage.

The idea is this: Create some number of worker threads. The first task of each thread is to enter a loop controlled by *WaitForSingleObject* and wait for the event to be signaled. As client requests come in via a WinSock connection, the event is signaled. One of the threads is notified that the event has been signaled. This thread gets the socket, signals the dispatch thread that it has done so, and goes about its work. After the work for that client request is finished, the worker thread returns to the top of the loop and again waits for the event to become signaled. The worker threads wait without using a great deal of system-processing power.

This approach offers two advantages. First, the threads are created as the service begins, and they run throughout the life of the service. This saves the processing load caused by the constant creation and destruction of threads. Thread creation is less costly than process creation, but it is not free. Second, this approach allows us to control the number of threads. In some cases clients might need to wait while threads finish up other requests. This lag can be addressed by allowing the monitoring of thread usage and configuring thread usage to the level required to give acceptable performance while causing the least inconvenience to clients waiting for service.

The disadvantage of this approach is that as written, there is no allowance for a growing number of threads. This could be solved by controlling the maximum number of threads with a dynamically configurable value. While in practice adding threads would be easy, killing off running threads might be a bit more difficult.

CommService.h and CommService.cpp—shown in Listings 12-1 and 12-2, respectively—define a class that uses *CppService* as a base class and adds support for receiving and dispatching requests received via WinSock.

**CommService.h**

```
#define NUM_WORKERS 4

class CCommService : public CPPService
{
private:
    void WSCommDispatcher(THREADPROC Proc);
    void SetLastSocket(SOCKET s);
```

**Listing 12-1** *(continued)*

**Listing 12-1** *continued*

```
    SOCKET GetLastSocket();
    HANDLE m_hGotSocket;
    HANDLE m_hEvent;
    HANDLE m_hThreads[NUM_WORKERS];
    DWORD m_dwThreadIDs[NUM_WORKERS];
public:
    static DWORD __stdcall Thread(LPVOID t);
    virtual void DoWork(SOCKET s, WORD ThreadNum);
    int GetServerPort();
    void SetServerPort(int tServerPort);
    int m_ServerPort;
    SOCKET LastSocket;
    CCommService(char *tsvcName, char *tdispName,
        DWORD tsvcStart = SERVICE_DEMAND_START,
        bool CreateMsgPump = true);
    ~CCommService();
    virtual void Run();
    virtual void OnInstall();
};
```

**CommService.cpp**

```
// CommService.cpp : Communications service, using TCP/IP
//  and Events
//

#include "stdafx.h"

//---------------------------------------------------------------------
// Example simple main routine
int main(int argc, char* argv[])
{
    CCommService MyCommService("CommService",
        "Communications Test Service");

    // We could do something like the following if we needed to.
    // MyCommService.SetServerPort(5555);
    // This example uses the default.

    // Have we handled the arguments and done an
    //  install or uninstall?
    if (MyCommService.ParseArguments(argc, argv) == false)
    {
        // If not, start the service running.
        MyCommService.StartService();
    }
    return 0;
}
```

**Listing 12-2**

```
//------------------------------------------------------------------
// The heart of the class, the WinSock dispatcher
void CCommService::WSCommDispatcher(THREADPROC Proc)
{
    // Declare and initialize.
    BOOL    fConnected = FALSE;
    DWORD   dwThreadID = (DWORD)0;
    HANDLE  hThread    = INVALID_HANDLE_VALUE;
    int     addrLen;
    int     error;
    struct  sockaddr_in srvSocketAddr;
    struct  sockaddr_in cliSocketAddr;
    char    diag[255];
    WSADATA wsaData;
    SOCKET  srvSocket;
    SOCKET  cliSocket;

    error = WSAStartup(WS_VERSION_REQD, &wsaData);
    if (error != 0)
    {
        return;
    }

    if (LOBYTE(wsaData.wVersion) < 2)
    {
        sprintf(diag, "\nVersion %d.%d not supported",
            LOBYTE(wsaData.wVersion),
            HIBYTE(wsaData.wVersion));
        LogEvent(EVENTLOG_ERROR_TYPE, EVMSG_DEBUG, diag);
        return;
    }

    srvSocket = socket(AF_INET, SOCK_STREAM, 0);
    if (srvSocket == INVALID_SOCKET)
    {
        sprintf(diag, "SERVER: Windows Socket Error %d - "
            "Couldn't create socket",
            WSAGetLastError());
        LogEvent(EVENTLOG_ERROR_TYPE, EVMSG_DEBUG, diag);
        WSACleanup();
        return;
    }

    srvSocketAddr.sin_family = AF_INET;
    srvSocketAddr.sin_addr.s_addr = INADDR_ANY;
    srvSocketAddr.sin_port = GetServerPort();
```

*(continued)*

**Listing 12-2** *continued*

```
    if (bind(srvSocket, (LPSOCKADDR)&srvSocketAddr,
        sizeof(srvSocketAddr)) == SOCKET_ERROR)
    {
        sprintf(diag, "SERVER: Windows Socket Error %d - "
            "Couldn't bind socket",
            WSAGetLastError());

        LogEvent(EVENTLOG_ERROR_TYPE, EVMSG_DEBUG, diag);
        WSACleanup();
        return;
    }

    if (listen(srvSocket, SOMAXCONN) == SOCKET_ERROR)
    {
        sprintf(diag, "SERVER: Windows Socket Error %d - "
            "Couldn't listen on socket",
            WSAGetLastError());
        LogEvent(EVENTLOG_ERROR_TYPE, EVMSG_DEBUG, diag);
        WSACleanup();
        return;
    }

    while ((IsRunning()))
    {
        addrLen = (sizeof(cliSocketAddr));

        cliSocket = accept(srvSocket,
            (LPSOCKADDR)&cliSocketAddr, &addrLen);

        if (cliSocket == INVALID_SOCKET)
        {
            sprintf(diag,
                "SERVER: Windows Socket Error %d - "
                "accept() got invalid socket",
                WSAGetLastError());

            LogEvent(EVENTLOG_ERROR_TYPE, EVMSG_DEBUG, diag);
            WSACleanup();
            return;
        }

        SetLastSocket(cliSocket);
        SetEvent(m_hEvent);
```

```
        while (WaitForSingleObject(m_hGotSocket,
            1000) == WAIT_TIMEOUT)
        {
            if (!IsRunning())
            {
                WSACleanup();
                sprintf(diag, "SERVER: Exiting");
                LogEvent(EVENTLOG_INFORMATION_TYPE,
                    EVMSG_DEBUG, diag);
                return;
            }
        }
        ResetEvent(m_hGotSocket);
    }
    WSACleanup();
    sprintf(diag, "SERVER: Exiting");
    LogEvent(EVENTLOG_INFORMATION_TYPE, EVMSG_DEBUG, diag);

    return;
}

//--------------------------------------------------------------------
// The constructor
CCommService::CCommService(char *tsvcName,
                           char *tdispName,
                           DWORD tsvcStart,
                           bool  CreateMsgPump)
:CPPService(tsvcName, tdispName, tsvcStart, CreateMsgPump)
{
    DWORD dwCreationFlags = 0;
    // Create the event; default security, NOT manual Reset,
    //  NON signaled originally, NOT named, since just used by
    //  this process.
    m_hEvent = CreateEvent(NULL, FALSE, FALSE, NULL);
    if (m_hEvent == NULL)
    {
        LogEvent(EVENTLOG_ERROR_TYPE,
            EVMSG_DEBUG,
            "Can't create event!");
    }
    // Create the event; default security, Manual Reset,
    //  NON signaled originally, NOT named, since just
    //  used by this process.
```

*(continued)*

**Listing 12-2** *continued*

```
    m_hGotSocket = CreateEvent(NULL, TRUE, FALSE, NULL);
    if (m_hEvent == NULL)
    {
        LogEvent(EVENTLOG_ERROR_TYPE,
            EVMSG_DEBUG,
            "Can't create Got Socket event!");
    }

    m_ServerPort = 5043;  // a default port

    for (WORD loop = 0 ; loop < NUM_WORKERS ; loop++)
    {
        if ((m_hThreads[loop] = CreateThread(NULL,
            0, Thread, (LPVOID)loop,
            dwCreationFlags,
            &m_dwThreadIDs[loop])) == NULL)
        {
            LogEvent(EVENTLOG_ERROR_TYPE,
                EVMSG_DEBUG,
                "Can't create thread!");
        }
    }
}

CCommService::~CCommService()
{
    if (m_hEvent != NULL)
    {
        CloseHandle(m_hEvent);
    }
    if (m_hGotSocket != NULL)
    {
        CloseHandle(m_hGotSocket);
    }
    for (WORD loop = 0; loop < NUM_WORKERS; loop++)
    {
        if (m_hThreads[loop] != NULL)
        {
            CloseHandle(m_hThreads[loop]);
        }
    }
}

//-----------------------------------------------------------------
// Used to pass a socket from the dispatcher to the worker thread
```

```
SOCKET CCommService::GetLastSocket()
{
    return LastSocket;
}

//--------------------------------------------------------------------
// Used to pass a socket from the dispatcher to the worker thread
void CCommService::SetLastSocket(SOCKET s)
{
    LastSocket = s;
}

//--------------------------------------------------------------------
// Set the port number the server should use.
void CCommService::SetServerPort(int tServerPort)
{
    m_ServerPort = tServerPort;
}

//--------------------------------------------------------------------
// Get the port number the server is using.
int CCommService::GetServerPort()
{
    return m_ServerPort;
}

//--------------------------------------------------------------------
// The routine called to run the service
void CCommService::Run()
{
    WSCommDispatcher(Thread);

    m_isRunning = false;
    // Give threads a chance to die.
    Sleep(2000);
    return;
}

//--------------------------------------------------------------------
// Start the service upon installation.
void CCommService::OnInstall()
{
    ::StartThisService(ServiceName());
}
```

*(continued)*

**Listing 12-2** *continued*

```
//-----------------------------------------------------------------
// The function that does the actual work; this should be overridden
void CCommService::DoWork(SOCKET s, WORD ThreadNum)
{
    char diag[255];
    char data[1024];
    BOOL fSuccess;
    int len;
    static int blksSent = 0;
    int bytesRead;
    int maxData = 512;

    bytesRead = 0L;
    do {
        memset((void *)data, '\0', 1024);
        if ((len = recv(s,
            ((char *)data)+bytesRead,
            maxData, 0)) == SOCKET_ERROR)
        {
            fSuccess = FALSE;
            wsprintf(diag, "SOCKET ERROR", data);
            LogEvent(EVENTLOG_ERROR_TYPE,
                EVMSG_DEBUG, diag);
        }
        else
        {
            if (len)
            {
                fSuccess = TRUE;
                bytesRead += (DWORD)len;
                blksSent++;
                data[200] = '\0';          // Only try to log the first
                                           //  200 characters or less.
                wsprintf(diag,
                    "Client says: %s to Thread %d",
                    data, ThreadNum);
                LogEvent(EVENTLOG_INFORMATION_TYPE,
                    EVMSG_DEBUG, diag);
            }
        }
    } while (IsRunning() && len != SOCKET_ERROR && len != 0);

    // This is just to simulate doing something that takes 2 seconds.
    Sleep(2000);
    closesocket(s);
}
```

```
//---------------------------------------------------------------------
// The thread routine; used to call DoWork correctly
DWORD __stdcall CCommService::Thread(LPVOID t)
{
    DWORD ret;
    WORD ThreadNum;
    SOCKET s;
    CCommService *p_this;

    p_this = (CCommService *)m_this;
    ThreadNum = (WORD)(t);

    do {
        while ((ret = WaitForSingleObject(
            p_this->m_hEvent, 1000)) == WAIT_TIMEOUT &&
            p_this->IsRunning() == TRUE)
        {
            ;
        }
        if (p_this->IsRunning() == FALSE)
        {
            break;
        }
        if (ret == WAIT_OBJECT_0)
        {
            s = p_this->GetLastSocket();
            SetEvent(p_this->m_hGotSocket);
            p_this->DoWork(s, ThreadNum);
        }
    } while (ret == WAIT_TIMEOUT || ret == WAIT_OBJECT_0);
    return(0);

}
```

This example required only minor changes to *CppService*. For convenience, I added a simple function, *IsRunning*. This is just an access function for the *m_isRunning* member variable implemented in CppService.h as follows. (The full source for this version of *CppService* is on the companion CD-ROM.)

```
// Added for Chapter 12
BOOL IsRunning()
{
        if (m_CreateMsgPump)
        {
            MessagePump(&m_isRunning);
        }
    return (m_isRunning != 0);
}
```

**An overview of new class members** Take a look at CommService.h in Listing 12-1. You'll see several new functions and data members. *WSCommDispatcher* is the function used to receive TCP/IP requests from clients and dispatch them to the worker threads. *SetLastSocket* and *GetLastSocket* work together to allow the newly dispatched thread to get the socket that it needs to handle the request. There are two event handles declared. The event handle *m_gotSocket* is used to signal that the worker thread has gotten the socket associated with the request, and the event handle *m_hEvent* is used to dispatch just a single thread. Two arrays, *m_hThreads* and *m_dwThreadIDs*, are dimensioned based on the number of worker threads to be used. These two arrays hold the thread handles and thread IDs, respectively.

*Thread* is a static member function that is the main routine for the worker threads. Recall that C++ class member functions always pass an implicit *this* pointer as the first unseen parameter. To allow the *Thread* function to be used as a thread procedure, we must declare it as a static function. *DoWork* is declared as virtual and is the function that actually performs the work of the server. This function accepts as a parameter the socket that resulted in the thread being dispatched and the thread number that called the function. The thread number is used in this case to permit the *DoWork* function to place the thread number in the event log.

**The *CCommService* constructor** The constructor for *CCommService* first creates the two event handles. The first event handle, *m_hEvent*, is created with default security and automatic reset. It is originally nonsignaled and not named. The automatic reset is important. If multiple threads are waiting on the event handle and automatic reset is enabled, only one thread will be notified when the event is signaled. The second event handle, *m_hGotService*, is created with the same parameters, except that it will be manually reset.

Next a default server port is set. This is an arbitrary value above 5000; in our example that value is 5043. Port numbers below 5000 are reserved for other uses. Finally, the constructor calls *CreateThread* in a loop until NUM_WORKERS threads are started. The destructor simply closes the handles opened in the constructor.

**Other class member functions** *Run* is overridden to actually control what the service does. In this case what *Run* does is quite simple:

```
void CCommService::Run()
{
    WSCommDispatcher(Thread);

    m_isRunning = false;
    // Give threads a chance to die.
    Sleep(2000);
    return;
}
```

The main task of *Run* is to call *WSCommDispatcher*. *WSCommDispatcher* is responsible for virtually all of the WinSock functionality. The following series of steps is required for acting as a WinSock server:

- WinSock must be initialized by calling *WSAStartup*.
- The server socket must be created using *socket*.
- The server socket must be bound, calling *bind*.
- The server must call *listen* to initiate listening on the port.
- The server must call *accept*, returning the socket to be used for sending and receiving data.

*WSCommDispatcher* first calls *WSAStartup*:

```
int WSAStartup(
    WORD wVersionRequested,
    LPWSADATA lpWSAData
);
```

This function initiates the WinSock library. It also allows you to specify the highest version of WinSock that the program can accept in the first parameter, *wVersionRequested*. You should place the minor version in the high-order byte of *wVersionRequested* and the major version in the low-order byte. The second parameter is a pointer to a WSADATA structure:

```
typedef struct WSAData {
    WORD           wVersion;
    WORD           wHighVersion;
    char           szDescription[WSADESCRIPTION_LEN+1];
    char           szSystemStatus[WSASYS_STATUS_LEN+1];
    unsigned short iMaxSockets;
    unsigned short iMaxUdpDg;
    char FAR *     lpVendorInfo;
} WSADATA;
```

Generally, you can ignore most of this information. The first and second data members are the WinSock version that the WinSock library expects the caller to use and the highest version supported. These are often the same value. The character arrays can be filled with somewhat useful information, though I was at one point surprised to find an implementation that reported "Running (Duh!)" in *szSystemStatus*. After that episode, I generally avoided doing anything with these values. You should ignore the last three members of this structure for WinSock 2 and greater; these members are not used for Windows 2000 or Windows NT 4. *WSCommDispatcher* checks the version of WinSock and verifies that it is version 2 or later.

Next the server socket is obtained through a call to *socket*:

```
SOCKET socket (
    int af,
    int type,
    int protocol
);
```

The first parameter, *af*, is the address family. This is normally the constant AF_INET. WinSock 2 supports other address families, such as AF_IPX and AF_APPLETALK. The second parameter is *type*, which can be SOCK_STREAM or SOCK_DGRAM. SOCK_STREAM provides a sequenced, reliable communication medium between the client and server. SOCK_DGRAM supports connectionless, unreliable communication. In most cases SOCK_STREAM is appropriate. The final parameter, *protocol*, is set to 0 in *CCommService* to use the default protocol. The protocol selected by default depends on the value passed in *type*.

> **NOTE** Calling one type of communication reliable and the other unreliable is not a value judgment. Reliable means that the packets are sequenced and that there is a mechanism for retrying failed communication. Unreliable communication does not provide this, and is appropriate for brief, stateless communication.

*WSCommDispatcher* next calls the WinSock function *bind*.

```
int bind (
    SOCKET s,
    const struct sockaddr FAR *name,
    int namelen
);
```

The first parameter to *bind* is the socket obtained with the call to *socket*. In the case of a TCP/IP socket, the second parameter is a pointer to a *sockaddr_in* structure:

```
struct sockaddr_in {
    short   sin_family;
    u_short sin_port;
    struct  in_addr sin_addr;
    char    sin_zero[8];
};
```

*WSCommDispatcher* sets *sin_family* to AF_INET, *sin_port* to the return from the *CCommService* member function *GetServerPort*, and *sin_addr* to INADDR_ANY, meaning that any address on the host can be used, in the case of a multihomed host (a host with more than one address). The last parameter to *bind* is *namelen*, which is set to the size of the *sockaddr_in* structure.

If *bind* succeeds, the next step is for *WSCommDispatcher* to call *listen* to place the server socket in a state to allow it to listen for incoming connections.

```
int listen(
    SOCKET s,
    int backlog
);
```

The first parameter is the server socket previously obtained through a call to *socket*. The second parameter, *backlog*, specifies the maximum length of the queue for incoming connections. In Listing 12-2, *backlog* is set to SOMAXCONN to allow the maximum number of backlogged connections to be set by the underlying service provider. If the number specified for *backlog* is out of range, the valid number nearest the requested value is used.

Once the socket has been set to listen for connections, the *WSCommDispatcher* function enters the loop shown in the following code fragment:

```
while ((IsRunning()))
{
    addrLen = (sizeof(cliSocketAddr));

    cliSocket = accept(srvSocket,
        (LPSOCKADDR)&cliSocketAddr, &addrLen);

    if (cliSocket == INVALID_SOCKET)
    {
        sprintf(diag, "SERVER: Windows Socket Error %d - "
            "accept() got invalid socket",
                WSAGetLastError());

        LogEvent(EVENTLOG_ERROR_TYPE, EVMSG_DEBUG, diag);
        WSACleanup();
        return;
    }

    SetLastSocket(cliSocket);
    SetEvent(m_hEvent);

    while (WaitForSingleObject(m_hGotSocket,
        1000) == WAIT_TIMEOUT)
    {
        if (!IsRunning())
        {
            return;
        }
    }
    ResetEvent(m_hGotSocket);
}
```

This loop is the controlling loop for the WinSock monitoring program. The loop is controlled by the return from *IsRunning*, a Boolean function that returns *false* if the service is stopped. At the top of the loop, *accept* is called:

```
SOCKET accept(
    SOCKET s,
    struct sockaddr FAR *addr,
    int FAR *addrlen
);
```

This call is similar to *bind*. The second parameter is a pointer to a buffer that is filled with address information about the client. This is the socket that will be used for further communication with the client.

At this point, the problem is this: How do we activate a waiting worker thread and make that thread aware of the socket? Recall that the dispatch mechanism that we use has all worker threads initially wait on *m_hEvent*, the event handle set for automatic reset. When we signal *m_hEvent*, one of the threads waiting on that object will be activated. Thus, rather than polling for an available thread, the thread is assigned by virtue of being one of the threads waiting on this event. We still need to get the socket to the worker thread. Since we do not know which worker thread might be activated, we need to have a way to pass the socket to whatever thread becomes active.

To do this, we call *SetLastSocket*, a method of *CCommService*. This method quickly sets a member of the class to the socket passed and sets the *m_hEvent* event. This is the signal for one of the worker threads to be fired. The worker thread is sitting in the loop in the following code fragment:

```
do {
    while ((ret = WaitForSingleObject(
        p_this->m_hEvent,
        1000)) == WAIT_TIMEOUT &&
        p_this->IsRunning() == TRUE)
    {
        ;
    }
    if (p_this->IsRunning() == FALSE)
    {
        break;
    }
    if (ret == WAIT_OBJECT_0)
    {
        s = p_this->GetLastSocket();
        SetEvent(p_this->m_hGotSocket);
        p_this->DoWork(s, ThreadNum);
    }
} while (ret == WAIT_TIMEOUT || ret == WAIT_OBJECT_0);
```

Once *m_hEvent* is signaled, the thread tests several conditions. If the return from *WaitForSingleObject* indicates the event was signaled, the thread gets the last socket by calling the *GetLastSocket* method. The thread then sets the *m_hGotSocket* event, which acts as a signal for the loop in *WSCommDispatcher* to reset *m_hGotSocket* and continue trying to accept connections.

At the bottom of the loop inside the *Thread* function in Listing 12-2 is a call to *DoWork*, the function that actually does the processing. In this simple example, all that *DoWork* does is read from the socket passed from *Thread* and log the text in the event log. To read from the socket, the WinSock function *recv* is called.

```
int recv (
    SOCKET s,
    char FAR *buf,
    int len,
    int flags
);
```

The first parameter is the socket to receive data on. The data is written to *buf* for a maximum length of *len* bytes. The final parameter, *flags*, can be MSG_PEEK to read the incoming data but not remove it, or MSG_OOB, meaning that *recv* should process out-of-band data.

**Possible enhancements to *CCommService*** While *CCommService* is a workable solution, we can enhance it in several ways. First, if *WSCommDispatcher* signals *m_hEvent* and no worker threads are available, the processing in that method will stop, possibly losing incoming connections. A solution that would also solve another problem—the need to grow the worker thread pool—would be to create a semaphore that would be incremented each time a worker thread starts operation and decremented as the thread begins to await another task. If *WSCommDispatcher* notices that an incoming connection arrives and no thread is waiting (determined by checking the semaphore), it could create an additional thread.

Another optimization would be to further isolate the protocol within the class. Currently two methods of the class use the WinSock functions. By abstracting the communication in a class (as we will do shortly for client-side communication), all WinSock-specific functionality could be isolated within the external class, thus allowing a single class to support (for example) both WinSock and named pipes.

### Scenario 2: Using I/O Completion Ports

I/O Completion Ports (IOCPs) are an alternative to the approach used in Listing 12-2. IOCPs have a well-deserved reputation for being difficult to implement. Part of the complexity comes from the fact that the preparation of an operation and the handling of the results occur in two different places. Adding to this complexity are the obscure techniques required to mix synchronous I/O and IOCPs and ensure that the threads handling I/O can get the proper context.

Listings 12-3 and 12-4 contain NPService.h and NPService.cpp, respectively. The service created by compiling these modules communicates with a client by using named pipes and IOCPs. The purpose of the communication in this case is to change the duration, timing, and frequency of a beep that is part of the main processing loop for the service. What's most important about this example is that it demonstrates a way to allow the operating parameters of a service to be modified either on the same machine or on any machine that is accessible across the network.

**NPService.h**

```
#define REQ_DURATION        1
#define REQ_FREQ            2
#define REQ_PAUSE           3

typedef struct _DATA_PACKET {
    WORD ServerHandle;
    WORD ServiceCode;
    WORD ReturnCode;
    DWORD DataLen;
    DWORD BufLen;
    char Buffer[1024];
} DATA_PACKET;

struct OVERLAPPED_PLUS {
    OVERLAPPED overlapped;
    DATA_PACKET dataPacket;
};

class CNPService : public CPPService
{
private:
    CRITICAL_SECTION m_cs;
    DWORD m_dwPause;
    DWORD m_dwDuration;
    DWORD m_dwFreq;
    char m_szPipeName[128];
public:
    HANDLE InitializeThreads(void);
    static DWORD __stdcall NPCommDispatcher(LPVOID Proc);
    static DWORD __stdcall Thread(LPVOID h);
    virtual void DoWork(HANDLE hPipe, WORD ThreadNum);
    LPSTR GetPipeName(LPSTR szBuffer)
    {
        strcpy(szBuffer, m_szPipeName);
        return(szBuffer);
    }
```

**Listing 12-3**

```
    void SetPipeName(LPSTR szNewPipeName)
    {
        strncpy(m_szPipeName, szNewPipeName, 128);
    }
    CNPService(char *tsvcName, char *tdispName,
        DWORD tsvcStart = SERVICE_DEMAND_START,
        bool CreateMsgPump = true);
    ~CNPService();
    virtual void Run();
    virtual void OnInstall();
};
```

Listing 12-3 first defines some constants used by the client to specify the service requested. In this case, setting the duration of the beep, the frequency of the beep, and the length of the pause are each separate operations. It is important to minimize round trips to the service, especially when communicating across a network. In a production application, all variables would be changed in a single operation.

Next is a definition of a structure named DATA_PACKET. This structure contains information that allows us to establish a client's context on the server, as well as allowing us to establish a service code for a particular request. OVERLAPPED_PLUS requires some explanation.

When we perform asynchronous I/O operations, we use a structure named OVERLAPPED to allow the operating system to complete the operation asynchronously.

```
typedef struct _OVERLAPPED {
    DWORD  Internal;
    DWORD  InternalHigh;
    DWORD  Offset;
    DWORD  OffsetHigh;
    HANDLE hEvent;
} OVERLAPPED;
```

The first two members are used internally and should not be touched. The third and fourth members, *Offset* and *OffsetHigh*, specify where in a file the operation should take place. These offsets are ignored when the OVERLAPPED structure is used for named pipes or completion ports. The final member, *hEvent*, must be set to an event object created with *CreateEvent*. The event object must be a manual-reset event.

The OVERLAPPED_PLUS structure contains an OVERLAPPED structure plus a DATA_PACKET structure. This is a fairly common trick to allow asynchronous operations to keep track of a context. Often, only a pointer to a context object is placed after the OVERLAPPED structure. I decided for illustrative purposes to include the entire structure.

The class declaration for the *CNPService* class contains some new elements over and above those in the *CPPService* class. The first is *m_cs*, a critical section object. This critical section will be used to serialize access to the next three data members, *m_dwPause*, *m_dwDuration*, and *m_dwFreq*. These data members are used to control the portion of the *Run* method that performs the simple task of looping around a *Beep* function call. The pipe name is stored in *m_szPipeName*. Several new methods are also added to the class declaration. These are fleshed out in Listing 12-4.

**NPService.cpp**

```
// NPService.cpp : Defines the entry point for the console application
//

#include "stdafx.h"

#define MAX_CLIENTS 100
#define MAX_DATA_SIZE 4096

int main(int argc, char* argv[])
{
    CNPService MyNPService("NPService", "Named Pipe Service");
    MyNPService.SetPipeName("NPServiceTest");

    MyNPService.m_isRunning = true;
    // Have we handled the arguments and done an
    //  install or uninstall?
    if (MyNPService.ParseArguments(argc, argv) == false)
    {
        // If not, start the service running.
        MyNPService.StartService();
    }
    return 0;
}

CNPService::CNPService(char *tsvcName, char *tdispName,
    DWORD tsvcStart, bool CreateMsgPump) : CPPService(tsvcName,
    tdispName, tsvcStart, CreateMsgPump)
{
    strcpy(m_szPipeName, "NPServiceTest");
    InitializeCriticalSection(&m_cs);
    m_dwFreq = 2000;
    m_dwDuration = 200;
    m_dwPause = 1000;
}
```

**Listing 12-4**

```
CNPService::~CNPService()
{
    DeleteCriticalSection(&m_cs);
}

//------------------------------------------------------------------
// The routine that causes requests to be dispatched
DWORD CNPService::NPCommDispatcher(LPVOID NotUsed)
{
    char szPipeName[255];
    bool fConnected = false;
    BOOL fSuccess;
    CNPService *p_this;
    HANDLE hPipe;
    OVERLAPPED_PLUS *overlapped;

    p_this = (CNPService *)m_this;

    SECURITY_ATTRIBUTES  sa;        // Security attributes.
    PSECURITY_DESCRIPTOR pSD;       // Pointer to SD.
    // Allocate memory for the security descriptor.
    pSD = (PSECURITY_DESCRIPTOR) LocalAlloc(LPTR,
        SECURITY_DESCRIPTOR_MIN_LENGTH);

    // Initialize the new security descriptor.
    InitializeSecurityDescriptor(pSD, SECURITY_DESCRIPTOR_REVISION);

    // Add a NULL descriptor ACL to the security descriptor.
    //  See MS KB articles Q126645 and Q102798.
    // Note that the NULL DACL means that ALL rights
    //  are allowed.
    SetSecurityDescriptorDacl(pSD, TRUE, (PACL) NULL, FALSE);
    sa.nLength = sizeof(sa);
    sa.lpSecurityDescriptor = pSD;
    sa.bInheritHandle = TRUE;

    HANDLE hCompletionPort = p_this->InitializeThreads();

    while (p_this->m_isRunning)
    {
        if (p_this->m_isPaused)
        {
            Sleep(1000);
        }
```

*(continued)*

**Listing 12-4** *continued*

```
        else
        {
            strcpy(szPipeName, "\\\\.\\pipe\\");
            strcat(szPipeName, "NPServiceTest");

            hPipe = CreateNamedPipe(szPipeName, // Name of the pipe
                PIPE_ACCESS_DUPLEX |        // Pipe is bidirectional
                FILE_FLAG_OVERLAPPED,
                PIPE_TYPE_MESSAGE |         // Each write = message
                PIPE_READMODE_MESSAGE |
                PIPE_WAIT,
                MAX_CLIENTS,               // Maximum 100 instances
                MAX_DATA_SIZE,
                MAX_DATA_SIZE,
                NMPWAIT_USE_DEFAULT_WAIT,
                &sa);

            hCompletionPort = CreateIoCompletionPort(
                hPipe,
                hCompletionPort,
                (DWORD)hPipe, 0);

            overlapped = new OVERLAPPED_PLUS;
            memset((void *)overlapped, '\0',
                sizeof(OVERLAPPED_PLUS));
            overlapped->overlapped.hEvent =
                CreateEvent(NULL, TRUE, FALSE, NULL);
            fSuccess = ConnectNamedPipe(hPipe,
                (LPOVERLAPPED)overlapped);
            while ((WaitForSingleObject(
                overlapped->overlapped.hEvent,
                1000)) == WAIT_TIMEOUT)
            {
                ;
            }
        }

    }
    return 0;
}

//-------------------------------------------------------------------
// The routine called to run the service
void CNPService::Run()
```

```
{
    DWORD tPause;
    DWORD tFreq;
    DWORD tDuration;
    DWORD dwThreadId;

    HANDLE hThreadHandle = CreateThread(
        NULL,
        0,
        NPCommDispatcher,
        0,
        0,
        &dwThreadId
        );

    // Close handle, thread will continue.
    CloseHandle(hThreadHandle);

    // This will call MessagePump if needed.
    while (IsRunning())
    {
        // Get a consistent set of values...
        EnterCriticalSection(&m_cs);
        tPause = m_dwPause;
        tFreq = m_dwFreq;
        tDuration = m_dwDuration;
        LeaveCriticalSection(&m_cs);
        // ...then use them OUTSIDE the critical section.

        Beep(tFreq, tDuration);
        Sleep(m_dwPause);
    }

    m_isRunning = false;
    // Give threads a chance to die.
    Sleep(2000);
    return;
}

//---------------------------------------------------------------
// Start the service upon installation.
void CNPService::OnInstall()
```

*(continued)*

**Listing 12-4** *continued*

```
{
    char szKey[256];
    char szBuffer[255];
    HKEY hKey = NULL;
    BYTE data[4096];
    DWORD cData = 4096;
    DWORD loop;
    BOOL foundIt = FALSE;
    long ret;
    DWORD type = REG_BINARY;

    char diag[255];
    strcpy(diag, "Handling Named Pipe Installation Issues");
    LogEvent(EVENTLOG_INFORMATION_TYPE, EVMSG_DEBUG, diag);

    // Make registry entries to support named pipes without
    //  requiring a user session. See MS KB articles Q126645 and
    //  Q102798.
    strcpy(szKey,
        "SYSTEM\\CurrentControlSet\\Services\\"
        "LanmanServer\\Parameters\\");
    ret = RegOpenKeyEx(HKEY_LOCAL_MACHINE,
        szKey, 0, KEY_ALL_ACCESS, &hKey);

    strcpy(szKey, "NullSessionPipes");
    if ((ret = RegQueryValueEx(hKey, szKey,
        NULL, &type, &data[0], &cData)) == ERROR_SUCCESS)
    {
        for (loop = 0, foundIt = FALSE ; loop < cData ;)
        {
            if (strlen((char *)&data[loop]) &&
                !(stricmp((const char *)&data[loop],
                GetPipeName(szBuffer))))
            {
                foundIt = TRUE;
            }
            loop += strlen((char *)&data[loop])+1;
        }
        // If we found it, this was previously installed.
        //  We can walk away.
        if (foundIt == FALSE)
        {
            if (cData < 4080)
```

```
            {
                strcpy((char *)&data[cData-1],
                    GetPipeName(szBuffer));
                cData += strlen(szBuffer);
                data[cData] = '\0';
                data[cData+1] = '\0';
                strcpy(szKey, "NullSessionPipes");
                SetLastError(0);

                ret = RegSetValueEx(
                hKey,        // Handle to key to set value for
                    szKey,  // Address of subkey name
                    0,      // Reserved
                    type,   // Type of value
                    // Address of value data
                    (const unsigned char *)data,
                    cData+1); // Size of value data
                if (ret != ERROR_SUCCESS)
                {
                    printf(
                        "\nGetLastError returns %d on "
                        "registry save...",
                        GetLastError());
                }

            }
        }
    }
    RegCloseKey(hKey);
    strcpy(diag, "About to start service in installer...");
    LogEvent(EVENTLOG_INFORMATION_TYPE, EVMSG_DEBUG, diag);
    printf("\nAbout to start service...");

    ::StartThisService(ServiceName());
    return;
}

//-----------------------------------------------------------------
// The function that initializes threads and completion port
HANDLE CNPService::InitializeThreads()
{

    DWORD loop;
    HANDLE hCompletionPort;
```

*(continued)*

**Listing 12-4** *continued*

```
    HANDLE hThreadHandle;
    DWORD dwThreadId;
    SYSTEM_INFO systemInfo;
    bool fConnected = false;
    DWORD dwCompletionKey = 0;

    // Create completion port to be associated with pipes.
    hCompletionPort = CreateIoCompletionPort(INVALID_HANDLE_VALUE,
        NULL, 0, 0);
    if (hCompletionPort == NULL)
    {
        return NULL;
    }

    // Get number of processors.
    GetSystemInfo(&systemInfo);

    // Create two threads per processor.
    for (loop = 0;
        loop < systemInfo.dwNumberOfProcessors*2;
        loop++)
    {

        hThreadHandle = CreateThread(
            NULL,
            0,
            Thread,
            hCompletionPort,
            0,
            &dwThreadId);
        if (hThreadHandle == NULL) {
            CloseHandle(hCompletionPort);
            return NULL;
        }
        // Close the handle, the thread will continue.
        CloseHandle(hThreadHandle);
    }

    // Return successfully.
    return hCompletionPort;

} // InitializeThreads

//-----------------------------------------------------------------
```

```
// The thread routine
DWORD __stdcall CNPService::Thread(LPVOID Context)
{
    HANDLE hCompletionPort = Context;
    BOOL bSuccess;
    DWORD dwIoSize;
    OVERLAPPED_PLUS *lpOverlapped;
    DWORD cbRead;
    HANDLE hPipe;
    CNPService *p_this;

    p_this = (CNPService *)m_this;

    while (p_this->m_isRunning)
    {
        bSuccess = GetQueuedCompletionStatus(
            hCompletionPort,
            &dwIoSize,
            (LPDWORD)&hPipe,
            (LPOVERLAPPED *)&lpOverlapped,
            (DWORD)1000);

        if (!bSuccess) {
            CloseHandle(hPipe);
            continue;
        }

        // This odd behavior is required to make
        //  the handle act as synchronous.
        lpOverlapped->overlapped.hEvent =
            ((HANDLE) ((DWORD)lpOverlapped->overlapped.hEvent|0x1));

        printf("\nSuccess!");

        ReadFile(hPipe, &lpOverlapped->dataPacket,
            (sizeof(DATA_PACKET)), &cbRead,
            (LPOVERLAPPED)lpOverlapped);

        DWORD dwNewValue =
            *((DWORD *)&lpOverlapped->dataPacket.Buffer[0]);
        switch (lpOverlapped->dataPacket.ServiceCode)
        {
        case REQ_DURATION:
            EnterCriticalSection(&p_this->m_cs);
```

*(continued)*

**Listing 12-4** *continued*

```
            p_this->m_dwDuration = dwNewValue;
            LeaveCriticalSection(&p_this->m_cs);
            break;
        case REQ_PAUSE:
            EnterCriticalSection(&p_this->m_cs);
            p_this->m_dwPause = dwNewValue;
            LeaveCriticalSection(&p_this->m_cs);
            break;
        case REQ_FREQ:
            EnterCriticalSection(&p_this->m_cs);
            p_this->m_dwFreq = dwNewValue;
            LeaveCriticalSection(&p_this->m_cs);
            break;
        }

        strcpy(lpOverlapped->dataPacket.Buffer,
            "Message Received!");
        lpOverlapped->dataPacket.DataLen =
            strlen(lpOverlapped->dataPacket.Buffer);
        lpOverlapped->dataPacket.BufLen =
            sizeof(lpOverlapped->dataPacket.Buffer);

        while (WriteFile(hPipe, &lpOverlapped->dataPacket,
            (sizeof(DATA_PACKET)),
            &cbRead,
            (LPOVERLAPPED)lpOverlapped) == FALSE &&
            GetLastError() == ERROR_IO_PENDING)
        {
            Sleep(1);
        }

        DisconnectNamedPipe(hPipe);
        CloseHandle(hPipe);
        hPipe = NULL;
        CloseHandle(lpOverlapped->overlapped.hEvent);
        delete lpOverlapped;
    }
    return(0);

}
```

**Installation issues** *OnInstall* solves a problem that occurs because named pipes is an authenticated protocol. When initially testing a named pipes server converted from a console mode application to a service, I discovered that I was unable to connect to any pipe; I received access-denied errors every time I tried to make the connection. The service was starting under the security of the System account, and therefore should have had rights to do what it pleased, as long as it was not accessing resources off the server. As I often do when I encounter access-denied errors on a service, I changed the security context of the service and had it start under my user ID and password (my account was in the *domain admins* group). Not surprisingly, the service correctly connected to the client when I started it this way.

This is not an ideal situation. When distributing a service application, requiring a service to run under a user account can be a pain. I understood the issue: a named pipes server could impersonate the named pipes client, possibly allowing an errant service to do widespread damage. I was confident that the service in question would not do any damage and in fact was not using impersonation.

I found the solution in two Microsoft Knowledgebase articles, Q102798 and Q126645, available on the companion CD-ROM. The first article suggested that creating a security descriptor would resolve the problem. This step is required and included in the method *NPCommDispatcher*, but it is not sufficient to allow the service to connect to named pipes clients. The second article correctly described a registry change required to enable the service to connect to a named pipes client. A registry entry, *NullSessionPipes* (located at *HKLM\System\CurrentControlset\Services\LanManServer\Parameters*), is a double-null terminated binary entry. Each service that needs to connect to a null session pipe must be listed in this entry, separated by NULLs. The final entry is followed by two NULLs. Figure 12-1 shows the end of the *NullSessionPipes* entry with *NPService* as the last entry.

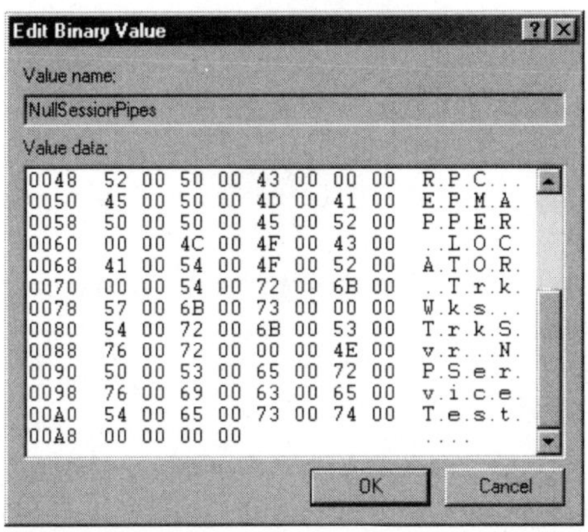


**Figure 12-1** *The registry entry that allows a service running under the System account to connect to named pipes clients.*

**The operation of the service** Once the service is installed it can be run. The *Run* method first creates a thread to run the *NPCommDispatcher* method. This method is declared static so that it can be used as a thread procedure. *NPCommDispatcher* first creates a security descriptor to be used when creating named pipes to allow the service to connect using the System account.

Next the method *InitializeThreads* is called. This function creates a completion port using the Win32 function *CreateIoCompletionPort*:

```
HANDLE CreateIoCompletionPort (
    HANDLE FileHandle,              // File handle to associate with
                                    //  the I/O completion port
    HANDLE ExistingCompletionPort,  // Handle to the I/O completion
                                    //  port
    DWORD CompletionKey,            // Per-file completion key for I/O
                                    //  completion packets
    DWORD NumberOfConcurrentThreads // Number of threads allowed to
                                    //  execute concurrently
)
```

The first parameter, *FileHandle*, is the file handle to associate with the IOCP or the value INVALID_HANDLE_VALUE if the port should be created without associating it with a handle. This handle can be a file or pipe handle or a WinSock socket. In this case, this parameter is passed as INVALID_HANDLE_VALUE because no pipes are currently active. *ExistingCompletionPort* associates a new instance of the completion port with an existing completion port. *NPService* passes NULL for the *ExistingCompletionPort* value in *InitializeThreads* because there is no existing IOCP. *CompletionKey* is a context value that is often used to send the I/O handle to the routine that will service the IOCP. In this case, it is passed as 0. The final parameter, *NumberOfConcurrentThreads*, is the number of I/O threads the system allows to run. Passing a value of 0—as in the *NPService* example—tells the system to allow one I/O thread per processor on the system. Whenever a thread processing an IOCP enters a wait state, that thread is no longer considered in the thread count. Therefore when that previously waiting thread begins processing again, momentarily more threads than specified will be running. The number will be reduced as other IOCP threads terminate.

*InitializeThreads* next calls *GetSystemInfo* to obtain the number of processors on the system. This number is used to create two threads to monitor IOCPs for each processor. (I'll discuss the *Thread* method shortly.) Once the threads are created, *InitializeThreads* returns the handle to the completion port.

Once *InitializeThreads* returns, *NPCommDispatcher* enters a loop controlled by the value of *m_isRunning*. This is to allow this thread to properly shut down when the service is stopped. If the service is not paused, a named pipe is created using the Win32 *CreateNamedPipe* function. *CreateNamedPipe* is a server-side only function:

```
HANDLE CreateNamedPipe(
    LPCTSTR lpName,         // Pointer to pipe name
    DWORD dwOpenMode,       // Pipe open mode
    DWORD dwPipeMode,       // Pipe-specific modes
```

```
    DWORD nMaxInstances,      // Maximum number of instances
    DWORD nOutBufferSize,     // Output buffer size, in bytes
    DWORD nInBufferSize,      // Input buffer size, in bytes
    DWORD nDefaultTimeOut,    // Time-out time, in milliseconds
    // Pointer to security attributes
    LPSECURITY_ATTRIBUTES lpSecurityAttributes
);
```

The first parameter, *lpName*, is a pointer to the name of the pipe. This is a UNC name, in the form \\\\.*pipe**PipeName*. The dot (.) indicates the pipe is on the current machine. The pipe exists on the logical share *pipe*. The final portion of the name is used to uniquely identify the pipe to clients and when the server creates additional instances of the pipe.

The open mode, passed as *dwOpenMode*, accepts three different classes of flags. The first type refers to the type of access the pipe will allow:

- PIPE_ACCESS_DUPLEX means the pipe allows bidirectional communication.
- PIPE_ACCESS_INBOUND means the pipe will allow only incoming data.
- PIPE_ACCESS_OUTBOUND means that from the server's perspective, this is a write-only pipe.

A second type of flag that can be passed to *dwOpenMode* has two values:

- FILE_FLAG_WRITE_THROUGH causes writes to be completed across a network before a write operation returns. This flag is only valid for byte mode pipes (which I'll discuss shortly).
- FILE_FLAG_OVERLAPPED enables overlapped, or asynchronous, operation mode. This flag allows the operation of the pipe using IOCPs.

A third type of flag that can be passed to *dwOpenMode* relates to security:

- WRITE_DAC means the caller will have write access to the named pipe's Discretionary Access Control List (DACL).
- WRITE_OWNER means the caller will have write access to the named pipe's owner.
- ACCESS_SYSTEM_SECURITY means the caller will have rights to the named pipe's System Access Control List (SACL).

In Listing 12-4, *CreateNamedPipe* is called with PIPE_ACCESS_DUPLEX to create a named pipe for reading and writing and FILE_FLAG_OVERLAPPED to allow the pipe to be used with IOCPs.

The next parameter, *dwPipeMode*, also has three general types of flags. The first type controls the way data is accessed from the pipe:

- PIPE_TYPE_BYTE creates a pipe in which data is written as a stream of bytes and is the default.
- PIPE_TYPE_MESSAGE creates a pipe in which data written to the pipe in a single operation is considered a message. The same value must be passed for each instance of the named pipe.

Another pair of flags controls how data is read from the pipe:

- PIPE_READMODE_BYTE is the default and creates a pipe in which data is read as a stream of bytes.
- PIPE_READMODE_MESSAGE creates a pipe that reads one message at a time. The message mode for writing and reading is preferred unless you want to have your program manually terminate messages so that the byte stream can be parsed as it is read.

The final pair of flags that can be passed as part of *dwPipeMode* is the most misunderstood:

- PIPE_WAIT sets the blocking mode for the pipe being created.
- PIPE_NOWAIT sets the nonblocking mode for the pipe being created.

In a situation in which you might need to test for other conditions while waiting, your natural inclination is to use PIPE_NOWAIT, as with a server-based application. This is not the case—PIPE_NOWAIT is provided only for compatibility with LAN Manager version 2. Using PIPE_WAIT in a combination with *dwOpenMode* that includes FILE_FLAG_OVERLAPPED provides the correct mix for use with IOCPs.

The *nMaxInstances* parameter passed to *CreateNamedPipe* controls the maximum number of instances of the named pipe that will be allowed. In Listing 12-4, *nMaxInstances* is set to a constant that evaluates to 100. In the real world, the number of concurrently active instances of a named pipe implemented as this application is likely to be lower. PIPE_UNLIMITED_INSTANCES allows the number of pipes to be limited only by the amount of memory present.

The next two parameters, *nOutBufferSize* and *nInBufferSize*, are advisory in nature. The actual size of the buffers can be the system-defined minimum, the system-defined maximum, or the specified size. The default timeout is specified in *nDefaultTimeout*, which specifies the timeout in milliseconds if *WaitNamedPipe* is called using NMPWAIT_USE_DEFAULT_WAIT. The final parameter is the security attribute, set in accordance with the requirements in Microsoft Knowledge Base article Q102798.

Next an IOCP is created through a call to *CreateIoCompletionPort*. In Listing 12-4, unlike the call in *InitializeThreads*, the pipe handle is passed and the existing completion port handle returns from *InitializeThreads*. The pipe handle, *hPipe*, is cast as a DWORD and sent in the *CompletionKey* parameter to *CreateIoCompletionPort*. When we look at the *Thread* method of *CNPService*, we'll see that this is passed in to *GetQueuedCompletionStatus*.

An OVERLAPPED_PLUS structure is then allocated and filled in, as in the following code fragment:

```
overlapped = new OVERLAPPED_PLUS;
memset((void *)overlapped, '\0',
    sizeof(OVERLAPPED_PLUS));
overlapped->overlapped.hEvent =
    CreateEvent(NULL, TRUE, FALSE, NULL);
fSuccess = ConnectNamedPipe(hPipe,
    (LPOVERLAPPED)overlapped);
while ((WaitForSingleObject(
    overlapped->overlapped.hEvent,
    1000)) == WAIT_TIMEOUT)
{
    if (!(p_this->m_isRunning))
    {
        break;
    }
}
```

The OVERLAPPED_PLUS structure is allocated with *new*. The *hEvent* member of the embedded OVERLAPPED structure is set to a handle created with *CreateEvent*. *ConnectNamedPipe* is called with the pipe handle and a pointer to the OVERLAPPED_PLUS structure cast as an OVERLAPPED. Next we wait on the event handle. When this is signaled, the pipe will be connected. While we wait, every second we break from *WaitForSingleObject* and test the Boolean flag *m_isRunning*. We break out of the loop if the flag is TRUE.

Interestingly, the pipe has been created, we know the connection has been made, but no reading or processing has been done. That is done in the *Thread* member function. Two instances of the thread per processor start in *InitializeThreads*. The beginning of the *Thread* method is shown in the following code fragment:

```
p_this = (CNPService *)m_this;

while (p_this->m_isRunning)
{
    bSuccess = GetQueuedCompletionStatus(
        hCompletionPort,
        &dwIoSize,
```

*(continued)*

```
            (LPDWORD)&hPipe,
            (LPOVERLAPPED *)&lpOverlapped,
            (DWORD)1000);

        if (!bSuccess) {
            continue;
        }
}
```

Recall that *Thread* is a static member function; it can only directly access static members of *CNPService*. As with a static member function of the base class, we use a pointer to the class—held in *m_this* to get to nonstatic members. After a check at the top of the *while* loop to confirm the service is still running, we call *GetQueuedCompletionStatus*. This is the function that acts as a gateway to the IOCP. If we run the service without any clients attaching, this function will wait the amount of time specified in the timeout parameter and return indicating a failure. The prototype for *GetQueuedCompletionStatus* is as follows:

```
BOOL GetQueuedCompletionStatus(
    HANDLE CompletionPort,          // The I/O completion port
                                    //  of interest
    LPDWORD lpNumberOfBytesTransferred,
                                    // To receive number of bytes
                                    //  transferred during I/O
    LPDWORD lpCompletionKey,        // To receive file's completion key
    LPOVERLAPPED *lpOverlapped,     // To receive pointer to OVERLAPPED
                                    //  structure
    DWORD dwMilliseconds            // Optional timeout value
);
```

The first parameter is the handle of the completion port. The number of bytes transferred is passed in *lpNumberOfBytesTransferred*. The third parameter is *lpCompletionKey*. Recall that this parameter contains the pipe handle that we set when we created the IOCP in *NPCommDispatcher*. This will be used for further operation on the pipe. The fourth parameter is *lpOverlapped*, a pointer to an OVERLAPPED structure. Recall that when connecting to the pipe using *ConnectNamedPipe*, we passed an OVERLAPPED_PLUS structure rather than a simple OVERLAPPED structure. This OVERLAPPED_PLUS structure can be used for additional context, if needed. One example of this is a server that uses IOCPs for all I/O operations. When *GetQueuedCompletionStatus* returns, the current thread might need to know whether the operation that completed was a read or a write operation. Information about the operation that triggered the queued completion status can allow the server to act appropriately.

When *GetQueuedCompletionStatus* returns indicating success, the next step is to actually read some data. The queued completion status that the program has been notified of is the connection to a named pipes client. *ReadFile* must be used to actually get the data.

There is a complication here. What happens if we read the data in the pipe using *ReadFile*? This function would return immediately and fire another completion when done. This is not what we're looking for. Further, we know that future requests from the client and writes to the client will be short in duration and will come as fast as the client can process them. In this case, we'd like to use the normal overlapped operations rather than the IOCP mechanism. The method to make this happen is somewhat odd and depends on the fact that Win32 treats the low 2 bits of a handled value specially. These bits are not set on normal handles. *ReadFile* and *WriteFile* are designed to see the low bit of a handle as a magic flag that says normal IOCP mechanisms should not be used. This is the reason for the following odd bit of code:

```
lpOverlapped->overlapped.hEvent =
    ((HANDLE)((DWORD)lpOverlapped->overlapped.hEvent|0x1));
```

Through all the casts, we simply set that magic bit of the handle so that IOCP notifications are not used. The call to *ReadFile* allows us to read information about the reason for the call in the *ServiceCode* member of DATA_PACKET. The call to *ReadFile* also allows us to read information from the buffer. We cast the first element in the buffer to a DWORD and use this value as a parameter to set the duration, pause, or frequency used to allow the system to control the service's beep.

The code to set the *m_dwDuration*, *m_dwPause*, and *m_dwFreq* variables is straightforward, including a call to *EnterCriticalSection* and *LeaveCriticalSection* to control access to these variables as they are set. Finally, for demonstration purposes only, a message, "Message Received!", is sent back to the client. Once the message is sent, *DisconnectNamedPipe* is called with the pipe handle and the handle is closed with a call to *CloseHandle*. The event handle previously created and sent in the OVERLAPPED structure is also closed.

The *Run* method is the last part of Listing 12-4 left to describe. It is similar to other examples, but in this case the calls to *Beep* and *Sleep* use the members of the class that control the duration, pause, and frequency.

### A New Option: *QueueUserWorkItem*

Several new functions in Windows 2000 allow work items to be queued for processing. *QueueUserWorkItem* allows a unit of work to be queued:

```
BOOL QueueUserWorkItem(
    LPTHREAD_START_ROUTINE Function,
    PVOID Context,
    ULONG Flags
);
```

The first parameter is *Function*, the function that will be executed. *Context* is the 4-byte value that will be passed to *Function* when it is called. *Flags* is a bit-flag that can be set to the values described in Table 12-1.

**TABLE 12-1**
**VALUES FOR THE *FLAGS* PARAMETER OF *QUEUEUSERWORKITEM***

| *Value* | *Meaning* |
|---|---|
| WT_EXECUTEDEFAULT | The function is queued to a non-I/O thread. |
| WT_EXECUTEINIOTHREAD | The function is executed in an I/O worker thread. This flag should be used to ensure that the function will be executed in a thread that will not terminate with pending asynchronous I/O requests. |
| WT_EXECUTEINPERSISTENTIOTHREAD | The documentation indicates that this flag causes the function to run in a thread that never terminates. The documentation also says that no worker threads are persistent. |
| WT_EXECUTELONGFUNCTION | This is a hint to the system that the function being called could wait for a long time. The system uses this information to decide if new threads should be created. This flag can be used only with WT_EXECUTEINIOTHREAD. |

An alternative to explicitly calling *QueueUserWorkItem* is to use the Win32 API function *BindIoCompletionCallback*, also new to Windows 2000:

```
BOOL BindIoCompletionCallback(
    HANDLE FileHandle,
    LPOVERLAPPED_COMPLETION_ROUTINE Function,
    ULONG Flags
);
```

This function greatly simplifies the use of I/O completion ports, a complex operation in prior Windows versions. *FileHandle* is the handle to a file opened with the FILE_FLAG_OVERLAPPED flag. *Function* is a pointer to a routine to be called when the I/O on the file is complete. The last parameter, *Flags*, is unused and must be 0. The prototype for *Function* is:

```
VOID CALLBACK FileIOCompletionRoutine(
    DWORD dwErrorCode,                  // Completion code
    DWORD dwNumberOfBytesTransfered,    // Number of bytes transferred
    LPOVERLAPPED lpOverlapped           // Pointer to structure with
                                        //  I/O information
);
```

The first parameter, *dwErrorCode*, is the completion code, which will be 0 if the I/O was successful or ERROR_HANDLE_EOF if the operation fails. The second parameter, *dwNumberOfBytesTransfered*, specifies the number of bytes transferred or returns 0 if an error occurs. The last parameter, *lpOverlapped*, is a pointer to an OVERLAPPED structure.

Most of the overlapped structure can be ignored when we use it for named pipe access and completion callbacks. The last member, *hEvent*, is often used as a way to pass context to the *FileIOCompletionRoutine*. If we were using a file handle rather than a named pipe handle, we could simply allocate additional memory after the OVERLAPPED structure and place context information there, as we did in Listing 12-4.

The advantage of *QueueUserWorkItem* and *BindIoCompletionCallback* should be clear: much of the work is done for you. The disadvantage is that you as a developer have no real control over the number of threads created. Thus, it is possible that one server-based application on a shared machine can monopolize the processor.

## WinSock vs. Named Pipes

Both WinSock and named pipes have their advantages. If you need to create a server-like application that must run on a Windows 9x machine, WinSock is all that you really can use, since Windows 9x can be a named pipes client but not a named pipes server. Note that many of the functions used for the WinSock service in Listings 12-1 and 12-2 and for the named pipes service in Listings 12-3 and 12-4 use functions that are available only on Windows 2000 and Windows NT.

If you need to impersonate a client in order to enforce security, named pipes wins hands down. *ImpersonateNamedPipeClient* is a relatively easy way to allow your server to act under the authority of the connected client. If you need to connect over wide-area networks or the Internet, WinSock is a better choice.

## Events vs. I/O Completion Ports vs. *QueueUserWorkItem*

Choosing the overall structure of a server-based application is perhaps a bigger decision than choosing a communication protocol. In both the WinSock example and the named pipes example, the details of the one protocol could be easily ripped out and replaced with those of the other protocol. It is much more difficult to replace one architecture for handling client requests with another.

The WinSock example using an event handle to control access to a set of worker threads was in many ways easier to create than the IOCP example or the named pipes example. The structure seems clear and it seems to offer reasonable control over the number of threads and over how work is performed. IOCPs have the advantage of being standardized with operating system support. Once you have created one IOCP-based service, you will more easily be able to create a second. IOCPs also ensure that the most recently used worker thread will be used first, giving the best chance that its memory will not have been paged out to disk. There are no guarantees when using the automatic reset event handle with multiple threads running. Both IOCPs and named pipes hold up under reasonable loads with a small number of clients simulating a larger number of clients.

*QueueUserWorkItem* offers great promise, though with too little developer control for my comfort. In theory, *BindIoCompletionCallback* seems like another step in the right direction for creating high performance servers to handle large numbers of clients.

In practice, a number of the server-based applications I have created have used the simpler one-thread-per-client model. Of course, I've limited these applications to small numbers of clients with each interaction comprised of a short query and response, but for some simpler requirements this model can suffice.

## A GENERALIZED CLIENT COMMUNICATION CLASS

In order to communicate with the client applications created in this chapter, we need to create some client software.

One way to allow clients to communicate using the protocol decided at run time is to create a couple of layers of DLLs. One layer can act as a generic interface. That layer can call down to a protocol-specific DLL when you make the decision about the protocol to use. This is the approach I take in my book, *Windows Client/Server Developer's Guide*. The protocol-independent DLLs documented in that book are still in use today. They've been used by C++, Borland Delphi, and Microsoft Visual Basic clients. Since then, I've thought about other ways to create protocol independence. Creating a C++ class hierarchy is one way to enable an application to work using WinSock or named pipes as appropriate.

Listing 12-5 shows the header file for the client communication, ClientComm.h. A base class, *CClientComm*, defines the basic operations required for any communication to take place. *Open*, *Read*, *Write*, and *Close* are virtual functions in the base class. There are two descendant classes, one for WinSock and one for named pipes.

Both implement the virtual functions declared in the base class and both have any protocol-specific properties set by the constructor. Protocol-specific properties include naming information, named pipe handle, or WinSock socket. The server name is in the base class.

**ClientComm.h**

```
typedef struct _DATA_PACKET {
    WORD ServerHandle;
    WORD ServiceCode;
    WORD ReturnCode;
    DWORD DataLen;
    DWORD BufLen;
    char Buffer[1024];
} DATA_PACKET;

class CClientComm {
public:
    bool fConnected;
    void ShowError(LPSTR doingWhat);
    LPSTR GetServerName(LPSTR buffer);
    CClientComm(LPCSTR szServerParam)
    {
        fConnected = FALSE;
        strncpy(szServer, szServerParam, 255);
    }
    virtual DWORD Open();
    virtual DWORD Read(LPSTR data,
        DWORD cBytesToRead,
        LPDWORD cBytesRead);
    virtual DWORD Write(LPSTR data,
        DWORD cBytesToWrite,
        LPDWORD cBytesWritten);
    virtual DWORD Close();
private:
    char szServer[255];
};

class CWinSockClientComm : public virtual CClientComm {
public:
    CWinSockClientComm(LPSTR szServerParam, int port);
    DWORD Open();
    DWORD Read(LPSTR data,
        DWORD cBytesToRead,
        LPDWORD cBytesRead);
```

**Listing 12-5** *(continued)*

**Listing 12-5** *continued*

```
    DWORD Write(LPSTR data,
        DWORD cBytesToWrite,
        LPDWORD cBytesWritten);
    DWORD Close();
private:
    WSADATA wsaData;
    SOCKET m_cliSocket;
    int m_iPort;
};

class CNPClientComm : public virtual CClientComm {
public:
    ~CNPClientComm();
    CNPClientComm(LPCSTR szServerParam, LPCSTR szPipeNameParem);
    DWORD Open();
    DWORD Read(LPSTR data,
        DWORD cBytesToRead,
        LPDWORD cBytesRead);
    DWORD Write(LPSTR data,
        DWORD cBytesToWrite,
        LPDWORD cBytesWritten);
    DWORD Close();
private:
    char m_szPipeName[255];
    HANDLE m_hPipe;
};
```

It is important to note that this is a client communication class. The details of implementing the server side of each protocol are different from the client-side implementation. For one thing, providing separate threads for communication is usually not important in a client. The client simply waits while the communication takes place.

You'll find both class implementations on the accompanying CD-ROM, but I will describe the named pipe implementation, *CNPClientComm*. The constructor simply sends the server name to the base constructor and sets the pipe name. The fragment below is the *CNPClientComm* implementation of *Open*.

```
DWORD CNPClientComm::Open()
{
    char szFullPipeName[255];
    char buffer[255];
    int ret = -1;

    wsprintf(
        szFullPipeName,
        "\\\\%s\\pipe\\%s",
```

```
        GetServerName(buffer),
        m_szPipeName);

    m_hPipe = CreateFile(szFullPipeName, // The pipe name
        GENERIC_READ|GENERIC_WRITE,      // Read and write
        0,                               // Don't share
        NULL,                            // Default security
        OPEN_EXISTING,                   // Open an existing pipe
        0,                               // Default attributes
        NULL);                           // No template file

    if (m_hPipe == INVALID_HANDLE_VALUE)
    {
        char buffer[255];
        sprintf(buffer, "CreateFile (%s)", szFullPipeName);
        if (GetLastError() != 2)
        {
            ShowError(buffer);
        }
        ret = -1;
    }
    else
    {
        fConnected = TRUE;
    }
    return(fConnected == TRUE);
}
```

The pipe name is built up from the server name and the pipe name. Instead of a named pipes–specific function, *CreateFile* is called to open the pipe:

```
HANDLE CreateFile(
    LPCTSTR lpFileName,           // Pointer to name of the file
    DWORD dwDesiredAccess,        // Access (read-write) mode
    DWORD dwShareMode,            // Share mode
    LPSECURITY_ATTRIBUTES lpSecurityAttributes,
                                  // Pointer to security attributes
    DWORD dwCreationDisposition,  // How to create
    DWORD dwFlagsAndAttributes,   // File attributes
    HANDLE hTemplateFile          // Handle to file with attributes
                                  //  to copy
);
```

Most of the parameters are used exactly as you would expect. Table 12-2 describes some additional flags for named pipes for *dwFlagsAndAttributes*.

**TABLE 12-2**
**ADDITIONAL FLAGS FOR OPENING CLIENT-SIDE NAMED PIPES**

| *Flag* | *Meaning* |
|---|---|
| SECURITY_ANONYMOUS | Client impersonated at Anonymous level |
| SECURITY_IDENTIFICATION | Impersonate client at the Identification impersonation level |
| SECURITY_IMPERSONATION | Impersonate client at the Impersonation level |
| SECURITY_DELEGATION | Impersonate client at the Delegation impersonation level |
| SECURITY_CONTEST_TRACKING | Specifies that security tracking mode is dynamic; default is static |
| SECURITY_EFFECTIVE_ONLY | Only enabled aspects of the client's security context are available (This allows the client to limit the groups and privileges the server can impersonate.) |

The balance of the *Open* method of *NPClientComm* checks for errors. The *Read* method uses *PeekNamedPipe* to test for data being available and pauses briefly if no data is waiting to give it a chance to arrive.

```
BOOL PeekNamedPipe(
    HANDLE hNamedPipe,                // Handle to pipe to copy from
    LPVOID lpBuffer,                  // Pointer to data buffer
    DWORD nBufferSize,                // Size, in bytes, of data buffer
    LPDWORD lpBytesRead,              // Pointer to number of bytes read
    LPDWORD lpTotalBytesAvail,        // Pointer to total number of
                                      //  bytes available
    LPDWORD lpBytesLeftThisMessage    // Pointer to unread bytes in
                                      //  this message
);
```

The pipe handle is passed as *hNamedPipe*. The second parameter, *lpBuffer*, points to a buffer to accept the data if available, and *nBufferSize* is the size of that buffer. The last three parameters are pointers to DWORDs that accept the number of bytes read, total bytes available, and bytes left in this message. If the function succeeds and data is available, the return value is nonzero. In any case, the function returns immediately. The actual reading and writing of data is done exactly as it would be for a normal file—using *ReadFile* and *WriteFile*.

Figure 12-2 at the top of the next page shows a simple MFC client program. The first three fields require entry. When you click on Connect, the last field will be filled in with the text "Message Received!" if everything works.

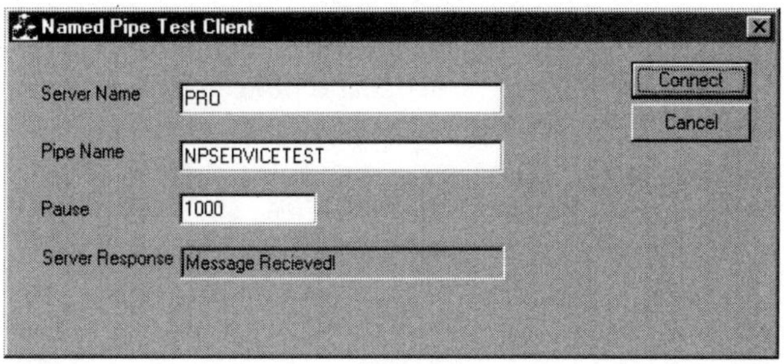


**Figure 12-2** *A simple MFC dialog client that connects with* NPService *from Listing 12-4.*

The code attached to the Connect button is simple:

```
void CNPClientDlg::OnOK()
{
    DWORD dwValue;
    DWORD dwBytes;
    DATA_PACKET data;
    CString strServer;
    CString strPipe;
    CString strPause;
    CString strServerResponse;
    m_ctlServer.GetWindowText(strServer);
    m_ctlPipe.GetWindowText(strPipe);
    m_ctlPause.GetWindowText(strPause);

    m_OK.EnableWindow(FALSE);

    dwValue = atol(strPause);
    data.ServiceCode = 1;
    data.BufLen = sizeof(DATA_PACKET);
    data.DataLen = sizeof(DWORD);

    memcpy(&data.Buffer[0], (void *)&dwValue, sizeof(DWORD));

    CNPClientComm MyClient((LPCSTR)strServer, (LPCSTR)strPipe);

    MyClient.Open();
    MyClient.Write((char *)&data, sizeof(DATA_PACKET), &dwBytes);

    dwBytes = sizeof(DATA_PACKET);
    MyClient.Read((char *)&data, sizeof(DATA_PACKET), &dwBytes);

    m_ctlServerResp.SetWindowText(data.Buffer);

    MyClient.Close();

    m_OK.EnableWindow(TRUE);
    //CDialog::OnOK();
}
```

After setting the value of the *data* variable, an instance of *CNPClientComm* is declared. *Open* is called with the server name and pipe as entered in the dialog. *Write* is called with the *data* variable, followed by a call to *Read* to get the response. The result, returned in *data.Buffer*, is then placed into the final read-only edit box with the response from the server.

## CONCLUSION

In this chapter, we have looked at several different communication protocols as well as the different methods to manage interaction with clients. The implications of dealing with clients are much greater than you might think. Often what limits a server is not pure processing power but the server's ability to handle the I/O. Using an event handle or IOCP can go a long way toward opening up that bottleneck.

In the next chapter, we will look at further integration with Microsoft SQL Server, making full use of the server-side development possibilities of that environment. Then in Chapter 14 we will put it all together and create a server-based application that will use many of the techniques and APIs covered so far to create a reliable server that can monitor the health of other servers. This is a nontrivial application that will be further enhanced in Chapter 15 using the active Internet technologies Active Server Pages and ISAPI Extensions covered in Chapters 9 and 10.

*Chapter 13*

# Integrating with SQL Server

Almost everyone who uses a computer is aware of Microsoft Office, the suite of business applications that includes Microsoft Word, Microsoft Excel, Microsoft Access, and Microsoft PowerPoint. Fewer computer users might be aware that a similar product exists for servers. Microsoft BackOffice attempts to meet the basic needs of those who support and design server-based applications in the same way that Office meets the basic needs of desktop and laptop computer users. Like Office applications, BackOffice applications can be enhanced and extended by developers to allow these general tools to meet specific needs.

BackOffice consists of the following server-based applications:

- Microsoft SQL Server for database access
- Microsoft Exchange Server for messaging
- Microsoft Systems Management Server for client management
- Microsoft SNA server for connectivity to mainframe and midrange computers

In Chapter 7, I described how we use MAPI to send and receive mail. While other MAPI message sources are available, Exchange is the most common. This chapter will focus on SQL Server, which is a common data source for ODBC applications such as the one we saw in Chapter 8.

We could use SQL Server as just another data source, interchangeable with desktop databases such as Access and Borland Paradox. However, this would not even begin to touch its potential. Consider the following scenarios:

- You must design a system that uses Web clients for inquiry and simple data entry and also uses a Microsoft Visual Basic client for more sophisticated data entry and reporting. Both systems can insert records into the database. Inserting a record into one table should be accompanied by insertion of several records into another table.
- You need to create an order entry system that will notify a system administrator whenever a customer's outstanding balance exceeds predefined limits. You would also like to have quick and easy reporting of customer balances without having to read through the entire database.
- You need to create a system that will access the e-mail system, but not all client machines will have the e-mail client installed. Nor, for that matter, will all users have their own e-mail accounts.

These and many other system requirements can be handled using Microsoft SQL Server. We'll revisit these scenarios as we explore the capabilities of SQL Server.

# TRANSACT-SQL

In Chapter 8, I described the general structure of the SQL commands that allows client software to select, insert, update, and delete records in a SQL Server table. Of course, Transact-SQL (T-SQL)—the SQL dialect included with Microsoft SQL Server—supports that syntax. However, those simple statements barely scratch the surface of this rich programming environment.

Let's review briefly. Selecting data from a SQL data source uses a command in this form:

```
SELECT <field list>
    FROM <table name>
    WHERE <condition>
    ORDER BY <sort fields>
```

Of course, this command has many options, and not all the clauses of the statement are required. For instance, *SELECT * FROM tblPatients* is a perfectly valid T-SQL select statement. *SELECT TOP 5 * FROM tblPatients ORDER BY accountBalance* is also a valid T-SQL statement. We use the *TOP* keyword to specify a limit to the number of records that should be returned. *UPDATE, INSERT,* and *DELETE* statements also use the same kind of regular syntax.

T-SQL also supports a limited procedural language. This includes support for *IF*, *ELSE*, *WHILE*, and *CASE* statements. With these procedural statements, T-SQL goes far beyond the limits of non-server-based databases. T-SQL can be leveraged to support server-based development with three general features:

- *Triggers*. These are statements that are triggered by an event on the server.
- *Stored procedures*. These are sets of procedures that are precompiled and stored on the server. Stored procedures can perform actions or return record sets.
- *Extended stored procedures*. These are somewhat similar to stored procedures, but rather than using T-SQL code, extended stored procedures are created in C or C++ and compiled into DLLs in a specific format.

These three components of SQL Server allow you to create applications that meet all of the requirements listed in the scenarios mentioned earlier in the chapter. Before discussing those scenarios in detail, let's look at what each of these three features do.

## Triggers

Triggers are bits of T-SQL code that are fired off whenever a prescribed event takes place. SQL Server supports triggers on insert, update, and delete operations. Triggers can perform many functions. One of the most common is the enforcement of relational integrity. Triggers are fired after the operation that triggered them has taken place, but they have the ability to roll back the operation. Views are sometimes used to present users or client applications with restricted data from a single table or data from multiple tables joined together. Triggers are not fired on changes to a view, but if the underlying table that is part of a view has a trigger installed on the operation taking place via the view, the trigger on the table is fired.

Triggers can also perform other operations on the table that fired the trigger or on other tables. One other common use of triggers is to maintain a totals field in a header record. For instance, if triggers exist on the inserts, updates, or deletions of an order item table, those triggers could maintain a total stored in an order header table. From a purely relational standpoint this is generally not considered good form, but it is often a solution when you require instant, current information about order balances. Of course, an invoice built from such a system must add the order lines to ensure that the total is correct to the penny. However, for ad hoc reporting and other purposes, such a total might be invaluable. Triggers ensure that the totals stored will be accurate virtually all the time.

The T-SQL code in Listing 13-1 gives you an idea of what a trigger can do. The purpose of this trigger is to create a specialized transaction record whenever a new record is inserted into the target table.

```
CREATE TRIGGER EXC_CHARGE_INSERT ON dbo.EXC_CHARGE_CODE
FOR INSERT
AS

DECLARE
@ID int,
    @ChargeCode varchar(20),
    @ChargeQuantity int,
    @ServiceDate dateTime,
    @PatientAccount float,
    @UsrID varchar(255),
    @OverrideDescription varchar(50),
    @ExceptionDateID int,
    @deptCode char(10),
    @timeNow datetime,
    @ExceptionDate datetime,
    @EnteringArea char(7),
    @EnteringAreaID char(10)

SELECT @ID=ID, @ChargeCode=Charge_Code,
    @ChargeQuantity=Convert(int, CHARGE_QUANTITY),
    @ServiceDate=Convert(datetime, CHARGE_SERVICE_DATE),
    @PatientAccount=PATIENT_ACCOUNT_NUMBER,
    @exceptionDateID=PA_PROCESSING_EXCEPTION_DATE_I,
    @UsrID=Usr_ID,
    @OverrideDescription=Convert(varchar(50),
        OVERRIDE_DESCRIPTION),
    @EnteringAreaID=ENTERING_AREA
FROM Inserted

exec MySP_GetDeptCode @ChargeCode, @deptCode OUTPUT
exec MySP_GetEnteringArea @EnteringAreaID, @EnteringArea OUTPUT

    INSERT INTO tblExceptionsSummary
        (Type, TypeFileID, ChargeCode,
        ChargeQuantity,ServiceDate,
        PatientAccount, UsrID,
        OverrideDescription, Dept,
        ExceptionDateID, DeptCode,
        EnteringArea)
```

**Listing 13-1**

```
    VALUES('CHARGE', @ID, @ChargeCode,
        @ChargeQuantity,
        @ServiceDate,@PatientAccount,
        @UsrID,@OverrideDescription,
        SUBSTRING(@ChargeCode, 1, 3),
        @exceptionDateID,
        @DeptCode,@EnteringArea)
GO
```

The trigger in Listing 13-1 shows many of the features that make T-SQL a suitable development environment for enhancing both client and server applications. Briefly, the purpose of the trigger is to get several fields from the inserted record, retrieve some data from two other files, and create a new record in another table. In doing so, the trigger illustrates the strengths of T-SQL. The first line actually creates the stored procedure:

```
CREATE TRIGGER EXC_CHARGE_INSERT ON dbo.EXC_CHARGE_CODE
FOR INSERT
AS
```

This is the syntax for creating any stored procedure. Of course, the trigger name, table name, and type of operation that will fire this trigger (in this case, *INSERT*) will vary.

The first strength of T-SQL highlighted by the trigger is the broad support for many different types within the language. Of course there are integers, but there are also *char*, *varchar*, and *dateTime* types. Variables start with a leading "at" sign (@). While none are used here, there are system variables that start with "@@".

Once the variables are declared, the trigger uses a *SELECT* statement to get the fields from the record that is being inserted—available as fields in the *Inserted* pseudotable—into the variables just declared. Next the trigger calls two stored procedures.

```
exec MySP_GetDeptCode @ChargeCode, @deptCode OUTPUT
exec MySP_GetEnteringArea @EnteringAreaID, @EnteringArea OUTPUT
```

These two lines execute two stored procedures. (I'll cover stored procedures in detail in the next section.) What's important about this code is how the variables are used. Each of these stored procedures, *MySP_GetDeptCode* and *MySP_GetEnteringArea*, expects two parameters. The first parameter in each case is one of the variables just retrieved from the *Inserted* pseudotable. The second parameter for each of the stored procedures is marked as an *OUTPUT* parameter, meaning that a value will be returned in those variables.

Finally, the trigger inserts a record into another table, taking the values from the inserted record and those retrieved using stored procedures. In many cases a trigger for this type of operation could be performed using a compound statement that feeds the *INSERT* statement with values from a *SELECT* statement. This was not possible in the example trigger because some exotic field type transformations were required. Thankfully, T-SQL allowed the required operations to take place.

One complication that often occurs when we work within the SQL language is type incompatibility. T-SQL provides a convenient function named *CONVERT* that converts variables from one type to another:

```
CONVERT (data_type[(length)], expression [, style])
```

*CONVERT* accepts as parameters the data type and the expression to convert and, optionally, the style. This optional parameter is used for formatting when converting date/time types into strings. There is also a *CAST* function that performs a similar operation. Listing 13-1 shows several examples of *CONVERT*.

*SUBSTRING* is another function built into T-SQL:

```
SUBSTRING(expression, start, length)
```

*SUBSTRING* accepts three parameters. The first is *expression*, which should evaluate to a character string, binary string, text, image, or column. The return value is *length* bytes of *expression* starting at *start*. This function is used in Listing 13-1 to allow part of a field to be saved into a smaller field.

One advantage of triggers is their ability to offload required functionality from the client to the server. Recall the first scenario mentioned above.

> *You must design a system that uses Web clients for inquiry and simple data entry and also uses a Microsoft Visual Basic client for more sophisticated data entry and reporting. Both systems can insert records into the database. Inserting a record into one table should be accompanied by insertion of several records into another table.*

How can triggers help you in this scenario? A common challenge of developing multiple clients to act on a single database is ensuring that each client behaves the same way for the same operation.

For example, I created a document-tracking system that allowed documents to be added from either a traditional fat client program or from a Web application. When a document was added to the tracking system, a series of operations needed to take place, depending on the document's attributes. One of those operations involved routing the documents to responsible parties. This required looking up document-responsibility information from a table and then creating routing records in another table. One of my concerns was ensuring that no matter which way the documents were entered they would create the same routing records. This is problematic even during initial implementation, but virtually impossible during updates, which might not always have the two types of client applications in synch.

Triggers provided me with a solution by moving functionality away from the clients to the server. The trigger was fired for all clients. Even if a third client came on board—perhaps a Microsoft Visual C++ application—the operation performed by the stored procedure would work exactly as it did for the existing clients.

Triggers can also help in situations in which totals need to be maintained, such as the second scenario described above.

> *You need to create an order entry system that will notify a system administrator whenever a customer's outstanding balance exceeds predefined limits. You would also like to have quick and easy reporting of customer balances without having to read through the entire database.*

Relational design dictates that totals should not be carried in records in which related records would allow calculation of the totals. This is a good rule, and one that I always followed before the advent of reliable systems with available triggers. While I still seldom violate that rule, I find that trigger-maintained totals can be a lifesaver for some situations, such as the scenario mentioned above. Properly written triggers allow us to maintain totals with reasonable reliability. They also have a 0 default value for the fields that contain the totals. For huge databases that require up-to-the-minute information about totals, triggers can be crucial.

## Stored Procedures

Stored procedures are another way to off-load processing and business logic to the server. In the example I just mentioned, where a trigger maintains totals, a stored procedure could allow standardized logic to calculate the totals no matter where they will be used or displayed. Any bit of business logic that needs to be used by multiple applications is a good candidate for stored procedures.

Listing 13-1 used two stored procedures. One of the stored procedures was named *MySP_GetEnteringArea*. Its source is shown in Listing 13-2:

```
CREATE PROCEDURE MySP_GetEnteringArea
    @EnteringAreaID char(10),
    @EnteringArea char(7) OUTPUT AS
    SELECT @EnteringArea = CHARGE_ENTERING_AREA.code
    FROM CHARGE_ENTERING_AREA
    WHERE CHARGE_ENTERING_AREA_ID =
        CONVERT(float, @EnteringAreaID)
```

**Listing 13-2**

This simple stored procedure does little more than call a *SELECT* statement and return a character string. The syntax for creating a stored procedure is similar to the syntax for creating a trigger. Why would such a simple *SELECT* statement not be called directly from the trigger? There are two reasons for this.

The first reason is that the function performed by this example stored procedure is a common requirement throughout the system I took it from. Placing this function in a stored procedure allows any changes required when looking up an entering area to be handled in the stored procedure. The importance of being able to hide the implementation was brought home to me when I recently needed to change the field type of *CHARGE_ENTERING_AREA_ID* in Listing 13-2. Dozens of other stored procedures and triggers used this stored procedure to get the entering area, passing in the *EnteringAreaID* as a 10-byte character string. A new release of the vendor's product changed *CHARGE_ENTERING_AREA_ID*'s type to a float field. Because the logic to return the entering area was encapsulated in this stored procedure, the stored procedure had to change—but little else did. In other situations, more than just a data type might change. Underlying business rules can be encoded and enforced in stored procedures. When these business rules change, as they often do, the stored procedure can change without requiring widespread changes throughout a SQL Server application.

The second reason is that stored procedures can be faster than calling *SELECT* statements scattered throughout code on the server or in the client application. *Inside Microsoft SQL Server 7.0* by Ron Soukup and Kalen Delaney (Microsoft Press, 1999) details the reasons why stored procedures offer a performance advantage. The advantage comes primarily from the fact that stored procedures are checked for syntax and compiled only the first time they are run.

Stored procedures provided with SQL Server conventionally use *sp_* as the first three characters of their names. In Listings 13-1 and 13-2, I prefixed my stored procedures with the somewhat unoriginal *mySP_*. Using a standard scheme to name your stored procedures is entirely optional. In some cases even the names of stored procedures that come with SQL Server are less than perfect. In at least one situation, a procedure beginning with *sp_* is not in fact a stored procedure but an extended stored procedure (covered in the next section). For multiprogrammer projects in which many programmers will be creating stored procedures, some naming conventions should be implemented to ensure consistency of stored procedure names.

## Extended Stored Procedures

As we have seen, T-SQL is a powerful language that is quite capable when manipulating databases. Unfortunately, not every object is a database. Devices and even other applications might require attention. SQL Server provides one more way to extend itself: extended stored procedures.

Extended stored procedures are created using any language capable of creating a DLL. Since stored procedures are in DLLs, you aren't required to create a new process when you call them. Rather, SQL Server loads the DLL into its own address space, and one of SQL Server's threads runs the extended stored procedure function. The implications of this structure should be obvious: Be sure that the function you intend to use as an extended stored procedure can handle exceptions and can follow all the other rules for multithreaded applications. One more important rule is to avoid changing anything related to the global state of the process. These changes affect not only your extended stored procedure, but SQL Server as well. While in theory an extended stored procedure could do all sorts of damage to SQL Server, in practice such damage seldom occurs.

Remember the third scenario mentioned at the beginning of the chapter?

> *You need to create a system that will access the e-mail system, but not all client machines will have the e-mail client installed. Nor, for that matter, will all users have their own e-mail accounts.*

The extended stored procedures that come standard with SQL Server can solve this problem. As I promised during the MAPI discussion in Chapter 7, there is a way to allow SQL Server to perform some simple e-mail operations. The machine on which SQL Server runs must meet two requirements. First the machine must have a valid MAPI profile. Second the administrator must configure SQL Mail on the server.

Figure 13-1 shows SQL Server Enterprise Manager with the Support Services folder open. If you right-click on SQL Mail and select Properties, the dialog in Figure 13-2 will appear. Select a profile from the drop-down list, and decide whether SQL Mail should start when SQL Server starts. Then click on Test to ensure SQL Mail is working. Click OK, and SQL Mail should be enabled.

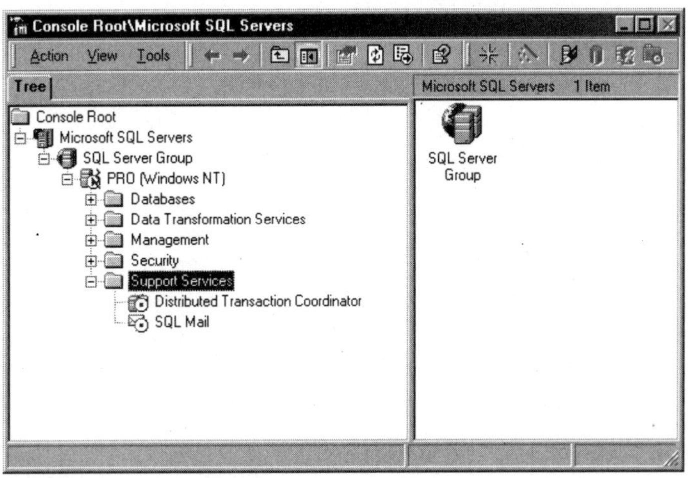


**Figure 13-1** *The SQL Server Enterprise Manager screen with the Support Services folder open.*

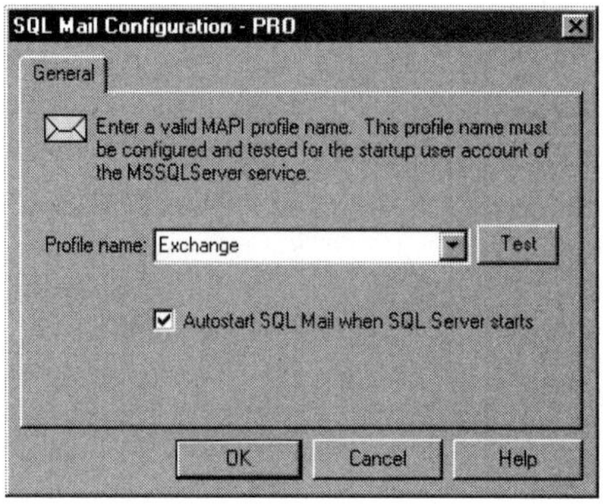


**Figure 13-2** *The dialog to set a SQL Mail profile.*

Using the extended stored procedures for sending and receiving mail is fairly straightforward if you use most of the defaults. The procedure to send mail is named *xp_sendmail.*

```
xp_sendmail {[@recipients =] 'recipients [;...n]'}
    [,[@message =] 'message']
    [,[@query =] 'query']
    [,[@attachments =] attachments]
    [,[@copy_recipients =] 'copy_recipients [;...n]'
    [,[@blind_copy_recipients =] 'blind_copy_recipients [;...n]'
    [,[@subject =] 'subject']
    [,[@type =] 'type']
    [,[@attach_results =] 'attach_value']
    [,[@no_output =] 'output_value']
    [,[@no_header =] 'header_value']
    [,[@width =] width]
    [,[@separator =] 'separator']
    [,[@echo_error =] 'echo_value']
    [,[@set_user =] 'user']
    [,[@dbuse =] 'database']
```

Most of these parameters are not needed. *Recipients*, *subject*, and *message* are often all that you'll need. For example, the Troubleshooter database used in Chapter 9 is used at a site where end users are allowed to enter new troubleshooting documents. The newly entered documents are placed in a pending state so that the subject matter expert can look the article over and verify that the information is correct. Rather than require subject matter area experts to search for pending documents, I had SQL Server use the Insert trigger to send e-mail whenever a record was added. The code to send the e-mail was simple:

```
exec xp_sendmail @recipients = 'DReilly@webspan.net',
    @subject = 'There is a new document waiting!',
    @message = 'A new document has been added.'
```

The other arguments for *xp_sendmail* are described fully in the MSDN documentation of the SQL Server Books Online.

Reading mail with SQL Mail is similar to reading mail with Simple MAPI, which I covered in Chapter 7. First *xp_findnextmsg* must be called, and then *xp_readmail* is called to actually read the mail. The syntax for these two extended stored procedures is listed here. Most of the arguments to the extended stored procedures mirror either Simple MAPI arguments or elements in the MAPI message structures.

```
xp_findnextmsg [[@msg_id =] 'message_number' [OUTPUT]]
    [,[@type =] type]
    [,[@unread_only =] 'unread_value'])

xp_readmail [[@msg_id =] 'message_number']
    [,[@type =] 'type' [OUTPUT]]
    [,[@peek =] 'peek']
    [,[@suppress_attach =] 'suppress_attach']
    [,[@originator =] 'sender' OUTPUT]
    [,[@subject =] 'subject' OUTPUT]
    [,[@message =] 'message' OUTPUT]
    [,[@recipients =] 'recipients [;...n]' OUTPUT]
    [,[@cc_list =] 'copy_recipients [;...n]' OUTPUT]
    [,[@bcc_list =] 'blind_copy_recipients [;...n]' OUTPUT]
    [,[@date_received =] 'date' OUTPUT]
    [,[@unread =] 'unread_value' OUTPUT]
    [,[@attachments =] 'attachments [;...n]' OUTPUT])
    [,[@skip_bytes =] bytes_to_skip OUTPUT]
    [,[@msg_length =] length_in_bytes OUTPUT]
    [,[@originator_address =] 'sender_address' OUTPUT]]
```

Of course, using extended stored procedures to send and receive mail with SQL Server is a primitive operation. All of the limitations of Simple MAPI are present, including the inability to delete messages in folders other than the Inbox. Even with all of these limitations, however, using extended stored procedures this way has some advantages:

- Mail can originate as a by-product of a database operation.
- Users who do not have e-mail access can indirectly send mail.
- There are ways to use e-mail to send query requests and return result sets. MSDN and SQL Server Books Online provide much more information on this feature.

### Creating a custom extended stored procedure

The extended stored procedures that come with SQL Server are a good start. Since extended stored procedures are functions exported from a DLL, can we create our own extended stored procedure? Thankfully, the answer is yes.

The Open Data Services API (ODSAPI) provides the tools required to build a DLL that can contain functions exported as extended stored procedures. ODSAPI provides more than 60 functions that support the creation of extended stored procedures. Our example will use just a few of these functions, but all are documented in SQL Server Books Online.

The steps required to create an extended stored procedure using Visual C++ 6 are as follows:

1. Create a new Win32 DLL project.
2. Add an include line for Srv.h to the StdAfx.h file.
3. Add Opends60.lib to the project's libraries.
4. Add the \mssql7\devtools\include directory to the include directories list, and add \mssql7\devtools\lib to the library directories list.
5. A 1-KB copy of Srv.h is included with Microsoft Visual Studio 6. It appears to be missing some crucial information that is included with the 17-KB Srv.h included with SQL Server. Rename the smaller file, or arrange the include directory order so that the larger one is read first. If you are creating a C++ program and you receive unresolved externals on mangled function names while linking, you are probably finding the wrong header.
6. A 39-KB copy of Opends60.lib is included with Visual Studio 6. It appears to be missing some crucial information that is included with the 84-KB Opends60.lib included with SQL Server. Rename the smaller file, or arrange the library directory order so that the larger one is read first. If you are creating a C++ program and you receive error messages about unresolved externals on function names that are exactly as they appear in the header—especially *srv_paraminfo*—while linking, you are probably finding the wrong library.
7. Create a function named *__GetXpVersion*. Note the two underscores. This function must be exported by your DLL. The function needs to have only a single line of code:

```
ULONG APIENTRY __GetXpVersion(void)
{
    return ODS_VERSION;
}
```

If trace flag -7260 is set, SQL Server calls this function to determine the version of ODSAPI used. If this callback is not present, or if the version reported is less than what the server requires, a warning message is returned when the function is called.

A great deal of code is required in an extended stored procedure simply to get to the arguments and return a value. From a SQL Server perspective, the function exposed as a stored procedure does not directly accept the number of arguments the extended stored procedure accepts. For instance, if we wanted SQL Server to initiate a call to a beeper, the extended stored procedure would accept two parameters. The first parameter is the beeper number, and the second is the number to be beeped, just like the *CallBeeper* function in Listing 7-2 in Chapter 7.

Listing 13-3 shows Xp_beep.cpp—the code that creates the stored procedure *xp_beep*.

**Xp_beep.cpp**

```
// xp_beep.cpp : xp_beep stored procedure
//

#include "stdafx.h"
#define XP_NOERROR 0
#define XP_ERROR   1
char *ReportTAPIError(LONG ret, char *op, char *buff)
{
    switch (ret)
    {
    case LINEERR_INVALAPPNAME:
        wsprintf(buff, "\nop=%s Ret=LINEERR_INVALAPPNAME", op);
        break;
    case LINEERR_OPERATIONFAILED:
        wsprintf(buff, "\nop=%s Ret=LINEERR_OPERATIONFAILED", op);
        break;
    case LINEERR_INIFILECORRUPT:
        wsprintf(buff, "\nop=%s Ret=LINEERR_INIFILECORRUPT", op);
        break;
    case LINEERR_INVALPOINTER:
        wsprintf(buff, "\nop=%s Ret=LINEERR_INVALPOINTER", op);
        break;
    case LINEERR_REINIT:
        wsprintf(buff, "\nop=%s Ret=LINEERR_REINIT", op);
        break;
    case LINEERR_NOMEM:
        wsprintf(buff, "\nop=%s Ret=LINEERR_NOMEM", op);
        break;
```

**Listing 13-3** *(continued)*

**Listing 13-3** *continued*

```
    case LINEERR_INVALPARAM:
        wsprintf(buff, "\nop=%s Ret=LINEERR_INVALPARAM", op);
        break;
    case LINEERR_BADDEVICEID:
        wsprintf(buff, "\nop=%s Ret=LINEERR_BADDEVICEID", op);
        break;
    case LINEERR_NODRIVER:
        wsprintf(buff, "\nop=%s Ret=LINEERR_NODRIVER", op);
        break;
    case LINEERR_INCOMPATIBLEAPIVERSION:
        wsprintf(buff, "\nop=%s Ret=LINEERR_INCOMPATIBLEAPIVERSION",
            op);
        break;
    case LINEERR_INVALAPPHANDLE:
        wsprintf(buff, "\nop=%s Ret=LINEERR_INVALAPPHANDLE", op);
        break;
    case LINEERR_RESOURCEUNAVAIL:
        wsprintf(buff, "\nop=%s Ret=LINEERR_RESOURCEUNAVAIL", op);
        break;
    case LINEERR_UNINITIALIZED:
        wsprintf(buff, "\nop=%s Ret=LINEERR_UNINITIALIZED", op);
        break;
    case LINEERR_OPERATIONUNAVAIL:
        wsprintf(buff, "\nop=%s Ret=LINEERR_OPERATIONUNAVAIL", op);
        break;
    case LINEERR_NODEVICE:
        wsprintf(buff, "\nop=%s Ret=LINEERR_NODEVICE", op);
        break;
    case LINEERR_ALLOCATED:
        wsprintf(buff, "\nop=%s Ret=LINEERR_ALLOCATED", op);
        break;
    case LINEERR_LINEMAPPERFAILED:
        wsprintf(buff, "\nop=%s Ret=LINEERR_LINEMAPPERFAILED", op);
        break;
    case LINEERR_INCOMPATIBLEEXTVERSION:
        wsprintf(buff, "\nop=%s Ret=LINEERR_INCOMPATIBLEEXTVERSION",
            op);
        break;
    case LINEERR_INVALMEDIAMODE:
        wsprintf(buff, "\nop=%s Ret=LINEERR_INVALMEDIAMODE", op);
        break;
    case LINEERR_STRUCTURETOOSMALL:
        wsprintf(buff,"\nop=%s Ret=LINEERR_STRUCTURETOOSMALL", op);
        break;
```

```
    case LINEERR_INVALPRIVSELECT:
        wsprintf(buff, "\nop=%s Ret=LINEERR_INVALPRIVSELECT", op);
        break;
    case LINEERR_ADDRESSBLOCKED:
        wsprintf(buff, "\nop=%s Ret=LINEERR_ADDRESSBLOCKED", op);
        break;
    case LINEERR_DIALBILLING:
        wsprintf(buff, "\nop=%s Ret=LINEERR_DIALBILLING", op);
        break;
    case LINEERR_DIALDIALTONE:
        wsprintf(buff,"\nop=%s Ret=LINEERR_DIALDIALTONE", op);
        break;
    case LINEERR_NOTOWNER:
        wsprintf(buff, "\nop=%s Ret=LINEERR_NOTOWNER", op);
        break;
    case LINEERR_DIALPROMPT:
        wsprintf(buff, "\nop=%s Ret=LINEERR_DIALPROMPT", op);
        break;
    case LINEERR_DIALQUIET:
        wsprintf(buff, "\nop=%s Ret=LINEERR_DIALQUIET", op);
        break;
    case LINEERR_INVALCALLHANDLE:
        wsprintf(buff, "\nop=%s Ret=LINEERR_INVALCALLHANDLE", op);
        break;
    case LINEERR_INVALCALLSTATE:
        wsprintf(buff, "\nop=%s Ret=LINEERR_INVALCALLSTATE", op);
        break;
    case LINEERR_INVALCOUNTRYCODE:
        wsprintf(buff, "\nop=%s Ret=LINEERR_INVALCOUNTRYCODE", op);
        break;
    }
    return (buff);
}
int CallBeeper(char *beeperNumber, char *beepTo, char *retBuffer)
{
    HLINEAPP hLineApp;
    HLINE hLine;
    char szFriendlyAppName[255];
    char szAddress[255];
    DWORD dwNumDevs = 0;
    DWORD dwAPIVersion = 0x00020000;
    DWORD dwCallbackInstance = 43;
    DWORD dwStatus;
    DWORD dwDeviceID = 0;
```

*(continued)*

**Listing 13-3** *continued*

```
LONG ret;
int funcRet = -1;
LINEINITIALIZEEXPARAMS LineInitializeExParams;
LINEEXTENSIONID ExtensionID;
LPLINEDEVCAPS DevCaps = NULL;

strcpy(szFriendlyAppName,
    "TAPI Beeper Extended Stored Procedure");
memset((void *)&LineInitializeExParams,
    0, sizeof(LINEINITIALIZEEXPARAMS));
LineInitializeExParams.dwTotalSize =
    sizeof(LINEINITIALIZEEXPARAMS);
LineInitializeExParams.dwOptions =
    LINEINITIALIZEEXOPTION_USEEVENT;

ret = lineInitializeEx(&hLineApp, NULL, NULL, szFriendlyAppName,
    &dwNumDevs, &dwAPIVersion, &LineInitializeExParams);
ReportTAPIError(ret, "lineInitializeEx", retBuffer);
if (ret == 0)
{
    // It worked!
    // Loop through available devices until we find a good one.
    for (dwDeviceID = 0; dwDeviceID < dwNumDevs; dwDeviceID++)
    {
        ret = lineNegotiateAPIVersion(
            hLineApp,
            dwDeviceID,
            0x00020000,
            0x00020001,
            &dwAPIVersion,
            &ExtensionID);
        if (ret == 0)
        {
            ret = lineOpen(hLineApp, dwDeviceID, &hLine,
                dwAPIVersion, 0, dwCallbackInstance,
                LINECALLPRIVILEGE_NONE, 0, 0);
            ReportTAPIError(ret, "lineOpen", retBuffer);
            if (ret == 0)
            {
                break;
            }
        }
    }
```

```
        ReportTAPIError(ret, "lineNegotiateAPIVersion", retBuffer);
        if (ret == 0)
        {

            HCALL hCall;
            char szLineName[255];

            DevCaps = (LPLINEDEVCAPS)new char[1024];
            DevCaps->dwTotalSize = 1024;
            ret = lineGetDevCaps(hLineApp,
                dwDeviceID, dwAPIVersion, 0, DevCaps);
            ReportTAPIError(ret, "lineGetDevCaps", retBuffer);
            if (ret >= 0 && DevCaps->dwLineNameSize > 0)
            {
                if (DevCaps->dwLineNameSize > (254))
                {
                    strncpy (szLineName,
                        (LPSTR) DevCaps +
                        DevCaps->dwLineNameOffset,
                        254);
                    szLineName[254] = '\0';
                }
                else
                {
                    lstrcpy(szLineName,
                        (LPSTR) DevCaps +
                        DevCaps->dwLineNameOffset);
                }
            }
            delete (char *)DevCaps;

            // Set the address, which is really a phone number.
            wsprintf(szAddress, "%s,,,%s#", beeperNumber, beepTo);
            ret = lineMakeCall(hLine, &hCall, szAddress, 0, 0);
            if (ret > 0)
            {
                wsprintf(retBuffer, "lineMakeCall returned %d", ret);
            }
            else
            {
                funcRet = 0;
            }
            ReportTAPIError(ret, "lineMakeCall", retBuffer);
```

*(continued)*

**Listing 13-3** *continued*

```
            while ((dwStatus = WaitForSingleObject(
            LineInitializeExParams.Handles.hEvent,
                20000)) == WAIT_OBJECT_0)
            {
                LINEMESSAGE lm;
                // TAPI's returning some information...
                if ((ret = lineGetMessage(hLineApp, &lm, 0)) != 0)
                {
                ReportTAPIError(ret, "lineGetMessage", retBuffer);
                    return (ret);
                }
                switch (lm.dwMessageID)
                {
                case LINE_REPLY:
                    if ((long)lm.dwParam2 < 0)
                    {
                        wsprintf(retBuffer,
                            "\nError occured...Request ID %d",
                            lm.dwParam1);
                    }
                    break;
                case LINE_CALLSTATE:
                    if (LINECALLSTATE_DISCONNECTED&lm.dwParam1)
                    {
                        lineClose(hLine);
                    }

                    if (LINECALLSTATE_IDLE&lm.dwParam1)
                    {
                        lineClose(hLine);
                    }
                } //...switch (lm.dwMessageID)
            }//...while ((dwStatus = WaitForSingleObject(
        }//...if (ret == 0)
    }
    lineShutdown(hLineApp);
    return 0;
}

BOOL APIENTRY DllMain(HANDLE hModule,
                      DWORD  ul_reason_for_call,
                      LPVOID lpReserved
                     )
```

```
{
    return TRUE;
}

ULONG APIENTRY __GetXpVersion(void)
{
    return ODS_VERSION;
}
// We expect this function to receive 2 parameters.
SRVRETCODE xp_beep(SRV_PROC *pSrvProc)
{
    int paramCount;
    int ret;
    BYTE cType;
    unsigned long cbMaxLen = 255;
    unsigned long cbActualLen = 255;
    BOOL bNull;
    char beeperNumber[255];
    char beepTo[255];
    char szText[255];

    memset(beeperNumber, '\0', 255);
    memset(beepTo, '\0', 255);
    memset(szText, '\0', 255);

    paramCount = srv_rpcparams(pSrvProc);

    if (paramCount != 2)
    {
        return (XP_ERROR);
    }

    ret = srv_paraminfo(pSrvProc,
        1,
        &cType,
        &cbMaxLen,
        &cbActualLen,
        (BYTE *)&beeperNumber[0],
        &bNull);

    if (cType != SRVBIGCHAR &&
        cType != SRVBIGVARCHAR &&
        cType != SRVVARCHAR)
```

*(continued)*

**Listing 13-3** *continued*

```
    {
        return (XP_ERROR);
    }
    if (cbActualLen > 255)
    {
        return (XP_ERROR);
    }

    cbMaxLen = cbActualLen = 255;

    ret = srv_paraminfo(pSrvProc,
        2,
        &cType,
        &cbMaxLen,
        &cbActualLen,
        (BYTE *)&beepTo[0],
        &bNull);

    if (cType != SRVBIGCHAR &&
        cType != SRVBIGVARCHAR &&
        cType != SRVVARCHAR)
    {
        return (XP_ERROR);
    }
    if (cbActualLen > 255)
    {
        return (XP_ERROR);
    }

    __try
    {
        __try
        {
            if (CallBeeper(beeperNumber, beepTo, szText) == 0)
            {
                wsprintf(szText, "Calling %s with %s",
                    beeperNumber, beepTo);
            }
        }
        __except(EXCEPTION_EXECUTE_HANDLER)
        {
            strcpy(szText, "Exception in XP_BEEP");
        }
    }
```

```
    __finally
    {
        ret = srv_describe(pSrvProc, 1,
            "Message", SRV_NULLTERM,
            SRVBIGVARCHAR, strlen(szText),
            SRVBIGVARCHAR, strlen(szText),
            szText);
        ret = srv_sendrow(pSrvProc);

        ret = srv_senddone(pSrvProc,
            (SRV_DONE_COUNT | SRV_DONE_MORE),
            0, 1);
    }

    return (XP_NOERROR);
}
```

At the top of the listing two constants are defined that will signal success or failure as the return code. Next come several functions that are similar to the functions in Listing 7-2. There are a couple of changes. First *ReportTAPIError* accepts three parameters, the third being a buffer that will accept the translated error. Next *CallBuffer* accepts an additional parameter—the return buffer that will receive a string reporting on the success or failure of the operation.

The *__GetXpVersion* function is as described on page 476. The heart of the stored procedure is *xp_beep*, the last procedure defined in Listing 13-3. The prototype for this procedure is common to all extended stored procedures.

```
SRVRETCODE xp_beep(SRV_PROC *pSrvProc)
```

The *pSrvProc* parameter is used as a handle for other functions related to creating an extended stored procedure. From this handle, the stored procedure code can discover the type and number of parameters passed to the extended stored procedure. The parameter count is returned by a call to *srv_rpcparams*, a function that accepts as a single parameter *pSrvProc*, the parameter to the stored procedure. The parameter count is tested against the number required. If too few were sent, an error is returned.

Once the parameter count is retrieved, the next step is to retrieve the parameters and validate that the parameter types are correct. For each expected parameter, *srv_paraminfo* is called.

```
int srv_paraminfo (
    SRV_PROC * srvproc,
    int n,
    BYTE * pbType,
    ULONG * pcbMaxLen,
    ULONG * pcbActualLen,
    BYTE * pbData,
    BOOL * pfNull);
```

The first parameter is the pointer passed to the extended stored procedure. The second parameter, *n*, is the parameter number. Parameters are counted starting with 1, so the first parameter is 1, the second 2, and so on. The type of parameter is returned in the variable pointed to by *pbType*. The maximum and actual lengths are returned in *pcbMaxLen* and *pcbActualLen*, respectively. The actual parameter data is passed back in the buffer pointed to by *bpData*. If the parameter is NULL, the variable pointed to by *pfNull* is set to TRUE.

For each of the two expected parameters we perform two checks, one to verify the correct type and one to verify the maximum length. The code to do this is as follows:

```
if (cType != SRVBIGCHAR &&
    cType != SRVBIGVARCHAR &&
    cType != SRVVARCHAR)
{
    return (XP_ERROR);
}
if (cbActualLen > 255)
{
    return (XP_ERROR);
}
```

The possible data types are covered in MSDN in the Open Data Services Reference. In this example, I am filtering to ensure a normal character type is passed. Once the parameters have been validated, *CallBeeper* is called inside a *__try*/*__except* block. This is to ensure that any exception thrown by *CallBeeper* does not bubble up beyond the extended stored procedure DLL.

To return a result to SQL Server, we create a single column to be part of the result set. This requires three steps. First we call *srv_describe*:

```
int srv_describe (
    SRV_PROC * srvproc,
    int colnumber,
    DBCHAR * column_name,
    int namelen,
    DBINT desttype,
    DBINT destlen,
    DBINT srctype,
    DBINT srclen,
    void * srcdata);
```

The first parameter is the pointer passed as the parameter to the extended stored procedure. The second parameter is *colnumber*, the column number of this parameter in the result set. The name of the column is sent as *column_name*. The balance of the parameters are self-explanatory. The *desttype* and *srctype* parameters contain Open Data Services data types, the same type passed in to *srv_paraminfo* as *pbType*. In the second step, after the row is described and set, we call *srv_sendrow* with a single parameter, *pSrvProc*—the parameter passed to the extended stored procedure. Third we call *srv_senddone*.

```
int srv_senddone (
    SRV_PROC * srvproc,
    DBUSMALLINT status,
    DBUSMALLINT info,
    DBINT count);
```

The first parameter is the same pointer passed to all Open Data Services functions. The *status* parameter can contain one or more of the flags described in Table 13-1.

**TABLE 13-1**
**FLAG VALUES FOR STATUS PARAMETER OF *SRV_SENDDONE***

| *Status Flag* | *Meaning* |
|---|---|
| SRV_DONE_FINAL | The current result set is the final result. |
| SRV_DONE_MORE | The current result set is not the final result. |
| SRV_DONE_COUNT | The count parameter contains a valid count. |
| SRV_DONE_ERROR | The current client command receives an error. |
| SRV_DONE_RPC_IN_BATCH | The current results are the final results in this batch of remote stored procedures. |

In the example, *status* is set to SRV_DONE_FINAL | SRV_DONE_COUNT, meaning that this is the last result and the *count* parameter has a valid record count—1. The third parameter is unused, and 0 should be passed.

### Installing and using our extended stored procedure

Once we create our extended stored procedure, we should copy it to a directory where SQL Server can find it. When we've done that, the easiest way to interactively test the extended stored procedure is to load the SQL Server Query Analyzer. A stored procedure, *sp_addextendedproc*, is used to install the extended stored procedure. This stored procedure expects two parameters, the name of the extended stored procedure function (which is case-sensitive) and the name of the DLL (which has the DLL extension). Optionally, the name of the extended stored procedure can be prefixed by the owner name in the form *owner.function*. Figure 13-3 shows the screen after *xp_beep* has been installed.

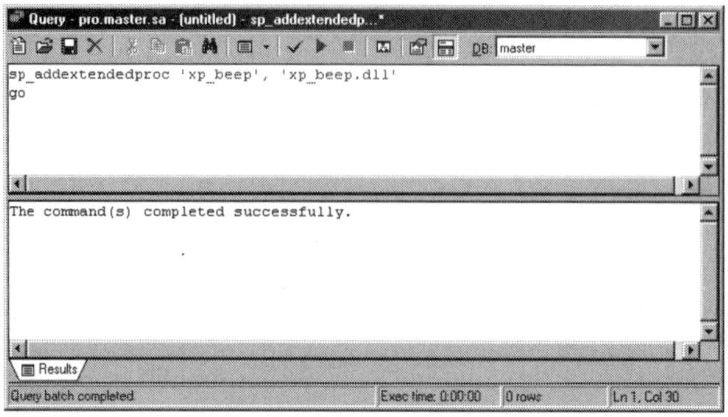


**Figure 13-3** *SQL Server Query Analyzer showing* xp_beep *being installed.*

Figure 13-4 shows how the extended stored procedure is called and the results returned. To remove the extended stored procedure, *sp_dropextendedproc* can be called with the name of the extended stored procedure as its single parameter.

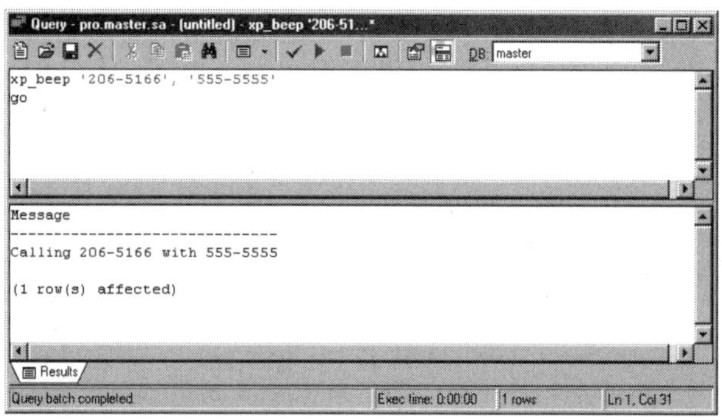


**Figure 13-4** *Running* xp_beep *in the SQL Server Query Analyzer.*

# CONCLUSION

Choosing to use the flexibility of SQL Server is a smart and easy decision. What is surprising is the ease of use offered by today's developer tools. In years past, developing triggers and stored procedures was difficult work, and the tools available were not terribly helpful. SQL Server 6.5's Enterprise Manager offered developers little in the way of assistance when they edited SQL code.

Times have changed. Both SQL Server 7 and Microsoft Visual Studio offer tools for developing SQL code; these tools will seem familiar to developers who use integrated development environments for other languages. Niceties such as color-coded syntax highlighting have been joined by source-level debugging abilities.

While the server world has changed, the client world has not been standing still. Though supporting multiple types of clients has always been a problem, the Web has made that task an even more familiar scenario. This greater need to support multiple clients increases the need to offload processing to servers. Encapsulating business rules inside the database server is a natural solution.

Long-time SQL Server developers are already well aware of the joys of business logic residing on the server. These same developers might not be aware of extended stored procedures. Even those who know about extended stored procedures might have shied away from using them for fear of degrading SQL Server reliability. Unlike many of the projects for this book, the extended stored procedure *xp_beep* worked the first time and never caused any problem with SQL Server. Of course, an extended stored procedure could still damage SQL Server, but that fear has been overhyped. For SQL Server programmers who have hit the wall programming in T-SQL, extended stored procedures offer a flexible solution.

Part III

# Building Windows 2000 Server Applications

*Chapter 14*

# A Traditional Service Application

Thus far I have given you short examples that show how to implement a particular aspect of a server-based application. In this chapter, we will create a server-based application from soup to nuts. The final application will have some concessions to make it a better teaching tool, but it will be a workable server-based application. In Chapter 15, we will further enhance the application by adding support for Internet monitoring and management. This sample application uses many of the features that we've examined throughout the book.

## A Network Monitor

One thing that becomes apparent as you create and use more server-based applications is that keeping track of what is running and what is not running becomes an ever-increasing part of your job. Your organization might have an operations staff responsible for monitoring the performance of server-based applications. Even with this support, however, failures can be missed and not caught until the worst possible time.

Network monitoring is a real-life problem that looks a lot like a common programming problem: poll vs. interrupt. Using an operations staff to monitor your servers is a lot like having a program that constantly checks on the state of a variable or a system setting—often called polling. Asynchronous operations, or interrupts, often make more efficient use of system resources. Allowing your server-based applications to interrupt—rather than having a human being constantly poll their status—can be very useful.

## What Is a Network Monitor?

A network monitor is a dedicated workstation or server that tests the state of equipment and services on the network. The system checks for failures and then uses available resources to notify the responsible person. These notifications can be sent via e-mail, pager, or any other notification method on hand.

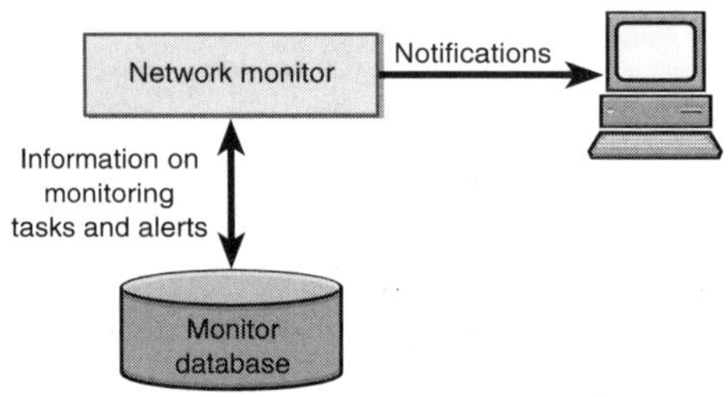


**Figure 14-1** *The relationship between the network monitor, the monitor database, and the user.*

Figure 14-1 shows the relationship between the network monitor, the monitor database, and end users. The network monitor periodically queries the monitor database to determine what tasks should be performed. If a failure occurs, an alert message is written back to the monitor database, and depending upon the criteria, a notification will be sent to the user. The monitor database could be something as simple as an INI file or as complex as a complete Microsoft SQL Server database. For this example I use a SQL Server database. The structure of the database is outlined in the SQL creation script presented in Listing 14-1.

**CreateTables.sql**

```
CREATE TABLE [dbo].[TblAlerts] (
    [AlertID] [int] IDENTITY (1, 1) NOT NULL ,
    [TaskID] [int] NOT NULL ,
    [DateTimeOfAlert] [datetime] NULL ,
    [DateTimeReset] [datetime] NULL ,
    [DateTimeIntervention] [datetime] NULL ,
    [ResetTypeID] [int] NULL ,
    [AlertComment] [varchar] (255) NULL,
    [ResetComment] [varchar] (255) NULL
)
GO
```

**Listing 14-1**

```
CREATE TABLE [dbo].[TblResetType] (
    [ResetTypeID] [int] IDENTITY (1, 1) NOT NULL ,
    [Description] [char] (50) NULL
)  ON [PRIMARY]
GO

CREATE TABLE [dbo].[TblTasks] (
    [TaskID] [int] IDENTITY (1, 1) NOT NULL ,
    [Name] [char] (50) NOT NULL ,
    [ExecuteType] [int] NULL ,
    [Executable] [varchar] (50) NULL ,
    [Function] [varchar] (255) NULL ,
    [Parameter1] [varchar] (50) NULL ,
    [Parameter2] [varchar] (50) NULL ,
    [Parameter3] [varchar] (50) NULL ,
    [Parameter4] [varchar] (50) NULL ,
    [DateTimeLastRun] [datetime] NULL ,
    [AtOrEvery] [char] (1) NULL ,
    [EveryType] [char] (30) NULL ,
    [RunAtTime] [datetime] NULL ,
    [DateTimeNextRun] [datetime] NULL ,
    [RunEveryInterval] [int] NULL
    [Beeper] varchar(50) NULL,
    [Email] varchar(128) NULL) ON [PRIMARY]
GO

ALTER TABLE [dbo].[TblAlerts] WITH NOCHECK ADD
    CONSTRAINT [PK_TblAlerts]
PRIMARY KEY  CLUSTERED
    (
        [AlertID]
    )  ON [PRIMARY]
GO

ALTER TABLE [dbo].[TblResetType] WITH NOCHECK ADD
    CONSTRAINT [PK_TblResetType]
PRIMARY KEY  NONCLUSTERED
    (
        [ResetTypeID]
    )  ON [PRIMARY]
GO

ALTER TABLE [dbo].[TblTasks] WITH NOCHECK ADD
    CONSTRAINT [PK_TblTasks]
```

*(continued)*

**Listing 14-1** *continued*

```
PRIMARY KEY  NONCLUSTERED
    (
        [TaskID]
    )  ON [PRIMARY]
GO

CREATE  INDEX [IX_TblAlerts] ON
    [dbo].[TblAlerts]([TaskID]) ON [PRIMARY]
GO

CREATE  INDEX [IX_TblAlerts_1] ON
    [dbo].[TblAlerts]([DateTimeOfAlert]) ON [PRIMARY]
GO

CREATE  INDEX [IX_TblTasks] ON
    [dbo].[TblTasks]([Name]) ON [PRIMARY]
GO

CREATE  INDEX [IX_TblTasks_1] ON
    [dbo].[TblTasks]([DateTimeNextRun]) ON [PRIMARY]
GO
```

The primary tables in the monitor database are as follows:

- *TblTasks*. The list of tasks—including the DLL or EXE file to run—along with functional information, the date and time of the last run, and when the next run is due
- *TblAlerts*. The list of alerts, with fields to hold the TaskID that the alert refers to, the date and time the alert occurred, and, if applicable, the date and time the alert was reset and the reset type
- *TblResetType*. The type of reset, which can be a manual reset—meaning someone intervened and reset it—or a self-corrected reset, meaning that the next time the task was run it succeeded

In *MonitorService*, all alerts will be sent to a single person. The address information for that person is located in each record in *TblTasks*. In a real-world application, at least one additional table would contain responsible-party information. This table would be related to the task information table, allowing the failure of each task to result in alerts to a different person, as appropriate. We could also specify an amount of time to give the responsible person to reset the error or assign that value within the task. Different environments require different actions—an obscure system used for nightly processing is quite different from a line of business system that affects an entire enterprise.

## The Network Monitor's Structure

The network monitor's requirements fit nicely into the structure of a Microsoft Windows 2000 service. To see if we need to do processing, we can simply add a test to the processing loop contained in *Run*. The actual processing can take place in a separate thread. We do this test with an ODBC connection, using the classes I described in Chapter 8.

At least two other threads run on the network monitor. The monitor uses the same mechanism for communicating with clients as does the *CCommService* example from Chapter 12. The service creates the requested number of worker communication threads in its constructor. There is also a thread running to follow up on alerts. This thread allows the service to track unhandled alerts, again notifying those involved if needed. *TblAlerts* contains the field *DateTimeIntervention*, which contains the date and the time the system last tried to notify the responsible party of the problem. The time of the last intervention, if any, is used to determine whether an alert should be escalated. In *CMonitorService*, escalation is a two-step process, moving from e-mailing to beeping. A more elaborate process could include backup people related to the task or responsible party.

The actual tests that probe the network are implemented as separate DLL or executable files. The database contains information on the type of file—a DLL or an EXE file—as well as the function name for DLLs. The task file, which contains information about who is responsible for each task, also contains parameters, which are later packaged to be sent to the DLL or passed directly to the EXE file. Any DLL function to be used by *CMonitorService* must accept a single parameter—a pointer to a class that gives context to the DLL function and returns information on the success or failure of the operation. The network monitor supports EXE files because they allow us to use existing programs that cannot be modified. In this case, the only detail returned to *CMonitorService* is a return code from the executable. For this reason, custom DLL functions are the preferred way to call tests.

This structure allows the greatest flexibility possible. The sample DLL will ping a server using TCP/IP, determine the status of a service, test an ODBC data source, and perform a more complete test on a SQL Server database. We can add new functions as needed without requiring changes to the base executable.

## The *CMonitorService* Class

The *CMonitorService* class is based upon the *CPPService* class. It uses some of the same functions as *CTAPIMAPIService*, which we created in Chapter 7. I made only one change to the base class. You can see the change to the *CPPService* class at the bottom of the *ParseArguments* method shown in the following code fragment:

```
BOOL CPPService::ParseArguments(int argc, char **argv)
{
    BOOL result = false;
    if (argc > 1 && !(_strnicmp(argv[1], "-i", 2)))
    {
        if ((Install()))
        {
            printf("\n%s installed!", ServiceName());
        }
        else
        {
            printf("\n%s NOT installed! Last error %d",
            ServiceName(), GetLastError());
        }
        result = true;
    }
    else if (argc > 1 && !(_strnicmp(argv[1], "-u", 2)))
    {
        if ((UnInstall()))
        {
            printf("\n%s uninstalled!", ServiceName());
        }
        else
        {
            printf(
                "\n%s NOT uninstalled! Last error "
                "%d", ServiceName(), GetLastError());
        }
        result = true;
    }
    // Added for Chapter 14
    else if (argc > 1 && !(_strnicmp(argv[1], "-d", 2)))
    {
        m_isRunning = true;
        Run();
        result = true;
    }
    return result;
}
```

This change adds support for a *–d* parameter. This parameter allows the program to run as a standard console mode application. This is tremendously useful for debugging. Of course, not all problems can be diagnosed using the *–d* mode because some problems can be caused by the security context under which the service operates.

> **NOTE** *MonitorService* must be run under the context of a specific user rather than under the context of the System account. If you run the service under the System account, you will find no mail profile. This will cause the service to not run.
>
> One other possible problem is the use of the default mail profile. If there is no default mail profile, or if the default mail profile is not appropriate, mail might not be sent. You can modify the code, passing an actual mail profile name rather than NULL to accept the default. Making the mail profile a parameter would make the service even more flexible.

Listing 14-2 contains the StdAfx.h file, the standard header for *CMonitorService*. This header includes files to support the base class, TAPI, MAPI, and ODBC.

**StdAfx.h**

```
// StdAfx.h : include file for standard system include files,
//  or project-specific include files that are used frequently, but
//  are changed infrequently
//

#if !defined(AFX_STDAFX_H__7327D38D_5E17_11D3_B4B6_00C04F79B510__
INCLUDED_)
#define AFX_STDAFX_H__7327D38D_5E17_11D3_B4B6_00C04F79B510__INCLUDED_

#if _MSC_VER > 1000
#pragma once
#endif // _MSC_VER > 1000

#define WS_VERSION_REQD    0x0202
// Exclude rarely used stuff from Windows headers.
#define WIN32_LEAN_AND_MEAN

#include <windows.h>
#include <stdio.h>
#include <stdlib.h>
#include <winsock2.h>
#include <string.h>
#include <tapi.h>
#include <mapi.h>
#include <mapix.h>
#include "mapiinit.h"
```

**Listing 14-2** *(continued)*

**Listing 14-2** *continued*

```
#include <initguid.h>
#include <mapitags.h>
#include "SQL.H"
#include "sqlext.h"
#include "odbclass.h"
#include "time.h"

typedef DWORD (WINAPI *THREADPROC)(LPVOID lpParameter);
#include "CppSvcMsg.h"
#include "CPPService.h"
#include "MonitorService.h"

// TODO: Reference additional headers your program requires here.

//{{AFX_INSERT_LOCATION}}
// Microsoft Visual C++ will insert additional
//  declarations immediately before the previous line.

#endif //!defined(AFX_STDAFX_H__7327D38D_5E17_11D3_B4B6_00C04F79B510__
INCLUDED_)
```

Listing 14-3 shows MonitorService.h, the header for the *CMonitorService* class. First note that the number of worker threads specified by the NUM_WORKERS *#define* is two rather than four as in some previous examples. This service will interact less with remote clients and do more dynamic thread creation. Two enums are defined for the type of executable the monitor runs to perform network tests. The MONITOR_CONTEXT structure is a general-purpose structure that allows information on a current task to be passed from thread to thread and to the testing functions called in an outlying DLL. Many of the other methods of the class are similar to earlier examples, such as *CTAPIMAPIService* from Chapter 7. Additional data members of the class include the name, user name, and password used to connect to the monitoring database. These default to "Monitoring", "sa", and " ", respectively, and can be changed after the class is constructed.

**MonitorService.h**

```
#define NUM_WORKERS 2

enum ExecutableType {
    ExecutableFile = 1,
    DLLFile = 2
};
```

**Listing 14-3**

```
enum OperationType {
    ProcessClient = 1,
    ProcessTask = 2
};

typedef struct _MONITOR_CONTEXT {
    OperationType Operation;
    ExecutableType exeType;
    LPVOID CommHandle;
    char szExecutable[255];
    char szFunction[255];
    char szParameters[4][132];
    char szTaskName[255];
    DWORD dwTaskID;
    DWORD dwRunEveryInterval;
    char atOrEvery;
    char szReturnMsg[512];
    long returnCode;
    bool fSuccess;
} MONITOR_CONTEXT;

typedef DWORD (FAR PASCAL *PFNTESTFUNC)
    (MONITOR_CONTEXT *pContext);

class CMonitorService : public CPPService
{
private:
    static DWORD __stdcall DoTask(LPVOID v);
    static DWORD __stdcall WSCommDispatcher(LPVOID v);
    static DWORD __stdcall MonitorAlerts(LPVOID v);
    int CallBeeper(char *beeperNumber, char *beepTo);
    int SendMapiMessage(char *szTo, char *szSubject,
        char *szNoteText);
    bool GetRootFolder(void);
    bool GetFoldersHierarchy(char *name,
        IMAPIFolder *pfolder, short int depth);
    void ReportTAPIError(LONG ret, char *op);
    void SetLastSocket(SOCKET s);
    int InitMAPI();
    int DeInitMAPI();
    SOCKET GetLastSocket();
    HANDLE m_hGotContext;
    HANDLE m_hEvent;
    HANDLE m_hThreads[NUM_WORKERS];
```

*(continued)*

**Listing 14-3** *continued*

```
    DWORD m_dwThreadIDs[NUM_WORKERS];
    SOCKET LastSocket;
    int m_ServerPort;
    CRITICAL_SECTION csMapi;
public:
    char m_dbPassword[255];
    char m_dbUser[255];
    char m_database[255];
    static DWORD __stdcall Thread(LPVOID t);
    virtual void DoWork(SOCKET s, WORD ThreadNum);
    int GetServerPort();
    void SetServerPort(int tServerPort);
    CMonitorService(char *tsvcName, char *tdispName,
        DWORD tsvcStart = SERVICE_DEMAND_START,
        bool CreateMsgPump = true);
    ~CMonitorService();
   virtual void Run();
   virtual void OnInstall();
};
```

Listing 14-4 contains MonitorService.cpp, which defines most methods of the *CMonitorService* class. The TAPI- and MAPI-related functions are located in TAPI-MAPISupport.cpp in the companion CD-ROM. I made modest changes to the MAPI functions because of the relatively high volume of e-mail that could be sent by this application. Most of the setup and breakdown of the MAPI environment is contained in *InitMapi* and *DeInitMapi*, respectively. In earlier examples these functions did no more than load and unload the MAPI DLL.

**MonitorService.cpp**

```
// MonitorService.cpp : Communications service, using TCP/IP
//  and Events.
//
#include "stdafx.h"
#include <mapiguid.h>

//-------------------------------------------------------------------
// Example simple main routine.
int main(int argc, char* argv[])
{
    CMonitorService MyMonitorService("MonitorService",
        "Monitor Test Service");
```

```
    // We could do something like the following if we needed to.
    // MyCommService.SetServerPort(5555);
    // This example uses the default.

    // Have we handled the arguments and done an install
    //  or an uninstall?
    if (MyMonitorService.ParseArguments(argc, argv) == false)
    {
        // If not, start the service running.
        MyMonitorService.StartService();
    }
    return 0;
}

//---------------------------------------------------------------------
// Utility function.
LPSTR DeleteTrsp(LPSTR s)
{
    int loop;
    loop = strlen(s);
    loop--;

    while (loop && (s[loop] == ' ' || s[loop] == '\t'))
    {
        s[loop] = '\0';
        loop--;
    }
    return(s);
}

//---------------------------------------------------------------------
// The heart of the class, the WinSock dispatcher
DWORD __stdcall CMonitorService::WSCommDispatcher(LPVOID v)
{
    // Declare and initialize.
    BOOL    fConnected = FALSE;
    DWORD   dwThreadID = (DWORD)0;
    HANDLE  hThread = INVALID_HANDLE_VALUE;
    int     addrLen;
    int     error;
    struct  sockaddr_in srvSocketAddr;
    struct  sockaddr_in cliSocketAddr;
    char    diag[255];
    WSADATA wsaData;
```

*(continued)*

```
SOCKET  srvSocket;
SOCKET  cliSocket;
CMonitorService *p_this;

p_this = (CMonitorService *)m_this;

error = WSAStartup(WS_VERSION_REQD, &wsaData);
if (error != 0)
{
    return 0;
}

if (LOBYTE(wsaData.wVersion) < 2)
{
    sprintf(diag, "\nVersion %d.%d not supported",
        LOBYTE(wsaData.wVersion),
        HIBYTE(wsaData.wVersion));
    p_this->LogEvent(EVENTLOG_ERROR_TYPE, EVMSG_DEBUG, diag);
    return 0;
}

srvSocket = socket(AF_INET, SOCK_STREAM, 0);
if (srvSocket == INVALID_SOCKET)
{
    sprintf(diag, "SERVER: Windows Socket Error %d - "
        "Couldn't create socket",
        WSAGetLastError());
    p_this->LogEvent(EVENTLOG_ERROR_TYPE, EVMSG_DEBUG, diag);
    WSACleanup();
    return 0;
}

srvSocketAddr.sin_family = AF_INET;
srvSocketAddr.sin_addr.s_addr = INADDR_ANY;
srvSocketAddr.sin_port = p_this->GetServerPort();

if (bind(srvSocket, (LPSOCKADDR)&srvSocketAddr,
    sizeof(srvSocketAddr)) == SOCKET_ERROR)
{
    sprintf(diag, "SERVER: Windows Socket Error %d - "
        "Couldn't bind socket",
        WSAGetLastError());
```

```
        p_this->LogEvent(EVENTLOG_ERROR_TYPE, EVMSG_DEBUG, diag);
        WSACleanup();
        return 0;
    }

    if (listen(srvSocket, SOMAXCONN) == SOCKET_ERROR)
    {
        sprintf(diag, "SERVER: Windows Socket Error %d - "
            "Couldn't listen on socket",
            WSAGetLastError());

        p_this->LogEvent(EVENTLOG_ERROR_TYPE, EVMSG_DEBUG, diag);
        WSACleanup();
        return 0;

    }

    while ((p_this->IsRunning()))
    {
        addrLen = (sizeof(cliSocketAddr));

        cliSocket = accept(srvSocket,
            (LPSOCKADDR)&cliSocketAddr, &addrLen);

        if (cliSocket == INVALID_SOCKET)
        {
            wsprintf(diag,
                "SERVER: Windows Socket Error %d - "
                "accept() got invalid socket",
                WSAGetLastError());

            p_this->LogEvent(EVENTLOG_ERROR_TYPE, EVMSG_DEBUG, diag);
            WSACleanup();
            return 0;
        }

        p_this->SetLastSocket(cliSocket);
        SetEvent(p_this->m_hEvent);

        while (WaitForSingleObject(p_this->m_hGotContext,
            1000) == WAIT_TIMEOUT)
```

*(continued)*

```
        {
            if (!p_this->IsRunning())
            {
                WSACleanup();
                wsprintf(diag, "SERVER: Exiting");
                p_this->LogEvent(EVENTLOG_INFORMATION_TYPE,
                    EVMSG_DEBUG, diag);
                return 0;
            }
        }
        ResetEvent(p_this->m_hGotContext);
    }
    WSACleanup();
    sprintf(diag, "SERVER: Exiting");
    p_this->LogEvent(EVENTLOG_INFORMATION_TYPE, EVMSG_DEBUG, diag);

    return 0;
}

//-------------------------------------------------------------------
// The constructor.
CMonitorService::CMonitorService(char *tsvcName,
                                 char *tdispName,
                                 DWORD tsvcStart,
                                 bool CreateMsgPump)
:CPPService(tsvcName, tdispName, tsvcStart, CreateMsgPump)
{
    DWORD dwCreationFlags = 0;
    // Create the event, default security,
    //  NOT manual Reset,
    //  NON signaled originally,
    //  NOT named, since just used by this process.
    m_hEvent = CreateEvent(NULL, FALSE, FALSE, NULL);
    if (m_hEvent == NULL)
    {
        LogEvent(EVENTLOG_ERROR_TYPE,
            EVMSG_DEBUG,
            "Can't create event!");
    }
    // Create the event, default security,
    //  Manual Reset,
    //  NON signaled originally,
    //  NOT named, since just used by this process.
```

```
    m_hGotContext = CreateEvent(NULL, TRUE, FALSE, NULL);
    if (m_hEvent == NULL)
    {
        LogEvent(EVENTLOG_ERROR_TYPE,
            EVMSG_DEBUG,
            "Can't create Got Socket event!");
    }

    m_ServerPort = 5043;                    // A default port
    strcpy(m_database, "Monitoring");       // Default values
    strcpy(m_dbUser, "sa");
    strcpy(m_dbPassword, "");

    for (WORD loop = 0 ; loop < NUM_WORKERS ; loop++)
    {
        if ((m_hThreads[loop] = CreateThread(NULL,
                0, Thread, (LPVOID)loop,
                dwCreationFlags,
                &m_dwThreadIDs[loop])) == NULL)
        {
            LogEvent(EVENTLOG_ERROR_TYPE,
                EVMSG_DEBUG,
                "Can't create thread!");
        }
    }
}

CMonitorService::~CMonitorService()
{
    if (m_hEvent != NULL)
    {
        CloseHandle(m_hEvent);
    }
    if (m_hGotContext != NULL)
    {
        CloseHandle(m_hGotContext);
    }
    for (WORD loop = 0 ; loop < NUM_WORKERS ; loop++)
    {
        if (m_hThreads[loop] != NULL)
        {
            CloseHandle(m_hThreads[loop]);
        }
    }
}
```

*(continued)*

```
//-----------------------------------------------------------------
// Used to pass a socket from the dispatcher to the worker thread
SOCKET CMonitorService::GetLastSocket()
{
    return LastSocket;
}

//-----------------------------------------------------------------
// Used to pass a socket from the dispatcher to the worker thread
void CMonitorService::SetLastSocket(SOCKET s)
{
    LastSocket = s;
}

//-----------------------------------------------------------------
// Set the port number the server should use.
void CMonitorService::SetServerPort(int tServerPort)
{
    m_ServerPort = tServerPort;
}

//-----------------------------------------------------------------
// Get the port number the server is using.
int CMonitorService::GetServerPort()
{
    return m_ServerPort;
}

//-----------------------------------------------------------------
// The routine called to run the service
void CMonitorService::Run()
{
    DWORD dwThreadID;
    DWORD dwSleepCount = 0;
    HANDLE hThread;
    RETCODE rc;
    MONITOR_CONTEXT Context;

    ::InitializeCriticalSection(&csMapi);

    ::EnterCriticalSection(&csMapi);
    InitMAPI();
    ::LeaveCriticalSection(&csMapi);
```

```
CODBCDatabase::InitCriticalSection();

CODBCDatabase *db;

db = new CODBCDatabase(m_database, m_dbUser, m_dbPassword);

if ((hThread = CreateThread(NULL, 0, WSCommDispatcher,
    (LPVOID)0, 0, &dwThreadID)) != NULL)
{
    CloseHandle(hThread);
}

Sleep(1);

if ((hThread = CreateThread(NULL, 0, MonitorAlerts,
    (LPVOID)0, 0, &dwThreadID)) != NULL)
{
    CloseHandle(hThread);
}

while (m_isRunning)
{
    if (!(dwSleepCount%30))
    {
        UWORD col = 1;
        CODBCCursor *curs;
        SQL_TIMESTAMP_STRUCT Date;
        SQL_TIMESTAMP_STRUCT tsNow;
        char szDate[255];
        char szDateNext[255];
        char szBuffer[255];
        char szSql[1024];

        curs = new CODBCCursor(db);
        curs->setTables("tblTasks");

        curs->bindColumn(col, "TaskID",
            255, SQL_C_ULONG);
        curs->bindColumn(col, "Executable", 255);
        curs->bindColumn(col, "Function", 255);
        curs->bindColumn(col, "ExecuteType",
            255, SQL_C_ULONG);
        curs->bindColumn(col, "DateTimeLastRun",
            255, SQL_C_TYPE_TIMESTAMP);
```

*(continued)*

```
curs->bindColumn(col, "Parameter1", 255);
curs->bindColumn(col, "Parameter2", 255);
curs->bindColumn(col, "Parameter3", 255);
curs->bindColumn(col, "Parameter4", 255);
curs->bindColumn(col, "Name", 255);
curs->bindColumn(col, "atOrEvery", 2);
curs->bindColumn(col, "RunEveryInterval",
    255, SQL_C_ULONG);

curs->BuildSQLTimestamp(&tsNow, szDate);
wsprintf(szBuffer,
    " WHERE DateTimeNextRun<='%04d-%02d-%02d %02d:%02d'",
    tsNow.year, tsNow.month, tsNow.day,
    tsNow.hour, tsNow.minute);

curs->setRestrict(szBuffer);
curs->setOrderBy(" DateTimeNextRun ");

curs->doSelect();
if ((rc = curs->fetch()) == SQL_SUCCESS ||
     (rc == SQL_SUCCESS_WITH_INFO))
{

    memcpy((void *)&Date,
        (SQL_TIMESTAMP_STRUCT *)
        (*curs)["DateTimeLastRun"],
        sizeof(SQL_TIMESTAMP_STRUCT));

    Context.dwTaskID = *(int *)(*curs)[1];
    Context.exeType =
        *(ExecutableType *)(*curs)["ExecuteType"];
    Context.dwRunEveryInterval =
        *(int *)(*curs)["RunEveryInterval"];
    strcpy(Context.szExecutable,
        (char *)(*curs)["Executable"]);
    strcpy(Context.szFunction,
        (char *)(*curs)["Function"]);
    strcpy(Context.szParameters[0],
        (char *)(*curs)["Parameter1"]);
    strcpy(Context.szParameters[1],
        (char *)(*curs)["Parameter2"]);
    strcpy(Context.szParameters[2],
        (char *)(*curs)["Parameter3"]);
```

```
strcpy(Context.szParameters[3],
    (char *)(*curs)["Parameter4"]);
strcpy(Context.szTaskName,
    (char *)(*curs)["Name"]);
Context.atOrEvery = *(char *)(*curs)["atOrEvery"];

curs->BuildSQLTimestamp(&tsNow, szDate);

if (Context.atOrEvery == 'E')
{
    curs->IncrementSQLTimestamp(&tsNow,
        Context.dwRunEveryInterval);
}
else
{
    curs->IncrementSQLTimestamp(&tsNow,
        (60*24));
}
wsprintf(szDateNext, "%04d-%02d-%02d %02d:%02d",
    tsNow.year,
    tsNow.month,
    tsNow.day,
    tsNow.hour,
    tsNow.minute);

// Delete this cursor so that the outstanding
//  statement is cleared and the update can take place.
//  This limits us to one event per minute,
//  not an unreasonable limit for an example.
delete curs;

wsprintf(szSql, "UPDATE tblTasks SET "
    "DateTimeLastRun='%s', DateTimeNextRun='%s'"
    " WHERE TaskID=%d",
    szDate, szDateNext, Context.dwTaskID);

db->ExecuteSQL(szSql);

hThread = CreateThread(NULL, 0, DoTask,
    (LPVOID)&Context, 0,
    &dwThreadID);
if (hThread != NULL)
```

*(continued)*

```
                {
                    CloseHandle(hThread);
                }
                else
                {
                    LogEvent(EVENTLOG_ERROR_TYPE, EVMSG_ERROR,
                        DeleteTrsp(Context.szTaskName),
                        "Could not create thread");
                    wsprintf(szSql,
                        "INSERT TblAlerts(DateTimeOfAlert,"
                        "TaskID,AlertComment)"
                        "VALUES('%s',%d,'Unable to create thread')",
                        szDate, Context.dwTaskID);
                    db->ExecuteSQL(szSql);
                }

            }
            else
            {
                delete curs;
            }
            dwSleepCount = 0;
        }
        dwSleepCount++;
        Sleep(1000);
    }

    m_isRunning = false;
    // Give threads a chance to die.
    Sleep(2000);

    delete db;
    DeInitMAPI();

    CODBCDatabase::DelCriticalSection();
    ::DeleteCriticalSection(&csMapi);

    return;
}

//------------------------------------------------------------------
// Start the service upon installation.
void CMonitorService::OnInstall()
```

```
{
    ::StartThisService(ServiceName());
}

//-----------------------------------------------------------------------
// The function that does the actual work. This should be overridden.
void CMonitorService::DoWork(SOCKET s, WORD ThreadNum)
{
    char diag[255];
    char data[1024];
    BOOL fSuccess;
    int len;
    static int blksSent = 0;
    int bytesRead;
    int maxData = 512;

    bytesRead = 0L;

    do {
        memset((void *)data, '\0', 1024);
        if ((len = recv(s,
            ((char *)data)+bytesRead,
            maxData, 0)) == SOCKET_ERROR)
        {
            fSuccess = FALSE;
            wsprintf(diag, "SOCKET ERROR", data);
            LogEvent(EVENTLOG_ERROR_TYPE,
                EVMSG_DEBUG, diag);
        }
        else
        {
            if (len)
            {
                fSuccess = TRUE;
                bytesRead += (DWORD)len;
                blksSent++;
                data[200] = '\0';       // Only try to log the
                                // first 200 characters or fewer.
                wsprintf(diag,
                    "Client says: %s to Thread %d",
                    data, ThreadNum);
                LogEvent(EVENTLOG_INFORMATION_TYPE,
                    EVMSG_DEBUG, diag);
            }
```

*(continued)*

**Listing 14-4** *continued*

```
        }
    } while (IsRunning() && len != SOCKET_ERROR && len != 0);
    closesocket(s);

}

//-----------------------------------------------------------------
// The thread routine;  used to call DoWork correctly
DWORD __stdcall CMonitorService::Thread(LPVOID t)
{
    DWORD ret;
    WORD ThreadNum;
    SOCKET s;
    CMonitorService *p_this;

    p_this = (CMonitorService *)m_this;
    ThreadNum = (WORD)(t);

    do {
        while ((ret = WaitForSingleObject(p_this->m_hEvent,
                1000)) == WAIT_TIMEOUT &&
                p_this->IsRunning() == TRUE)
        {
            ;
        }
        if (p_this->IsRunning() == FALSE)
        {
            break;
        }
        if (ret == WAIT_OBJECT_0)
        {
            s = p_this->GetLastSocket();
            SetEvent(p_this->m_hGotContext);
            p_this->DoWork(s, ThreadNum);
        }
    } while (ret == WAIT_TIMEOUT || ret == WAIT_OBJECT_0);
    return(0);
}

DWORD __stdcall CMonitorService::DoTask(LPVOID v)
{
    MONITOR_CONTEXT *Context;
    STARTUPINFO StartupInfo;
    PROCESS_INFORMATION ProcessInfo;
    BOOL RetVal;
    DWORD dw;
```

```
SQL_TIMESTAMP_STRUCT tsNow;
char szCommandLine[512];
char szDate[255];
char szSql[1024];
HMODULE hLibrary;
PFNTESTFUNC pfnTestFunc;
CODBCDatabase *db;
CODBCCursor *curs;
CMonitorService *p_this;

p_this = (CMonitorService *)m_this;

Context = (MONITOR_CONTEXT *)v;

db = new CODBCDatabase("Monitoring", "sa", "");
if (!(db->isConnected()))
{
    return(0);
}

curs = new CODBCCursor(db);

curs->BuildSQLTimestamp(&tsNow, szDate);

// Now we do the loadlibrary or createprocess.
switch (Context->exeType)
{
case DLLFile:
    Context->fSuccess = false;
    wsprintf(Context->szReturnMsg,
        "Function %s in Library %s not loaded",
        DeleteTrsp(Context->szFunction),
        DeleteTrsp(Context->szExecutable));
    hLibrary = LoadLibrary(Context->szExecutable);
    if (hLibrary != NULL)
    {
        pfnTestFunc = (PFNTESTFUNC)GetProcAddress(hLibrary,
            Context->szFunction);
        if ((pfnTestFunc != NULL))
        {
            pfnTestFunc(Context);
        }
        FreeLibrary(hLibrary);
    }
    if (!Context->fSuccess)
```

*(continued)*

**Listing 14-4** *continued*

```
        {
            LPVOID szMsgBuf;
            FormatMessage(
                FORMAT_MESSAGE_ALLOCATE_BUFFER |
                FORMAT_MESSAGE_FROM_SYSTEM |
                FORMAT_MESSAGE_IGNORE_INSERTS,
                NULL,
                GetLastError(),
                MAKELANGID(LANG_NEUTRAL, SUBLANG_DEFAULT),
                (LPTSTR) &szMsgBuf,
                0,
                NULL);
            strcat(Context->szReturnMsg, "  ");
            strcat(Context->szReturnMsg, (const char *)szMsgBuf);
            // Free the buffer.
            LocalFree(szMsgBuf);
        }

        break;
    case ExecutableFile:
        memset((void *)&StartupInfo, '\0', sizeof(StartupInfo));
        memset((void *)&ProcessInfo, '\0', sizeof(ProcessInfo));
        StartupInfo.cb = sizeof(StartupInfo);
        StartupInfo.cbReserved2 = 0;
        StartupInfo.dwFillAttribute = 0;
        StartupInfo.dwFlags = 0;
        StartupInfo.dwX = 0;
        StartupInfo.dwXCountChars = 0;
        StartupInfo.dwY = 0;
        StartupInfo.dwYCountChars = 0;
        StartupInfo.lpDesktop = NULL;
        StartupInfo.lpReserved = NULL;
        StartupInfo.lpReserved2 = NULL;
        StartupInfo.lpTitle = "";
        StartupInfo.wShowWindow = SW_HIDE;
        sprintf(szCommandLine, "%s %s %s %s %s",
            Context->szExecutable,
            Context->szParameters[0],
            Context->szParameters[1],
            Context->szParameters[2],
            Context->szParameters[3]);
        RetVal = CreateProcess(NULL, szCommandLine, NULL, NULL,
            FALSE, 0, NULL, NULL,
```

```
            &StartupInfo,
            &ProcessInfo);
        if (!RetVal)
        {
            LPVOID szMsgBuf;
            FormatMessage(
                FORMAT_MESSAGE_ALLOCATE_BUFFER |
                FORMAT_MESSAGE_FROM_SYSTEM |
                FORMAT_MESSAGE_IGNORE_INSERTS,
                NULL,
                GetLastError(),
                MAKELANGID(LANG_NEUTRAL, SUBLANG_DEFAULT),
                (LPTSTR) &szMsgBuf,
                0,
                NULL);
            wsprintf(Context->szReturnMsg,
                "Error creating process: %s ", szMsgBuf);
            LocalFree(szMsgBuf);
        }
        else
        {
            DWORD dwExitCode;
            do {
                dw = WaitForSingleObject(ProcessInfo.hProcess, 1000);
            } while (dw == WAIT_TIMEOUT && p_this->IsRunning());
            GetExitCodeProcess(ProcessInfo.hProcess, &dwExitCode);
            wsprintf(Context->szReturnMsg,
                "Process %s Returned %d",
                szCommandLine, dwExitCode);
            Context->fSuccess = (dwExitCode == 0);
            CloseHandle(ProcessInfo.hProcess);
            CloseHandle(ProcessInfo.hThread);
        }
        break;
    }

    if (!Context->fSuccess)
    {
        curs->BuildSQLTimestamp(&tsNow, szDate);
        p_this->LogEvent(EVENTLOG_ERROR_TYPE, EVMSG_ALERT,
            DeleteTrsp(Context->szTaskName),
            DeleteTrsp(Context->szReturnMsg));
        wsprintf(szSql,
            "INSERT TblAlerts(DateTimeOfAlert,"
```

*(continued)*

**Listing 14-4** *continued*

```
            "TaskID,alertComment)"
            "VALUES('%s',%d,'%s')",
            szDate,Context->dwTaskID,
            Context->szReturnMsg);
        db->ExecuteSQL(szSql);
    }
    else
    {
        // Clear any alert.
        wsprintf(szSql,
            "UPDATE TblAlerts SET DateTimeReset='%s',"
            "ResetTypeID="
            "(SELECT resetTypeId FROM TblResetType "
            "WHERE Description LIKE 'Self Corrected%%') "
            "WHERE TaskID=%d",
            szDate, Context->dwTaskID);
        db->ExecuteSQL(szSql);
    }
    delete curs;
    delete db;
    return(0);
}

//--------------------------------------------------------------------------
// This is used to monitor alerts.
DWORD __stdcall CMonitorService::MonitorAlerts(LPVOID t)
{
    DWORD dwSleepCount = 0;
    RETCODE rc;
    char szRestrict[1024];
    char szDate[255];
    char szBuffer[255];
    CMonitorService *p_this;
    CODBCDatabase *db;
    CODBCCursor *curs;
    SQL_TIMESTAMP_STRUCT ts;

    p_this = (CMonitorService *)m_this;

    db = new CODBCDatabase(p_this->m_database,
        p_this->m_dbUser,
        p_this->m_dbPassword);
```

```
    if (!db->isConnected())
    {
        char diag[255];
        wsprintf(diag,
            "Cannot Connect to %s database",
            p_this->m_database);
        p_this->LogEvent(EVENTLOG_ERROR_TYPE,
            EVMSG_DEBUG, diag);
        dwSleepCount = 0;
        return 0;
    }

    while (p_this->IsRunning())
    {
        if ((dwSleepCount%180) == 0)
        {
            UWORD col;
            do {
                curs = new CODBCCursor(db);

                curs->setTables("tblAlerts");
                curs->bindColumn(col, "AlertID", 255,
                    SQL_C_ULONG);
                curs->bindColumn(col, "TaskID", 255,
                    SQL_C_ULONG);
                curs->bindColumn(col, "DateTimeReset", 255,
                    SQL_C_TYPE_TIMESTAMP);
                curs->bindColumn(col, "DateTimeIntervention", 255,
                    SQL_C_TYPE_TIMESTAMP);
                curs->bindColumn(col, "AlertComment", 255);

                curs->BuildSQLTimestamp(&ts, szDate);
                curs->DecrementSQLTimestamp(&ts, 15);

                wsprintf(szRestrict,
                    " WHERE DateTimeReset IS NULL "
                    "AND (DateTimeIntervention IS NULL OR "
                    "DateTimeIntervention<"
                    "'%04d-%02d-%02d %02d:%02d')",
                    ts.year, ts.month, ts.day, ts.hour, ts.day);

                curs->setRestrict(szRestrict);

                curs->doSelect();
```

*(continued)*

**Listing 14-4** *continued*

```
                rc = curs->fetch();
                if (rc == SQL_SUCCESS ||
                    rc == SQL_SUCCESS_WITH_INFO)
                {
                    DWORD dwAlertID;
                    DWORD dwTaskID;
                    char szDate[255];
                    char szAlertComment[512];
                    // We declare these in here to
                    //  allow us to use a separate
                    //  connection to the db.
                    CODBCCursor *taskCurs;
                    CODBCDatabase *db;

                    dwAlertID = *(int *)(*curs)["AlertID"];
                    dwTaskID = *(int *)(*curs)["TaskID"];
                    strcpy(szAlertComment,
                        (char *)(*curs)["AlertComment"]);
                    SQL_TIMESTAMP_STRUCT tsNotify;
                    memset((void *)&tsNotify, '\0', sizeof(tsNotify));
                    memcpy((void *)&tsNotify,
                        (SQL_TIMESTAMP_STRUCT *)
                        (*curs)["DateTimeIntervention"],
                        sizeof(SQL_TIMESTAMP_STRUCT));

                    db = new CODBCDatabase(p_this->m_database,
                        p_this->m_dbUser,
                        p_this->m_dbPassword);

                    taskCurs = new CODBCCursor(db);

                    taskCurs->setTables("tblTasks");
                    taskCurs->bindColumn(col, "Name", 255);
                    taskCurs->bindColumn(col, "EMail", 255);
                    taskCurs->bindColumn(col, "Beeper", 255);

                    wsprintf(szRestrict, " WHERE TaskID=%d", dwTaskID);
                    taskCurs->setRestrict(szRestrict);

                    taskCurs->doSelect();
                    taskCurs->fetch();

                    // Notify the responsible party.
                    if (tsNotify.year == 0)
```

```
                {
                    // First time? Use e-mail.
                    sprintf(szBuffer,
                        "Error executing task number %d (%s). "
                        "\nMessage: %s",
                        dwTaskID,
                        DeleteTrsp(
                            (char *)(*taskCurs)["Name"]),
                        DeleteTrsp(szAlertComment));

                    EnterCriticalSection(&p_this->csMapi);
                    if ((p_this->SendMapiMessage(
                        (char *)(*taskCurs)["EMail"],
                        "Monitor error!",
                        szBuffer)) == -1)
                    {
                        char diag[255];
                        wsprintf(diag,
                            "Cannot send E-Mail to %s",
                            (char *)(*taskCurs)["EMail"]);
                        p_this->LogEvent(
                            EVENTLOG_ERROR_TYPE,
                            EVMSG_DEBUG, diag);

                    }
                    LeaveCriticalSection(&p_this->csMapi);
                }
                else
                {
                    // Second time? Beep'em.
                    wsprintf(szBuffer, "%04d",
                        dwTaskID);
                    // Uncomment this code if you want to beep
                    //  the person in tblTasks. This can be
                    //  quite annoying during testing.
/*                  p_this->CallBeeper(
                        (char *)(*taskCurs)["Beeper"],
                        szBuffer);*/
                }
                delete taskCurs;
                taskCurs = NULL;

                // Change intervention time.
                curs->BuildSQLTimestamp(&tsNotify, szDate);
```

*(continued)*

**Listing 14-4** *continued*

```
                        delete curs;
                        curs = 0;
                        wsprintf(szRestrict, "UPDATE tblAlerts "
                            "SET DateTimeIntervention='%s' "
                            "WHERE alertID=%d",
                            szDate, dwAlertID);
                        db->ExecuteSQL(szRestrict);
                        delete db;
                        db = NULL;
                    }
                    else
                    {
                        delete curs;
                        curs = NULL;
                    }
                } while (p_this->IsRunning() &&
                    (rc == SQL_SUCCESS ||
                    rc == SQL_SUCCESS_WITH_INFO));
            }
            Sleep(1000);
            dwSleepCount++;
        }
        if (db)
        {
            delete db;
            db = NULL;
        }
        if (curs)
        {
            delete curs;
            curs = NULL;
        }
        return 0;
    }
```

To describe the way that *CMonitorService* works, I will step through the code starting at the *Run* method, describing the functions used by *Run* as they occur.

The *Run* method of *CMonitorService* first declares some variables, including two variables from the ODBC classes we first saw in Chapter 8, *CODBCDatabase* and *CODBCCursor*. I create a critical section to serialize access to the MAPI functions, which use some global variables. I call the modified version of *InitMapi* that is now a method of *CMonitorService*, which loads the MAPI DLL and sets up the MAPI session. Next I create two threads. First I use *CreateThread* to create a thread running *WSCommDispatcher*. This thread dispatches client requests; we first saw it in the *CCommService* example in Chapter 12. Next I create a thread to run the *MonitorAlerts* static method of the class.

The *MonitorAlerts* method polls the *TblAlerts* file periodically—every 3 minutes in *CMonitorService*. I create local copies of the *CODBCDatabase* and *CODBCCursor* objects to allow *MonitorAlerts* to search the alerts table for unresolved alerts. Next I create a *while* loop controlled by the *IsRunning* method of *CMonitorService*. This method will manage alerts for the duration of the operation of the service.

A variable named *dwSleepCount* keeps track of the number of calls to *Sleep* with an argument specifying a 1000-millisecond sleep. This allows *MonitorAlert* to enter a section of code used to read the alerts in the *TblAlerts* file. I create a cursor pointing to the *TblAlerts* table. The two fields only get alerts with no date in the *DateTimeReset* field (meaning that they are current alerts) and that have been outstanding for at least 15 minutes, based on the value in *DateTimeOfAlert*. To select these alerts, I use one of several new methods added to *CODBCCursor* designed to work with ODBC's Timestamp type. These types are returned in a SQL_TIMESTAMP_STRUCT that contains members for year, month, day, hour, minute, second, and fraction of a second. For instance, the *BuildSQLTimestamp* method of *CODBCCursor* creates a SQL_TIMESTAMP_STRUCT and a string suitable to be placed in a SQL statement and places in each respective variables pointed to by the two arguments. *IncrementSQLTimestamp* increments the timestamp by the specified number of minutes, both values passed as parameters. These methods handle timestamp changes that cause the day to change. There are also methods to decrement timestamps; I use them here to create a timestamp for 15 minutes prior to the current system time.

For each alert that meets the specified criteria, I gather information about the task that failed, using a separate cursor and connection so that the existing connection remains at the proper position. Using information contained in the task record, *MonitorAlerts* either e-mails the responsible person with details of the problem or beeps the user with the task ID referred to by the alert. Finally the intervention time is stored in the alert's record. At the bottom of the loop, *Sleep* is called for 1000 milliseconds and *dwSleepCount* is incremented.

Let's go back to *Run* in *CMonitorService*. Once the *MonitorAlerts* thread begins, *Run* enters a loop controlled by *IsRunning*. As in *MonitorAlerts*, a variable named *dwSleepCount* allows processing to occur only after some number of calls to *Sleep*—in this case, 30 calls, meaning that the processing occurs for only 30 seconds. Times in the system are kept only to the minute, so this resolution is adequate. The number of times the thread calls *Sleep* is another item that might be stored in the registry and thus be configurable in a production application.

Each record in *TblTasks* contains a field called *DateTimeNextRun*. This field allows a relatively simple query to handle tasks that should be run every *n* minutes or each day at a given time. This is the field I used in the query in *Run* to determine which tasks should be run. This implementation has an artificial limit that allows only one task to be run per minute. This limit could be eliminated in one of two ways: either establish two connections to the database so that changes on one cursor would not disturb the results from the initial query, or cache the task ID of all tasks waiting to run in an array of DWORDs and then process the ID.

For records in *TblTasks* that meet the criteria, information from the record is placed into the appropriate fields in a MONITOR_CONTEXT structure. The elements stored there include the name of the DLL or executable program to run, the function name, and parameters to pass. Depending upon the type of task—one performed every *n* minutes or one performed at a certain time—*DateTimeNextRun* and *DateTimeLastRun* are set. Of course, at this point it is uncertain that the program will actually be run, but failures will be logged in the Windows 2000 event log and in *TblAlerts*. Finally I create a thread to run *DoTask*, the function that actually runs the task specified in *TblTasks*. I fill in a MONITOR_CONTEXT structure based upon information in *TblTask* and send a pointer to the structure as the argument to the thread.

*DoTask* opens some ODBC connections and then enters a *switch* statement controlled by the *exeType* member of the context pointer passed to *DoTask*. If a DLL is specified and the DLL can be loaded using *LoadLibrary*, and if the function specified in *TblTasks* can be located using *GetProcAddress*, I call the specified function and pass it the same pointer to MONITOR_CONTEXT that was passed to *DoTask*. If an error occurs—either in loading the DLL or in the operation of the function in the DLL—an alert is inserted into *TblAlerts*.

If an EXE file is specified, I call *CreateProcess* and pass the parameters found in *TblTasks* on the command line. I check the return code from the newly created process to determine success or failure; 0 indicating success and any other value indicating failure. In a production system, the parameters might allow keywords that would be replaced at run time. For instance, a parameter of @today might be replaced with today's date and @now might be replaced with the current time.

## MONITORING TASK FUNCTIONS

The framework I've built allows you to add network monitoring functions by creating extension DLLs that accept as their lone parameter a pointer to a MONITOR_CONTEXT structure. These extension DLLs can do whatever you need them to do, allowing for tremendous flexibility. I've provided four functions as examples.

- *Ping* uses TCP/IP and "pings" another machine on the network.
- *TestServiceStatus* checks the status of a service on a specified server.
- *TestODBCConnection* tests an ODBC connection.
- *TestSQLServerStatus* does more extensive, SQL Server–specific testing.

These four example functions are implemented in Listing 14-5, TestMonitor.cpp. When compiled, this listing creates TestMonitor.dll.

**TestMonitor.cpp**

```
// TestMonitor.cpp : entry point for the example DLL called by
//  MonitorService
//

#include "stdafx.h"

BOOL APIENTRY DllMain(HANDLE hModule,
                      DWORD  ul_reason_for_call,
                      LPVOID lpReserved
                     )
{
    return TRUE;
}

// This should really be in a shared header file used by
//  the service and this DLL.
typedef struct _MONITOR_CONTEXT {
    OperationType Operation;
    ExecutableType exeType;
    LPVOID CommHandle;
    char szExecutable[255];
    char szFunction[255];
    char szParameters[4][132];
    char szTaskName[255];
    DWORD dwTaskID;
    DWORD dwRunEveryInterval;
    char atOrEvery;
    char szReturnMsg[512];
    long returnCode;
    bool fSuccess;
} MONITOR_CONTEXT;

// Declarations and definitions for Ping

// This is an adaptation of the Ping included in the
//  Platform SDK.

#define ICMP_ECHO 8
#define ICMP_ECHOREPLY 0

#define ICMP_MIN 8 // Minimum 8-byte icmp packet (just header)
#define STATUS_FAILED 0xFFFF
#define DEF_PACKET_SIZE 32
#define MAX_PACKET 1024
```

**Listing 14-5** *(continued)*

**Listing 14-5** *continued*

```
#pragma pack(4)

/* The IP header */
typedef struct iphdr {
    unsigned int h_len:4;          // Length of the header
    unsigned int version:4;        // Version of IP
    unsigned char tos;             // Type of service
    unsigned short total_len;      // Total length of the packet
    unsigned short ident;          // Unique identifier
    unsigned short frag_and_flags; // Flags
    unsigned char ttl;
    unsigned char proto;           // Protocol (TCP, UDP, etc.)
    unsigned short checksum;       // IP checksum

    unsigned int sourceIP;
    unsigned int destIP;
}IpHeader;

// ICMP header
typedef struct _ihdr {
    BYTE i_type;
    BYTE i_code; /* type sub code */
    USHORT i_cksum;
    USHORT i_id;
    USHORT i_seq;
    // This is not the std header, but
    //  we reserve space for time. This is
    //  used to get the elapsed time.
    ULONG timestamp;
}IcmpHeader;

//-----------------------------------------------------------------
// Tests service status; considers RUNNING to be
//  success.
DWORD APIENTRY TestServiceStatus(LPVOID v)
{
    MONITOR_CONTEXT *Context;
    char szServer[255];
    char szService[255];
    DWORD cbNeeded, dwServicesReturned, dwResumeHandle;
    SC_HANDLE scm;
    ENUM_SERVICE_STATUS *ess;
```

```
    ess = new ENUM_SERVICE_STATUS[1000];

    Context = (MONITOR_CONTEXT *)v;

    strcpy(szServer, Context->szParameters[0]);
    strcpy(szService, Context->szParameters[1]);

    scm = OpenSCManager(szServer, NULL,
        SC_MANAGER_ENUMERATE_SERVICE);

    dwServicesReturned = dwResumeHandle = 0;
    if (EnumServicesStatus(scm, SERVICE_WIN32, SERVICE_STATE_ALL,
        ess, sizeof(ENUM_SERVICE_STATUS)*1000,
        &cbNeeded, &dwServicesReturned, &dwResumeHandle) == 0)
    {
        return Context->fSuccess == true? 1 : 0;
    }

    for (DWORD loop = 0 ; loop < dwServicesReturned ; loop++)
    {
        if (!(stricmp(ess[loop].lpDisplayName, szService)))
        {
            if (ess[loop].ServiceStatus.dwCurrentState ==
                SERVICE_RUNNING)
            {
                Context->fSuccess = true;
                strcpy(Context->szReturnMsg, "Service is running");
            }
            else
            {
                Context->fSuccess = false;
                switch (ess[loop].ServiceStatus.dwCurrentState)
                {
                case SERVICE_START_PENDING:
                    strcpy(Context->szReturnMsg,
                        "Service is starting");
                    break;
                case SERVICE_STOPPED:
                    strcpy(Context->szReturnMsg,
                        "Service is stopped");
                    break;
                case SERVICE_PAUSE_PENDING:
                    strcpy(Context->szReturnMsg,
                        "Service is pausing");
                    break;
```

*(continued)*

**Listing 14-5** *continued*

```
                default:
                    strcpy(Context->szReturnMsg,
                        "Service NOT running");
                    break;
                }
            }
            break;
        }
    }
    CloseServiceHandle(scm);
    return Context->fSuccess == true? 1 : 0;
}

//-----------------------------------------------------------------
// Calculates checksum for Ping
USHORT Checksum(USHORT *buffer, int size) {

    unsigned long cksum = 0;

    while(size > 1)
    {
        cksum += *buffer++;
        size -= sizeof(USHORT);
    }

    if (size)
    {
        cksum += *(UCHAR*)buffer;
    }

    cksum = (cksum >> 16) + (cksum & 0xffff);
    cksum += (cksum >> 16);
    return (USHORT)(~cksum);
}

//-----------------------------------------------------------------
// Fills in default ICMP header information
void fill_icmp_data(char * icmp_data, int datasize)
{

    static int nCounter = 1;
    IcmpHeader *icmp_hdr;
```

```
    char *datapart;

    icmp_hdr = (IcmpHeader*)icmp_data;

    icmp_hdr->i_type = ICMP_ECHO;
    icmp_hdr->i_code = 0;
    icmp_hdr->i_id = (nCounter++);
    icmp_hdr->i_cksum = 0;
    icmp_hdr->i_seq = 0;

    datapart = icmp_data + sizeof(IcmpHeader);
    memset(datapart, 'D', datasize - sizeof(IcmpHeader));

}

//-------------------------------------------------------------------
// Used really just to determine the time it took for response
int decode_resp(char *buf, int bytes, struct sockaddr_in *from) {

    IpHeader *iphdr;
    IcmpHeader *icmphdr;
    unsigned short iphdrlen;

    iphdr = (IpHeader *)buf;

    iphdrlen = iphdr->h_len * 4 ; // Number of 32-bit words
                                  //  * 4 = bytes

    icmphdr = (IcmpHeader*)(buf + iphdrlen);

    if (icmphdr->i_type != ICMP_ECHOREPLY)
    {
        return 0;
    }

    return(GetTickCount()-icmphdr->timestamp);

}

//-------------------------------------------------------------------
// Exported Ping function.
// Note that this function will NOT work on Microsoft Windows 95;
//  it should work on Windows 98, Windows NT, and Windows 2000.
int APIENTRY Ping(LPVOID v)
```

*(continued)*

**Listing 14-5** *continued*

```
{
    MONITOR_CONTEXT *Context;
    char            szServer[255];
    SOCKET          rawSocket;
    LPHOSTENT       lpHost;
    struct          sockaddr_in saDest;
    struct          sockaddr_in saSrc;
    int             nRet;
    int             result = 0;
    int             iTimeout = 1000;
    int             datasize;
    int             recvLen;
    WSADATA         wsaData;
    WORD            wVerReq;
    char            *icmp_data;
    char            *recvbuf;

    Context = (MONITOR_CONTEXT *)v;
    Context->fSuccess = false;  // Default.

    strcpy(szServer, Context->szParameters[0]);

    wVerReq = MAKEWORD(2, 1);
    WSAStartup(wVerReq, &wsaData);

    rawSocket = WSASocket (AF_INET,
        SOCK_RAW,
        IPPROTO_ICMP,
        NULL, 0, 0);

    if (rawSocket == INVALID_SOCKET)
    {
        WSACleanup();
        wsprintf(Context->szReturnMsg,
            "Error creating Raw socket");
        return(result);
    }

    iTimeout = 1000;
    nRet = setsockopt(rawSocket, SOL_SOCKET, SO_RCVTIMEO,
        (char*)&iTimeout, sizeof(iTimeout));
    if (nRet == SOCKET_ERROR)
```

```
{
    WSACleanup();
    wsprintf(Context->szReturnMsg,
        "Error setting socket option receive timeout");
    return(result);
}

iTimeout = 1000;
nRet = setsockopt(rawSocket, SOL_SOCKET, SO_SNDTIMEO,
    (char*)&iTimeout, sizeof(iTimeout));
if (nRet == SOCKET_ERROR)
{
    WSACleanup();
    wsprintf(Context->szReturnMsg,
        "Error setting socket option send timeout");
    return(result);
}

memset(&saDest, 0, sizeof(saDest));

// Look up host.
lpHost = gethostbyname(szServer);
if (lpHost == NULL)
{
    wsprintf(Context->szReturnMsg,
        "Error Getting host (%s) by name",
        szServer);
    return(result);
}

// Set up destination socket address.
saDest.sin_addr.s_addr = *((u_long FAR *) (lpHost->h_addr));
saDest.sin_family = AF_INET;
saDest.sin_port = 0;

datasize = DEF_PACKET_SIZE;
datasize += sizeof(IcmpHeader);

icmp_data = (char *)HeapAlloc(
    GetProcessHeap(), HEAP_ZERO_MEMORY, MAX_PACKET);
recvbuf = (char *)HeapAlloc(
    GetProcessHeap(), HEAP_ZERO_MEMORY, MAX_PACKET);
```

*(continued)*

**Listing 14-5** *continued*

```
    if (icmp_data == NULL || recvbuf == NULL)
    {
        wsprintf(Context->szReturnMsg,
            "Error Getting memory");
        return(result);
    }

    memset(icmp_data, 0, MAX_PACKET);
    fill_icmp_data(icmp_data, datasize);

    ((IcmpHeader*)icmp_data)->i_cksum = 0;
    ((IcmpHeader*)icmp_data)->timestamp = GetTickCount();

    ((IcmpHeader*)icmp_data)->i_seq = 1;
    ((IcmpHeader*)icmp_data)->i_cksum = Checksum((USHORT*)icmp_data,
        datasize);

    nRet = sendto(rawSocket, icmp_data,
        datasize, 0,
        (struct sockaddr*)&saDest,
        sizeof(saDest));
    if (nRet == SOCKET_ERROR)
    {
        if (WSAGetLastError() == WSAETIMEDOUT)
        {
            wsprintf(Context->szReturnMsg,
                "Timeout in Ping");
            return(result);
        }
        else
        {
            wsprintf(Context->szReturnMsg,
                "Error %d in Ping",
                WSAGetLastError());
            return(result);
        }
    }
    recvLen = sizeof(saSrc);
    nRet = recvfrom(rawSocket,
        recvbuf, MAX_PACKET, 0,
        (struct sockaddr*)&saSrc,
        &recvLen);

    if (nRet == SOCKET_ERROR)
```

```
    {
        if (WSAGetLastError() == WSAETIMEDOUT)
        {
            wsprintf(Context->szReturnMsg,
                "Timeout in Ping");
            return(result);
        }
        else
        {
            wsprintf(Context->szReturnMsg,
                "Error %d in Ping",
                WSAGetLastError());
            return(result);
        }
    }

    // Decode Response returns the time
    //  in milliseconds the ping took.
    wsprintf(Context->szReturnMsg,
        "Ping succeeded - time: %d ms",
        decode_resp(recvbuf, nRet, &saSrc));

    Context->returnCode =
        decode_resp(recvbuf, nRet, &saSrc);
    Context->fSuccess = true;

    HeapFree (GetProcessHeap(), 0, icmp_data);
    HeapFree (GetProcessHeap(), 0, recvbuf);
    if (rawSocket != INVALID_SOCKET)
    {
        closesocket(rawSocket);
    }
    WSACleanup();
    return(1);
}

//-----------------------------------------------------------------
// Exported function to test generic ODBC connection.
//  Data source must be defined in ODBC administrator.
int APIENTRY TestODBCConnection(PVOID v)
{
    MONITOR_CONTEXT *Context;
    CODBCDatabase *db;
    int result = 0;
```

*(continued)*

**Listing 14-5** *continued*

```
    Context = (MONITOR_CONTEXT *)v;
    CODBCDatabase::InitCriticalSection();

    db = new CODBCDatabase(Context->szParameters[0],
        Context->szParameters[1],
        Context->szParameters[2]);

    if (db->isConnected())
    {
        result = 1;
        wsprintf(Context->szReturnMsg,
            "Connect to %s Succeeded!",
            Context->szParameters[0]);
        Context->fSuccess = true;
    }
    else
    {
        char diag[512];
        char temp[512];
        wsprintf(Context->szReturnMsg,
            "Error connecting to %s! Last error was: %s",
            Context->szParameters[0], db->getLastErrorString(diag));

        // Quote quotes.
        for (int loop = 0, skip = 0;
            Context->szReturnMsg[loop] != '\0' ; loop++)
        {
            if (Context->szReturnMsg[loop] == '\'')
            {
                temp[loop+skip] = '\'';
                skip++;
            }
            temp[loop+skip] = Context->szReturnMsg[loop];
            temp[loop+skip+1] = '\0';
        }
        strcpy(Context->szReturnMsg, temp);
        Context->fSuccess = false;
    }

    delete db;
    CODBCDatabase::DelCriticalSection();

    return result;
}
```

```
//-------------------------------------------------------------------
// Tests SQL Server database, with enhancements based upon
//  what we know about SQL Server
int APIENTRY TestSQLServerStatus(PVOID v)
{
    MONITOR_CONTEXT *Context;
    CODBCDatabase *db;
    char szTemp[512];
    int result = 0;

    Context = (MONITOR_CONTEXT *)v;
    CODBCDatabase::InitCriticalSection();

    sprintf(szTemp, "DRIVER={SQL Server};Server=%s;"
        "database=%s;uid=%s;pwd=%s",
        Context->szParameters[0],
        Context->szParameters[1],
        Context->szParameters[2],
        Context->szParameters[3]);

    db = new CODBCDatabase(szTemp);

    if (db->isConnected())
    {
        result = 1;
        wsprintf(Context->szReturnMsg,
            "Connect to %s Succeeded!",
            Context->szParameters[0]);
        Context->fSuccess = true;
    }
    else
    {
        char diag[512];
        char temp[512];
        MONITOR_CONTEXT ctx;
        Context->fSuccess = false;

        // Since we know the name of the server, try to ping it.
        strcpy(ctx.szParameters[0], Context->szParameters[0]);
        Ping(&ctx);
        wsprintf(Context->szReturnMsg,
            "Error connecting to %s/%s!  "
            "Last error was: %s. Pinged and %s",
```

*(continued)*

**Listing 14-5** *continued*

```
                Context->szParameters[0],
                Context->szParameters[1],
                db->getLastErrorString(diag),
                ctx.szReturnMsg);
            // Quote quotes.
            for (int loop = 0, skip = 0;
                Context->szReturnMsg[loop] != '\0' ; loop++)
            {
                if (Context->szReturnMsg[loop] == '\'')
                {
                    temp[loop+skip] = '\'';
                    skip++;
                }
                temp[loop+skip] = Context->szReturnMsg[loop];
                temp[loop+skip+1] = '\0';
            }
            strcpy(Context->szReturnMsg, temp);
            if (ctx.fSuccess)
            {
                ctx.fSuccess = false;
                strcpy(ctx.szParameters[0], Context->szParameters[0]);
                strcpy(ctx.szParameters[1], "MSSQLServer");
                TestServiceStatus(&ctx);
                if (ctx.fSuccess)
                {
                    strcat(Context->szReturnMsg,
                        "  MSSQLServer Service is running.");
                }
                else
                {
                    strcat(Context->szReturnMsg,
                        "  MSSQLServer Service is NOT running.");
                }
            }
        }

        delete db;
        CODBCDatabase::DelCriticalSection();

        return result;
    }
```

*Ping* uses the standard TCP/IP method to open a raw socket to evoke an echo from a remote server. The *Ping* function as I implement it here is based upon the Ping.c sample included with the MSDN Platform SDK. I've made several adaptations.

Most notably, there is no screen I/O associated with the operation of *Ping*. As with all DLL monitoring functions called by *CMonitorService*, all feedback is passed in the *szReturnMsg* parameter of the MONITOR_CONTEXT structure passed to the function. Additionally, I make only a single attempt to ping the server rather than multiple attempts.

At a high level, *Ping* opens a raw TCP/IP socket, finds the host based upon the name passed in *szParameters[0]* of the MONITOR_CONTEXT structure, and then sends a block of data and determines the amount of time the response took. *Ping* sets a timeout of 1 second. In real-world testing, connecting to local servers across a 100-Base-T network reports a send-receive interval between 0 and 14 milliseconds. *Ping* generally returns times of between 125 and 160 milliseconds over a RAS connection.

The details of implementing *Ping* are beyond the scope of this book. However, you will find it useful to understand the implications and use of *Ping*. *Ping* can provide additional information in the event of some other network failure. For example, in the event of a failure, *TestSQLServerStatus*—which I'll describe more fully in a moment—uses its knowledge of the server name to call *Ping* to connect to the SQL Server database. The failed SQL Server connection—combined with the results of a ping of the server—can tell you a lot about the underlying cause of a reported problem.

*TestServiceStatus* is the second exported function in TestMonitor.dll. The purpose of *TestServiceStatus* is to determine whether a particular service is running on a given server. The server name and the service to check are passed in *szParameters[0]* and *szParameters[1]*, respectively. Since creating services is one of this book's major topics, *TestServiceStatus* deserves a more detailed explanation.

Recall that when we install a service, we first call the Win32 function *OpenSCManager*, which has the following prototype:

```
SC_HANDLE OpenSCManager (
    LPCTSTR lpMachineName,    // Pointer to machine name string
    LPCTSTR lpDatabaseName,   // Pointer to database name string
    DWORD dwDesiredAccess     // Type of access
);
```

The first parameter is the machine name. When we modify a service on the local machine, we can pass NULL for this parameter. If we want to check on the status of services running on another machine, *lpMachineName* must be the name of the other machine. NULL can be passed as the database name in *lpDatabaseName* because the default is currently the only allowed value. When all we need to do is check on existing services, we can pass SC_MANAGER_ENUMERATE_SERVICES as *dwDesiredAccess*.

Once *OpenSCManager* returns the handle to the SCM, we need to call *EnumServicesStatus* to check the status of services on the specified machine. The prototype for *EnumServicesStatus* is as follows:

```
BOOL EnumServicesStatus(
    SC_HANDLE hSCManager,     // Handle to service control manager
                              //  database
    DWORD dwServiceType,      // Type of services to enumerate
    DWORD dwServiceState,     // State of services to enumerate
    LPENUM_SERVICE_STATUS lpServices,
                              // Pointer to service status buffer
    DWORD cbBufSize,          // Size of service status buffer
    LPDWORD pcbBytesNeeded,   // Pointer to variable for bytes needed
    LPDWORD lpServicesReturned,
                              // Pointer to variable for number
                              //  returned
    LPDWORD lpResumeHandle    // Pointer to variable for next entry
);
```

*EnumServicesStatus* does not return a single service's status, but rather reports on the status of all services. The first parameter is the SCM handle returned from *OpenSCManager*. The type of service to enumerate is passed in the second parameter, *dwServiceType*. This parameter can be SERVICE_WIN32 or SERVICE_DRIVER. In *TestMonitor*, this parameter is always SERVICE_WIN32. One complication of passing back the status of all services is the need to allocate a relatively large buffer to pass as *lpServices*. One alternative is to call the function first with a small buffer, as specified in *cbBuffSize*, and check the return code for an error. If *GetLastError* returns ERROR_MORE_DATA, *pcbBytesNeeded* will point to the number of bytes required to retrieve the remaining service entries.

The entries returned in *lpServices* are structures with an embedded structure. Both structures are shown here.

```
typedef struct _ENUM_SERVICE_STATUS {
    LPTSTR lpServiceName;
    LPTSTR lpDisplayName;
    SERVICE_STATUS ServiceStatus;
} ENUM_SERVICE_STATUS;

typedef struct _SERVICE_STATUS {
    DWORD dwServiceType;
    DWORD dwCurrentState;
    DWORD dwControlsAccepted;
    DWORD dwWin32ExitCode;
    DWORD dwServiceSpecificExitCode;
    DWORD dwCheckPoint;
    DWORD dwWaitHint;
} SERVICE_STATUS
```

*TestServiceStatus* in *TestMonitor* uses only two elements. First I test the *lpServiceName* member of ENUM_SERVICE_STATUS to find the requested service. Once I've found the correct ENUM_SERVICE_STATUS structure, I check *dwCurrentState* in *ServiceStatus*. The possible values include SERVICE_STOPPED, SERVICE_STOP_PENDING, SERVICE_START_PENDING, SERVICE_PAUSED, and SERVICE_RUNNING. From the perspective of *TestServiceStatus*, any value for *dwCurrentState* except SERVICE_RUNNING is considered a failure. For most of the common status codes, I place a friendly representation of the service code in the *szReturnMsg* member of the MONITOR_CONTEXT structure passed to *TestServiceStatus*. This service code allows *MonitorService* to pass more useful information to the user. Appendix B discusses another way to use the Service Control Manager to monitor services running on Windows 2000 servers.

*TestODBCConnection* attempts to create a connection to an ODBC database by creating a *CODBCDatabase* object. It passes the ODBC data source name in *szParameters[0]*, and the user name and password in *szParameters[1]* and *szParameters[2]*, respectively. If the connection fails, a newly added *GetLastError* member of *CODBCDatabase* provides the *SQLState* and other descriptive information on any error that occurs during the attempt to connect. You'll find the modified ODBClass.cpp and ODBClass.h with the *TestMonitor* project on the companion CD-ROM.

There is one seemingly odd code fragment in *TestODBCConnection*.

```
// Quote quotes.
for (int loop = 0, skip = 0;
    Context->szReturnMsg[loop] != '\0'; loop++)
{
    if (Context->szReturnMsg[loop] == '\'')
    {
        temp[loop+skip] = '\'';
        skip++;
    }
    temp[loop+skip] = Context->szReturnMsg[loop];
    temp[loop+skip+1] = '\0';
}
strcpy(Context->szReturnMsg, temp);
```

The purpose of this code is to replace each original single-quote character with two single-quote characters. Messages from the SQL Server ODBC driver commonly contain single quotes. It is important to duplicate single-quote characters because the string will eventually be passed to SQL Server as part of an insert operation. (SQL Server considers a single-quote character to be the end of a quoted string unless the single quote is followed immediately by another single quote.)

*TestSQLServerStatus* is the last of the four functions exported by *TestMonitor*. *TestSQLServerStatus* takes advantage of knowledge we have about SQL Server connections. Rather than using *szParameters[0]* as the ODBC data source name, *szParameters[0]* is the server name, *szParameters[1]* is the name of the database on the server, and *szParameters[2]* and *szParameters[3]* should hold the user name and password, respectively.

*CODBCDatabase* required a change to accommodate using *SQLDriverConnect* rather than *SQLConnect* to connect. *SQLDriverConnect* allows a connection that does not directly link to a predefined ODBC data source.

```
SQLRETURN SQLDriverConnect(
    SQLHDBC ConnectionHandle,
    SQLHWND WindowHandle,
    SQLCHAR *InConnectionString,
    SQLSMALLINT StringLength1,
    SQLCHAR *OutConnectionString,
    SQLSMALLINT BufferLength,
    SQLSMALLINT *StringLength2Ptr,
    SQLUSMALLING DriverCompletion);
```

Only a couple of the parameters to *SQLDriverConnect* are significant for this discussion. *WindowHandle* is passed as 0 in *CODBCDatabase* since our goal is to avoid any user interface. *InConnectionString* is a string that for SQL Server looks like this: "DRIVER={SQL Server};Server=<ServerName>;database=<DatabaseName>;-uid=<UserName>;password=<password>". In *TestSQLServerStatus*, SQL_DRIVER_NOPROMPT is sent in the *DriverCompletion* parameter to ensure that no dialogs are displayed.

If the connection fails, *TestSQLServerStatus* tests connectivity to the server using *Ping*. If *Ping* succeeds, I call *TestServiceStatus* passing the server name and "MSSQL-Server" in *szParameters[0]* and *szParameters[1]*, respectively. I copy details of the success or failure of these additional tests to *szReturnMsg* to allow *MonitorService* to give the user more details of the failure.

## CONCLUSION

The *MonitorService* example presented in this chapter represents a real program designed to meet specific needs and accommodate future requirements. Several features of the program enable this flexibility.

First SQL Server tables let the underlying engine know what to do. As we will see in Chapter 15, we can add further flexibility by allowing Web clients to view and modify this information store.

Second the tables control virtually all of the program's operation, even down to the functions called by the underlying *MonitorService* engine. The four sample functions in *TestMonitor* barely scratch the surface of what we can do using *MonitorService*. For example, we can add functions that test connectivity to IPX and APPC machines the same way that *Ping* allows us to determine the status of a TCP/IP client. We can add more functions to *TestMonitor* to allow it to perform tasks similar to those performed by *TestSQLServerStatus* against other database servers. Mail monitoring is another natural extension. We can create mail messages with return receipt capabilities, generating pinglike abilities to connect to mail servers.

It's important to remember that a program like *MonitorService* can do much more than monitor network activity. Any process that can live within the restrictions dictated by the MONITOR_CONTEXT structure can operate as part of this service, allowing any operation that needs to be performed periodically—perhaps once per day—to operate reliably, logging activities and notifying users of failure.

Of course, the version of *MonitorService* covered in this chapter does not allow easy monitoring of output by people who are uncomfortable using a tool that allows them to look into a SQL Server database. In Chapter 15, I will add the ability to interact with the service in interesting and powerful ways.

*Chapter 15*

# Administering a Service Application on the Web

One of the most important parts of a service application is its ease of administration. No matter how much you like the way a service application functions, you're going to have problems if it's difficult to administer. Using the Web to administer an application can give your server-based application an edge on the competition.

There are several ways to communicate with a service application over the Web. Let's take the MonitorService network monitoring application from Chapter 14 as our example. First, much of the application is table-driven. You can modify those tables to change the behavior of the application.

A second way to interact with the service application over the Web is to create a process on the Web server that uses some of the techniques outlined in Chapter 12. Recall that MonitorService from Chapter 14 created two worker threads to interact with TCP/IP clients. These worker threads allow an application to call into the service and request information or change parameters. I'll discuss this process later in this chapter.

Modifying the tables that drive the application is a task best suited to Active Server Pages (ASP) scripts, covered in Chapter 9. These server-side scripts can contain VBScript code that has access to server-side components. These components allow easy access to data sources through Active Data Objects (ADO). ASP has the advantages of being flexible, relatively fast, and available on Internet Information Server (IIS), which is included with Microsoft Windows 2000 as well as several other platforms. The slight disadvantage with ASP is that it is a script that is interpreted at run time. This feature has some performance implications. Since scripts contain the source code for the application, they might not be appropriate for some commercial applications. A developer might not want an application's source code distributed to customers. You can mitigate this problem somewhat by encapsulating crucial business logic in server-side ActiveX components, as demonstrated in the HTMLUtil example in Chapter 9.

# USING ASP TO MONITOR MONITORSERVICE

Listings 15-1 and 15-2 show Global.asa and Default.asp, the application file and initial script used in the ASP section of the Web monitoring example presented in this chapter. Global.asa contains only one of the four possible event handlers, *SessionOnStart*. *SessionOnStart* sets a session variable that defines the parameters required to log on to the monitoring ODBC data source and then redirects the application to Default.asp. Doing so ensures that all users start at the same place in the application. Another possible reason to force all users through a single entry screen is to ensure that users enter through an application login screen. While a network monitoring system should be restricted in some way, this chapter's ISAPIMonitor program is an example of an application that is best secured using the user authentication options present in IIS. Appendix A discusses setting up virtual directories in IIS and details ways of securing IIS applications.

**Global.asa**

```
<SCRIPT LANGUAGE="VBScript" RUNAT="Server">

'You can add special event handlers in this file that will run
' automatically when special ASP events occur. To create these
' handlers, create a subroutine with a name from the
' list below that corresponds to the event you want to use. For
' example, to create an event handler for Session_OnStart,
' put the following code into this file (without the comments):
Sub Session_OnStart
    session("SQLLOGIN")="UID=sa;PWD=;DSN=Monitoring"
    Response.Redirect("Default.asp")
End Sub
```

**Listing 15-1**

```
'Sub Session_OnEnd
'End Sub
'Application_OnStart ' Runs once when the first page of your
                     '  application is run for the first time (by
                     '  any user)
'Application
_OnEnd   ' Runs once when the Web server shuts down

</SCRIPT>
```

**Default.asp**

```
<%@ Language=VBScript %>
<HTML>
<HEAD>
<META NAME="GENERATOR" Content="Microsoft Visual Studio 6.0">
<TITLE>Monitoring Main Screen</TITLE>
</HEAD>
<BODY>
<%
dim rstAlerts
dim db
dim strSQL
dim link

Set db=Server.CreateObject("ADODB.Connection")
db.Open(Session("SQLLOGIN"))

    strSQL="Select MIN(DateTimeOfAlert) as FirstAlert, "
    strSQL=strSQL & "MAX(DateTimeOfAlert) as LastAlert, "
    strSQL=strSQL & " COUNT(DateTimeOfAlert) as CountAlerts, "
    strSQL=strSQL & " MAX(AlertComment) as Comment, "
    strSQL=strSQL & " MAX(Name) as TaskName, "
    strSQL=strSQL & " MAX(TaskID) as MaxTaskID "
    strSQL=strSQL & " from QryAlertsAndTasks "
    strSQL=strSQL & " WHERE DateTimeReset is NULL "
    strSQL=strSQL & " GROUP BY TaskID "
    strSQL=strSQL & " ORDER BY TaskName "
    set rstAlerts = db.Execute(strSQL)

    Response.Write("<CENTER>")
```

**Listing 15-2** *(continued)*

**Listing 15-2** *continued*

```
    link="<CENTER><A HREF=SelectTask.asp"
    link=link&">Add, Edit or Delete Tasks</A><BR>"
    link=link&"<A HREF=ISAPIMonitor.dll?"
    link=link&">Monitor Trace</A><BR>"
    if rstAlerts.EOF then
        Response.Write("<H2>No Alerts</H2>")
        Response.Write(link)
    else
        Response.Write("<H2>Alerts</H2><BR>")
        Response.Write(link)
        Response.Write("Click on task name to see details of ")
        Response.Write("all active alerts for that task.<BR>  ")
        rstAlerts.MoveFirst
        Response.Write("<TABLE WIDTH=85% BORDER=1 CELLSPACING=1")
        Response.Write(" CELLPADDING=1><TR>")
        Response.Write("<TD BGCOLOR=aqua><B><CENTER>")
        Response.Write("Task Name</CENTER></B></TD>")
        Response.Write("<TD BGCOLOR=aqua><B><CENTER>")
        Response.Write("First/Last<BR>Alert</CENTER></B></TD>")
        Response.Write("<TD BGCOLOR=aqua><B><CENTER># Alerts")
        Response.Write("</CENTER></B></TD>")
        Response.Write("<TD BGCOLOR=aqua><B><CENTER>Alert Comment")
        Response.Write("</CENTER></B></TD>")
        Response.Write("</TR>"&vbcrlf)
        Do While Not rstAlerts.EOF
            Response.Write("<TR BGCOLOR=WHITE>")
            link="<CENTER><A HREF=TaskAlerts.asp?TaskID="
            link=link & rstAlerts("MaxTaskID")
            link=link&">"&rstAlerts("TaskName")&"</CENTER></A>"
            Response.Write("<TD BGCOLOR=white><B>" & link & "</B>")
            Response.Write("</TD><TD BGCOLOR=white><B><CENTER>")
            Response.Write(rstAlerts("FirstAlert"))
            Response.Write("<BR>" & rstAlerts("LastAlert"))
            Response.Write("</CENTER></B></TD>")
            Response.Write("<TD BGCOLOR=white><B><CENTER>")
            Response.Write(rstAlerts("CountAlerts") & "</CENTER>")
            Response.Write("</B></TD><TD BGCOLOR=white><B>")
            Response.Write(rstAlerts("Comment") & "</B></TD>")
            Response.Write("</TR>"&vbcrlf)
            rstAlerts.MoveNext
```

```
        loop
        Response.Write("</CENTER>")
    end if
    set rstAlerts=nothing
    set db=nothing

%>
</BODY>
</HTML>
```

## Interacting with Alerts

The general structure of all ASP source files in the Web monitoring example is similar to Default.asp in Listing 15-1, so I'll explain the Default.asp listing in detail with only differences explained when describing other ASP source file listings. Default.asp creates the main screen of this chapter's Web monitoring application. From this screen—directly or indirectly—a user can get to the rest of the application. First I create an ADODB connection by calling the *CreateObject* method of the *Server* object. With the connection string set in the *SessionOnStart* method in Global.asa, I call the *Open* method of the database connection object returned from *CreateObject*.

Next I create a SQL string to get a list of the tasks that have outstanding alerts. To do this, I create a SELECT query with a GROUP BY clause on a SQL Server view I created in the monitoring database first described in Chapter 14. While it is a good idea to use relational design when you create tables, sometimes it is useful to look at the data with tables joined. In this case, it is convenient to have *TblTasks* and *TblAlerts* joined. Using the joined tables in a view offers better performance and better network utilization than separately getting records from *TblAlerts* and *TblTasks* and manually linking them on the client side. While you don't need to modify the fields in the view we create here, a view can also modify data types or sizes. This can be useful when you need to combine data from several databases with similar but not identical information.

Listing 15-3 shows the code to create the view named *QryAlertsAndTasks*. Using a GROUP BY clause allows me to get one record returned per task that has outstanding alerts, with the first and most recent alert time and the count of the number of alerts.

**SQL script for *QryAlertsAndTasks***

```
if exists (select * from sysobjects where id =
    object_id(N'[dbo].[QryAlertsAndTasks]') and
    OBJECTPROPERTY(id, N'IsView') = 1)
drop view [dbo].[QryAlertsAndTasks]
GO

SET QUOTED_IDENTIFIER  ON    SET ANSI_NULLS  ON
GO

CREATE VIEW dbo.QryAlertsAndTasks
AS
SELECT TblAlerts.DateTimeOfAlert, TblAlerts.DateTimeReset,
    TblAlerts.DateTimeIntervention, TblAlerts.ResetComment,
    TblTasks.Name, TblTasks.DateTimeLastRun,
    TblTasks.DateTimeNextRun, TblTasks.Beeper,
    TblTasks.EMail, TblResetType.Description,
    TblAlerts.AlertComment, TblAlerts.TaskID
FROM TblAlerts INNER JOIN
    TblTasks ON
    TblAlerts.TaskID = TblTasks.TaskID LEFT OUTER JOIN
    TblResetType ON
    TblAlerts.ResetTypeID = TblResetType.ResetTypeID

GO
SET QUOTED_IDENTIFIER  OFF    SET ANSI_NULLS  ON
GO
```

**Listing 15-3**

The SQL string created in Default.asp is passed to the *Execute* method of *db*, returning a recordset object, saved into *rstAlerts*. If this recordset contains any records, *EOF* will be *false*, and an HTML table to list the tasks with exceptions will be created.

Default.asp creates a link for each task in the table so that the user can click on the task name to see details of the task. The resulting screen is shown in Figure 15-1.

Each task's hyperlink in the table shown in Figure 15-1 serves as a link to TaskAlerts.asp. TaskAlerts.asp shows the details for each task, including all active alerts related to the task. This information can be used to pick out the details of each alert, including the alert comments that contain information specific to the failure, such as the *AlertComment* for each alert. Default.asp uses the SQL MAX keyword to select the *AlertComment* field from one of the alerts. All returned values in a GROUP BY query must be returned by an aggregate function, such as MAX, MIN, COUNT SUM, or AVG. The decision to use MAX is arbitrary. Microsoft Jet SQL supports an aggregate

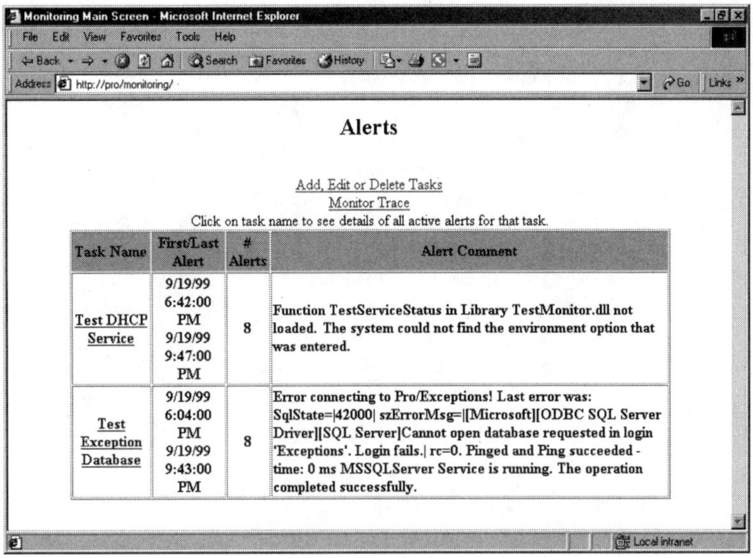


**Figure 15-1** *The default screen for the Web monitoring ASP application.*

function, LAST, that seems more appropriate, but LAST is not supported by SQL Server. Listing 15-4 shows the code for TaskAlerts.asp, and Figure 15-2 shows the page that script creates.

**TaskAlerts.asp**

```
<%@ Language=VBScript %>
<HTML>
<HEAD>
<META NAME="GENERATOR" Content="Microsoft Visual Studio 6.0">
<TITLE>Task Alert Details Screen</TITLE>
</HEAD>
<BODY>
<%
dim rstAlerts
dim db
dim strSQL
dim link
dim task

task=request("TaskID")
```

**Listing 15-4** *(continued)*

**Listing 15-4** *continued*

```
Set db=Server.CreateObject("ADODB.Connection")
db.Open(Session("SQLLOGIN"))

    strSQL="Select DateTimeOfAlert, "
    strSQL=strSQL & " AlertComment, "
    strSQL=strSQL & " DateTimeIntervention, "
    strSQL=strSQL & " Name, "
    strSQL=strSQL & " TaskID "
    strSQL=strSQL & " from QryAlertsAndTasks "
    strSQL=strSQL & " WHERE TaskID="&CStr(Task)
    strSQL=strSQL & " AND DateTimeReset is NULL"
    strSQL=strSQL & " ORDER BY DateTimeOfAlert DESC "
    set rstAlerts = db.Execute(strSQL)

    Response.Write("<CENTER>")

    if rstAlerts.EOF then
        Response.Write("<H2>No Alerts active for this task.</H2>")
    else
        rstAlerts.MoveFirst
        Response.Write("<H2>Alerts for ")
        Response.Write(rstAlerts("Name")&"</H2><BR>")
        link="<CENTER><A HREF=ResetAlerts.asp?TaskID=" & _
            rstAlerts("TaskID")
        link=link&">Reset All Alerts for this Task</CENTER></A>"
        Response.Write(link)
        Response.Write("<TABLE WIDTH=85% BORDER=1 CELLSPACING=1")
        Response.Write(" CELLPADDING=1><TR>")
        Response.Write("<TD BGCOLOR=aqua><B><CENTER>Date/Time<BR>")
        Response.Write("of Alert</CENTER></B></TD>")
        Response.Write("<TD BGCOLOR=aqua><B><CENTER>Date/Time<BR>")
        Response.Write("of Notification</CENTER></B></TD>")
        Response.Write("<TD BGCOLOR=aqua><B><CENTER>Alert Comment")
        Response.Write("</CENTER></B></TD>")
        Response.Write("</TR>"&vbcrlf)
        Do While Not rstAlerts.EOF
            Response.Write("<TR BGCOLOR=WHITE>")
            Response.Write("<TD BGCOLOR=white><B>")
            Response.Write(rstAlerts("DateTimeOfAlert") & "</B></TD>")
            Response.Write("<TD BGCOLOR=white><B>")
            Response.Write(rstAlerts("DateTimeIntervention") & "</B>")
            Response.Write("</TD><TD BGCOLOR=white><B>")
            Response.Write(rstAlerts("AlertComment") & "</B></TD>")
            Response.Write("</TR>"&vbcrlf)
            rstAlerts.MoveNext
```

```
        loop
        Response.Write("</CENTER>")

    end if
    set rstAlerts=nothing
    set db=nothing

%>
</BODY>
</HTML>
```

At the top of Figure 15-2 you'll see a hyperlink, Reset All Alerts For This Task. This hyperlink calls ResetAlerts.asp to allow the user to reset all alerts associated with the task displayed in TaskAlerts.asp. Clicking on this hyperlink displays the screen shown in Figure 15-3. This screen allows the user to enter a reset comment to be placed in the record in *tblAlerts*. One comment is used as a comment for all reset alerts. Allowing each alert to be reset with its own reset comment could be a useful addition, especially in a case in which multiple failure types cause a single alert. Listing 15-5 shows the source for ResetAlerts.asp.

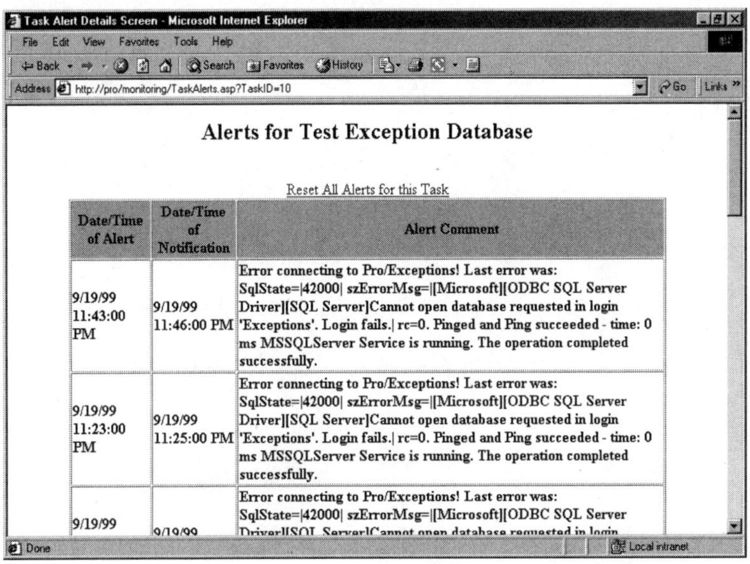


**Figure 15-2** *The Task Alert Details Screen created by TaskAlerts.asp.*

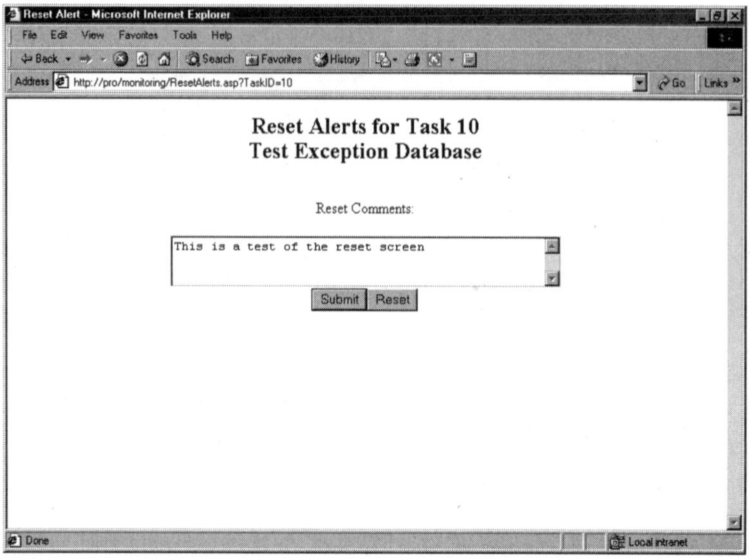


**Figure 15-3** *Reset Alert screen created by ResetAlerts.asp.*

**ResetAlerts.asp**

```
<%@ Language=VBScript %>
<HTML>
<HEAD>
<META NAME="GENERATOR" Content="Microsoft Visual Studio 6.0">
<TITLE>Reset Alert</TITLE>
</HEAD>
<BODY>

<%
dim rstTasks
dim db
dim strSQL
dim taskID

taskID=request("taskID")

Set db=Server.CreateObject("ADODB.Connection")
db.Open(Session("SQLLOGIN"))

strSQL="SELECT * FROM tblTasks WHERE taskID="&taskID

set rstTasks=db.Execute(strSQL)
```

**Listing 15-5**

```
Response.Write("<CENTER>")
if rstTasks.eof then
    Response.Write("<H2>Sorry, Task "&taskID&" was deleted")
    Response.Write(" by another workstation!</H2>")
    Response.Write("<FORM action=""Default.asp"" ")
    Response.Write("method=POST id=form1 name=form1>")
    Response.Write("<INPUT type=""submit"" ")
    Response.Write("value=""Return to Main Screen"" ")
    Response.Write("id=submit1 name=submit1>")
    Response.Write("</FORM>    ")
else
    Response.Write("<H2>Reset Alerts for Task "&taskID&"<BR>")
    Response.Write(rstTasks("Name")&"</H2>")
    Response.Write("<BR>Reset Comments:<BR>")
    Response.Write("<FORM action=""ProcessReset.asp?TaskID=")
    Response.Write(""&taskID&""" method=POST id=form1 name=form1>")
    Response.Write("<TEXTAREA rows=3 cols=50 ")
    Response.Write("id=ResetComments name=ResetComments>")
    Response.Write("</TEXTAREA><BR>    ")
    Response.Write("<INPUT type=""submit"" ")
    Response.Write("value=""Submit"" ")
    Response.Write("id=submit1 name=submit1>")
    Response.Write("<INPUT type=""Reset"" ")
    Response.Write("value=""Reset"" ")
    Response.Write("id=Reset1 name=Reset1>")
    Response.Write("</FORM>    ")
end if

set rstTasks=nothing
set db=nothing

%>
</BODY>
</HTML>
```

Once the user enters a reset comment on the screen shown in Figure 15-3, he or she can click on the Submit button to reset the alerts in the database. Clicking on the Submit button calls ProcessReset.asp, shown in Listing 15-6. This is a short routine that creates and executes a SQL UPDATE command to set a reset date, reset comment, and reset type. A SQL UPDATE returns no records, so I need to pass an additional parameter to the *Execute* method of the database connection object *db*. The parameter value, *adExecuteNoRecords*, is passed as the third parameter. Since I don't need to use the second parameter, it is passed as an empty parameter represented by two consecutive commas, as in the following fragment:

```
db.Execute strSQL,,adExecuteNoRecords
```

ProcessReset.asp does not return a page to the browser but instead redirects the browser back to Default.asp. Unless an additional alert arrives after the SQL UPDATE command that resets all of the outstanding alerts for the task involved, returning to Default.asp will present the user with a screen without an entry for the task whose alerts were just reset.

**ProcessReset.asp**

```
<%@ Language=VBScript %>
<%
Response.Buffer=true
dim db
dim strSQL
dim taskID
dim recs
dim rstResetType
dim userReset

taskID=request("taskID")

Set db=Server.CreateObject("ADODB.Connection")
db.Open(Session("SQLLOGIN"))

' We try to determine the User Intervention
'  reset type ID, but default to 2 if we fail.
strSQL="SELECT ResetTypeID FROM tblResetType "
strSQL=strSQL&"WHERE Description LIKE 'User Intervention%'"

set rstResetType=db.Execute(strSQL)

if not rstResetType.EOF then
    userReset=rstResetType("ResetTypeID")
else
    userReset=2
end if

strSQL="UPDATE tblAlerts SET ResetTypeID="&userReset&", "
strSQL=strSQL&"ResetComment='"&request("ResetComments")&"', "
strSQL=strSQL&"DateTimeReset='"&Now()&"'"
strSQL=strSQL&" WHERE taskID="&taskID

db.Execute strSQL,,adExecuteNoRecords

set db=nothing
Response.Redirect("Default.asp")

%>
```

**Listing 15-6**

## Interacting with Tasks

One last ability is required to allow complete Web maintenance of the tables that drive MonitorService. While working with alerts is all that is needed most of the time, the ability to add, edit, or delete tasks from the Web is sometimes necessary. Take a look back at the screen created by Default.asp, shown in Figure 15-1. There is a hyperlink at the top of the page: Add, Edit, Or Delete Tasks. Clicking on this link brings you to a screen created by SelectTask.asp, shown in Figure 15-4.

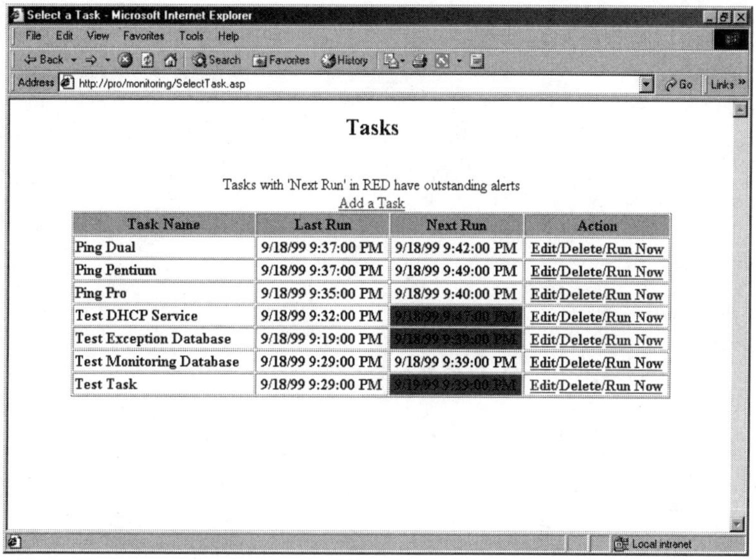


**Figure 15-4** *The Select A Task screen created by SelectTask.asp.*

SelectTask.asp presents all tasks in alphabetical order in an HTML table. The Next Run column of tasks that have outstanding alerts are highlighted in red. The last column of the table contains hyperlinks that allow the tasks to be edited, deleted, or run. Listing 15-7 shows the code for SelectTask.asp.

**SelectTask.asp**

```
<%@ Language=VBScript %>
<HTML>
<HEAD>
<META NAME="GENERATOR" Content="Microsoft Visual Studio 6.0">
<TITLE>Select a Task</TITLE>
</HEAD>
<BODY>
```

**Listing 15-7** *(continued)*

**Listing 15-7** *continued*

```
<%
Response.Buffer=true
dim db
dim strSQL
dim taskID
dim recs
dim rstTasks
dim rstAlerts

Set db=Server.CreateObject("ADODB.Connection")
db.Open(Session("SQLLOGIN"))

' We try to determine the User Intervention
'   reset type ID, but default to 2 if we fail.
strSQL="SELECT * FROM tblTasks ORDER BY Name"

set rstTasks=db.Execute(strSQL)

    Response.Write("<CENTER>")
    if rstTasks.EOF then
        Response.Write("<H2>No Tasks Defined</H2>")
    else
        Response.Write("<H2>Tasks</H2><BR>")
        Response.Write("Tasks with 'Next Run' in RED have")
        Response.Write(" outstanding alerts")
        link=link &"<BR><A HREF=EditTask.asp?TaskID=0"
        link=link&">Add a Task</A>"
        Response.Write(link)
        rstTasks.MoveFirst
        Response.Write("<TABLE WIDTH=85% BORDER=1 CELLSPACING=1")
        Response.Write(" CELLPADDING=1><TR>")
        Response.Write("<TD BGCOLOR=aqua><B><CENTER>")
        Response.Write("Task Name</CENTER></B></TD>")
        Response.Write("<TD BGCOLOR=aqua><B><CENTER>Last Run")
        Response.Write("</CENTER></B></TD>")
        Response.Write("<TD BGCOLOR=aqua><B><CENTER>Next Run")
        Response.Write("</CENTER></B></TD>")
        Response.Write("<TD BGCOLOR=aqua><B><CENTER>Action")
        Response.Write("</CENTER></B></TD>")
        Response.Write("</TR>"&vbcrlf)
        Do While Not rstTasks.EOF
            Response.Write("<TR BGCOLOR=WHITE>")
            Response.Write("<TD BGCOLOR=white><B>")
            Response.Write(rstTasks("Name")&"</B></TD>")
```

```
            Response.Write("<TD BGCOLOR=white><B><CENTER>")
            Response.Write(rstTasks("DateTimeLastRun"))
            Response.Write("</CENTER></B></TD>")
            strSQL="SELECT AlertID FROM tblAlerts "
            strSQL=strSQL&"WHERE TaskID="&rstTasks("TaskID")
            strSQL=strSQL&" AND DateTimeReset IS NULL"

            set rstAlerts=db.Execute(strSQL)
            if rstAlerts.EOF then
                Response.Write("<TD BGCOLOR=WHITE><B><CENTER>")
            else
                Response.Write("<TD BGCOLOR=RED><B><CENTER>")
            end if
            Response.Write(rstTasks("DateTimeNextRun"))
            Response.Write("</CENTER></B></TD>")
            Response.Write("<TD BGCOLOR=white><B><CENTER>")
            link="<A HREF=EditTask.asp?TaskID="
            link=link & rstTasks("TaskID")
            link=link &">Edit</A>/"
            link=link &"<A HREF=DeleteTask.asp?TaskID="
            link=link & rstTasks("TaskID")
            link=link&">Delete</A>/"
            link=link &"<A HREF=RunNow.asp?TaskID="
            link=link & rstTasks("TaskID")
            link=link&">Run Now</A>"
            Response.Write(link)
            Response.Write("</CENTER></B></TD>")
            Response.Write("</TR>"&vbcrlf)
            rstTasks.MoveNext
        loop
    end if
    Response.Write("</CENTER>")
    set rstTasks=nothing
    set db=nothing


%>

</BODY>
</HTML>
```

EditTask.asp allows users to edit most elements of the task. Figure 15-5 shows the screen produced by EditTask.asp that results when you click on the Edit hyperlink in the screen shown in Figure 15-4. The current values are placed in each of the fields and can be left alone or edited. For the *ExecuteType* and *AtOrEvery* fields, combo boxes are provided to restrict entries to valid values. Listing 15-8 shows EditTask.asp.

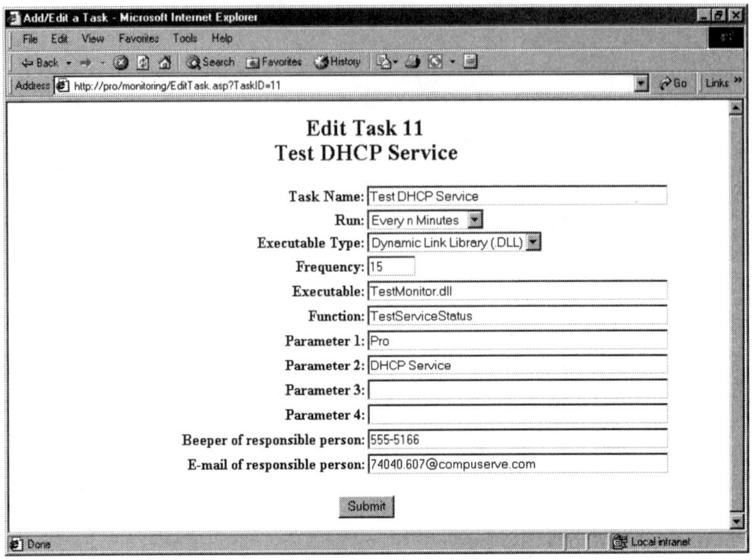


**Figure 15-5** *Add/Edit A Task screen created by EditTask.asp.*

**EditTask.asp**

```
<%@ Language=VBScript %>
<HTML>
<HEAD>
<META NAME="GENERATOR" Content="Microsoft Visual Studio 6.0">
<TITLE>Add/Edit a Task</TITLE>
</HEAD>
<BODY>

<%
dim rstTasks
dim db
dim strSQL
dim taskID
dim cbStr

taskID=request("taskID")

Set db=Server.CreateObject("ADODB.Connection")
db.Open(Session("SQLLOGIN"))
```

**Listing 15-8**

```
strSQL="SELECT * FROM tblTasks WHERE taskID="&taskID

set rstTasks=db.Execute(strSQL)

Response.Write("<CENTER>")
if taskID<>0 AND rstTasks.eof then
    Response.Write("<H2>Sorry, Task "&taskID&" was deleted")
    Response.Write(" by another workstation!</H2>")
    Response.Write("<FORM action=""SelectTask.asp"" ")
    Response.Write("method=POST id=form1 name=form1>")
    Response.Write("<INPUT type=""submit"" ")
    Response.Write("value=""Return to Task Selction Screen"" ")
    Response.Write("id=submit1 name=submit1>")
    Response.Write("</FORM>   ")
else
    if taskID<>0 then
        rstTasks.MoveFirst
    end if
    Response.Write("<H2>Edit Task ")
    if taskID<>0 then
        Response.Write(taskID)
    end if
    Response.Write("<BR>")
    if taskID<>0 then
        Response.Write(rstTasks("Name")&"</H2>")
    else
        Response.Write("New Task</H2>")
    end if

    Response.Write("<FORM method=POST ")
    Response.Write("action=savetask.asp?TaskID=" & taskID)
    Response.Write(" id=form1 name=form1><P>")
    Response.Write("<P><TABLE BORDER=0 cellspacing=0><TR>")
    Response.Write("<TD  width=""50%%""><B></B></TD>")
    Response.Write("<TD ><B></B></TD>")
    Response.Write("</TR>")
    Response.Write("<TR BGCOLOR=WHITE>")

    Response.Write("<TD align=right width=""50%%"">")
    Response.Write("<B>Task Name:</B></TD>")
    Response.Write("<TD><B><INPUT type=text NAME=Name ")
    if taskID<>0 then
        Response.Write("SIZE=50 VALUE="""&rstTasks("Name")&""">")
```

*(continued)*

**Listing 15-8** *continued*

```
else
    Response.Write("SIZE=50>")
end if
Response.Write("</B></TD></TR><TR BGCOLOR=WHITE>")

Response.Write("<TD align=right width=""50%%""><B>Run:</B></TD>")
cbStr="<SELECT id=cbRunType name=cbRunType>"
if taskID<>0 then
    if rstTasks("AtOrEvery")="E" then
        cbStr=cbStr+"<OPTION VALUE=E SELECTED>Every n Minutes"
        cbStr=cbStr+"</OPTION><OPTION VALUE=A>At a specific time"
        cbStr=cbStr+"</OPTION>"
    else
        cbStr=cbStr+"<OPTION VALUE=E>Every n Minutes</OPTION>"
        cbStr=cbStr+"<OPTION VALUE=A SELECTED>At a specific time"
        cbStr=cbStr+"</OPTION>"
    end if
else
    cbStr=cbStr+"<OPTION VALUE=E>Every n Minutes</OPTION>"
    cbStr=cbStr+"<OPTION VALUE=A>At a specific time</OPTION>"
end if
cbStr=cbStr+"</SELECT>"
Response.Write("<TD><B>"+cbStr+"</B></TD>")
Response.Write("</TR><TR BGCOLOR=WHITE>")

Response.Write("<TD align=right width=""50%%"">")
Response.Write("<B>Executable Type:</B></TD>")
cbStr="<SELECT id=cbExeType name=cbExeType>"
if taskID<>0 then
    if rstTasks("ExecuteType")=1 then
        cbStr=cbStr+"<OPTION VALUE=1 SELECTED>"
        cbStr=cbStr+"Executable (.EXE)</OPTION>"
        cbStr=cbStr+"<OPTION VALUE=2>Dynamic Link "
        cbStr=cbStr+"Library (.DLL)</OPTION>"
    else
        cbStr=cbStr+"<OPTION VALUE=1>Executable "
        cbStr=cbStr+"(.EXE)</OPTION>"
        cbStr=cbStr+"<OPTION VALUE=2 SELECTED>"
        cbStr=cbStr+"Dynamic Link Library "
        cbStr=cbStr+"(.DLL)</OPTION>"
    end if
else
    cbStr=cbStr+"<OPTION VALUE=1>Executable "
    cbStr=cbStr+"(.EXE)</OPTION>"
```

```
        cbStr=cbStr+"<OPTION VALUE=2>Dynamic Link Library "
        cbStr=cbStr+"(.DLL)</OPTION>"
    end if
    cbStr=cbStr+"</SELECT>"
    Response.Write("<TD><B>"+cbStr+"</B></TD>")
    Response.Write("</TR><TR BGCOLOR=WHITE>")

    Response.Write("<TD align=right width=""50%%"">")
    Response.Write("<B>Frequency:</B></TD>")
    Response.Write("<TD><B><INPUT type=text NAME=Interval ")
    if taskID<>0 then
        Response.Write("SIZE=5 VALUE=")
        Response.Write(rstTasks("RunEveryInterval")&">")
    else
        Response.Write("SIZE=5>")
    end if
    Response.Write("</B></TD></TR><TR BGCOLOR=WHITE>")

    Response.Write("<TD align=right width=""50%%"">")
    Response.Write("<B>Executable:</B></TD>")
    Response.Write("<TD><B><INPUT type=text NAME=Executable ")
    if taskID<>0 then
        Response.Write("SIZE=50 VALUE=""")
        Response.Write(rstTasks("Executable")&""">")
    else
        Response.Write("SIZE=50>")
    end if
    Response.Write("</B></TD></TR><TR BGCOLOR=WHITE>")

    Response.Write("<TD align=right width=""50%%"">")
    Response.Write("<B>Function:</B></TD>")
    Response.Write("<TD><B><INPUT type=text NAME=Function ")
    if taskID<>0 then
        Response.Write("SIZE=50 VALUE="""&rstTasks("Function")&""">")
    else
        Response.Write("SIZE=50>")
    end if
    Response.Write("</B></TD></TR><TR BGCOLOR=WHITE>")

    Response.Write("<TD align=right width=""50%%"">")
    Response.Write("<B>Parameter 1:</B></TD>")
    Response.Write("<TD><B><INPUT type=text ")
    Response.Write("MAXLENGTH=255 NAME=Parameter1 ")
    if taskID<>0 then
        Response.Write("SIZE=50 VALUE=""" & _
            rstTasks("Parameter1")&""">")
```

*(continued)*

**Listing 15-8** *continued*

```
else
    Response.Write("SIZE=50>")
end if
Response.Write("</B></TD></TR><TR BGCOLOR=WHITE>")

Response.Write("<TD align=right width=""50%%"">")
Response.Write("<B>Parameter 2:</B></TD>")
Response.Write("<TD><B><INPUT type=text ")
Response.Write("MAXLENGTH=255 NAME=Parameter2 ")
if taskID<>0 then
    Response.Write("SIZE=50 VALUE=""" & _
        rstTasks("Parameter2")&""">")
else
    Response.Write("SIZE=50>")
end if
Response.Write("</B></TD></TR><TR BGCOLOR=WHITE>")

Response.Write("<TD align=right width=""50%%"">")
Response.Write("<B>Parameter 3:</B></TD>")
Response.Write("<TD><B><INPUT type=text ")
Response.Write("MAXLENGTH=255 NAME=Parameter3 ")
if taskID<>0 then
    Response.Write("SIZE=50 VALUE=""" & _
        rstTasks("Parameter3")&""">")
else
    Response.Write("SIZE=50>")
end if
Response.Write("</B></TD></TR><TR BGCOLOR=WHITE>")

Response.Write("<TD align=right width=""50%%"">")
Response.Write("<B>Parameter 4:</B></TD>")
Response.Write("<TD><B><INPUT type=text ")
Response.Write("MAXLENGTH=255 NAME=Parameter4 ")
if taskID<>0 then
    Response.Write("SIZE=50 VALUE=""" & _
        rstTasks("Parameter4")&""">")
else
    Response.Write("SIZE=50>")
end if
Response.Write("</B></TD></TR><TR BGCOLOR=WHITE>")

Response.Write("<TD align=right width=""50%%"">")
Response.Write("<B>Beeper of Responsible person:</B></TD>")
```

```
    Response.Write("<TD><B><INPUT type=text MAXLENGTH=255")
    Response.Write(" NAME=Beeper ")
    if taskID<>0 then
        Response.Write("SIZE=50 VALUE=""" & _
            rstTasks("Beeper")&""">")
    else
        Response.Write("SIZE=50>")
    end if
    Response.Write("</B></TD></TR><TR BGCOLOR=WHITE>")

    Response.Write("<TD align=right width=""50%"">")
    Response.Write("<B>E-mail of Responsible person:</B></TD>")
    Response.Write("<TD><B><INPUT type=text MAXLENGTH=255 ")
    Response.Write("NAME=email ")
    if taskID<>0 then
        Response.Write("SIZE=50 VALUE="""&rstTasks("email")&""">")
    else
        Response.Write("SIZE=50>")
    end if
    Response.Write("</B></TD></TR><TR BGCOLOR=WHITE>")

    Response.Write("</TR></TABLE><BR>")

    Response.Write("<INPUT type=""submit"" ")
    Response.Write("value=""Submit"" ")
    Response.Write("id=submit1 name=submit1>")

    Response.Write("</FORM>    ")
end if

set rstTasks=nothing
set db=nothing

%>
</BODY>
</HTML>
```

EditTask.asp creates an invisible table to properly align elements on the form. If a *TaskID* of 0 is passed to EditTask.asp, a new record is added. Look back at Figure 15-4, which shows the screen produced by SelectTask.asp, and notice the hyperlink Add A Task at the top of the screen. When you select Add A Task, EditTask.asp is called with a *TaskID* of 0. When you click on the Submit button on the screen in Figure 15-5, SaveTask.asp is called. SaveTask.asp can be called with a nonzero *TaskID* parameter to update an existing task or with the *TaskID* parameter set to zero to insert a new record. Listing 15-9 shows SaveTask.asp.

**SaveTask.asp**

```
<%@ Language=VBScript %>
<HTML>
<HEAD>
<META NAME="GENERATOR" Content="Microsoft Visual Studio 6.0">
<TITLE>Save a Task</TITLE>
</HEAD>
<BODY>
<%
function nullSafe(s)
    if len(s)>0 then
        nullSafe="'"&s&"'"
    else
        nullSafe="null"
    end if
end function

dim db
dim strSQL
dim taskID
dim cbStr
dim numRecs

taskID=request("taskID")

Set db=Server.CreateObject("ADODB.Connection")
db.Open(Session("SQLLOGIN"))

if taskID then
    strSQL="UPDATE tblTasks SET "
    strSQL=strSQL&" Name="&NullSafe(request("Name"))&","
    strSQL=strSQL&" AtOrEvery='"&request("cbRunType")&"',"
    strSQL=strSQL&" ExecuteType="&request("cbExeType")&","
    if CLng(request("Interval"))>0 then
        strSQL=strSQL&" RunEveryInterval="&request("Interval")&","
    end if

    strSQL=strSQL&" Executable="&NullSafe(request("Executable"))&","
    strSQL=strSQL&" Function="&NullSafe(request("Function"))&","
    strSQL=strSQL&" Parameter1="&NullSafe(request("Parameter1"))&","
    strSQL=strSQL&" Parameter2="&NullSafe(request("Parameter2"))&","
    strSQL=strSQL&" Parameter3="&NullSafe(request("Parameter3"))&","
    strSQL=strSQL&" Parameter4="&NullSafe(request("Parameter4"))&","
    strSQL=strSQL&" Beeper="&NullSafe(request("beeper"))&","
    strSQL=strSQL&" email="&NullSafe(request("email"))
    strSQL=strSQL&" WHERE TaskID="&taskID
```

**Listing 15-9**

```
else
    strSQL="INSERT INTO tblTasks(Name,AtOrEvery,ExecuteType,"
    if CLng(request("Interval"))>0 then
        strSQL=strSQL&"RunEveryInterval,"
    end if
    strSQL=strSQL&"Executable,parameter1,parameter2,parameter3,"
    strSQL=strSQL&"parameter4,beeper,email,DateTimeNextRun) VALUES("
    strSQL=strSQL&NullSafe(request("Name"))&","
    strSQL=strSQL&NullSafe(request("AtOrEvery"))&","
    strSQL=strSQL&request("cbExeType")&","
    if CLng(request("Interval"))>0 then
        strSQL=strSQL&request("Interval")&","
    end if
    strSQL=strSQL&NullSafe(request("Executable"))&","
    strSQL=strSQL&NullSafe(request("Function"))&","
    strSQL=strSQL&NullSafe(request("Parameter1"))&","
    strSQL=strSQL&NullSafe(request("Parameter2"))&","
    strSQL=strSQL&NullSafe(request("Parameter3"))&","
    strSQL=strSQL&NullSafe(request("Parameter4"))&","
    strSQL=strSQL&NullSafe(request("beeper"))&","
    strSQL=strSQL&NullSafe(request("email"))&","
    strSQL=strSQL&"'"&Now()&"')"
end if
numRecs=0
db.Execute strSQL,numRecs,adExecuteNoRecords

Response.Write("<CENTER>")
if numRecs>0 then
    Response.Write("<H2>Changes Recorded!</H2>")
else
    Response.Write("<H2>An error has occured</H2>")
end if

Response.Write("<FORM action=""SelectTask.asp"" ")
Response.Write("method=POST id=form1 name=form1>")
Response.Write("<INPUT type=""submit"" value=")
Response.Write("""Return to Task List"" id=submit1 name=submit1>")
Response.Write("</FORM>")

Response.Write("</CENTER>")
%>

</BODY>
</HTML>
```

In addition to the main line of code, Listing 15-9 contains one function, *nullSafe*, declared at the top of the listing. This function allows us to safely set string fields in a SQL query, even if the value we are setting is a null. The string returned by *nullSafe* is either the string enclosed in single quotes or the literal string *null*.

When someone deletes a task we have a dilemma. What should happen with the alerts out there for the deleted task? There are two possible options. The first is to cascade the deletes, deleting all alert records related to the task. In the Web monitoring example I have taken a different tack. Rather than delete the record, I set the reset type to 3 (which happens to be the *ResetTypeID* for "Task Deleted" in my version of the *tblResetType* file). I do this using a delete trigger on *TblTasks*, which is shown in the following code fragment:

```
CREATE TRIGGER DelTblTasks ON [TblTasks]
FOR DELETE
AS

UPDATE tblAlerts SET ResetTypeID = 3
    WHERE TaskID = (SELECT TaskID FROM Deleted)
```

Triggers have pseudotables available to them named *Inserted* or *Deleted*, depending upon the type of trigger. I use a subquery to retrieve the *TaskID* from the deleted record and use that in the WHERE clause of the UPDATE statement to update *TblAlerts*.

If you select the Run Now hyperlink for a task, the *DateTimeNextRun* column in the underlying table *tblTasks* is set to the system date and time. RunNow.asp, shown in Listing 15-10, is the ASP page called when you click on this hyperlink. There are a couple of things to remember about this function.

- Setting *DateTimeNextRun* does not directly run the task, but rather causes MonitorService to run the task as part of its normal processing, generally within 30 seconds.
- *DateTimeNextRun* is set using the system date and time on the server on which IIS is running. While this is often the same server on which MonitorService is running, if the service is running on another server and the system clocks on the two servers are not synchronized, setting *DateTimeNextRun* might not actually force the task to run immediately.

**RunNow.asp**

```
<%@ Language=VBScript %>
<%
Response.Buffer=true
dim db
```

**Listing 15-10**

```
dim strSQL
dim taskID

taskID=request("taskID")

Set db=Server.CreateObject("ADODB.Connection")
db.Open(Session("SQLLOGIN"))

' We try to determine the User Intervention
'  reset type ID but default to 2 if we fail.
strSQL="UPDATE tblTasks SET DateTimeNextRun='"&Now()&"' "
strSQL=strSQL&"WHERE TaskID="&taskID

db.Execute strSQL,,adExecuteNoRecords

set db=nothing
Response.Redirect("SelectTask.asp")

%>
```

Taken together, the eight ASP files allow virtually complete access to the tables that drive the MonitorService application. The user can, over the intranet or the Internet, monitor and reset alerts as well as modify, add, and delete tasks. This is 90 percent of what an administrator needs to know about the running monitor.

The other 10 percent that is useful if not essential is the ability to look at the activities taking place on the server. For instance, in addition to seeing that a task has succeeded or failed, you might find it useful to get to the feedback of an operation and see exactly when it was performed within the context of the application. Multiple threads run tasks and monitor tasks at any given moment. How useful is it to be able to look at what amounts to a trace of the application's progress? Answering that question is the goal of the section that follows.

# USING ISAPI TO MONITOR MONITORSERVICE

MonitorService knows quite a bit more about what is going on within the program than it actually logs to a file. Much of this information is state information that might not even make sense out of context. Simply knowing that one or another thread of the program is working can be at the very least interesting. And when you're debugging a multithreaded application, understanding the interactions between threads can be critical to understanding failures.

## *CMonitorService* Modifications

To implement the ability to get real-time trace information, I have added several data members and methods to the base class for *CMonitorService*, *CPPService*. These members and methods are

- CRITICAL_SECTION *m_csTrace*. A critical section object used to control access by multiple threads to the trace-related variables.
- BOOL *m_debugging*. Set when the *–D* flag is passed on the command line. This causes trace messages to be immediately printed to the console.
- LONG *m_traceHead*. Used to point to the logical start of messages within an array of messages used in round-robin fashion.
- LONG *m_traceTail*. Used to point to the logical end of messages in conjunction with *m_traceHead*.
- char * *m_traces[]*. Holds the pointers to the actual trace messages.
- DWORD *Trace(LPCSTR traceStr)*. A virtual method that places trace messages into the *m_traces* array.

You'll find the complete source for CPPService.h and CPPService.cpp on the companion CD-ROM. The *Trace* method is at the core of the changes to *CPPService*. *Trace* is shown in Listing 15-11.

**CPPService.cpp**

```
DWORD CPPService::Trace(LPCSTR traceStr)
{
    char szTs[255];
    struct tm *time_now;
    time_t secs_now;

    time(&secs_now);
    time_now = localtime(&secs_now);

    strftime(szTs, 30,
        "%Y-%m-%d %H:%M",
        time_now);
    EnterCriticalSection(&m_csTrace);
    // Loop back, so we keep 100 in memory
    if (m_traceTail == MAX_TRACES)
```

**Listing 15-11**

```
    {
        m_traceTail = 0;
        m_traceHead = 1;
    }
    if (m_traces[m_traceTail] != 0)
    {
        delete[] m_traces[m_traceTail];
    }
    m_traces[m_traceTail] = new char[strlen(traceStr) +
        strlen(szTs)+10];

        // Trace string contains timestamp followed
        //  by the message text.
    strcpy(m_traces[m_traceTail], szTs);
    strcat(m_traces[m_traceTail], ": ");
    strcat(m_traces[m_traceTail], traceStr);

    if (m_debugging)
    {
        printf("\n%s ", m_traces[m_traceTail]);
    }
    if (m_traceHead > m_traceTail)
    {
        m_traceHead++;
        if (m_traceHead == MAX_TRACES)
        {
            m_traceHead = 0;
        }
    }
    m_traceTail++;
    LeaveCriticalSection(&m_csTrace);
    return((DWORD)m_traceHead);
}
```

The job of *Trace* is to place the string passed as *traceStr* into the *m_traces* pointer array. Before managing the *m_traceHead*, *m_traceTail*, and *m_traces* variables, the function enters a critical section object, *m_csTrace*. In classes derived from *CPPService*, other threads will manipulate the *m_traceHead*, *m_traceTail*, and *m_traces* variables, so we must serialize access to these variables. The critical section object is initialized and deleted in the constructor and destructor, respectively. The first and last messages are pointed to by *m_traceHead* and *m_traceTail*, respectively. These pointers are manipulated so that the most recent MAX_TRACES messages in the array are always available. These traces could have also been placed in a SQL Server table; however, making the trace messages available in this way presents a more interesting example. Finally, if the service is being debugged and run as a console mode application rather than as a service, the message is displayed on the console using *printf*.

I made changes to *CMonitorService* in two areas. First, the trace statements must be placed in the appropriate functions of the service. You'll find the complete code for the modified *CMonitorService* on the companion CD-ROM, and you'll find calls to the new *Trace* method of *CPPService* in *DoTask* and *MonitorAlerts*. The second area changed in *CMonitorService* is *DoWork*, shown in Listing 15-12.

**MonitorService.cpp**

```
void CMonitorService::DoWork(SOCKET s, WORD ThreadNum)
{
    char diag[255];
    char data[2048];
    BOOL fSuccess;
    int len;
    static int blksSent = 0;
    int bytesRead;
    int maxData = 512;
    int numSent = 0;
    bool finalSent = false;

    bytesRead = 0L;

    memset((void *)data, '\0', 1024);
    do {
        if ((len = recv(s,
            ((char *)data),
            maxData, 0)) == SOCKET_ERROR)
        {
            fSuccess = FALSE;
            wsprintf(diag, "SOCKET ERROR", data);
            LogEvent(EVENTLOG_ERROR_TYPE,
                EVMSG_DEBUG, diag);
        }
        else
        {
            EnterCriticalSection(&m_csTrace);
            long curPacket = m_traceHead;
            while (len != SOCKET_ERROR && IsRunning())
            {
                DATA_PACKET *d;
                d = (DATA_PACKET *)&data[0];
                switch (d->ServiceCode)
```

**Listing 15-12**

```
                {
                case REQ_FIRST_TRACE:
                    curPacket = m_traceHead+1;
                    numSent = 0;
//                    break;  // Step through this.
                case REQ_NEXT_TRACE:
                    if (curPacket >= MAX_TRACES)
                    {
                        curPacket = 0;
                    }
                    if (m_traces[curPacket] == 0 ||
                        curPacket == (m_traceTail) ||
                        (curPacket == MAX_TRACES-1 &&
                        m_traceHead == 0) &&
                        numSent < MAX_TRACES)
                    {
                        // Send a signal that we are done.
                        d->DataLen = 0;
                        len = send(s, (const char *)d,
                            (14+d->DataLen)+1, 0);
                        finalSent = true;
                    }
                    else
                    {
                        d->DataLen = strlen(m_traces[curPacket])+1;
                        strncpy(d->Buffer,
                            m_traces[curPacket], d->BufLen);
                        d->Buffer[d->DataLen+1] = '\0';
                        len = send(s, (const char *)d,
                            (14+d->DataLen)+1, 0);
                        curPacket++;
                        numSent++;
                    }
                    break;
                default:
                    d->DataLen = 0;
                    break;
                }
                if (!finalSent && len != SOCKET_ERROR)
                {
                    // Get the next message from the client.
```

*(continued)*

**Listing 15-12** *continued*

```
                    do {
                        len = recv(s,
                            ((char *)data),
                            maxData, 0);
                        if (IsRunning() && len == 0)
                        {
                            Sleep(100);
                        }
                    } while (len == 0 && IsRunning());
                }
                else
                {
                    len = SOCKET_ERROR;
                }
            }
            LeaveCriticalSection(&m_csTrace);
        }
    } while (!(finalSent) && IsRunning() &&
        len != SOCKET_ERROR && len != 0);
    closesocket(s);
}
```

*DoWork* first tries to receive a package on the socket passed as the first parameter. Recall that this is a socket that has been retrieved by *WSCommDispatcher* and *Thread*, first described in the CommService example in Chapter 12. The buffer received should be a DATA_PACKET structure, also first described in Chapter 12. DATA_PACKET is shown here:

```
typedef struct _DATA_PACKET {
    WORD ServerHandle;
    WORD ServiceCode;
    WORD ReturnCode;
    DWORD DataLen;
    DWORD BufLen;
    char Buffer[MAX_DATA_SIZE];
} DATA_PACKET;
```

*ServiceCode* can be set to one of two values, *REQ_FIRST_TRACE* or *REQ_NEXT_TRACE*, requesting the first trace message or the next trace message, respectively. *ServiceCode* controls a *switch* statement. If the first trace message is requested, I set the local variable *curPacket* to *m_traceHead* and pass through to the second case statement (note the commented-out *break* after the *REQ_FIRST_TRACE* case). Depending on whether there is another message to send, I either send the message—setting *DataLen* to the length of the message—or I send a DATA_PACKET with *DataLen* set to 0. If there is no message to send, the local Boolean variable *finalSent* is set to *true*. After the *switch* statement, I try to receive another request from the client, breaking out only if *recv* returns SOCKET_ERROR or the *IsRunning* method of *CPPService* returns false. Finally, after all messages are sent, I leave the *m_csTrace* critical section and close the socket.

Look at the code in Listing 15-12. You can see that every loop is controlled by the return value of *IsRunning*, in addition to whatever other logic controls the loop. For instance, rather than just testing *len* to see if a socket error has occurred, the fragment below checks *len* as well as the return value of *IsRunning*.

```
while (len != SOCKET_ERROR && IsRunning())
{
    // Continue looping
```

This makes for a somewhat more complicated function, but it is essential to ensure that the function will return to *DoWork* whenever the service is stopped so that the thread running *DoWork* can terminate normally.

## The ISAPIMonitor ISAPI Extension

Once the service is running and tracing its operation, we need to get at the information. An ideal way to do this is from the Web. Look back at the Monitor Trace link in Figure 15-1. Clicking on this link leads to the screen shown in Figure 15-6. The screen displays all of the trace statements currently cached in the service.

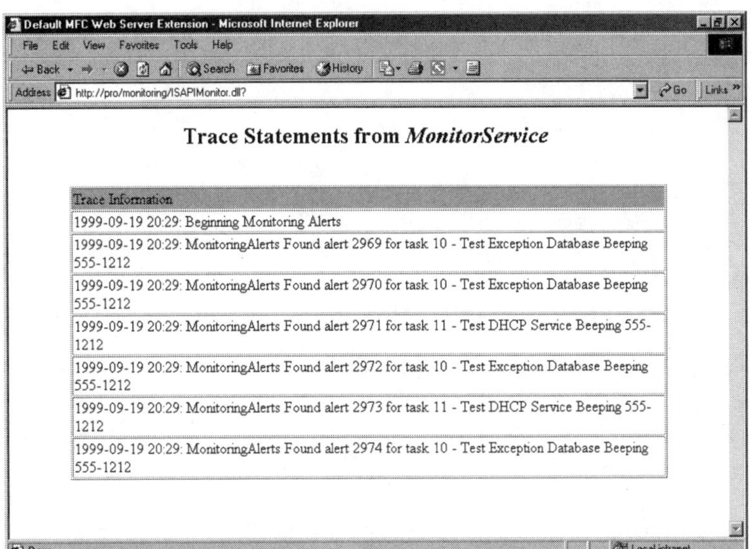


**Figure 15-6** *The trace statements screen.*

The information in this screen can be generated in a couple of ways. A server-side ActiveX control can generate the table information for an ASP page, using TCP/IP to communicate to *CMonitorService*. An alternative is to use an ISAPI extension. For this example, I will use ISAPI to create the entire page. Listing 15-13 shows *ISAPIMonitor*, the ISAPI extension I created to display the monitor trace information.

**ISAPIMonitor.cpp**

```
// ISAPIMONITOR.CPP - Implementation file Monitor Trace
//  display

#include "stdafx.h"
#include "ISAPIMonitor.h"

///////////////////////////////////////////////////////////////////////
// The one and only CWinApp object
// NOTE: You can remove this object if you alter your project to no
//  longer use MFC in a DLL.

//CWinApp theApp;

///////////////////////////////////////////////////////////////////////
// command-parsing map

BEGIN_PARSE_MAP(CISAPIMonitorExtension, CHttpServer)
    // TODO: insert your ON_PARSE_COMMAND() and
    //  ON_PARSE_COMMAND_PARAMS() here to hook up your commands.
    // For example:

    ON_PARSE_COMMAND(Default, CISAPIMonitorExtension, ITS_EMPTY)
    DEFAULT_PARSE_COMMAND(Default, CISAPIMonitorExtension)
END_PARSE_MAP(CISAPIMonitorExtension)

///////////////////////////////////////////////////////////////////////
// The one and only CISAPIMonitorExtension object

CISAPIMonitorExtension theExtension;

///////////////////////////////////////////////////////////////////////
// CISAPIMonitorExtension implementation

CISAPIMonitorExtension::CISAPIMonitorExtension()
{
}
```

**Listing 15-13**

```
CISAPIMonitorExtension::~CISAPIMonitorExtension()
{
}

BOOL CISAPIMonitorExtension::GetExtensionVersion(
    HSE_VERSION_INFO* pVer)
{
    // Call default implementation for initialization.
    CHttpServer::GetExtensionVersion(pVer);

    // Load description string.
    TCHAR sz[HSE_MAX_EXT_DLL_NAME_LEN+1];
    ISAPIVERIFY(::LoadString(AfxGetResourceHandle(),
        IDS_SERVER, sz, HSE_MAX_EXT_DLL_NAME_LEN));
    _tcscpy(pVer->lpszExtensionDesc, sz);
    return TRUE;
}

BOOL CISAPIMonitorExtension::TerminateExtension(DWORD dwFlags)
{
    // Extension is being terminated
    // TODO: Clean up any per-instance resources.
    return TRUE;
}

///////////////////////////////////////////////////////////////////////
// CISAPIMonitorExtension command handlers

void CISAPIMonitorExtension::Default(CHttpServerContext* pCtxt)
{
    DWORD dwBytes = 0;
    DATA_PACKET d;

    StartContent(pCtxt);
    WriteTitle(pCtxt);

    memset((char *)&d, '\0', sizeof(DATA_PACKET));
    // Of course, this should be a parameter, a
    //  registry entry, or at least modified
    //  in the source for your environment.
    CWinSockClientComm MyClient("DUAL", 5043);
    if (MyClient.Open() == -1)
    {
        *pCtxt << _T("<CENTER><H2>Sorry. Can't connect to ");
        *pCtxt << _T("CMonitorService<CENTER></H2>");
        return;
    }
```

*(continued)*

**Listing 15-13** *continued*

```
    *pCtxt << _T("<CENTER><H2>Trace Statements ");
    *pCtxt << _T("from <I>MonitorService</I></H2><BR>");
    *pCtxt <<
        _T("<TABLE WIDTH=85% BORDER=1 CELLSPACING=1 CELLPADDING=1>");
    *pCtxt << _T("<TR><TD BGCOLOR=AQUA> ");
    *pCtxt << _T("Trace Information </TR></TD> ");

    // Initialize these.
    d.ServiceCode = REQ_FIRST_TRACE;
    d.DataLen = 16;
    do {
        d.BufLen = 1024;
        MyClient.Write((char *)&d, sizeof(d), &dwBytes);
        // Initialize this.
        d.DataLen = 0;
        memset(d.Buffer, '\0', sizeof(d.Buffer));
        MyClient.Read((char *)&d, sizeof(d), &dwBytes);
         if (d.DataLen)
        {
            *pCtxt << _T("<TR><TD> ");
            *pCtxt << _T(d.Buffer);
            *pCtxt << _T("</TD></TR>");
            d.ServiceCode = REQ_NEXT_TRACE;
            d.DataLen = 16;
        }
    } while (d.DataLen && dwBytes);
    MyClient.Close();

    *pCtxt << _T("</TABLE> ");

    *pCtxt << _T("<FORM action=\"Default.asp\" ");
    *pCtxt << _T("method=POST id=form1 name=form1>");
    *pCtxt << _T("<INPUT type=\"submit\" ");
    *pCtxt << _T("value=\"Return to Alert List\" ");
    *pCtxt << _T(" id=submit1 name=submit1>");
    *pCtxt << _T("</FORM>");
    EndContent(pCtxt);
}
// Do not edit the following lines, which are needed by ClassWizard.
#if 0
BEGIN_MESSAGE_MAP(CISAPIMonitorExtension, CHttpServer)
    //{{AFX_MSG_MAP(CISAPIMonitorExtension)
    //}}AFX_MSG_MAP
END_MESSAGE_MAP()
#endif    // 0
```

```
///////////////////////////////////////////////////////////////////////
// If your extension will not use MFC, you'll need this code to make
//  sure the extension objects can find the resource handle for the
//  module. If you convert your extension to not be dependent on MFC,
//  remove the comments around the following AfxGetResourceHandle()
//  and DllMain() functions, as well as the g_hInstance global.

/****/

static HINSTANCE g_hInstance;

HINSTANCE AFXISAPI AfxGetResourceHandle()
{
    return g_hInstance;
}

BOOL WINAPI DllMain(HINSTANCE hInst, ULONG ulReason,
    LPVOID lpReserved)
{
    if (ulReason == DLL_PROCESS_ATTACH)
    {
        g_hInstance = hInst;
    }

    return TRUE;
}

/****/
```

The majority of Listing 15-13 is the Wizard-generated code. I have removed the reliance on MFC classes outside the MFC ISAPI classes, following the instructions in the source code as well as the extra steps described in Chapter 10.

The *Default* method is used to generate the HTML code required to display the monitor trace in the user's browser. Recall that *Default* is created by the MFC ISAPI Extension Wizard as the entry point called when no specific function is requested on an incoming URL. If you need your ISAPI extension to do more than one thing, you should add other class members and change the parse map macros, as we saw in Chapter 10.

*Default* creates the headers for the table by streaming the HTML code through the *pCtxt* pointer passed as the sole parameter to *Default*. *Default* relies upon the *CWinSockClientComm* class first described in Chapter 12. Recall that this class descends from *CClientComm*, a generic base class. If *CMonitorService* used named pipes instead of WinSock, I could have used the same method calls after creating a

*CNPClientComm* object rather than a *CWinSockClientComm* object. The constructor for *CWinSockClientComm* is called with the name of the server and the port number. The server must be running *CMonitorService*, and the port must match the port used by *CMonitorService*. I call the *Open* method of *CWinSockClientComm* to actually create the socket. If *Open* fails and returns –1, a message is written to the HTML output stream and the function exits.

The key to getting any communication working reliably between a client and server program is to ensure that both programs observe a known protocol. As with communication between people, if both parties talk or listen at once they aren't likely to be as productive as if they talked and listened in turn. *Default* ensures that the protocol is followed by calling the *Write* and *Read* methods in a loop in the opposite order *CMonitorService* calls them. As each message is read, *Default* creates a table row and cell to contain the message. After all messages are read, I call the *Close* method of *CWinSockClientComm* to end the connection. Finally I stream out the code to create a button at the bottom of the page that allows the user to return to the default screen, which shows tasks with active alerts.

# CONCLUSION

I have covered four major types of server-side systems in this book:

- Traditional Windows 2000 service applications
- ASP applications
- ISAPI applications and filters
- SQL Server integration

Each of these systems has its own strengths and weaknesses. Traditional Windows 2000 service applications are the basis of many server-side applications. Services can be configured to run whenever the system they are on is running. There are virtually no limits to what these services can do within the constraints of the Win32 environment. Each of the other three types of server-side development depends upon Windows 2000 services.

ASP and ISAPI extensions allow you as a server-side developer to integrate with IIS to create applications available over an intranet or the Internet. Of course, IIS itself is a Windows 2000 service. ASP and ISAPI extensions can do much of the same work, and the decision to use one or the other can depend upon the application's end user as well as the application's performance requirements. As we have seen, you can take steps to allow ASP applications to scale up beyond what might be possible with just scripting. ISAPI applications allow you the freedom to do virtually anything that Windows 2000 can do, and you can use them over the Web.

SQL Server provides persistent storage that can be used by both server-side applications and client applications. While SQL Server can be used as just another data source, doing so would be a mistake. A SQL Server database allows you to create stored procedures and triggers that can encapsulate and enforce business logic at the server. In this multiclient world, with traditional fat clients and thin browser clients both interacting with the database, having this business logic on the server can greatly simplify client software design.

The Web monitoring sample in this chapter integrates all of these server-side systems. Building on the MonitorService example created in Chapter 14, I used ASP to add a Web interface that monitors and modifies the SQL Server database. To allow Web users even more information about the inner workings of the MonitorService application, I created ISAPIMonitoring, an ISAPI extension that communicates using WinSock. ISAPIMonitoring shows ISAPI's potential to open up the entire server world to Web-based clients.

There you have it. I hope you have enjoyed this inside look at service-based applications. What you do with server-based applications is limited only by your imagination. As Windows 2000 and its successors expand the role of server-based applications, new technologies will undoubtedly arise and build on what I've covered in this book. I hope I have provided the foundation that will allow you to grow with those changes.

# Appendix A

# Setting Up Virtual Directories in IIS

How you set up a virtual directory affects how you create and secure a Web application. While some Web applications that require security will require you to create custom security, a properly configured virtual directory can suffice in many cases.

To create a new virtual directory, open the Internet Services Manager and select Default Web Site, as shown in Figure A-1.

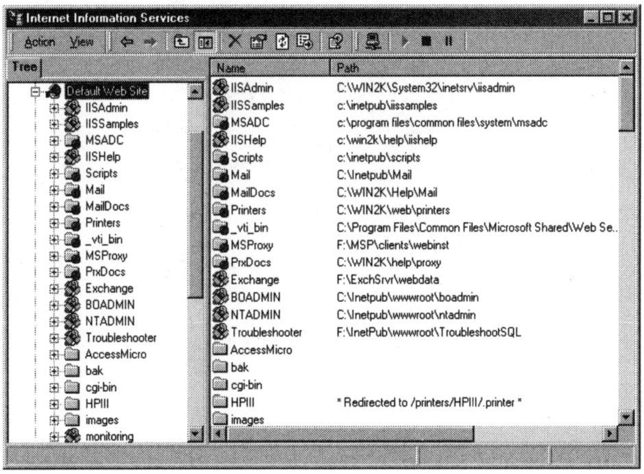


**Figure A-1** *The Internet Services Manager.*

Right-click on Default Web Site, select New, and then select Virtual Directory. The Virtual Directory Creation Wizard will appear. In the screens that follow, the wizard will request, in turn, the following pieces of information:

- **Site Alias.** This is the name that will follow the site name in a URL. For example, if you enter NewSite on a server named PRO, intranet users can access the site using *http://PRO/NewSite*.

- **Directory.** This is the physical directory where the files used by this virtual directory will reside. The directory can be on the local drives or on a remote drive. Most often, the directory is a local drive under the *\InetPub\wwwRoot* directory.
- **Access Permissions.** These specify what can be done in the directory. Figure A-2 shows the possible permission settings. Note the distinction between running scripts and executing ISAPI applications or CGI programs. Failure to allow execute rights in a directory in which an ISAPI DLL is called will result in the failure of that call, possibly allowing the user to download the DLL—something you likely don't want to allow. Write and Browse rights are virtually never given, except in a development environment.

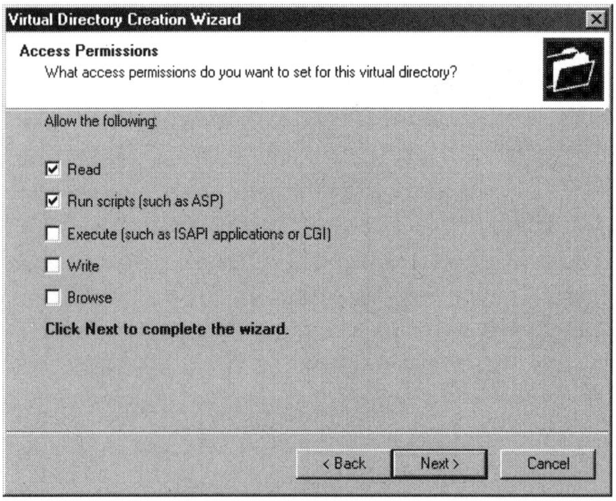


**Figure A-2** *Setting access permissions in the Virtual Directory Creation Wizard.*

Once you've created the virtual directory, you can right-click on the directory in the Internet Services Manager and select Properties. This brings up a dialog like the one shown in Figure A-3. The Virtual Directory tab allows you to change some of the information requested by the wizard. The radio button group at the top of the tab controls where files for the virtual directory will reside. As the selected radio button changes, the balance of the controls in the dialog changes to reflect appropriate questions for the type of file source indicated.

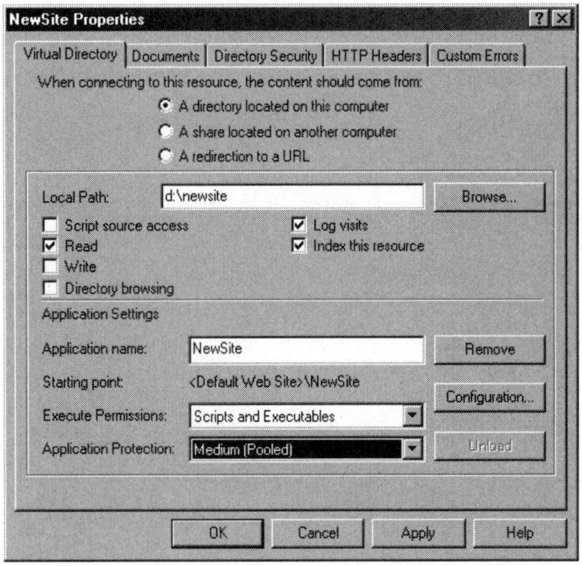


**Figure A-3** *Setting virtual directory properties.*

One setting that the wizard does not allow you to set is Application Protection, shown at the bottom of the dialog in Figure A-3. Changing the Application Protection level allows you to control how your application will run, whether in the same process as other Web services (Low), pooled in a process with other Web applications (Medium—the default), or in its own process (High). In a production environment, you should start an application at a high protection level and move it to less restrictive levels as the application proves itself trustworthy.

Clicking on the Configuration button shown in Figure A-3 brings up a dialog with three tabs. The first tab controls the DLL that individual file extensions are bound to. For example, requesting a file with an *asp* extension calls Asp.dll. The second tab allows you to control session state management and timeouts as well as the default language for ASP files. The third tab, shown in Figure A-4, allows you to control debugging of ASP applications. You can enable client-side script debugging, server-side script debugging, or both. You can also control the information returned to the client when an error occurs. The default error information is important while debugging the application, but you might want to hide error information when the application is in production.

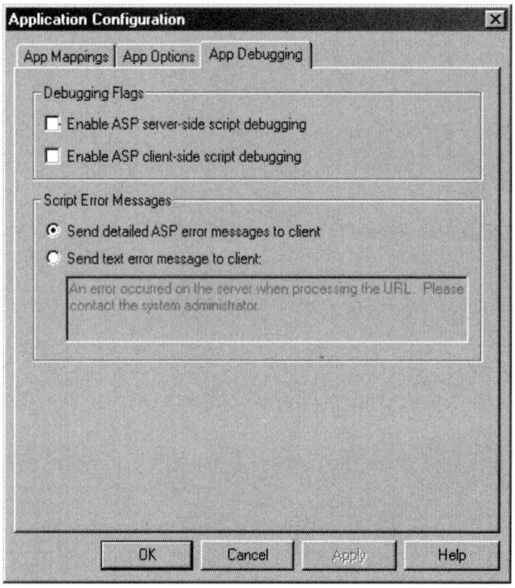


**Figure A-4** *The Application Configuration dialog.*

Take a look back at the dialog in Figure A-3 .You'll notice several other tabs. Figure A-5 shows the Documents tab. From this screen, you can control the default form of the application. I commonly remove all but Default.asp, or whatever is the name of the first page I want visitors to see. Allowing multiple default documents makes the site vulnerable to the possibility of alternate paths to the application.

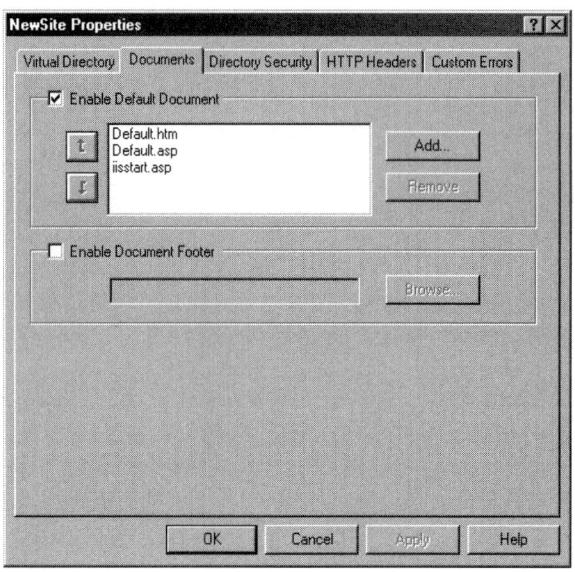


**Figure A-5** *The Documents tab of the NewSite Properties dialog.*

The third tab of the NewSite Properties dialog from Figure A-3 is Directory Security, shown in Figure A-6. The first button on that tab brings up the dialog shown in Figure A-7.

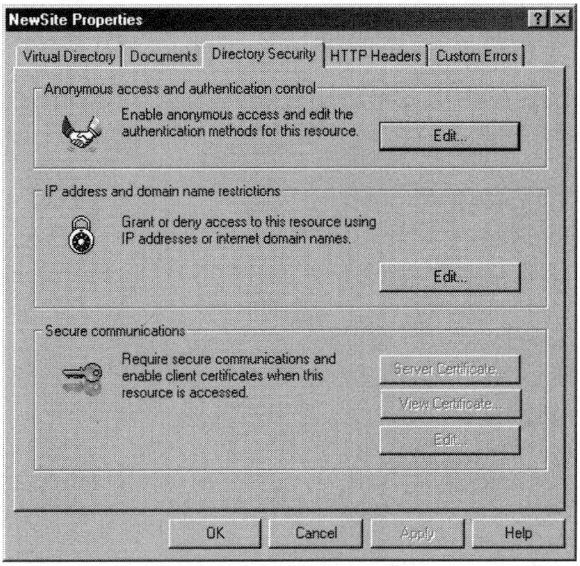


**Figure A-6** *The Directory Security tab of the NewSite Properties dialog.*

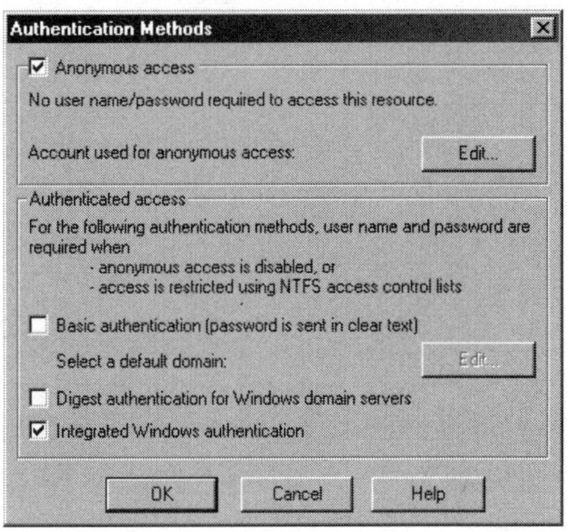


**Figure A-7** *The Authentication Methods dialog.*

When checked, the first check box in Figure A-7 allows anonymous access to the Web site. In fact, allowing anonymous access really allows all visitors who are not otherwise authenticated to access the site using an account that can be set by clicking on the Edit button labeled Account Used for Anonymous Access. Commonly, this account is named *IUSR_servername*. For instance, on my server named Pro, the user name is *IUSR_PRO*.

The second group box shown in Figure A-7 allows you to control other authentication methods. Basic Authentication sends the user name and password in clear text. The user names and passwords are then authenticated against a domain's user database. Obviously, this option has security implications. It is not an optimal authentication method if your site requires high security or the domain that will be used to authenticate the password has other resources that require bulletproof security. The Edit button to the right of the Basic Authentication check box allows you to select the default domain to use when authenticating the user names and passwords.

Digest Authentication sends a hash value representing the password—rather than the clear text password—across the wire. This option is new to IIS 5. The final authentication method is Integrated Windows Authentication. When you select this option, a relatively secure method is used to establish the user's identity. This more secure method is only used if anonymous access is disabled or if Windows file security has been set on the requested file. In practice, this authentication method is perfectly appropriate for an intranet application, but less so for an Internet application.

Looking again to Figure A-3, you'll see that the fourth tab, HTTP Headers, allows you to enable content expiration, add custom HTTP headers, set content ratings, and control MIME file types. The last tab, Custom Errors, allows you to set a page to be displayed to the user when certain HTTP errors occur. Thus you can control what the user sees when HTTP errors occur while the user is accessing the page. Rather than displaying the default "Forbidden-Directory Access Denied" for a 403.14 error, you can display a page of your choice.

## CONCLUSION

Given the extensive configuration options of practically all aspects of the virtual directory, sometimes the choices can almost be too much. For developers of Web-based applications, the most important considerations involve the site's security. IIS offers the flexibility to do all of the security work for you. Alternatively, you can do it all on your own by allowing anonymous users access and then providing your own security by forcing users through a login screen.

*Appendix B*

# Reacting to Service Failures

In Chapter 14, I created a service that monitors other services, servers, and databases on a network. During the discussion of network monitoring, I noted that having an operations person periodically check the status of various servers was much like a computer program that polled, or looked for input periodically in a somewhat inefficient way. I then described the MonitorService program that, in effect, did the polling for the operations people and interrupted them when needed.

Microsoft Windows 2000 offers one additional way to monitor a service that is closer to a true interrupt model. Using the new Win32 API function *ChangeServiceConfig2*, you can let Windows 2000 know what it should do if a service fails. The meaning of a service failing is straightforward and somewhat limited. For purposes of *ChangeServiceConfig2*, a service has failed if it terminates without reporting a SERVICE_STOPPED status. Thus, the method of monitoring service failure covered in this appendix is of no value if the entire server has failed. Nonetheless, *ChangeServiceConfig2* can be useful in monitoring services that are failing in the way the function defines failure.

Let's take a look at *ChangeServiceConfig2*.

```
BOOL ChangeServiceConfig2(
    SC_HANDLE hService,
    DWORD dwInfoLevel,
    LPVOID lpInfo
);
```

The first parameter is a handle opened using *OpenService* or *CreateService*. The second parameter, *dwInfoLevel*, can be one of two constants:

- SERVICE_CONFIG_DESCRIPTION allows the description for the specified service to be changed. In this case, the third parameter, *lpInfo*, points to a SERVICE_DESCRIPTION structure. This structure contains a single member, *lpDescription*.

- SERVICE_CONFIG_FAILURE_ACTIONS allows the actions taken when the service fails (as defined above). In this case, *lpInfo* points to a SERVICE_FAILURE_ACTIONS structure, which is defined as follows:

```
typedef struct _SERVICE_FAILURE_ACTIONS {
    DWORD       dwResetPeriod;
    LPTSTR      lpRebootMsg;
    LPTSTR      lpCommand;
    DWORD       cActions;
    SC_ACTION * lpsaActions;
} SERVICE_FAILURE_ACTIONS;
```

The first member, *dwResetPeriod*, indicates the number of seconds that must elapse before the failure count is reset to 0. Setting *dwResetPeriod* to INFINITE means that the failure count is never reset. If you choose to have the server reboot as the result of a failure (using the method described below), *lpRebootMsg* is the message broadcast to all users. If *lpRebootMsg* is NULL, the reboot message is not changed, and if it points to an empty string, the reboot message is deleted and no message will be broadcast.

You can also choose to have the command specified in *lpCommand* run when a service fails. If *lpCommand* is NULL, the command is unchanged, and if *lpCommand* points to an empty string, the command is removed.

The last two members of the structure are *cActions* and *lpsaActions*. You can specify any number of actions to take place when a failure occurs, with the number of actions specified in *cActions*. An array of SC_ACTION structures pointed to by *lpsaActions* is used by the Service Control Manager (SCM) to determine what actions to perform when a failure takes place. The offset within the array indicates which action should take place. For example, when the service fails for the first time, the SC_ACTION structure at offset 0 (the number of failures minus one) takes place. The second failure causes the SCM to look at action 1 and so on. The SC_ACTION structure is defined as follows:

```
typedef struct _SC_ACTION {
    SC_ACTION_TYPE  Type;
    DWORD           Delay;
} SC_ACTION;
```

The first parameter, *Type*, can be one of the following values:

| | |
|---|---|
| SC_ACTION_NONE | No action is taken. |
| SC_ACTION_REBOOT | Reboot the server. |
| SC_ACTION_RESTART | Restart the service. |
| SC_ACTION_RUN_COMMAND | Run a command. |

The second member of SC_ACTION is *Delay*, used to specify the time to wait, in milliseconds, before performing the action. When rebooting the server or restarting the service, a delay is generally specified. For the reboot, to allow users to try to save their work, and for restarting the service, the delay may allow the service to recover before the restart is attempted.

One approach would be to allow the first failure to run a command, perhaps running a program notifying an administrator of a failure and attempting to restart the service from within the program run on the command line. The command could also trigger a message to some network monitoring software, such as the MonitorService example from Chapter 14. A second failure might cause a reboot of the server if the service that failed was critical.

Another new Win32 API function that retrieves information about the service description of failure behavior is *QueryServiceConfig2*. Its prototype is:

```
BOOL QueryServiceConfig2(
    SC_HANDLE hService,
    DWORD dwInfoLevel,
    LPBYTE lpBuffer,
    DWORD cbBufSize,
    LPDWORD pcbBytesNeeded
);
```

The meanings of the first three parameters are similar to the meanings of the parameters for *ChangeServiceConfig2*. The fourth parameter, *cbBufSize*, is the size of the buffer pointed to by *lpBuffer*. The final parameter, *pcbBytesNeeded*, is a pointer to a DWORD that will contain the size the buffer must be if *ChangeServiceConfig2* fails with *GetLastError* returning ERROR_INSUFFICENT_BUFFER. Because the size of the data returned in *lpBuffer* is variable and cannot be determined in advance, one strategy is to call the function one time with a zero-length buffer to get the length required and then again using the length returned in *pcbBytesNeeded*.

For example, the following code gets the length required, allocates a buffer of the correct size, and then calls *QueryServiceConfig2* with a properly sized buffer:

```
DWORD dwRequired = 0;
SERVICE_FAILURE_ACTIONS *pActions = NULL;

hService=OpenService(hSCM, "MonitorService", SERVICE_ALL_ACCESS);
QueryServiceConfig2(hService, SERVICE_CONFIG_FAILURE_ACTIONS,
    NULL,0,&dwRequired);
if (GetLastError() == ERROR_INSUFFICENT_BUFFER)
{
    pActions = (SERVICE_FAILURE_ACTIONS *)BYTE[dwRequired];
    if (pActions)
    {
        QueryServiceConfig2(hService,
            SERVICE_CONFIG_FAILURE_ACTIONS,
            pActions,dwRequired,&dwRequired);
        // Do something...
    }
}
```

# Bibliography

**Eddon, Guy, and Henry Eddon. *Inside Distributed COM.* Redmond, Wash.: Microsoft Press, 1998.**

This is the classic on Distributed COM (DCOM) and is a pretty good introduction to COM in general. For situations in which it is important to have transparent location independence for the server, DCOM or remote procedure calls (RPC) are the best options. DCOM is somewhat easier to implement, and having *Inside Distributed COM* available will make the learning process much easier. Beyond what is commonly considered DCOM topics, the book also includes useful coverage of Microsoft Transaction Server and the upcoming COM+ technology.

**Flanagan, David. *JavaScript: The Definitive Guide.* Sebastopol, Calif.: O'Reilly & Associates, 1998.**

If you need to use JavaScript and you don't know where to start, *JavaScript: The Definitive Guide* is a good place to look. Part II of this book discusses in detail the client-side JavaScript in the browser—something I covered briefly in Chapter 9.

**Microsoft Corporation. Microsoft Developer Network. Redmond, Wash.: Microsoft, 1999.**

No matter what other resource materials you have available, the Microsoft Developer Network (MSDN) is essential. Especially when you need to have the latest information about new technologies, nothing can beat the quarterly library updates on CD. Of course, much of the same information is available on line at the MSDN Web site (*http://msdn.microsoft.com*), but having the CDs makes finding the information more convenient. The searching capabilities alone can justify the cost of the MSDN Library. Even if you have many of the resources in hard copy format (as I do), finding exactly what you need is ever so much easier with the MSDN CDs.

**Microsoft Corporation. *Microsoft Internet Information Server Resource Kit.* Redmond, Wash.: Microsoft Press, 1998.**

Although this book covers IIS only through version 4, it is the most recent book of its kind available. The MSDN documentation covers most of the differences between IIS 4 and IIS 5, allowing you to use this book in conjunction with the more recent MSDN coverage of IIS. *Microsoft Internet Information Server Resource Kit* is intended for system administrators rather than developers, but even developers will likely need to administer their own development IIS system.

**Microsoft Corporation. *Microsoft ODBC 3.0 Software Development Kit and Programmer's Reference,* Volume 2. Redmond, Wash.: Microsoft Press, 1997.**
This book is another essential bit of documentation that any programmer should have. Even if you intend to use other data access methods, such as ADO, in many cases ADO calls into an ODBC driver. If, like me, you need to call the ODBC API directly, the *ODBC 3.0 Software Development Kit and Programmer's Reference* is a must-have.

**Evans, Nicholas D., Ken Miller, and Ken Spencer. *Programming Microsoft Visual InterDev 6.0.* Redmond, Wash.: Microsoft Press, 1999.**
Very much an introductory book, *Programming Microsoft Visual InterDev 6.0* focuses on using Microsoft Visual InterDev as it was intended to be used. If you have read this book, you probably noticed that I don't use Visual InterDev in the way Evans et al. describe. Prior to Visual InterDev, I used a simple text editor to edit my ASP files. I moved to Visual InterDev as a text editor only because of the syntax color coding. If you want to use Visual InterDev to its full potential, this is the book for you. Even if you are like me and use Visual InterDev as only a text editor, the book offers many tips and tricks that you will find useful.

**Murray, James D., and Debby Russell. *Windows NT Event Logging.* Sebastopol, Calif.: O'Reilly & Associates, 1998.**
This book is really aimed at administrators, but the relatively short section for programmers is quite helpful. Event logging is a great deal more complex than you might initially think, and this book helps you cut through that complexity.

**Musciano, Chuck, and Bill Kennedy. *HTML: The Definitive Guide,* 3d ed. Sebastopol, Calif.: O'Reilly & Associates, 1998.**
When I went to review this book, I couldn't find it in the stack of books that I had set aside for this bibliography. The reason is simple: I'd needed it earlier and it was at the top of the stack on my desk. I originally purchased the first edition and currently have the third edition. (Thanks, Sue!) I primarily use the book as a reference. My only disappointment with the third edition is the authors chose to remove the information on every element reference that clearly showed browser dependencies.

**Napper, Lewis. *WinSock 2.0.* Foster City, Calif.: IDG Books Worldwide, 1997.**
I had hoped that my inclusion of this book would spur a number of people to purchase it, but according to Amazon.com (and several postings on WinSock UseNet

news groups), *WinSock 2.0* is out of stock and unavailable. That is a shame. *You can't have mine!* This is one of only a couple of good books on WinSock. The fact that I own this one is due more to relative cost than to any special merit of this book over the others. Having purchased *WinSock 2.0,* I never had any need to purchase another WinSock resource. This book does contain a bit too much coverage of older WinSock features that make more sense in the 16-bit world than in the 32-bit world, but it is still one of those books I wish you could get your hands on.

**Okuntseff, Nik. *Windows NT Security: Programming Easy-to-Use Security Options.* Lawrence, Kans.: R & D Books, 1997.**

This is a less-than-easy-to-read book about a less-than-easy-to-use feature of Microsoft Windows 2000. That said, I have not found a better source for this information, including the MSDN documentation. Security is not my favorite feature of Windows 2000, but when I am presented with a security-related problem, this is the book I will pick up.

**Reilly, Douglas J. *Win32 Client/Server Developer's Guide.* Reading, Mass.: Addison-Wesley, 1996.**

What can I say about this book? Much of what I discussed in *Win32 Client/Server Developer's Guide* is still valid today. This book did not adequately cover developing server-side applications. In fact, it did not cover server-side applications at all. However, several parts of this book still make owning it worthwhile.

First the book describes a DLL-based, protocol-independent, client-side communication toolkit. I have called this toolkit from many different programming languages, and it is still in production. This allows one of my applications to decide at run time whether to use named pipes or WinSock.

Second this book covers remote procedure calls (RPC). While much attention these days is paid to Distributed COM rather than RPC, RPC can still be a valuable tool.

**Solomon, David A. *Inside Windows NT,* 2d ed. Redmond, Wash.: Microsoft Press, 1998.**

This book is one of those essential books for folks interested in serious Windows 2000/NT development. Because of its date of publication, the book refers to Windows NT 5 rather than Windows 2000, and some features of what was known as Windows NT 5 when this book was published—for example, 64-bit Alpha support—have been cut from the final product. More than technical details, *Inside Windows NT* gives you an insider's view of Windows 2000/NT. Sometimes understanding these perspectives can help foster a greater understanding of the operating system as a whole.

**Soukup, Ron, and Kalen Delaney. *Inside Microsoft SQL Server 7.0.* Redmond, Wash.: Microsoft Press, 1999.**

Even experienced SQL Server administrators and programmers will have this book by their sides. While it is not in a reference format and it omits coverage of many of the tools included with SQL Server 7.0, this book is a worthwhile read for the historical context it gives to SQL Server and for the low-level insights it offers into what makes SQL Server tick. I have spent only a little time with this volume, but based on the quality of Ron Soukup's original volume, I am looking forward to reading more of the current edition.

If you can have only a single book on SQL Server, you might be better off with one of the books that is oriented a bit more toward providing a reference tool for SQL Server. The purpose of *Inside Microsoft SQL Server 7.0* is different, and it in no way attempts to duplicate the online documentation. But if your library has room for a couple of books on SQL Server, I would certainly recommend this title.

**Tanenbaum, Andrew S. *Modern Operating Systems.* Englewood Cliffs, N.J.: Prentice Hall, 1992.**

I had never considered reading a book like *Modern Operating Systems* until I was faced with the prospect of writing about client/server systems. I realized that some of the issues raised in *Modern Operating Systems* were crucial to understanding what it takes to create world-class server-based software. Don't wait until you are about to write a book to read this classic.

*Modern Operating Systems* contains a great deal of detail on creating distributed operating systems. This information carries over directly to any system that will run on more than a single machine at a time. Even for systems that work on a single machine at a time, the discussions about multithreaded applications and the implications of threading are timeless and crucial to creating server-based software. The section on classical interprocess communication problems alone is likely worth the cost of the book.

**Thai, Thuan L. *Learning DCOM.* Cambridge, Mass.: O'Reilly & Associates, 1999.**

This is the one other DCOM book I own besides *Inside Distributed COM,* by Eddon and Eddon. Given only one book about DCOM, I would choose *Inside Distributed COM,* but as with many topics this complex, there's benefit from having more than a single source. *Learning DCOM* is a reasonable second source.

**Weissinger, A. Keyton. *ASP in a Nutshell: A Desktop Quick Reference.* Sebastopol, Calif.: O'Reilly & Associates, 1999.**

This is a very high-level look at ASP that is rich in short examples but would be helped by at least one significant example. I sometimes take information gained from this broad overview and use it to target specific information in the MSDN documentation.

# Index

*Italic page number references indicate figures or tables.*

## Special Characters



## A

## J–K



## L



## M

## N

## O



## P

## U

## V



## W

## X

## Douglas J. Reilly

Ever since he convinced his wife to spend what seemed like far too much money for an Atari 800, Douglas J. Reilly has loved to play with computers. For many years before buying the Atari, he made a living repairing photocopiers and early personal computers. After a while, the software became more fun than the hardware.

Doug is the owner of Access Microsystems, Inc., a small consulting firm that develops software, using Microsoft Visual C++, Borland Delphi, Microsoft Access, and many of the APIs and technologies covered in this book. He has created applications to electronically test job applicants, track retailers' inventory, and repair damaged databases. Currently he is working on a variety of health care applications for the St. Barnabas Health Care System and, most recently, Home Care Information Systems, both in New Jersey. In addition to developing software, Doug has written articles for *Dr. Dobb's Journal* and *Software Development,* and he also wrote a column for the *Pervasive Software Developer's Journal.*

Doug lives with his wife, Jean, and two children, Tim and Erin. When not programming, he enjoys music, reading, and bicycle riding, although book writing and other concerns have conspired against serious riding this year. Maybe next year.

Doug can be reached by e-mail at *doug@accessmicrosystems.com*.

The manuscript for this book was prepared using Microsoft Word 2000. Pages were composed by Microsoft Press using Adobe PageMaker 6.52 for Windows, with text in Garamond and display type in Helvetica Black. Composed pages were delivered to the printer as electronic prepress files.

***Cover Graphic Designer***

Girvin | Strategic Branding & Design

***Cover Illustrator***

Glenn Mitsui

***Interior Graphic Artist***

Michael Kloepfer

***Principal Compositor***

Barb Runyan

***Indexer***

Lynn Armstrong

# Serve up **powerfully scalable** *business solutions*

**U.S.A.** **$59.99**
U.K. £38.99 [V.A.T. included]
Canada $89.99
ISBN 0-7356-0517-3

**W**ith the innovations in Microsoft® SQL Server™ 7.0, organizations like yours get a powerfully enhanced tool for turning enterprise information into business results. In this essential companion to version 7.0, two of the most knowledgeable authorities on SQL Server technology step inside the reengineered SQL Server engine to reveal how underlying system structure and behavior affect application development. Use this in-depth, expert investigation—plus the ready-to-load evaluation copy of SQL Server 7.0—to understand how to create high-performance data warehousing, transaction processing, and decision-support applications that scale as far as your vision for the enterprise.

Microsoft Press® products are available worldwide wherever quality computer books are sold. For more information, contact your book or computer retailer, software reseller, or local Microsoft Sales Office, or visit our Web site at mspress.microsoft.com. To locate your nearest source for Microsoft Press products, or to order directly, call 1-800-MSPRESS in the U.S. (in Canada, call 1-800-268-2222).

Prices and availability dates are subject to change.

**Microsoft**®
**mspress.microsoft.com**

# MICROSOFT LICENSE AGREEMENT

Book Companion CD

**IMPORTANT—READ CAREFULLY:** This Microsoft End-User License Agreement ("EULA") is a legal agreement between you (either an individual or an entity) and Microsoft Corporation for the Microsoft product identified above, which includes computer software and may include associated media, printed materials, and "on-line" or electronic documentation ("SOFTWARE PRODUCT"). Any component included within the SOFTWARE PRODUCT that is accompanied by a separate End-User License Agreement shall be governed by such agreement and not the terms set forth below. By installing, copying, or otherwise using the SOFTWARE PRODUCT, you agree to be bound by the terms of this EULA. If you do not agree to the terms of this EULA, you are not authorized to install, copy, or otherwise use the SOFTWARE PRODUCT; you may, however, return the SOFTWARE PRODUCT, along with all printed materials and other items that form a part of the Microsoft product that includes the SOFTWARE PRODUCT, to the place you obtained them for a full refund.

## SOFTWARE PRODUCT LICENSE

The SOFTWARE PRODUCT is protected by United States copyright laws and international copyright treaties, as well as other intellectual property laws and treaties. The SOFTWARE PRODUCT is licensed, not sold.

1. **GRANT OF LICENSE.** This EULA grants you the following rights:

   a. **Software Product.** You may install and use one copy of the SOFTWARE PRODUCT on a single computer. The primary user of the computer on which the SOFTWARE PRODUCT is installed may make a second copy for his or her exclusive use on a portable computer.

   b. **Storage/Network Use.** You may also store or install a copy of the SOFTWARE PRODUCT on a storage device, such as a network server, used only to install or run the SOFTWARE PRODUCT on your other computers over an internal network; however, you must acquire and dedicate a license for each separate computer on which the SOFTWARE PRODUCT is installed or run from the storage device. A license for the SOFTWARE PRODUCT may not be shared or used concurrently on different computers.

   c. **License Pak.** If you have acquired this EULA in a Microsoft License Pak, you may make the number of additional copies of the computer software portion of the SOFTWARE PRODUCT authorized on the printed copy of this EULA, and you may use each copy in the manner specified above. You are also entitled to make a corresponding number of secondary copies for portable computer use as specified above.

   d. **Sample Code.** Solely with respect to portions, if any, of the SOFTWARE PRODUCT that are identified within the SOFTWARE PRODUCT as sample code (the "SAMPLE CODE"):

      i. **Use and Modification.** Microsoft grants you the right to use and modify the source code version of the SAMPLE CODE, *provided* you comply with subsection (d)(iii) below. You may not distribute the SAMPLE CODE, or any modified version of the SAMPLE CODE, in source code form.

      ii. **Redistributable Files.** Provided you comply with subsection (d)(iii) below, Microsoft grants you a nonexclusive, royalty-free right to reproduce and distribute the object code version of the SAMPLE CODE and of any modified SAMPLE CODE, other than SAMPLE CODE (or any modified version thereof) designated as not redistributable in the Readme file that forms a part of the SOFTWARE PRODUCT (the "Non-Redistributable Sample Code"). All SAMPLE CODE other than the Non-Redistributable Sample Code is collectively referred to as the "REDISTRIBUTABLES."

      iii. **Redistribution Requirements.** If you redistribute the REDISTRIBUTABLES, you agree to: (i) distribute the REDISTRIBUTABLES in object code form only in conjunction with and as a part of your software application product; (ii) not use Microsoft's name, logo, or trademarks to market your software application product; (iii) include a valid copyright notice on your software application product; (iv) indemnify, hold harmless, and defend Microsoft from and against any claims or lawsuits, including attorney's fees, that arise or result from the use or distribution of your software application product; and (v) not permit further distribution of the REDISTRIBUTABLES by your end user. Contact Microsoft for the applicable royalties due and other licensing terms for all other uses and/or distribution of the REDISTRIBUTABLES.

2. **DESCRIPTION OF OTHER RIGHTS AND LIMITATIONS.**

- **Limitations on Reverse Engineering, Decompilation, and Disassembly.** You may not reverse engineer, decompile, or disassemble the SOFTWARE PRODUCT, except and only to the extent that such activity is expressly permitted by applicable law notwithstanding this limitation.
- **Separation of Components.** The SOFTWARE PRODUCT is licensed as a single product. Its component parts may not be separated for use on more than one computer.
- **Rental.** You may not rent, lease, or lend the SOFTWARE PRODUCT.
- **Support Services.** Microsoft may, but is not obligated to, provide you with support services related to the SOFTWARE PRODUCT ("Support Services"). Use of Support Services is governed by the Microsoft policies and programs described in the user manual, in "on-line" documentation, and/or in other Microsoft-provided materials. Any supplemental software code provided to you as part of the Support Services shall be considered part of the SOFTWARE PRODUCT and subject to the terms and conditions of this EULA. With respect to technical information you provide to Microsoft as part of the Support Services, Microsoft may use such information for its business purposes, including for product support and development. Microsoft will not utilize such technical information in a form that personally identifies you.

- **Software Transfer.** You may permanently transfer all of your rights under this EULA, provided you retain no copies, you transfer all of the SOFTWARE PRODUCT (including all component parts, the media and printed materials, any upgrades, this EULA, and, if applicable, the Certificate of Authenticity), **and** the recipient agrees to the terms of this EULA.
- **Termination.** Without prejudice to any other rights, Microsoft may terminate this EULA if you fail to comply with the terms and conditions of this EULA. In such event, you must destroy all copies of the SOFTWARE PRODUCT and all of its component parts.

3. **COPYRIGHT.** All title and copyrights in and to the SOFTWARE PRODUCT (including but not limited to any images, photographs, animations, video, audio, music, text, SAMPLE CODE, REDISTRIBUTABLES, and "applets" incorporated into the SOFTWARE PRODUCT) and any copies of the SOFTWARE PRODUCT are owned by Microsoft or its suppliers. The SOFTWARE PRODUCT is protected by copyright laws and international treaty provisions. Therefore, you must treat the SOFTWARE PRODUCT like any other copyrighted material **except** that you may install the SOFTWARE PRODUCT on a single computer provided you keep the original solely for backup or archival purposes. You may not copy the printed materials accompanying the SOFTWARE PRODUCT.
4. **U.S. GOVERNMENT RESTRICTED RIGHTS.** The SOFTWARE PRODUCT and documentation are provided with RESTRICTED RIGHTS. Use, duplication, or disclosure by the Government is subject to restrictions as set forth in subparagraph (c)(1)(ii) of the Rights in Technical Data and Computer Software clause at DFARS 252.227-7013 or subparagraphs (c)(1) and (2) of the Commercial Computer Software—Restricted Rights at 48 CFR 52.227-19, as applicable. Manufacturer is Microsoft Corporation/One Microsoft Way/Redmond, WA 98052-6399.
5. **EXPORT RESTRICTIONS.** You agree that you will not export or re-export the SOFTWARE PRODUCT, any part thereof, or any process or service that is the direct product of the SOFTWARE PRODUCT (the foregoing collectively referred to as the "Restricted Components"), to any country, person, entity, or end user subject to U.S. export restrictions. You specifically agree not to export or re-export any of the Restricted Components (i) to any country to which the U.S. has embargoed or restricted the export of goods or services, which currently include, but are not necessarily limited to, Cuba, Iran, Iraq, Libya, North Korea, Sudan, and Syria, or to any national of any such country, wherever located, who intends to transmit or transport the Restricted Components back to such country; (ii) to any end user who you know or have reason to know will utilize the Restricted Components in the design, development, or production of nuclear, chemical, or biological weapons; or (iii) to any end user who has been prohibited from participating in U.S. export transactions by any federal agency of the U.S. government. You warrant and represent that neither the BXA nor any other U.S. federal agency has suspended, revoked, or denied your export privileges.
6. **NOTE ON JAVA SUPPORT.** THE SOFTWARE PRODUCT MAY CONTAIN SUPPORT FOR PROGRAMS WRITTEN IN JAVA. JAVA TECHNOLOGY IS NOT FAULT TOLERANT AND IS NOT DESIGNED, MANUFACTURED, OR INTENDED FOR USE OR RESALE AS ON-LINE CONTROL EQUIPMENT IN HAZARDOUS ENVIRONMENTS REQUIRING FAIL-SAFE PERFORMANCE, SUCH AS IN THE OPERATION OF NUCLEAR FACILITIES, AIRCRAFT NAVIGATION OR COMMUNICATION SYSTEMS, AIR TRAFFIC CONTROL, DIRECT LIFE SUPPORT MACHINES, OR WEAPONS SYSTEMS, IN WHICH THE FAILURE OF JAVA TECHNOLOGY COULD LEAD DIRECTLY TO DEATH, PERSONAL INJURY, OR SEVERE PHYSICAL OR ENVIRONMENTAL DAMAGE. SUN MICROSYSTEMS, INC. HAS CONTRACTUALLY OBLIGATED MICROSOFT TO MAKE THIS DISCLAIMER.

## DISCLAIMER OF WARRANTY

**NO WARRANTIES OR CONDITIONS.** MICROSOFT EXPRESSLY DISCLAIMS ANY WARRANTY OR CONDITION FOR THE SOFTWARE PRODUCT. THE SOFTWARE PRODUCT AND ANY RELATED DOCUMENTATION ARE PROVIDED "AS IS" WITHOUT WARRANTY OR CONDITION OF ANY KIND, EITHER EXPRESS OR IMPLIED, INCLUDING, WITHOUT LIMITATION, THE IMPLIED WARRANTIES OF MERCHANTABILITY, FITNESS FOR A PARTICULAR PURPOSE, OR NONINFRINGEMENT. THE ENTIRE RISK ARISING OUT OF USE OR PERFORMANCE OF THE SOFTWARE PRODUCT REMAINS WITH YOU.

**LIMITATION OF LIABILITY.** TO THE MAXIMUM EXTENT PERMITTED BY APPLICABLE LAW, IN NO EVENT SHALL MICROSOFT OR ITS SUPPLIERS BE LIABLE FOR ANY SPECIAL, INCIDENTAL, INDIRECT, OR CONSEQUENTIAL DAMAGES WHATSOEVER (INCLUDING, WITHOUT LIMITATION, DAMAGES FOR LOSS OF BUSINESS PROFITS, BUSINESS INTERRUPTION, LOSS OF BUSINESS INFORMATION, OR ANY OTHER PECUNIARY LOSS) ARISING OUT OF THE USE OF OR INABILITY TO USE THE SOFTWARE PRODUCT OR THE PROVISION OF OR FAILURE TO PROVIDE SUPPORT SERVICES, EVEN IF MICROSOFT HAS BEEN ADVISED OF THE POSSIBILITY OF SUCH DAMAGES. IN ANY CASE, MICROSOFT'S ENTIRE LIABILITY UNDER ANY PROVISION OF THIS EULA SHALL BE LIMITED TO THE GREATER OF THE AMOUNT ACTUALLY PAID BY YOU FOR THE SOFTWARE PRODUCT OR US$5.00; PROVIDED, HOWEVER, IF YOU HAVE ENTERED INTO A MICROSOFT SUPPORT SERVICES AGREEMENT, MICROSOFT'S ENTIRE LIABILITY REGARDING SUPPORT SERVICES SHALL BE GOVERNED BY THE TERMS OF THAT AGREEMENT. BECAUSE SOME STATES AND JURISDICTIONS DO NOT ALLOW THE EXCLUSION OR LIMITATION OF LIABILITY, THE ABOVE LIMITATION MAY NOT APPLY TO YOU.

## MISCELLANEOUS

This EULA is governed by the laws of the State of Washington USA, except and only to the extent that applicable law mandates governing law of a different jurisdiction.

Should you have any questions concerning this EULA, or if you desire to contact Microsoft for any reason, please contact the Microsoft subsidiary serving your country, or write: Microsoft Sales Information Center/One Microsoft Way/Redmond, WA 98052-6399.

PN 097-0002297